Fodor's Thirteenth Edition

Pacific
Northwest

The complete guide, thoroughly up-to-date

Packed with details that will make your trip

The must-see sights, off and on the beaten path

What to see, what to skip

Vacation itineraries, walking tours, day trips

Smart lodging and dining options

Essential local dos and taboos

Transportation tips

Key contacts, savvy travel advice

When to go, what to pack

Clear, accurate, easy-to-use maps

D1127468

Fodor's Pacific Northwest

EDITOR: Constance Jones

Editorial Contributors: Jeffrey Boswell, John Doerper, Julie Fay, Melisse Gelula, Sue Kernaghan, Jeff Kuechle, Donald S. Olson, Don Pitcher, Glenn W. Sheehan, Don Thacker

Editorial Production: Stacey Kulig

Maps: David Lindroth, Inc., *cartographer*; Rebecca Baer and Robert Blake, *map editors*

Design: Fabrizio La Rocca, *creative director*; Guido Caroti, *art director*; Jolie Novak, *photo editor*

Cover Design: Pentagram

Production/Manufacturing: Mike Costa

Cover Photograph: J. A. Kraulis/Masterfile

Database Production: Janet Foley, Mark Laroche, Julie Tomasz, Martin Walsh

Copyright

Thirteenth Edition

ISBN 0–679–00373–8

ISSN 1098–6774

Special Sales

Fodor's Travel Publications are available at special discounts for bulk purchases for sales promotions or premiums. Special editions, including personalized covers, excerpts of existing guides, and corporate imprints, can be created in large quantities for special needs. For more information, contact your local bookseller or write to Special Markets, Fodor's Travel Publications, 201 East 50th Street, New York, NY 10022. Inquiries from Canada should be directed to your local Canadian bookseller or sent to Random House of Canada, Ltd., Marketing Department, 2775 Matheson Boulevard East, Mississauga, Ontario L4W 4P7. Inquiries from the United Kingdom should be sent to Fodor's Travel Publications, 20 Vauxhall Bridge Road, London SW1V 2SA, England.

PRINTED IN THE UNITED STATES OF AMERICA

10 9 8 7 6 5 4 3 2 1

Important Tip

Although all prices, opening times, and other details in this book are based on information supplied to us at press time, changes occur all the time in the travel world, and Fodor's cannot accept responsibility for facts that become outdated or for inadvertent errors or omissions. So **always confirm information when it matters,** especially if you're making a detour to visit a specific place.

CONTENTS

Maps

ON THE ROAD WITH FODOR'S

THE TRIPS YOU TAKE THIS YEAR and next are going to be significant trips, if only because they'll be your first in the new millennium. Acutely aware of that fact, we've pulled out all stops in preparing *Fodor's Pacific Northwest*. To guide you in putting together your Pacific Northwest experience, we've created multiday itineraries and neighborhood walks. And to direct you to the places that are truly worth your time and money, we've rallied the team of endearingly picky know-it-alls we're pleased to call our writers. Having seen all corners of the Pacific Northwest, they're real. If you knew them, you'd poll them for tips yourself.

Jeffrey Boswell, who revised the Oregon and Portland chapters, fled the *San Francisco Examiner* newsroom in 1995 to take up life as a freelance editor in the Great Northwest. He lives in Portland, exploring its growing restaurant scene and hiking in the surrounding countryside, and travels frequently to Oregon's coast, Seattle, and Vancouver.

Updater of the Washington chapter, Bellingham resident **John Doerper** has explored Washington State and the Pacific Northwest for more than 25 years. A former food editor for *Washington, Pacific Northwest,* and *Seattle,* he has written extensively about this fascinating region. He is also the author of several guidebooks.

Freelance writer **Julie Fay,** updater of the Seattle chapter, is a Seattle native and fifth-generation Washingtonian. She spends much of each summer at her family's beach cabin in the San Juan Islands, revisiting favorite haunts and combing the north Puget Sound region for new ones.

Vancouver-born freelance writer **Sue Kernaghan,** a fourth-generation British Columbian, pestered elderly relatives for historical insights and covered a lot of dirt roads, open water, and country pubs while researching the Vancouver and British Columbia chapters.

Novelist and playwright **Donald S. Olson,** who wrote the Portland and Oregon chapters, has written on Oregon for the *New York Times, Travel & Leisure,* and *Diversion.*

Don Pitcher's knowledge of Southeast Alaska comes from a dozen seasons spent guiding visitors through the region. He is the author of guidebooks on Alaska, Wyoming, Washington, and Berkeley, California, and today lives in Anchorage.

Don Thacker is an Edmonton-based geographer and writer who particularly enjoys the rugged beauty of the Canadian Rockies. His special focus in the British Columbia chapter this year was the British Columbia Rockies.

Don't Forget to Write

Keeping a travel guide fresh and up-to-date is a big job. So we love your feedback—positive and negative—and follow up on all suggestions. Contact the Pacific Northwest editor at editors@fodors.com or c/o Fodor's, 201 East 50th Street, New York, NY 10022. And have a wonderful trip!

Karen Cure

Karen Cure
Editorial Director

The Pacific Northwest

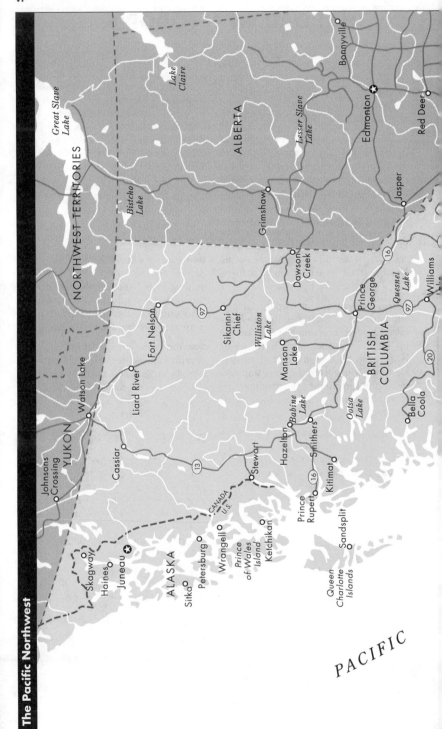

NORTHWEST TERRITORIES

Great Slave Lake

Lake Claire

ALBERTA

Bistcho Lake

Lesser Slave Lake

Edmonton

Bonnyville

Red Deer

Jasper

Grimshaw

Dawson Creek

Prince George

16

Quesnel Lake

97

Williams

YUKON

Johnsons Crossing

Watson Lake

Fort Nelson

97

Sikanni Chief

Williston Lake

Manson Lake

BRITISH COLUMBIA

20

Liard River

Cassiar

13

Stewart

Hazelton

Babine Lake

Smithers

16

Ootsa Lake

Bella Coola

Skagway

Haines

Juneau

ALASKA

Sitka

Petersburg

Wrangell

Prince of Wales Island

Ketchikan

CANADA U.S.

Prince Rupert

Kitimat

Sandsplit

Queen Charlotte Islands

PACIFIC

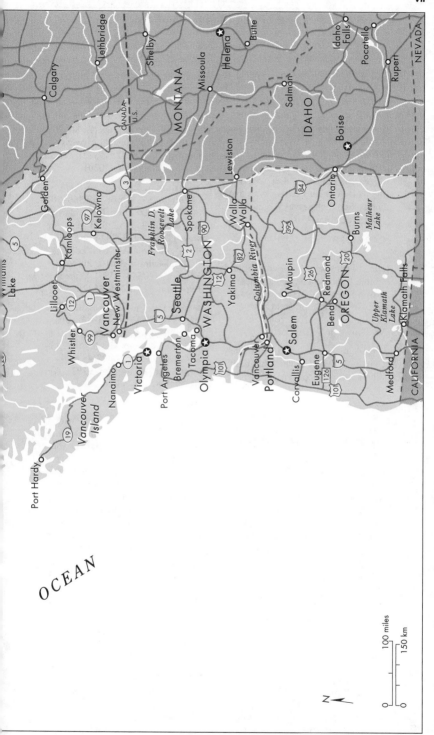

SMART TRAVEL TIPS A TO Z

Basic Information on Traveling in the Pacific Northwest, Savvy Tips to Make Your Trip a Breeze, and Companies and Organizations to Contact

AIR TRAVEL

BOOKING YOUR FLIGHT

When you book **look for nonstop flights** and **remember that "direct" flights stop at least once.** Try to avoid connecting flights, which require a change of plane.

CARRIERS

Leading regional carriers in the Pacific Northwest are Horizon Air and United Express. The two airlines provide frequent service between cities in Washington and Oregon. Horizon Air also flies from Seattle to Vancouver and Victoria.

The major regional carrier in western Canada is Air B.C., which has daily flights from Vancouver and Victoria into Seattle. Air B.C. also has several daily flights between Vancouver and Portland. Helijet Airways provides jet helicopter service from Vancouver and Seattle's Boeing Field to Victoria.

In addition to its regular airport service, Air B.C. has floatplane service between Vancouver and Victoria harbors. Kenmore Air has scheduled flights from Seattle's Lake Union to Victoria and points in the San Juan Islands. Along with several other floatplane companies, Kenmore provides fly-in service to remote fishing resorts along the coast of British Columbia.

➤ MAJOR AIRLINES: **Air B.C.** (☎ 604/688–5515 or 250/360–9074; 800/776–3000 in the U.S.). **Air Canada** (☎ 800/776–3000). **Air North Ltd.** (☎ 800/764–0407). **Alaska** (☎ 800/252–7522). **American** (☎ 800/433–7300). **British Airways** (☎ 800/247–9297). **Continental** (☎ 800/523–3273). **Delta** (☎ 800/221–1212). **EVA Airways** (☎ 800/695–1188). **Hawaiian** (☎ 800/367–5320). **Japan** (☎ 800/525–3663). **Northwest** (☎ 800/225–2525). **Thai** (☎ 800/426–5204). **TWA** (☎ 800/221–2000).

United/United Express (☎ 800/241–6522). **US Airways/US Airways Express** (☎ 800/428–4322). **Western Pacific** (☎ 800/930–3030).

➤ REGIONAL AIRLINES: **Air B.C.** (☎ 604/688–5515 or 250/360–9074; 800/776–3000 in the U.S.). **Harbor Air** (☎ 800/359–3220). **Helijet Airways** (☎ 604/273–1414 or 800/665–4354). **Horizon Air** (☎ 800/547–9308). **Kenmore Air** (☎ 206/486–8400 or 800/543–9595). **United Express** (☎ 800/241–6522).

➤ SMALLER AIRLINES: **America West** (☎ 888/615–8556). **Canadian** (☎ 800/426–7000). **Horizon Air** (☎ 800/547–9308). **Reno Air** (☎ 800/736–6247). **Skywest** (☎ 800/453–9417). **Southwest** (☎ 800/435–9792). **Westjet** (☎ 800/538–5696).

CHECK-IN & BOARDING

Assuming that not everyone with a ticket will show up, airlines routinely overbook planes. When that happens, airlines ask for volunteers to give up their seats. In return these volunteers usually get a certificate for a free flight and are rebooked on the next flight out. If there are not enough volunteers, the airline must choose who will be denied boarding. The first to get bumped are passengers who checked in late and those flying on discounted tickets, so **get to the gate and check in as early as possible,** especially during peak periods.

Always **bring a government-issued photo I.D. to the airport.** You may be asked to show it before you are allowed to check in.

CUTTING COSTS

The least-expensive airfares to the Pacific Northwest must usually be purchased in advance and are nonrefundable. It's smart to **call a number of airlines, and when you are quoted a good price, book it on the spot**—the same fare may not be available the next day. Always **check different routings** and look into using different airports. Travel agents, especially low-fare specialists (☞ Discounts & Deals, *below*), are helpful.

Consolidators are another good source. They buy tickets for scheduled international flights at reduced rates from the airlines, then sell them at prices that beat the best fare available directly from the airlines, usually without restrictions. Sometimes you can even get your money back if you need to return the ticket. Carefully read the fine print detailing penalties for changes and cancellations, and **confirm your consolidator reservation with the airline.**

When you **fly as a courier** you trade your checked-luggage space for a ticket deeply subsidized by a courier service. There are restrictions on when you can book and how long you can stay.

➤ CONSOLIDATORS: **Cheap Tickets** (☎ 800/377–1000). **Discount Airline Ticket Service** (☎ 800/576–1600). **Unitravel** (☎ 800/325–2222). **Up & Away Travel** (☎ 212/889–2345). **World Travel Network** (☎ 800/409–6753).

ENJOYING THE FLIGHT

For more legroom **request an emergency-aisle seat.** Don't sit in the row in front of the emergency aisle or in front of a bulkhead, where seats may not recline. If you have dietary concerns, **ask for special meals when booking.** These can be vegetarian, low-cholesterol, or kosher, for example. On long flights, try to maintain a normal routine, to help fight jet lag. At night **get some sleep.** By day **eat light meals, drink water** (not alcohol), and **move around the cabin** to stretch your legs.

FLYING TIMES

It takes about 5 hours to fly nonstop to Seattle or Portland from New York, about 4 hours from Chicago, and 2 hours from Los Angeles. Flights from New York to Vancouver take about 8 hours with connections; from Chicago, about 4½ hours nonstop; and from Los Angeles, about 3 hours nonstop. To reach destinations in Alaska you must connect to a regional carrier, such as

Alaska Airlines, in Seattle; it takes about 2½ hours to fly from there to Anchorage and about 1½ hours to Juneau.

HOW TO COMPLAIN

If your baggage goes astray or your flight goes awry, complain right away. Most carriers require that you **file a claim immediately.**

➤ AIRLINE COMPLAINTS: U.S. Department of Transportation **Aviation Consumer Protection Division** (✉ C-75, Room 4107, Washington, DC 20590, ☎ 202/366–2220). Federal Aviation Administration Consumer Hotline (☎ 800/322–7873).

AIRPORTS &TRANSFERS

➤ AIRPORT INFORMATION: The major gateways are **Portland International Airport** (✉ N.E. Airport Way at I-205, ☎ 888/739–4636) **Sea-Tac International Airport** (☎ 206/431–4444). **Vancouver International Airport** (☎ 604/276–6101).

TRANSFERS

See the A to Z sections at the end of the Portland, Seattle, and Vancouver chapters for information about airport transfers to the center of each city.

BOAT & FERRY TRAVEL

Ferries play an important part in the transportation network of the Pacific Northwest. In some areas ferries provide the only form of access into and out of communities. In other places ferries transport thousands of commuters a day to and from work in the cities. Ferries are one of the best ways for visitors to get a feel for the region and its ties to the sea.

WASHINGTON

If you are planning to use the Washington State Ferry System, try to **avoid peak commuter hours.** The heaviest traffic flows are eastbound in the mornings and on Sunday evening, and westbound on Saturday morning and weekday afternoons. The best times for travel are 9–3 and after 7 PM on weekdays. In July and August you may have to wait up to three hours to take a car aboard one of the popular San Juan Islands ferries. Walk-on space is always available; if possible, **leave your car behind.**

SMART TRAVEL TIPS

The vessels of **Washington State Ferries** carry more than 23 million passengers a year between points on Puget Sound and the San Juan Islands. Reservations are not available on any domestic routes.

BRITISH COLUMBIA

B.C. Ferries operates ferries between the mainland and Vancouver Island and elsewhere, carrying passengers, cars, campers, RVs, trucks, and buses. Peak traffic times are Friday afternoon, Saturday morning, and Sunday afternoon, especially during summer months and holiday weekends.

Black Ball Transport's MV *Coho* makes daily crossings year-round, from Port Angeles to Victoria. The *Coho* can carry 800 passengers and 100 cars across the Strait of Juan de Fuca in 1½ hours. Advance reservations are not accepted.

Clipper Navigation operates three passenger-only jet catamarans between Seattle and Victoria. One makes the trip in two hours, another makes it in three hours, and the third, which takes the scenic route, makes it in five hours. The company also operates the *Princess Marguerite III* car and passenger ferry between Seattle and Victoria, with one round-trip daily from mid-May to mid-September. The sailing time is 4½ hours each way.

SOUTHEAST ALASKA

The ferries of the **Alaska Marine Highway** system travel within Alaska and between Bellingham, Washington, and the towns of the Inside Passage. The Marine Highway links up with British Columbia Ferries in Prince Rupert.

➤ BOAT & FERRY INFORMATION: **Alaska Marine Highway** (✉ Box 25535, Juneau 99802-5535, ☎ 907/465-3941 or 800/642-0066, FAX 907/277-4829). **Black Ball Transport** (✉ 430 Belleville St., Victoria, BC V8V 1W9, ☎ 604/386-2202 in Victoria or 360/457-4491 in Port Angeles). **British Columbia Ferries** (✉ 1112 Fort St., Victoria, BC V8V 4V2, ☎ 250/386-3431, FAX 250/381-5452). **Victoria Clipper** (✉ 2701 Alaskan Way, Pier 69, Seattle, WA 98121, ☎ 250/480-5555 in Victoria;

206/448-5000 in Seattle; 800/888-2535 in the U.S. only). **Washington State Ferries** (✉ Colman Dock, Pier 52, Seattle, WA 98104, ☎ 206/464-6400; 800/843-3779 in WA).

DISCOUNT PASSES

The **AlaskaPass Travelpass** (✉ Box 351, Vashon Island, WA 98070, ☎ 800/248-7598) provides transportation aboard any Alaska or British Columbia ferry as well as many connecting bus and train services. Passes of varying lengths enable the independent traveler to exercise a high degree of flexibility in choosing an itinerary.

BUS TRAVEL

Greyhound Lines operates regular intercity bus routes to points throughout the region. **Gray Line of Seattle** has daily bus service between Seattle and Victoria via the Washington State ferry at Anacortes. **Gray Line** companies in Portland, Seattle, Vancouver, and Victoria operate charter bus service and scheduled sightseeing tours that last from a few hours to several days.

➤ BUS AND SIGHTSEEING COMPANIES: **Gray Line** (☎ 503/285-9845 or 800/422-7042 in Portland; 206/624-5077 or 800/544-0739 in Seattle; 604/681-8687 or [from the U.S. only] 800/663-0667 in Vancouver; 250/388-5248 or [from the U.S. only] 800/663-8390 in Victoria; 907/277-5581 or 800/544-2206 in AKP). **Greyhound** (☎ 800/231-2222). **Pacific Coach Lines** (☎ 800/661-1725, for travel from Vancouver to Victoria).

➤ CHARTER COMPANIES: **Gray Line** (☎ 503/285-9845 or 800/422-7042 in Portland; ☎ 206/624-5077 in Seattle; ☎ 604/681-8687 in Vancouver; ☎ 250/388-5248 in Victoria). **Evergreen Gray Line** (☎ 503/285-9845 or 800/422-7042).

DISCOUNT PASSES

The **AlaskaPass Travelpass** provides transportation aboard any Alaska or British Columbia ferry as well as many connecting bus and train services. Greyhound's **Ameripass**, valid on all U.S. routes, allows unlimited bus travel within a 7-, 15-, 30-, or 60-day period. Greyhound Lines of

Canada offers the **CanPass,** valid for 7, 15, 30, or 60 days of unlimited bus travel within Canada.

➤ PASSES: **AlaskaPass Travelpass** (☎ 800/248–7598). **Greyhound Ameripass** (☎ 800/231–2222).

CAMERAS & PHOTOGRAPHY

➤ PHOTO HELP: **Kodak Information Center** (☎ 800/242–2424). *Kodak Guide to Shooting Great Travel Pictures,* available in bookstores or from Fodor's Travel Publications (☎ 800/533–6478; $16.50 plus $4 shipping).

EQUIPMENT PRECAUTIONS

Always **keep your film and tape out of the sun.** Carry an extra supply of batteries, and **be prepared to turn on your camera or camcorder** to prove to security personnel that the device is real. Always **ask for hand inspection of film,** which becomes clouded after successive exposures to airport X-ray machines, and **keep videotapes away from metal detectors.**

CAR RENTAL

Rates in Portland begin at $33 a day and $145 a week. Rates in Seattle begin at $50 a day and $155 a week. Rates in Vancouver begin at US$25 a day and US$130 a week. This does not include tax on car rentals, which is 15% in Vancouver and 18.3% in Seattle.

➤ MAJOR AGENCIES: **Alamo** (☎ 800/327–9633; 020/8759–6200 in the U.K.). **Avis** (☎ 800/331–1212; 800/879–2847 in Canada; 02/9353–9000 in Australia; 09/525–1982 in New Zealand). **Budget** (☎ 800/527–0700; 0144/227–6266 in the U.K.). **Dollar** (☎ 800/800–4000; 020/8897–0811 in the U.K., where it is known as Eurodollar; 02/9223–1444 in Australia). **Hertz** (☎ 800/654–3131; 800/263–0600 in Canada; 0990/90–60–90 in the U.K.; 02/9669–2444 in Australia; 03/358–6777 in New Zealand). **National InterRent** (☎ 800/227–7368; 0345/222525 in the U.K., where it is known as Europcar InterRent).

CUTTING COSTS

To get the best deal **book through a travel agent, who will shop around.** Also **price local car-rental companies,** although the service and maintenance may not be as good as those of a major player. Remember to ask about required deposits, cancellation penalties, and drop-off charges if you're planning to pick up the car in one city and leave it in another. If you're traveling during a holiday period, also make sure that a confirmed reservation guarantees you a car.

Do **look into wholesalers,** companies that do not own fleets but rent in bulk from those that do and often offer better rates than traditional car-rental operations.

➤ LOCAL AGENCIES: **Lo-Cost Rent-a-Car** ☎ (604/689–9664).

➤ WHOLESALERS: **Auto Europe** (☎ 207/842–2000 or 800/223–5555, FAX 800/235–6321).

INSURANCE

When driving a rented car you are generally responsible for any damage to or loss of the vehicle as well as for any property damage or personal injury that you may cause. Before you rent see what coverage your personal auto-insurance policy and credit cards already provide.

For about $15 to $20 per day, rental companies sell protection, known as a collision- or loss-damage waiver (CDW or LDW), that eliminates your liability for damage to the car.

In most states you don't need a CDW if you have personal auto insurance or other liability insurance. However, **make sure you have enough coverage to pay for the car.** If you do not have auto insurance or an umbrella policy that covers damage to third parties, purchasing liability insurance and a CDW or LDW is highly recommended.

REQUIREMENTS & RESTRICTIONS

In the Pacific Northwest you must be 21 to rent a car, and rates may be higher if you're under 25. You'll pay extra for child seats (about $3 per day), which are compulsory for children under five, and for additional drivers (about $2 per day). Non-U.S. residents will need a reservation voucher, a passport, a driver's license, and a travel policy that covers each driver, in order to pick up a car.

SURCHARGES

Before you pick up a car in one city and leave it in another **ask about drop-off charges or one-way service fees,** which can be substantial. Note, too, that some rental agencies charge extra if you return the car before the time specified in your contract. To avoid a hefty refueling fee **fill the tank just before you turn in the car,** but be aware that gas stations near the rental outlet may overcharge.

CAR TRAVEL

FROM THE U.S.

The main entry point into Canada by car is on I–5 at Blaine, Washington, 30 mi south of Vancouver. Border-crossing procedures are usually quick and simple (☞ Passports & Visas, *below*). The I–5 border crossing at Blaine is open 24 hours. The peak traffic time northbound into Canada is 4 PM. Southbound, delays can be expected evenings and weekend mornings. Try to plan on reaching the border at off-peak times. There are smaller highway border stations at various other points between Washington and British Columbia but they may be closed at night.

WITHIN THE PACIFIC NORTHWEST

Except for a short distance north of Vancouver, there are no roads along the rugged mainland coast of British Columbia and Southeast Alaska.

Alaskan cities such as Juneau have no direct access by road; cars must be brought in by ferry. Skagway and Haines are the only towns in Southeast Alaska accessible directly by road. The trip—a grueling 1,650 mi from Seattle—passes through British Columbia and the Yukon Territory.

AUTO CLUBS

The American Automobile Association (AAA) and the Canadian Automobile Association (CAA) provide full services to members of any of the Commonwealth Motoring Conference (CMC) clubs, including the Automobile Association, the Royal Automobile Club, and the Royal Scottish Automobile Club. Services are also available to members of the Alliance Internationale de l'Automobile (AIT), the Fédération Internationale de l'Automobile (FIA), and the Federation of Interamerican Touring and Automobile Clubs (FITAC). Members receive travel information, itineraries, maps, tour books, information about road and weather conditions, emergency road services, and travel-agency services.

➤ IN AUSTRALIA: **Australian Automobile Association** (☎ 02/6247–7311).

➤ IN CANADA: **Canadian Automobile Association** (CAA, ☎ 613/247–0117).

➤ IN NEW ZEALAND: **New Zealand Automobile Association** (☎ 09/377–4660).

➤ IN THE U.K.: **Automobile Association** (AA, ☎ 0990/500–600). **Royal Automobile Club** (RAC, ☎ 0990/722–722 for membership; 0345/121–345 for insurance).

➤ IN THE U.S.: **American Automobile Association** (AAA, ☎ 800/564–6222).

GASOLINE

Gasoline prices are higher in Washington and Oregon than anywhere else in the U.S: At press time unleaded averaged about $1.55 a gallon. In Alaska, prices are somewhat lower. In Canada gasoline sells for about 55¢ per liter.

ROAD CONDITIONS

Winter driving in the Pacific Northwest can sometimes present some real challenges. In coastal areas the mild, damp climate contributes to roadways that are frequently wet. Winter snowfalls are not common (generally only once or twice a year), but when snow does fall, traffic grinds to a halt and the roadways become treacherous and stay that way until the snow melts.

Tire chains, studs, or snow tires are essential equipment for winter travel in mountain areas. If you're planning to drive into high elevations, be sure to check the weather forecast beforehand. Even the main-highway mountain passes can be forced to close because of snow conditions. During the winter months state and provincial highway departments operate snow advisory telephone lines that give pass conditions.

RULES OF THE ROAD

The speed limit on U.S. interstate highways is generally 65 mph in rural areas and 55 mph in urban zones and on secondary highways. In Canada (where the metric system is used), the speed limit is usually 100 kph (62 mph) on expressways and 80 kph (50 mph) on secondary roads.

CHILDREN IN THE PACIFIC NORTHWEST

There is a wide range of activities for children at destinations in the Pacific Northwest. Seattle, Portland, and Vancouver have zoos and many parks with playgrounds. Indoor ice-skating rinks, ocean beaches, and aquatic centers are other child-friendly options.

If you are renting a car don't forget to **arrange for a car seat** when you reserve.

FLYING

If your children are two or older **ask about children's airfares.** As a general rule, infants under two not occupying a seat fly at greatly reduced fares or even for free.

Experts agree that it's a good idea to use safety seats aloft for children weighing less than 40 pounds. Airlines set their own policies: U.S. carriers usually require that the child be ticketed, even if he or she is young enough to ride free, since the seats must be strapped into regular seats. Do **check your airline's policy about using safety seats during takeoff and landing.** And since safety seats are not allowed just everywhere in the plane, get your seat assignments early.

When reserving, **request children's meals or a freestanding bassinet** if you need them. But note that bulkhead seats, where you must sit to use the bassinet, may lack an overhead bin or storage space on the floor.

LODGING

Most hotels in the Pacific Northwest allow children under a certain age to stay in their parents' room at no extra charge, but others charge for them as extra adults; be sure to **find out the cutoff age for children's discounts.**

SIGHTS & ATTRACTIONS

Places that are especially good for children are indicated by a rubber duckie icon in the margin.

CONSUMER PROTECTION

Whenever shopping or buying travel services in the Pacific Northwest, **pay with a major credit card** so you can cancel payment or get reimbursed if there's a problem. If you're doing business with a particular company for the first time, **contact your local Better Business Bureau and the attorney general's offices** in your state and the company's home state, as well. Have any complaints been filed? Finally, if you're buying a package or tour, always **consider travel insurance** that includes default coverage (☞ Insurance, *below*).

➤ LOCAL BBBs: **Alaska Better Business Bureau** (✉ 2805 Bering St., Suite 2, Anchorage 99503-3819, ☎ 907/562–0704). **British Columbia Better Business Bureaus** (✉ 788 Beatty St., Suite 404, Vancouver V6B 2M1, ☎ 604/682–2711 for mainland British Columbia; ✉ 1005 Langley St., Room 201, Victoria V8W 1V7, ☎ 250/386–6348 for Vancouver Island). **Oregon Better Business Bureau** (✉ 333 S.W. 5th Ave., Suite 300, Portland 97204, ☎ 503/226–3981). **Washington Better Business Bureau** (✉ Box 68926, Sea-Tac 98168-0926, ☎ 206/431–2222). **Council of Better Business Bureaus** (✉ 4200 Wilson Blvd., Suite 800, Arlington, VA 22203, ☎ 703/276–0100, ℻ 703/525–8277).

CRUISE TRAVEL

More than 30 ships, of all sizes, offer cruises to Alaska. You can sail the Inside Passage on a small ship carrying a handful of passengers or cross the Gulf of Alaska in the company of more than 1,000 other people. For the latest information on which cruise lines and ships are sailing to Alaska, see *Fodor's Alaska Ports of Call* or *Fodor's Alaska.*

Cruise ships travel the Inside Passage and Gulf of Alaska from mid-May through late September. The most popular ports of embarkation are Vancouver and Seward (port city for Anchorage), but cruises also leave from San Francisco and Seattle. One of the best ways to see the state is to **combine your cruise with a land tour.**

To get the best deal on a cruise, **consult a cruise-only travel agency.** For a low-priced cruise alternative, **consider traveling by ferry.**

➤ CRUISE LINES: **Cruise Lines International Association** (✉ 500 5th Ave., Suite 1407, New York, NY 10110, ☎ 212/921–0066).

CUSTOMS & DUTIES

When shopping, **keep receipts** for all purchases. Upon reentering the country, **be ready to show customs officials what you've bought.** If you feel a duty is incorrect or object to the way your clearance was handled, note the inspector's badge number and ask to see a supervisor. If the problem isn't resolved, write to the appropriate authorities, beginning with the port director at your point of entry.

IN AUSTRALIA

Australia residents who are 18 or older may bring home $A400 worth of souvenirs and gifts (including jewelry), 250 cigarettes or 250 grams of tobacco, and 1,125 ml of alcohol (including wine, beer, and spirits). Residents under 18 may bring back $A200 worth of goods. Prohibited items include meat products. Seeds, plants, and fruits need to be declared upon arrival.

➤ INFORMATION: **Australian Customs Service** (Regional Director, ✉ Box 8, Sydney, NSW 2001, ☎ 02/9213–2000, FAX 02/9213–4000).

IN CANADA

Canadian residents who have been out of Canada for at least 7 days may bring home C$500 worth of goods duty-free. If you've been away less than 7 days but more than 48 hours, the duty-free allowance drops to C$200; if your trip lasts 24–48 hours, the allowance is C$50. You may not pool allowances with family members. Goods claimed under the C$500 exemption may follow you by mail; those claimed under the lesser exemptions must accompany you. Alcohol and tobacco products may be included in the 7-day and 48-hour exemptions but not in the 24-hour exemption. If you meet the age requirements of the province or territory through which you reenter Canada, you may bring in, duty-free, 1.14 liters (40 imperial ounces) of wine or liquor *or* 24 12-ounce cans or bottles of beer or ale. If you are 16 or older you may bring in, duty-free, 200 cigarettes and 50 cigars. Check ahead of time with Revenue Canada or the Department of Agriculture for policies regarding meat products, seeds, plants, and fruits.

You may send an unlimited number of gifts worth up to C$60 each duty-free to Canada. Label the package UNSOLICITED GIFT—VALUE UNDER $60. Alcohol and tobacco are excluded.

➤ INFORMATION: **Revenue Canada** (✉ 2265 St. Laurent Blvd. S, Ottawa, Ontario K1G 4K3, ☎ 613/993–0534; 800/461–9999 in Canada).

IN NEW ZEALAND

Homeward-bound residents 17 or older may bring back $700 worth of souvenirs and gifts. Your duty-free allowance also includes 4.5 liters of wine or beer; one 1,125-ml bottle of spirits; and either 200 cigarettes, 250 grams of tobacco, 50 cigars, or a combination of the three up to 250 grams. Prohibited items include meat products, seeds, plants, and fruits.

➤ INFORMATION: **New Zealand Customs** (Custom House, ✉ 50 Anzac Ave., Box 29, Auckland, New Zealand, ☎ 09/359–6655, FAX 09/359–6732).

IN THE U.K.

From countries outside the EU, including the United States, you may bring home, duty-free, 200 cigarettes or 50 cigars; 1 liter of spirits or 2 liters of fortified or sparkling wine or liqueurs; 2 liters of still table wine; 60 ml of perfume; 250 ml of toilet water; plus £136 worth of other goods, including gifts and souvenirs. If you're returning from outside the EU, prohibited items include meat products, seeds, plants, and fruits.

➤ INFORMATION: **HM Customs and Excise** (✉ Dorset House, Stamford

St., Bromley Kent BR1 1XX, ☎ 020/
7202–4227).

IN THE U.S.

Non-U.S. residents ages 21 and older
may import into the United States 200
cigarettes or 50 cigars or 2 kilograms
of tobacco, 1 liter of alcohol, and gifts
worth $100. Meat products, seeds,
plants, and fruits are prohibited.

➤ INFORMATION: **U.S. Customs Service**
(inquiries, ✉ 1300 Pennsylvania Ave.
NW, Washington, DC 20229, ☎ 202/
927–6724; complaints, ✉ Office of
Regulations and Rulings, 1300 Pennsylvania Ave. NW, Washington, DC
20229; registration of equipment, ✉
Registration Information, 1300 Pennsylvania Ave. NW, Washington, DC
20229, ☎ 202/927–0540).

DINING

You'll find almost any type of cuisine
in Seattle, Portland, and Vancouver.
Pacific Northwest cuisine, which
features regional seafood and produce,
often prepared in styles that reflect an
Asian influence, is a highlight. Vancouver has a large Chinese community
and many Asian restaurants. The
restaurants we list are the cream of the
crop in each price category.

RESERVATIONS & DRESS

Reservations are always a good idea:
we mention them only when they're
essential or are not accepted. Book as
far ahead as you can, and reconfirm
as soon as you arrive. We mention
dress only when men are required to
wear a jacket or a jacket and tie.

WINE, BEER & SPIRITS

You must be 21 to buy alcohol in
Washington, Oregon, and Alaska.
The legal age to purchase liquor in
British Columbia is 19.

DISABILITIES & ACCESSIBILITY

ACCESS IN THE
PACIFIC NORTHWEST

The **Easter Seal Society** publishes
Access Seattle, a free guide to the
city's services for people with disabilities. **Tourism British Columbia's**
accommodations guide describes the
accessibility of lodging facilities
throughout the province. If you drop
by the **Vancouver Tourist Information**

Centre, you can look in the center's
General Information binder for the
list of area attractions that are wheelchair accessible. **Access Alaska** provides information and referral to
visitors with disabilities. **Challenge
Alaska** provides recreational opportunities for people with disabilities.
Activities include downhill and cross-
country skiing, sea kayaking, canoeing, camping, fishing, swimming,
dogsledding, and backpacking.

➤ LOCAL RESOURCES: **Access Alaska**
(✉ 3710 Woodland Dr., Suite 900,
Anchorage, AK 99517, ☎ 907/248–
4777). **Challenge Alaska** (✉ 1132 E.
74th Ave., No. 107, Anchorage, AK
99518, ☎ 907/344–7399). **Easter
Seal Society** (✉ 521 2nd Ave. W,
Seattle, WA 98119, ☎ 206/281–
5700). **Vancouver Tourist Information Centre** (✉ 200 Burrard St.,
Vancouver, BC Z6C 3L6, ☎ 604/
683–2000).

LODGING

When discussing accessibility with an
operator or reservations agent **ask
hard questions.** Are there any stairs,
inside *or* out? Are there grab bars next
to the toilet *and* in the shower/tub?
How wide is the doorway to the
room? To the bathroom? For the most
extensive facilities meeting the latest
legal specifications **opt for newer
accommodations.**

SIGHTS & ATTRACTIONS

In compliance with the Americans
with Disabilities Act, major attractions and zoos in Oregon, Washington, and Alaska are accessible to
persons with disabilities via wheelchair ramps, elevators, and automatic
doors.

TRANSPORTATION

Portland's Tri-Met buses and MAX
light-rail trains, Seattle's Metro buses,
and Vancouver's BC Transit buses
and SkyTrain rapid-transit trains all
operate accessible public transit
vehicles for persons with physical
disabilities.

➤ COMPLAINTS: **Disability Rights
Section** (✉ U.S. Department of Justice, Civil Rights Division, Box
66738, Washington, DC 20035-6738,
☎ 202/514–0301; 800/514–0301;

202/514–0301 TTY; 800/514–0301 TTY, FAX 202/307–1198) for general complaints. **Aviation Consumer Protection Division** (☞ Air Travel, *above*) for airline-related problems. **Civil Rights Office** (✉ U.S. Department of Transportation, Departmental Office of Civil Rights, S-30, 400 7th St. SW, Room 10215, Washington, DC 20590, ☎ 202/366–4648, FAX 202/366–9371) for problems with surface transportation.

TRAVEL AGENCIES

In the United States, although the Americans with Disabilities Act requires that travel firms serve the needs of all travelers, some agencies specialize in working with people with disabilities.

➤ TRAVELERS WITH MOBILITY PROBLEMS: **Access Adventures** (✉ 206 Chestnut Ridge Rd., Rochester, NY 14624, ☎ 716/889–9096), run by a former physical-rehabilitation counselor. **CareVacations** (✉ 5-5110 50th Ave., Leduc, Alberta T9E 6V4, ☎ 780/986–6404 or 877/478–7827, FAX 780/986–8332) has group tours and is especially helpful with cruise vacations. **Flying Wheels Travel** (✉ 143 W. Bridge St., Box 382, Owatonna, MN 55060, ☎ 507/451–5005 or 800/535–6790, FAX 507/451–1685). **Hinsdale Travel Service** (✉ 201 E. Ogden Ave., Suite 100, Hinsdale, IL 60521, ☎ 630/325–1335, FAX 630/325–1342).

➤ TRAVELERS WITH DEVELOPMENTAL DISABILITIES: **New Directions** (✉ 5276 Hollister Ave., Suite 207, Santa Barbara, CA 93111, ☎ 805/967–2841 or 888/967–2841, FAX 805/964–7344).

ECOTOURISM

The citizens of Washington, Oregon, Alaska, and British Columbia tend to be actively interested in preserving their environment. Protection of marine mammals is of particular concern, and whale-watching is a big business here.

As anywhere, be careful to discard cigarette butts in designated receptacles to help prevent forest fires.

EMERGENCIES

➤ CONTACTS: For **police, ambulance,** or **other emergencies** in Alaska, Oregon, and Washington, dial 911.

For **police, fire** and **ambulance** in Vancouver and Victoria, B.C., dial 911; dial 0 elsewhere in the province.

MEDICAL PLANS

No one plans to get sick while traveling, but it happens, so **consider signing up with a medical-assistance company.** Members get doctor referrals, emergency evacuation or repatriation, hot lines for medical consultation, cash for emergencies, and other assistance.

➤ MEDICAL-ASSISTANCE COMPANIES: **AEA International SOS** (✉ 8 Neshaminy Interplex, Suite 207, Trevose, PA 19053, ☎ 215/245–4707 or 800/523–6586, FAX 215/244–9617; ✉ 12 Chemin Riantbosson, 1217 Meyrin 1, Geneva, Switzerland, ☎ 4122/785–6464, FAX 4122/785–6424; ✉ 331 N. Bridge Rd., 17-00, Odeon Towers, Singapore 188720, ☎ 65/338–7800, FAX 65/338–7611).

GAY & LESBIAN TRAVEL

➤ COMMUNITY RESOURCES: Portland: **Hotline** (☎ 800/777–2437). Seattle: **Greater Seattle Business Association** (☎ 206/363–9188). Vancouver: **Prideline B.C.** (✉ 1170 Bute St., ☎ 604/684–6869); **Vancouver Lesbian Connection** (✉ 876 Commercial Dr., ☎ 604/254–8458).

➤ PUBLICATIONS: Portland: *Just Out* (☎ 503/236–1252). Seattle: *Seattle Gay News* (☎ 206/324–4297).

➤ GAY- AND LESBIAN-FRIENDLY TRAVEL AGENCIES: **Different Roads Travel** (✉ 8383 Wilshire Blvd., Suite 902, Beverly Hills, CA 90211, ☎ 323/651–5557 or 800/429–8747, FAX 323/651–3678). **Kennedy Travel** (✉ 314 Jericho Turnpike, Floral Park, NY 11001, ☎ 516/352–4888 or 800/237–7433, FAX 516/354–8849). **Now Voyager** (✉ 4406 18th St., San Francisco, CA 94114, ☎ 415/626–1169 or 800/255–6951, FAX 415/626–8626). **Skylink Travel and Tour** (✉ 1006 Mendocino Ave., Santa Rosa, CA 95401, ☎ 707/546–9888 or 800/225–5759, FAX 707/546–9891), serving lesbian travelers.

HOLIDAYS

Major national holidays include New Year's Day; Martin Luther King Jr. Day (U.S., 3rd Mon. in Jan.); President's Day (U.S., 3rd Mon. in Feb.); Victoria Day (Canada, 4th Mon. in May); Memorial Day (U.S., last Mon. in May); Canada Day (Canada, July 1); Independence Day (U.S., July 4); Labor Day (1st Mon. in Sept.); Thanksgiving Day (Canada: 2nd Mon. in Oct., U.S.: 4th Thurs. in Nov.); Remembrance Day (Canada, 2nd Thurs. in Nov); Christmas Eve and Christmas Day; Boxing Day (Canada, Dec. 26); and New Year's Eve.

INSURANCE

The most useful travel insurance plan is a comprehensive policy that includes coverage for trip cancellation and interruption, default, trip delay, and medical expenses (with a waiver for preexisting conditions).

Without insurance you will lose all or most of your money if you cancel your trip, regardless of the reason. Default insurance covers you if your tour operator, airline, or cruise line goes out of business. Trip-delay covers expenses that arise because of bad weather or mechanical delays. Study the fine print when comparing policies.

British and Australian citizens need extra medical coverage when traveling overseas. Always **buy travel policies directly from the insurance company**; if you buy it from a cruise line, airline, or tour operator that goes out of business you probably will not be covered for the agency or operator's default, a major risk. Before you make any purchase **review your existing health and home-owner's policies** to find what they cover away from home.

➤ TRAVEL INSURERS: In the U.S. Access America (✉ 6600 W. Broad St., Richmond, VA 23230, ☎ 804/285–3300 or 800/284–8300), **Travel Guard International** (✉ 1145 Clark St., Stevens Point, WI 54481, ☎ 715/345–0505 or 800/826–1300). In Canada **Voyager Insurance** (✉ 44 Peel Center Dr., Brampton, Ontario L6T 4M8, ☎ 905/791–8700; 800/668–4342 in Canada).

➤ INSURANCE INFORMATION: In the U.K. the **Association of British Insurers** (✉ 51–55 Gresham St., London EC2V 7HQ, ☎ 020/7600–3333, FAX 020/7696–8999). In Australia the **Insurance Council of Australia** (☎ 03/9614–1077, FAX 03/9614–7924).

LODGING

The lodgings we list are the cream of the crop in each price category. We always list the facilities that are available—but we don't specify whether they cost extra: When pricing accommodations, always ask what's included and what costs extra.

Assume that hotels operate on the European Plan (EP, with no meals) unless we specify that they use the Continental Plan (CP, with a Continental breakfast daily), Modified American Plan (MAP, with breakfast and dinner daily), or the Full American Plan (FAP, with all meals).

APARTMENT & VILLA RENTALS

If you want a home base that's roomy enough for a family and comes with cooking facilities **consider a furnished rental.** These can save you money, especially if you're traveling with a group. Home-exchange directories sometimes list rentals as well as exchanges.

➤ INTERNATIONAL AGENTS: **Rent-a-Home International** (✉ 7200 34th Ave. NW, Seattle, WA 98117, ☎ 206/789–9377 or 800/964–1891, FAX 206/789–9379). **Hideaways International** (✉ 767 Islington St., Portsmouth, NH 03801, ☎ 603/430–4433 or 800/843–4433, FAX 603/430–4444; membership $99).

➤ LOCAL AGENTS: Portland: **French Home Rentals** (☎ 503/219–9190); Seattle: **Vacation Getaways** (☎ 206/283–5829).

➤ RENTAL LISTINGS: **Web Vacations** (☎ 800/937–4401) handles rentals in Washington, Oregon, Alaska, and British Columbia. You can also search for available rentals on the Internet: www.webvacations.com.

B&BS

The Pacific Northwest is known for its wide range of bed-and-breakfast options in urban areas, in country settings, and along the coast. Most B&B's provide Continental breakfasts, some offer full breakfasts, and some have kitchens that guests can use.

➤ BED&BREAKFAST GUILDS: Regional B&B organizations can provide information on reputable establishments: **Oregon** (☎ 800/944–6196); **Washington** (☎ 800/647–2918); **British Columbia** (☎ 800/239–1141).

➤ RESERVATION SERVICES: **A Northwest Bed & Breakfast Reservation Service** (✉ 610 S.W. Broadway, Portland, OR 97205, ☎ 503/243–7616). **A Traveller's Reservation Service** (✉ 720 Bonnie View Acres Rd., Oak Harbor, WA 98227, ☎ 206/232–2345). **Best Canadian Bed & Breakfast Network** (✉ 1090 W. King Edward Ave., Vancouver, BC V6H 1Z4, ☎ 604/738–7207). Before leaving the United Kingdom, you can book a B&B through **American Bed & Breakfast, Inter-Bed Network** (✉ 31 Ernest Rd., Colchester, Essex CO7 9LQ, ☎ 0206/223162).

CAMPING

Oregon, Washington, Alaska, and British Columbia have excellent government-run campgrounds. A few accept advance camping reservations, but most do not. Privately operated campgrounds sometimes have extra amenities such as laundry rooms and swimming pools. For more information, contact the state or provincial tourism department.

HOME EXCHANGES

If you would like to exchange your home for someone else's **join a home-exchange organization,** which will send you its updated listings of available exchanges for a year and will include your own listing in at least one of them. It's up to you to make specific arrangements.

➤ EXCHANGE CLUBS: **HomeLink International** (✉ Box 650, Key West, FL 33041, ☎ 305/294–7766 or 800/638–3841, ☎ 305/294–1448; $93 per year). **Intervac U.S.** (✉ Box 590504, San Francisco, CA 94159, ☎ 800/756–4663, ☎ 415/435–7440; $83 for catalogs).

HOSTELS

No matter what your age you can **save on lodging costs by staying at hostels.** In some 5,000 locations in more than 70 countries around the world, Hostelling International (HI), the umbrella group for a number of national youth-hostel associations, offers single-sex, dorm-style beds and, at many hostels, couples rooms and family accommodations. Membership in any HI national hostel association, open to travelers of all ages, allows you to stay in HI-affiliated hostels at member rates (one-year membership is about $25 for adults; hostels run about $10–$25 per night). Members also have priority if the hostel is full; they're eligible for discounts around the world, even on rail and bus travel in some countries.

➤ ORGANIZATIONS: **Australian Youth Hostel Association** (✉ 10 Mallett St., Camperdown, NSW 2050, ☎ 02/9565–1699, ☎ 02/9565–1325). **Hostelling International—American Youth Hostels** (✉ 733 15th St. NW, Suite 840, Washington, DC 20005, ☎ 202/783–6161, ☎ 202/783–6171). **Hostelling International—Canada** (✉ 400–205 Catherine St., Ottawa, Ontario K2P 1C3, ☎ 613/237–7884, ☎ 613/237–7868). **Youth Hostel Association of England and Wales** (✉ Trevelyan House, 8 St. Stephen's Hill, St. Albans, Hertfordshire AL1 2DY, ☎ 01727/855215 or 01727/845047, ☎ 01727/844126). **Youth Hostels Association of New Zealand** (✉ Box 436, Christchurch, New Zealand, ☎ 03/379–9970, ☎ 03/365–4476). Membership in the U.S. is $25, in Canada C$26.75, in the U.K. £9.30, in Australia $44, in New Zealand $24.

HOTELS

When booking a room, always **call the hotel's local toll-free number** (if one is available) rather than the central reservations number—you'll often get a better price. Always ask about special packages or corporate rates. Many properties offer special weekend rates, sometimes up to 50% off regular prices. However, these deals are usually not extended during peak summer months, when hotels are normally full. All hotels listed have private bath unless otherwise noted.

➤ TOLL-FREE NUMBERS: **Baymont Inns** (☎ 800/428–3438). **Best Western** (☎ 800/528–1234). **Canadian Pacific**

(☎ 800/441–1414). **Choice** (☎ 800/221–2222). **Clarion** (☎ 800/252–7466). **Colony** (☎ 800/777–1700). **Comfort** (☎ 800/228–5150). **Courtyard by Marriott** (☎ 800/321–2211). **Delta** (☎ 800/877–1133). **Doubletree and Red Lion Hotels** (☎ 800/222–8733). **Embassy Suites** (☎ 800/362–2779). **Fairfield Inn** (☎ 800/228–2800). **Forte** (☎ 800/225–5843). **Four Seasons** (☎ 800/332–3442). **Hilton** (☎ 800/445–8667). **Holiday Inn** (☎ 800/465–4329). **Howard Johnson** (☎ 800/654–4656). **Hyatt Hotels & Resorts** (☎ 800/233–1234). **Inter-Continental** (☎ 800/327–0200). **Le Meridien** (☎ 800/543–4300). **Marriott** (☎ 800/228–9290). **Nikko Hotels International** (☎ 800/645–5687). **Omni** (☎ 800/843–6664). **Radisson** (☎ 800/333–3333). **Ramada** (☎ 800/228–2828). **Renaissance Hotels & Resorts** (☎ 800/468–3571). **Ritz-Carlton** (☎ 800/241–3333). **Sheraton** (☎ 800/325–3535). **Sleep Inn** (☎ 800/221–2222). **Stouffer** (☎ 800/468–3571). **West Coast Hotels/Coast Hotels** (☎ 800/426–0670). **Westin Hotels & Resorts** (☎ 800/228–3000). **Wyndham Hotels & Resorts** (☎ 800/822–4200).

MOTELS/MOTOR INNS

➤ NATIONAL CHAINS: **Best Western** (☎ 800/528–1234), **Days Inn** (☎ 800/329–7466), **La Quinta Inns** (☎ 800/531–5900), **Motel 6** (☎ 800/466–8356), **Quality Inns** (☎ 800/291–8860), **Super 8 Motels** (☎ 800/848–8888), and **Travelodge** (☎ 800/578–7878).

Nendel's (☎ 800/547–0106), **Sandman Inns** (☎ 800/726–3626), and **Shilo Inns** (☎ 800/222–2244) are regional chains.

MAIL & SHIPPING

At press time, it cost 33¢ to mail a standard letter anywhere within the United States, 20¢ for a standard-size postcard. Mail to Canada costs 40¢ per first ounce, and 23¢ for each additional ounce; mail to Great Britain and other foreign countries costs 50¢ per half ounce.

First-class rates in Canada are 46¢ for up to 30 grams of mail delivered within Canada, 52¢ for up to 30 grams delivered to the United States, 70¢ for 30 to 50 grams. International mail and postcards run 92¢ for up to 20 grams, $1.26 for 20–50 grams.

RECEIVING MAIL

Visitors can have letters or parcels sent to them while they are traveling by using the following address: Name of addressee, c/o General Delivery, Main Post Office, City and State/Province, U.S./Canada, Zip Code (U.S.) or Postal Code (Canada). Contact the nearest post office for further details. Any item mailed to "General Delivery" must be picked up by the addressee in person within 15 days or it will be returned to the sender.

MONEY MATTERS

Prices for meals and accommodations in the Pacific Northwest are generally lower than in other major North American regions. Prices for first-class hotel rooms in major cities (Seattle, Portland, Vancouver, and Victoria) range from $100 to $200 a night, although you can still find some "value" hotel rooms for $65 to $90 a night.

As a rule, costs outside the major cities are lower, but prices for rooms and meals at some of the major deluxe resorts can rival or exceed those at the best big-city hotels. In Alaska, food costs are higher because the state has to import virtually all of its produce, as well as its manufactured goods, from the "lower" 48 states.

Prices in Canada are always quoted in Canadian dollars. When you are comparing prices with those in the United States, costs should be calculated via the current rate of exchange. At press time (fall 1999) the exchange rate was US$1 to C$1.48 and C$1 to US$.68, but this exchange rate can vary considerably. Check with a bank or other financial institution for the current rate. A good way to be sure you're getting the best exchange rate is by using your credit card. The issuing bank will convert your bill at the current rate. Prices throughout this guide are given for adults. Substantially reduced fees are almost always available for children, students, and senior citizens. For information on taxes, *see* Taxes, *below*.

SMART TRAVEL TIPS

ATMS

➤ ATM LOCATIONS: **Cirrus** (☎ 800/424–7787). **Plus** (☎ 800/843–7587).

CREDIT CARDS

Throughout this guide, the following abbreviations are used: **AE**, American Express; **D**, Discover; **DC**, Diners Club; **MC**, MasterCard; and **V**, Visa.

➤ REPORTING LOST CARDS: To report a stolen or lost credit card contact **American Express** (☎ 800/300–8765); **Diner's Club** (☎ 800/234–6377); **Discover** (☎ 800/347–2683); **MasterCard** (☎ 800/826–2181); **Visa** (☎ 800/336–8472).

CURRENCY

The United States and Canada both use the same currency denominations—dollars and cents—although each currency has a different value on the world market. In the United States, the most common paper currency comes in $1, $5, $10, and $20 bills. Common notes in Canada include the $2, $5, $10, and $20 bills. (Canada replaced its $1 bill with a $1 gold-colored coin nicknamed the "loonie" by Canadians because it contains a picture of a loon on one side.) Coins in both countries come in denominations of 1¢ (penny), 5¢ (nickel), 10¢ (dime), 25¢ (quarter), and 50¢ (half-dollar).

NATIONAL PARKS

Look into discount passes to save money on park entrance fees. The Golden Eagle Pass ($50) gets you and your companions free admission to all parks for one year. (Camping and parking are extra.) Both the Golden Age Passport ($10), for those 62 and older, and the Golden Access Passport (free), for travelers with disabilities, entitle holders to free entry to all national parks, plus 50% off fees for the use of many park facilities and services. You must show proof of age and of U.S. citizenship or permanent residency (such as a U.S. passport, driver's license, or birth certificate) and, if requesting Golden Access, proof of disability. All three passes are available at all national park entrances where entrance fees are charged. Golden Eagle Passes are also available by mail.

Canada's national park system does not offer vacation passes, only annual passes. For $35, the Great Western Pass grants one adult a year's admission to the Canadian national parks.

➤ PARK INFORMATION: **National Park Service** (✉ National Capitol Area Office, 1100 Ohio Dr. SW, Washington, DC 20242, ☎ 202/208–4747). **Parks Canada** (✉ 25 Eddy St., Hull, Quebec K1A 0M5, ☎ 888/773–8888, operator 999).

OUTDOORS & SPORTS

BICYCLING

➤ ASSOCIATIONS: **Portland Wheelmen Touring Club** (☎ 503/257–7982) and **Cascade Bicycle Club** (Seattle; ☎ 206/522–3222).

CLIMBING/MOUNTAINEERING

➤ INFORMATION: **Mazama Club** (Portland; ☎ 503/227–2345). **The Mountaineers** (Seattle; ☎ 800/553–4453). **Alpine Club of Canada** (✉ Box 2040, Canmore, Alberta T0L 0M0, ☎ 403/678–3200).

FISHING

➤ INFORMATION/LICENSES: **Oregon Department of Fish and Wildlife** (✉ Box 59, Portland, OR 97207, ☎ 503/229–5551). **Washington Department of Fish and Wildlife** (✉ 600 Capitol Way, Olympia, WA 98501–0091, ☎ 206/753–5700). **Alaska Department of Fish and Game** (✉ Box 25526, Juneau, AK 99802, ☎ 907/465–4180). For saltwater fishing: **Department of Fisheries and Oceans** (✉ 555 W. Hastings St., Suite 400, Vancouver, BC V6B 5G3, ☎ 604/666–0384). For freshwater fishing: **Ministry of Environment, Fish and Wildlife Information** (✉ Parliament Bldgs., Victoria, BC V8V 1X5, ☎ 604/387–9740).

HIKING

➤ INFORMATION: **Washington Trails Association** (✉ 1305 4th Ave., Suite 512, Seattle, WA 98101, ☎ 206/625–1367). **American Long Distance Hikers Association–West** (✉ Box 651, Vancouver, WA 98666, ☎ no phone).

SKIING

➤ PASSES & INFORMATION: **Oregon Department of Transportation** (☎ 800/977–6368 for information and Sno-Park permits). **Office of Winter**

Recreation, Parks and Recreation Commission (✉ 7150 Cleanwater La., Olympia, WA 98504, ☎ 360/902–8500 for information and Sno-Park permits). **Canada West Ski Areas Association** (✉ 3313 32nd Ave., Suite 103, Vernon V1T 2M8, ☎ 250/542–9020). **Alaska Parks and Recreation Department** (☎ 907/586–5226 for information).

PACKING

Residents of the Pacific Northwest are generally informal by nature and wear clothing that reflects their disposition. Summer days are warm but evenings can cool off substantially. Your best bet is to **dress in layers**—sweatshirts, sweaters, and jackets are removed or put on as the day progresses. If you plan to explore the region's cities on foot, or if you choose to hike along mountain trails or beaches, take comfortable walking shoes. Locals tend to dress conservatively when going to the theater or symphony, but it's not uncommon to see some patrons wearing jeans. In other words, almost anything is acceptable for most occasions.

If you're heading for Alaska, **take a collapsible umbrella or a rain slicker.** Passengers aboard Alaska-bound cruise ships should check with their travel agents about the dress code on board. Some vessels expect formal attire for dinner, while others do not. In all cases, you will need a waterproof coat and warm clothes if you plan to spend time on deck.

If you plan on hiking or camping during the summer, insect repellent is a must.

In your carry-on luggage **bring an extra pair of eyeglasses or contact lenses** and **enough of any medication you take** to last the entire trip. You may also want your doctor to write a spare prescription using the drug's generic name, since brand names may vary from country to country. In luggage to be checked, **never pack prescription drugs or valuables.** To avoid customs delays, carry medications in their original packaging. And don't forget to copy down and carry addresses of offices that handle refunds of lost traveler's checks.

CHECKING LUGGAGE

How many carry-on bags you can bring with you is up to the airline. Most allow two, but not always, so make sure that everything you carry aboard will fit under your seat, and get to the gate early. Note that if you have a seat at the back of the plane, you'll probably board first, while the overhead bins are still empty.

If you are flying internationally, note that baggage allowances may be determined not by piece but by weight—generally 88 pounds (40 kilograms) in first class, 66 pounds (30 kilograms) in business class, and 44 pounds (20 kilograms) in economy.

Airline liability for baggage is limited to $1,250 per person on flights within the United States. On international flights it amounts to $9.07 per pound or $20 per kilogram for checked baggage (roughly $640 per 70-pound bag) and $400 per passenger for unchecked baggage. You can buy additional coverage at check-in for about $10 per $1,000 of coverage, but it excludes a rather extensive list of items, shown on your airline ticket.

Before departure **itemize your bags' contents** and their worth, and label the bags with your name, address, and phone number. (If you use your home address, cover it so that potential thieves can't see it readily.) Inside each bag **pack a copy of your itinerary.** At check-in **make sure that each bag is correctly tagged** with the destination airport's three-letter code. If your bags arrive damaged or fail to arrive at all, file a written report with the airline before leaving the airport.

PASSPORTS & VISAS

U.S. & CANADIAN CITIZENS

Canadian and U.S. citizens do not need a passport to travel between the United States and Canada.

➤ U.K. CITIZENS: **U.S. Embassy Visa Information Line** (☎ 01891/200–290; calls cost 49p per minute, 39p per minute cheap rate) for U.S. visa information. **U.S. Embassy Visa Branch** (✉ 5 Upper Grosvenor Sq., London W1A 1AE) for U.S. visa information; send a self-addressed, stamped envelope.

SMART TRAVEL TIPS

SMART TRAVEL TIPS

Write the **U.S. Consulate General** (⊠ Queen's House, Queen St., Belfast BTI 6EO) if you live in Northern Ireland. Write the **Office of Australia Affairs** (⊠ 59th floor, MLC Centre, 19-29 Martin Pl., Sydney NSW 2000) if you live in Australia. Write the **Office of New Zealand Affairs** (⊠ 29 Fitzherbert Terr., Thorndon, Wellington) if you live in New Zealand.

PASSPORT OFFICES

The best time to apply for a passport or to renew is during the fall and winter. Before any trip, check your passport's expiration date, and, if necessary, renew it as soon as possible.

➤ AUSTRALIAN CITIZENS: **Australian Passport Office** (☎ 131–232).

➤ NEW ZEALAND CITIZENS: **New Zealand Passport Office** (☎ 04/494–0700 for information on how to apply; 04/474–8000 or 0800/225–050 in New Zealand for information on applications already submitted).

➤ U.K. CITIZENS: **London Passport Office** (☎ 0990/210–410) for fees and documentation requirements and to request an emergency passport.

SENIOR-CITIZEN TRAVEL

To qualify for age-related discounts **mention your senior-citizen status up front** when booking hotel reservations (not when checking out) and before you're seated in restaurants (not when paying the bill). When renting a car ask about promotional car-rental discounts, which can be cheaper than senior-citizen rates.

➤ EDUCATIONAL PROGRAMS: **Elderhostel** (⊠ 75 Federal St., 3rd floor, Boston, MA 02110, ☎ 877/426–8056, FAX 877/426–2166).

STUDENTS IN THE PACIFIC NORTHWEST

➤ STUDENT IDs & SERVICES: **Council on International Educational Exchange** (CIEE, ⊠ 205 E. 42nd St., 14th floor, New York, NY 10017, ☎ 212/822–2600 or 888/268–6245, FAX 212/822–2699) for mail orders only, in the United States **Travel Cuts** (⊠ 187 College St., Toronto, Ontario M5T 1P7, ☎ 416/979–2406 or 800/667–2887) in Canada.

TAXES

SALES TAX

Sales tax varies among areas. Oregon and Alaska have no sales tax, although most cities levy a tax on hotel rooms. Portland, for example, has a 9% room tax. The sales tax in Washington is 7%–8.2%, depending on the municipality. Seattle adds 5% to the rate for hotel rooms. Canada's 7% Goods & Services Tax (GST) is added to hotel bills but will be rebated to foreign visitors. In British Columbia, consumers pay an 8%–10% provincial and municipal tax. The percentage varies from one municipality to another.

GST

Canada's Goods and Services Tax (GST) is 7%, applicable on virtually every purchase except basic groceries and a small number of other items. Visitors to Canada may claim a full rebate of the GST on any goods taken out of the country as well as on short-term accommodations. Rebates can be claimed either immediately on departure from Canada at participating duty-free shops or by mail. Rebate forms can be obtained at most stores and hotels in Canada or by writing to Revenue Canada (⊠ Visitor's Rebate Program, Ottawa, Ontario K1A 1J5, ☎ 902/432–5608; 800/668–4748 in Canada). Claims must be for a minimum of $7 worth of tax and can be submitted up to a year from the date of purchase. Purchases made during multiple visits to Canada can be grouped together for rebate purposes.

TELEPHONES

The area code for Portland and surrounding areas is 503; current plans call for the addition of a new area code (971) in Portland in October 2001. Area code 541 is used in the rest of Oregon. The metropolitan Seattle area code is 206; 253, 425, and 360 are used in the rest of western Washington, and 509 is used for eastern Washington. Area codes for British Columbia are 604 and 250. Alaska uses 907, except for the town of Hyder in Southeast Alaska, which uses the 604 area code.

Pay telephone calls generally cost 35¢ for local calls. Charge phones are also found in many locations. These phones can be used to charge a call to a telephone-company credit card, your home phone, or the party you are calling: You do not need to deposit coins. For directory assistance, dial 1, the area code, and 555–1212. For local directory assistance, dial 1 followed by 555–1212. You can dial most international calls directly. Dial 0 to reach an operator.

Many hotels place a surcharge on local calls made from your room and include a service charge on long-distance calls. It may be cheaper for you to make your calls from a pay phone in the hotel lobby rather than from your room.

TIME

Washington, Oregon, and British Columbia are in the Pacific time zone. Alaska is in the Alaska time zone, which is one hour behind the Pacific zone. All observe Daylight Saving Time from early April to late October.

TIPPING

Tips and service charges are usually not automatically added to a bill in the United States or Canada. If service is satisfactory, customers generally give waiters, waitresses, taxi drivers, barbers, hairdressers, and so forth a tip of 15%–20% of the total bill. Bellhops, doormen, and porters at airports and railway stations are generally tipped $1 for each item of luggage.

TOURS & PACKAGES

On a prepackaged tour or independent vacation everything is prearranged so you'll spend less time planning—and often get it all at a good price.

BOOKING WITH AN AGENT

Travel agents are excellent resources. But it's a good idea to collect brochures from several agencies because some agents' suggestions may be influenced by relationships with tour and package firms that reward them for volume sales. If you have a special interest **find an agent with expertise in that area**; ASTA (☞ Travel Agencies, *below*) has a database of specialists worldwide.

Make sure your travel agent knows the accommodations and other services of the place he or she is recommending. Ask about the hotel's location, room size, beds, and the availability of a pool, room service, or programs for children, if you care about these. Has your agent been there in person or sent others whom you can contact?

Do some homework on your own, too: Local tourism boards can provide information about lesser-known and small-niche operators, some of which may sell only direct.

BUYER BEWARE

Each year consumers are stranded or lose their money when tour operators—even large ones with excellent reputations—go out of business. So **check out the operator.** Ask several travel agents about its reputation, and try to **book with a company that has a consumer-protection program.** (Look for information in the company's brochure.) In the United States, members of the National Tour Association and United States Tour Operators Association are required to set aside funds to cover your payments and travel arrangements in case the company defaults. It's also a good idea to choose a company that participates in the American Society of Travel Agent's Tour Operator Program (TOP); ASTA will act as mediator in any disputes between you and your tour operator.

Remember that the more your package or tour includes the better you can predict the ultimate cost of your vacation. Make sure you know exactly what is covered, and **beware of hidden costs.** Are taxes, tips, and transfers included? Entertainment and excursions? These can add up.

➤ TOUR-OPERATOR RECOMMENDATIONS: **American Society of Travel Agents** (☞ Travel Agencies, *below*). **National Tour Association** (NTA, ⌧ 546 E. Main St., Lexington, KY 40508, ☏ 606/226–4444 or 800/682–8886). **United States Tour Operators Association** (USTOA, ⌧ 342 Madison Ave., Suite 1522, New York, NY 10173, ☏ 212/599–6599 or 800/468–7862, FAX 212/599–6744).

SMART TRAVEL TIPS

TRAIN TRAVEL

Amtrak, the U.S. passenger rail system, has daily service to the Pacific Northwest from the Midwest and California. The *Empire Builder* takes a northern route from Chicago to Spokane, whence separate legs continue to Seattle and Portland. The *Coast Starlight* begins in Los Angeles, makes stops throughout western Oregon and Washington, and terminates in Seattle.

Canada's passenger service, **VIA Rail Canada,** operates transcontinental routes on the *Canadian* three times weekly between eastern Canada and Vancouver. A second train, the *Skeena,* runs three times weekly between Jasper, Alberta, to the British Columbia port city of Prince Rupert.

WITHIN THE PACIFIC NORTHWEST

Amtrak's *Cascades* trains travel between Seattle and Vancouver, and between Seattle, Portland, and Eugene. The **Great Canadian Railtour Co., Ltd.,** operates the *Rocky Mountaineer,* a two-day rail cruise between Vancouver and the Canadian Rockies that runs from May to October. There are two routes—one to Banff/Calgary and the other to Jasper—through landscapes considered to be the most spectacular in the world. An overnight hotel stop is made in Kamloops.

On Vancouver Island, **VIA Rail** runs the *E&N Railway* daily from Victoria north to Courtenay. **B.C. Rail** operates daily service from its North Vancouver terminal to the town of Prince George. At Prince George, it is possible to connect with VIA Rail's *Skeena* service east to Jasper and Alberta or west to Prince Rupert.

The Seattle-based **American Orient Express Railway Company** operates several trips in the Northwest aboard its luxury cars, including one that travels from Portland through Washington and into Idaho before terminating at Glacier Mountain National Park.

➤ RAILWAY COMPANIES: **American Orient Express Railway Company** (☎ 888/759–3944). **Amtrak** (☎ 800/ 872–7245). **B.C. Rail** (☎ 604/631– 3500 or 800/663–8238). **Great Canadian Railtour Co., Ltd.** (☎ 800/665– 7245). **VIA Rail Canada** (☎ 604/ 383–4324 or 800/561–3949).

RAIL PASSES

VIA Rail Canada (☞ *above*) offers a Canrailpass that is good for 30 days. System-wide passes cost $379 (good from January to May and mid-October to December) and $589 (good from June to mid-October). Youth passes (age 24 and under) are $529 in peak season and $345 during the off-season. Prices are quoted in Canadian dollars. Tickets can be purchased in the United States or the United Kingdom from a travel agent, from **Long Haul Leisurail** (✉ Box 113, Peterborough PE1 1LE, ☎ 0733/51780), or upon arrival in Canada. This offer does not apply to Canadian citizens.

TRAVEL AGENCIES

A good travel agent puts your needs first. Look for an agency that has been in business at least five years, emphasizes customer service, and has someone on staff who specializes in your destination. In addition **make sure the agency belongs to a professional trade organization.** The American Society of Travel Agents (ASTA), with 27,000 agents in some 170 countries, is the largest and most influential in the field. Operating under the motto "Integrity in Travel," it maintains and enforces a strict code of ethics and will step in to help mediate any agent-client disputes if necessary. ASTA also maintains a Web site that includes a directory of agents. Note that if a travel agency is also acting as your tour operator, *see* Buyer Beware *in* Tours & Packages, *above*.

➤ LOCAL AGENT REFERRALS: **American Society of Travel Agents** (ASTA, ☎ 800/965–2782 24-hr hot line, FAX 703/ 684–8319, www.astanet.com). **Association of British Travel Agents** (✉ 68– 271 Newman St., London W1P 4AH, ☎ 020/7637–2444, FAX 020/7637– 0713). **Association of Canadian Travel Agents** (✉ 1729 Bank St., Suite 201, Ottawa, Ontario K1V 7Z5, ☎ 613/521–0474, FAX 613/521–0805). **Australian Federation of Travel Agents** (✉ Level 3, 309 Pitt St., Sydney 2000, ☎ 02/9264–3299, FAX 02/ 9264–1085). **Travel Agents' Association of New Zealand** (✉ Box 1888,

Wellington 10033, ☎ 04/499–0104, FAX 04/499–0786).

VISITOR INFORMATION

➤ ALASKA: **Alaska Division of Tourism** (⊠ Box 110801, Juneau 99811-0801, ☎ 907/465–2010 or 800/762–5275).

➤ BRITISH COLUMBIA: **Tourism British Columbia** (⊠ Parliament Building, Victoria, BC V8V 1X4, ☎ 800/663–6000). **Vancouver Tourist Info Centre** (⊠ 200 Broward St., Vancouver, BC Z6C 3L6, ☎ 604/683–2000).

➤ OREGON: **Portland/Oregon Visitors Association** (⊠ 28 World Trade Center, 26 S.W. Salmon St., 97204, ☎ 503/222–2223 or 800/962–3700).

➤ WASHINGTON: **Visitors Information Center** (⊠ Washington State Convention Center, 800 Convention Pl., Seattle, WA 98104, ☎ 206/461–5840). **Washington State Tourism** (⊠ 101 General Administration Bldg., Olympia 98504, ☎ 800/544–1800).

WEB SITES

Do **check out the World Wide Web** when you're planning. You'll find everything from up-to-date weather forecasts to virtual tours of famous cities. Fodor's Web site, www.fodors.com, is a great place to start your on-line travels. For more information specifically on the Pacific Northwest, visit **Alaska** at www.commerce.state.ak.us/tourism; **British Columbia** at travel.bc.ca; **Washington** at www.tourism.wa.gov; and **Oregon** at www.traveloregon.com.

WHEN TO GO

The Pacific Northwest's mild climate is best from June through September.

Hotels in the major tourist destinations are often filled in July and August, so it's important to book reservations in advance. Spring and fall are also excellent times to visit. The weather usually remains quite good, and the prices for accommodations, transportation, and tours can be lower (and the crowds much smaller!) in the most popular destinations. In winter, snow is uncommon in the lowland areas but abundant in the nearby mountains, making the region a skier's dream.

CLIMATE

Average daytime summer highs are in the 70s; winter temperatures are generally in the 40s. Rainfall varies greatly from one locale to another. In the coastal mountains, for example, 160 inches of rain falls annually, creating temperate rain forests. In eastern Oregon, Washington, and British Columbia, near-desert conditions prevail, with rainfall as low as 6 inches per year. Seattle has an average of only 36 inches of rainfall a year—less than New York, Chicago, or Miami. Throughout the Pacific Northwest, however, most rain falls during the winter months, when cloudy skies and drizzly weather persist. More than 75% of Seattle's annual precipitation occurs from October through March.

➤ FORECASTS: **Weather Channel Connection** (☎ 900/932–8437), 95¢ per minute from a Touch-Tone phone.

The following are average daily maximum and minimum temperatures for major cities in the Pacific Northwest region.

Climate in the Pacific Northwest

PORTLAND

Jan.	44F	7C	May	67F	19C	Sept.	74F	23C
	33	1		46	8		51	10
Feb.	50F	10C	June	72F	22C	Oct.	63F	17C
	36	2		52	11		45	7
Mar.	54F	12C	July	79F	26C	Nov.	52F	11C
	37	3		55	13		39	4
Apr.	60F	15C	Aug.	78F	25C	Dec.	46F	8C
	41	5		55	13		35	2

SMART TRAVEL TIPS

SEATTLE

Jan.	45F	7C	May	66F	19C	Sept.	69F	20C
	35	2		47	8		52	11
Feb.	50F	10C	June	70F	21C	Oct.	62F	16C
	37	3		52	11		47	8
Mar.	53F	12C	July	76F	24C	Nov.	51F	10C
	38	3		56	13		40	4
Apr.	59F	13C	Aug.	75F	24C	Dec.	47F	8C
	42	5		55	13		37	3

VANCOUVER

Jan.	41F	5C	May	63F	17C	Sept.	64F	18C
	32	0		46	8		50	10
Feb.	46F	8C	June	66F	19C	Oct.	57F	14C
	34	1		52	11		43	6
Mar.	48F	9C	July	72F	22C	Nov.	48F	9C
	36	2		55	13		37	3
Apr.	55F	13C	Aug.	72F	22C	Dec.	45F	7C
	41	5		55	13		34	1

JUNEAU

Jan.	29F	−2C	May	55F	13C	Sept.	56F	13C
	18	−8		38	3		42	6
Feb.	34F	1C	June	62F	16C	Oct.	47F	8C
	22	−6		44	7		36	2
Mar.	38F	3C	July	64F	18C	Nov.	37F	3C
	26	−4		48	9		28	−2
Apr.	47F	8C	Aug.	62F	17C	Dec.	32F	0C
	31	−1		46	8		23	−5

1 DESTINATION: PACIFIC NORTHWEST

THE LAY OF THE LAND

IGH IN THE Oregon Cascades near a small, isolated lake, the peaks, wrapped in an autumn snow, are blurred by the dusk. As the sun sinks in the west, darkness falls over the dense forest. A wispy fog from the upper basin slips over the lake; the tall firs creak in the wind and to the east, barely visible, three rugged peaks shrug in the distance. Farther away hundreds of tiny lakes like this one await, all empty and quiet in their own seldom explored basins.

Up here you feel yourself connect with nature; you meld with it. Things of the world, below the meadows, canyons, and forests, simply do not exist. The sensation of being alone with nature, of being in the very cup of her hands, is familiar to those who live in the Pacific Northwest. There are certainly more remote areas, but here people seem to have found their niche in the ecosystem and, more or less, are as pleased with their failure to conquer nature as they are with their occasional, temporary successes.

To understand the people of the Pacific Northwest—there are roughly 13 million in an area about the size of Western Europe—one has to understand the land and the climate and how the two combine to cast their spell. For even in the cities of the Pacific Northwest, nature is never far away. In Seattle, Mount Rainier and the Olympic Mountains enchant commuters stuck in traffic; in Vancouver, British Columbia, the Coast Range juts out over downtown, keeping the metropolis in line; and in Portland, 5,000 acres of forestland in the hills north of the city center harbor deer, elk, and the odd bear and cougar. It's not a zoo, it's just there, a piece of almost primeval forest. No matter how many planes Seattle's Boeing Company churns out, or how many chips come out of Oregon's high-tech Silicon Forest, or how many shares of stock change hands in the volatile Vancouver Stock Exchange, the relationship with nature and the wilds is not altered. There is always this mixture of respect and

love, fear and admiration, topped off with simple awe.

These feelings come naturally when you survey the landscape, but still there are the simultaneous sensations of solitude and inclusion. To understand, look at the far corners of this land: southern Alaska and southeastern Oregon.

Swathed in sitka spruce, the islands scattered below the Alaskan mountains are like small worlds. Roads and people are few. The intrepid can kayak through the inlets and fjords for days on end, catching salmon or watching the glaciers peel majestically off into the sea, sheet by sheet. Roughly in the middle of this region is Juneau, the only state capital that is inaccessible by road. Here it is common for legislative aides to live in makeshift camps in the hills above town and to ski to the state's modest capitol building. Behind the coast ranges are deep, remote river canyons and lakes that stretch all the way east to where the mighty Rockies dribble off into a few bumps on the tundra. As you move south along coastal British Columbia, the terrain is no less steep, but the glaciers shrink back into the hanging valleys, leaving only a few waterfalls. Other than fishing vessels and the occasional cruise ship, this is lonely country, beautiful, but often pelted with wild rain storms and blizzards that blast straight across the north Pacific.

Likewise, southeastern Oregon is solitary country. It is a land of extremes, a high desert where it is not at all uncommon, especially in the spring or fall, to find the highest and lowest temperature reading in the lower 48 states in the same county. A 100-mi drive across the desert and scrubland is not likely to turn up another soul. What people there are here—many of them descendants of Basque settlers who arrived a century ago—tend to their stock on the arid plains. The land is dominated by Steens Mountain, a 60-mi-long slab of desert floor that through the millennia gradually tilted upward. From the west, the gain in elevation is barely noticeable at first, just a steppe rolling into the distance. But after 30 mi of bad road, the mountain simply breaks off into space, the Alvord Desert a gasping 5,000 ft below. And beyond, the gray horizon fades into Nevada and Idaho.

Whether it is the cathedral-like island forests of southern Alaska or the sagebrush-covered frontier of southeastern Oregon, the awe is there in the Pacific Northwest—subtle yet omnipresent. In many ways, the land here shapes people, mellowing and hypnotizing them until other ways of life seem improbably complicated.

RECREATIONAL CHOICES abound in the Pacific Northwest. Raft a river. Hike to the top of a butte you've never climbed before. Or bicycle a road in the baking deserts of eastern Oregon or Washington to see the mirages disappear as you approach them. However you choose to enjoy the landscape, you'll be in good company with the locals, who often seem more interested in day tripping than in day trading.

Pacific Northwesterners may come across a bit flaky—carefree, perhaps—but some say this contagious attitude simply comes with the land. The Native Americans of the Pacific Northwest had it pretty easy compared with their cousins on the Great Plains. Whereas a family of Sioux may have needed to scour 100 square mi of land to find enough food to live on, West Coast Indians only needed to dip into the river for fish or take a few steps out of the village for game. Sure, the weather was damp, but wood for shelter and warmth was plentiful, and the time not spent gathering food went toward monumental projects of art, such as the totems of Coastal British Columbia.

In the Pacific Northwest, being rich is defined as living a clean life; nature deals the bonuses. People here have the opportunity to hike, fish, hunt, or just wake up every morning with a view of a forest. Some might call this simple living; others just call it wacky. Some examples: Portland twice elected as mayor a local tavern owner who bikes around the city in lederhosen and calls out "Whoop, whoop" at the drop of a photo opportunity. And a few years ago there was a strong effort (serious does not seem to be the right word)

to make the rock-and-roll classic "Louie, Louie" the state song of Washington.

Is there some sort of pattern here? Is it that the dampness warps great and creative minds? When the explorers Lewis and Clark arrived almost 200 years ago, the rain almost drove them crazy, and that was after only one winter! Imagine a lifetime of gray winters; you look out of your window in November at a line of dark clouds rolling in from the west and know there will be only a handful of clear days (probably below freezing) until April. Northwest author Ken Kesey has blamed everything from impotence to union problems on this drizzly season. True, residents of the Pacific Northwest drink more and are more likely to commit suicide than many other Americans, but perhaps the weather also helps them maintain a sense of the absurd. In Portland's Oregon Convention Center, for instance, the men's rooms have etchings of Oregon waterfalls perched above the urinals.

So people here are a little eccentric. But remember, when an impulse sends you ripping down an untracked ski run or landing a thrashing steelhead in a river at flood stage, the humdrum details of daily life become pretty ridiculous. When dental appointments and traffic jams seem like some sort of cosmic joke, you're freed of so much. You can fade back from the human fray to a peaceful place, to your personal lake beneath the peaks, and watch dusk fall.

— By Tom Gaunt

NEW AND NOTEWORTHY

Traffic, previously not a problem in Portland, has increased significantly due to a building boom, prompting the extension of the city's **MAX light-rail** system to Hillsboro; an extension to the Portland airport is under construction. The city is also bringing back **streetcars:** In 2001 a new line will connect Nob Hill, downtown, and Portland State University.

Commuter rail service between Seattle and Tacoma began in 1999 and service to Everett is to begin in 2000. Another transit project, the **Link light-rail system,** will use surface streets, elevated tracks, and tunnels to connect the University District, Capitol Hill, downtown Seattle, Tukwila, and Sea-Tac Airport. It is projected to be complete by 2004. Vancouver has also announced plans to expand its **SkyTrain** rapid transit system.

New daily Amtrak service links Vancouver and Seattle. A ride on the European-built **Cascades train,** which follows the coast most of the way, is a truly glorious way to take in the region's scenery. The *Cascades* also travels between Seattle, Portland, and Eugene on tracks that have been overhauled to allow higher-speed travel.

The Seattle Mariners baseball team moved from the Kingdome in 1999 into the state-of-the-art **Safeco Field,** and the Seattle Seahawks football team will move into a new stadium in the new century. The **Experience Music Project,** to open near the Space Needle in 2000, will serve as a museum, school, and library that will present live performances. It will also house artifacts of well-known Seattle area musicians, including Jimi Hendrix and Pearl Jam. Pike Place Market now has a **Heritage Center** devoted to the history and people that have made the market a city landmark. In Alaska, Juneau's **Mount Roberts Tram** complex has expanded to include an observatory, a theater, a cultural center, shops, and a restaurant.

WHAT'S WHERE

Oregon

Although the climate and landscape of Oregon vary dramatically from place to place, much of the state enjoys a constant level of natural splendor. The Pacific coast is a wild and rocky 300-mi stretch dotted with small towns. In the north are the Columbia River Gorge and Mount Hood, dramatic examples of the power of earth and water. On the gentler side, the Willamette Valley is a lush wine-producing region and home to Eugene and other laid-back cities. Oregon's largest city, Portland, in the northwest part of the state, is among the nation's most livable—not surprising given its unspoiled setting and host of urban amenities.

Washington

From the islands that dot Puget Sound to the peak of Mount Rainier to the Yakima Valley's vineyards, Washington presents hundreds of opportunities to appreciate the great outdoors. Watch whales from coastal lighthouses, dine on fresh seafood in waterside towns, tramp through dripping rain forests, hike high mountains—or head straight to Seattle, the Pacific Northwest's hippest city, where the green hills and bay views are best appreciated from a coffee bar and the music and art scenes change as frequently as the tides.

British Columbia

Canada's westernmost province contains Pacific beaches, forested islands, year-round skiing, and world-class fishing—a wealth of outdoor action and beauty. Its towns and cities, from Anglophile Victoria to the placid Gulf Islands, reflect the diversity of its inhabitants. Cosmopolitan Vancouver, with its many modern skyscrapers, enjoys a spectacular setting. Tall fir trees stand practically downtown, rock spires tower close by, the ocean is at your doorstep, and residents who have come from every corner of the earth create a young and vibrant atmosphere.

Southeast Alaska

The glacier-filled fjords of the Inside Passage are Southeast Alaska's most famous attraction; what a century ago was the route to the Klondike goldfields is today the centerpiece of many Alaskan cruises. Juneau, the state's capital, is also in the Southeast, as are a number of interesting small towns. Petersburg and Ketchikan (which is also known for its totem-pole carving) are traditional fishing villages; an onion-dome cathedral accents Sitka, the capital of Russian America; and each fall up to 4,000 eagles gather outside Haines.

PLEASURES AND PASTIMES

Beaches

The coasts of Oregon, Washington, and British Columbia have long, sandy beaches that run for miles at a stretch. But the waters are generally too cold or treacherous for swimming. Even in summertime, beach-goers must be prepared to dress warmly. The most accessible ocean beaches in the Pacific Northwest are in Oregon. Those in Washington and on western Vancouver Island are more remote; even in summer the beaches are never crowded. The gravel shores of Washington's Puget Sound and British Columbia's Inside Passage attract few swimmers or sunbathers but are popular for beachcombing and viewing marine life.

Canoeing and Rafting

The area's swift rivers provide challenges to canoeists and kayakers. Many of these rivers should be attempted only by experienced boaters. June through September are prime months for white-water rafting.

Charters

Cruising and deep-sea-fishing charters are available from many ports throughout the Pacific Northwest. Campbell River on British Columbia's Vancouver Island, Neah Bay and Port Angeles on Washington's Olympic Peninsula, Westport on the Long Beach Peninsula in southern Washington, and Depoe Bay in Oregon are leading ports.

Climbing and Mountaineering

The mountains of the Pacific Northwest have given many an adventurer quite a challenge. It is no coincidence that many members of the U.S. expedition teams to Mount Everest come from this region.

Dining

Many restaurants in the Northwest serve local specialties—salmon, crab, oysters, and other seafood delicacies—in dishes that, reflecting the region's ties to Asia and the Pacific Islands, often incorporate the ingredients and techniques of Japanese, Korean, Thai, and other cuisines. Unless otherwise noted, casual but neat dress is appropriate at all of the restaurants reviewed.

Fishing

The coastal regions and inland lakes and rivers of the Pacific Northwest are known for excellent fishing. Lodges, many of which are accessible only by seaplane, cater to anglers in search of the ultimate fishing experience. Visiting sportsmen must possess a nonresident license for the state or province in which they plan to fish. Licenses are easily obtainable at sporting-goods stores, bait shops, and other outlets in fishing areas.

Golf

The Northwest has many excellent golf courses, but not all of them are open to the public. Consequently, visitors may find it difficult to arrange a tee time at a popular course. If you are a member of a golf club at home, check to see if your club has a reciprocal playing arrangement with private clubs in the areas that you will be visiting.

Lodging

You'll find a broad range of noteworthy lodging options in the Pacific Northwest, from elegant, full-service downtown hotels to remote, get-away-from-it-all lodges. Bed-and-breakfasts are an especially popular lodging choice, with distinctive properties offering memorable experiences in cities, coastal towns, and mountaintop villages.

Sailboarding

The Columbia River, particularly at Hood River, Oregon, is one of the world's premier locations for windsurfing. Puget Sound and some of the inland lakes in Washington are other venues for the sport. Sailboard rentals and lessons are available from local specialty shops. In British Columbia, the town of Squamish is quickly becoming another major windsurfing destination.

Skiing

Moist air off the Pacific Ocean dumps snow on the coastal mountains, providing excellent skiing from November through the end of March and sometimes into April. Resort and lift-ticket prices tend to be less expensive here than at the internationally known ski destinations, but the slopes, especially on weekends, can be crowded. Winter driving in these high elevations usually requires a four-wheel-drive vehicle or tire chains.

Wildlife Viewing

Sea lions, seals, dolphins, and whales are a few of the marine mammals that can be observed in bays, near headlands, and along the coast. In the spring and summer thousands of gray whales pass by the British Columbia, Washington, and Oregon coasts on their seasonal migration from Alaska to Baja California in Mexico. One of the easiest and most exciting ways to see them is by taking a whale-watching boat excursion. In the forests and along coastal rivers and estuaries deer, bald eagles, herons, and egrets are commonly seen. The dedicated birders who annually trek to the Northwest find that their efforts are amply rewarded.

FODOR'S CHOICE

Portland

Sights and Attractions

⭐ **International Rose Test Garden.** Three breathtaking terraced gardens on 4 acres high above the city are planted with 10,000 rosebushes in more than 400 varieties.

⭐ **Japanese Garden.** Considered the most authentic Japanese garden outside Japan, this serene oasis provides a peaceful retreat only minutes from city traffic.

⭐ **Nob Hill** The fine old Victorian homes of the Nob Hill neighborhood surround Portland's trendiest shopping streets—Northwest 21st and 23rd avenues—which are chockablock with boutiques, restaurants, and coffee bars.

⭐ **Oregon Museum of Science and Industry.** A great place for children, the museum houses the Northwest's largest astronomy center (with an Omnimax theater and a 200-seat planetarium), a hands-on computer facility, a space wing with a mission-control center, and even its own submarine, the USS *Blueback*.

⭐ **Pioneer Courthouse Square.** Downtown Portland's heart and soul, a broad brick plaza with a purple tile fountain and whimsical weather vane, is surrounded by department stores and handsome office towers.

⭐ **Pittock Mansion.** The opulent French Renaissance–style mansion, completed in 1914, is perched above the city on landscaped grounds with vistas of the city and the Cascade Range.

⭐ **Portland Saturday Market.** Vendors at North America's largest open-air handicraft market sell crystals, beaded hats, stained glass, jewelry, flags, rubber stamps, decorative boots, and other handmade items. Street entertainers and food booths enhance the festive atmosphere.

Flavors

⭐ **Couvron.** Portland's finest restaurant for contemporary French cuisine has a casual but elegant interior and a menu high on charm and creativity. $$$–$$$$

⭐ **Wildwood.** A stainless-steel open kitchen anchors this restaurant serving award-winning fresh Pacific Northwest cuisine on trendy Northwest 21st Avenue. $$$–$$$$

⭐ **Zefiro.** The chef at this attractive restaurant combines Southeast Asian and Mediterranean ingredients and cooking techniques. $$$–$$$$

⭐ **The Heathman.** The French-trained chef of this sophisticated hotel dining room changes his menu with the season to make use of fresh Northwest fish, game, wild mushrooms, and produce. $$–$$$$

⭐ **Assaggio.** Authentic Italian cuisine is cooked to perfection at this small Sellwood trattoria painted in burnt-sienna colors and decorated in classical motifs. $–$$

Comforts

⭐ **Governor Hotel.** Small and quiet, the Governor is the most atmospherically "Northwestern" of Portland's many renovated luxury accommodations, more like an Arts and Crafts–style club than a bustling downtown hotel. $$$$

⭐ **Heathman Hotel.** Superior service, an award-winning restaurant, and elegant public areas have earned this centrally located hotel a reputation for quality. $$$$

⭐ **Doubletree Hotel/Lloyd Center.** Within walking distance of the Lloyd Center shopping mall, the MAX light-rail system, and the Oregon Convention Center, this business-oriented hotel offers well-appointed accommodations. $$–$$$$

⭐ **MacMaster House.** Less than 10 minutes by foot from fashionable Northwest 23rd Avenue, this 17-room Colonial Revival mansion built in 1886 is a comfortable, funky, and fascinating bed-and-breakfast inn. $$–$$$

Oregon

Sights and Attractions

⭐ **Cape Perpetua.** The highest lookout point on the Oregon coast is part of a 2,700-acre scenic area with a visitor center and several hiking trails, including one that winds through a rain forest to an enormous 500-year-old Sitka spruce.

★ **Columbia River Gorge.** From Crown Point, a 730-ft-high bluff, there's an unparalleled 30-mi view down the gorge created by America's second-largest river.

★ **Columbia River Maritime Museum, Astoria.** The observation tower of a World War II submarine and the personal belongings of the passengers of area shipwrecks are among the exhibits here.

★ **Crater Lake National Park.** Rain and snowmelt have filled the caldera left by the eruption of Mount Mazama, creating a sapphire-blue lake—at a depth of 1,900 ft, the nation's deepest—so clear that sunlight penetrates 400 ft.

★ **Fort Clatsop National Memorial, Astoria.** Lewis and Clark's humble winter fort, a log stockade built in 1805 at the conclusion of their trailblazing journey across North America, has been faithfully reconstructed on what is believed to be its original site.

★ **John Day Fossil Beds National Monument.** Three high-desert sites in central Oregon's scenic John Day Valley contain the richest collection of prehistoric plant and animal fossils in the world.

★ **Mount Hood.** The majestic Cascade Range peak is less than an hour's drive from Portland.

★ **Oregon Coast Aquarium, Newport.** The home of Keiko, the orca who starred in *Free Willy,* is part of a 4½-acre complex with re-creations of Pacific marine habitats.

★ **Oregon Shakespeare Festival, Ashland.** More than 100,000 theater lovers come to the Rogue Valley every year to see some of the finest Shakespearean productions this side of Stratford-upon-Avon—plus works by Ibsen, Williams, and other playwrights.

★ **Wildlife Safari, Winston.** Come face to face with free-roaming animals from the comfort of your car at this 600-acre, drive-through wildlife park.

Flavors

★ **Chateaulin, Ashland.** An ivy-covered storefront houses this romantic restaurant, which dispenses French food, local wines, and gracious service with equal facility. *$$$*

★ **Chez Jeanette, Gleneden Beach.** Fresh seafood and local produce receive a sophisticated Parisian spin at this whitewashed cottage-restaurant near Lincoln City. *$$$*

★ **Nick's Italian Café, McMinnville.** Ask any wine maker in the valley to name his or her favorite wine-country restaurant, and chances are that Nick's will head the list. *$$$*

★ **The Bistro, Cannon Beach.** A profusion of flowers and candlelight makes this 12-table restaurant a most romantic dining establishment. *$$*

★ **Blue Heron Bistro, Coos Bay.** Subtle preparations of local seafood and homemade pasta with an international flair are the highlights of the far-ranging menu at this busy bistro. *$$*

★ **La Serre, Yachats.** The chef at what many consider to be the best restaurant on the Oregon coast has a deft touch with seafood, which is always impeccably fresh and never deep fried. *$$*

Comforts

★ **Tu Tu Tun Lodge, near Gold Beach.** Famous for its food, fishing, and hospitality, this rustically elegant fishing resort sits on the fabled Rogue River. *$$$$*

★ **Valley River Inn, Eugene.** The southern Willamette Valley's premier hotel is pleasantly set on the banks of the Willamette River. *$$$–$$$$*

★ **Timberline Lodge, Mount Hood.** A National Historic Landmark that has withstood howling winter storms for more than six decades, the lodge warms its guests with hospitality, hearty food, and rustic rooms. *$$$*

★ **Under the Greenwood Tree, Medford-Ashland.** Luxurious rooms, stunning 10-acre gardens, and breakfasts cooked by the owner, a Cordon Bleu–trained chef, make a visit here memorable. *$$$*

★ **Flying M Ranch, Yamhill.** "Daniel Boone–eclectic" might be the best description of the decor at this great log lodge, the centerpiece of a 625-acre complex of cabins and riverside hotel units. *$$–$$$*

★ **Mt. Ashland Inn, Ashland.** Cedar logged on the property was used to build this lodge. The views of Mount Shasta are as magnificent as the forested setting. *$$–$$$$*

⭐ **The Steamboat Inn, Steamboat.** A veritable Who's Who of the world's top fly fishermen have visited Oregon's most famous fishing lodge; others come simply to relax in the reading nooks or on the broad decks of the riverside cabins. $$–$$$

⭐ **Chetco River Inn, near Brookings.** Acres of forest surround this splendidly remote inn where guests hike, hunt wild mushrooms, or relax in front of the fireplace. $$

⭐ **Mattey House Bed & Breakfast, Lafayette.** Antiques and hand-screened wallpapers decorate this 100-year-old Victorian home, which is now a favorite wine-country B&B. $$

⭐ **Sylvia Beach Hotel, Newport.** This 1912 beachfront hotel has a literary theme—each of the antiques-filled rooms is named for a famous writer, and no two are decorated alike. $$–$$$

Seattle

Sights and Attractions

⭐ **Ballard Locks.** Follow the fascinating progress of fishing boats and pleasure craft through the locks, part of the Lake Washington Ship Canal; then watch as salmon and trout make the same journey via a ladder that allows migrating fish to swim upstream on a gradual incline.

⭐ **Experience Music Project.** Slated to open in mid-2000, this interactive museum will celebrate American popular music. Exhibits will include a Jimi Hendrix gallery and a gallery featuring Bob Dylan, Hank Williams, Kurt Cobain, and Pearl Jam.

⭐ **Museum of Flight.** Exhibits on the history of human flight fill the Red Barn, Boeing's original airplane factory, and the Great Gallery contains more than 20 classic airplanes, dating from the Wright brothers to the jet era.

⭐ **Pike Place Market.** It's fun here anytime, but there's no place in the world quite like the Pike Place Market in full swing on a Saturday afternoon. "If we get separated, I'll meet you by the pig in an hour." But watch for low-flying fish!

⭐ **Space Needle.** There's nothing like the view of the city at night from the observation deck of this Seattle landmark.

Flavors

⭐ **Fullers.** Consistently ranked at or near the top of Seattle's restaurants in local and national publications, Fullers delivers a rare commodity: a dining experience of exceptional poise and restraint, born out of unconventional, even visionary, risk-taking. $$$$

⭐ **Lampreia.** The subtle beige-and-gold interior of this Belltown restaurant is the perfect backdrop for chef-owner Scott Carsberg's clean, sophisticated cuisine. $$$$

⭐ **Rover's.** An intimate escape from the energy of downtown, Rover's offers exceptional French cooking with a menu (changing daily) founded on fresh, locally available ingredients, selected and prepared by chef-owner Thierry Rautureau. $$$$

⭐ **Dahlia Lounge.** The easygoing ambience of the Dahlia Lounge perfectly suits chef Tom Douglas's penchant for simple, if uncommon, preparations. His signature Dungeness crab cakes lead an ever-evolving menu focused on regional ingredients. $$$

⭐ **Metropolitan Grill.** Dripping with classic steak-house atmosphere, this clubby downtown spot serves custom-aged mesquite-broiled steaks—the best in Seattle. $$$

⭐ **Palace Kitchen.** Northwest ingredients are again the centerpiece of Tom Douglas's latest venture, which has a gorgeous curved bar and an open kitchen. $$$

⭐ **Ray's Boathouse.** The view of Puget Sound may be the drawing card, but the seafood is fresh, well prepared, and complemented by one of the area's finest wine lists. $$$

⭐ **Saigon Gourmet.** This small café in the International District is about as plain as they get, but the Vietnamese food is superb and the prices are incredibly low. $

Comforts

⭐ **Alexis Hotel.** Attentive service and fine amenities distinguish the European-style Alexis, which occupies two restored buildings near the waterfront. Rooms are decorated with imported Italian and French fabrics and antiques. $$$$

★ **Bellevue Club Hotel.** The locally produced fine, decorative, and applied artworks that adorn its public and private spaces are among the standout features of this boutique hotel, winner of numerous awards for its design. $$$$

★ **Four Seasons Olympic Hotel.** Seattle's most elegant hotel has a 1920s Renaissance Revival–style grandeur; public rooms are appointed with marble, wood paneling, potted plants, and thick rugs and furnished with plush armchairs. $$$$

★ **Hotel Monaco.** Goldfish in your room are among the fun touches at this luxury hotel inside a former office building in the heart of the Financial District. The light and whimsical lobby has high ceilings and hand-painted nautical murals inspired by the fresco at the Palace of Knossos in Crete. $$$$

★ **Sorrento.** Sitting high on First Hill, this deluxe European-style hotel, designed to look like an Italian villa, has wonderful views overlooking downtown and the waterfront. $$$$

★ **Woodmark Hotel.** This is the only hotel on the shores of Lake Washington. Its contemporary-style rooms, done in exquisite shades of café au lait, taupe, and ecru, come with amenities such as terrycloth bathrobes, coffeemakers, irons, hair dryers, complimentary shoe shines, and the morning paper. $$$$

★ **Inn at Harbor Steps.** Rooms here are commodious, with high ceilings, gas fireplaces, and tidy kitchenettes. The bathrooms accommodate large tubs (some of them whirlpools) and oversize glass-enclosed shower stalls. $$$–$$$$

★ **Inn at the Market.** Sophisticated but unpretentious, this hotel right up the street from the Pike Place Market combines the best aspects of a small French country inn with the informality of the Pacific Northwest. $$$–$$$$

★ **Gaslight Inn.** Rooms at this Capitol Hill bed-and-breakfast inn range from a cozy crow's nest to large rooms and suites with gas fireplaces, carved antique beds, and ceiling fans. $$–$$$

★ **Marriott Sea-Tac.** The luxurious Marriott near the airport has a five-story tropical atrium that's complete with a waterfall, a dining area, an indoor pool, and a lounge. $$–$$$

Washington

Sights and Attractions

★ **A ferry ride through the San Juan Islands.** Nothing beats the view of the islands from the waters of Puget Sound.

★ **Mount Rainier National Park.** Magnificent Mount Rainier is the centerpiece of a park with hiking and cross-country ski trails, lakes and rivers, and ample camping facilities.

★ **Point Defiance Zoo and Aquarium, Tacoma.** The zoo's re-creations of natural habitats provide close-up views of whales, walruses, sharks, polar bears, octopuses, apes, reptiles, and birds.

★ **Snoqualmie Falls.** Spring and summer snowmelt turns the Snoqualmie River into a thundering torrent as it cascades through a 268-ft rock gorge to a deep pool below.

★ **Whale-watching on Long Beach Peninsula.** Climb the North Head Lighthouse and watch for a whale blow—the vapor that spouts into the air when a whale exhales—as gray whales pass by on their way back and forth from breeding grounds in warmer waters.

Flavors

★ **The Ark, Nahcotta.** The oysters at the Ark couldn't be fresher—they're raised in beds behind the restaurant. $$$

★ **Christina's.** The modern decor at the premier Orcas restaurant includes original artwork and copper-top tables. The seasonal menu changes daily but generally emphasizes fresh local fish and seafood. $$$

★ **Birchfield Manor, Yakima.** All entrées at the Yakima wine country's best restaurant come with an exotic homemade bread of the day. $$–$$$

★ **Alice's Restaurant, Tenino.** Homey and intimate, this restaurant in a rural farmhouse serves six-course, prix-fixe dinners of innovative yet classic American cuisine. $$

Comforts

★ **Domaine Madeleine, Port Angeles.** The rooms at this small and romantic inn have views of the water, fireplaces, Jacuzzis, TVs with VCRs, and CD/tape players. Breakfast is a feast. $$$–$$$$

☆ **Majestic Hotel, Anacortes.** An old mercantile building in the San Juan Islands has been turned into one of the finest small hotels in the Northwest. $$$–$$$$

☆ **Spring Bay Inn, Orcas Island.** Former park rangers run this B&B on acres of woodland. All the rooms have bay views, wood-burning fireplaces, feather beds, and private sitting areas. $$$–$$$$

☆ **Inn at Langley, Whidbey Island.** Built of concrete and wood, this Frank Lloyd Wright–inspired structure rests on the edge of a bluff that descends to a beach. $$$$

☆ **Salish Lodge, Snoqualmie.** The rooms at this favorite getaway of Seattleites have views of Snoqualmie Falls or the Snoqualmie River. Elaborate Saturday and Sunday brunches include eggs, bacon, fish, fresh fruit, pancakes, and a locally renowned oatmeal. $$$$

☆ **Shelburne Inn, Seaview.** Impeccably maintained, this antiques-filled inn retains an air of refinement. The gourmet breakfast is unforgettable. $$–$$$

Vancouver

Sights and Attractions

☆ **Dr. Sun Yat-Sen Classical Chinese Garden.** The first authentic Ming Dynasty–style garden outside of China, this garden was built in 1986 by 52 artisans from Suzhou, known as the "garden city" of the People's Republic.

☆ **Granville Island.** This small sandbar was a derelict factory district, but its industrial buildings and tin sheds, painted in upbeat primary colors, now house restaurants, a public market, marine activities, and artists' studios.

☆ **Museum of Anthropology.** Vancouver's most spectacular museum displays aboriginal art from the Pacific Northwest and around the world—dramatic totem poles and canoes; exquisite carvings of gold, silver, and argillite; and masks, tools, and textiles.

☆ **Stanley Park.** An afternoon in this 1,000-acre wilderness park, only blocks from downtown, can include beaches, the ocean, the harbor, Douglas fir and cedar forests, and a good look at the North Shore mountains.

Flavors

☆ **C.** Its marina-side location overlooking False Creek is a perfect setting for this innovative seafood restaurant. $$$–$$$$

☆ **Bacchus.** Low lighting, heavy velvet drapes, and Venetian glass lamps create a mildly decadent feel at this sensuous Italian restaurant inside the Wedgewood Hotel. $$–$$$$

☆ **Il Giardino di Umberto.** Come to this little yellow house at the end of Hornby Street to savor Tuscan favorites in an attractive jumble of terra-cotta-tiled rooms. The vine-draped courtyard with a wood-burning oven is especially romantic. $$–$$$$

☆ **Liliget Feast House.** Tucked into an intimate downstairs longhouse near English Bay is one of the few places in the world that serve original Northwest Coast native cuisine. $$–$$$$

☆ **Imperial Chinese Seafood.** This Cantonese restaurant in the Art Deco Marine Building has two-story floor-to-ceiling windows with stupendous views of Stanley Park and the North Shore mountains across Burrard Inlet. $$–$$$

☆ **Tojo's.** Hidekazu Tojo is a sushi-making legend, with more than 2,000 preparations tucked away in his creative mind. $$$

☆ **Vij's.** Vikram Vij, who calls his elegant South Granville restaurant a "curry art gallery," brings together the best of the subcontinent and the Pacific Northwest for some exciting new interpretations of Indian cuisine. $$

Comforts

☆ **Hotel Vancouver.** The copper roof of this grand château-style hotel dominates Vancouver's skyline. The hotel itself, opened in 1939 by the Canadian National Railway, commands a regal position in the center of town. $$$$

☆ **Pan Pacific Hotel.** A centerpiece of Vancouver's Trade and Convention Centre, located on top of the Canada Place complex on the city's stunning waterfront, the luxurious Pan Pacific has a dramatic three-story atrium lobby and expansive views of the harbor and mountains. $$$$

★ **Listel Vancouver.** This Robson Street hotel doubles as an art gallery, with about half of its guest rooms displaying the works of well-known contemporary artists. *$$$–$$$$*

★ **Sutton Place.** Not far from the Robson Street shops is this modern 21-story hotel, which looks and feels more like an exclusive European guest house. Guest rooms are furnished with rich, dark woods and the service is gracious and attentive. *$$$–$$$$*

★ **English Bay Inn.** In this renovated 1930s Tudor house a block from the ocean and Stanley Park, the guest rooms have wonderful sleigh beds with matching armoires. *$$–$$$*

★ **West End Guest House.** Built in 1906, this lovely Victorian house is a true "painted lady," from its gracious front parlor, cozy fireplace, and early 1900s furniture to its bright pink exterior. *$$–$$$*

British Columbia

Sights and Attractions

★ **Butchart Gardens, Victoria.** This world-class horticultural collection grows more than 700 varieties of flowers and has Italian, Japanese, and English rose gardens.

★ **Craigdarroch Castle.** The lavish mansion of British Columbia's first millionaire is now a museum that surveys life at the end of the 19th century.

★ **Minter Gardens, Rosedale.** Here you will find beautifully presented theme gardens—Chinese, rose, English, fern, fragrance, and more—along with aviaries and ponds.

★ **O'Keefe Historic Ranch, Vernon.** For a window on cattle-ranch life at the turn of the century, visit the O'Keefe house, a late-19th-century Victorian mansion opulently furnished with original antiques.

★ **Pacific Rim National Park, Vancouver Island.** The first national marine park in Canada comprises a hard-packed white-sand beach, a group of islands, and a demanding coastal hiking trail.

Flavors

★ **The Marina Restaurant, Victoria.** Locals love this round restaurant overlooking the Oak Bay Marina; imaginative seafood dishes are the highlights of the diverse menu. *$$–$$$*

★ **Mahle House, Nanaimo.** The intimate setting and innovative Northwest cuisine make a visit here one of the finest dining experiences in the region. *$$*

★ **The Old House Restaurant, Courtenay.** This bilevel restaurant offers casual dining in a restored 1938 house with large cedar beams and a stone fireplace. *$$*

★ **Royal Coachman Inn, Campbell River, Vancouver Island.** Informal, blackboard-menu restaurants like this one dot the landscape of the island, but here the menu, which changes daily, is surprisingly daring. *$–$$*

Comforts

★ **Hastings House, Saltspring Island.** You'll feel more than pampered at one of the finest country inns in North America. *$$$$*

★ **April Point Lodge and Fishing Resort, Campbell River, Vancouver Island.** Spread across a point of Quadra Island and stretching into Discovery Passage, the 1944 cedar lodge is surrounded by refurbished fishermen's cabins and guest houses. *$$$–$$$$*

★ **Ocean Pointe Resort, Victoria.** Public rooms and half the guest rooms have views of downtown Victoria and the parliament buildings. *$$$*

Southeast Alaska

Sights and Attractions

★ **Glacier Bay National Park and Preserve.** This is one of the jewels of the entire national park system. Visiting Glacier Bay is like stepping back into the Little Ice Age.

★ **Saxman Native Village.** At this village named for a missionary who helped native Alaskans settle here before 1900, you'll find a tribal dwelling believed to be the largest of its kind in the world.

★ **Tlingit Fort.** On its way to a former battlefield, this trail in Sitka National Historical Park wends past some of the most skillfully carved totem poles in Alaska.

Flavors

★ **Channel Club, Sitka.** If you've never dined on halibut cheeks, you don't know what you're missing. The decor is nautical, with fishnet floats, whale baleen, and whalebone carvings hanging on the walls. *$$–$$$*

★ **Gold Creek Salmon Bake, Juneau.** Dine outdoors (May–September) on fresh-caught salmon cooked over an alder fire, and after dinner pan for gold in a nearby stream. *$$*

★ **Salmon Falls Resort, Ketchikan.** The dining area of the resort overlooks the waters of Clover Passage, where sunsets are often a vivid red. Seafood fresh from adjacent waters is especially good; try the halibut and the prawns stuffed with crabmeat. *$$*

★ **The Fiddlehead, Juneau.** Probably Juneau's favorite restaurant, this is a delightful place where healthful dishes come in generous portions. *$–$$*

★ **Beachcomber Inn, Petersburg.** Seafood with a distinctly Norwegian flair is the specialty in this restored cannery building on the shores of Wrangell Narrows. *$*

Comforts

★ **Glacier Bay Country Inn, Gustavus.** All rooms in this picturesque, rambling log structure have views of the Chilkat Mountains. *$$$$*

★ **Gustavus Inn, Gustavus.** Many guests at this inn, which continues a tradition of gracious Alaska rural living, prefer to do nothing but enjoy the inn's tranquillity and its notable family-style meals. *$$$$*

★ **Westmark Shee Atika, Sitka.** Stay here for a night or two and you'll come away with an increased appreciation for Southeast Alaskan native art and culture. Many rooms overlook Crescent Harbor and the islands in the waters beyond; others have mountain and forest views. *$$$$*

★ **The Prospector, Juneau.** Business travelers and legislators favor this small, modern hotel. Very large rooms have contemporary furnishings, bright watercolors of Alaskan nature, and views of the channel, mountains, or city. *$$$–$$$$*

★ **Inn at the Waterfront, Juneau.** Rooms here are comfortable and bright. The Inn is home to the Summit, an intimate, candlelit restaurant with a separate, copper-topped bar. *$$–$$$$*

★ **Ingersoll Hotel, Ketchikan.** Patterned wallpaper, wood wainscoting, and etched-glass windows on the oak registration desk set an old-fashioned mood for this three-story downtown hotel, built in the 1920s. The rooms are standard, but the views are sublime. *$$$*

★ **Alaskan Hotel, Juneau.** Guest rooms at this historic 1913 hotel in the heart of downtown Juneau have turn-of-the-century antiques and iron beds. The decor is reminiscent of the hotel's original gold rush–era opulence. *$$*

FESTIVALS AND SEASONAL EVENTS

Listed below are some of the major annual events that take place in the Pacific Northwest.

OREGON

MID-FEB.–EARLY NOV.➤ The **Oregon Shakespeare Festival** (☎ 541/482–4331) in Ashland presents classic and contemporary plays in repertory.

APR.➤ The **Hood River Valley Blossom Festival** (☎ 541/386–2000 or 800/366–3530) is a springtime floral spectacle.

MAY➤ The **Cinco de Mayo Festival** (☎ 503/222–9807) in Portland is one of the largest such celebrations this side of Guadalajara. In late May, the **Brookings Azalea Festival** (☎ 541/469–3181) shows off the azaleas of Oregon's southern coast.

JUNE➤ The **Portland Rose Festival** (☎ 503/227–2681) packs diverse events—an air show, three parades, auto racing, and a riverside carnival among them—into 25 days. Also this month, **Sandcastle Day** (☎ 503/436–2623) transforms Cannon Beach into a sculptured fantasyland.

MID-JUNE–EARLY SEPT.➤ The **Britt Festivals** (☎ 541/773–6077 or 800/882–7488) present concerts, musical theater, and dance at an outdoor amphitheater in historic Jacksonville.

LATE JUNE–MID-JULY➤ The **Oregon Bach Festival** (☎ 541/346–5666) in Eugene celebrates the works of the great composer.

JULY➤ The **Oregon Coast Music Festival** (☎ 541/267–0938) in Coos Bay,

North Bend, and Charleston presents classical bluegrass, jazz, and other concerts. The **Oregon Brewer's Festival** (☎ 503/295–1862), a beer-lover's delight, is held in Portland.

MID-JULY➤ The **Salem Art Fair and Festival** (☎ 503/581–2228), Oregon's biggest art fair, includes exhibits, food, entertainment, and tours of historic mansions.

AUG.➤ The **Mount Hood Festival of Jazz** (☎ 503/224–4400) brings nationally acclaimed jazz musicians to Gresham for performances in an outdoor setting.

LATE AUG.–EARLY SEPT.➤ The **Oregon State Fair** (☎ 503/378–3247) takes place in Salem the 11 days before Labor Day.

MID-SEPT.➤ **Oktoberfest** (☎ no phone) draws half a million people to Mount Angel for an extravaganza of Bavarian food, beer, wine, and cabaret.

WASHINGTON

LATE MAR.–MID-APR.➤ The **Skagit Valley Tulip Festival** (☎ 360/428–5959) is a showcase of millions of colorful tulips and daffodils.

MAY➤ The **Viking Fest** (☎ 360/779–4999) celebrates the Norwegian community of Poulsbo's proud heritage.

MEMORIAL DAY WEEKEND➤ The **Northwest Folklife Festival** (☎ 206/684–7300) in Seattle is one of the nation's largest folk-music festivals.

LATE JUNE–EARLY JULY➤ **Fort Vancouver Days** (☎ 877/600–0800) in Vancouver include a chili cook-

off, musical events, and fireworks.

JULY➤ **Bite of Seattle** (☎ 206/784–9705) an event at the Seattle Center, showcases the fare at the city's finest restaurants. The **Pacific Northwest Arts Fair** (☎ 425/454–3322) a juried show in Bellevue, presents the works of several hundred artists.

MID-JULY–EARLY AUG.➤ **Seafair** (☎ 206/728–0123) in Seattle begins with a torchlight parade and ends with a Blue Angels air show and hydroplane races.

LATE AUG.➤ The **Washington State International Kite Festival** (☎ 800/451–2542) sends kites of all shapes and sizes flying above Long Beach.

LATE AUG.–EARLY SEPT.➤ **Bumbershoot—The Seattle Arts Festival** (☎ 206/281–7788) is a beloved Seattle showcase for music, dance, theater, comedy, and the visual and literary arts.

EARLY SEPT.➤ The **Wooden Boat Festival** (☎ 360/385–3628) of Port Townsend includes historic boat displays, demonstrations, and a street fair.

EARLY–MID-SEPT.➤ The **Western Washington Fair** (☎ 253/845–6755) brings top entertainment, animals, food, exhibits, and rides to the town of Puyallup.

BRITISH COLUMBIA

JAN.➤ The **Polar Bear Swim** (☎ 604/683–2000) on New Year's Day in Vancouver is said to bring good luck all year. **Skiing competitions** take place at most alpine ski resorts (through February).

MAR.➤ The **Pacific Rim Whale Festival** (☎ 250/726–4641) on Vancouver Island's west coast celebrates the spring migration of gray whales with guided tours by whale experts and accompanying music and dancing. Northwest vintages take center stage at the **Vancouver International Wine Festival** (☎ 604/873–3311).

APR.➤ The **TerrifVic Jazz Party** (☎ 250/953–2011) in Victoria presents top international Dixieland bands.

MAY➤ **Cloverdale Rodeo** (☎ 604/576–9461) in Surrey is rated sixth in the world by the Pro Rodeo Association. **Vancouver Children's Festival** (☎ 604/708–5655) provides free open-air stage performances.

JUNE➤ **Canadian International Dragon Boat Festival** (☎ 604/688–2382) in Vancouver includes entertainment, exotic foods, and the ancient "awakening the dragons" ritual of long, slender boats decorated with huge dragon heads.

JUNE–SEPT.➤ **Whistler Summer Festivals** (☎ 604/932–5528) present daily street entertainment and music festivals at the international ski and summer resort.

JULY 1➤ **Canada Day** inspires celebrations around the country in honor of Canada's birthday. In Vancouver, **Canada Place** (☎ 604/666–7200) hosts an entire day of free outdoor concerts followed by a fireworks display in the inner

harbor. Victoria stages the daylong **Great Canadian Family Picnic** (☎ 250/389–0528) in Beacon Hill Park. The event usually includes children's games, bands, food booths, and fireworks.

JULY➤ The **Harrison Festival of the Arts** (☎ 604/796–3664) focuses on ethnic music, dance, and theater, such as African, Caribbean, or Central American. The **Vancouver Sea Festival** (☎ no phone) celebrates the city's nautical heritage with the World Championship Bathtub Race, sailing regattas, and windsurfing races.

AUG.➤ The **Abbotsford International Airshow** (☎ 604/852–8511) is three days of flight performances and a large-aircraft display. The **Pacific National Exhibition** (☎ 604/253–2311) in Vancouver has parades, exhibits, sports, entertainment, and logging contests. The **Squamish Days Loggers Sports Festival** (☎ 604/892–9877) draws loggers from around the world to compete in a series of incredible feats.

SEPT.➤ Cars speed through downtown Vancouver in the **Molson Indy Formula** (☎ 604/280–4639).

OCT.➤ The **Okanagan Wine Festivals** (☎ 800/972–5151) take place in the Okanagan-Similkameen area. The **Vancouver International Film Festival** (☎ 604/685–0260) brings top directors and films to the city.

DEC.➤ The **Carol Ships** (☎ 604/688–7246), sailboats full of carolers and decorated with colored lights, ply the waters of the Vancouver harbor.

ALASKA

EARLY FEB.➤ The **Tent City Winter Festival** (☎ 907/874–3901) in Wrangell captures the flavor of Alaska's early days.

LATE MAR.➤ **Seward's Day,** which commemorates the signing of the 1867 treaty purchasing Alaska from Russia, is celebrated around the state on the last Monday in March.

EARLY APR.➤ The **Alaska Folk Festival** (☎ 907/463–3316) in Juneau is a mix of music, handmade crafts, and foods.

MAY➤ The **Little Norway Festival** (☎ 907/772–4636) in picturesque Petersburg celebrates the town's Scandinavian heritage. The **Juneau Jazz and Classics Festival** (☎ 907/463–3378) presents nationally known musicians.

JUNE➤ The **Sitka Summer Music Festival** (☎ 907/747–6774) is a monthlong series of chamber-music performances.

MID-OCT.➤ The **Alaska Day Celebration** (☎ 800/423–0568) brings out the whole town of Sitka to celebrate the day—October 18—the United States acquired Alaska from Russia. The weeklong festival includes a period costume ball and a parade.

2 PORTLAND

Oregon's largest city is among America's most livable—not surprising, given its verdant natural setting and host of urban amenities. To find out the secret to Portland's allure, stroll through the city's parks and gardens, explore its intriguing neighborhoods and lively downtown, peruse the galleries and museums, or just sit back and enjoy the buzz at any of the dozens of coffeehouses, cafés, and microbreweries.

By Donald S.
Olson

Updated by
Jeffrey Boswell

PORTLAND IS LOADED WITH ENERGY. For decades this inland port on the Willamette River was the undiscovered gem of the West Coast, often overlooked by visitors seeking more sophisticated milieus. But in the past decade, people have begun flocking here in unprecedented numbers—to visit and to live.

The city's proximity to mountains, ocean, and desert adds an element of natural grandeur to its urban character. Majestic Mount Hood, about 70 mi to the east, acts as a kind of mascot, and on a clear day several peaks of the Cascade Range are visible, including Mount St. Helen's, which dusted the city with ash when it erupted in 1980. The west side of town is built on a series of forested hills that descend to the downtown area, the Willamette River, and the flatter east side. Filled with stately late-19th-century and modern architecture, linked by an effective and intelligent transit system, and home to a vital arts scene, Portland is a place where there's much to do day or night, rain or shine.

The quality of life remains a high and constant priority here. As far back as 1852, Portland began setting aside city land as parks. This legacy has added immeasurably to the city's attractiveness and environmental mystique. Included among Portland's 250 parks, public gardens, and greenways are the nation's largest urban wilderness, the world's smallest park, and the only extinct volcano in the lower 48 states within a city's limits.

A temperate climate and plenty of precipitation keep Portland green year-round and make it a paradise for gardeners. The City of Roses, as it's known, celebrates its favorite flower with a monthlong Rose Festival—a June extravaganza with auto and boat races, visiting navy ships, and a grand parade second in size only to Pasadena's Rose Parade. But the floral spectacle really starts three months earlier, when streets and gardens bloom with the colors of flowering trees, camellias, rhododendrons, and azaleas.

Portland, which began as an Indian clearing of about 1 square mi, has become a metropolis of 2 million people; within its now 132-square-mi borders are 90 diverse and distinct neighborhoods. A center for sports and sportswear makers, the Portland metropolitan area, which includes the burgeoning city of Vancouver across the state line in Washington, contains the headquarters and factories of Jantzen, Nike, Columbia Sportswear, and Pendleton. The city's western suburbs of Beaverton and Hillsboro have been called the Silicon Forest because of their high concentration of high-tech manufacturing plants, including those of Intel, Tektronix, and Fujitsu. High-tech shipbuilding, furniture, fabricated-metals, and other manufacturers have broadened the region's economic base even further. And its prime location at the confluence of the Columbia and Willamette rivers has helped Portland become the third-largest port on the West Coast. Five main terminals export automobiles, steel, livestock, grain, and timber products. Shipyards repair tankers, tugboats, cruise ships, and navy vessels.

The arts here flourish in unexpected places: You'll find artwork in police stations, office towers, banks, playgrounds, and on the sides of buildings. The brick-paved transit mall downtown is a veritable outdoor gallery of fountains and sculptures. As for the performing arts, Portland is home to several professional theater companies, the Oregon Symphony, the Portland Opera, and Chamber Music Northwest, to name a few. Those into nightlife will also find some of the best live-band and club action in the country. Families have plenty of kid-friendly attractions to enjoy, including the Oregon Zoo, Oaks Amusement Park, and Oregon Museum of Science and Industry. Although Portland is now one of the largest metropolitan areas in the nation, it has only one major-league sports team—the National Basketball Association's Portland Trail Blazers. There is a community effort under way to renovate downtown's Civic Stadium and model it after Baltimore's Oriole Park at Camden Yards, in hopes of attracting a major-league baseball team.

For all its focus on the future, though, Portland has not forgotten its past. Architectural preservation is a major preoccupation, particularly when it comes to the 1860s brick buildings with cast-iron columns and the 1890s ornate terra-cotta designs that grace areas like the Skidmore Old Town, Yamhill, and Glazed Terra-Cotta national historic districts. In the Pearl District, older industrial buildings are being given new life as residential lofts, restaurants, office space, galleries, and boutiques.

With so much going on, the future will undoubtedly bring more people to Portland. To curb urban sprawl the city has instituted an urban growth boundary and is actively promoting urban density controls within the inner city. In the process it has revitalized several older neighborhoods and created some entirely new ones. Not all Portlanders are happy with the results, which have brought increased traffic congestion and constant construction. But the new century will bring a renewed emphasis on mass transit, with an extension of the MAX light-rail line to Portland International Airport, as well as a new streetcar line connecting Portland State University, downtown, and the popular Nob Hill neighborhood to the northwest. The city's farsighted approach to growth and its pitfalls means it reaps all of the benefits and few of the problems of its boom. As a result, Portland is better than ever, cultivating a new level of sophistication, building on enhanced prosperity, and bursting with fresh energy.

Pleasures and Pastimes

Dining
Portland's restaurant scene has improved dramatically during the past decade. Many new eateries specializing in regional Pacific Northwest cuisine have opened downtown and in the popular Nob Hill neighborhood northwest of downtown. You'll find excellent seafood in Portland, including fresh fish (particularly salmon), sweet Dungeness crab, mussels, shrimp, and oysters; other good choices are local lamb and beef and seasonal game dishes. Desserts made with local fruits such as huckleberries and marionberries are always worth trying.

Lodging
Portland's long-standing shortage of rooms has been relieved some in the past year with the addition of several new high-rise downtown hotels, including the Marriott City Center. In addition, a few low-rise inns have opened on the metro area's fast-growing west side to serve business travelers in the technology sector. You'll also find some cozy bed-and-breakfasts outside the downtown area.

Parks and Gardens
Portland is a very green city, with a liberal dose of color—flowers, particularly roses, are everywhere. Forest Park, at 5,000 acres, is the nation's largest urban wilderness; hiking is the prime activity here. Washington Park is home to the Japanese Garden, the International Rose Test Garden, and the ever-expanding Oregon Zoo and on clear days has a spectacular view of Mt. Hood.

When to Go

A great time to visit is June (if you can get a hotel room), when Portland hosts the annual Rose Festival with its many events, including the Grand Floral Parade, Rose Festival Air Show, and Fleet Week. The roses are in full bloom at this time—indeed, the city landscape is resplendent with wildflowers and gardens abloom with rhododendrons and azaleas. Portland also hosts world-class summer music festivals. Clear days are more frequent in late summer and early fall, and fall is spectacular, with leaves at their colorful peak in late October. Winters are usually mild, but they can be relentlessly rainy.

EXPLORING PORTLAND

The Willamette River is Portland's east-west dividing line. Burnside Street separates north from south. The city's 200-ft-long blocks make them easy to walk, but you can also explore the downtown core by either MAX light rail or Tri-Met bus (☞ Getting Around *in* Portland A to Z, *below*).

Great Itineraries

IF YOU HAVE 1 DAY
Spend the morning exploring the parks, museums, and historic districts in downtown Portland. To get the flavor of a Portland neighborhood, stroll along Northwest 23rd Avenue and through Nob Hill in the early afternoon. From there, drive up into the northwest hills to the Pittock Mansion. Just minutes away, in the southwest hills, are the famous rose gardens and Japanese Garden in Washington Park.

IF YOU HAVE 3 DAYS
On your first day, explore downtown Portland, Northwest 23rd Avenue and Nob Hill, the Pittock Mansion, and the gardens in Washington Park. On the second morning, visit the Oregon Museum of Science and Industry (OMSI), have lunch in Sellwood, and then head to Hoyt Arboretum, Forest Park, or both. Head back to east Portland on your third day to check out the Hawthorne District. Then, to gain a historical perspective, drive to Oregon City or Fort Vancouver.

Downtown

Portland has one of the most attractive downtown urban cores in America. Clean, compact, and filled with parks, plazas, and fountains, it holds a mix of new and historic buildings. Hotels, shops, museums, restaurants, and entertainment can all be found here, and the entire downtown area is part of the Tri-Met transit system's Fareless Square, within which you can ride MAX or any bus for free.

Numbers in the text correspond to numbers in the margin and on the Downtown, Skidmore, and Chinatown map.

A Good Walk

Begin at Southwest Morrison Street and Southwest 6th Avenue at **Pioneer Courthouse Square** ①. If it's not January or February, you'll probably notice the **vintage trolley cars** that pull up to the MAX stop here; they run to Lloyd Center. From the square, walk south on 6th Avenue for two blocks. At the corner of 6th Avenue and Salmon Street is **Nike-Town** ②. Continue one block south to Main Street and one block west to Broadway and the **Portland Center for the Performing Arts** ③. Behind the center are the tree-lined **South Park Blocks** along Park Avenue from Market to Salmon Street. On the east side of Park at Jefferson Street, a mural of Lewis and Clark and the Oregon Trail rises above

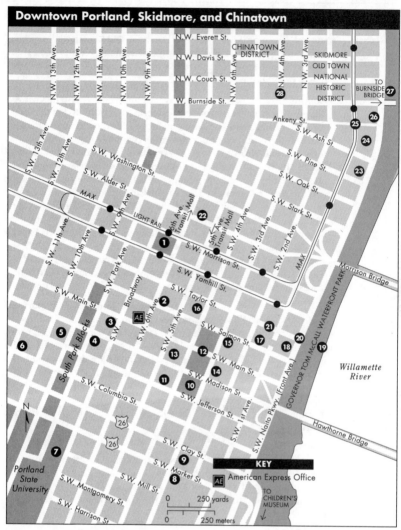

Downtown Portland, Skidmore, and Chinatown

KEY

AE American Express Office

Chapman and
Lownsdale Squares, **12**

Chinatown Gate, **28**

City Hall, **11**

Civic Auditorium, **8**

Glazed Terra-Cotta
Nat. Hist. Dist., **22**

Gov. Tom McCall
Waterfront Park, **19**

Japanese-American
Historical Plaza, **27**

Jeff Morris Memorial
Fire Museum, **24**

Justice Center, **14**

KOIN Center, **9**

Mark O. Hatfield
U.S. Courthouse, **15**

Mill Ends Park, **20**

NikeTown, **2**

Old Church, **6**

Oregon History
Center, **4**

Oregon Maritime
Center and
Museum, **23**

Pioneer Courthouse
Square, **1**

Portland Art
Museum, **5**

Portland Building, **13**

Portland Center for
the Performing Arts, **3**

Portland/Oregon
Visitors Assoc., **18**

Portland Saturday
Market, **26**

Portland State
University, **7**

Skidmore Fountain, **25**

State of Oregon
Sports Hall of Fame, **16**

Terry Schrunk
Plaza, **10**

World Trade
Center, **17**

Yamhill Nat. Hist.
Dist., **21**

the entrance to the **Oregon History Center** ④. West on Jefferson across the Park Blocks is the **Portland Art Museum** ⑤. Walk west on Jefferson and south on 11th Avenue to reach the **Old Church** ⑥. Loop back east to the South Park Blocks along Columbia Street and head south on Park Avenue to Market Street, where the campus of **Portland State University** ⑦ begins.

Continue east on Market to 3rd Avenue and you'll reach the **Civic Auditorium** ⑧, which has a massive waterfall fountain. **KOIN Center** ⑨, the most distinctive high-rise in downtown Portland, occupies the next block to the north. Continue north for two blocks on 3rd Avenue to **Terry Schrunk Plaza** ⑩. On the west side of the plaza is Portland's restored **City Hall** ⑪. The adjacent **Chapman and Lownsdale squares** ⑫ are flanked by the blue, postmodern **Portland Building** ⑬ to the west and the **Justice Center** ⑭ to the east. Rising beside the Justice Center, between Main and Salmon streets, is the **Mark O. Hatfield U.S. Courthouse** ⑮. The **State of Oregon Sports Hall of Fame** ⑯ is north of Chapman Square on 4th Avenue, between Salmon and Taylor streets. Head east on Salmon to the **World Trade Center** ⑰ on 2nd Avenue; the **Portland/Oregon Visitors Association** ⑱ occupies the building on Naito Parkway, a street most locals still call Front Avenue, the name it had before it was changed to honor a local real-estate mogul.

Cross Naito Parkway and enter **Governor Tom McCall Waterfront Park** ⑲, where you'll see **Salmon Street Fountain.** The park extends north for about a mile to Burnside Street. Follow the park one block north to Taylor Street, where **Mill Ends Park** ⑳ sits in the middle of a traffic island on Naito Parkway. You are now in the **Yamhill National Historic District** ㉑ of cast-iron and other buildings. If you are interested in art and architecture, zigzag back and forth between Southwest 5th and Southwest 6th avenues and the intersecting streets of Oak and Yamhill. This is the heart of the **Glazed Terra-Cotta National Historic District** ㉒.

TIMING

The entire downtown walk can be accomplished in about 90 minutes. If you're planning to stop at the Oregon History Center or Portland Art Museum (both closed on Monday), add at least one to two hours for each. Allot 15 or 30 minutes for the Sports Hall of Fame, which is closed on Sunday.

Sights to See

⑫ **Chapman and Lownsdale squares.** During the 1920s, these parks were segregated by sex: Chapman, between Madison and Main streets, was reserved for women, and Lownsdale, between Main and Salmon streets, was for men. The elk statue on Main Street, which separates the parks, was given to the city by former mayor David Thompson. It supposedly honors an elk that grazed here in the 1850s.

OFF THE
BEATEN PATH
CHILDREN'S MUSEUM – Hands-on play is the order of the day at this museum with exhibits, a clay shop, and a child-size grocery store. In late 2000 the museum will move into a new home in Washington Park across from the zoo. ⊠ 3037 S.W. 2nd Ave., between S.W. Barbour Blvd. and S.W. Woods St. near the Ross Island Bridge, ☎ 503/823–2227. ☞ $4. ☉ Daily 9–5.

⑪ **City Hall.** Portland's four-story, granite-faced City Hall, which was completed in 1895, is an example of the Renaissance Revival style popular in the late 19th century. Italian influences can be seen in the porch, the pink scagliola columns, the cornice embellishments, and other details. ⊠ 1220 S.W. 5th Ave., ☎ 503/823–4000. ☉ Weekdays 8–5.

8 **Civic Auditorium.** Home base for the Portland Opera, the Civic Auditorium also hosts traveling musicals and other theatrical extravaganzas. The building itself, part of the Portland Center for the Performing Arts (☞ *below*), is not particularly distinctive, but the **Ira Keller Fountain,** a series of 18-ft-high stone waterfalls across from the front entrance, is worth a look. ⊠ *S.W. 3rd Ave. and Clay St.,* ☎ *503/274–6560.*

22 **Glazed Terra-Cotta National Historic District.** A century ago terra-cotta was often used in construction because of its availability and low cost; it could also be easily molded into the decorative details that were popular at the time. Elaborate lions' heads, griffins, floral displays, and other classical motifs adorn the rooflines of the district's many buildings that date from the late 1890s to the mid-1910s. Public art lines 5th and 6th avenues. On 5th you'll find a sculpture that reflects light and changing colors, a nude woman made of bronze, a copper and redwood creation inspired by the Norse god Thor, and a large limestone cat in repose. Sixth Avenue has a steel-and-concrete matrix, a granite-and-brick fountain, and an abstract modern depiction of an ancient Greek defending Crete. ⊠ *S.W. 5th and S.W. 6th Aves. between S.W. Oak and S.W. Yamhill Sts.*

NEED A BREAK? The **Rock Bottom Brewing Co.** (⊠ 210 S.W. Morrison St., at S.W. 2nd Ave., ☎ 503/796–2739) is one of the ritzier examples of that authentically Portland experience, the brew pub. Have a pint of ale—brewed on the premises, of course—and sample the fine pub foods and snacks.

19 **Governor Tom McCall Waterfront Park.** The park named for a former governor of Oregon revered for his statewide land-use planning initiatives stretches north along the Willamette River for about a mile to Burnside Street. Broad and grassy, it yields what may be the finest ground-level view of downtown Portland's bridges and skyline. The park, on the site of a former expressway, hosts many events, among them the Rose Festival, classical and blues concerts, and the Oregon Brewers Festival. The five-day **Cinco de Mayo Festival** (☎ 503/222–9807) in early May celebrates Portland's sister-city relationship with Guadalajara, Mexico. Next to the Rose Festival, this is one of Portland's biggest get-togethers. Food and arts-and-crafts booths, stages with mariachi bands, and a carnival complete with a Ferris wheel line the riverfront for the event. Bikers, joggers, and roller and in-line skaters enjoy the area year-round. The arching jets of water at the **Salmon Street Fountain** change configuration every few hours and are a favorite cooling-off spot during the dog days of summer. ⊠ *S.W. Naito Pkwy. (Front Ave.) from just south of the Hawthorne Bridge to the Burnside Bridge.*

14 **Justice Center.** This modern building houses the county courts and support offices and, on the 16th floor, the **Police Museum,** which has uniforms, guns, and badges worn by the Portland Police Bureau. Thanks to a city ordinance requiring that 1% of the development costs of new buildings be allotted to the arts, the center's hallways are lined with travertine sculptures, ceiling mosaics, stained-glass windows, and photographic murals. Visitors are welcome to peruse the works of art. ⊠ *1111 S.W. 2nd Ave.,* ☎ *503/823–0019.* ☞ *Free.* ☉ *Mon.–Thurs. 10–3.*

9 **KOIN Center.** An instant landmark after its completion in 1984, this handsome tower with a tapering form and a pyramidal top takes its design cues from early art deco skyscrapers. Made of brick with limestone trim and a blue metal roof, the tower houses offices (including those of a local television and radio station), a multiplex cinema, and,

COMING UP ROSES

EVERY JUNE since 1905, Portland, the City of Roses, has rolled out its rosy red carpet and welcomed thousands of visitors from around the world to its annual Rose Festival. The monthlong extravaganza now draws a total of some 2 million people, making it *the* event of Portland's year. During the festival, the roses in the 4½-acre International Rose Test Garden—and all over the city—are at their finest.

The festivities begin on the first Friday in June, with the naming and coronation of a rose queen, chosen each year from among candidates representing 14 Portland high schools. The ceremony is held at the Arlene Schnitzer Concert Hall. In honor of each rose queen, a bronze star is embedded in a sidewalk in the International Rose Test Garden and there is a fireworks spectacular downtown over the Willamette River after the coronation. On the day after the coronation, about 350,000 people turn out to see the dozens of illuminated floats in the **Starlight Parade** downtown.

The highlight of the 25 days of events and festivities is the **Grand Floral Parade** on the second Saturday in June, when around half a million people jam downtown streets to watch dozens of all-floral floats, marching bands, and equestrian performers. The parade is the second-largest all-floral parade in North America, second only to the Tournament of Roses Parade in Pasadena, California. Many people camp out overnight on downtown streets to hold a good spot along the parade route, but you can reserve a paid seat ($10–$20) in special viewing areas.

The Rose Festival coincides with **Fleet Week,** which usually gets under way around June 10. Thousands of sailors and marines cruise into town on dozens of military ships

that dock downtown, along the seawall on the west side of the Willamette River. Tens of thousands of people board the various cutters, destroyers, and frigates of the U.S. Navy, U.S. Coast Guard, and Royal Canadian Navy for free tours. On the Up River/Down River Cruises you can pay about $20 to ride a U.S. Navy or U.S. Coast Guard ship along the Columbia River from Longview, Washington, to Portland (cruises restricted to those age 8 and over).

In late June the **Rose Festival Airshow,** one of the nation's best, draws huge crowds to the Hillsboro Airport in suburban Portland. Dozens of aircraft, from biplanes to fighter jets, buzz the west side of town during the three-day event. The U.S. Air Force's Thunderbirds have appeared in past shows. The show costs about $10 for general admission, but reserved seating is also available.

Contending with the glory of the roses, the works of 125 juried artists from Oregon and around the U.S. appear at the **Portland Arts Festival** during three days in late June. Sculpture, jewelry, paintings, and photography fill the South Park Blocks near Portland State University, amid live music and food booths. The Portland Rose Society's **Annual Spring Rose Show** at Lloyd Center's Ice Chalet is the largest and longest-running rose show in the country. Local growers show off their best buds and compete for trophies on the Thursday and Friday before the Grand Floral Parade.

For more information on the Rose Festival and related events, check the official Web site, www.rosefestival.org, E-mail info@rosefestival.org, call ☎ 503/227–2681, or write ✉ 202 N.W. 2nd Ave., Portland 97209.

on its top floors, some of the most expensive condominiums in Portland. ⊠ *S.W. Columbia St. and S.W. 3rd Ave.*.

⑮ Mark O. Hatfield U.S. Courthouse. The New York architectural firm Kohn Pedersen Fox designed Portland's newest skyscraper, which was completed in 1997. The sophisticated exterior is clad in Indiana limestone, and the courtroom lobbies have expansive glass walls. Public rooftop terraces yield grand city views. ⊠ *S.W. 3rd Ave. between Main and Salmon Sts.*

⑳ Mill Ends Park. Sitting in the middle of a traffic island on Naito Parkway, this patch of urban tranquillity, at 24 inches in diameter, has been recognized by the *Guinness Book of Records* as the world's smallest official city park. ⊠ *S.W. Naito Pkwy. at Taylor St.*

② NikeTown. This futuristic F. A. O. Schwarz for the athletically inclined is a showplace for Nike, the international sportswear giant headquartered in suburban Beaverton. A life-size plaster cast of Michael Jordan captured in mid-jump dangles from the ceiling near the basketball shoes. Autographed sports memorabilia, video monitors, and statuary compete for your attention with the many products for sale. But don't expect any bargains: Prices are full retail and the word "sale" is almost as taboo around here as the name Reebok. ⊠ *930 S.W. 6th Ave.*, ☎ *503/221–6453.* ⊘ *Mon.–Thurs. and Sat. 10–7, Fri. 10–8, Sun. 11:30–6:30.*

⑥ Old Church. This building erected in 1882 is a prime example of Carpenter Gothic architecture. Tall spires and original stained-glass windows enhance its exterior of rough-cut lumber. The acoustically resonant church hosts free classical concerts at noon each Wednesday. If you're lucky, you'll get to hear one of the few operating Hook and Hastings tracker pipe organs. ⊠ *1422 S.W. 11th Ave.*, ☎ *503/222–2031.* 🎫 *Free.* ⊘ *Weekdays 11–3, Sat. by appointment.*

④ Oregon History Center. Impressive eight-story-high trompe l'oeil murals of Lewis and Clark and the Oregon Trail (the route the two pioneers took from the Midwest to the Oregon Territory) cover two sides of this downtown museum, which follows the state's story from prehistoric times to the present. The multisensory, hands-on "Portland!" exhibit presents a vivid slice of city life. Archaeological and anthropological artifacts, ship models, and memorabilia from the Oregon Trail are also on display in a series of dramatic galleries. The center's research library is open to the public; its bookstore is a good source for maps and publications on Pacific Northwest history. ⊠ *1200 S.W. Park Ave.*, ☎ *503/222–1741.* 🎫 *$6.* ⊘ *Tues.–Sat. 10–5, Sun. noon–5.*

★ ① Pioneer Courthouse Square. Downtown Portland's public heart and commercial soul are centered in this amphitheatrical brick piazza, whose design echoes the classic central plazas of European cities. Special events often take place in this premier people-watching venue, where the neatly dressed office crowd mingles with some of the city's stranger elements. The best time to be here is at noon, when a goofy weather machine blasts a fanfare and a shining sun, stormy dragon, or blue heron rises out of a misty cloud to confirm the day's weather. Four **vintage trolley** cars run from the MAX station here to Lloyd Center, with free service every half hour daily (10–6 weekends, 9:30–3 weekdays) from May to December and on weekends only in March and April (no service in January and February). Directly across the street is one of downtown Portland's most familiar landmarks, the classically sedate **Pioneer Courthouse.** Built in 1869, it's the oldest public building in the Pacific Northwest. ⊠ *701 S.W. 6th Ave.*, ☎ *503/223–1613.*

⑤ Portland Art Museum. The treasures at the Pacific Northwest's oldest visual- and media-arts facility span 35 centuries of Asian, European, and American art, with collections of Native American, regional, and contemporary art. The film center presents the annual Portland International Film Festival in February and March and the Northwest Film Festival in early November. ⊠ *1219 S.W. Park Ave.,* ☎ *503/226–2811; 503/221–1156 for film schedule.* 🎟 *$7.50.* ⊙ *Tues.–Sun. 10–5.*

⑬ Portland Building. *Portlandia,* the second-largest hammered-copper statue in the world, surpassed only by the Statue of Liberty, kneels on the second-story balcony of one of the first postmodern buildings in the United States. The building itself generates strong feelings; chances are you'll either love it or hate it. The controversial structure, architect Michael Graves's first major design commission, is buff colored with brown and blue trim and exterior decorative touches. The interior spaces are dark and clumsily executed. A permanent exhibit of public art includes a huge fiberglass mold of Portlandia's face and original works by local artists. ⊠ *1120 S.W. 5th Ave.* 🎟 *Free.* ⊙ *Weekdays 8–6.*

⑨ Portland Center for the Performing Arts. The "old building" and the hub of activity here is the **Arlene Schnitzer Concert Hall,** host to the Oregon Symphony, musical events of many genres, and lectures. Across Main Street, but still part of the center, is the 292-seat **Delores Winningstad Theater,** used for plays and special performances. Its stage design and dimensions are based on those of an Elizabethan-era stage. The 916-seat **Newmark Theater,** which houses Portland Center Stage, a highly regarded resident theater company, is also part of the complex. The section of the street connecting the old and new buildings is sometimes blocked off for food fairs, art shows, and other events. ⊠ *S.W. Broadway and S.W. Main St.,* ☎ *503/796–9293.*

⑱ Portland/Oregon Visitors Association. You can pick up maps and literature about the city and the state at this agency inside World Trade Center Two. ⊠ *28 S.W. Salmon St.,* ☎ *503/222–2223 or 800/962–3700.* ⊙ *Weekdays 9–5, Sat. 9–4.*

⑦ Portland State University. The state's only university in a major metropolitan area takes advantage of downtown's South Park Blocks to provide trees and greenery for its 15,000 students. The compact campus, located between Market Street and I–405, spreads west from the Park Blocks to 12th Avenue and east to 5th Avenue. Seven schools offer undergraduate, master's, and doctoral degrees.

⑯ State of Oregon Sports Hall of Fame. This museum houses sports memorabilia associated with prominent Oregonian athletes and organizations such as Heisman Trophy winner Terry Baker, the Portland Trail Blazers professional basketball team, and baseball player Mickey Lolich, who pitched for the Detroit Tigers in three World Series. ⊠ *321 S.W. Salmon St.,* ☎ *503/227–7466.* 🎟 *$3.* ⊙ *Tues.–Sun. 10–6.*

⑩ Terry Schrunk Plaza. A terraced amphitheater of green lawn and brick, shaded by flowering cherry trees, the plaza is a popular lunch spot for the office crowd. ⊠ *Between S.W. 3rd and 4th Aves. and S.W. Madison and Jefferson Sts.*

⑰ World Trade Center. The three sleek, handsome World Trade Center buildings, designed by the Portland architectural firm Zimmer Gunsel Frasca, are connected by sky bridges. Retail stores, a restaurant, coffee shops, banks, and travel agencies occupy the ground floors. ⊠ *Salmon St. between S.W. 2nd Ave. and S.W. Naito Pkwy.*

★ **㉑ Yamhill National Historic District.** Many examples of 19th-century cast-iron architecture have been preserved within this district's six square blocks. Because the cast-iron facade helped support the main structure, these buildings traditionally did not need big, heavy walls to bear the weight; the interior spaces could therefore be larger and more open. North and west of this area, along 2nd Avenue, galleries exhibit fine art, ceramics, photography, and posters. On the first Thursday of each month, new shows are unveiled and most galleries stay open until 9 PM. Call the Portland Art Museum at 503/226–2811 for details. ✉ *Between S.W. Naito Pkwy. and S.W. 3rd Ave., and S.W. Morrison and S.W. Taylor Sts.*

The Skidmore District and Chinatown

The Skidmore Old Town National Historic District, commonly called the Skidmore District or Old Town, is where Portland was born. The 20-square-block section, bounded by Oak Street to the south and Everett Street to the north, includes buildings of varying ages and architectural designs. Before it was renovated, this was skid row, and vestiges of that condition remain. In addition to many Chinese restaurants and gift shops, the area is home to an increasing number of gay bars and restaurants. MAX serves the area with a stop at the Old Town/Chinatown station.

Numbers in the text correspond to numbers in the margin and on the Downtown, Skidmore, and Chinatown map.

A Good Walk

Begin on Southwest Naito Parkway at the **Oregon Maritime Center and Museum** ㉓. Across Southwest Ash Street at the far northern corner of the Central Fire Station is the **Jeff Morris Memorial Fire Museum** ㉔. **Skidmore Fountain** ㉕, the centerpiece of Ankeny Square, is adjacent to the museum. On Saturday and Sunday the area west of the fountain near 2nd Avenue is home to the **Portland Saturday Market** ㉖. Walk north one block on Naito Parkway past the Burnside Bridge to the **Japanese-American Historical Plaza** ㉗. Walk west on Burnside Street to Northwest 4th Avenue and the **Chinatown Gate** ㉘, the official entrance to the **Chinatown District.**

TIMING

Sights in the Skidmore District and Chinatown can be easily seen in an hour or less. Add a half hour if you're interested in the American Advertising Museum. It's best to do this walk during daylight hours because the street scene here can be intimidating.

Sights to See

❷❽ **Chinatown Gate.** Recognizable by its five roofs, 64 dragons, and two huge lions, the Chinatown Gate is the official entrance to the **Chinatown District.** During the 1890s, Portland had the second-largest Chinese community in the United States. Today's Chinatown is compressed into several blocks with restaurants (though many locals prefer Chinese eateries outside the district), shops, and grocery stores. ✉ *N.W. 4th Ave. and Burnside St.*

❷❼ **Japanese-American Historical Plaza.** Take a moment to study the evocative figures cast into the bronze columns at the plaza's entrance; they show Japanese-Americans before, during, and after World War II—living daily life, fighting in battle for the United States, marching off to internment camps. More than 110,000 Japanese-Americans were interned by the American government during the war. This park, an oasis of meticulous landscaping and flowering cherry trees, was created to commemorate their experience and contributions. Simple blocks of granite carved with haiku poems describing the war experience powerfully evoke this dark episode in American history. ✉ *East of Naito Pkwy. between W. Burnside and N.W. Couch Sts.*

24 **Jeff Morris Memorial Fire Museum.** This is not a museum you enter: The antique horse-drawn pumps and other fire-fighting equipment on display are visible through large plate-glass windows on the north side of the Central Fire Station building. Cast-iron medallions, capitals, and grillwork taken from other buildings decorate the wall; cast-iron columns mark the border of Ankeny Square, beside the museum. ⊠ *111 S.W. Naito Pkwy.*

NEED A
BREAK?

For a break from sightseeing and shopping, settle into cool, dark **Kell's Irish Restaurant & Pub** (⊠ 112 S.W. 2nd Ave., between S.W. Ash and S.W. Pine Sts., ☎ 503/227–4057) for a pint of Guinness and authentic Irish pub fare—and be sure to ask the bartender how all those folded-up dollar bills got stuck to the ceiling.

👆 **23** **Oregon Maritime Center and Museum.** Local model makers created most of this museum's models of ships that plied the Columbia River. Prime street-level examples of cast-iron architecture grace the building's exterior. The admission fee includes entrance aboard the last operating stern-wheel steam tug in the United States, which is docked across the street. ⊠ *113 S.W. Naito Pkwy.*, ☎ *503/224–7724.* ⊡ *$4.* ☉ *Memorial Day–Labor Day, Fri.–Sun. 11–4; Labor Day–Memorial Day, Thurs.–Sun. 11–4.*

★ **26** **Portland Saturday Market.** On Saturday and Sunday from March to Christmas, the west side of the Burnside Bridge and the Skidmore Fountain environs is home to North America's largest open-air handicraft market. This is not upscale shopping by any means, but if you're looking for crystals, yard goods, beaded hats, stained glass, birdhouses, jewelry, flags, wood and rubber stamps, or custom footwear and decorative boots, you stand a good chance of finding them. Entertainers and food and produce booths add to the festive atmosphere. ⊠ *Under west end of the Burnside Bridge, from S.W. Naito Pkwy. to Ankeny Sq.*, ☎ *503/222–6072.* ☉ *Mar.–Dec., Sat. 10–5, Sun. 11–4:30.*

25 **Skidmore Fountain.** This unusually graceful fountain built in 1888 is the centerpiece of **Ankeny Square,** a plaza around which many community activities take place. Two nymphs uphold the brimming basin on top; citizens once quenched their thirst from the spouting lions' heads below, and horses drank from the granite troughs at the base of the fountain. ⊠ *S.W. Ankeny St. at S.W. Naito Pkwy.*

Nob Hill and Vicinity

The showiest example of Portland's newly acquired urban chic is Northwest 23rd Avenue, a 20-block thoroughfare that cuts north–south through the neighborhood known as Nob Hill. Fashionable since the 1880s and still filled with Victorian residential architecture, the neighborhood is a mixed-use cornucopia of old Portland charm and new Portland trendiness. With its cafés, restaurants, galleries, and boutiques, it's a delightful place to stroll, shop, and people-watch. More trendy restaurants, shops, and nightspots can be found on Northwest 21st Avenue, a few blocks away. Finding parking in this neighborhood has become such a challenge that the city has decided to put in a streetcar line. Now under construction, it will run from Legacy Good Samaritan Hospital in Nob Hill, connect with MAX light rail near Pioneer Courthouse Square downtown, and then continue up 10th Avenue to Portland State University.

Numbers in the text correspond to numbers in the margin and on the Nob Hill and Vicinity map.

Two Good Walks

Northwest 23rd Avenue between West Burnside Street and Northwest Lovejoy Street—the east–west-running streets are in alphabetical order—is the heart of Nob Hill. There's such a profusion of coffee bars and cafés along the avenue that some locals call it Latte-land Central. You don't need a map of the avenue, just cash or credit cards. Some of the shops and restaurants are in newly designed quarters, and others are tucked into restored Victorian and other century-old homes and buildings. As it continues north past Lovejoy Street, the avenue begins to quiet down. Between Overton and Pettygrove streets, a block of open-porch frame houses converted into shops typifies the alternative, New Age side of Portland. The **Pettygrove House** ㉙, a Victorian gingerbread on the corner of 23rd Avenue and Pettygrove Street, was built by the man who gave Portland its name. Continue on 23rd Avenue past Pettygrove to Quimby Street to reach the **Clear Creek Distillery** ㉚.

There's much more to Nob Hill than Northwest 21st and 23rd avenues, something you'll discover if you walk among the neighborhood's Victorian residences. Most of the noteworthy structures are private residences and do not have identifying plaques, nor do they admit visitors. Begin at 23rd Avenue and Flanders Street, with the 1891 **Trevett-Nunn House** ㉛, an excellent example of the Colonial Revival style. Continue east to the 1907 **Day Building** ㉜, an apartment building fronted by Corinthian columns. Farther east is the Byzantine **Temple Beth Israel** ㉝, completed in 1928. At Flanders and 17th Avenue head north (to the left) to Irving Street. The **Campbell Townhouses** ㉞ are the only known example of brick row-house construction in Oregon. Continue west on Irving and north (to the right) on 18th Avenue to the **Ayer-Shea House** ㉟, an elegant Colonial Revival house.

Heading west on Johnson Street, you'll pass the Italianate-style **Sprague-Marshall-Bowie House** (⊠ 2234 N.W. Johnson St.), built in 1882. A few doors away is the 1893 **Albert Tanner House** (⊠ 2248 N.W. Johnson St.), a rare Stick-style residence with a wraparound porch and richly decorated front gables. The 2½-story **Mary Smith House** ㊱ offers an unusual variation on the Colonial Revival style. At 22nd Avenue, turn south (left) to reach the **Nathan Loeb House** ㊲, a fine late-19th-century Queen Anne–style structure. Continue south on 22nd Avenue and turn east (left) on Hoyt Street to reach the **Joseph Bergman House** (⊠ 2134 N.W. Hoyt St.), a High Victorian Italianate–style home built in 1885. Head two blocks east to 20th Avenue and two blocks south (to the right) to reach the rare, Shingle-style **George Huesner House** ㊳.

TIMING

Strolling along 23rd Avenue from Burnside Street to Pettygrove Street can take a half hour or half a day, depending on how many eateries or shops lure you in along the way. The tour of neighborhood Victorian residences can be done in about an hour.

Sights to See

㉟ **Ayer-Shea House.** This Colonial Revival house was built in 1892 by Whidden and Lewis, who also designed Portland's City Hall. ⊠ *1809 N.W. Johnson St.*

㉞ **Campbell Townhouses.** These six attached buildings with Queen Anne–style detailing, reminiscent of row houses in San Francisco and along the East Coast, have undergone virtually no structural modification since they were built in 1893. ⊠ *1705–1719 N.W. Irving St.*

㉚ **Clear Creek Distillery.** The distillery keeps such a low profile that it's practically invisible. But ring the bell and someone will unlock the wrought-iron gate and let you into a dim, quiet tasting room where

28

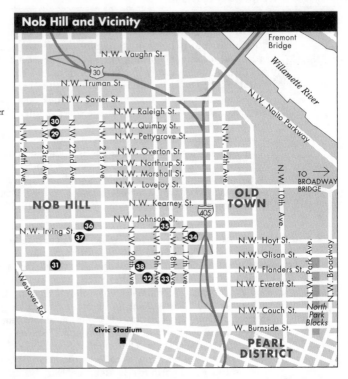

Nob Hill and Vicinity

you can sample Clear Creek's world-famous Oregon apple and pear brandies and grappas. ⊠ *1430 N.W. 23rd Ave., near Quimby St.,* ☎ *503/248–9470.* ☺ *Weekdays 8–4:30 or by appointment.*

㉜ Day Building. A 1907 example of the Colonial Revival style offers a front facade of large, fluted columns rising more than 30 ft to ornate Corinthian capitals. ⊠ *2068 N.W. Flanders St.*

㊳ George Huesner House. Typical of the Shingle style that came into vogue in the 1890s, this home was designed by Edgar Lazarus, architect of landmarks such as Vista House in the Columbia River Gorge. ⊠ *333 N.W. 20th Ave.*

NEED A BREAK?

You won't have any trouble finding a place to sit and caffeinate on Northwest 23rd. Two of Portland's largest coffee competitors, Coffee People and Starbucks, face each other on opposite sides of Hoyt Street. The best of the smaller cafés is **Torrefazione Italia** (⊠ 838 N.W. 23rd Ave., ☎ 503/228–1255), which exudes a bright Italian charm and serves delicious coffee (none of it flavored) in Deruta ceramic cups.

㊱ Mary Smith House. Dating from 1906, this home has a central second-story bow window and a full-length veranda with a central bowed portico supported by Ionic columns. ⊠ *2256 N.W. Johnson St.*

㊲ Nathan Loeb House. One of the most ornate Victorians in Portland, the Loeb House has turned-wood posts, wood arches with central pendants and sunburst spandrel patterns, and a projecting ground-floor section with an ornamental three-bay round-arch window. ⊠ *726 N.W. 22nd Ave.*

㉙ Pettygrove House. Back in 1845, after he'd bought much of what is now downtown Portland for $50, Francis Pettygrove and his partner,

Asa Lovejoy, flipped a coin to decide who would name the still unbuilt city. Pettygrove won and chose Portland, after a town in his native Maine. His beautifully restored Victorian gingerbread house was built in 1892. ⊠ *2287 N.W. Pettygrove St.*

㉝ Temple Beth Israel. The imposing sandstone, brick, and stone structure with a massive domed roof and Byzantine styling was completed in 1928 and still serves a congregation first organized in 1858. ⊠ *1972 N.W. Flanders St.*

㉛ Trevett-Nunn House. Built in 1891, this Colonial Revival home is the oldest extant residence designed by Whidden and Lewis, Portland's most distinguished late-19th-century architectural firm. ⊠ *2347 N.W. Flanders St.*

Washington Park and Forest Park

Numbers in the text correspond to numbers in the margin and on the Washington Park and Forest Park map.

A Good Tour
The best way to get to Washington Park is via MAX light rail, which travels through a tunnel deep beneath the city's West Hills. Be sure to walk through the Washington Park station, the deepest (260 ft) transit station in North America. Graphics on the walls depict life in the Portland area over the past 17 million years. There's also a core sample of the bedrock. If you're driving, head west of downtown on West Burnside Street and south (turn left) on Southwest Tichner Drive to reach 322-acre Washington Park, home to the **Hoyt Arboretum** ㊴, the **International Rose Test Garden** ㊵, and the **Japanese Garden** ㊶. By car, the **Oregon Zoo** ㊷ and the **World Forestry Center** ㊸ can best be reached by heading west on U.S. 26. North of the park is the opulent **Pittock Mansion** ㊹. Also north of Washington Park is **Forest Park** ㊺.

TIMING

You could easily spend a day at either Washington Park or Forest Park; plan on at least two hours at the zoo, an hour or more at the arboretum, rose garden, and Japanese Garden, and an hour to tour the Pittock Mansion and its grounds.

Sights to See
㊺ Forest Park. The nation's largest (5,000 acres) urban wilderness, this city-owned oasis, home to more than 100 species of birds and 50 species of mammals, contains more than 50 mi of trails. The **Portland Audubon Society** (⊠ 5151 N.W. Cornell Rd., ☎ 503/292–9453) supplies free maps and sponsors a bevy of bird-related activities in the heart of the only old-growth forest in a major U.S. city. Programs include guided bird-watching events, a hospital for injured and orphaned birds, and a gift shop stocked with books, feeders, and bird-lovers' paraphernalia. ⊠ *Take N.W. Lovejoy St. west to where it becomes Cornell Rd. and follow to the park,* ☎ *503/823–7529.* ⊑ *Free.* ☺ *Dawn–dusk.*

㊴ Hoyt Arboretum. Ten miles of trails wind through the arboretum, which has more than 800 species of plants and one of the nation's largest collections of coniferous trees; pick up trail maps at the visitor center. Also here are the Winter Garden and a memorial to veterans of the Vietnam War. ⊠ *4000 S.W. Fairview Blvd.,* ☎ *503/228–8733.* ⊑ *Free.* ☺ *Arboretum daily dawn–dusk, visitor center most days 9–4.*

★ **㊵ International Rose Test Garden.** Despite the name, these grounds are not an experimental greenhouse laboratory but three breathtaking terraced gardens, set on 4 acres, where 10,000 bushes and 400 varieties of roses grow. The flowers, many of them new varieties, are at their

30

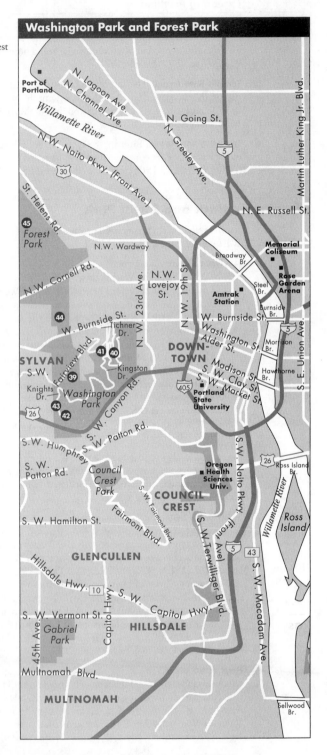

Washington Park and Forest Park

peak in June and July and September and October. From the gardens, there are highly photogenic views of the downtown skyline and, on fine days, the Fuji-shape slopes of Mount Hood, 50 mi to the east. Summer concerts take place in the garden's amphitheater. Take MAX light rail to Washington Park station and transfer to Bus No. 63. ⊠ *400 S.W. Kingston Ave.,* ☎ *503/823–3636.* 🖾 *Free.* ☉ *Dawn–dusk.*

★ ㊶ **Japanese Garden.** The most authentic Japanese garden outside Japan is nestled among 5½ acres of Washington Park above the International Rose Test Garden. This serene oasis, designed by a Japanese landscape master and opened to the public in 1967, represents five separate garden styles: Strolling Pond Garden, Tea Garden, Natural Garden, Sand and Stone Garden, and Flat Garden. The Tea House was built in Japan and reconstructed here. The west side of the Pavilion has a majestic view of Portland and Mount Hood. Take MAX light rail to Washington Park station and transfer to Bus No. 63. ⊠ *611 S.W. Kingston Ave.,* ☎ *503/223–1321.* 🖾 *$6.* ☉ *Apr.–May and Sept., daily 10–6; June– Aug., daily 9–8; Oct.–Mar., daily 10–4.*

🐾 ㊷ **Oregon Zoo.** The zoo, which was established in 1887, has been a prolific breeding ground for Asian elephants. Major exhibits include an African section with rhinos, hippos, zebras, and pythons, plus an aviary with 15 species of birds. Other popular attractions include an Alaska Tundra exhibit, with wolves and grizzly bears, a penguinarium, and habitats for beavers, otters, and reptiles native to the west side of the Cascade Range. During the summer a 4-mi round-trip narrow-gauge train operates from the zoo, chugging through the woods to a station near the International Rose Test Garden and the Japanese Garden. Take the MAX light rail to Washington Park station. ⊠ *4001 S.W. Canyon Rd.,* ☎ *503/226–7627.* 🖾 *$5.50; free 2nd Tues. of month after 3 PM.* ☉ *Labor Day–Memorial Day, daily 9:30–6; Memorial Day–Labor Day, daily 9:30–4.*

★ ㊹ **Pittock Mansion.** Henry Pittock, the founder and publisher of the *Oregonian* newspaper, built this mansion, which combines French Renaissance and Victorian styles. The opulent manor, erected in 1914, is filled with art and antiques of the 1880s. The grounds, north of Washington Park and 1,000 ft above the city, have superb views of the skyline, rivers, and the Cascade Range. ⊠ *3229 N.W. Pittock Dr.; from W. Burnside St. heading west, turn right on N.W. Barnes Rd. and follow signs,* ☎ *503/823–3624.* 🖾 *$4.50.* ☉ *Daily noon–4.*

🐾 ㊸ **World Forestry Center.** The center, across from the Oregon Zoo, takes its arboreal interests seriously—its spokesperson is a 70-ft-tall talking tree! Outside, a 1909 locomotive and antique logging equipment are displayed, and inside are two floors of exhibits, a multi-image "Forests of the World," a collection of 100-year-old wood, and a gift shop. ⊠ *4033 S.W. Canyon Rd.,* ☎ *503/228–1367.* 🖾 *$3.50.* ☉ *Daily 10–5.*

East of the Willamette River

Portland is known as the City of Roses, but the 10 distinctive bridges spanning the Willamette River have also earned it the name Bridgetown. The older drawbridges, near downtown, open several times a day to allow passage of large cargo ships and freighters.

Numbers in the text correspond to numbers in the margin and on the East of the Willamette River map.

A Good Tour

Most people visit Portland's east-side destinations separately, and by car rather than public transportation. **Laurelhurst Park** ㊻ is a stately enclave. Busy Hawthorne Boulevard in the **Hawthorne District** ㊼ offers some interesting shopping and abuts **Mount Tabor Park** ㊽ at its eastern end. At the western end of Hawthorne Boulevard, on the banks of the Willamette River, is the **Oregon Museum of Science and Industry** ㊾. Head south and east to the **American Advertising Museum** ㊿ and **Crystal Springs Rhododendron Garden** �; then make your way back toward the river and the shops of the **Sellwood District** �652. At river's edge stands **Oaks Amusement Park** �653, a good spot for kids; another option is to drive a little farther south to **North Clackamas Aquatic Park** �654, where you can all unwind in the wave pool.

TIMING

You could spend a pleasant hour or so strolling each of the parks, gardens, and neighborhoods here. Plan to spend one to two hours at the Oregon Museum of Science and Industry or the amusement park.

Sights to See

㊿ **American Advertising Museum.** This museum is devoted solely to advertising. Exhibits celebrate memorable campaigns, print advertisements, radio and TV commercials, and novelty and specialty products. ⊠ *5035 S.E. 24th Ave.,* ☎ *503/226–0000.* ⊡ *$3.* ☉ *Sat. noon–5.*

� **Crystal Springs Rhododendron Garden.** For much of the year this 7-acre retreat near Reed College is used by bird-watchers and those who want a restful stroll. But starting in April, thousands of rhododendron bushes and azaleas burst into flower. The peak blooming season for these woody shrubs is May; by late June the show is over. ⊠ *S.E. 28th Ave. (west side, 1 block north of Woodstock Blvd.),* ☎ *503/777–1734.* ⊡ *$3 Mar.–Labor Day, Thurs.–Mon.; otherwise free.* ☉ *Daily dawn–dusk.*

OFF THE
BEATEN PATH

THE GROTTO – Owned by the Catholic Church, the Sanctuary of Our Sorrowful Mother, as it's officially known, displays more than 100 statues and shrines in 62 acre of woods. The grotto was carved into the base of a 110-ft cliff and features a replica of Michelangelo's *Pietà*. From this vantage point you'll get a fantastic view of the Columbia River and the Cascades. There's a dazzling Festival of Lights at Christmastime (late November through December), with 250,000 lights, and holiday concerts in the 600-seat chapel. Sunday masses are held here, too. ⊠ *Sandy Blvd. at N.E. 85th Ave.,* ☎ *503/254–7371.* ⊡ *Grotto free, upper garden level $2.* ☉ *Spring–fall 9–6:30, closes at sunset in winter; call for details.*

�647 **Hawthorne District.** Though it's quickly becoming more upscale, this neighborhood near the foot of Mount Tabor still has a countercultural feel. The popularity of the many bookstores, coffeehouses, taverns, restaurants, antiques stores, used CD shops, and boutiques here sometimes makes finding a parking space a challenge. ⊠ *S.E. Hawthorne Blvd., between 30th and 42nd Aves.*

NEED A
BREAK?

For a good and reasonably priced meal, try the **Tabor Hill Cafe** (⊠ 3766 S.E. Hawthorne Blvd., ☎ 503/230–1231) for breakfast, lunch, or brunch. At the **Bagdad Theater** (⊠ 3702 S.E. Hawthorne Blvd., ☎ 503/230–0895) you can buy a pint of beer and a slice of pizza and watch a movie. **Pastaworks** (⊠ 3731 S.E. Hawthorne Blvd., ☎ 503/232–1010) sells cookware, gourmet deli food, organic produce, beer, wine, and pasta.

㊿ �646 **Laurelhurst Park.** Manicured lawns, stately trees, and a wildfowl pond make this 25-acre southeast Portland park a favorite urban hangout. Laurelhurst, one of the city's most beautiful neighborhoods, surrounds the park. ⊠ *S.E. 39th Ave. between S.E. Ankeny and Oak Sts.* ☉ *Daily dawn–dusk.*

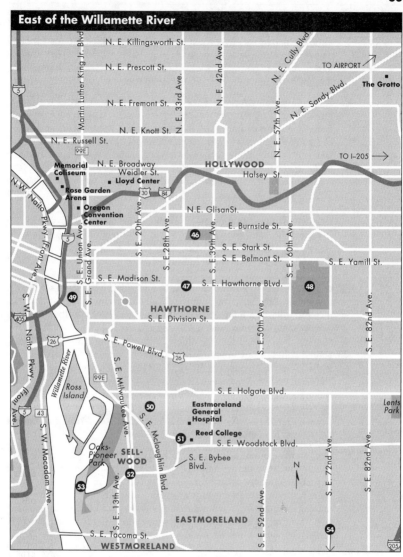

East of the Willamette River

N. E. Killingsworth St.

N. E. Prescott St.

Martin Luther King Jr. Blvd

N. E. Cully Blvd.

TO AIRPORT

The Grotto

N. E. Fremont St.

N. E. 42nd Ave.

N. E. Sandy Blvd.

N. E. 33rd Ave.

N. E. Knott St.

N. E. 57th Ave.

N. E. Russell St.

99E

TO I-205 →

Memorial Coliseum

N. E. Broadway
Weidler St.

HOLLYWOOD

Halsey St.

Rose Garden Arena

Lloyd Center

30 84

Oregon Convention Center

N.E. GlisanSt.

E. Burnside St.

46

S. E. Stark St.

S. E. 20th Ave.

S. E. 28th Ave.

S. E. 39th Ave.

S. E. Belmont St.

S. E. 60th Ave.

S. E. Yamill St.

S. E. Madison St.

47

S. E. Hawthorne Blvd.

48

49

HAWTHORNE
S. E. Division St.

S. E.50th Ave.

S. E. 82nd Ave.

405

S. E. Powell Blvd.

26

26

Willamette River

99E

S. E. Holgate Blvd.

Lents Park

Ross Island

S. E. Milwaukee Ave.

50

Eastmoreland General Hospital

43

S. E. Mcloughlin Blvd.

51

Reed College

S. E. Woodstock Blvd.

S. W. Macadam Ave.

Oaks Pioneer Park

SELL-WOOD

S. E. Bybee Blvd.

N

S. E. 72nd Ave.

S. E. 82nd Ave.

53

52

S. E. 13th Ave.

S. E. 52nd Ave.

EASTMORELAND

54

S. E. Tacoma St.
WESTMORELAND

205

American Advertising Museum, **50**

Crystal Springs Rhododendron Garden, **51**

Hawthorne District, **47**

Laurelhurst Park, **46**

Mount Tabor Park, **48**

North Clackamas Aquatic Park, **54**

Oaks Amusement Park, **53**

Oregon Museum of Science and Industry, **49**

Sellwood District, **52**

🖑 ㊽ **Mount Tabor Park.** Dirt trails and an asphalt road wind through forested hillsides and past good picnic areas to the top of Mount Tabor, which looks out toward Portland's West Hills. Mount Tabor is an extinct volcano; the buttes and conical hills east of the park are evidence of the gigantic eruptions that formed the Cascade Range millions of years ago. ⊠ *S.E. 60th Ave. and Salmon St.,* ☎ *503/823–7529.*

🖑 ㊾ **North Clackamas Aquatic Park.** If you're visiting Portland with kids any time of the year and are looking for a great way to cool off—especially on one of Portland's notoriously hot July or August days—check out this all-indoor attraction, whose pool has 4-ft waves and super slides. A family rate is available on Sunday and Wednesday. Children under age 8 must be accompanied by someone 13 or older. ⊠ *7300 S.E. Harmony Rd., Milwaukie,* ☎ *503/557–7873.* 🎫 *$9.50.* ☉ *Mon., Wed., and Fri. 4–8; weekends 11–8 (no open swim Sat., Sun. 3–4).*

OFF THE   **NORTHWEST ALPACAS RANCH –** The kids can pet the llama-like animals
BEATEN PATH   at this ranch southwest of Portland. There's also a gift shop that sells
              sweaters made from alpaca wool. ⊠ *11785 S.W. River Rd., Scholls,* ☎
              503/628–3089. 🎫 *Free.* ☉ *Fri.–Sun. 10–5.*

🖑 ㊽ **Oaks Amusement Park.** It may not be Disneyland, but there's a small-town charm to this park with thrill rides and miniature golf in summer and roller-skating year-round. In summer 1999 Oaks Park opened Acorn Acres, complete with a 360-degree loop roller coaster. The skating rink, built in 1905, is the oldest continuously operating one in the United States. There are outdoor concerts in summer. Also in the park is the **Ladybug Theater** (☎ *503/232–2346*), which presents shows for children. ⊠ *S.E. Spokane St. east of the Willamette River (from east side of Sellwood Bridge, take Grand Ave. north and Spokane west),* ☎ *503/233–5777.* 🎫 *Park free, 5-hr ride passes $8.50–$11.* ☉ *Mid-June–Labor Day, Tues.–Sun. noon–5; late Mar.–mid-June and Labor Day–Oct., weekends only, noon–5.*

★ 🖑 ㊾ **Oregon Museum of Science and Industry** (OMSI). An Omnimax theater and planetarium are among the main attractions at the Northwest's largest astronomy educational facility, which also has a hands-on computer center, a space wing with a mission-control center, and many permanent and touring scientific exhibits. Moored in the Willamette as part of the museum is a 240-ft submarine, the USS *Blueback*. ⊠ *1945 S.E. Water Ave., south of the Morrison Bridge,* ☎ *503/797–4000.* 🎫 *Museum and planetarium $6.50; Omnimax $5.50; USS Blueback $3.50.* ☉ *Memorial Day–Labor Day, daily 9:30–7 (Thurs. until 8); Labor Day–Memorial Day, daily 9:30–5:30 (Thurs. until 8).*

㊼ **Sellwood District.** The browsable neighborhood that begins east of the Sellwood Bridge was once a separate town. Annexed by Portland in the 1890s, it retains a modest charm. On weekends the antiques stores along 13th Avenue do a brisk business. Each store is identified by a plaque that tells the date of construction and what the building was originally used for. ⊠ *S.E. 13th Ave. between Malden and Clatsop Sts.*

DINING

First-time visitors to Portland are often surprised by the diversity of restaurants and the low prices. Lovers of ethnic foods can choose from restaurants serving Chinese, French, Indian, Italian, Japanese, Middle Eastern, Tex-Mex, Thai, and Vietnamese specialties. There's also Pacific Northwest cuisine, which incorporates regional fish and game plus locally grown wild mushrooms and other produce.

Restaurants are arranged first by neighborhood and then by type of cuisine served.

CATEGORY	COST*
$$$$	over $35
$$$	$25–$35
$$	$15–$25
$	under $15

per person for a three-course meal, excluding drinks and service

Downtown and the Pearl District

American

$$$$ ✕ **Atwater's.** Perched on the 30th floor of the U.S. Bancorp Tower, Atwater's has an outstanding view of the Willamette River, the Cascade Range, and the city's skyline. The cuisine is American but relies almost exclusively on ingredients indigenous to the Pacific Northwest—depending on the season everything from fresh seafood (ahi, Pacific salmon, Dungeness crab, sturgeon) to chicken and game. An 18,000-bottle enclosed "wine cellar" with labels from every wine-producing region in the world is a prominent feature of the dining room. Dansk linens, silver cutlery, crystal glasses, and an orchid on every table lend a touch of elegance. Musicians perform in the adjoining bar from Wednesday to Saturday. ⊠ *111 S.W. 5th Ave.,* ☎ *503/275–3600. Reservations essential. AE, D, DC, MC, V. No lunch.*

$$–$$$$ ✕ **Jake's Grill.** Not to be confused with the Jake's (☞ *below*) of seafood fame, this eatery in the Governor Hotel is famous for its fare of turf rather than surf. Steaks and the Sunday brunch are popular draws. ⊠ *611 S.W. 10th Ave.,* ☎ *503/220–1850. AE, D, DC, MC, V.*

$$$ ✕ **Esplanade at RiverPlace.** Tall windows frame a dramatic view of the sailboat-filled marina and the Willamette River at this restaurant in the RiverPlace Hotel (☞ Lodging, *below*). The cuisine is gourmet Pacific Northwest—Dungeness crab cakes; plump scallops seared with fennel, red onion, and oyster mushrooms; duck with blackberry sauce—and the wine list includes many hard-to-find Pacific Northwest vintages. ⊠ *1510 S.W. Harbor Way,* ☎ *503/228–3233. AE, D, DC, MC, V.*

$$–$$$ ✕ **Red Star Tavern & Roast House.** Cooked in a wood-burning oven, smoker, rotisserie, or grill, the cuisine at Red Star can best be described as American comfort food inspired by the bounty of the Pacific Northwest. Spit-roasted leg of lamb, maple-fired baby back ribs with a brown-ale glaze, and charred salmon with fennel sausage and Manila clams are some of the better entrées. The wine list includes regional and international vintages, and 12 local microbrews are on tap. The spacious restaurant, part of the Fifth Avenue Suites Hotel, has a lodge-style ambience, with tufted leather booths, murals, and copper accents. ⊠ *503 S.W. Alder St.,* ☎ *503/222–0005. AE, D, DC, MC, V.*

American/Casual

$ ✕ **Bridgeport BrewPub & Restaurant.** The only food on the menu here is thick, hand-thrown pizza on sourdough crust, served inside a cool, ivy-covered, century-old industrial building. The boisterous crowds wash down the pizza with frothing pints of Bridgeport's English-style ale, brewed on the premises. During the summer the flower-festooned loading dock is transformed into a beer garden. ⊠ *1313 N.W. Marshall St.,* ☎ *503/241–3612. MC, V.*

Chinese

$–$$ **Fong Chong.** Considered by many locals to be Chinatown's best Chinese restaurant, Fong Chong serves dim sum every day. The family-style eatery features dumplings, which are filled with shrimp, pork, or vegetables and are accompanied by plenty of different sauces. If you haven't

36

Abou Karim, **29**

Alexis, **27**

Assaggio, **43**

Atwater's, **26**

Bangkok Kitchen, **39**

Bastas, **8**

Bima, **18**

Bridgeport BrewPub, **1**

Couvron, **15**

Dan & Louis's Oyster Bar, **25**

Esparza's Tex-Mex Cafe, **36**

Esplanade at RiverPlace, **31**

Fong Chong, **28**

Fujin, **41**

Genoa, **37**

The Heathman, **16**

Higgins, **24**

Hokkaido Japanese Cuisine and Sushi Bar, **35**

Indigine, **40**

Jake's Famous Crawfish, **11**

Jake's Grill, **19**

Kornblatt's, **4**

Mayas Taqueria, **20**

McCormick and Schmick's, **30**

Misohapi, **2**

Montage, **44**

Murata, **17**

Newport Bay at RiverPlace, **32**

Paley's Place, **6**

Papa Haydn, **3**

Pazzo, **13**

Piatti on Broadway, **21**

Pizzicato, **12**

Plainfield's Mayur, **10**

Red Star Tavern & Roast House, **14**

The Ringside, **9**

Saigon Kitchen, **33**

Southpark, **23**

Tennessee Red's, **42**

Typhoon!, **22**

Wild Abandon, **38**

Wildwood, **5**

Yen Ha, **34**

Zefiro, **7**

Portland Dining

Willamette River

N.W. Naito Parkway (Front Ave.)

N.E. River

Fremont Bridge

N.W. Vaughn St.

30

N.W. Thurman St.

N.W. Savier St.

N.W. Raleigh St.

N.W. Quimby St.

N.W. Pettygrove St.

N.W. Naito Parkw

N.W. 24th Ave.

N.W. 23rd Ave.

N.W. 22nd Ave.

N.W. 21st Ave.

N.W. 15th Ave.

N.W. 14th Ave.

N.W. 10th Ave.

N.W. Overton St.

N.W. Northrup St.

N.W. Marshall St.

N.W. Lovejoy St.

Amtra

NOB HILL

N.W. Kearney St.

405

N.W. Johnson St.

N.W. 20th Ave.

N.W. 19th Ave.

N.W. 18th Ave.

N.W. 17th Ave.

N.W. Irving St.

N.W. Hoyt St.

N.W. Glisan St.

N.W. Flanders St.

N.W. Everett St.

N.W. Park Ave.

Westover Rd.

N.W. Couch St.

S.W. Vista Ave.

PEARL DISTRICT

S.W. Morrison St.

15th Ave.

S.W. 20th Ave.

S.W. 18th Ave.

S.W. 16th Ave.

S.W. 14th Ave.

S.W. Taylor St.

S.W. Salmon St.

S.W. Yar

S.W.

TO WASHINGTON PARK

26

Portland Art Museum

12th Ave.

S.W. 10th Ave.

S.W. Park Ave.

S.W. Broadway

S.W. Mai

S.W. Madi

S.W. Jeffers

S.W. Columbi

S.W. Clay St.

S.W. Market St.

N

KEY

AE American Express Office

0 ——— 750 yards

0 ——— 750 meters

S.W. Harrison St.

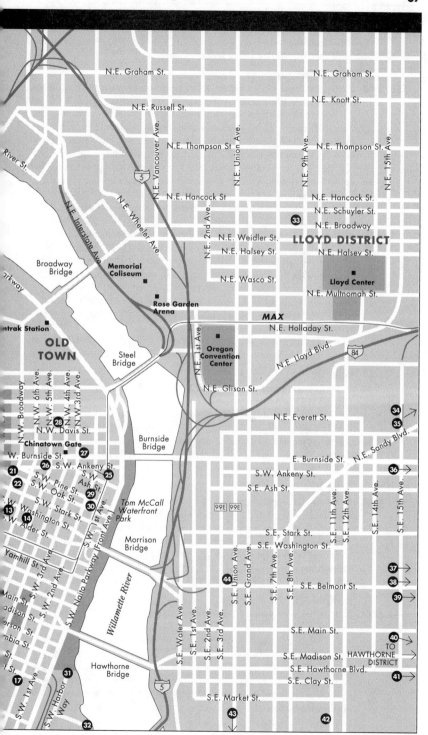

eaten dim sum before, just take a seat: the food is brought to you on carts. Pick what you want as the carts come by and pass the plates among your companions at large tables with tops that rotate like a lazy susan. ⊠ *301 N.W. 4th Ave.,* ☎ *503/220–0235. AE, D, DC, MC.*

Contemporary

$$$–$$$$ ✕ **Higgins.** Chef Greg Higgins, former executive chef at the Heathman Hotel, opened this restaurant near the Arlene Schnitzer Concert Hall in 1994. He focuses on Pacific Northwest ingredients but incorporates traditional French cooking styles and other international influences into his menu. Start with the country-style terrine of venison, chicken, and pork with dried sour cherries and a roasted-garlic mustard. For an entrée, try the Alaskan spot prawns, Totten Inlet mussels, and halibut simmered together in a tomato-saffron broth and served with spring vegetables. Fresh seafood dishes are standouts. Higgins is dedicated to organic herbs and produce—he grows his own. A bistro menu is also available. ⊠ *1239 S.W. Broadway,* ☎ *503/222–9070. AE, MC, V. No lunch weekends.*

$$–$$$$ ✕ **The Heathman.** Chef Philippe Boulot, the French-trained former
★ head chef at New York's Mark Hotel, revels in the fresh fish, game, wild mushrooms, and other ingredients of the Pacific Northwest. His menu changes with the season and may include seared ahi tuna wrapped in locally cured prosciutto and served with Oregon-truffle risotto; Normandy-style braised rabbit in apple cider and mustard sauce, served with sage white-wine gnocchi; or roasted pesto salmon with red onion-caper relish. The dining room, scented with wood smoke and adorned with Andy Warhol prints, is a favorite for special occasions. ⊠ *Heathman Hotel, 1001 S.W. Broadway,* ☎ *503/790–7752. AE, D, DC, MC, V.*

Eclectic

$$ ✕ **Bima Restaurant and Bar.** A restored warehouse in the artsy Pearl District contains one of the city's most popular restaurants and bars. The cuisine takes its cue from the gulf coast of Mexico, the southern United States, and the Caribbean. Pecan-crusted catfish, assorted fish and meat skewers, fish tacos, and luscious ribs are some of the specialties. There's a bar menu as well. ⊠ *1338 N.W. Hoyt St.,* ☎ *503/ 241–3465. AE, MC, V. Closed Sun.*

Greek

$–$$ ✕ **Alexis.** The Mediterranean decor here consists only of white walls and basic furnishings, but the authentic Greek flavor keeps the crowds coming for *kalamarakia* (deep-fried squid served with *tzatziki,* a yogurt dip), *horiatiki* (a Greek salad combination with feta cheese and kalamata olives), and other traditional dishes. If you have trouble making up your mind, the gigantic Alexis platter includes a little of everything. ⊠ *215 W. Burnside St.,* ☎ *503/224–8577. AE, D, MC, V. No lunch weekends.*

Italian

$$–$$$$ ✕ **Piatti on Broadway.** Chefs turn out flavorful Italian dishes from an open kitchen at this trattoria inside the Benson Hotel. Pizzas and other specialties are baked in a wood-burning oven. The menu includes antipasti, soups, salads, focaccia sandwiches, and pastas, including the cannelloni: crab-and-cheese-stuffed red pepper pasta with champagne cream sauce and sautéed spinach. Try the zenzenro—tiger prawns sautéed with fresh ginger, garlic, black currants, pine nuts, and Calabrian chilies, tossed with linguine. Although this is part of a California-based chain, the chef uses local and seasonal produce, seafood, and meats. The happy hour bar menu is a bargain. ⊠ *319 S.W. Broadway,* ☎ *503/525–0945. AE, MC, V. No lunch Sun.*

$$–$$$ ✕ **Pazzo.** The aromas of roasted garlic and wood smoke greet patrons of the bustling, street-level dining room of the Hotel Vintage Plaza (☞ *below*). Pazzo's frequently changing menu relies on deceptively sim-

ple new Italian cuisine—pastas, risottos, and grilled meats, fish, and poultry. Try the lamb chops with fennel and the artichoke risotto if they're being prepared. The decor is a mix of dark wood, terra-cotta, and dangling Parma hams. ⊠ *627 S.W. Washington,* ☏ *503/228–1515. AE, D, DC, MC, V.*

Japanese

$–$$$ ✗ **Murata.** It's tiny and the prices are steep, but Murata has the finest sushi in town. *Uni* (sea urchin), *hamachi* (yellowtail tuna), *saba* (mackerel), *aji* (Spanish mackerel), and *kasu* (cod) are all outstanding. Reserve a day ahead for *kaiseki,* several courses assembled by the chef. ⊠ *200 S.W. Market St.,* ☏ *503/227–0080. AE, MC, V. Closed Sun. No lunch Sat.*

Lebanese

$–$$ ✗ **Abou Karim.** More than half the menu is vegetarian, but the leg of lamb served on a bed of rice with lentil soup or a full salad is a favorite here. Health-conscious diners will find a special menu of meals low in saturated fats, and there is an outside area for dining in summer. A few plants and a Lebanese sword or two hanging on the wall are the only nods to atmosphere. This is a smoke-free environment. ⊠ *221 S.W. Pine St.,* ☏ *503/223–5058. AE, MC, V. Closed Sun.*

Mexican

$ ✗ **Mayas Taqueria.** This downtown outpost of a popular local chain serves up good Mexican food at very reasonable prices. The taco, with a generous heap of your choice of grilled meat and beans, and served with fresh salsa and tortilla chips, is probably the best deal in town. It's convenient to the MAX light rail and within walking distance of many downtown shopping areas. ⊠ *1000 S.W. Morrison,* ☏ *503/226–1946. MC, V.*

Pizza

$ ✗ **Pizzicato.** This local chain serves up gourmet pizzas topped by inventive combinations such as red potato and prosciutto. The restaurant interiors are clean, bright, and modern. Beer and wine are available. ⊠ *705 S.W. Alder St.,* ☏ *503/226–1007;* ⊠ *505 N.W. 23rd Ave.,* ☏ *503/242–0023. AE, MC, V.*

Seafood

$$–$$$$ ✗ **Jake's Famous Crawfish.** Diners have been enjoying fresh Pacific Northwest seafood in Jake's warren of wood-paneled dining rooms for more than a century—the back bar came around Cape Horn during the 1880s, and the chandeliers hanging from the high ceilings date from 1881. But it wasn't until 1920, when crawfish was added to the menu, that the restaurant began to get a national reputation. White-coated waiters can take your order from a lengthy sheet of daily seafood specials year-round, but try to come during crawfish season, from May to September, when you can sample the tasty crustacean in pie, cooked Creole style, or in a Cajun-style stew over rice. ⊠ *401 S.W. 12th Ave.,* ☏ *503/226–1419. AE, D, DC, MC, V. No lunch weekends.*

$$–$$$$ ✗ **McCormick & Schmick's.** This is the place to come in Portland if you love seafood and single-malt scotches—41 varieties are listed on the bar menu, including a 25-year-old The Macallan at $31.25 a glass. The seafood is flawless at this lively restaurant, where you can dine in a cozy wooden booth downstairs or upstairs overlooking the bar. Fresh Pacific Northwest oysters and Alaskan halibut are favorites; specialties include Dungeness crab cakes with roasted red pepper sauce. A new menu is printed daily with a list of more than two dozen fresh seasonal choices. Oregon and California vineyards take center stage on the wine list. ⊠ *235 S.W. 1st Ave.,* ☏ *503/224–7522. AE, D, DC, MC, V. No lunch weekends.*

$$–$$$$ ✗ **Southpark.** One of Portland's newest fine restaurants, Southpark specializes in wood-fired Mediterranean seafood in a comfortable, art deco–tinged room with two bars. Executive chef Paul Ornstein's menu includes grilled grape leaf–wrapped salmon with pomegranate and sherry glaze, and tuna au poivre with mashed potatoes and red wine demi-glace. There's a wide selection of fresh Pacific Northwest oysters and fine regional wines available by the glass. Some of the desserts are baked to order. Southpark is conveniently located near the Arlene Schnitzer Concert Hall and the Portland Art Museum. This is a no-smoking environment. ⊠ *901 S.W. Salmon St.,* ☎ *503/326–1300. AE, D, DC, MC, V.*

$$–$$$ ✗ **Newport Bay at RiverPlace.** When it comes to river, bridge, and city-skyline views, there's not a bad seat in this circular glass dining room that floats on the Willamette River. Newport Bay seeks out whatever is in season worldwide, which might include Oregon spring salmon, Maine lobster, Australian lobster tail, Alaskan halibut, sturgeon, or New Zealand roughy, as well as swordfish, marlin, and shark. ⊠ *RiverPlace, 0425 S.W. Montgomery St.,* ☎ *503/227–3474. AE, D, DC, MC, V.*

$–$$ ✗ **Dan & Louis's Oyster Bar.** Oysters here come fried, stewed, or on the half shell. Crab stew—virtually impossible to find elsewhere in town—is also a specialty. Founder Louis Wachsmuth, who started his restaurant in 1907, was an avid collector of steins, plates, and marine art. The collection has grown over the years to fill beams, nooks, crannies, and nearly every inch of wall. ⊠ *208 S.W. Ankeny St.,* ☎ *503/227–5906. AE, D, DC, MC, V.*

Thai

$–$$$ ✗ **Typhoon!** A Buddha with burning incense watches over diners at this trendy restaurant in the Imperial Hotel. Come here for excellent Thai food at reasonable prices in a cozy but lively atmosphere. The spicy chicken or shrimp with crispy basil, the curry and noodle dishes, and the vegetarian spring rolls are standouts. It's packed for lunch but never uncomfortable. ⊠ *400 S.W. Broadway,* ☎ *503/224–8285. AE, D, DC, MC, V. No lunch weekends.*

Nob Hill and Vicinity

American

$$$–$$$$ ✗ **The Ringside.** If you're in the mood for a juicy steak, head for this Portland institution without further ado. There are other things on the menu, but the Ringside has been famous for beef for more than 50 years. The onion rings, made with Walla Walla sweets, are equally renowned. ⊠ *2165 N.W. Burnside St.,* ☎ *503/223–1513. AE, D, DC, MC, V. No lunch.*

Contemporary

$$$–$$$$ ✗ **Wildwood.** Executive chef Cory Schreiber won a James Beard Foundation Award in 1998, the first Portland area restaurateur to do so. Blond wood chairs and a stainless-steel open kitchen set the tone at this restaurant, serving fresh Pacific Northwest cuisine on trendy Northwest 21st Avenue. The entrée choices are plentiful, including dishes made with quail, lamb, pork loin, chicken, steak, and fish. There's also a gourmet vegetarian selection. For an appetizer, try the skillet-roasted Washington mussels with garlic, tomato, saffron, and grilled bread. Wildwood also has a Sunday brunch and a family-style Sunday supper menu with selections for two or more people. The place is a bit cramped and pricey, but it's worth it. ⊠ *1221 N.W. 21st Ave.,* ☎ *503/248–9663. AE, MC, V.*

Delicatessens

$ ✗ **Kornblatt's.** Come to Kornblatt's for the best bagel in Portland. The decor at this kosher deli is reminiscent of a 1950s diner; the fresh-cooked pastrami, corned beef, and tongue are lean and tender, and the home-smoked salmon and sablefish are simply the best. For breakfast, try the poached eggs with spicy corned-beef hash. ⊠ *628 N.W. 23rd Ave.,* ☎ *503/242–0055. MC, V.*

Eclectic

$$$–$$$$ ✕ **Zefiro.** Blond floors, pale green walls, lots of windows, and archi-
★   tectural lighting fixtures set the mood at Zefiro, where clarity and attractive detail are the thematic touchstones of the dining room and kitchen. The ever-changing menu combines Southeast Asian and Mediterranean elements with gratifying results. Try the oysters with Thai sauce or any of the grilled fish dishes; the Caesar salad is justly popular. This is a place to see and be seen. ⊠ *500 N.W. 21st Ave.,* ☎ *503/226–3394. Reservations essential. AE, DC, MC, V. Closed Sun. No lunch Sat.*

$$ ✕ **Papa Haydn.** Many patrons come here just for the luscious desserts, but this corner restaurant also makes a convenient lunch or dinner stop. Top sandwiches include Gruyère cheese and Black Forest ham grilled on rustic Italian bread and the mesquite-grilled chicken breast on a roll with bacon, avocado, basil, and tomato. Favorite dinner entrées are the Bresola filet mignon and the pan-seared pork medallions with a pear-tarragon demi-glace. More versions of meat, fish, and poultry, grilled or cooked on a rotisserie, are available next door at the trendy Jo Bar. ⊠ *701 N.W. 23rd Ave.,* ☎ *503/228–7317. Reservations essential for Sun. brunch. AE, MC, V.*

French

$$$–$$$$ ✕ **Couvron.** Casual yet elegant Couvron is Portland's finest restaurant
★   for contemporary French cuisine. Chef Anthony Demes's signature dishes include a honey-glazed Oregon duck breast with curry and anise, a pan-roasted foie gras with summer truffles and diced organic root vegetables in a red wine sauce, a thyme-roasted Alaskan halibut, and sautéed salmon mignon on a chiffonade potato cake with stewed leeks. The Grand Marnier soufflé is otherworldly. ⊠ *1126 S.W. 18th Ave.,* ☎ *503/225–1844. Reservations essential. AE, MC, V. Closed Sun.–Mon. No lunch.*

$$$–$$$$ ✕ **Paley's Place.** This charming bistro restaurant on trendy Northwest 21st Avenue features Pacific Northwest–style French cuisine. There are two dining rooms and, weather permitting, seating on the front porch and back patio. For a starter, try the spring asparagus and sautéed duck liver with farm-fresh egg and warm applewood-smoked bacon vinaigrette. Among the entrées are dishes featuring duck, New York steak, chicken, pork tenderloin, and halibut. A vegetarian dish is also available. The dessert menu includes banana cream pie with a thick chocolate base and topped with hot buttered rum glaze. Paley's has a fine selection of Willamette Valley and French wines. ⊠ *1204 N.W. 21st Ave.,* ☎ *503/243–2403. AE, MC, V. Closed Sun.–Mon. No lunch Sat.*

Indian

$$–$$$ ✕ **Plainfield's Mayur.** Portland's finest Indian cuisine is served in a Victorian house amid quietly elegant surroundings. The tomato-curry soup and vegetarian dishes such as *dahi wadi* (crispy fried lentil croquettes) and basmati rice *biryani* (with silver leaf) are popular. Other specialties include lobster in brown onion sauce and lamb shanks in sandalwood sauce. For bread, try the garlic nan. This is one of the few Indian restaurants in North America to win an award from *Wine Spectator.* ⊠ *852 S.W. 21st Ave.,* ☎ *503/223–2995. AE, D, DC, MC, V. No lunch.*

Italian

$$ ✕ **Bastas.** Whoever thought a former Tastee-Freeze could be converted into an Italian restaurant with such stylish results? The walls at Bastas are painted with Italian earth shades and there's a small side garden for alfresco dining in good weather. The menu, drawn from all over Italy, includes pasta, fish, and meat dishes. ⊠ *410 N.W. 21st Ave.,* ☎ *503/274–1572. AE, MC, V.*

Pan-Asian

$ ✕ **Misohapi.** The interior is hip, tongue-in-chic '90s modern with pastel walls, white fabric clouds supported by stainless-steel rods, and unusual lighting fixtures. The food is a mixture of Thai and Vietnamese with a sushi bar thrown in for good measure. Try the hot-and-sour seafood soup, the lemongrass seafood dish, or the peanutty pad thai noodles with shrimp. ⊠ *1123 N.W. 23rd Ave.,* ☎ *503/796–2012. MC, V. Closed Sun.*

East of the Willamette

Barbecue

$ ✕ **Tennessee Red's Barbecue Company.** The best barbecue is usually found in raw, out of the way places, and that's what you'll find at this corner rib joint in a laid-back Portland neighborhood. There's a choice of five sauces, including a hazelnut sauce called "Oregon," but the hot "Texas" is the best. Be sure to pick your sauce when ordering or you'll get the "Memphis," which is sweeter. The portions here are more than generous, and tasty cornbread is served with all meals. In addition to the requisite ribs and brisket, Tennessee Red's offers chicken, sausage, and blackened catfish. You get your choice of two home-style side dishes. Top it all off with a huge slice of key lime pie or sweet potato pie. ⊠ *2133 S.E. 11th Ave.,* ☎ *503/231–1710. MC, V. Closed Sun.–Mon.*

Cajun/Creole

$–$$ ✕ **Montage.** Spicy Cajun is the jumping-off point for the chef at this sassy bistro under the Morrison Bridge on Portland's east side. Jambalayas, blackened pork and catfish, hoppin' John, rabbit sausage, and old-fashioned macaroni dishes are served up from around noon until the wee hours in an atmosphere that's loud, crowded, and casually hip. ⊠ *301 S.E. Morrison St.,* ☎ *503/234–1324. Reservations not accepted. No credit cards. No lunch weekends.*

Chinese

$ ✕ **Fujin.** This family-owned restaurant serves consistently good Cantonese food at very reasonable prices. In addition to the regular menu, there are special dishes that change daily. Try the sesame shrimp; they'll make it for you even if it's not on the specials board. Fujin's a great place for lunch on a Saturday afternoon. There's nothing fancy about the atmosphere, but the service is great. ⊠ *3549 S.E. Hawthorne Blvd..* ☎ *503/231–3753. MC, V. Closed Sun.*

Contemporary

$$–$$$ ✕ **Wild Abandon.** This small alternative restaurant serves daring dishes—but it works. The inventive menu includes such offerings as "Udon Dream," a bowl of udon noodles tossed with smoked salmon, caramelized red onions, and carrots in smoked pear-apple cream sauce with brandy. Fresh fish, pork tenderloin, beef, and vegetarian items are available as well. For an appetizer, try the shrimp cocktail, a creation of chili-marinated prawns, baby greens, and fresh vegetables with lime-cumin aioli. Sunday brunch includes omelets that many consider the best in town. ⊠ *2411 S.E. Belmont,* ☎ *503/232–4458. AE, D, DC, MC, V. No lunch.*

Eclectic

$$ ✕ **Indigine.** Chef-owner Millie Howe wows regulars with her unique cuisine, which draws on the flavors of India, Latin America, Indonesia, and Europe. Saturday features an all-Indian menu, and there's a Sunday brunch. The intimate room, accented with flowers and natural wood, has a pleasingly spare look. The small garden deck out back

is a great place for a romantic dinner on a summer evening. ✉ *3723 S.E. Division St.,* ☎ *503/238–1470. AE, MC, V. Closed Mon. No lunch.*

Italian

$$$$ ✗ **Genoa.** Widely regarded as the finest Italian restaurant in Portland, ★ Genoa serves a prix-fixe menu (seven-courses on Friday and Saturday evenings, four courses on weekdays). The menu, which changes every two weeks, focuses on the authentic Italian cuisine. In a space that evokes Tuscany, seating is limited to a few dozen diners, so service is excellent. Smoking is permitted only in a separate sitting room. This will probably be one of the best, most leisurely dining experiences you'll have in the Pacific Northwest. ✉ *2822 S.E. Belmont,* ☎ *503/238–1464. Reservations essential. AE, D, MC, V. No lunch.*

$–$$ ✗ **Assaggio.** In an age of canned music it's pleasant to enter a restau- ★ rant and hear Maria Callas singing opera arias. But, then, everything about this Sellwood trattoria (food, decor, price) is extraordinarily pleasant. Many dishes are available as family-style samplers. Farfalle, fusilli, penne, and spaghetti dishes are properly cooked al dente and not overly sauced. For starters try the salad sampler or any of the *bruschette* (grilled garlic bread with various toppings). An excellent wine cellar favors Italian vintages. The interior, painted in a burnt-sienna shade and accented with classical architectural motifs, lovingly evokes Italy. ✉ *7742 S.E. 13th Ave.,* ☎ *503/232–6151. MC, V. Closed Sun.–Mon. No lunch.*

Japanese

$$ ✗ **Hokkaido Japanese Cuisine and Sushi Bar.** The soothing sound of water flowing through a rock fountain greets diners at this restaurant with very reasonable prices. The sushi and sashimi are impeccably fresh and show occasional flashes of inspiration. Try the spider roll, a whole soft-shell crab surrounded by seaweed, rice, and wasabi. ✉ *6744 N.E. Sandy Blvd.,* ☎ *503/288–3731. MC, V. Closed Mon. No lunch Sun.*

Pan-Asian

$ ✗ **Saigon Kitchen.** Consistently good Vietnamese and Thai food and friendly service have made Saigon Kitchen a neighborhood favorite. Fried salted calamari and fiery chili noodles with prawns or chicken are delectable standouts on the wide-ranging menu. The decor is no-nonsense diner, but don't let that deter you. ✉ *835 N.E. Broadway,* ☎ *503/281–3669. AE, D, MC, V.*

Southwestern

$$ ✗ **Esparza's Tex-Mex Cafe.** Be prepared for south-of-the-border crazi-ness at this beloved local eatery. Wild West kitsch festoons the walls, but it isn't any wilder than some of the entrées that emerge from chef-owner Joe Esparza's kitchen. Look for offerings like lean smoked-sir-loin tacos—Esparza's is renowned for its smoked meats—and, for the truly adventurous diner, ostrich enchiladas. ✉ *2725 S.E. Ankeny St., at S.E. 28th Ave.,* ☎ *503/234–7909. AE, MC, V. Closed Sun.–Mon.*

Thai

$ ✗ **Bangkok Kitchen.** Chef-owner Srichan Miller juggles the lime, cilantro, coconut milk, lemongrass, curry, and hot peppers of classic Thai cui-sine with virtuosity. Pay no attention to the '60s diner decor, and be sure to try one of the noodle dishes—the tender rice-stick noodles with shrimp, egg, fresh mint, chilies, and coconut are memorable. Order your dishes mild or medium-hot unless you have an asbestos tongue, and don't forget the cold Singha beer. ✉ *2534 S.E. Belmont St.,* ☎ *503/236–7349. No credit cards. Closed Sun.–Mon. No lunch Sat.*

Vietnamese

$ ✗ **Yen Ha.** The vibrant flavors of Vietnam find full expression at crowded Yen Ha. Superb rice-paper rolls—translucent cylinders filled with pungent bean threads, fresh mint, and shrimp, then dipped in peanut sauce—and wonderful noodle dishes are among the star attractions. ⊠ *6820 N.E. Sandy Blvd.,* ☎ *503/287–3698. MC, V.*

LODGING

Many of the elegant hotels near the city center and waterfront appeal because of their proximity to the city's attractions. The all-suites hotels in the southwest suburbs provide space without requiring you to give up the extras. Budget travelers will need to sacrifice convenience to the airport or downtown. Some establishments offer senior-citizen discounts and family plans.

CATEGORY	COST*
$$$$	over $170
$$$	$110–$170
$$	$60–$110
$	under $60

All prices are for a standard double room, excluding 9% room tax.

Downtown

$$$$ ⚇ **Benson Hotel.** Portland's grandest hotel was built in 1912. The hand-carved Russian Circassian walnut paneling and the Italian white-marble staircase are among the noteworthy design touches in the public areas. In the guest rooms expect to find small crystal chandeliers, inlaid mahogany doors, and the original ceilings. ⊠ *309 S.W. Broadway, 97205,* ☎ *503/228–2000 or 800/426–0670,* ℻ *503/226–4603. 287 rooms. 2 restaurants, bar, coffee shop, in-room data ports, minibars, room service, exercise room, laundry service, concierge, airport shuttle, parking (fee). AE, D, DC, MC, V.*

$$$$ ⚇ **Governor Hotel.** With its mahogany walls and mural of Pacific
★ Northwest Indians fishing in Celilo Falls, the clubby lobby of the distinctive Governor sets the overall tone for the hotel's 1920s Arts and Crafts style. Painted in soothing earth tones, the guest rooms have large windows and whirlpool tubs; some have fireplaces and balconies. Jake's Grill is located off the lobby. ⊠ *611 S.W. 10th Ave., 97205,* ☎ *503/224–3400 or 800/554–3456,* ℻ *503/241–2122. 100 rooms. 2 restaurants, bars, sports bar, in-room data ports, minibars, no-smoking rooms, room service, indoor lap pool, sauna, steam room, aerobics, exercise room, health club, indoor track, video games, laundry service and dry cleaning, concierge, business services, meeting rooms, parking (fee). AE, D, DC, MC, V.*

$$$$ ⚇ **Heathman Hotel.** Superior service, an award-winning restaurant, a cen-
★ tral downtown location (adjoining the Performing Arts Center), and swank public areas have earned the Heathman its reputation for quality. From the teak-panel lobby hung with Warhol prints to the rosewood elevators and marble fireplaces, this hotel exudes refinement. The guest rooms are luxuriously comfortable, if not overly spacious, and the bathrooms have plenty of marble and mirrors. Afternoon tea is served in the high-ceiling Tea Court, which becomes a popular gathering spot in the evenings. ⊠ *1009 S.W. Broadway, 97205,* ☎ *503/241–4100 or 800/551–0011,* ℻ *503/790–7110. 151 rooms. Restaurant, 2 bars, in-room data ports, minibars, no-smoking floor, room service, exercise room, library, laundry service and dry cleaning, concierge, parking (fee). AE, D, DC, MC, V.*

$$$$ ⚇ **Hotel Vintage Plaza.** This historic landmark takes its theme from the area's vineyards. Guests can fall asleep counting stars in top-floor rooms, where skylights and wall-to-wall conservatory-style windows rate highly among the special details. Hospitality suites have extralarge rooms with a full living area, and the deluxe rooms have a bar. All rooms are appointed in hunter green, deep plum, cerise, taupe, and gold; some rooms have hot tubs. Complimentary coffee and newspapers are available in the morning; wine is served in the evening; and an extensive collection of Oregon vintages is displayed in the tasting room. Two-story town-house suites are named after local wineries. ⊠ *422 S.W. Broadway, 97205, ☎ 503/228–1212 or 800/243–0555, ℻ 503/228–3598. 107 rooms, 21 suites. Restaurant, piano bar, in-room data ports, minibars, room service, exercise room, concierge, business services, meeting rooms, parking (fee). AE, D, DC, MC, V.*

$$$$ 🏨 **RiverPlace Hotel.** With its bright rooms, wing chairs, teak tables, and feather pillows, this hotel has the feeling of a private home. It has one of the best views in Portland, overlooking the river, the marina, and the city skyline. Amenities include a complimentary Continental breakfast, the morning newspaper, and valet parking in a locked garage. ⊠ *1510 S.W. Harbor Way, 97201, ☎ 503/228–3233 or 800/227–1333, ℻ 503/295–6161. 39 rooms, 44 suites. 2 restaurants, bar, in-room data ports, minibars, no-smoking rooms, room service, hot tub, sauna, concierge, business services, meeting rooms, parking (fee). AE, D, DC, MC, V.*

$$$–$$$$ 🏨 **Embassy Suites.** Recently renovated, this Old Town property in the Historic Multnomah Hotel building is within walking distance of the riverfront and MAX light rail. The cozy accommodations in the all-suite property have large windows and sofa beds, wet bars, and three telephones. Amenities include hair dryers, irons, bathrobes, and umbrellas, plus a complimentary van that will take you anywhere within a 2-mi radius. A full breakfast, cooked to order, is included in the room rate. ⊠ *319 S.W. Pine, 97204, ☎ 503/279–9000 or 800/362–2779. 276 suites. Refrigerators, in-room data ports, indoor pool, exercise room, baby-sitting, laundry service, concierge, business services, meeting rooms, valet parking. AE, D, DC, MC, V.*

$$$–$$$$ 🏨 **Fifth Avenue Suites Hotel.** The 1912 Lipman Wolfe Department Store reopened as a boutique hotel in 1997. A tall vestibule with a marble mosaic floor leads to the art-filled lobby, where guests gather by the fireplace for an early evening glass of wine or a complimentary Continental breakfast. Curtained sliding doors divide the 10-story property's 550-square-ft suites. Upholstered chairs, fringed ottomans, and other appointments in the sitting areas will make you feel right at home (or wish you had one like this). The large bathrooms are stocked with every amenity. ⊠ *506 S.W. Washington St., 97205, ☎ 503/222–0001 or 800/711–2971, ℻ 503/222–0004. 221 suites. Restaurant, bar, in-room data ports, minibars, no-smoking floor, room service, massage, health club, laundry service and dry cleaning, business services, meeting rooms, parking (fee). AE, D, DC, MC, V.*

$$$–$$$$ 🏨 **Hilton Portland.** Opened in 1963, the Hilton was Portland's first large, full-service business and convention hotel. The property, which recently underwent a major renovation, is located within walking distance of the Performing Arts Center, Pioneer Courthouse Square, the Portland Art Museum, and MAX light rail. The typical Hilton-style rooms have coffeemakers, hair dryers, irons, and voice mail. Alexander's restaurant, specializing in Pacific Northwest cuisine, offers a panoramic view of the Portland metro area from the 23rd floor. More than 60 restaurants are within three blocks. ⊠ *921 S.W. 6th Ave., 97204, ☎ 503/226–1611 or 800/774–1500, ℻ 503/220–2565. 455 rooms. 2 restaurants, bar, in-room data ports, no-smoking rooms, indoor pool, hot tub, massage, steam room, exercise room, business services, meeting rooms, parking (fee). AE, D, DC, MC, V.*

$$$–$$$$ 🏨 **Marriott City Center.** Portland's newest major hotel opened in July 1999. The lobby of the 20-story property, which is in the heart of Portland's downtown arts and dining area, is accented with a grand staircase,

46

Benson Hotel, **9**

Best Western Inn at the Convention Center, **22**

Courtyard by Marriott, **26**

Doubletree Hotel Jantzen Beach, **19**

Doubletree Hotel Portland—Lloyd Center, **24**

Embassy Suites, **15**

Fifth Avenue Suites Hotel, **12**

Governor Hotel, **8**

Greenwood Inn, **4**

Heathman Hotel, **13**

Heron Haus, **1**

Hilton Garden Inn, **5**

Hilton Portland, **14**

Hotel Vintage Plaza, **10**

Lamplighter Inn, **3**

MacMaster House, **2**

Mallory Hotel, **7**

Marriott City Center, **11**

Marriott Hotel Downtown, **17**

Portland Guest House, **23**

Portland's White House, **28**

Ramada Inn Airport, **27**

Ramada Plaza Hotel, **21**

Red Lion Inn Coliseum, **20**

Residence Inn by Marriott, **6**

RiverPlace Hotel, **18**

The Riverside, **16**

Shilo Inn Suites Hotel, **25**

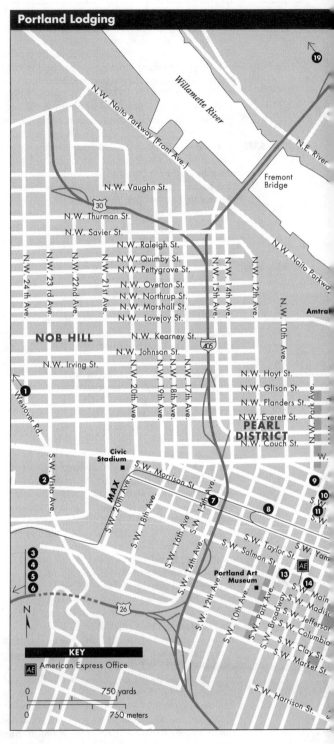

Portland Lodging

maple paneling, marble floors, and a large chandelier. Rooms, designed for business travelers, have voice mail, coffeemakers, hair dryers, and irons. The Chinook Grill is a bistro-style restaurant featuring Pacific Northwest cuisine. MAX light rail is two blocks away. ⊠ *520 S.W. Broadway, 97205,* ☎ *503/226–6300 or 800/228–9290,* 𝔽𝔸𝕏 *503/227–7515. 238 rooms, 11 suites. Restaurant, bar, in-room data ports, room service, hot tub, exercise room, gift shop, laundry service, concierge, business services, meeting rooms, parking (fee). AE, D, DC, MC, V.*

$$$–$$$$ 🏨 **Marriott Hotel Downtown.** The large rooms here are decorated in off-whites; the best ones look east to the Willamette and the Cascades. All have coffeemakers, irons, hair dryers, and voice mail. Champions Lounge, filled with sports memorabilia, is a singles' hot spot on weekends. The hotel, which is located on the Willametter River, recently underwent a major renovation. It's a few blocks from MAX light rail. ⊠ *1401 S.W. Naito Pkwy., 97201,* ☎ *503/226–7600,* 𝔽𝔸𝕏 *503/221–1789. 503 rooms, 6 suites. Restaurant, bar, in-room data ports, no-smoking rooms, room service, indoor pool, hot tub, health club, coin laundry, laundry service and dry cleaning, concierge, business services, meeting rooms, parking (fee). AE, D, DC, MC, V.*

$$$ 🏨 **The Riverside.** If you're concerned about location and value, consider this scrupulously maintained five-story hotel on the MAX lightrail line. East-facing rooms have a good view of the Willamette River and the Governor Tom McCall Waterfront Park; rooms on the west side, a trifle quieter, face downtown. Amenities here include coffeemakers and irons, and guests have privileges at a nearby health club. ⊠ *50 S.W. Morrison St., 97204,* ☎ *503/221–0711 or 800/899–0247,* 𝔽𝔸𝕏 *503/274–0312. 140 rooms. Restaurant, bar, no-smoking rooms, room service, dry cleaning, business services, meeting rooms, parking (fee). AE, D, DC, MC, V.*

$$–$$$ 🏨 **Mallory Hotel.** The years have been kind to this 1920s-vintage hotel eight blocks from the downtown core. Its gilt-ceiling lobby has fresh white paint and floral carpeting; crystal chandeliers and a leaded-glass skylight hark back to a more genteel era. The rooms are old-fashioned but clean and cheerful and have been refurbished; corner suites and rooms on the east side of the building have impressive skyline views. The hotel is a favorite with visiting singers, writers, and artists of every stripe. The staff is friendly and knowledgeable. Pets are allowed for $10 extra. ⊠ *729 S.W. 15th Ave., 97205,* ☎ *503/223–6311 or 800/228–8657,* 𝔽𝔸𝕏 *503/223–0522. 136 rooms. Restaurant, bar. AE, D, DC, MC, V.*

East of the Willamette

$$–$$$$ 🏨 **Doubletree Hotel Portland—Lloyd Center.** This busy and well-ap★ pointed business-oriented hotel maintains a huge traffic in meetings and special events. The public areas are a tasteful mix of marble, rose-and-green carpet, and antique-style furnishings. The large rooms, many with balconies, have views of the mountains or the city center. Lloyd Center and the MAX light-rail line are across the street; the Oregon Convention Center is a five-minute walk away. ⊠ *1000 N.E. Multnomah St., 97232,* ☎ *503/281–6111 or 800/222–8733,* 𝔽𝔸𝕏 *503/284–8553. 476 rooms. 3 restaurants, 2 bars, in-room data ports, room service, pool, exercise room, laundry service and dry cleaning, business services, meeting rooms, airport shuttle, parking (fee). AE, D, DC, MC, V.*

$$–$$$ 🏨 **Portland's White House.** Hardwood floors with Oriental rugs, chandeliers, antiques, and fountains create a warm and romantic mood at this elegant bed-and-breakfast inn in a Greek Revival mansion in the historic Irvington district. The mansion, built in 1911 and on the National Register of Historic Landmarks, was remodeled in 1997. Rooms have private baths and mahogany canopy or four-poster queen- and king-size

beds. The Garden Room overlooks a courtyard from its own portico. A full gourmet breakfast is included in the room rate, and the owners even provide vegetarian or low-fat options. The signature dish is salmon eggs Benedict with orange hollandaise sauce. Smoking and pets are not permitted at this special find in Northeast Portland. ⊠ *1914 N.E. 22nd Ave., 97212,* ☎ *503/287–7131 or 800/272–7131,* ℻ *503/249–1641. 9 rooms. Dining room, in-room data ports, library, free parking. AE, D, MC, V.*

$$ ⊞ **Best Western Inn at the Convention Center.** Rooms here are done in pleasing creams and rusts; those with king-size beds usually come with wet bars. The inn is four blocks west of Lloyd Center, directly across the street from the Portland Convention Center, and on the MAX line. ⊠ *420 N.E. Holladay St., 97232,* ☎ *503/233–6331,* ℻ *503/233–2677. 97 rooms. Coffee shop, no-smoking floor, coin laundry, dry cleaning, meeting room, free parking. AE, D, DC, MC, V.*

$$ ⊞ **Portland Guest House.** Inside a Northeast Portland working-class Victorian home with a dusty heather exterior paint job, this cozy B&B near the Lloyd Center contains rooms with antique walnut furniture, original Pacific Northwest artwork, and phones. The rates include a gourmet breakfast. No smoking is permitted at this inn. ⊠ *1720 N.E. 15th St., 97212,* ☎ *503/282–1402. 7 rooms, 5 with bath. Free parking. AE, DC, MC, V.*

$$ ⊞ **Ramada Plaza Hotel.** Rooms here come with king- or queen-size beds and sofas, plus full-length mirrors, irons, coffeemakers, and hair dryers. The Rose Garden arena, Memorial Coliseum, and Oregon Convention Center are within walking distance. ⊠ *1441 N.E. 2nd Ave., 97232,* ☎ *503/233–2401,* ℻ *503/238–7016. 238 rooms. Restaurant, bar, no-smoking floor, room service, pool, exercise room, dry cleaning and laundry service, business services, airport shuttle, free parking. AE, D, DC, MC, V.*

$$ ⊞ **Red Lion Inn Coliseum.** The restaurant and many of the rooms at the Red Lion overlook the Willamette River. A railroad line lies between the river and the hotel, making courtside rooms the better choice if you want peace and quiet. The rooms are standard but pleasing enough; decorated in pinks, whites, mauve, and sea-foam green, they have queen-size beds and modern oak furnishings. You can walk to the Rose Garden arena and MAX light rail. ⊠ *1225 N. Thunderbird Way, 97227,* ☎ *503/235–8311,* ℻ *503/232–2670. 212 rooms. Restaurant, bar, no-smoking rooms, room service, pool, hot tub, exercise room, laundry service and dry cleaning, meeting rooms, airport shuttle, free parking. AE, D, DC, MC, V.*

West of Downtown

$$$–$$$$ ⊞ **Hilton Garden Inn.** This new Hilton in suburban Beaverton brings a much-needed lodging option to Portland's west side. The property is in a suburban setting and offers bright rooms with plush dark green carpeting and work desks as well as microwaves and coffeemakers. It's conveniently located just off U.S. 26. ⊠ *15520 N.W. Gateway Ct., Beaverton,* ☎ *503/439–1717, 800/445–8667,* ℻ *503/439–1818. 150 rooms. Indoor pool, hot tub, in-room refrigerators, in-room data ports, 24-hr business center. AE, D, DC, MC, V.*

$$$ ⊞ **Heron Haus.** This lovely B&B is inside a stately, 90-year-old Tudor-style mansion near Forest Park. Special features include a tulip-shape bathtub in one room and a tiled, seven-headed antique shower in another. All rooms have phones, work desks, and fireplaces. Breakfast, included in the room rate, is a gourmet Continental affair. No smoking is allowed at Heron Haus. ⊠ *2545 N.W. Westover Rd., 97210,* ☎ *503/274–1846,* ℻ *503/248–4055. 6 rooms. Breakfast room, in-room data ports, business services, free parking. MC, V.*

$$$ 🏨 **Residence Inn by Marriott.** Located near the West Side's many high-tech offices and fabrication plants, this all-suites motel is popular with people relocating to Portland. It's within walking distance of several restaurants, a shopping center, and a multiplex theater. The homey suites, some with fireplaces, have full kitchens, two phone lines, voice mail, coffeemakers, irons, and hair dryers. Complimentary Continental breakfast is included. There's also a Courtyard by Marriott right next door (☒ 3050 N.W. Stucki, ☏ 503/690–1800) with 155 rooms ($99) and six suites ($124). The Courtyard has a restaurant, indoor pool, and hot tub. ☒ *18855 N.W. Tanasbourne Dr., Hillsboro 97124, ☏ 503/531–3200 or 800/331–3131, FAX 503/645–1581. 122 suites. In-room data ports, no-smoking rooms, pool, hot tub, tennis court, exercise room, coin laundry, laundry service, business services, meeting rooms, free parking. AE, D, DC, MC, V.*

$$–$$$ 🏨 **MacMaster House.** On King's Hill, less than 10 minutes by foot from
★ fashionable Northwest 23rd Avenue, this 17-room Colonial Revival mansion built in 1886 is comfortable, funky, and fascinating. A hybrid assortment of Victorian furniture and antiques fills the parlors, and the guest rooms on the second and third floors are charming without being too cute. The two suites with large, private, old-fashioned baths are the ones to choose, especially the spacious Artist's Studio, tucked garretlike under the dormers, with a high brass bed and fireplace. Patrick Long, who was Perry Ellis's private chef, prepares a justly renowned gourmet breakfast. ☒ *1041 S.W. Vista Ave., 97205, ☏ 503/223–7362 or 800/774–9523, FAX 503/224–8808. 5 rooms share 2½ baths, 2 suites. Free parking. AE, D, DC, MC, V.*

$$ 🏨 **Greenwood Inn.** Rooms at this hotel in suburban Portland, a 10-minute drive west of downtown, are decorated with custom wood furnishings, original works of art, and southwestern shades of sand, ocher, pale green, and red; ask for one with a courtyard view and avoid the noisier rooms on the hotel's west side. You can dance to live bands three nights a week. The Pavilion restaurant, set among Japanese-style gardens beneath an atrium, serves Pacific Northwest cuisine and has an extensive wine cellar. ☒ *10700 S.W. Allen Blvd., Beaverton 97005, ☏ 503/643–7444 or 800/289–1300, FAX 503/626–4553. 250 rooms. Restaurant, 2 bars, kitchenettes, no-smoking rooms, 2 pools, outdoor hot tub, exercise room, free parking. AE, D, DC, MC, V.*

$ 🏨 **Lamplighter Inn.** Although the inn is close to the freeway, noise coming into the hotel is muffled by highway embankments. The Lamplighter's color scheme runs to blues and mauves. The small shopping mall across the street has a supermarket, lounge, and sporting-goods and equipment stores; a Mongolian restaurant is nearby. There's a walkway over U.S. 26 to the Sunset Transit Center, which is served by MAX light rail and many bus lines. ☒ *10207 S.W. Parkway Ave., Beaverton 97225, ☏ 503/297–2211, FAX 503/297–0915. 56 rooms. Kitchenettes, free parking. AE, D, DC, MC, V.*

Portland International Airport Area

$$$–$$$$ 🏨 **Doubletree Hotel Jantzen Beach.** The four-story Doubletree has larger-than-average guest rooms, many with balconies and good views of the Columbia River and Vancouver, Washington. Standard amenities include coffeemakers and irons. Public areas glitter with brass and bright lights that accentuate the greenery and the burgundy, green, and rose color scheme. The seasonal menu at Maxi's Seafood Restaurant highlights ingredients fresh from Pacific Northwest fields, farms, and waters. ☒ *909 N. Hayden Island Dr. (east of I–5's Jantzen Beach exit), 97217, ☏ 503/283–4466 or 800/222–8733, FAX 503/283–4743. 320 rooms. Restaurant, bar, coffee shop, in-room data ports, no-smoking*

rooms, room service, pool, outdoor hot tub, tennis court, exercise room, coin laundry, dry cleaning, concierge, business services, meeting rooms, airport shuttle, free parking. AE, D, DC, MC, V.

$$$–$$$$ 🏨 **Shilo Inn Suites Hotel.** Each room at this all-suites hotel has three TVs, a microwave, four telephones, a wet bar, and two oversize beds; the rates include a Continental breakfast as well. The contemporary decor runs to soothing pale blues, light pinks, and light grays in both the public and private areas. ✉ *11707 N.E. Airport Way, 97220,* ☎ *503/252–7500 or 800/222–2244,* ℻ *503/254–0794. 200 rooms. Restaurant, bar, in-room data ports, no-smoking floor, refrigerators, room service, in-room VCRs, indoor pool, hot tub, steam room, exercise room, coin laundry, laundry service and dry cleaning, concierge, business services, meeting rooms, airport shuttle, parking (fee). AE, D, DC, MC, V.*

$$–$$$ 🏨 **Ramada Inn Airport.** The business center at this facility has computers, fax machines, and individual workstations. The 108 executive suites have microwaves, wet bars, coffeemakers, and sitting areas. Spacious one- and two-bedroom suites have whirlpool tubs; standard rooms, with king-size beds, are decorated in quiet grays, browns, and pinks. ✉ *6221 N.E. 82nd Ave., 97220,* ☎ *503/255–6511 or 800/272–6232,* ℻ *503/255–8417. 202 rooms. Restaurant, bar, no-smoking rooms, refrigerators, room service, pool, outdoor hot tub, sauna, exercise room, coin laundry, laundry service and dry cleaning, business services, airport shuttle, free parking. AE, D, DC, MC, V.*

$$ 🏨 **Courtyard by Marriott.** This modern six-story hotel is conveniently located ¾ mi from I–205. The average-size rooms are brightly decorated in teals and maroons and have coffeemakers, irons, and voice mail. ✉ *11550 N.E. Airport Way, 97220,* ☎ *503/252–3200 or 800/321–2211,* ℻ *503/252–8921. 150 rooms, 10 suites. Restaurant, bar, in-room data ports, no-smoking rooms, room service, outdoor pool, outdoor hot tub, exercise room, coin laundry, laundry service and dry cleaning, business services, airport shuttle, free parking. AE, D, DC, MC, V.*

NIGHTLIFE AND THE ARTS

"A&E, The Arts and Entertainment Guide," published each Friday in the *Oregonian,* contains listings of performers, productions, events, and club entertainment. *Willamette Week,* published free each Wednesday and widely available throughout the metropolitan area, contains similar, but hipper, listings. *Just Out,* the city's gay and lesbian newspaper, is published bimonthly.

Nightlife

Portland's flourishing music scene encompasses everything from classical concerts to the latest permutations of rock and roll and hip-hop. The city has become something of a mecca for young rock bands, which perform in dance clubs scattered throughout the metropolitan area. Good jazz groups perform nightly in clubs and bars. Top-name musicians and performers in every genre regularly appear at the city's larger venues.

Bars and Lounges

DOWNTOWN

Many of the best bars and lounges in Portland are found in its restaurants. **Atwater's** (✉ 111 S.W. 5th Ave., ☎ 503/275–3600) is the place to go to enjoy a panoramic city view and live music with your cocktail. The Pearl District's **Bima** (✉ 1338 N.W. Hoyt St., ☎ 503/241–3465) has a large lounge with a good bar menu. **Brasserie Montmarte** (✉ 626 S.W. Park Ave., ☎ 503/224–5552) is a popular late-night spot with free jazz and nightclublike decor. At the **Heathman Hotel** (✉ 1001 S.W. Broadway, ☎ 503/241–4100) you can sit in the marble bar or the wood-panel Tea Court. **Huber's** (⊠ 411 S.W. 3rd Ave., ☎ 503/ 228–5686), the city's oldest restaurant, is noted for its Spanish coffee and old-fashioned ambience. The young and eclectic crowd at the **Lotus Cardroom and Cafe** (⊠ 932 S.W. 3rd Ave., ☎ 503/227–6185) comes to drink, dance, and play pool.

NOB HILL

Boisterous **Gypsy** (⊠ 625 N.W. 21st Ave., ☎ 503/796–1859) has a 1950s-like atmosphere. In the winter, you can sit by the fireplace in the softly lit bar at **L'Auberge** (⊠ 2601 N.W. Vaughn St., ☎ 503/223– 3302); in the summer, tables are set out on the back deck. **Wildwood** (⊠ 1221 N.W. 21st Ave., ☎ 503/248–9663) is casually chic. At **Zefiro** (⊠ 500 N.W. 21st Ave., ☎ 503/226–3394) the atmosphere is likewise informally upscale.

Brew Pubs, Brew Theaters, and Microbreweries

Dozens of small breweries operating in the metropolitan area produce pale ales, bitters, bocks, barley wines, and stouts. Some have attached pub operations, where you can sample a foaming pint of house ale. An especially interesting facet of the microbrewery phenomenon is the "brew theaters"—former neighborhood movie houses, lovingly restored, whose patrons enjoy food, suds, and recent theatrical releases.

The **Bagdad Theatre and Pub** (⊠ 3702 S.E. Hawthorne Blvd., ☎ 503/ 230–0895) screens recent Hollywood films and serves microbrews. Portland Brewing's **Brewhouse Tap Room and Grille** (⊠ 2730 N.W. 31st Ave., ☎ 503/228–5269), part of a 27,000-square-ft brewery complex, has a large restaurant. **Bridgeport BrewPub** (⊠ 1313 N.W. Marshall St., ☎ 503/241–3612), Portland's oldest microbrewery, prepares hand-tossed pizza (☞ Dining, *above*) to accompany its ales. The **Mission Theater** (⊠ 1624 N.W. Glisan St., ☎ 503/223–4031) was the first brew theater to show recent Hollywood offerings and serve locally brewed McMenamins ales.

The McMenamins chain of microbreweries includes some pubs in restored historic buildings. **Ringlers** (⊠ 1332 W. Burnside St., ☎ 503/ 225–0627) occupies the first floor of the building that houses the famous **Crystal Ballroom** (☞ Dancing, *below*). **Ringlers Annex** (⊠ 1223 S.W. Stark St., ☎ 503/525–0520), one block away from Ringlers, is a pie-shape corner pub where you can puff a cigar while drinking beer, port, or a single-malt scotch. **Widmer Brewing and Gasthaus** (⊠ 955 N. Russell St., ☎ 503/281–3333) brews German-style beers and has a full menu; you can tour the adjacent brewery during the daytime except on Sunday.

Coffeehouses and Teahouses

DOWNTOWN

Traditional English teas, complete with scones and Devonshire cream, are served with authentic English accents at the **British Tea Garden** (⊠ 725 S.W. 10th Ave., ☎ 503/221–7817). **Giant Steps** (⊠ 1208 N.W. Glisan St., ☎ 503/226–2547), with its stark, angular modern decor, is the artsy Pearl District's coffeehouse of choice. **Starbucks** (⊠ 720 S.W. Broadway, ☎ 503/223–2488) has cloned itself in just about every section of Portland; its main downtown store at Pioneer Courthouse Square is a good place to sip a latte and people-watch.

NOB HILL AND VICINITY

Coffee People (⊠ 533 N.W. 23rd Ave., ☎ 503/221–0235) and **Starbucks** (⊠ 605 N.W. 23rd Ave., ☎ 503/223–1747) are the largest coffee emporiums in Nob Hill, drawing crowds from early in the morning until late in the evening. **Torrefazione Italia** (⊠ 838 N.W. 23rd Ave.,

☎ 503/228–1255), a smaller coffeehouse with the individualized charm the larger chains lack, serves the best cappuccino in town.

EAST PORTLAND

Common Grounds (✉ 4321 S.E. Hawthorne Blvd., ☎ 503/236–4835) has plush couches, desserts, and light meals. Sippers lounge on sofas and overstuffed chairs at **Pied Cow** (✉ 3244 S.E. Belmont St., ☎ 503/230–4866), a laid-back alternative to more yuppified establishments. **Rimsky-Korsakoffee House** (✉ 707 S.E. 12th Ave., ☎ 503/232–2640), one of the city's first coffeehouses, is still one of the best, especially when it comes to desserts. **Torrefazione Italia** (✉ 1403 N.E. Weidler St., ☎ 503/288–1608) has an east-side location in a busy area near Lloyd Center.

Comedy

Harvey's Comedy Club (✉ 436 N.W. 6th Ave., ☎ 503/241–0338) presents stand-up comics nightly except Monday.

Dancing

McMenamins Crystal Ballroom (✉ 1332 W. Burnside St., ☎ 503/225–0047), a famous Portland dance hall that dates from 1914, sat empty for three decades until being completely refurbished in 1997. Rudolph Valentino danced the tango here in 1923, and you may feel like doing the same once you step out onto the 7,500-square-ft "elastic" floor (it's built on ball bearings) and feel it bouncing beneath your feet. Bands perform everything from swing to hillbilly rock nightly except Monday.

Gay and Lesbian Clubs

Boxxes/Panorama (✉ Stark St. between 10th and 11th Aves., ☎ 503/221–7262), a bar-disco-restaurant complex, is usually packed on weekends. Boxxes features music videos and has video poker machines and keno. Panorama, a cavernous space, has a large dance floor that's popular with gay men, lesbians, and straights. The Fish Grotto specializes in seafood, and the Red Cap Cafe has a light menu.

C. C. Slaughters (✉ 200 N.W. 3rd Ave., ☎ 503/248–9135) is a casual male-oriented bar with a dance floor and restaurant. The bar menu features an excellent halibut-and-chips served with garlic toast and slaw.

Egyptian Room (✉ 3701 S.E. Division St., ☎ 503/236–8689), Portland's most popular lesbian bar-disco, has pool tables and video poker games up front and a medium-size dance floor with a DJ spinning cool music in the back.

Scandals (✉ 1038 S.W. Stark St., ☎ 503/227–5887), a cruisy, male-oriented neighborhood bar and restaurant, has a quiet, low-key atmosphere with plate-glass windows that look out onto the street. The bar has video poker machines and keno.

Twelfth Avenue Grille (✉ 1135 S.W. Washington St., ☎ 503/243–2181), Portland's newest gay bar and restaurant, appeals to an upscale male crowd. There's a pool table and video poker machines on a lower level.

Live Music

BLUES, FOLK, AND ROCK

Candlelight Room (✉ 2032 S.W. 5th Ave., ☎ 503/222–3378) presents blues nightly.

Dublin Pub (✉ 6821 S.W. Beaverton–Hillsdale Hwy., ☎ 503/297–2889) pours more than 100 beers on tap and hosts Irish bands and rock groups.

Kell's (✉ 112 S.W. 2nd Ave., ☎ 503/227–4057) serves up terrific Irish food and Celtic music nightly.

Key Largo Restaurant and Nightclub (✉ 31 N.W. 1st Ave., ☎ 503/223–9919) is in a historic building with brick walls, an outdoor courtyard, and a dance floor. The club serves Cajun food and books top-drawer rock, blues, and folk acts.

La Luna (✉ 215 S.E. 9th Ave., ☎ 503/241–5862) hosts hot rock acts—and occasional world beat, blues, and ethnic-music performers—in a nightclub setting.

Moody's (✉ 424 S.W. 4th Ave., ☎ 503/223–4241) is the place to go for hard rock.

The **North by Northwest Music Festival** (☎ 512/467–7979), an annual new music conference, spotlights hundreds of up-and-coming musicians from around the West in late September. The focus is on alternative rock, but other musical genres are represented as well. One admission price gets you into about two dozen downtown clubs during the three-day event. There are also panels, workshops, and a music trade show.

Satyricon (✉ 125 N.W. 6th Ave., ☎ 503/243–2380) is Portland's leading outlet for grunge, punk, and other alternative rock music.

During the Rose Festival–dominated month of June, **A Taste of Beaverton** (✉ Griffith Park, at the intersection of Hwys. 10 and 217, Beaverton, ☎ 503/644–0123) attracts big-name entertainers to a three-day bash in suburban Beaverton. A food pavilion presents Pacific Northwest specialties while the bands play on.

COUNTRY AND WESTERN

The **Drum** (✉ 14601 S.E. Division St., ☎ 503/760–1400), Portland's top country club, books traditional country and contemporary country-rock performers.

Jubitz Truck Stop (✉ 10210 N. Vancouver Way, ☎ 503/283–1111) presents live country music nightly.

JAZZ

Brasserie Montmartre (✉ 626 S.W. Park Ave., ☎ 503/224–5552) presents duos on weeknights and quartets and larger groups on weekends.

Jazz de Opus (✉ 33 N.W. 2nd Ave., ☎ 503/222–6077) books local musicians with national reputations seven nights a week.

Since 1982 the **Mount Hood Jazz Festival** (✉ 26000 S.E. Stark, Gresham, ☎ 503/224–4400) has drawn big names as well as new talent to this three-day event in August. Past years have seen appearances by Ella Fitzgerald, Sarah Vaughan, and George Benson. The festival is held on the campus of Mount Hood Community College in suburban Gresham. You can take MAX light rail to Gresham Transit Center and transfer to Bus 26.

Parchman Farm (✉ 1204 S.E. Clay St., ☎ 503/235–7831) showcases prominent local jazz performers nightly.

The Arts

When it comes to public arts funding, Oregon ranks very low compared with other states, yet Portland is home to a symphony orchestra, opera and dance companies, and a number of theater companies. Most Portland-based performing arts groups have their own box-office numbers; *see* individual listings. For other events, the main ticket outlets are **Ticketmaster** (☎ 503/224–4400) and **Fastixx** (☎ 503/224–8499).

Dance

Oregon Ballet Theatre (☎ 503/222–5538 or 888/922–5538) produces five classical and contemporary works a year, including a much-loved holiday *Nutcracker*. Most performances are at the Portland Center for the Performing Arts.

Film

Cinema 21 (⊠ 616 N.W. 21st Ave., ☎ 503/223–4515), in the Nob Hill area, and **Cinemagic** (⊠ 2021 S.E. Hawthorne, ☎ 503/231–7919), in the Hawthorne District, are the city's most progressive art-movie houses; both also host the annual gay and lesbian film festival. For Hollywood blockbusters, new foreign films, and interesting low-budget sleepers, check out **Center Cinemas** (⊠ S.W. 3rd Ave. and Clay St., ☎ 503/225–5555, ext. 4608) downtown. The **Movie House** (⊠ 1220 S.W. Taylor St., ☎ 503/225–5555, ext. 4609), a restored theater in the former Portland Women's Club, shows critically acclaimed first-run British and American films. The **Northwest Film and Video Center** (⊠ S.W. 9th Ave. and Taylor St., ☎ 503/221–1156), a branch of the Portland Art Museum, screens all manner of art films, documentaries, and independent features and presents the three-week Portland International Film Festival in February and March.

Classical Music

CHAMBER MUSIC

Chamber Music Northwest (☎ 503/223–3202) presents some of the most sought-after soloists, chamber musicians, and recording artists from the Portland area and abroad for a five-week summer concert series; performances take place at Reed College and Catlin Gabel School.

ORCHESTRAS

The **Oregon Symphony** (☎ 503/228–1353 or 800/228–7343) presents more than 40 classical, pop, children's, and family concerts each year at the Arlene Schnitzer Concert Hall. The **Portland Baroque Orchestra** (☎ 503/222–6000) performs works on period instruments in a season that runs from October to April. Performances are held in the city at Trinity Episcopal Church (⊠ 147 N.W. 19th Ave.) and at St. Anne's Chapel, Marylhurst College (⊠ Hwy. 43, 1 mi east of Lake Oswego), a half-hour drive from downtown.

Opera

Portland Opera (☎ 503/241–1802) and its orchestra and chorus stage five productions annually at the Portland Civic Auditorium (☞ *below*).

Performance Venues

Arlene Schnitzer Concert Hall (⊠ Portland Center for the Performing Arts, S.W. Broadway and Main St., ☎ 503/796–9293) hosts rock stars, choral groups, lectures, and concerts by the Oregon Symphony and others.

The 23,000-seat **Civic Stadium** (⊠ 1844 S.W. Morrison, ☎ 503/248–4345) hosts concerts and sporting events.

Memorial Coliseum (⊠ 1 Center Ct., Rose Quarter, ☎ 503/321–3211), a 12,000-seat venue in northeast Portland on the MAX light-rail line, books rock groups, touring shows, the Ringling Brothers circus, ice-skating extravaganzas, and sporting events.

Portland Center for the Performing Arts (⊠ 1111 S.W. Broadway, ☎ 503/796–9293) schedules rock shows, symphony performances, lectures, and Broadway musicals (☞ Downtown *in* Exploring Portland, *above*).

Portland Civic Auditorium (⊠ 222 S.W. Clay St., ☎ 503/796–9293), with 3,000 seats and outstanding acoustics, presents opera, ballet, country and rock concerts, and touring shows.

The 21,000-seat **Rose Garden Arena** (⊠ 1 Center Ct., Broadway and N. Interstate Ave., ☎ 503/235–8771) replaced Memorial Coliseum as Portland's biggest indoor venue in 1995. It's home to the Portland Trail Blazers basketball team and the site of major rock concerts. It's on the MAX light-rail line.

Roseland Theater (⊠ 8 N.W. 6th Ave., ☎ 503/224–2038), which holds 1,400 people, specializes in rock and blues.

Theater

Artists Repertory Theatre (⊠ 1516 S.W. Alder St., ☎ 503/241–1278) stages five productions a year—regional premieres, occasional commissioned works, and selected classics.

Oregon Puppet Theater (☎ 503/236–4034) stages five children's productions a year at different locations in town.

Portland Center Stage (⊠ 1111 S.W. Broadway, ☎ 503/274–6588) produces six contemporary and classical works between October and April in the 800-seat Newmark Theater.

Portland Repertory Theater (⊠ 2 World Trade Center, 26 S.W. Salmon St., 3rd floor, ☎ 503/224–4491), the region's oldest professional theatrical company, presents five productions each year.

Tygres Heart Shakespeare Co. (⊠ 309 S.W. 6th Ave., ☎ 503/222–9220) mounts a fall, winter, and spring Shakespearean production in the intimate, court-style Winningstad Theatre.

OUTDOOR ACTIVITIES AND SPORTS

Portlanders are definitely oriented to the outdoors. Hikers, joggers, and mountain bikers take to the city's hundreds of miles of parks, paths, and trails. The Willamette and Columbia rivers are used for boating and water sports; unfortunately, it's not easy to rent any kind of boat for casual use. Big-sports fervor is reserved for Trail Blazer games, held at the Rose Quarter arena on the east side. The Portland/Oregon Visitors Association (☞ Visitor Information *in* Portland A to Z, *below*) provides information on sports events and outdoor activities in the city.

Participant Sports

Ballooning

From April through October, check out **Vista Balloon Adventures** (701 S.E. Sherk Pl., Sherwood 97140, ☎ 503/625–7385 or 800/622–2309, FAX 503/625–3845), just south of Portland, for a bird's-eye view of the northern Willamette Valley. Five balloons take off daily, weather permitting, and float up to 3,000 ft over wine country. From I–5, take the Tualatin exit (No. 289), then go west on Tualatin-Sherwood Road to Highway 99 W, turn left, and continue to Newberg.

Bicycling

Cyclists are common on Portland's streets. Many major streets have designated bike lanes, and numerous bike paths meander through parks and along the shoreline of the Willamette River. Designated routes include a 30-mi path northwest of downtown Portland along U.S. 30 and a path through northwest and southwest Portland on Terwilliger Boulevard to Lake Oswego. Other options are the 5½ mi of promenade along the Willamette River between the Broadway and Sellwood bridges and an east-side riverfront path between the Hawthorne and Burnside bridges. There is extensive off-road riding in Forest Park. Bikes can be rented downtown at **Bike Central** (⊠ 732 S.W. 1st Ave., ☎ 503/227–4439).

Fishing

The Columbia and Willamette rivers are major sportfishing streams with opportunities for angling virtually year-round. Unfortunately, though salmon can still be caught here, runs have been greatly reduced in both rivers in recent years, and the Willamette River is still plagued by pollution. Nevertheless, the Willamette still offers prime fishing for bass, channel catfish, sturgeon, crappies, perch, panfish, and crayfish. It is also a good winter steelhead stream. June is the top shad month, with some of the best fishing occurring below Willamette Falls at Oregon City. The Columbia River is known for its salmon, sturgeon, walleye, and smelt. The Sandy and Clackamas rivers, near Mount Hood, are smaller waterways popular with local fishermen.

OUTFITTERS

Outfitters throughout Portland operate guide services, including **G.I. Joe's** (⊠ 1140 N. Hayden Meadows Dr., ☎ 503/283–0312) and **Stewart Fly Shop** (⊠ 23830 N.E. Halsey St., ☎ 503/666–2471). Few outfitters rent equipment, so bring your own or be prepared to buy.

REGULATIONS

Local sport shops are the best sources of information on current fishing hot spots, which change from year to year. Detailed fishing regulations are available at local tackle shops or from the **Oregon Department of Fish and Wildlife** (⊠ 2501 S.W. 1st Ave., Portland 97201, ☎ 503/872–5263).

Golf

Broadmoor Golf Course (⊠ 3509 N.E. Columbia Blvd., ☎ 503/281–1337) is an 18-hole, par-72 course where the greens fee ranges from $20 to $22 and an optional cart costs $22.

At the 18-hole, par-70 **Colwood National Golf Club** (⊠ 7313 N.E. Columbia Blvd., ☎ 503/254–5515), the greens fee runs from $18 to $31, plus $22 for an optional cart. On mornings and weekends, the $31 greens fee includes a cart.

Heron Lakes Golf Course (⊠ 3500 N. Victory Blvd., ☎ 503/289–1818) consists of two 18-hole, par-72 courses: the less challenging Greenback, and the Great Blue, generally acknowledged to be the most difficult links in the greater Portland area. The greens fee at the Green, as it is locally known, ranges from $18 to $20, while the fee at the Blue is $29 at all times. An optional cart at either course costs $24.

Pumpkin Ridge Golf Course (⊠ 12930 N.W. Old Pumpkin Ridge Rd., Cornelius 97113, ☎ 503/647–4747) has 36 holes, with the 18-hole Ghost Creek par-71 course open to the public. When it opened in 1992 *Golf Digest* named it the best new public course in the nation. Greens fees are high, ranging from $50 to $110; cart rental is $15.

Ice-Skating

Ice Chalet at Lloyd Center (⊠ Multnomah St. and N.E. 9th Ave., ☎ 503/288–6073) and **Ice Chalet at Clackamas Town Center** (⊠ 12000 S.E. 82nd Ave., ☎ 503/786–6000) have open skating and skate rentals ($8.50 admission includes skate rental). The rinks, inside the shopping malls, are open year-round.

Swimming and Sunbathing

Blue Lake Regional Park (⊠ 20500 N.E. Marine Dr., Troutdale, ☎ 503/665–4995) has a swimming beach that's packed on hot summer days. You can also fish and rent small boats here. This is a great place to take a hike on the surrounding trails or to have a picnic.

If you feel like tanning au naturel, drive about a half hour northwest of downtown to **Sauvie Island,** a wildlife refuge with a secluded beachfront that's popular (and legal with) nude sunbathers. If the sky is clear, you'll get a spectacular view from the riverbank of three Cascade mountains—Hood, St. Helens, and Adams. Huge oceangoing vessels cruise by on their way to and from the Port of Portland. To get here, take U.S. 30 north to Sauvie Island bridge, turn right, and follow Reeder Road until you hit gravel. Look for the Collins Beach signs. There's plenty of parking, but a permit is required. You can buy it ($3.50 for a one-day permit, $10.50 for an annual permit) at the Cracker Barrel country store just over the bridge on the left side of the road.

Skiing

For information about permits for cross-country and downhill skiing, *see* Oregon A to Z *in* Chapter 3. Two places in Portland that rent skis and equipment are the **Mountain Shop** (⊠ 628 N.E. Broadway, ☎ 503/288–6768) and **REI** (⊠ 1798 Jantzen Beach Center, ☎ 503/283–1300).

Tennis

Glendoveer Golf Course (⊠ 14015 N.E. Glisan St., ☎ 503/253–7507) and the **Lake Oswego Indoor Tennis Center** (⊠ 2900 S.W. Diane Dr., ☎ 503/635–5550) have indoor tennis courts. The **Portland Tennis Center** (⊠ 324 N.E. 12th Ave., ☎ 503/823–3189) operates four indoor courts and eight lighted outdoor courts. The **St. John's Racquet Center** (⊠ 7519 N. Burlington Ave., ☎ 503/823–3629) has three indoor courts.

Portland Parks and Recreation (☎ 503/823–7529) operates 117 outdoor tennis courts (many with night lighting) at Washington Park, Grant Park, and many other locations. The courts are open on a first-come, first-served basis year-round, but you can reserve one, starting in March, for play from May to September.

Spectator Sports

Auto Racing

Portland International Raceway (⊠ West Delta Park, 1940 N. Victory Blvd., ☎ 503/823–7223) presents bicycle and drag racing and motocross on weeknights, and sports-car, motorcycle, and go-cart racing on weekends from April to September.

Portland Speedway (⊠ 9727 N. Martin Luther King Jr. Blvd., ☎ 503/285–9511) hosts demolition derbies and NASCAR and stock-car races from April to September. In June, it hosts the Budweiser Indy Car World Series, a 200-mi race that lures the top names on the Indy Car circuit.

Baseball

The **Portland Rockies** (⊠ 1844 S.W. Morrison, ☎ 503/223–2837), an affiliate of the Colorado Rockies, play at Civic Stadium from June to September.

Basketball

The **Rose Garden** (⊠ 1 Center Ct., ☎ 503/797–9617) is the 21,700-seat home court of the Portland Trail Blazers of the National Basketball Association.

Horse Racing

Thoroughbred and quarter horses race, rain or shine, at **Portland Meadows** (⊠ 1001 N. Schmeer Rd., ☎ 503/285–9144) from October to April.

Ice Hockey

The **Portland Winter Hawks** (☎ 503/238–6366) of the Western Hockey League play home games at **Memorial Coliseum** (⊠ 300 N. Winning Way) and at the **Rose Garden** (⊠ 1 Center Ct.).

SHOPPING

There's no sales tax in Oregon, so you can save a few dollars on items you buy and can carry back home. Portland's main shopping area is **downtown,** between Southwest 2nd and 10th avenues and between Southwest Stark and Morrison streets. **Nob Hill,** north of downtown along Northwest 21st and 23rd avenues, is home to eclectic clothing, gift, book, and food shops. Most of the city's fine-art galleries are concentrated in the **Pearl District,** north from Burnside Street to Marshall Street between Northwest 8th and 15th avenues, along with furniture and design stores. **Sellwood,** 5 mi from the city center, south on Naito Parkway and east across the Sellwood Bridge, has more than 50 antiques and collectibles shops along Southeast 13th Avenue, plus specialty shops and outlet stores for sporting goods. **Hawthorne Boulevard** between 30th and 42nd avenues has an often countercultural array of bookstores, coffeehouses, antiques stores, and boutiques.

The **Portland Saturday Market** (⊠ Burnside Bridge, underneath west end, ☎ 503/222–6072), open on Saturday and Sunday, is a good place to find handcrafted items. *See* The Skidmore District and Chinatown *in* Exploring Portland, *above.*

Portland merchants are generally open from Monday to Saturday between 9 or 10 AM and 6 PM and on Sunday between 11 AM or noon and 4 PM. Most shops in downtown's Pioneer Place, the east side's Lloyd Center, and the outlying malls are open until 9 PM every night.

Malls and Department Stores

Downtown/City Center

Meier and Frank (⊠ 621 S.W. 5th Ave., ☎ 503/223–0512), a department store that dates from 1857, has 10 floors of general merchandise at its main location downtown.

Nordstrom (⊠ 701 S.W. Broadway, ☎ 503/224–6666) sells fine-quality apparel and accessories and has a large footwear department. Bargain lovers should head for the **Nordstrom Rack** (⊠ 401 S.W. Morrison St., ☎ 503/299–1815) outlet across from Pioneer Place Mall.

Pioneer Place (⊠ 700 S.W. 5th Ave., ☎ 503/228–5800) holds 70 upscale specialty shops (including Williams-Sonoma, Coach, J. Crew, Godiva, and Caswell-Massey) in a three-story glass-roof atrium setting. You'll find good, inexpensive ethnic foods from 18 vendors in the Cascades Food Court in the basement.

Saks Fifth Avenue (⊠ 850 S.W. 5th Ave., ☎ 503/226–3200) has two floors of men's and women's clothing, jewelry, and other merchandise.

Beyond Downtown

NORTHEAST PORTLAND

Lloyd Center (⊠ N.E. Multnomah St. at N.E. 9th Ave., ☎ 503/282–2511), which is on the MAX light-rail line, contains more than 170 shops, including Nordstrom and Meier and Frank, a large food court, a multiscreen cinema, and an ice-skating pavilion.

SOUTHEAST PORTLAND

Clackamas Town Center (⊠ Sunnyside Rd. at I–205's Exit 14, ☎ 503/653–6913) has five major department stores, more than 180 shops, and an ice-skating rink.

Washington Square (✉ 9585 S.W. Washington Sq. Rd., at S.W. Hall Blvd. and Hwy. 217, Tigard, ☎ 503/639–8860) contains five major department stores and 120 specialty shops.

The **Water Tower** (✉ 5331 S.W. MacAdam Ave., ☎ 503/228–9431), in the John's Landing neighborhood, is a pleasant smaller mall with 35 specialty shops and six restaurants.

Specialty Stores

Antiques
Portland Antique Company (✉ 1211 N.W. Glisan St., ☎ 503/223–0999) spreads over 35,000 square ft in the Pearl District. It houses the Pacific Northwest's largest selection of European and English antiques.

Shogun's Gallery (✉ 206 N.W. 23rd Ave., ☎ 503/224–0328) specializes in Japanese and Chinese furniture, especially the lightweight wooden Japanese cabinets known as *tansu*. Also here are chairs, tea tables, altar tables, armoires, ikebana baskets, and Chinese wooden picnic boxes, all of them at least 100 years old and at extremely reasonable prices.

Stars Antique Mall (✉ 305 N.W. 21st Ave., ☎ 503/220–8180) rents out its 10,000-square-ft space in Nob Hill to a variety of antiques dealers; you might find anything from low-end 1950s kitsch to high-end treasures.

Art Dealers and Galleries
Butters Gallery, Ltd. (✉ 223 N.W. 9th Ave., ☎ 503/248–9378) has monthly exhibits of the works of nationally known and local artists in its Pearl District space.

In Her Image Gallery (✉ 3208 S.E. Hawthorne Blvd., ☎ 503/231–3726) specializes in statues, totems, and works of art dedicated to the great earth goddesses.

Photographic Image Gallery (✉ 240 S.W. 1st Ave., ☎ 503/224–3543) carries prints by nationally known nature photographers Christopher Burkett and Joseph Holmes, among others, and has a large supply of photography posters.

Pulliam/Deffenbaugh Gallery (✉ 522 N.W. 12th Ave., ☎ 503/228–6665) generally shows contemporary figurative and expressionistic works by Pacific Northwest artists.

Quintana's Galleries of Native American Art (✉ 501 S.W. Broadway, ☎ 503/223–1729 or 800/321–1729) focuses on Pacific Northwest coast, Navajo, and Hopi art and jewelry, along with photogravures by Edward Curtis.

Twist (✉ 30 N.W. 23rd Pl., ☎ 503/224–0334; ✉ Pioneer Place, ☎ 503/222–3137) has a huge space in Nob Hill and a smaller shop downtown. In Nob Hill you'll find contemporary American ceramics, glass, furniture, sculpture, and handcrafted jewelry; downtown carries an assortment of objects, often with a pop, whimsical touch.

Books
New Renaissance Bookshop (✉ 1338 N.W. 23rd Ave., ☎ 503/224–4929), between Overton and Pettygrove, is dedicated to New Age and metaphysical books and tapes.

Powell's City of Books (✉ 1005 W. Burnside St., ☎ 503/228–4651), the largest used and new retail bookstore in the world (more than 1.5 million volumes), covers an entire city block. It also carries rare and hard-to-find editions. There's also a **Powell's for Cooks and Garden-**

ers on the east side (✉ 3747 Hawthorne Ave., ☎ 503/235–3802) and a small store located in the Portland International Airport.

Clothing

Elizabeth Street and Zelda's Shoe Bar (✉ 635 N.W. 23rd Ave., ☎ 503/243–2456), two connected boutiques in Nob Hill, carry a sophisticated, highly eclectic line of women's clothes, accessories, and shoes.

Jane's Obsession (✉ 728 N.W. 23rd Ave., ☎ 503/221–1490), a porch-level shop in one of Northwest 23rd Avenue's "house boutiques," sells luxurious French and Italian lingerie.

Mario's (✉ 921 S.W. Morrison St., ☎ 503/227–3477), Portland's best store for fine men's clothing, carries designer lines by Canali, Armani, Vestimenta, Donna Karan, and Calvin Klein, among others.

Mario's for Women (✉ 811 S.W. Morrison St., ☎ 503/241–8111) stocks Armani, Calvin Klein, and Vesti.

Nob Hill Shoes and Repair (✉ 921 N.W. 23rd Ave., ☎ 503/224–8682), a tiny spot, sells men and women's Naot sandals from Israel and Swedish Bastad clogs. (These are big in Portland, which has entered its post-Birkenstock phase.)

Norm Thompson Outfitters (✉ 1805 N.W. Thurman St., ☎ 503/221–0764) carries classic fashions for men and women, innovative footwear, and one-of-a-kind gifts.

Portland Outdoor Store (✉ 304 S.W. 3rd Ave., ☎ 503/222–1051) stubbornly resists all that is trendy, both in clothes and decor, but if you want authentic western gear—saddles, Stetsons, boots, or cowboy shirts—head here.

Portland Pendleton Shop (✉ S.W. 4th Ave. and Salmon St., ☎ 503/242–0037) stocks clothing by the famous local apparel maker.

Gifts

Christmas at the Zoo (✉ 118 N.W. 23rd Ave., ☎ 503/223–4048 or 800/223–5886) is crammed year-round with decorated trees and has Portland's best selection of European handblown glass ornaments and plush animals.

Gai-Pied (✉ 2544 N.E. Broadway, ☎ 503/331–1125) carries periodicals, books, gifts, and videos of interest to the gay community.

Kathmandu to You (✉ 511 N.W. 21st Ave., ☎ 503/221–9986) has clothing, incense, and Eastern religious artifacts and gifts.

Made in Oregon (☎ 800/828–9673), which sells books, smoked salmon, local wines, Pendleton woolen goods, carvings made of myrtle wood, and other products made in the state, has shops at Portland International Airport, the Lloyd Center, the Galleria, Old Town, Washington Square, and Clackamas Town Center.

Jewelry

Carl Greve (✉ 731 S.W. Morrison St., ☎ 503/223–7121), in business since 1922, carries exclusive designer lines of fine jewelry, such as Mikimoto pearls, and has the state's only Tiffany boutique. The second floor is reserved for china, stemware, and housewares.

Music

Django Records (✉ 1111 S.W. Stark St., ☎ 503/227–4381) is a must for collectors of tapes, compact discs, 45s, and vintage albums.

Music Millennium Northwest (✉ 801 N.W. 23rd Ave., ☎ 503/248–0163) stocks a huge selection of CDs and tapes in every possible musical category, from local punk to classical. **Classical Millennium** (✉ 3144 E. Burnside St., ☎ 503/231–8909), the company's east-side location, has the best selection of classical CDs and tapes in Oregon.

Perfume
Aveda Lifestyle Store and Spa (✉ 500 S.W. 5th Ave., ☎ 503/248–0615) sells the flower-based Aveda line of scents and skin-care products.

Perfume House (✉ 3328 S.E. Hawthorne Blvd., ☎ 503/234–5375) carries hundreds of brand-name fragrances for women and men.

Toys
Finnegan's Toys and Gifts (✉ 922 S.W. Yamhill St., ☎ 503/221–0306), downtown Portland's largest toy store, stocks artistic, creative, educational, and other types of toys.

PORTLAND A TO Z

Arriving and Departing

By Bus
From the **Greyhound** terminal (✉ 550 N.W. 6th Ave., ☎ 503/243–2357 or 800/231–2222) next to the Amtrak station in Old Town, buses arrive at and depart from points throughout the nation.

By Car
I–5 enters Portland from the north and south. **I–84,** the city's major eastern corridor, terminates in Portland. **U.S. 26** and **U.S. 30** are primary east–west thoroughfares. Bypass routes are **I–205**, which links I–5 and I–84 before crossing the Columbia River into Washington, and **I–405**, which arcs around western downtown.

By Plane
Portland International Airport (✉ N.E. Airport Way at I–205, ☎ 877/739–4636), about 12 mi from downtown in northeast Portland, is served by Air Canada, Alaska, American, America West, Continental, Delta, Hawaiian, Horizon, Northwest, Reno, Southwest Airlines, TWA, United, and Western Pacific. *See* Air Travel *in* Smart Travel Tips A to Z for airline phone numbers.

BETWEEN THE AIRPORT AND CITY CENTER

By Bus: Tri-Met (☎ 503/238–7433) Bus 12 runs about every 15 minutes to and from the airport. The fare is $1.10. An extension of the MAX light-rail line, running from the Gateway Transit Center (at the intersection of I–84 and I–205) directly to the airport, is scheduled to open in fall 2001. **Evergreen Gray Line** (☎ 503/285–9845) buses leave from the airport every 30 minutes and serve most major downtown hotels. The fare is $12 one-way and $22 round-trip.

By Car: From the airport, take I–205 south to westbound I–84. Drive west over the Willamette River and take the City Center exit. Going to the airport, take I–84 east to I–205 north; follow I–205 to the airport exit.

By Taxi: The trip between downtown Portland and the airport takes about 30 minutes by taxi. The fare is about $30.

By Train
Amtrak (☎ 800/872–7245) serves Union Station (✉ 800 N.W. 6th Ave.). The *Coast Starlight* operates daily between Seattle, Portland, and Los Angeles. The *Empire Builder* travels between Portland and Chicago. The *Cascades,* modern European trains, operate daily between Eugene, Portland, Seattle, and Vancouver, B.C.

Getting Around

By Bus
Tri-Met operates bus service throughout the greater Portland area. The fares are the same for Tri-Met and the MAX light-rail system (☞ *below*), and tickets can be used on either system. Buses are free throughout the entire downtown "Fareless Square," whose borders are Northwest Irving Street to the north, I–405 to the west and south, and the Willamette River to the east. The Tri-Met information office at Pioneer Courthouse Square (✉ 6th Ave. and Morrison St., ☎ 503/238–7433) is open on weekdays from 9 to 5.

By Car
Numbered roads in Portland are avenues. Most city-center streets are one-way only, and Southwest 5th and 6th avenues between Burnside and Southwest Madison streets are limited to bus traffic. It is legal to turn right on a red light at most intersections (check the signs). Left turns from a one-way street onto another one-way street on a red light are also legal. Most parking meters are patrolled from 8 AM to 6 PM; many streets have posted rush-hour regulations. Meter parking is free on Sunday and most major holidays.

By Light Rail
Metropolitan Area Express (☎ 503/228–7246), or MAX, links the eastern and western Portland suburbs with downtown, Washington Park and the Oregon Zoo, the Lloyd Center district, the Convention Center, and the Rose Quarter. From downtown, trains operate daily from 5:30 AM to 1 AM, with a fare of $1.10 for travel through one or two zones, $1.40 for three zones, and $3.50 for an unlimited all-day ticket. Trains run about every 10 minutes from Monday through Saturday and every 15 minutes on Sunday and holidays.

By Taxi
Taxi fare is $2.50 at flag drop plus $1.50 per mile. The first person pays by the meter, and each additional passenger pays $1. Cabs cruise the city streets, but it's better to phone for one. The major companies are **Broadway Cab** (☎ 503/227–1234), **New Rose City Cab** (☎ 503/282–7707), **Portland Taxi Company** (☎ 503/256–5400), and **Radio Cab** (☎ 503/227–1212).

Contacts and Resources

Emergencies
Ambulance (☎ 911). **Fire** (☎ 911). **Police** (☎ 911).

Eastmoreland Hospital (✉ 2900 S.E. Steele St., ☎ 503/234–0411). **Legacy Emanuel Hospital and Health Center** (✉ 2801 N.W. Gantenbien Ave., ☎ 503/413–2200). **Legacy Good Samaritan Hospital & Medical Center** (✉ 1015 N.W. 22nd Ave., ☎ 503/413–7711). **Providence Portland Medical Center** (✉ 805 N.E. Glisan St., ☎ 503/215–1111). **Providence St. Vincent Hospital** (✉ 9205 S.W. Barnes Rd., ☎ 503/216–1234).

Willamette Dental Group PC (✉ 1933 S.W. Jefferson St., ☎ 503/644–3200) has offices throughout the metropolitan area and is open Saturday.

Guided Tours
ORIENTATION
Gray Line Sightseeing (☎ 503/285–9845) operates city tours year-round and scheduled service to Chinook Winds Casino in Lincoln City; call for departure times.

Sternwheeler Riverboat Tours (☎ 503/223–3928). The *Columbia Gorge* departs year-round from Tom McCall Waterfront Park (⊠ S.W. Naito Parkway and Stark St.) on two-hour excursions of the Willamette River; there are also Friday-night dinner cruises. During the summer the stern-wheeler travels up the Columbia River. **Yachts-O-Fun Riverboat Cruises** (☎ 503/234–6665) operates dinner and Sunday-brunch cruises, Portland harbor excursions, and historical tours.

Willamette Shore Trolley (⊠ 311 N. State St.; Portland: south of River-Place Marina, at Sheridan and Moody Sts., Lake Oswego, ☎ 503/222–2226). Vintage double-decker trolleys provide scenic round-trips between suburban Lake Oswego and downtown, along the west shore of the Willamette River. The 7-mi route, which the trolley traverses in 45 minutes, passes over trestles and through Elk Rock tunnel along one of the most scenic stretches of the river. The line, opened in 1885, was electrified in 1914, and Southern Pacific Railway operated dozens of trips daily along this route in the 1920s. Passenger service ended in 1929 and the line was taken over by the Oregon Electric Railway Historical Society. Reservations are recommended. The trolley ($6 round trip) departs Lake Oswego at noon and 2 PM and Portland at 1 and 3 on Friday, Saturday, and Sunday.

The **Portland/Oregon Visitors Association** (☞ Visitor Information, *below*), which is open on weekdays from 9 to 5 and Saturday from 9 to 4, has brochures, maps, and guides to art galleries and select neighborhoods.

Late-Night Pharmacies

Walgreens has a 24-hour pharmacy with drive-through service in the Hawthorne District (⊠ 940 S.E. 39th Ave., ☎ 503/238–6053).

Visitor Information

Portland/Oregon Visitors Association (⊠ 2 World Trade Center, 28 S.W. Salmon St., 97204, ☎ 503/222–2223 or 800/962–3700) is open weekdays 9–5, Saturday 9–2.

3 OREGON

Welcome to Oregon, where natural splendor is the rule, not the exception. The bounty includes the rocky Pacific coast, the wild Rogue and McKenzie rivers, and scenic knockouts like the Columbia River Gorge, Mount Hood, and Crater Lake. Old West memories linger on amid the vast grandeur of eastern Oregon's high desert, forests, and mountains. On the gentler side, the Willamette Valley is a lush wine-producing region, home to attractions commemorating the state's pioneer history and world-renowned cultural events.

By Donald S.
Olson

Updated by
Jeffrey Boswell

NO **MATTER WHAT** you're looking for in a vacation, no other state can offer more than Oregon. Within a 90-minute drive from Portland or Eugene you can lose yourself in the recreational landscape of your choice: uncrowded ocean beaches, snow-silvered mountain wilderness, or a monolith-studded desert that has served as the backdrop for many a Hollywood western. In the Willamette Valley wine country, scores of tasting rooms offer up the fruit of the vine. Food lovers find that Oregon produces some of the nation's best fruits, vegetables, and seafood, all of which can be enjoyed in the growing number of fine restaurants throughout the state. Plenty of attractions keep the kids busy, too, from the Enchanted Forest near Salem to the Oregon Coast Aquarium in Newport. And shoppers take note—there's no sales tax in Oregon.

Although the state has a notorious reputation for being rainy, and winters can be wet and dreary, the rest of the year more than makes up for it. Much of the state is actually a desert, and most of the precipitation falls west of the Cascades. At its eastern end, Oregon begins in a high, sage-scented desert plateau that covers nearly two-thirds of the state's 96,000 square mi. As you move west, the landscape rises to 11,000-ft-high alpine peaks, meadows, and lakes; plunges to fertile farmland and forest; and ends at the cold, tumultuous Pacific.

Oregon's beneficent climate and landscape have supported human residents for a very long time. Evidence of Oregon's earliest Native American inhabitants is tantalizingly rare, but what does exist suggests that tribes of nomadic hunter-gatherers established themselves throughout the region many centuries before the first white explorers and settlers arrived. In eastern Oregon, a pair of 9,000-year-old sagebrush sandals (now in the Oregon Museum of Natural History in Eugene) and nets woven from reeds have been discovered; on the coast, ancient shell middens indicate that even the earliest Oregonians feasted on seafood. In the Columbia River Gorge, a recently unearthed male skeleton has archaeologists revising their time lines.

Whites arrived in 1792, when Robert Gray, an American trading captain, followed a trail of debris and muddy water inland and came upon the Columbia River. Shortly thereafter, British Army lieutenant William Broughton was dispatched to investigate Gray's find, and he sailed as far upriver as the rapids-choked mouth of the Columbia River Gorge. Within a few years, a thriving seaborne fur trade sprang up, with American and British entrepreneurs exchanging baubles, cloth, tools, weapons, and liquor with the native peoples for high-quality beaver and sea-otter pelts.

In 1805, American explorers Meriwether Lewis and William Clark reached the site of present-day Astoria after their epic overland journey, spurring an influx of white pioneers—mostly fur trappers and traders sent by John Jacob Astor's Pacific Fur Company in 1811 to do business and claim the land for the United States. The English disputed American claims to the territory on the basis of Broughton's earlier exploration, and after the War of 1812 began, they negotiated the purchase of Astoria from Astor's company. It wasn't until 1846, with the signing of the Oregon Treaty, that the British formally renounced their claims in the region.

Oregon Country, as it was called, grew tremendously between 1841 and 1860, as more than 50,000 settlers from the eastern United States made the journey westward over the plains in their covered wagons. There is a story, never confirmed, that early pioneers arriving at a crossroads of the Oregon Trail found a pile of gold quartz or pyrite pointing the way south to California. The way north was marked by a hand-lettered sign: TO OREGON, and Oregonians like to think that the more literate of the pioneers found their way here, while the fortune hunters continued south. As settlers capitalized on gold-rush San Francisco's need for provisions and other supplies, Oregon reaped its own riches, and the lawless frontier gradually acquired a semblance of civilization. Most white pioneers settled in the Willamette Valley, where the bulk of Oregon's 3.2 million residents still live. The territory's residents voted down the idea of statehood three times, but in 1859, Oregon became the 33rd U.S. state.

The state still attracts many newcomers every year, and it's no wonder, since it has so much to offer. Not only do Oregonians take full advantage of the outdoors, making them some of the hardest-playing Americans, but they have also been called the hardest-working Americans. Rural Oregon's economy is still dependent on timber (the state is America's largest producer of softwood), agriculture (hazelnuts, fruit, berries, wine, seed crops, livestock, and dairy products), and fishing. A major high-tech center known as the Silicon Forest, producing high-speed computer hardware and sophisticated instruments, has taken root west of Portland in the Tualatin Valley, side by side with the wine industry.

In the meantime, tourism grows in importance every year, as visitors from all over the world discover the scenic and recreational treasures that so thrill Oregonians themselves. A sophisticated hospitality industry has appeared, making Oregon more accessible than ever before. You'll feel more than welcome here, but when you visit, expect a little ribbing if locals catch you mispronouncing the state's name: it's "Ore-ee-gun" not "Ore-uh-gone."

Pleasures and Pastimes

Dining

Fresh foods grown, caught, and harvested in the Northwest are standard fare in gourmet restaurants throughout Oregon. Outside urban areas and resorts, most restaurants tend to be low-key and unpretentious, both in ambience and cuisine. On the coast, look for regional specialties—clam chowder, fresh fish (particularly salmon), sweet Dungeness crab, mussels, shrimp, and oysters. Elsewhere in the state fresh river fish, local lamb and beef, and seasonal game dishes appear on many menus. Desserts made with local fruits such as huckleberries and marionberries are always worth trying.

CATEGORY	COST*
$$$$	over $35
$$$	$25–$35
$$	$15–$25
$	under $15

per person for a three-course meal, excluding drinks and service

Lodging

Luxury hotels, sophisticated resorts, historic lodges, Old West hotels, and rustic inns are among Oregon's diverse accommodations. Cozy bed-and-breakfasts, many of them in Victorian-era houses in small towns, are often real finds.

Oregon

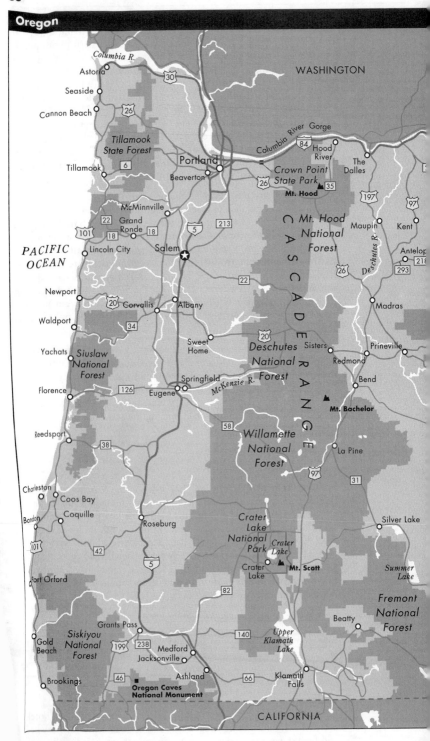

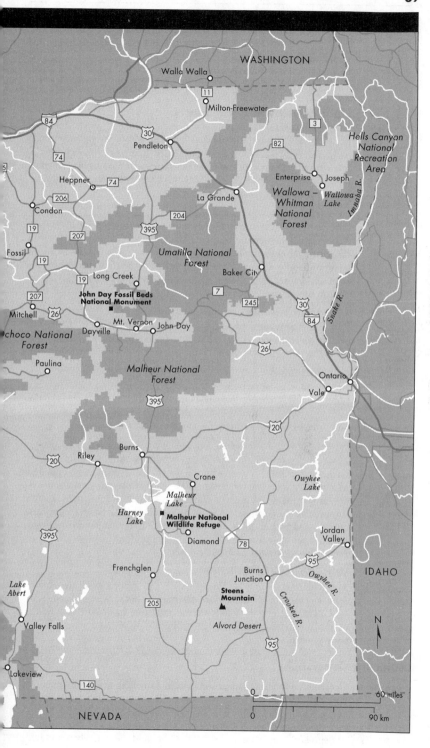

CATEGORY	COST*
$$$$	over $170
$$$	$110–$170
$$	$60–$110
$	under $60

All prices are for a standard double room, excluding room tax, which varies from 6% to 9½% depending on location.

Outdoor Activities and Sports

BIKING AND HIKING

For the past 20 years, Oregon has set aside 1% of its highway funds for the development and maintenance of bikeways throughout the state, resulting in one of the most extensive networks of bicycle trails in the country. The system of hiking trails through state-park and national-forest lands is equally comprehensive.

BOATING, FISHING, AND RAFTING

Oregon's many waterways afford limitless opportunities for adventure. Many companies operate boating and white-water rafting tours, or you can rent equipment and head out on your own. The Deschutes River north of Bend is a popular white-water rafting destination. Fishing requires a license. *See* Fishing *in* Oregon A to Z, *below,* for advice on how to obtain one.

HOT-AIR BALLOONING

If you've ever wanted to float over a verdant landscape in the basket of a hot-air balloon, come to the Willamette Valley in the warmer months for an aerial view of Oregon's wine country.

ROCKHOUNDING

Rockhounding—searching for semiprecious or unusual rocks—is very popular in the Ochocos in central Oregon and Harney County and the Stinkingwater Mountains in eastern Oregon. Agate, obsidian, jasper, and thunder eggs are among the sought-after stones.

SKIING

Most Oregon downhillers congregate around Mount Hood and Mount Bachelor, but there is also skiing to the south, at Willamette Pass and Mount Ashland. The temperate Willamette Valley generally receives only a few inches of snow a year, but the Coast Range, the Cascade Range, and the Siskiyou Mountains are all Nordic skiers' paradises, crisscrossed by hundreds of miles of trails. Every major downhill ski resort in the state also has Nordic skiing, but don't rule out the many Forest Service trails and logging roads.

Wine Tasting

The Willamette Valley is Oregon's main region for viticulture—many area wineries are open for tours, tastings, or both. Wineries near Forest Grove can be toured in a afternoon outing from Portland. South of the Willamette Valley are the Umpqua Valley and Rogue River wine-growing regions.

Exploring Oregon

Oregon's coastline stretches south from Astoria to the California border. Inland a bit, the fertile Willamette River valley also runs north–south. The mighty Columbia River travels west of the Cascade Range past the Mount Hood Wilderness Area to Astoria. The resort towns of Bend and Sisters are in Central Oregon, and the sparsely populated desert region is east of the Cascades.

Oregon tourist-information centers are marked with blue "I" signs from main roads. Opening and closing times vary, depending on the season and the individual office; call ahead for hours (☞ *Visitor Information* in *Oregon A to Z,* below).

Numbers in the text correspond to numbers in the margin and on the Oregon Coast and Willamette Valley/Wine Country; Salem; Eugene; Crater Lake National Park; Columbia River Gorge, the Cascades, and Central Oregon; and Eastern Oregon maps.

Great Itineraries

IF YOU HAVE 3 OR 4 DAYS

On your first day take U.S. 101 to the coastal resort town of **Cannon Beach** ②, and then continue south to **Newport** ⑥ and visit the **Oregon Coast Aquarium.** On day two drive east on U.S. 20, stopping briefly in **Corvallis** before continuing east on U.S. 20 and north on Interstate 5 (I–5) to **Salem** ⑬–⑰, the state capital. After touring Salem, visit one or more of the **Willamette Valley vineyards** around Forest Grove, Newberg, and Dundee before stopping in **McMinnville** ⑫ for the night. On day three take Highway 99 W north toward Portland and connect with I–5 heading north to I–84. The interstate winds eastward to the **Columbia Gorge.** At Troutdale, get on the **Historic Columbia River Highway,** which passes **Multnomah Falls** ㉙ before rejoining I–84. Continue east to the **Bonneville Dam** ㉛ and **The Dalles.** If you'll be staying in the area four days, spend night three in **Hood River** ㉜ and swing down to **Mount Hood** ㉝ the next morning.

IF YOU HAVE 7 OR 8 DAYS

Begin in Oregon's northwest, in **Astoria** ①, where the Columbia River meets the Pacific Ocean. From there, continue south on U.S. 101 to **Cannon Beach** ②. On day two head south from Cannon Beach to **Tillamook** ③ and the oceanfront parks on the **Three Capes Loop** ④. Continue south to **Newport** ⑥, where the **Oregon Coast Aquarium** is a must-see attraction. Spend the night south of Newport in the **Florence** ⑨ area. Drive south on day three to **Coos Bay** ⑩ and **Bandon** ⑪, then east on Highway 42 over the Coast Range to pick up I–5 heading south to **Ashland** ㉗. On day four backtrack north on I–5 to **Medford,** where you can pick up Highway 62 heading north and then east to **Crater Lake National Park** ㉔. Spend the night at the park, or backtrack west on Highway 62 and pick up Highway 230 north to Highway 138 west to I–5, which leads north to **Eugene** ⑲–㉒. (If you're not going to stay at Crater Lake, you'll need to get an early start from Medford.) If you've stayed at Crater Lake, on day five take Highway 138 east from the north end of the park to U.S. 97, which travels north past the **Newberry Volcanic National Monument** to **Bend** ㉟. If you've spent the night in Eugene, travel east along the McKenzie River on Highway 126 to Highway 242 (closed in winter, in which case stay on 126) to U.S. 20. This route travels past the western-theme town of **Sisters** to **Bend** ㉟. On day six head north on U.S. 97 and east on Highway 126 and U.S. 26 past the **Ochoco National Forest** ㊱ and the **John Day Fossil Beds National Monument** ㊸. You have three options for lodgings, depending on how much time you spend at the fossil beds: **Mitchell** and **John Day** ㊷ are both on U.S. 26; farther east on Highway 7 is **Baker City** ㊶. On day seven, take scenic U.S. 30 north from Baker City to North Powder, and then continue north on I–84 to **La Grande** ㊳ and **Pendleton** ㊲. If you have the time, spend the night in Pendleton, and on day eight drive west on I–84 to the **Columbia Gorge,** stopping at the **Bonneville Dam** ㉛ and **Multnomah Falls** ㉙.

When to Tour Oregon

When's the best time to take advantage of Oregon's wealth of beauty and activities? Winters in western Oregon are usually mild, but they can be relentlessly rainy. To the east of the Cascade Range, winters are clearer, drier, and colder. February–May are the best months for whale-watching along the coast and bird-watching at the Malheur National Wildlife Refuge in southeastern Oregon. Spring weather is changeable on both sides of the Cascades, but the landscape is a Technicolor wonder of wildflowers, flowering fruit trees (in the Hood River valley), and gardens bursting with rhododendrons and azaleas.

Jacksonville and Eugene host world-class summer music festivals, and the theater season in Ashland lasts from February to October. July and August are the prime months for visiting Crater Lake National Park, which is often snowed in for the rest of the year. Those months are predictably dry east of the Cascades, where it can get downright hot, but you can make a quick escape to the coast, where even summer weather can be cool and foggy. If you're looking for clear days along the coast, however, late summer and early fall are your best bets; these are also the best times to visit the many wineries in the Willamette Valley. Fall is spectacular throughout the state, with leaves at their colorful peak in late October.

THE OREGON COAST

Oregon has 300 mi of white-sand beaches, not a grain of which is privately owned. U.S. 101, called Highway 101 by most Oregonians (it sometimes appears this way in addresses as well), parallels the coast along the length of the state. It winds past sea-tortured rocks, brooding headlands, hidden beaches, historic lighthouses, and tiny ports, with the gleaming gun-metal-gray Pacific Ocean always in view. With its seaside hamlets and small hotels and resorts, the coast seems to have been created with pleasure in mind. South of Newport, the pace slows. The scenery and fishing and outdoor activities are just as rich as those in the towns to the north, but the area is less crowded and the commercialism less obvious.

Astoria and Vicinity

❶ *96 mi northwest of Portland on U.S. 30.*

The mighty Columbia River meets the Pacific at Astoria, which was founded in 1811. The city was named for John Jacob Astor, then America's wealthiest man, who financed the original fur-trading colony here. Modern Astoria is a placid amalgamation of small town and hardworking port city. Settlers built sprawling Victorian houses on the flanks of **Coxcomb Hill.** Many of the homes have since been restored and are no less splendid as bed-and-breakfast inns. With so many museums, inns, and recreational offerings, Astoria should be one of the Northwest's prime tourist destinations. Yet the town remains relatively undiscovered, even by Portlanders.

★ ○ The **Columbia River Maritime Museum,** on the downtown waterfront, is one of the two most interesting man-made tourist attractions on the Oregon coast (Newport's aquarium is the other). Beguiling exhibits range from the observation tower of the World War II submarine USS *Rasher* (complete with working periscopes) and the fully operational U.S. Coast Guard Lightship *Columbia* to the personal belongings of some of the ill-fated passengers of the 2,000 ships that have foundered here since 1811. ✉ *1792 Marine Dr., at 17th St.,* ☎ *503/325–2323.* ☞ *$5.* ○ *Daily 9:30–5.*

The **Astoria Column,** a 125-ft monolith atop Coxcomb Hill that was patterned after Trajan's Column in Rome, rewards the 164-step, spiral-stair climb with breathtaking views over Astoria, the Columbia River,

Oregon Coast and Willamette Valley/Wine Country

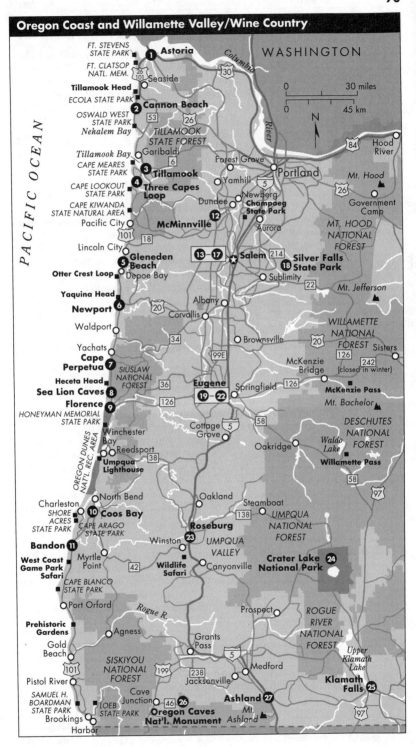

the Coast Range, and the Pacific. ⊠ *From U.S. 30 downtown take 16th St. south 1 mi to the top of Coxcomb Hill.* ☎ *Free.* ☉ *Daily 9–dusk.*

The prim and proper **Flavel House** was built between 1883 and 1885. Its Victorian-era furnishings, many selected by Captain George Flavel, yield insight into the lifestyle of a wealthy 19th-century shipping tycoon. The admission price also includes a visit to the **Heritage Museum.** Housed in the former City Hall, the museum surveys the history of Clatsop County, the oldest American settlement west of the Mississippi. ⊠ *441 8th St., at Duane St.,* ☎ *503/325–2203.* ☎ *$5.* ☉ *May–Sept., daily 10–5; Oct.–Apr., daily 11–4.*

★ ⅭS "Ocean in view! O! The joy!" recorded William Clark, standing on a spit of land south of present-day Astoria in the fall of 1805. After building a fort and wintering here, though, the explorers wrote "O! How horriable is the day waves brakeing with great violence against the shore . . . all wet and confined to our shelters." **Fort Clatsop National Memorial** is a faithful replica of the log stockade depicted in Clark's journal. Park rangers, who dress in period garb during the summer and perform early 19th-century tasks like making fire with flint and steel, lend an air of authenticity, as does the damp and lonely ambience of the fort itself. ⊠ *Fort Clatsop Loop Rd. (5 mi south of Astoria; from U.S. 101 cross Youngs Bay Bridge, turn east on Alt. U.S. 101, and follow signs),* ☎ *503/861–2471.* ☎ *$4 per vehicle.* ☉ *Mid-June–Labor Day, daily 8–6; Labor Day–mid-June, daily 8–5.*

ⅭS The earthworks of 37-acre **Fort Stevens,** at Oregon's northwestern tip, were mounded up during the Civil War to guard the Columbia against a Confederate attack. No such event occurred, but during World War II, Fort Stevens became the only mainland U.S. military installation to come under enemy (Japanese submarine) fire since the War of 1812. The fort's abandoned gun mounts and eerie subterranean bunkers are a memorable destination. The corroded skeleton of the *Peter Iredale,* a century-old English four-master ship, protrudes from the sand just west of the campground, a stark testament to the malevolence of the Pacific. ⊠ *Fort Stevens Hwy. (from Fort Clatsop, take Alt. U.S. 101 west past U.S. 101, turn north onto Main St.–Fort Stevens Hwy., and follow signs),* ☎ *503/861–2000.* ☎ *$3 per vehicle; park tours in summer $2.50; underground Battery Mishler $2.* ☉ *Mid-May–Sept., daily 10–6; Oct.–mid-May, daily 10–4.*

Dining and Lodging

$–$$ ✕ **Cannery Cafe.** Bright and contemporary, this restaurant in a 100-year-old renovated cannery has windows that look out onto the Columbia River. Fresh salads, large sandwiches, clam chowder, and crab cakes are lunch staples. The varied dinner menu emphasizes fresh seafood, including cioppino and oyster stew, and homemade southern Italian pasta dishes. ⊠ *1 6th St.,* ☎ *503/325–8642. MC, V. Closed Mon. No dinner Sun.*

$ ✕ **Columbian Cafe.** Locals love this unpretentious diner with a tongue-in-cheek south-of-the-border decor that's heavy on chili-pepper-shape Christmas lights and religious icons. Fresh, simple food—crepes with broccoli, cheese, and homemade salsa for lunch; grilled salmon and pasta with a lemon-cream sauce for dinner—is served by a staff that usually includes the owner. Come early; this place always draws a crowd. ⊠ *1114 Marine Dr.,* ☎ *503/325–2233. No credit cards. No dinner Sun.–Tues.*

$$–$$$ 🖫 **Franklin Street Station Bed & Breakfast.** Ticking grandfather clocks
★   and mellow marine light filtering through leaded-glass windows set the tone at this velvet-upholstered Victorian built in 1900 on the slopes above downtown Astoria. Breakfasts are huge, hot, and satisfying, and there's always a plate of goodies and a pot of coffee in the kitchen. ⊠

1140 Franklin St., 97103, ☎ *503/325–4314 or 800/448–1098. 6 rooms. MC, V.*

$$ 🏨 **Red Lion Inn.** The reliable chain's property sits right on the Columbia River, near the Astoria Bridge; the room balconies have views of the river, marina, and bridge. The small rooms and public areas are decorated in soothing earth tones. ✉ *400 Industry St., 97103,* ☎ *503/ 325–7373,* ℻ *503/325–5786. 124 rooms. Restaurant, bar, airport shuttle. AE, D, DC, MC, V.*

$–$$ 🏨 **Grandview Bed & Breakfast.** This turreted mansion lives up to its name—decks look out over Astoria, with the Columbia River and Washington State beyond. The interior is bright, with scrubbed hardwood floors and lace-filled rooms. The breakfast specialty is bagels with cream cheese and smoked salmon from Josephson's (☞ Shopping, *below*). ✉ *1574 Grand Ave., 97103,* ☎ *503/325–5555 or 800/488–3250. 9 rooms, 7 with bath. D, MC, V.*

Shopping
Josephson's (✉ 106 Marine Dr., ☎ 503/325–2190) is one of the Oregon coast's oldest commercial smokehouses, preparing Columbia River chinook salmon in the traditional alder-smoked and lox styles. Smoked shark, tuna, oysters, mussels, sturgeon, scallops, and prawns are also available by the pound or in sealed gift packs.

Seaside

12 mi south of Astoria on U.S. 101.

For years, Seaside had a reputation as a garish arcade-filled town. But it cleaned up its act and now supports a bustling tourist trade with hotels, condominiums, and restaurants surrounding a long beach. A 2-mi boardwalk parallels the shore and stately old beachfront homes. Only 90 mi from Portland, Seaside is often crowded, so it's not the place to come if you crave solitude. Peak times include February, during the Trail's End Marathon; mid-March, when hordes of teenagers descend on the town during spring break; and July, when the annual Miss Oregon Pageant is in full swing.

Dining and Lodging
$–$$ ✕ **Doogers.** The original branch of this Northwest chain is much loved by local families. The seafood is expertly prepared, and the creamy clam chowder may be the best on the coast. ✉ *505 Broadway,* ☎ *503/738– 3773. Reservations not accepted. AE, D, MC, V.*

$$$–$$$$ 🏨 **Shilo Inn.** Located right on the beach at Seaside's circle, this midrise hotel provides spectacular views of the Pacific, though the rooms (with coffeemakers) are nothing fancy. ✉ *30 N. Prom, 97138,* ☎ *503/738–9571 or 800/222–2244,* ℻ *503/738–0674. 112 rooms. Restaurant, indoor pool, sauna, spa, steam room, exercise room, coin laundry, airport shuttle. AE, D, DC, MC, V.*

En Route A brisk 2-mi hike from U.S. 101 south of Seaside leads to the 1,100-ft-high viewing point atop **Tillamook Head.** The view from here takes in the **Tillamook Rock Light Station,** which stands a mile or so out to sea. The lonely beacon, built in 1881 on a straight-sided rock, towers 41 ft above the surrounding ocean. In 1957 the lighthouse was abandoned; it is now a columbarium.

Eight miles south of Seaside, U.S. 101 passes the entrance to **Ecola State Park,** a playground of sea-sculpted rocks, sandy shoreline, green headlands, and panoramic views. The park's main beach can be crowded in summer, but the **Indian Beach** area contains an often deserted cove and explorable tide pools. ☎ *800/551–6949.* 🎟 *$3 per vehicle.* ☉ *Daily dawn–dusk.*

Cannon Beach

2 *10 mi south of Seaside on U.S. 101; 80 mi west of Portland on U.S. 26.*

Cannon Beach is Seaside's refined, artistic alter ego, a more mellow yet trendy place (population 1,200) for Portlanders to take the sea air. One of the most charming hamlets on the coast, the town contains beach-front homes and hotels and a weathered-cedar downtown shopping district. On the downside, the Carmel of the Oregon coast is expensive, crowded, and afflicted with a subtle, moneyed hauteur (such as the town's ban on vacation-home rentals) that may grate on more plebeian nerves.

The town got its name when a cannon from the wrecked schooner USS *Shark* washed ashore in 1846 (the piece is on display a mile east of town on U.S. 101). Towering over the broad, sandy beach is **Haystack Rock,** a 235-ft-high monolith that is supposedly the most-photographed feature of the Oregon coast. The rock is temptingly accessible during some low tides, but the coast guard regularly airlifts stranded climbers from its precipitous sides, and falls have claimed numerous lives over the years. Every May the town hosts the Cannon Beach Sandcastle Contest, for which thousands throng the beach to view imaginative and often startling works in this most transient of art forms.

Shops and galleries selling kites, upscale clothing, local art, wine, coffee, and food line **Hemlock Street,** Cannon Beach's main thoroughfare.

Dining and Lodging

$$ ✕ **The Bistro.** Flowers, candlelight, and classical music create a romantic
★ atmosphere at this 12-table restaurant. The three-course prix-fixe menu includes imaginative Continental-influenced renditions of fresh local seafood dishes; monstrous scampi and a Pacific seafood stew often appear as specials. ⊠ *263 N. Hemlock St.,* ☎ *503/436–2661. Reservations essential. MC, V. Closed Tues.–Wed. Nov.–Jan. No lunch.*

$$ ✕ **Blue Sky Cafe.** Stained glass, a jungle of plants, and butcher-paper-covered tables lend a quirky air to this hole-in-the-wall café, which is 13 mi south of Cannon Beach in Manzanita. Specialties include crab and rock shrimp baked in parchment, Thai coconut-curry soup, feta-mushroom-rosemary soup, and memorably rich desserts. ⊠ *154 Laneda St., off U.S. 101, Manzanita,* ☎ *503/368–5712. No credit cards. Closed Mon.–Tues. Oct.–June. No lunch.*

$–$$ ✕ **Doogers.** Like the original Doogers in Seaside, the Cannon Beach branch serves superb seafood in a casual, contemporary setting. Don't pass up the clam chowder. ⊠ *1371 S. Hemlock St.,* ☎ *503/436–2225. AE, D, MC, V.*

$ ✕ **Lazy Susan Cafe.** Entrées at this laid-back spot—*the* place to come for breakfast in Cannon Beach—include quiche, omelets, hot cereal, and a substantial order of waffles topped with fruit and orange syrup. Don't leave without tasting the fresh-baked scones and the home fries. ⊠ *Coaster Sq., 126 N. Hemlock St.,* ☎ *503/436–2816. Reservations not accepted. No credit cards. Closed Tues. No dinner Mon., Wed.*

$$$–$$$$ ✕⊞ **Stephanie Inn.** Superior service, luxurious rooms, and tastefully
★ decorated public areas make this three-story inn the premier ocean-front hotel in Cannon Beach. Impeccably maintained, with country-style furnishings, fireplaces, large bathrooms with whirlpool tubs, and balconies commanding outstanding views of Haystack Rock, the rooms are so comfortable you may never want to leave—except perhaps to enjoy the four-course prix-fixe dinners (reservations essential) of in-

novative Pacific Northwest cuisine. Generous country breakfasts are included in the tariff, as are evening wine and hors d'oeuvres. ⊠ *2740 S. Pacific, 97110,* ☎ *503/436–2221 or 800/633–3466,* FAX *503/436– 9711. 50 rooms. Dining room, minibars, refrigerators, in-room VCRs, massage, library. AE, D, DC, MC, V.*

$–$$$$ ☒ **Hallmark Resort at Cannon Beach.** Large suites with fireplaces, whirlpool tubs, kitchenettes, and great views make this triple-decker oceanfront resort a good choice for families or couples looking for a romantic splurge. The rooms, all with spacious balconies and oak-tile baths, have soothing color schemes. The least expensive units do not have views. Pets are welcome with a $10 charge. ⊠ *1400 S. Hemlock St., 97110,* ☎ *503/436–1566 or 888/448–4449,* FAX *503/436–0324. 132 rooms, 4 rental homes, 24 units in town. Restaurant, bar, in-room data ports, refrigerators, indoor pool, wading pool, sauna, exercise room, laundry service, business services, meeting rooms. AE, D, DC, MC, V.*

$$–$$$ ☒ **Webb's Scenic Surf.** Small and family-operated, this beachfront hotel is a throwback to simpler times in Cannon Beach, before trendiness translated into big resorts and $500 weekends. Many of the tidy rooms have kitchens and fireplaces. This is one of the best deals in town, but reservations are a must. ⊠ *255 N. Larch St., 97110,* ☎ *503/436– 2706 or 800/374–9322,* FAX *503/436–1229. 14 rooms. MC, V.*

En Route   South of Cannon Beach, U.S. 101 climbs 700 ft above the Pacific, providing dramatic views and often hair-raising curves as it winds along the flank of **Neahkahnie Mountain.** Cryptic carvings on beach rocks near here and centuries-old Native American legends of shipwrecked Europeans gave rise to a tale that the survivors of a sunken Spanish galleon buried a fortune in doubloons somewhere on the side of the 1,661-ft-high mountain.

Oswald West State Park

10 mi south of Cannon Beach on U.S. 101.

Adventurous travelers will enjoy a sojourn at one of the best-kept secrets on the Pacific coast, **Oswald West State Park,** at the base of Neahkahnie Mountain. Park in one of the two lots on U.S. 101 and use a park-provided wheelbarrow to trundle your camping gear down a ½-mi trail. An old-growth forest surrounds the 36 primitive campsites (reservations not accepted), and the spectacular beach contains caves and tide pools.

The trail to the summit, on the left about 2 mi south of the parking lots for Oswald West State Park (marked only by a HIKERS sign), rewards the intrepid with unobstructed views over surf, sand, forest, and mountain. Come in December or April and you might spot pods of gray whales. ☎ *503/368–5943; 800/551–6949 for campground information.* ⊠ *Day use free, campsite $10–$14.* ☉ *Day use year-round, daily dawn–dusk; camping Mar.–Oct.*

En Route   After passing through several small fishing, logging, and resort towns, U.S. 101 skirts around **Tillamook Bay,** where the Miami, Kilchis, Wilson, Trask, and Tillamook rivers enter the Pacific. The bay is a sportfishing mecca where the quarry includes sea-run cutthroat trout, bottom fish, and silver, chinook, and steelhead salmon, along with mussels, oysters, clams, and the delectable Dungeness crab. Charter-fishing services operate out of the **Garibaldi** fishing harbor 10 mi north of Tillamook. For some of the best rock fishing in the state, try Tillamook Bay's North Jetty.

Tillamook

❸ *30 mi south of Oswald State Park and Neahkahnie Mountain on U.S. 101.*

Tillamook County is something of a wet Wisconsin-on-the-Pacific. Though it lacks the sophisticated charm of Cannon Beach, the town of Tillamook, about 2 mi inland from the ocean, is a quiet, natural retreat. Surrounded by rich dairy land and blessed with abundant freshwater and saltwater fishing, it has some of the finest scenery on the Oregon coast.

The **Pioneer Museum** in Tillamook's 1905 county courthouse has an intriguing if old-fashioned hodgepodge of Native American, pioneer, logging, and natural-history exhibits, along with antique vehicles and military artifacts. ⊠ *2106 2nd St.,* ☎ *503/842–4553.* ☜ *$2.* ☉ *May–Sept., Mon.–Sat. 8:30–5, Sun. 12:30–5. Oct.–Apr., closed Mon.*

More than 750,000 visitors annually press their noses against the spotlessly clean windows at the **Tillamook County Creamery,** the largest cheese-making plant on the West Coast. Here the rich milk from the area's thousands of Holstein and brown Swiss cows becomes ice cream, butter, and cheddar and Monterey Jack cheeses. Exhibits at the visitor center, where free samples are dispensed, explain the cheese-making process. ⊠ *4175 Hwy. 101 N, 2 mi north of Tillamook,* ☎ *503/842–4481.* ☜ *Free.* ☉ *Mid-Sept.–May, daily 8–6; June–mid-Sept., daily 8–8.*

The **Blue Heron French Cheese Company** specializes in French-style cheeses—Camembert, Brie, and others. There's a petting zoo for kids, a sit-down deli, and a gift shop that carries wines and jams, mustards, and other products from Oregon. ⊠ *2001 Blue Heron Dr. (watch for signs from U.S. 101),* ☎ *503/842–8281.* ☜ *Free.* ☉ *Memorial Day–Labor Day, daily 8–8; Labor Day–Memorial Day, daily 9–5.*

Housed in the world's largest wooden structure, a former blimp hangar south of town, the **Naval Air Station Museum** displays one of the finest private collections of vintage aircraft from World War II, including a B-25 Mitchell and an ME-109 Messerschmidt. The 20-story building is big enough to hold a dozen football fields. ⊠ *6030 Hangar Rd. (½ mi south of Tillamook; head east from U.S. 101 on Long Prairie Rd. and follow signs),* ☎ *503/842–1130.* ☜ *$8.* ☉ *Daily 10–5.*

Outdoor Activities and Sports

Alderbrook Golf Club (⊠ 7300 Alderbrook Rd., ☎ 503/842–6413) is an 18-hole, par-69 golf course. The greens fee is $24; an optional cart costs $20.

Three Capes Loop

★ ❹ *Starts south of downtown Tillamook off 3rd St.*

The Three Capes Loop, a 35-mi byway off U.S. 101, is one of the coast's most thrilling driving experiences. The loop winds along the coast between Tillamook and Pacific City, passing three distinctive headlands—Cape Meares, Cape Lookout, and Cape Kiwanda. Bayocean Road heading west from Tillamook passes what was the thriving resort town of Bay Ocean. More than 30 years ago, Bay Ocean washed into the sea—houses, a bowling alley, everything—during a raging Pacific storm.

Nine miles west of Tillamook, trails from the parking lot at the end of Bay Ocean Spit lead through the dunes to a usually uncrowded and highly walkable white-sand beach.

Cape Meares State Park is on the northern tip of the Three Capes Loop. Cape Meares was named for English navigator John Meares, who voyaged along this coast in 1788. The restored **Cape Meares Lighthouse,** built in 1890 and open to the public May–September, provides a sweeping view over the cliff to the caves and sea-lion rookery on the rocks below. A many-trunked Sitka spruce known as the Octopus Tree grows near the lighthouse parking lot. ⊠ *Three Capes Loop 10 mi west of Tillamook,* ☎ *800/551–6949.* ☞ *Free.* ☉ *Park daily dawn–dusk; lighthouse May–Sept., daily 11–4; Mar., Apr., and Oct., weekends 11–4.*

Cape Lookout State Park lies south of the beach towns of Oceanside and Netarts. A fairly easy 2-mi trail—marked on the highway as WILDLIFE VIEWING AREA—leads through giant spruces, western red cedars, and hemlocks to views of Cascade Head to the south and Cape Meares to the north. Wildflowers, more than 150 species of birds, and migrating whales passing by in early April make this trail a favorite with nature lovers. The park has a picnic area overlooking the sea and a year-round campground. ⊠ *Three Capes Loop 8 mi south of Cape Meares,* ☎ *800/551–6949.* ☞ *Day use $3, campsites $16.* ☉ *Daily dawn–9* PM.

Huge waves pound the jagged sandstone cliffs and caves at **Cape Kiwanda State Natural Area.** The much-photographed, 327-ft-high **Haystack Rock** juts out of Nestucca Bay just south of here. Surfers ride some of the longest waves on the coast, hang gliders soar above the shore, and beachcombers explore tide pools and take in unparalleled ocean views. ⊠ *Three Capes Loop 15 mi south of Cape Lookout,* ☎ *800/551–6949.* ☞ *Free.* ☉ *Daily dawn–dusk.*

Pacific City

1½ mi south of Cape Kiwanda on Three Capes Loop.

The beach at Pacific City, the town visible from Cape Kiwanda, is one of the only places in the state where fishing dories (flat-bottom boats with high, flaring sides) are launched directly into the surf instead of from harbors or docks. During the commercial salmon season in late summer, it's possible to buy salmon directly from the fishermen.

A walk along the flat white-sand beach at **Robert Straub State Park** leads down to the mouth of the Nestucca River, considered by many to be the best fishing river on the north coast. ⊠ *West from main intersection in downtown Pacific City across the Nestucca River (follow signs),* ☎ *800/551–6949.* ☞ *Free.* ☉ *Daily dawn–dusk.*

OFF THE
BEATEN PATH

NATURE CONSERVANCY CASCADE HEAD TRAIL – The trail at one of the most unusual headlands on the Oregon coast winds through a rain forest where 250-year-old Sitka spruces and a dense green undergrowth of mosses and ferns is nourished by 100-inch annual rainfalls. After the forest comes grassy and treeless Cascade Head, a rare example of a maritime prairie. Magnificent views down to the Salmon River and west to the Coast Range open up as you continue along the headland, where black-tailed deer often graze and turkey vultures soar in the strong winds. You need to be in fairly good shape for the first and steepest part of the hike, which can be done in about an hour. The 270-acre area has been named a United Nations Biosphere Reserve. ⊠ *Savage Rd., 6 mi south of Neskowin off U.S. 101 (turn west on Three Rocks Rd. and north on Savage),* ☎ *503/230–1221.* ☞ *Free.* ☉ *July–Dec., daily dawn–dusk.*

Lincoln City

16 mi south of Pacific City on U.S. 101; 78 mi west of Portland on Hwy. 99 W and Hwy. 18.

Once a series of small villages, Lincoln City is a sprawling, suburban-ish town without a center. But the endless tourist amenities make up for whatever it lacks in charm. Clustered like barnacles on the offshore reefs are fast-food restaurants, gift shops, supermarkets, candy stores, antiques markets, dozens of motels and hotels, a factory-outlet mall, and a busy casino. Lincoln City is the most popular destination city on the Oregon coast, but its only real claim to fame is the 445-ft-long **D River,** stretching from its source in Devil's Lake to the Pacific; the *Guinness Book of Records* lists the D as the world's shortest river.

Casino

Chinook Winds The only casino located directly on the beach in Oregon has slot machines, blackjack, poker, keno, and off-track betting. There's no hotel, but the Shilo Inn (☞ Dining and Lodging, *below*) is located right next door. The entry atrium is accented with a two-story waterfall and natural rocks, trees, and plants to replicate the fishing ground of the Confederated Tribes of the Siletz, who own the casino. The Siletz Room offers fine dining, and there is an all-you-can-eat buffet, a snack bar, and a lounge. An arcade will keep the kids busy while you are on the gambling floor. Big-name entertainers perform in the showroom. ⊠ *1777 N.W. 44th St., 97367,* ☎ *541/996–5825 or 888/244–6665.*

Dining and Lodging

$$–$$$ ✕ **Bay House.** This restaurant inside a charming bungalow serves meals to linger over while you enjoy views across sunset-gilded Siletz Bay. The seasonal Pacific Northwest cuisine includes Dungeness crab cakes with roasted-chili chutney, fresh halibut Parmesan, and roast duckling with cranberry compote. The wine list is extensive, the service impeccable. ⊠ *5911 S.W. Hwy. 101, about 5 mi south of Lincoln City,* ☎ *541/996–3222. AE, D, MC, V. Closed Mon.–Tues. Nov.–Apr. No lunch.*

$–$$ ✕ **Kyllo's.** Light-filled Kyllo's rests on stilts beside the D River, proudly called the world's shortest. It's one of the best places in Lincoln City to enjoy casual but well-prepared seafood, pasta, and meat dishes. ⊠ *1110 N.W. 1st Ct.,* ☎ *541/994–3179. AE, D, MC, V.*

$ ✕ **Lighthouse Brew Pub.** This westernmost outpost of the Portland-based McMenamin brothers' microbrewery empire has the same virtues as their other establishments: fresh local ales; good, unpretentious sandwiches, burgers, and salads; and cheerfully eccentric decor that includes psychedelic art by Pacific Northwest painters. Try the stout-ale milk shake. ⊠ *4157 N. Hwy. 101,* ☎ *541/994–7238. Reservations not accepted. AE, D, MC, V.*

$$–$$$ 🏨 **Ester Lee Motel.** On a bluff overlooking the cold Pacific, this small, whitewashed motel attracts much repeat business. The fine amenities include wood-burning fireplaces, cable TV, and, in most rooms, full kitchens. Request a unit in the older section; the rooms there are larger and have brick fireplaces and picture windows. ⊠ *3803 S.W. Hwy. 101, 97367,* ☎ *541/996–3606 or 888/996–3606. 53 rooms. D, MC, V.*

$$ 🏨 **Shilo Inn Oceanfront Resort.** Located on the beach and adjacent to Chinook Winds Casino, this basic motel is popular because of its location. The indoor pool, spas, and saunas provide warm escapes on rainy winter days. A newer building has suites with kitchenettes, fireplaces, balconies, and ocean views. ⊠ *1501 N.W. 40th Pl., 97367,* ☎ *541/994–3655 or 800/222–2244,* ꜰꜲꭕ *503/994–2199. 187 rooms, 61 suites. Restaurant, indoor pool, 2 hot tubs, 2 steam rooms, exercise room, coin laundry. AE, D, DC, MC, V.*

Outdoor Activities and Sports

The greens fee at the 18-hole, par-66 course at the **Lakeside Golf & Racquet Club** (⊠ 3245 Clubhouse Dr., ☎ 541/994–8442) is $32; an optional cart costs $25.

Shopping

The **Factory Stores at Lincoln City** has 65 outlet stores, including L. L. Bean, Reebok, Bose, Mikasa, and Oneida. Items are 20%–70% off regular retail prices. ⊠ *1500 S.E. Devil's Lake Rd., 97367, ☎ 541/ 996–5000.*

Gleneden Beach

❺ *7 mi south of Lincoln City on U.S. 101.*

Salishan, the most famous resort on the Oregon coast, perches high above placid Siletz Bay. This expensive collection of guest rooms, vacation homes, condominiums, restaurants, golf fairways, tennis courts, and covered walkways blends into a forest preserve; if not for the signs, you'd scarcely be able to find it.

Dining and Lodging

$$$–$$$$ ✕ **Dining Room at Salishan.** The Salishan resort's main dining room,
★ a multilevel expanse of hushed waiters, hillside ocean views, and snow-white linen, features Pacific Northwest cuisine. House specialties include fresh local fish, game, beef, and lamb. By all means make a selection from the wine cellar, which has more than 10,000 bottles. ⊠ *7760 N. Hwy. 101, ☎ 541/764–2371. Reservations essential. Jacket and tie. AE, D, DC, MC, V. No lunch.*

$$$ ✕ **Chez Jeanette.** This country-French cottage nestles in the shore
★ pines between U.S. 101 and the ocean and seems a continent away from frenetic downtown Lincoln City. The atmosphere is quiet, with a fireplace, antiques, and tables set with linen and crystal. Try the carpetbagger steak, a thick fillet stuffed with tiny local oysters, wrapped in bacon, and sauced with crème fraîche, scallions, spinach, and bacon. The rest of the menu puts a Parisian spin on local products from the sea, sky, and pasture. ⊠ *7150 Old Hwy. 101, Gleneden Beach (turn west from U.S. 101 at the Salishan entrance, then turn south and go ¼ mi), ☎ 541/764–3434. Reservations essential. AE, D, MC, V. Closed Sun.–Mon. Labor Day–June. No lunch.*

$$$$ ▥ **Westin Salishan Lodge and Golf Resort.** From the soothing, silvered-cedar ambience of its rooms, divided among eight units in a hillside forest preserve, Salishan embodies a uniquely Oregonian elegance. Each of the quiet rooms has a wood-burning fireplace, a balcony, and original works by Northwest artists. Given all this, plus fine dining (☞ *above*), you'll understand why the timeless atmosphere also carries what may well be the steepest price tag on the coast. ⊠ *7760 N. Hwy. 101, 97388, ☎ 541/764–3600 or 800/452–2300, ℻ 541/764–3681. 205 rooms. 2 restaurants, bar, in-room data ports, minibars, no-smoking rooms, room service, indoor lap pool, beauty salon, massage, sauna, driving range, 18-hole golf course, putting green, 4 tennis courts, exercise room, hiking, beach, billiards, piano, library, baby-sitting, playground, laundry service and dry cleaning, concierge. AE, D, DC, MC, V.*

Outdoor Activities and Sports

Salishan Golf Links (⊠ 7760 N. Hwy. 101, ☎ 541/764–3632) is an 18-hole, par-72, often windy seaside course. The greens fee is $35; an optional cart costs $26.

Depoe Bay

12 mi south of Lincoln City on U.S. 101.

Depoe Bay calls itself the whale-watching capital of the world. The tiny harbor here is among the world's smallest. With a narrow channel and deep water, it is also one of the most protected on the coast; it supports a thriving fleet of commercial- and charter-fishing boats. The **Spouting Horn,** a natural cleft in the basalt cliffs on the waterfront, blasts seawater skyward during heavy weather.

Dining and Lodging

$$–$$$$ 🏨 **Channel House.** Some of the rooms in this inn on a cliffside in charming Depoe Bay have whirlpool tubs with views of the Pacific, most have fireplaces and balconies, and all have private baths. Each of the rooms, such as the Admiral's Suite and the Crow's Nest, brings a different nautical theme to its contemporary decor. A buffet breakfast is included in the room rate. Smoking and pets are not permitted. ⊠ *35 Ellington St., Depoe Bay 97341,* ☎ *541/765–2140 or 800/447–2140,* ᖴᗅᕽ *541/765–2191. 15 rooms. AE, D, MC, V.*

$$–$$$$ ✕ **Sea Hag.** This friendly restaurant has been specializing in fresh seafood for more than 30 years. Friday night features a seafood buffet, while Saturday the focus is on prime rib with Yorkshire pudding. ⊠ *53 Hwy. 101,* ☎ *541/765–2734. AE, D, DC, MC, V.*

Outdoor Activities and Sports

Tradewinds (⊠ U.S. 101 near Coast Guard Boat Basin Rd., ☎ 541/765–2345 or 800/445–8730) operates $12 whale-watching cruises on the hour, when conditions permit, from 10 AM until 5 or 6 PM. The ticket office is at the north end of the Depoe Bay Bridge. There is a resident group of gray whales that stays in the Depoe Bay area year-round.

En Route Five miles south of Depoe Bay off U.S. 101 (watch for signs), the **Otter Crest Loop,** another scenic byway, winds along the cliff tops. British explorer Captain James Cook named the 500-ft-high **Cape Foulweather** on a blustery March day in 1778. Backward-leaning shore pines lend mute witness to the 100-mph winds that still strafe this exposed spot. At the viewing point at the **Devil's Punchbowl,** 1 mi south of Cape Foulweather, you can peer down into a collapsed sandstone sea cave carved out by the powerful waters of the Pacific. About 100 ft to the north in the rocky tide pools of the beach known as **Marine Gardens,** purple sea urchins and orange starfish can be seen at low tide. The Otter Crest Loop rejoins U.S. 101 about 4 mi south of Cape Foulweather near **Yaquina Head,** which has been designated an Outstanding Natural Area. Harbor seals, sea lions, cormorants, murres, puffins, and guillemots frolic in the water and on the rocks below **Yaquina Bay Lighthouse**—a gleaming white tower activated in 1873.

Newport

❻ *12 mi south of Depoe Bay on U.S. 101; 114 mi from Portland, south on I–5 and west on Hwy. 34 and U.S. 20.*

Newport was transformed after Keiko, the orca star of the movie *Free Willy,* arrived at the Oregon Coast Aquarium in 1996. The small harbor and fishing town with about 8,000 residents became one of the most visited places on the coast. The surge of tourists brought new prosperity to a town feeling the pinch of federally imposed fishing restrictions that had cut into its traditional economy. Keiko moved to Iceland in 1998, so the crowds have diminished.

Newport exists on two levels: the highway above, threading its way through the community's main business district, and the old **Bayfront** along Yaquina Bay below (watch for signs on U.S. 101). With its high-masted fishing fleet, well-worn buildings, seafood markets, and art galleries and shops, Newport's Bayfront is an ideal place for an afternoon stroll. So many male sea lions in Yaquina Bay loiter near crab pots and bark from the waterfront piers that locals call the area the Bachelor Club.

Nye Beach, a neighborhood to the east of the highway, preserves a few remnants of Newport's crusty past. Many old cottages have been gentrified, but you can still get an idea of the simple beach architecture that until very recently characterized most of the Oregon coast. The Sylvia Beach Hotel (☞ Dining and Lodging, *below*), built in 1913 on a sea wall above the beach, once was billed as the honeymoon capital of Oregon. The graceful **Yaquina Bay Bridge,** a Work Projects Administration structure completed in 1936, leads to Newport's southern section.

★ ☾ The **Oregon Coast Aquarium,** a 4½-acre complex, contains re-creations of offshore and near-shore Pacific marine habitats, all teeming with life: playful sea otters (rescued from the Exxon *Valdez* oil spill in Alaska), comical puffins, fragile jellyfish, and even a 60-pound octopus. A sequence of exhibits follows a drop of rain from the forested uplands of the Coast Range through the tidal estuary and out to sea. There's a hands-on interactive area for children, and North America's largest seabird aviary. For a few years the biggest attraction was Keiko, the 4-ton killer whale brought to the aquarium to be rehabilitated. This magnificent mammal, the star of the movie *Free Willy,* moved to Iceland in 1998, and the aquarium is now developing new attractions. In spring 1999 a new 35,000-gallon saltwater salmon and sturgeon exhibit opened. Large coho salmon and sturgeon can be viewed in a naturalistic setting through a window wall 9 ft high and 20 ft wide. Keiko's former home is being transformed into a deep-sea exhibit complete with a wrecked ship. Visitors will pass through underwater acrylic tunnels, coming face to face with large sharks, sunfish, and sea turtles swimming above and below. The exhibit will open in summer 2000. ✉ *2820 S.E. Ferry Slip Rd. (heading south from Newport, turn right at southern end of Yaquina Bay Bridge and follow signs),* ☎ *541/867–3474.* ✆ *$8.75.* ☉ *Memorial Day–Labor Day, daily 9–6; Labor Day–Memorial Day, daily 10–5.*

☾ Interactive and interpretive exhibits at Oregon State University's **Hatfield Marine Science Center,** which is connected by a trail to the Oregon Coast Aquarium, explain current marine research from a global, bird's-eye, eye-level, and microscopic perspective. The star of the show is a large octopus in a touch tank near the entrance. She seems as interested in human visitors as they are in her; guided by a staff volunteer, you can sometimes reach in to stroke her suction-tipped tentacles. ✉ *2030 S. Marine Science Dr. (heading south from Newport, cross Yaquina Bay Bridge on U.S. 101 S and follow signs),* ☎ *541/867–0100.* ✆ *Suggested donation $4.* ☉ *Memorial Day–Labor Day, daily 10–6; Labor Day–Memorial Day, Thurs.–Mon. 10–4.*

Mariner Square (✉ 250 S.W. Bay Blvd.) has a **Ripley's Believe It or Not** and **The Wax Works** (☎ 541/265–2206 for both) and, in a boat moored across the street, **Undersea Gardens** (☎ 541/265–2206), where divers put on underwater shows.

Marine Discovery Tours offers narrated whale-watching cruises in the bay. The 65-ft excursion boat *Discovery,* with inside seating for 49 and two viewing levels, departs from the Newport bayfront in the morning and afternoon. You can also watch from outside. The best viewing is March–October, though tours run year-round except during storms. While they can't guarantee you'll see a whale, 95% of outi~

are successful. There is a resident population of gray whales that stays near Newport year-round, including young mothers with calves who feed less than 1 mi from shore. During summer they often come right up to the boat. *Discovery* is wheelchair accessible. ⊠ *345 S.W. Bay Blvd., Newport 97365,* ☎ *800/903–2628.* 🖅 *$18. D, MC, V.*

Dining and Lodging

$$–$$$ ✕ **Canyon Way Restaurant and Bookstore.** Cod, Dungeness crab cakes, bouillabaisse, and Yaquina Bay oysters are among the specialties of this Newport dining spot up the hill from the center of the Bayfront. There's also a deli counter for takeout. The restaurant, which has an outdoor patio, is to one side of a well-stocked bookstore. ⊠ *S.W. Canyon Way off Bay Front Blvd.,* ☎ *541/265–8319. AE, MC, V. No dinner Mon.*

$$ ✕ **Tables of Content.** The well-plotted prix-fixe menu at the restaurant of the outstanding Sylvia Beach Hotel (☞ *below*) changes nightly. Chances are the main dish will be fresh local seafood, perhaps a moist grilled salmon fillet in a sauce Dijonnaise, served with sautéed vegetables, fresh-baked breads, rice pilaf, and a decadent dessert. The interior is functional and unadorned, with family-size tables, but decor isn't the reason to come here. ⊠ *267 N.W. Cliff St. (from U.S. 101 head west on 3rd St.),* ☎ *541/265–5428. Reservations essential. AE, MC, V. No lunch.*

$–$$ ✕ **Don Petrie's Italian Food Co.** A little hole-in-the-sand eatery in Nye Beach, Don Petrie's serves some of the best seafood lasagna you'll ever eat. Get here early, especially on weekends. ⊠ *613 N.W. 3rd St.,* ☎ *541/265–3663. Reservations not accepted. MC, V.*

$ ✕ **Whale's Tale.** The atmosphere is casual and family oriented at this Bayfront restaurant with a menu of fresh local seafood, thick clam chowder, fish-and-chips, burgers, and sandwiches. ⊠ *452 S.W. Bay Blvd.,* ☎ *541/265–8660. AE, D, DC, MC, V. Closed Wed. Nov.–Apr.*

$$$ ⌸ **The Embarcadero.** This resort of vacation rental condominiums at the east end of Bay Boulevard has great views of Yaquina Bay and its graceful bridge. The public areas have a casual ambience. Spacious suites have one or two bedrooms, with a bay-side deck, a fireplace, and a kitchen. ⊠ *1000 S.E. Bay Blvd., 97365,* ☎ *541/265–8521 or 800/547–4779,* FAX *541/265–7844. 85 units. Restaurant, bar, indoor pool, outdoor hot tub, sauna, exercise room, dock, boating, fishing. AE, D, MC, V.*

$$–$$$ ⌸ **Sylvia Beach Hotel.** Make reservations far in advance for this 1913-
★ vintage beachfront hotel, whose antiques-filled rooms are named for famous writers. A pendulum swings over the bed in the Poe room. The Christie, Twain, and Colette rooms are the most luxurious; all have fireplaces, decks, and great ocean views. The rooms have no phones or TVs. A well-stocked split-level upstairs library has decks, a fireplace, slumbering cats, and too-comfortable chairs. Complimentary mulled wine is served here nightly at 10. A full breakfast is included in the room rate. ⊠ *267 N.W. Cliff St., 97365,* ☎ *541/265–5428. 20 rooms. Restaurant, library. AE, MC, V.*

Outdoor Activities and Sports

Fossils, clams, mussels, and other aeons-old marine creatures, easily dug from soft sandstone cliffs, make **Beverly Beach State Park,** 5 mi north of Newport, a favorite with young beachcombers. Agate hunters regularly comb **Agate Beach,** just north of Newport, for these colorful quartz treasures.

Shopping

On Newport's **Bay Boulevard** you'll find the finest group of fresh seafood markets on the coast. **Englund Marine Supply** (⊠ S.W. Bay Blvd., ☎ 541/265–9275) carries nautical supplies. **Nature's Window** (⊠ 338

S.W. Bay Blvd., ☎ 541/265–3940) stocks interesting science- and na-ture-related gift items. **Wood Gallery** (✉ 818 S.W. Bay Blvd., ☎ 541/265–6843) sells wood crafts and paintings.

En Route Chain-saw sculpture—a peculiar Oregon art form—reaches its dubi-ous pinnacle at **Sea Gulch,** a full-size ghost town inhabited by more than 300 carved-wood figures. Ray Kowalski wields his Stihl chain saw to create cowboys, Indians, hillbillies, trolls, gnomes, and other humorous figures. ✉ *U.S. 101, 10 mi south of Newport,* ☎ *541/563–2727.* 🖅 *$4.50.* ⊗ *Weekdays 3–7.*

Waldport

15 mi south of Newport on U.S. 101; 67 mi west of Corvallis on Hwy. 34 and U.S. 20.

Long ago the base of the Alsi Indians, Waldport later became a gold-rush town and a logging center. In the 1980s it garnered national at-tention when local residents fought the timber industry and stopped the spraying of dioxin-based defoliants in the Coast Range forests. Wald-port attracts many retirees and those seeking an alternative to the ex-pensive beach resorts nearby.

The **Drift Creek Wilderness** east of Waldport holds some of the rare old-growth forest that has triggered battles between the timber industry and environmentalists. Hemlocks hundreds of years old grow in parts of this 9-square-mi area. The 2-mi **Harris Ranch Trail** winds through these ancient giants—you may even spot a spotted owl. The Siuslaw National Forest–Waldport Ranger Station provides directions and maps. ✉ *Risely Creek Rd. (from Waldport, take Hwy. 34 east for 7 mi to the Alsea River crossing),* ☎ *541/563–3211.* ⊗ *Daily 8–4.*

Lodging

$$$–$$$$ 🖼 **Cliff House Bed-and-Breakfast.** The view from Yaquina John Point, on which this B&B sits, is magnificent. An almost overwhelming as-sortment of Asian and European antiques—including a 500-year-old sleigh bed, lacquered screens, and Chinese porcelains—adorns the house, which in livelier days was a bordello. The plush rooms all have ocean views and color TVs and VCRs. Three have balconies and wood-burning stoves. A glass-fronted terrace looking out over 8 mi of white-sand beach leads down to the garden. A Continental breakfast is served weekdays and a full breakfast on weekends. ✉ *1450 Adahi Rd., 1 block west of U.S. 101, 97394,* ☎ *541/563–2506,* 🅵🅰🆇 *541/563–4393. 4 rooms. Hot tub, sauna. D, MC, V.*

Outdoor Activities and Sports

McKinley's Marina (✉ Hwy. 34, ☎ 541/563–4656) rents boats and crab pots to those who want to take advantage of the excellent crab-bing in Alsea Bay.

Yachats

8 mi south of Waldport on U.S. 101.

A tiny burg of 635 inhabitants, Yachats (pronounced "Ya-*hots*") has acquired a reputation among Oregon beach lovers that is dispropor-tionate to its size. A relaxed alternative to the more touristy commu-nities to the north, Yachats has all the coastal pleasures: B&Bs, good restaurants, deserted beaches, tide pools, surf-pounded crags, fishing, and crabbing. The town's name is a Native American word meaning "foot of the mountain."

Dining and Lodging

$$ ✕ **Adobe Restaurant.** The food at the dining room of the Adobe Hotel doesn't always measure up to the extraordinary ocean views, but if you stick to the fresh seafood, you'll come away satisfied. The "Baked Crab Pot" is a rich, bubbling casserole filled with Dungeness crab and cheese in a shallot cream sauce; best of all is the "Captain's Seafood Platter," heaped with prawns, scallops, grilled oysters, and razor clams. ⊠ *1555 Hwy. 101,* ☎ *541/547–3141. AE, D, DC, MC, V.*

$$ ✕ **La Serre.** Don't be dismayed by the vaguely steak-and-salad-bar am-
★ bience at this skylit, plant-filled restaurant—the chef's deft touch with fresh seafood attracts knowledgeable diners from as far away as Florence and Newport. Try the tender geoduck clam, breaded with Parmesan cheese and flash-fried in lemon-garlic butter. A reasonably priced wine list and mouthwatering desserts complete the package. La Serre also serves Sunday brunch. ⊠ *2nd and Beach Sts.,* ☎ *541/547–3420. AE, MC, V. Closed Jan. and Tues. No lunch.*

$$$ 🏨 **Ziggurat.** You have to see this four-story cedar-and-glass pyramid 6½ mi south of Yachats to believe it. And you need to spend a night or two, serenaded by the wind and sea, to fully appreciate it. Odd angles, contemporary furnishings, and works of art gathered on the owners' world travels lend a discerning, sophisticated air. Two first-floor suites open out to grassy cliffs; the smaller fourth-floor bedroom has two balconies and dramatic views. There are a few rules: Pets, smoking, and children under 14 are not permitted. A full breakfast is included. ⊠ *95320 Hwy. 101, 97498,* ☎ *541/547–3925. 3 rooms. No credit cards.*

$–$$$ 🏨 **The Adobe.** The knotty-pine rooms in this unassuming resort motel are on the smallish side but are warm and inviting. High-beam ceilings and picture windows frame majestic views. Many rooms have wood-burning fireplaces; all have cable TV and coffeemakers. ⊠ *1555 Hwy. 101, 97498,* ☎ *541/547–3141 or 800/522–3623,* 📠 *541/547–4234. 95 units, 6 suites. Restaurant, bar, in-room VCRs, refrigerators, hot tub, sauna. AE, D, DC, MC, V.*

Shopping

Sea Rose (⊠ Mile Post 171, 6 mi south of Yachats, ☎ 541/547–3005) sells seashells from Oregon and around the world at remarkably low prices.

Cape Perpetua

★ ❼ *9 mi south of Yachats town on U.S. 101.*

About 1 mi south of the bevy of upscale B&Bs at the southern boundary of Yachats (6 mi from the town itself), an easy trail leads down from the parking lot at **Devil's Churn State Park** (⊠ U.S. 101, east side, no phone) to the deep, tide-cut fissure for which the park was named. Surging waves funneled into this narrow cleft in the basaltic embankment explode into "spouting horns" and sea spray.

Cape Perpetua, which has the highest lookout point on the Oregon coast, towers 800 ft above the rocky shoreline. Named by Captain Cook on St. Perpetua's Day in 1778, the cape is part of a 2,700-acre scenic area popular with hikers, campers, beachcombers, and naturalists. General information and a map of 10 trails are available at the **Cape Perpetua Visitors Center,** on the east side of the highway, 2 mi south of Devil's Churn. The easy 1-mi **Giant Spruce Trail** passes through a fern-filled rain forest to an enormous 500-year-old Sitka spruce. Easier still is the marked Auto Tour; it begins about 2 mi north of the visitor center and winds through Siuslaw National Forest to the ¼-mi **Whispering Spruce Trail.** Views from the rustic rock shelter here extend 150 mi north and south and 37 mi out to sea. The **Cape Perpetua Interpretive Center,** in the visitor center, has educational movies and exhibits about the natural forces that shaped Cape Perpetua. ⊠ *U.S. 101,* ☎ *541/547–3289.* ⊡ *Visitor center free, interpretive center $3.* ☉ *Memorial Day–Labor Day, daily 9–5; Labor Day–Memorial Day, weekends 10–4.*

Heceta Head

10 mi south of Cape Perpetua on U.S. 101; 65 mi from Eugene, west on Hwy. 126 and north on U.S. 101.

A ½-mi trail from the beachside parking lot at **Devil's Elbow State Park** leads to **Heceta Head Lighthouse,** whose beacon, visible for more than 21 mi, is the most powerful on the Oregon coast. The trail passes **Heceta House,** a pristine white structure said to be haunted by the wife of a lighthouse keeper whose child fell to her death from the cliffs shortly after the beacon was lit in 1894. The house is one of Oregon's most remarkable bed-and-breakfasts (☞ Lodging, *below*). ⊠ *U.S. 101,* ☎ *541/997–3851.* ⊡ *Day use $3, lighthouse tours free.* ☉ *Lighthouse Mar.–Oct., daily noon–5; park daily dawn–dusk.*

In 1880 a sea captain named Cox rowed a small skiff into a fissure in a 300-ft-high sea cliff. Inside, he was startled to discover a vaulted chamber in the rock, 125 ft high and 2 acres in area. Hundreds of massive sea lions—the largest bulls weighing 2,000 pounds or more—covered every available horizontal surface. Cox had no way of knowing it, but his discovery would eventually become one of the Oregon coast's premier tourist attractions, **Sea Lion Caves.** An elevator near the cliff-top ticket office descends to the floor of the cavern, near sea level, where Stellar and California sea lions and their fuzzy pups can be viewed from behind a wire fence. This is the only known hauling area (lair) and rookery for wild sea lions on the American mainland, and it's an awesome— if aromatic—sight and sound. In the spring and summer the mammals stay on the rocky ledges outside the cave; in fall and winter they move inside. You'll also see several species of sea birds here, including migratory pigeon guillemots, cormorants, and three varieties of gulls. Gray whales are visible during their northern and southern migrations, from October to December and from March to May. ⊠ *91560 U.S. 101, 1 mi south of Heceta Head,* ☎ *541/547–3111.* ⊡ *$6.50.* ☉ *July–Aug., daily 8–dusk; Sept.–June, daily 9–dusk.*

★ ☾ ❽

Lodging

$$–$$$ 🖭 **Heceta House.** This unusual B&B perches on a windswept promontory in one of Oregon's most majestic settings. Surrounded by a white picket fence, the late-Victorian house, owned by the U.S. Forest Service, is managed by Mike and Carol Korgan, certified executive chefs who prepare a seven-course breakfast (included in the room rate) each morning. The nicest of the simply furnished rooms is the Mariner's, with a private bath and an awe-inspiring view. Filled with period detailing and antiques, the common areas are warm and inviting. If you're lucky, you may hear Rue, the resident ghost, in the middle of the night. ⊠ *92072 Hwy. 101 S, Yachats, 97498,* ☎ *541/547–3696.* *3 rooms, 1 with bath. MC, V.*

En Route   South of Heceta Head, U.S. 101 jogs inland and the frowning headlands and cliffs of the north coast give way to the beaches, lakes, rivers, tidal estuaries, and rolling dunes of the south. Historic bridges span many of the famous fishing rivers that draw anglers from around the world. **Darlingtona Botanical Wayside** (⊠ Mercer Lake Rd., ☎ no phone), 6 mi south of Sea Lion Caves on the east side of U.S. 101, is an example of the rich plant life found in the marshy terrain near the coast. It's also a surefire child pleaser. A short paved nature trail leads through clumps of insect-catching cobra lilies, so named because they look like spotted cobras ready to strike. This wayside area is the most interesting in May, when the lilies are in bloom. Admission is free.

Florence

❾ *12 mi south of Heceta Head on U.S. 101; 63 mi west of Eugene on Hwy. 126.*

Tourists and retirees have been flocking to Florence in ever greater numbers in recent years. Its restored waterfront Old Town holds restaurants, antiques stores, fish markets, and other diversions. But what really makes the town so appealing is its proximity to remarkable stretches of coastline.

Florence is the gateway to the **Oregon Dunes National Recreation Area,** a 41-mi swath of undulating camel-color sand. The dunes, formed by eroded sandstone pushed up from the sea floor millions of years ago, have forests growing on them, water running through them, and rivers that have been dammed by them to form lakes. **Honeyman Memorial State Park,** 522 acres within the recreation area, is a base camp for dune-buggy enthusiasts, mountain bikers, hikers, boaters, horseback riders, and dogsledders (the sandy hills are an excellent training ground). The dunes are a vast and exuberant playground for children, particularly the slopes surrounding cool **Cleawox Lake.** ⊠ *Oregon Dunes National Recreation Area office, 855 Hwy. 101, Reedsport 97467,* ☎ *541/271–3611.* ☑ *Day use $3.* ☉ *Daily dawn–dusk.*

Dining and Lodging

$–$$$ ✕ **Windward Inn.** One of the south coast's most elegant eateries, this tightly run ship prides itself on its vast menu, master wine list, home-baked breads and desserts, and fresh seafood. The chinook salmon fillets poached in Riesling and the shrimp and scallops sautéed in white wine are delectable. ⊠ *3757 Hwy. 101 N,* ☎ *541/997–8243. AE, D, DC, MC, V.*

$–$$ ✕ **Bridgewater Seafood Restaurant.** Freshly caught seafood—25 to 30 choices nightly—is the mainstay of this creaky-floored Victorian-era restaurant in Florence's Old Town. The cooking is plain and not exactly inspired, but the locals seem to like it that way. ⊠ *1297 Bay St.,* ☎ *541/997–9405. MC, V.*

$ ✕ **Mo's.** Come here for clear bayfront views and a creamy bowl of clam chowder. This coastal institution has been around for more than 40 years, consistently providing fresh seafood and down-home service. ⊠ *1436 Bay St.,* ☎ *541/997–2185. D, MC, V.*

$$–$$$ ☷ **Driftwood Shores Surfside Resort Inn.** The chief amenity of this resort is its location directly above Heceta Beach, one of the longest sand beaches on the south coast. The simple rooms have ocean views and kitchens; the three-bedroom suites have fireplaces and balconies. ⊠ *88416 1st Ave., 97439 (from U.S. 101 take Heceta Beach Rd. west about 3 mi north of Florence),* ☎ *541/997–8263 or 800/422–5091,* ℻ *541/997–7301. 127 rooms, 26 suites. Restaurant, bar, indoor pool, hot tub, beach. AE, D, DC, MC, V.*

⚐ Oregon Dunes National Recreation Area. The facilities in the recreation area (☞ *above*) include a boat ramp and campgrounds for tents, RVs, and off-highway vehicles; all sites are available on a first-come, first-served basis, except the ones for off-highway vehicles, for which reservations are essential on weekends and holidays mid-May–mid-September. ⊠ *U.S. 101 at Florence,* ☎ *541/271–3611; 800/280–2267 for reservations only. 381 sites (66 with full hookups).* ☑ *$3 per ve-*

hicle day use, $11–$15 camping. Flush toilets, potable water, show-ers. ☉ *Year-round.*

Outdoor Activities and Sports

Ocean Dunes Golf Links (⊠ 3345 Munsel Lake Rd., ☎ 541/997–3232) is an 18-hole, par-71 course. The greens fee is $28 (higher in summer); an optional cart costs $24. **Sandpines Golf Course** (⊠ 1201 35th St., ☎ 541/997–1940) is an 18-hole, par-72 course. The greens fee runs from $35 to $45; an optional cart costs $26.

Shopping

Incredible & Edible Oregon (⊠ 1350 Bay St., ☎ 541/997–7018) in Florence's Old Town is devoted to Oregon products: wine, fruit preserves, books, and gift items.

Reedsport

20 mi south of Florence on U.S. 101; 90 mi west of Eugene on I–5 and Hwy. 38.

The small town of Reedsport owes its existence to the Umpqua River, one of the state's great steelhead fishing streams. Exhibits at the **Umpqua Discovery Center** in the waterfront area give a good introduction to the Lower Umpqua estuary and surrounding region. The center's chief attraction is the *Hero,* the laboratory ship Admiral Byrd used on his expeditions to the Antarctic. ⊠ *409 Riverfront Way,* ☎ *541/271–4816.* ⊡ *Museum $3, tour of the Hero $3, $5 for both.* ☉ *May–Sept., daily 10–6; Oct.–Apr., daily 10–4.*

The natural forces that created the towering sand dunes along this section of the Oregon coast are explained in interpretive exhibits at the Reedsport **Oregon Dunes National Recreation Area Visitors Center.** The center, which also sells maps, books, and gifts, is a good place to pick up free literature on the area. ⊠ *855 Highway Ave., south side of Umpqua River Bridge,* ☎ *541/271–3611.* ⊡ *Free.* ☉ *Memorial Day–Labor Day, daily 8:30–5; hrs vary rest of yr.*

A herd of wild Roosevelt elk, Oregon's largest land mammal, roams within sight of the **Dean Creek Elk Viewing Area.** Abundant forage and a mild winter climate enable the elk to remain at Dean Creek year-round. The best viewing times are early morning and just before dusk. ⊠ *Hwy. 38, 3 mi east of Reedsport (watch for signs).* ⊡ *Free.* ☉ *Daily dawn–dusk.*

En Route A public pier at **Winchester Bay's Salmon Harbor,** 3¼ mi south of Reedsport, juts out over the bay and yields excellent results for crabbers and fishermen (especially those after rockfish). There's also a full-service marina with a fish market.

Umpqua Lighthouse Park

6 mi south of Reedsport on U.S. 101.

Some of the highest sand dunes in the country are found in the 50-acre Umpqua Lighthouse Park. The first **Umpqua River Lighthouse,** built on the dunes at the mouth of the Umpqua River in 1857, lasted only four years before it toppled over in a storm. It took local residents 33 years to build another one. The "new" lighthouse, built on a bluff overlooking the south side of Winchester Bay and operated by the U.S. Coast Guard, is still going strong, flashing a warning beacon out to sea every five seconds. The **Douglas County Coastal Visitors Center** adjacent to the lighthouse has a museum and can arrange lighthouse tours. ⊠ *Umpqua*

Hwy., west side of U.S. 101, ☎ *541/271–4118.* 💲 *Donations appreciated.* ⊙ *Lighthouse May–Sept., Wed.–Sat. 10–4, Sun. 1–4.*

Coos Bay Area

❿ *27 mi south of Reedsport on U.S. 101; 116 mi southwest of Eugene, I–5 to Hwy. 38 to U.S. 101.*

The Coos Bay–Charleston–North Bend metropolitan area, collectively known as the Bay Area (population 25,000), is the gateway to rewarding recreational experiences. The town of Coos Bay lies next to the largest natural harbor between San Francisco Bay and Seattle's Puget Sound. A century ago vast quantities of lumber cut from the Coast Range were milled in Coos Bay and shipped around the world. The mountainous piles of wood chips visible from the highway on the north side of town are Oregon's number one export. Coos Bay still has a reputation as a rough-and-ready port city, but with mill closures and dwindling lumber reserves it has begun to look in other directions, such as tourism, for economic prosperity. One former mill has even been converted into a casino.

To see the best of the Bay Area head west from Coos Bay on Newmark Avenue for about 7 mi to **Charleston.** Though it's a Bay Area community, this quiet fishing village at the mouth of Coos Bay is a world unto itself. As it loops into town the road becomes the Cape Arago Highway and leads to several oceanfront parks.

Sunset Bay State Park, a placid semicircular lagoon protected from the sea by overlapping fingers of rock and surrounded by reefs, is one of the few places along the Oregon coast where you can swim without worrying about the currents and undertows. Only the hardiest souls will want to brave the chilly water, however. ✉ *2 mi south of Charleston off Cape Arago Hwy.,* ☎ *800/551–6949.* 💲 *Free.* ⊙ *Daily dawn–dusk.*

At **Shore Acres State Park,** an observation building on a grassy bluff overlooking the Pacific marks the site that held the mansion of lumber baron Louis J. Simpson. The view over the rugged wave-smashed cliffs is splendid, but the real glory of Shore Acres lies a few hundred yards to the south, where an entrance gate leads into what was Simpson's private garden. Beautifully landscaped and meticulously maintained, the gardens incorporate formal English and Japanese designs. From March to mid-October the grounds are ablaze with blossoming daffodils, rhododendrons, azaleas, roses, and dahlias. In December the entire garden is decked out with a dazzling display of holiday lights. ✉ *10965 Cape Arago Hwy., 1 mi south of Sunset Bay State Park,* ☎ *800/551–6949.* 💲 *Day use $3 per vehicle.* ⊙ *Daily 8–dusk.*

The distant barking of sea lions echoes in the air at **Cape Arago State Park.** A trio of coves connected by short but steep trails, the park overlooks the **Oregon Islands National Wildlife Refuge,** where offshore rocks, beaches, islands, and reefs provide breeding grounds for seabirds and marine mammals. ✉ *End of Cape Arago Hwy., 1 mi south of Shore Acres State Park,* ☎ *800/551–6949.* 💲 *Free.* ⊙ *Daily dawn–dusk.*

The wreck of the *New Carissa* freighter in winter 1999 was considered a serious threat to the fragile ecosystem at **South Slough National Estuarine Research Reserve,** but fortunately not much leaking oil reached the slough. The mudflats and tidal estuaries of Coos Bay support everything from algae to bald eagles and black bears. More than 300 species of birds have been sighted at the reserve; an interpretive center, guided walks (summer only), and nature trails give you a chance to see things up close. ⊠ *Seven Devils Rd., 4 mi south of Charleston,* ☎ *800/551–6949.* 🎫 *Free.* ⊙ *Trails daily dawn–dusk; interpretive center daily 8:30–4:30.*

Casino

Mill Resort and Casino. This complex, located just north of Coos Bay, has a casino with 350 slots, blackjack, poker, and bingo. There's a waterfront restaurant, and big-name entertainers perform in the showroom. At press time a 112-room hotel was under construction. ⊠ *3201 Tremont Ave., North Bend 97459,* ☎ *541/756–8800 or 800/953–4800,* 🅕🅐🅧 *541/756–0431.*

Dining and Lodging

$$ ✕ **Blue Heron Bistro.** You'll find subtle preparations of local seafood,
★ chicken, and homemade pasta at this busy bistro. There are no flat spots on the far-ranging menu; even the innovative soups and desserts are excellent. The skylit tile-floor dining room seats about 70 amid natural wood and blue linen. The seating area outside has blue awnings and colorful Bavarian window boxes that add a festive touch. Espresso and 18 microbrewery beers are available. ⊠ *100 W. Commercial St.,* ☎ *541/267–3933. AE, D, MC, V. Closed Sun. Oct.–May.*

$$ ✕ **Portside Restaurant.** The fish at this gem of a restaurant overlooking the Charleston boat basin comes straight to the kitchen from the dock outside. Try the steamed Dungeness crab with drawn butter. On Friday night come for the all-you-can-eat seafood buffet. The nautical decor reinforces the view of the harbor through the restaurant's picture windows. ⊠ *8001 Kingfisher Rd. (follow Cape Arago Hwy. from Coos Bay),* ☎ *541/888–5544. AE, DC, MC, V.*

$ ✕ **Kum-Yon's.** The preparations at this small pan-Asian restaurant on Coos Bay's main drag are average, and the ambience resembles nothing so much as a Seoul Burger King, but the portions of sushi, kung-pao shrimp, and other dishes are satisfying, and the prices are ridiculously low. ⊠ *835 S. Broadway,* ☎ *541/269–2662. AE, D, MC, V.*

$$ 🏠 **Coos Bay Manor.** Built in 1912 on a quiet residential street in Coos Bay, this 15-room Colonial Revival manor is listed on the National Register of Historic Places. Hardwood floors, detailed woodwork, high ceilings, and antiques and period reproductions offset the red-and-gold flocked wallpaper. An unusual open balcony on the second floor leads to the large rooms. Innkeeper Patricia Williams serves breakfast (included in the rates) in the wainscoted dining room or, if the weather is fine, on the upper balcony. ⊠ *955 S. 5th St., 97420,* ☎ *541/269–1224 or 800/269–1224,* 🅕🅐🅧 *541/269–1224. 5 rooms, 3 with bath. Airport shuttle. D, MC, V.*

Outdoor Activities and Sports

Kentuck Golf Course (⊠ 675 Golf Course La., North Bend, ☎ 541/756–4464) is an 18-hole, par-70 course. The greens fee is $16 on weekdays, $18 on weekends; a cart costs $15. **Sunset Bay Golf Course** (⊠ 11001 Cape Arago Hwy., ☎ 541/888–9301) is a 9-hole, par-36 course. The greens fee is $17, plus $22 for a cart.

OFF THE **GOLDEN AND SILVER FALLS STATE PARK –** Deep in old-growth forest sprin-
BEATEN PATH kled with delicate maidenhair ferns, this park is home to two of the region's natural wonders. Silver Falls is an arresting sight as it pours over a 200-ft-high semicircular rock ledge. One-quarter mile to the northwest, Golden Falls, another giant cataract formed by the thundering waters of Glenn Creek, is even more impressive, especially in the spring. ⊠ *U.S. 101, 24 mi northeast of Coos Bay (follow signs),* ☎ *800/551–6949.* 🎫 *Free.* ⊙ *Daily dawn–dusk.*

Bandon

⓫ *25 mi south of Coos Bay on U.S. 101.*

It may seem odd that tiny Bandon, built above a beach notable for its gallery of photogenic seastacks, bills itself as the Cranberry Capital of Oregon. But 10 mi north of town lie acres of bogs and irrigated fields where tons of the tart berries are harvested every year. Each October a Cranberry Festival, complete with a parade and a fair, takes place.

The town, almost entirely rebuilt after a devastating fire in 1936, has fine restaurants, resort hotels, and a busy boat basin on the Coquille River estuary. A few of the buildings in the Old Town area a block north of the boat basin hark back to the early 20th century, when Bandon was a booming port of call for passengers traveling from San Francisco to Seattle by steamship.

The **Bandon Historical Society Museum,** in the old City Hall building, documents the town's past. ⊠ *270 Fillmore St.,* ☎ *541/347–2164.* ▨ *$1.* ⊘ *Mon.–Sat. 10–4, Sun. noon–3 in summer.*

Follow the signs from Bandon south along Beach Loop Road to **Face Rock Wayside** and descend a stairway to the sand. Here you can gaze out to sea through a veritable gallery of natural sculptures, including Elephant Rock, Table Rock, and Face Rock.

The octagonal **Coquille Lighthouse** at **Bullards Beach State Park,** built in 1896 and no longer in use, stands lonely sentinel at the mouth of the Coquille River. From the highway the 2-mi drive to reach it passes through the Bandon Marsh, a prime bird-watching and picnicking area. The beach beside the lighthouse is a good place to search for jasper, agate, and driftwood. ⊠ *U.S. 101, 2 mi north of Bandon,* ☎ *800/551–6949.* ▨ *Free.* ⊘ *Daily dawn–dusk.*

☾ **West Coast Game Park Safari** shelters 450 animals of 75 exotic species, some of which children can pet. It's the largest wild animal petting park in the United States. There are lions, bears, black panthers, bison, deer, camels, lynx, cougars, leopards, chimpanzees, llamas, elk, and tigers. ⊠ *U.S. 101, 7 mi south of Bandon,* ☎ *541/347–3106.* ▨ *$7.95.* ⊘ *Jan.–Feb., weekends 9–5; Mar.–Sept., daily 9–7; Oct.–Nov., daily 9–5.*

Dining and Lodging

$$ ✕ **Bandon Boatworks.** A local favorite, this romantic jetty-side eatery serves up its seafood, steaks, and prime rib with a view of the Coquille River harbor and lighthouse. Try the panfried oysters flamed with brandy and anisette or the quick-sautéed seafood combination, which is heavy on scampi and scallops. ⊠ *S. Jetty Rd. off 1st St.,* ☎ *541/347–2111. AE, D, MC, V.*

$$ ✕ **Lord Bennett's.** His lordship has a lot going for him: a cliff-top setting, modern decor, sunsets visible through picture windows overlooking Face Rock Beach, and musical performers on weekends. The rich dishes include prawns sautéed with sherry and garlic and steaks topped with shiitake mushrooms. A Sunday brunch is served. ⊠ *1695 Beach Loop Rd.,* ☎ *541/347–3663. AE, D, MC, V.*

$$–$$$ ⊞ **Inn at Face Rock.** This modern resort sits across Beach Loop Drive from Bandon's fabulous walking beach. The units, many suite-size and larger, are comfortably furnished in a cream-and-sand color scheme; nearly half have ocean views, and some have kitchenettes and fireplaces. ⊠ *3225 Beach Loop Rd., 97411,* ☎ *541/347–9441 or 800/638–3092,* ℻ *541/347–2532. 55 units. Restaurant, bar, hot tub, 9-hole golf course, coin laundry. AE, D, DC, MC, V.*

Shopping

Cranberry Sweets (⊠ 1005 Newmark Ave., ☎ 541/347–9475) specializes in delectable handmade candies—cranberry jellies, "lemon pies" (white chocolate around a lemon jelly center), and other delicacies.

Cape Blanco State Park

27 mi south of Bandon on U.S. 101.

Cape Blanco is the westernmost point in Oregon, and perhaps the windiest—gusts clocked at speeds as high as 184 mph have twisted and battered the Sitka spruces along the 6-mi road from U.S. 101 to the **Cape Blanco Lighthouse.** The lighthouse, atop a 245-ft headland, has been in continuous use since 1870, longer than any other in Oregon. No one knows why the Spaniards sailing past these reddish bluffs in 1603 called them *blanco* (white). One theory is that the name refers to the fossilized shells that glint in the cliff face. Campsites at the 1,880-acre **Cape Blanco State Park** are available on a first-come, first-served basis. Three-hour night tours are available for $50. ⊠ *Cape Blanco Rd. (follow signs from U.S. 101),* ☎ *541/332–6774 state park, 541/332–2750 lighthouse.* ⊡ *Day use free, campsites $13–$18.* ☉ *Park daily dawn–dusk; lighthouse Apr.–Oct., Thurs.–Mon. 10–3:30.*

En Route U.S. 101 between Port Orford and Brookings, often referred to as the "fabulous fifty miles," soars up green headlands, some of them hundreds of feet high, and past an awesome seascape of cliffs and seastacks. The ocean is bluer and clearer—though not appreciably warmer—than it is farther north, and the coastal countryside is dotted with farms, grazing cattle, and small rural communities. As you round a bend between Port Orford and Gold Beach you'll see one of those sights that make grownups groan and kids squeal with delight: a huge, open-jawed Tyrannosaurus rex, with a green brontosaurus peering out from the forest beside it. The **Prehistoric Gardens** (⊠ 36848 Hwy. 101, ☎ 541/332–4463) is filled with life-size replicas of these primeval giants. The complex is open daily 8 AM–dusk. Admission is $5 for adults, $4 ages 4–11.

Gold Beach

35 mi south of Cape Blanco on U.S. 101.

The fabled **Rogue River,** which empties into the Pacific at Gold Beach, has been luring anglers and outdoor enthusiasts for more than a century. Zane Grey, in books like *Rogue River Feud,* was among the writers who helped establish the Rogue's reputation as a world-class chinook salmon and steelhead stream. Celebrities as diverse as Winston Churchill, Clark Gable, George Bush, and Ginger Rogers, who had a home on the Rogue, have all fished here. It's one of the few U.S. rivers to merit Wild and Scenic status from the federal government.

From spring to late fall an estimated 50,000 visitors descend on the town to take one of the daily jet-boat excursions (☞ Outdoor Activities and Sports, *below*) that roar upstream from Wedderburn, Gold Beach's sister city across the bay, into the Rogue River Wilderness Area. Some of the boats go to Agness, 32 mi upstream, where the riverside road ends and the Wild and Scenic portions of the Rogue begin. Other boats penetrate farther, to the white-knuckle rapids at Blossom Bar, 52 mi upstream. Black bears, otters, beavers, ospreys, egrets, and bald eagles are regularly seen on these trips. From Grave Creek to Watson Creek, along the 40-mi stretch classified as Wild, there is a National Recreation Trail granting access to this "vestige of primitive America."

Gold Beach is very much a seasonal town, thriving in the summer and nearly deserted the rest of the year. It marks the entrance to Oregon's banana belt, where mild, California-like temperatures take the sting out of winter and encourage a blossoming trade in lilies and daffodils.

Dining and Lodging

$$ ✕ **Nor'Wester Seafood Restaurant.** This eatery on the waterfront overlooking the boat harbor at the the mouth of the Rogue River serves good seafood, steaks, and pasta. ⊠ *Port of Gold Beach,* ☎ *541/247– 2333. AE, MC, V. No lunch.*

$$$$ ⊞ **Tu Tu Tun Lodge.** This well-known fishing resort (pronounced "Too-
★ *too*-tin") sits right on the Rogue River, 7 mi upriver from Gold Beach. Salmon and steelhead fishing made the Tu Tu Tun's name, but jet-boat excursions, golf, and other activities take place. All the units in this small establishment are rustically elegant. Some have hot tubs, others have fireplaces, and a few have both; private decks overlook the river. Two deluxe rooms have tall picture windows, tile baths, and outdoor soaking tubs with river views. The restaurant (closed Nov.–Apr.) serves breakfast, lunch, and dinner; the last, open to nonguests, though reservations are hard to come by, consists of a five-course prix-fixe meal that changes nightly. Portions are dauntingly huge. ⊠ *96550 N. Bank Rogue, 97444,* ☎ *541/247–6664,* ℻ *541/247–0672. 18 rooms, 3-bedroom house. Restaurant, bar, outdoor pool, 4-hole golf course, hiking, horseshoes, dock, boating, fishing. D, MC, V.*

$–$$ ⊞ **Ireland's Rustic Lodges.** Seven original one- and two-bedroom cabins filled with rough-hewn charm, plus 28 newer motel rooms and two cabins, are available in a landscaped beachside setting. Some units have wood-burning fireplaces and decks overlooking the sea. For the price, you can't beat this accommodation. ⊠ *29330 Ellensburg Ave. (U.S. 101), 97444,* ☎ *541/247–7718,* ℻ *541/247–0225. 30 rooms, 7 cabins, 3 houses. No-smoking rooms. MC, V.*

Outdoor Activities and Sports

GOLF

Cedar Bend Golf Course (⊠ 34391 Squaw Valley Rd., ☎ 541/247–6911) is a 9-hole, par-36 course. The greens fee for 18 holes (play twice) is $18; a cart costs $18.

JET-BOAT EXCURSIONS

Jerry's Rogue Boats (⊠ 29985 Harbor Way, ☎ 541/247–4571 or 800/451–3645) and **Rogue River Mail Boat Trips** (⊠ 94294 Rogue River Rd., ☎ 541/247–7033 or 800/458–3511) operate jet-boat excursions out of the Port of Gold Beach from May through October. Rates range $30–$75; some tours include a lunch stop at a riverside inn.

En Route Between Gold Beach and Brookings, you'll cross Thomas Creek Bridge, the highest span in Oregon. Take advantage of the off-road coastal viewing points along the 10-mi-long **Samuel H. Boardman State Park**—especially in summer, when highway traffic becomes heavy and rubbernecking can be dangerous.

Brookings

27 mi south of Gold Beach on U.S. 101.

A startling 90% of the pot lilies grown in the United States come from a 500-acre area inland from Brookings. Strangely enough, these white symbols of peace probably wouldn't be grown here in such abundance if not for the fact that in 1942 Brookings experienced the only wartime aerial bombing attack on the U.S. mainland. A Japanese air raid set trees ablaze and understandably panicked the local residents; the imminent ban on Japanese flowers set them to work cultivating the Easter lilies that appear in stores across the country every April. Mild temperatures along this coastal plain provide ideal conditions for flowering plants of all kinds—even a few palm trees, a rare sight in Oregon.

The town is equally famous as a commercial and sportfishing port at the mouth of the turquoise-blue **Chetco River.** If anything, the Chetco is more highly esteemed among fishermen and wilderness lovers than is the Rogue. A short jetty, used by many local crabbers and fishermen, provides easy and productive access to the river's mouth; salmon and steelhead weighing 20 pounds or larger swim here.

Brookings celebrates its horticultural munificence on Memorial Day weekend with an Azalea Festival in **Azalea Park** (⊠ N. Bank Rd. off U.S. 101 downtown) amid blossoming wild azaleas, some of them hundreds of years old. Take the kids to Kidtown to play on its wooden playground equipment.

The **Chetco Valley Historical Museum,** inside a mid-19th-century stagecoach stop and trading post, has some unusual items and is worth a brief visit. An iron casting that bears a likeness to Queen Elizabeth I has led to speculation that it was left during an undocumented landing on the Oregon coast by Sir Francis Drake. On a hill near the museum stands the **World Champion Cypress Tree,** 99 ft tall and with a 27-ft circumference. ⊠ 5461 Museum Rd., ☎ 541/469–6651. ☜ $1. ☉ Memorial Day–Labor Day, Wed.–Sun. noon–5, Labor Day–Memorial Day, Fri.–Sun. noon–5.

Loeb State Park contains 53 riverside campsites and some fine hiking trails, including one that leads to a hidden redwood grove. There's also a grove of myrtlewood trees—impressive because the species grows nowhere else in the world. ⊠ North bank of the Chetco River, 10 mi east of Brookings (follow signs from U.S. 101), ☎ 541/469–2021. Reservations not accepted. ☜ Day use free, campsites $13–$16. ☉ Daily dawn–dusk.

Dining and Lodging

$$ ✕ **Starboard Tack.** Fishing vessels docked in the adjacent boat basin and picture windows looking out to the sea lend a salty ambience to this low-key restaurant. The daily seafood specials—usually halibut and salmon—are the best bets. For lunch try the fish-and-chips or the crab melt. ⊠ 16011 Boat Basin Rd., ☎ 541/469–6006. MC, V.

$$ ✕▥ **Chetco River Inn.** Thirty-five acres of private forest surround this
★ remote inn 17 mi up the Chetco River from Brookings. Guests come here to hike, hunt wild mushrooms, and relax in the library or in front of the fireplace in the common room. The host cooks delicious dinners that sometimes star a nickel-bright salmon fresh from the stream. Rooms have thick comforters and panoramic river and forest views. A full breakfast is included. ⊠ 21202 High Prairie Rd., off N. Bank Rd., 97415, ☎ 541/670–1645 or 800/327–2688, ☎ 541/469–4341. 4 rooms. MC, V.

$$–$$$ ▥ **Best Western Beachfront Inn.** The ocean is right outside your window at this inn with balconies closer to the water than those at any other hotel in southern Oregon. The large rooms have microwaves; some units also have kitchens, and 12 rooms have whirlpool tubs. ⊠ 16008 Boat Basin Rd., 97415, off Lower Harbor Rd. (south of Port of Brookings), ☎ 541/469–7779 or 800/468–4081, ☎ 541/469–0283. 102 rooms. Refrigerators, pool, outdoor hot tub, beach. AE, D, DC, MC, V.

The Oregon Coast Essentials

Arriving and Departing

BY BUS

Greyhound (☎ 800/231–2222) serves Astoria, Coos Bay, Newport, Florence, and other coastal cities.

BY CAR

U.S. 101 enters coastal Oregon from Washington State at Astoria and from California near Brookings. **U.S. 30** heads west from Portland to Astoria. **U.S. 20** travels west from Corvallis to Newport. **Highway 126** winds west to the coast from Eugene. **Highway 42** leads west from Roseburg toward Coos Bay.

Getting Around

BY CAR

U.S. 101 runs the length of the coast, sometimes turning inland for a few miles.

Visitor Information

Astoria-Warrenton Area Chamber of Commerce (✉ 143 S. Hwy. 101, Astoria 97103, ☎ 503/861–1031 or 800/875–6807). **Bay Area Chamber of Commerce** (✉ 50 E. Central St., Coos Bay 97420, ☎ 541/269–0215 or 800/824–8486). **Brookings Harbor Chamber of Commerce** (✉ 16330 Lower Harbor Rd., 97415, ☎ 541/469–3181 or 800/535–9469). **Cannon Beach Chamber of Commerce** (✉ 2nd and Spruce Sts., 97110, ☎ 503/436–2623). **Florence Area Chamber of Commerce** (✉ 270 Hwy. 101, 97439, ☎ 541/997–3128). **Greater Newport Chamber of Commerce** (✉ 555 S.W. Coast Hwy., 97365, ☎ 503/265–8801 or 800/262–7844). **Lincoln City Visitors Center** (✉ 801 S.W. Hwy. 101, Suite 1, 97367, ☎ 541/994–8378 or 800/452–2151). **Seaside Visitors Bureau** (✉ 7 N. Roosevelt Ave., 97138, ☎ 503/738–6391 or 800/444–6740). **Tillamook Chamber of Commerce** (✉ 3705 Hwy. 101 N, 97141, ☎ 503/842–7525). **Yachats Area Chamber of Commerce** (✉ U.S. 101 near 2nd St., 97498, ☎ 541/547–3530).

THE WILLAMETTE VALLEY AND THE WINE COUNTRY

During the 1940s and 1950s, researchers at Oregon State University concluded that the Willamette Valley—the wet, temperate trough between the Coast Range to the west and the Cascade Range to the east—had the wrong climate for the propagation of varietal wine grapes. The researchers' techniques were faulty, as has been proven by the success of Oregon's burgeoning wine industry. More than 60 wineries dot the Willamette (pronounced "Wil-*lam*-it") and Yamhill valleys in the northern part of the state. Two dozen more wineries are scattered among the Umpqua and Rogue valleys (near Roseburg and Ashland, respectively) to the south. Their products—mainly cool-climate varietals like Pinot Noir, Chardonnay, and Johannisberg Riesling—have won gold medals in blind tastings against the best wines of California and Europe.

For a bird's-eye view of the northern Willamette Valley, check out **Vista Balloon Adventures** (✉ 701 S.E. Sherk Pl., Sherwood 97140, ☎ 503/625–7385 or 800/622–2309, FAX 503/625–3845) just south of Portland. It's the Pacific Northwest's largest hot-air balloon company. From April through October five balloons take off daily, weather permitting, and float 3,000 ft over the northern Willamette Valley wine country. From I–5, take the Tualatin exit (No. 289), then go west on

Tualatin-Sherwood Road to Highway 99 W, turn left, and continue to Newberg.

Numbers in the margin correspond to points of interest on the Oregon Coast and Willamette Valley/Wine Country map.

Forest Grove Area

24 mi west of Portland on Hwy. 8.

Forest Grove, a quaint little city of about 14,000 people, is increasingly being absorbed into the Portland metropolitan area. It is home to Pacific University, and it's near several wineries. To get here, take U.S. 26 west to Highway 6 and go west to Forest Grove. For the wineries, head south from Forest Grove on Highway 47 and watch for the blue road signs between Forest Grove, Gaston, and Yamhill.

Several of the larger wineries include **Montinore Vineyards** (✉ 3663 S.W. Dilley Rd., Forest Grove, ☎ 503/359–5012); **Elk Cove Vineyards** (✉ 27751 N.W. Olson Rd., Gaston, ☎ 503/985–7760); and **Laurel Ridge Vineyards** (✉ 46350 N.W. David Hill Rd., Forest Grove, ☎ 503/359–5436).

If you're in the area in August, be sure to check out the **Elephant Garlic Festival** (✉ 311 Hillcrest, North Plains, ☎ 503/647–2207). Farmers from the surrounding Coast Range foothills bring their crop of the giant "stinking rose" to this rural community for a two-day food fest. Admission is free. *Take U.S. 26 to the North Plains exit.*

Dundee and Yamhill

6 mi southwest of Newberg on Hwy. 99 W.

The lion's share (up to 90%) of the U.S. hazelnut crop is grown in Dundee, a haven of produce stands and tasting rooms. The 25 mi of Highway 18 between Dundee and Grande Ronde, in the Coast Range, roll through the heart of the Yamhill Valley wine country; wide shoulders and relatively light traffic earned the route a "most suitable" rating from the "Oregon Bicycling Guide."

The tasting room of **Argyle Winery,** a producer of sparkling wines, is housed in a restored Victorian farmhouse in Dundee. ✉ *691 Hwy. 99 W,* ☎ *503/538–8520.* ⊙ *Tasting room daily 11–5, tours by appointment.*

Sokol Blosser, one of Oregon's oldest and largest wineries, has a tasting room and walk-through vineyard with a self-guided tour that explains the grape varieties—Pinot Noir and Chardonnay, among others. ✉ *5000 Sokol Blosser La. (3 mi west of Dundee off Hwy. 99 W),* ☎ *503/864–2282 or 800/582–6668.* ⊙ *Daily 11–5.*

Willakenzie Estate began operation of its ultramodern gravity-feed system in 1995. Its two inaugural wines, the 1995 Pinot Gris and Pinot Blanc, have enjoyed critical acclaim. ✉ *19143 N.E. Laughlin Rd., Yamhill (12 mi from Newberg; head west on Hwy. 240 and north on Laughlin),* ☎ *503/662–3280.* ⊙ *By appointment only.*

Newberg

38 mi southwest of Portland on Hwys. 99 W and 18.

Newberg, a graceful pioneer town at a broad bend in the Willamette River, marks the starting point of the North Willamette Valley's wine country.

The oldest and most significant of Newberg's original structures is the **Hoover-Minthorne House,** the boyhood home of President Herbert

Hoover. Built in 1881, the preserved frame house still contains many of the original furnishings. Outside is the woodshed that no doubt played an important role in shaping young "Bertie" Hoover's character. ⊠ *115 S. River St.,* ☎ *503/538–6629.* ⊡ *$2.* ☉ *Mar.–Nov., Wed.–Sun. 1–4; Dec. and Feb., weekends 1–4.*

Rex Hill Vineyards, on a hill east of Newberg, produces some of the best Pinot Noir wines in Oregon, wines that more than hold their own against ones from California, France, and other high-profile locales. Rex Hill bottles the house wines for Portland's trendy new Southpark restaurant. ⊠ *30835 N. Hwy. 99W,* ☎ *503/538–0666.* ☉ *Daily 11–5.*

Champoeg State Park

9 mi from Newberg, south on Hwy. 219 and east on Champoeg Rd.

Champoeg State Park (pronounced Sham-*poo*-ee) is on the site of a Hudson's Bay Company trading post, granary, and warehouse that was built in 1813. This was the seat of the first provisional government in the Northwest. The settlement was abandoned after a catastrophic flood in 1861, then rebuilt and abandoned again after the flood of 1890. The park's wide-open spaces, groves of oak and fir, modern visitor center, museum, and historic buildings yield vivid insight into pioneer life. ⊠ *8239 Champoeg Rd. NE, St. Paul 97137,* ☎ *800/551–6949.* ⊡ *$3 per vehicle.* ☉ *Memorial Day–Labor Day, daily 10–6; Labor Day–Memorial Day, weekdays 8–4, weekends noon–4.*

OFF THE
BEATEN PATH

OLD AURORA COLONY – A fascinating slice of Oregon's pioneer past, the colony was the only major 19th-century communal society in the Pacific Northwest. Created by Germans in 1856, this frontier society espoused a "Love thy neighbor" philosophy, shared labor and property, and was known for its hospitality. Aurora retains many white frame houses dating from the 1860s and 1870s. Several structures have been incorporated into the Old Aurora Colony Museum (⊠ 2nd and Liberty Sts., ☎ 503/678–5754), which provides an overview of the colony's way of life. Follow an easy self-guided tour of the historic district, or take the guided walking tour ($3.50) given on weekends at 1 and 3 PM. The colony is open Tuesday–Saturday 10–4, Sunday noon–4. ⊠ *About 14 mi from Champoeg State Park; take Champoeg Rd. east to Arndt Rd.; pass under I–5 and turn south onto Airport Rd., then east onto Ehlen Rd.*

McMinnville

❷ *14 mi south of Newberg on Hwy. 99W.*

McMinnville, the largest (population 20,000) and most sophisticated of the wine-country towns, has a fine collection of B&Bs, small hotels, and restaurants. It's also the home of Howard Hughes's famous airplane, the *Spruce Goose.*

Capt. Michael King Smith Evergreen Aviation Education Center and Museum. This attraction enjoys as its claim to fame the *Spruce Goose,* which will be on permanent display here when a new museum building opens in fall 2000. Also known as the Hughes Flying Boat, the famous plane, which eccentric millionaire Howard Hughes flew only once—on November 2, 1947—was moved here in 1992 from Long Beach, California. There are also about a dozen military planes on display here. ⊠ *3850 Three Mile La., 97128,* ☎ *503/472–9361.* ⊡ *Free (admission will be charged once the new building opens).* ☉ *Daily 9–4.*

Linfield College (⊠ Linfield Ave. east of Hwy. 18), a perennial football powerhouse, is an oasis of brick and ivy amid McMinnville's farmers'-

market bustle. The college, founded in 1849 and the second oldest in Oregon, hosts the **International Pinot Noir Celebration** (☎ 800/775–4762) at the end of July and beginning of August.

The Pinot Noir and Pinot Gris wines produced on the 300-acre estate of **Yamhill Valley Vineyards** have won prestigious awards. ⊠ *16250 S.W. Oldsville Rd. (5 mi from downtown McMinnville; take Hwy. 99 W south to Hwy. 18 south to Oldsville Rd. and make a right),* ☎ *800/ 825–4845.* ⊙ *Mid-Mar.–June, weekends 11–5; July–Thanksgiving, daily 11–5.*

Dining and Lodging

$$$ ✕ **Nick's Italian Cafe.** Modestly furnished but with a voluminous wine
★ cellar, Nick's is a favorite of area wine makers. The food is spirited and simple, reflecting the owner's northern Italian heritage. The five-course prix-fixe menu changes nightly. À la carte options are also available. ⊠ *521 E. 3rd St.,* ☎ *503/434–4471. Reservations essential. AE, DC, MC, V. Closed Mon. No lunch.*

$$–$$$ ✕ **Third Street Grill and Wine Shop.** This establishment in a historic downtown McMinnville Victorian house serves Pacific Northwest cuisine. Signature dishes include pork tenderloin stuffed with sun-dried cherries, and cherry-wood-smoked Carlton beef fillet. The menu also includes seafood. More than 600 wines, including 120 Oregon Pinot Noirs, are available in the restaurant or for sale in the adjoining wine shop. Many wines are also available by the glass. In warm months you can dine on the patio. ⊠ *729 E. 3rd St.,* ☎ *503/435–1745. MC, V. Closed Sun. No lunch Sat.*

$$–$$$ ⊞ **Flying M Ranch.** A great log lodge, decorated in a style best described
★ as Daniel Boone eclectic, is the centerpiece of the 625-acre Flying M Ranch, perched above the steelhead-filled Yamhill River. Choose between somewhat austere cabins (the cozy, hot-tub-equipped Honeymoon Cabin is the nicest) or riverside hotel units. In keeping with the rustic tone, there are no TVs or telephones. Book ahead for a Flying M specialty: the Steak Fry Ride, on which guests, aboard their choice of a horse or a tractor-drawn wagon, ride into the mountains for a feast of barbecued steak with all the trimmings. ⊠ *23029 N.W. Flying M Rd., Yamhill 97148 (from McMinnville, off Hwy. 99 W head north on North Baker Rd.—which becomes West Side Rd.—for 5 mi, head west on Meadowlake Rd., and follow signs),* ☎ *503/662–3222, FAX 503/ 662–3202. 24 units, 7 cabins, more than 100 campsites. Restaurant, bar, tennis court, basketball, hiking, horseback riding, horseshoes, fishing. AE, D, DC, MC, V.*

$$ ⊞ **Mattey House Bed & Breakfast.** This 100-year-old Victorian-style
★ home was built by English immigrant Joseph Mattey, a prosperous local butcher. Its cheerful faux-marble fireplace and gourmet breakfasts (poached pears with raspberry sauce, frittatas, and Dutch-apple pancakes are typical fare) have made this B&B an area favorite. ⊠ *10221 N.E. Mattey La. (off Hwy. 99 W, ¼ mi south of Lafayette), 97128,* ☎ *503/434–5058, FAX 503/434–6667. 4 rooms. MC, V.*

$ ⊞ **Safari Motor Inn.** More functional than its exotic name suggests, this motel on McMinnville's main drag has modest rates and clean accommodations with up-to-date furnishings. ⊠ *345 N. Hwy. 99 W, at 19th St., 97128,* ☎ *503/472–5187 or 800/321–5543, FAX 503/434–6380. 90 rooms. Restaurant, bar, hot tub, exercise room. AE, D, DC, MC, V.*

Outdoor Activities and Sports

Bayou Golf & Country Club (⊠ 9301 S.W. Bayou Dr., ☎ 503/472–4651), a 9-hole, par-36 course, has a $20 greens fee; a cart costs $12.

Shopping

A restored 1910 schoolhouse contains the **Lafayette Schoolhouse Antique Mall** (⊠ Hwy. 99 W, 5 mi north of McMinnville, ☎ 503/864–2720), Oregon's largest permanent antiques show.

Grand Ronde

24 mi southwest of McMinnville, on Hwy. 18.

There's not much to see in Grand Ronde, but thanks to its Indian-operated casino the town has become a busy stop en route to the coast.

Dining and Lodging

$$ ✕🏨 **Spirit Mountain Casino and Lodge.** Its location on Highway 18, one of the main routes from Portland to the ocean, makes this casino (owned and operated by the Confederated Tribes of the Grande Ronde Community of Oregon) a popular destination. Only 90 minutes from Portland and 45 minutes from Salem, this is the biggest casino resort in Oregon. The 183,000-square-ft casino has 1,100 slots, 15 poker tables, 35 blackjack tables, roulette, craps, Pai Gow poker, keno, bingo, and off-track betting. Big-name comedians and rock and country musicians perform in the 1,700-seat concert hall, and there's an arcade for the kids. Patrons can take advantage of complimentary shuttle service from Portland and Salem. Dining options include an all-you-can-eat buffet, a deli, and a café. A new hotel opened in 1998, with rooms decorated in Pacific Northwest and Native American themes. Beds have carved wooden headboards and Pendleton Woolen Mills bedding. ⊠ *27100 S.W. Hwy. 18, Grande Ronde 97396, ☎ 503/879–2350 or 800/760–7977. 100 rooms. 4 restaurants, lounge, room service, free valet parking. D, MC, V.*

Salem

24 mi from McMinnville, south on Hwy. 99 W, and east on Hwy. 22; 45 mi south of Portland on I–5.

Salem has a rich pioneer history, but before that it was the home of the Calapooyan Indians, who called it Chemeketa, which means "place of rest." The town was later settled by fur trappers, farmers, and missionaries. The Willamette River provided easy transport for lumber from nearby forests and produce grown on the fertile farmlands of the Central Valley. By 1842 the first university on the West Coast had been established; in 1862 the thriving river town of Salem became the capital of the new state of Oregon. The main attractions in the state's third-largest city are west of I–5 in and around the Capitol Mall.

Numbers in the text correspond to numbers in the margin and on the Salem map.

A Good Walk

Begin at Court Street and Oregon's **Capitol complex** ⑬. Behind the Capitol, just across State Street, is **Willamette University** ⑭. Cross over 12th Street to the **Mission Mill Village** ⑮. From there, stroll down 12th Street to **Deepwood Estate** ⑯, south of Salem's downtown district. West of here is **Bush's Pasture Park** ⑰.

TIMING

Without stopping for tours, this walk can be done in about two hours. Allot an additional half hour for a guided tour of the Capitol, two hours for a full tour of Mission Mill Village, and a half hour each for the house tours at Deepwood Estate and Bush's Pasture Park. If you're pressed for time, skip the Capitol and university and begin your tour at Mission Mill Village.

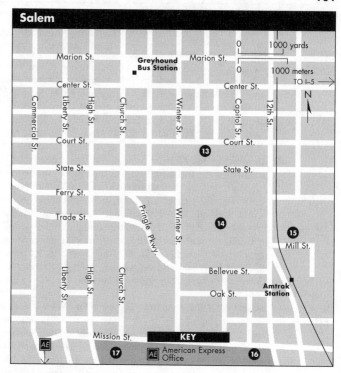

Sights to See

17 Bush's Pasture Park. These 105 acres of rolling lawn and formal English gardens include the remarkably well preserved **Bush House,** an 1878 Italianate mansion at the park's far western boundary. It has 10 marble fireplaces and virtually all of its original furnishings. The house and gardens are on the National Register of Historic Places. **Bush Barn Art Center,** behind the house, exhibits the work of Northwest artists and has a sales gallery. ⊠ *600 Mission St. SE,* ☎ *503/363–4714.* ☞ *$3.* ◷ *May–Sept., Tues.–Sun. noon–5; Oct.–Apr., Tues.–Sun. 2–5.*

16 Deepwood Estate. This fanciful 1894 Queen Anne–style house has splendid interior woodwork and original stained glass. An ornate gazebo from the 1905 Lewis and Clark expedition graces the fine gardens created in 1929 by landscape designers Elizabeth Lord and Edith Schryver. The estate is on the National Register of Historic Places. ⊠ *1116 Mission St. SE,* ☎ *503/363–1825.* ☞ *$4.* ◷ *May–Sept., Sun.–Fri. noon–4:30; Oct.–Apr., Sun.–Mon. and Wed.–Fri. 1–4.*

15 Mission Mill Village. The **Thomas Kay Woolen Mill Museum** complex (circa 1889), complete with working waterwheels and millstream, looks as if the workers have just stepped away for a lunch break. Teasel gigging, napper flock bins, and the patented Furber double-acting napper are but a few of the machines and processes on display. The **Jason Lee House,** the **John D. Boon Home,** and the **Methodist Parsonage** are also part of the village. There is nothing grandiose about these early pioneer homes, the oldest frame structures in the Northwest, but they reveal a great deal about domestic life in the wilds of Oregon in the 1840s. The adjacent **Marion County Historical Society Museum** (☎ 503/364–2128) displays pioneer and Calapooya Indian artifacts. ⊠ *Museum complex, 1313 Mill St. SE,* ☎ *503/585–7012.* ☞ *$5 (includes* *tour).* ☉ *Daily 10–4. Guided tours of houses and woolen mill museum leave from mill's admission booth every hr on the hr.*

OFF THE BEATEN PATH   **MOUNT ANGEL ABBEY –** This Benedictine monastery atop a 300-ft-high butte was founded in 1882. It's the site of one of two American buildings designed by Finnish architect Alvar Aalto. A masterpiece of serene and thoughtful design, Aalto's library opened its doors in 1970 and has become a place of pilgrimage for students and aficionados of modern architecture. ⊠ *18 mi from Salem, east on Hwy. 213 and north on Hwy. 214,* ☎ *503/845–3030.* 🎫 *Free.*

⑬ **Oregon Capitol.** A brightly gilded bronze statue of the Oregon Pioneer stands atop the 140-ft-high Capitol dome, looking north across the Capitol Mall. Built in 1939 with blocks of gray Vermont marble, Oregon's Capitol has an elegant yet austere neoclassical feel. New east and west wings were added in 1978. Relief sculptures and deft historical murals soften the interior. Tours of the rotunda, the house and senate chambers, and the governor's office leave from the information center under the dome. ⊠ *900 Court St.,* ☎ *503/986–1388.* 🎫 *Free.* ☉ *Weekdays 8–5, Sat. 9–4, Sun. noon–4. Guided tours Memorial Day–Labor Day, daily on the hr; rest of yr by appointment.*

OFF THE BEATEN PATH   **SCHREINER'S IRIS GARDENS –** Some call the Willamette Valley near Salem the "Bulb Basket of the Nation." Irises and tulips create fields of brilliant color in near-perfect growing conditions. Schreiner's Iris Gardens, established in 1925, ships bulbs all over the world; during the short spring growing season (mid-May–early June), the 10-acre display gardens are ablaze with fancifully named varieties such as Hello Darkness, Well Endowed, and Ringo. ⊠ *3625 Quinaby Rd. NE (north from Salem take I–5 to Exit 263, head west on Brooklake Rd., south on River Rd., and east on Quinaby),* ☎ *503/393–3232.* 🎫 *Free.* ☉ *8–dusk during blooming season only.*

⑭ **Willamette University.** Behind the Capitol, across State Street but half a world away, are the brick buildings and grounds of Willamette University, the oldest college in the West. Founded in 1842, Willamette has long been a mecca for aspiring politicians (former Oregon senators Mark O. Hatfield and Robert Packwood are alumni). **Hatfield Library,** built in 1986 on the banks of Mill Stream, is a handsome brick-and-glass building with a striking campanile; tall, prim **Waller Hall,** built in 1841, is one of the oldest buildings in the Pacific Northwest. ⊠ *Information Desk, Putnam University Center, Mill St.,* ☎ *503/370–6267.* ☉ *Weekdays 9–5.*

Dining and Lodging

$$–$$$ ✕ **DaVinci.** Salem politicos flock to this two-story downtown restaurant for Italian-inspired dishes cooked in a wood-burning oven. No shortcuts are taken in the preparation, so don't come if you're in a rush. But if you're in the mood to linger over seafood and fresh pasta that's made on the premises, you'll be more than content. The wine list is one of the most extensive in the Northwest; the staff is courteous and extremely professional. ⊠ *180 High St.,* ☎ *503/399–1413. AE, DC, MC, V. No lunch Sun.*

$ ✕ **Gerry Frank's Konditorei.** Furnished in the style of a European sidewalk café, this is *the* place to go in Salem for rich desserts. Sandwiches, salads, soup, and other simple entrées are served, but most people head straight for the display cases of homemade cakes, tortes, and cheesecakes with tempting names like "Orange Cloud" and "Blackout." ⊠ *310 Kearney St. SE,* ☎ *503/585–7070. D, MC, V.*

$ ✕ **Thompson Brewery & Public House.** The intimate rooms at this pub are decked out in a funky mix of '60s rock-and-roll memorabilia and hand-painted woodwork. India Pale Ale and Terminator Stout are among the beers made in a tiny brewery enlivened by colorful original art. The food—mostly hearty sandwiches, salads, and pasta dishes— is remarkably cheap. ✉ *3575 Liberty Rd. S,* ☎ *503/363–7286. AE, D, MC, V.*

$$ ▣ **Quality Inn.** The chief virtue of this clean, functional hotel is its location, about five minutes from the Capitol. ✉ *3301 Market St. NE, 97301,* ☎ *503/370–7888 or 800/228–5151,* ℻ *541/370–6305. 150 rooms. Restaurant, bar, no-smoking rooms, indoor pool, sauna, coin laundry, airport shuttle. AE, D, DC, MC, V.*

$$ ▣ **Ramada Inn.** This full-service hotel in downtown Salem is within walking distance of the Capitol. The comfortable rooms and suites have coffeemakers. Continental breakfast is complimentary. ✉ *200 Commercial St. SE, 97301,* ☎ *503/363–4123 or 800/272–6232,* ℻ *503/ 363–8993. 99 rooms, 15 suites. Restaurant, in-room data ports, no-smoking rooms, outdoor pool, hot tub, exercise room, laundry service and dry cleaning, meeting rooms, free parking. AE, D, DC, MC, V.*

$$ ▣ **Shilo Inn.** This all-suites inn near the Capitol features microwaves, coffeemakers, wet bars, hair dryers, voice mail, and irons. The generic rooms are comfortable, with sofas and writing tables. A complimentary Continental breakfast is included in the room rate. ✉ *3304 Market St., 97301,* ☎ *503/581–4001 or 800/222–2244,* ℻ *503/399–9385. 89 suites. Refrigerators, indoor pool, hot tub, steam room, exercise room, meeting rooms, airport shuttle, free parking. AE, D, DC, MC, V.*

$–$$ ▣ **State House Bed & Breakfast.** Twelve blocks from the Capitol Mall and Willamette University, this B&B has comfortable if smallish downstairs public areas and a hot tub that overlooks Mill Creek. The two simply furnished rooms on the second floor share a bath. The Grand Suite and the third-floor suite have kitchenettes. The noise level at this State Street property can be a bit high, but the convenient location and friendly proprietors are among the compensations. ✉ *2146 State St., 97301,* ☎ *503/363–2774,* ℻ *503/585–8812. 2 rooms share 1 bath, 2 suites. MC, V.*

Nightlife and the Arts

A flamboyant Tudor Gothic vaudeville house dating from 1926, the **Elsinore Theatre** (✉ 170 High St. SE, ☎ 503/375–3574) presents stage shows, concerts, and silent movies. The restored interior is worth seeing even if nothing is playing; call to arrange a tour.

Outdoor Activities and Sports

Battle Creek Golf Course (✉ 6161 Commercial St. SE, ☎ 503/585– 1402) is an 18-hole, par-72 course. The greens fee ranges $23–$25; a cart costs $20. The greens fee at the 18-hole, par-72 course at the **Salem Golf Club** (✉ 2025 Golf Course Rd., ☎ 503/363–6652) is $35 ($30 twilight); a cart costs $20.

En Route   South of Salem, the **Enchanted Forest** is the closest thing Oregon has to a major theme park. The park has several attractions in a forest setting, including the newest, the Big Timber Log Ride. On it, you ride logs through flumes that pass through a lumber mill and the woods. The ride—the biggest log ride in the Northwest—features a 25-ft roller-coaster dip and a 40-ft drop at the end. Other attractions include the Ice Mountain Bobsled roller coaster, the Haunted House, English Village, Storybook Lane, the Fantasy Fountains Water Light Show, Fort Fearless, and the western town of Tofteville. The park is located 7 mi south of Salem at Exit 248 off I–5. ✉ *8462 Enchanted Way SE, Turner 97392,* ☎ *503/363–3060.* ▱ *Adults $6.95 (some attractions cost* *extra).* ⊘ *Mar.–Labor Day, daily 9:30–6; Labor Day–Sept. 30, week-ends 9:30–6.*

Silver Falls State Park

★ ⓲ *26 mi east of Salem, Hwy. 22 to Hwy. 214.*

Hidden amid old-growth Douglas firs in the foothills of the Cascades, **Silver Falls** is the largest state park in Oregon (8,700 acres). South Falls, roaring over the lip of a mossy basalt bowl into a deep pool 177 ft below, is the main attraction here, but 13 other waterfalls—half of them more than 100 ft high—are accessible to hikers. The best time to visit is in the fall, when vine maples blaze with brilliant color, or early spring, when the forest floor is carpeted with trilliums and yellow violets. There are picnic facilities and a day lodge; during the winter you can cross-country ski. ⊠ *20024 Silver Falls Hwy. SE, Sublimity,* ☏ *800/551–6949.* 🄳 *$3 per vehicle.* ⊘ *Daily dawn–dusk.*

Albany

46 mi south of Silver Springs State Park on I–5 and Hwy. 20; 20 mi from Salem, south on I–5 and west on U.S. 20.

To see what a quintessential Willamette Valley river town looked like before the major highways were built, explore Albany, a former wheat and produce center. The town's 700 historic buildings, scattered over a 100-block area in three districts, include every major architectural style in the United States from 1850. Eight covered bridges can also be seen on a half-hour drive from Albany. Pamphlets and maps for self-guided walking and driving tours are available from the **Albany Visitors Association** (⊠ 300 S.W. 2nd Ave., ☏ 541/928–0911 or 800/526–2256), open weekdays from 9 to 5.

Dining

$$ ✕ **Novak's Hungarian Paprikas.** The Hungarian owners of this un-pretentious restaurant turn out native specialties such as *kolbasz* (home-made sausages with sweet-and-sour cabbage) and beef *szelet* (crispy batter-fried cutlets) with virtuosity. The restaurant's only drawback is its lack of a liquor license. ⊠ *2835 Santiam Hwy. SE,* ☏ *541/967–9488. MC, V. No lunch Sat.*

Corvallis

10 mi southwest of Albany on U.S. 20; 35 mi from Salem, south on I–5 and west on Hwy. 34.

The pioneers who settled Corvallis in 1847 named their town for its location in the "heart of the valley." About halfway between Salem and Eugene, Corvallis is not so much a sightseeing mecca as it is a good place to stop for a meal or spend the night. Driving or strolling through its quiet neighborhoods, along streets lined with stately trees, it's easy to get the impression that time here stopped sometime in the 1950s.

The pace quickens around the 500-acre campus of **Oregon State University** (⊠ 15th and Jefferson Sts., ☏ 541/737–0123), west of the city center. Established as a land-grant institution in 1868, OSU (or "Moo U" as it's sometimes called) is home to more than 15,000 students, many of them studying the agricultural sciences and engineering. Exhibits at the **Horner Museum** (⊠ Gill Coliseum, 26th and Washington Sts., ☏ 541/754–2951) detail Oregon's animal, mineral, and human history.

Dining and Lodging

$$-$$$ ✕ **Big River.** A former Greyhound bus depot holds one of Corvallis's most popular restaurants. The menu changes frequently but emphasizes foods from Oregon—pan-seared salmon, grilled chicken, and roasted lamb shanks. This is one of the few places in Corvallis to snag a good martini or single-malt Scotch. Musicians perform on Friday and Saturday night. ⊠ *101 N.W. Jackson St.,* ☎ *541/757–0694. AE, MC, V. Closed Sun. No lunch Sat.*

$$-$$$ ✕ **The Gables.** The most romantic restaurant in Corvallis has dark wood paneling and a straightforward menu of steaks, seafood, local lamb, and prime ribs. The portions are huge and satisfying. ⊠ *1121 N.W. 9th St.,* ☎ *541/752–3364. Reservations essential. AE, D, DC, MC, V. No lunch.*

$$ 🏨 **Ramada Inn.** This full-service motel is located near Oregon State University. The comfortable rooms have coffeemakers. ⊠ *1550 N.W. 9th St., 97330,* ☎ *541/753–9151,* ℻ *541/758–7089. 120 rooms. Restaurant, lounge, in-room data ports, no-smoking rooms, room service, outdoor pool, laundry service and dry cleaning, meeting rooms. AE, D, DC, MC, V.*

$$ 🏨 **Harrison House.** Maria Tomlinson runs this B&B in a 1939 Dutch Colonial–style home three blocks from the OSU campus. Chippendale, Queen Anne, and Colonial Williamsburg–era furniture fills the living and dining rooms. The three rooms on the second floor and one on the first are spacious and immaculate. The rates include a breakfast of Belgian waffles or eggs Benedict. ⊠ *2310 N.W. Harrison Rd., 97330,* ☎ *541/752–6248 or 800/233–6248,* ℻ *541/754–1353. 4 rooms, 2 with bath. AE, D, DC, MC, V.*

Outdoor Activities and Sports

GOLF

Trysting Tree Golf Club (⊠ 34028 Electric Rd., ☎ 541/752–3332) has an 18-hole, par-72 course. The greens fee is $28; a cart costs $22.

Brownsville

27 mi south of Corvallis off I–5.

Brownsville is another Willamette Valley town that has retained much of its original character. The **Linn County Historical Museum,** housed in Brownsville's 1890 railroad depot, has some noteworthy pioneer-era exhibits, including a covered wagon that arrived in 1865 after a trek along the Oregon Trail from Missouri. ⊠ *101 Park Ave.,* ☎ *541/ 466–3390.* 🎟 *Free.* ☉ *Mon.–Sat. 11–4, Sun. 1–5.*

Eugene

63 mi south of Corvallis on I–5.

Eugene was founded in 1846 when Eugene Skinner staked the first federal land-grant claim for pioneers. Back then it was called Skinner's Mudhole. Wedged between two landmark buttes—Skinner and Spencer—along the Willamette River, Eugene is the culinary, cultural, sports, and intellectual hub of the central Willamette Valley. The home of the University of Oregon is consistently given high marks for its "livability." A large student and former-student population lends Oregon's second-largest city a youthful vitality and countercultural edge. Full of parks and oriented to the outdoors, Eugene is a place where bike paths are used, pedestrians *always* have the right-of-way, and joggers are so plentiful that the city is known as the running capital of the world.

Past urban-renewal schemes helped to make downtown Eugene more pedestrian friendly but the area still lacks life—there are few exciting eateries, nightspots, or attractions. Shopping and commercial streets surround the Eugene Hilton and the world-class Hult Center for the Performing Arts (☞ Nightlife and the Arts, *below*), the two most prominent downtown buildings. Stock up on maps and information about the Eugene area at the **Lane County Convention and Visitors Association** (✉ 115 Olive St., between 7th and 8th Aves., ☎ 800/547–5445).

Numbers in the text correspond to numbers in the margin and on the Eugene map.

A Good Walk

From downtown Eugene, walk north across the Willamette River on the Autzen Footbridge and stroll through **Alton Baker Park.** Head north to the entertaining **Wistec** ⑲ science and technology museum, which is just outside the park to the west of Autzen Stadium. Or follow the path that leads west along the river. Walk back across the Willamette River via the Ferry Street Bridge to Gateway Park. Stay to the left at the end of the bridge and you'll eventually hit High Street. Head south on High to the **5th Street Public Market** ⑳ (which, despite its name, is on 5th Avenue). The market is a great place to have lunch. You'll need fortification for your next stop, **Skinner Butte Park** ㉑. From the market take 5th Avenue west and Lincoln Street north. If you're feeling hardy, you can climb to the top of Skinner Butte for a great view. The **George E. Owen Memorial Rose Garden** ㉒ is west of the park. Follow the bike path west from Skinner Butte Park along the Willamette River to the garden.

TIMING

This tour takes more than half a day unless you drive it. Plan to spend an hour or so at each stop, and add an extra hour if you visit the science center.

Sights to See

Alton Baker Park. There's fine hiking and biking at Alton Baker, the largest of three adjoining riverside parks—Gateway and Skinner Butte are the other two—on the banks of the Willamette River. A footpath along the river runs the length of the park. ✉ *Centennial Blvd. east of the Ferry St. Bridge.* ☉ *Daily dawn–dusk.*

⑳ 5th Street Public Market. A former chicken-processing plant houses this combination shopping mall and food court. The dining options range from sit-down restaurants to decadent bakeries (the Metropol Bakery on the building's lower level is especially fine) to the bewildering international diversity of the second-floor food esplanade. ✉ *5th Ave. and High St.,* ☎ *541/484–0383.* ☉ *Shops daily 10–6 (Fri. until 9), restaurants daily 7 AM–9 PM (weekends until 10).*

Hendricks Park. This quiet park east of the University of Oregon is at its most glorious in May, when its towering rhododendrons and azaleas blossom in shades of pink, yellow, red, and purple. From the university's Franklin Boulevard gate, head south on Agate Street, east on 19th Avenue, south on Fairmont Boulevard, and east on Summit Avenue. ✉ *Summit and Skyline Aves.*

Maude Kerns Art Center. The oldest church in Eugene, two blocks east of the university, houses this arts facility, which exhibits contemporary fine arts and crafts. ✉ *1910 E. 15th Ave.,* ☎ *541/345–1571.* 🎟 *Free.* ☉ *Mon.–Sat. 10–5, Sun. 1–5.*

㉒ George E. Owen Memorial Rose Garden. Three thousand roses bloom from June to September at this 9-acre garden west of Skinner Butte Park,

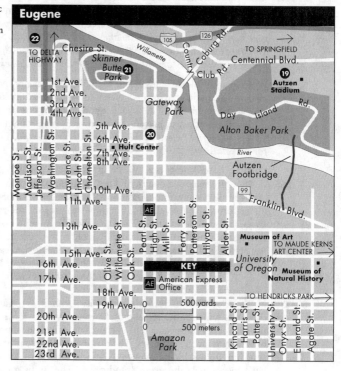

along the Willamette River. Magnolia, cherry, and oak trees dot the grounds. ✉ *300 N. Jefferson St.,* ☎ *541/682–4800.* 🎟 *Free.* ☉ *Daily 6 AM–11 PM.*

㉑ Skinner Butte Park. Eugene's parks and gardens are wonderfully diverse and add to the outdoor fabric of the city. Skinner Butte Park, rising from the south bank of the Willamette River, has the most historical cachet, since it was here that Eugene Skinner staked the claim that put Eugene on the map. Skinner Butte Loop leads to the top of Skinner Butte, from which **Spencer Butte,** 4 mi to the south, can be seen. The two main trails to the top of Skinner Butte traverse a sometimes difficult terrain through a mixed-conifer forest. ✉ *2nd Ave. and High St.,* ☎ *541/682–5521.* 🎟 *Free.* ☉ *Daily 10 AM–midnight.*

University of Oregon. The true heart of Eugene lies southeast of the city center at its university. Several fine old buildings can be seen on the 250-acre campus; **Deady Hall,** built in 1876, is the oldest. More than 400 varieties of trees grace the bucolic grounds, along with outdoor sculptures that include *Pioneer* and *Pioneer Mother.* The two bronze figures by Alexander Phimster Proctor were dedicated to the men and women who settled the Oregon Territory and less than a generation later founded the university. Track star Steve Prefontaine and Nike shoes founder Phil Knight attended school here and helped to establish Eugene's reputation as Tracktown, U.S.A.

Eugene's two best museums are affiliated with the university. The collection of Asian art at the **University of Oregon Museum of Art** (✉ 1430 Johnson La., ☎ 541/346–3027), next to the library, includes examples of Chinese imperial tomb figures, textiles, and furniture. Relics of a more localized nature are on display at the **University of Oregon Museum of Natural History** (✉ 1680 E. 15th Ave., ☎ 541/346–3024). Devoted to Pacific Northwest anthropology and the natural sciences, its highlights include the fossil collection of Thomas Condon, Oregon's first geologist, and a pair of 9,000-year-old sagebrush sandal. ⊠ *University of Oregon main entrance: Agate St. and Franklin Blvd.* ⌾ *$3 suggested donation for both museums.* ⊙ *Art museum Wed. noon–8, Thurs.–Sun. noon–5; natural history museum Wed.–Fri. noon–5, weekends 11–5.*

🅒 ⑲ **Wistec.** Eugene's imaginative, hands-on Willamette Science and Technology Center—Wistec to the locals—assembles rotating exhibits designed for curious young minds. The adjacent **planetarium**, one of the largest in the Pacific Northwest, presents star shows and entertainment events. ⊠ *2300 Leo Harris Pkwy.,* ☏ *541/682–3020 for museum; 541/687–7827 for planetarium.* ⌾ *$4.* ⊙ *Wed.–Fri. noon–5, weekends 11–5.*

Dining and Lodging

$$$ ✕ **Chanterelle.** Some diners find the European cuisine at this romantic 14-table restaurant old-fashioned, but the chef, Rolf Schmidt, sees no reason to go nouvelle. He continues to prepare the region's beef, lamb, and seafood in a traditional Old World manner. Crystal and fresh flowers fill Chanterelle, which is in an old warehouse across from the 5th Street Public Market. For several weeks during the year the restaurant is closed on Sunday and Monday. ⊠ *207 E. 5th Ave.,* ☏ *541/484–4065. AE, DC, MC, V. Closed Sun.–Mon., last 2 wks Mar., 1st wk Apr., last 2 wks Aug., 1st wk Sept. No lunch.*

$$–$$$ ✕ **Excelsior Café.** Its accomplished cuisine enhances the appealing Eu-
★   ropean elegance of this restaurant, bar, and bistro-style café across from the University of Oregon. The chef uses only fresh local produce, some of it grown on the premises. The menu changes according to the season, but staples include delicious salads and soups, gnocchi, grilled chicken, broiled salmon, and sandwiches. The dining room, shaded by blossoming cherry trees in the spring, has a quiet, understated atmosphere. There's outdoor seating on the front terrace or under a grape arbor in the back; in good weather both are fine places to take Sunday brunch. ⊠ *Excelsior Inn, 754 E. 13th Ave.,* ☏ *541/342–6963. AE, D, DC, MC, V.*

$$ ✕ **Zenon Cafe.** You never know what you'll find on the menu here—Thai, Indian, Italian, South American, or down-home barbecue—but it's sure to be memorable and expertly prepared. Slate floors, picture windows, Parisian-style street lamps, marble-top tables, and café chairs lend this eatery the feel of a romantic, open-air bistro. The desserts are formidable—two full-time bakers produce 20 to 30 daily. Look for the *zuccotto Fiorentino,* a dove-shape Italian wedding cake with rum, orange, and flavored whipped cream. ⊠ *898 Pearl St.,* ☏ *541/343–3005. Reservations not accepted. MC, V.*

$–$$ ✕ **Mekala's.** The emphasis at this eatery in the Fifth Street Public Market is on healthful yet zippy Thai staples such as pad thai and curries. ⊠ *296 E. 5th Ave.,* ☏ *541/342–4872. AE, MC, V.*

$ ✕ **Poppi's Anatolia.** The moussaka and *kalamarakia* (fried squid) at this home-style Greek restaurant are great; wash them down with retsina or Aegean beer. Except on Sunday nights, when the chef prepares only Greek dishes, you can also sample East Indian specialties. ⊠ *992 Willamette St.,* ☏ *541/343–9661. MC, V. No lunch Sun.*

$$$–$$$$ ✕🅣 **Valley River Inn.** Eugene's only four-star hotel, one of the few in
★   Oregon, is set on the banks of the Willamette River. Some rooms have an outdoor patio or balcony, some have river or pool views, and concierge rooms have access to a private lounge. All rooms have hair dryers, coffeemakers, and irons. In Sweetwaters restaurant overlooking the river, you can dine on Pacific Northwest cuisine such as salmon with Szechuan peppercorn crust and cranberry vinaigrette. Book the fishing package and the concierge will arrange a river or ocean fishing trip; when you get back the chef will prepare your catch just for you. ⊠ *1000 Val-*

ley River Way, Eugene 97401. ☎ 503/629–9465 or 800/543–8266. 257 rooms. Restaurant, bar, pool, hot tub, steam room, exercise room, bicycles, laundry service and dry cleaning, concierge, business services, meeting rooms, airport shuttle, free parking. AE, D, DC, MC, V.

$$–$$$$ 🏨 **Campbell House.** Built in 1892 on the east side of Skinner Butte, Campbell House is one of the oldest structures in Eugene. Restored with fastidious care, the luxurious B&B is surrounded by an acre of landscaped grounds. The parlor, library, and dining rooms have their original hardwood floors and curved-glass windows. Differing architectural details, building angles, and furnishings (a mixture of century-old antiques and reproductions) lend each of the rooms a distinctive personality. One suite has a whirlpool. The room rates include a breakfast of fresh-baked pastries and other items. ⊠ 252 Pearl St., 97401, ☎ 541/343–1119 or 800/264–2519, FAX 541/343–2258. 12 rooms, 6 suites. No-smoking rooms, in-room VCRs. AE, D, MC, V.

$$–$$$$ 🏨 **Excelsior Inn.** This small hotel in a former frat house manifests a
★ quiet sophistication more commonly found in Europe than in America. Crisply detailed, with cherry-wood doors and moldings, it has rooms furnished in a refreshingly understated manner, each with a marble-and-tile bath. The rates include a delicious breakfast. The ground-level Excelsior Café is one of Eugene's best restaurants. ⊠ 754 E. 13th Ave., 97401, ☎ 541/342–6963 or 800/321–6963, FAX 541/342–1417. 14 rooms. Restaurant, bar, café, in-room data ports, in-room VCRs, no-smoking rooms, free parking. AE, D, DC, MC, V.

$$–$$$ 🏨 **Eugene Hilton.** Location, amenities, and service make this downtown hotel Eugene's most convenient and comfortable. Sliding glass doors in each of the rooms open out to the city. The top-floor restaurant, Vistas, and CJ's, the adjacent bar, have the best butte-to-butte view in Eugene. The Hilton and its extensive convention facilities adjoin Eugene's Hult Center for the Performing Arts. Downtown shopping, the Willamette River, and more than 30 restaurants are within easy walking distance. ⊠ 66 E. 6th Ave., 97401, ☎ 541/342–2000 or 800/937–6660, FAX 541/342–6661. 272 rooms. 2 restaurants, 2 bars, indoor pool, beauty salon, hot tub, exercise room, free parking, airport shuttle. AE, D, DC, MC, V.

$$ 🏨 **New Oregon Best Western.** The plush furnishings and comprehensive amenities at this midsize motel near the University of Oregon come as a bit of a surprise, given the property's price range. ⊠ 1655 Franklin Blvd., 97403, ☎ 541/683–3669, FAX 541/484–5556. 129 rooms. In-room data ports, no-smoking floor, refrigerators, indoor pool, hot tub, sauna, exercise room, racquetball, laundry service and dry cleaning, free parking. AE, D, DC, MC, V.

Nightlife and the Arts

The **Hult Center For the Performing Arts** (⊠ 1 Eugene Centre, ☎ 541/682–5087), a spacious building of glass and native wood, is the locus of Eugene's cultural life. Renowned for the quality of their acoustics, the center's two theaters are home base for Eugene's symphony and opera companies (☞ below). There's nearly always something going on—ballets, major performers, traveling Broadway shows, and rock bands appear regularly.

Conductor Helmuth Rilling leads the internationally known **Oregon Bach Festival** (☎ 541/346–5666 or 800/457–1486) every summer. Concerts, chamber music, and social events—held mainly in Eugene at the Hult Center and the University of Oregon School of Music but also in Corvallis and Florence—are part of this 17-day event. In May and August, the **Oregon Festival of American Music** (☎ 541/687–6526 or 800/248–1615) presents concerts at the Hult Center and parks around Eugene. **Oregon Mozart Players** (☎ 541/345–6648), the state's premier professional chamber music orchestra, plays 20 concerts a year. The **Eugene Opera** (☎ 541/682–5000) produces three fully staged operas per season. The **Eugene Symphony** (☎ 541/687–9487) performs a full season of classical, family, and pops concerts.

Outdoor Activities and Sports

BASEBALL

The **Eugene Emeralds,** the Northwest League (Class A) affiliate of the Atlanta Braves, play at Civic Stadium (✉ 2077 Willamette St., ☎ 541/342–5367).

BASKETBALL

The **University of Oregon Ducks** play at MacArthur Court (✉ 1601 University St., ☎ 800/932–3668).

BIKING AND JOGGING

The **River Bank Bike Path,** originating in Alton Baker Park on the Willamette's north bank, is a level and leisurely introduction to Eugene's topography. It's one of 120 mi of trails in the area. **Prefontaine Trail,** used by area runners, travels through level fields and forests for 1½ mi. **Pedal Power** (✉ 535 High St., ☎ 541/687–1775) downtown rents bikes.

FOOTBALL

The **University of Oregon Ducks** play their home games at Autzen Stadium (✉ 2700 Centennial Blvd., ☎ 800/932–3668).

GOLF

Riveridge Golf Course (✉ 3800 N. Delta Hwy., ☎ 541/345–9160) is an 18-hole, par-71 course. The greens fee is $25; a cart costs $22.

SKIING

Willamette Pass (✉ Hwy. 58, 69 mi southeast of Eugene, ☎ 541/345–7669 or 800/444–5030), 6,666 ft high in the Cascades Range, packs an annual average snowfall of 300 inches atop 29 runs. The vertical drop is 1,563 ft. Four triple chairs and one double chair service the downhill ski areas, and 13 mi of Nordic trails lace the pass. Facilities here include a ski shop, day care, a bar, a restaurant, and Nordic and downhill rentals, repairs, and instruction.

Shopping

Valley River Center (✉ Delta Hwy. and Valley River Dr., 97401, ☎ 541/683–5511) is the largest shopping center between Portland and San Francisco. There are five department stores, including Bon Marché, Meier & Frank, and JCPenney, plus 144 specialty shops and a food court.

Every Saturday between April and Christmas, local craftspeople, farmers, and chefs come together from 10 to 5 to create the weekly **Eugene Saturday Market** (✉ 76 W. Broadway, ☎ 541/686–8885), a great people-watching event with cheap eats and nifty arts and crafts.

OFF THE
BEATEN PATH

HIGHWAY 126 WEST OF EUGENE – Westward toward the coast, Highway 126 curves past several wineries and the trout-filled Siuslaw River before ending in Florence (☞ The Oregon Coast, *above*).Two of the best-known wineries are **Hinman Vineyards** (✉ 27012 Briggs Hill Rd., south of Hwy. 126, Eugene, ☎ 541/345–1945) and **LaVelle Vineyards** (✉ 89697 Scheffler Rd., north of Hwy. 126, Elmira, ☎ 541/935–9406).

WALDO LAKE – Nestled in old-growth forest, Waldo Lake is thought by some to be the cleanest landlocked body of water in the world. The lake is only accessible after a short hike, so bring comfortable walking attire. ✉ *From Eugene take Hwy. 58 to Oakridge and continue toward Willamette Pass (follow signs north to Waldo Lake).*

McKenzie River Highway

East of Eugene on Hwy. 126 (52 mi to town of McKenzie Bridge).

Highway 126 as it heads east from Eugene is known as the McKenzie River Highway. Following the curves of the river, it passes grazing lands, fruit and nut orchards, and the small riverside hamlets of the McKenzie Valley. From the highway you can glimpse the bouncing, bubbling, blue-green **McKenzie River,** one of Oregon's top fishing, boating, and white-water rafting spots, against a backdrop of densely forested mountains, splashing waterfalls, and jet-black lava beds. The small town of McKenzie Bridge marks the end of the McKenzie River Highway and the beginning of the 26-mi **McKenzie River National Recreation Trail,** which heads north through the Willamette National Forest along portions of the Old Santiam Wagon Road.

Dining and Lodging

$$ ✕🏨 **Log Cabin Inn.** This inn on the banks of the wild, fish-filled McKenzie River is equally appropriate for a fishing vacation or a romantic weekend getaway. Antique furniture decorates log-cabin-style buildings; each room has a river view. Six riverfront tepees share a bath. Menu standouts at the delightful restaurant include wild boar, quail, salmon, a decadent homemade beer-cheese soup, and a locally famous marionberry cobbler. ✉ *56483 McKenzie Hwy., 97413,* ☎ *541/822–3432 or 800/355–3432,* 📠 *541/822–6173. 8 cabins, 6 tepees. Restaurant, bar, fishing. MC, V.*

Outdoor Activities and Sports

BOATING AND RAFTING

Oregon Whitewater Adventures (✉ 39620 Deerhorn Rd., Springfield, ☎ 541/746–5422 or 800/820–7238) operates half- to two-day rafting excursions on the river.

OFF THE
BEATEN PATH

McKENZIE PASS – Just beyond McKenzie Bridge, Highway 242 begins a steep, 22-mi eastward climb to McKenzie Pass in the Cascade Range. The scenic highway, which passes through the Mount Washington Wilderness Area and continues to the town of Sisters (☞ Central Oregon, *below*), is generally closed October–June because of heavy snow.

Roseburg and the Umpqua Valley

㉓ *73 mi south of Eugene on I–5 (to town of Roseburg).*

Roseburg is a name sacred to fishermen the world over. The town on the North Umpqua River is home to a dozen popular fish species, including bass, brown and brook trout, and chinook, coho, and sockeye salmon.

Sights to See

Douglas County Museum. One of the best county museums in the state, this museum surveys 8,000 years of human activity in the region. Its fossil collection, which includes a million-year-old saber-toothed tiger, is worth a stop. ✉ *123 Museum Dr.,* ☎ *541/957–7007.* 🎟 *$3.50.* ☉ *Weekdays 9–5, Sat. 10–5, Sun. 1–5.*

★ ☻ **Wildlife Safari.** Come face to face with free-roaming animals at this 600-acre, drive-through wildlife park. There's also a petting zoo, a miniature train, and elephant rides. The admission price includes two drive-throughs in the same day. From I–5 take Exit 119, follow Highway 42 west 3 mi to Lookingglass Road, and take a right on Safari Road. ✉ *Box 1600, Winston 97496,* ☎ *800/355–4848.* 🎟 *$11.95. AE, D, MC, V.* ☉ *Mar.–Oct., daily 9–7; Nov.–Feb., daily 10–4.*

Area Wineries

Admission to wineries is free. Some tasting rooms charge a nominal fee, but most offer complimentary samples.

Callahan Ridge Winery, which has won prizes for its Zinfandel and late-harvest Rieslings, hosts the Cure for the Summertime Blues Festival of music, crafts, food, and games each July. ⊠ *340 Busenbark La., Roseburg (from I–5's Exit 125 head northwest on Garden Valley Rd. and west on Melrose Rd.),* ☏ *541/673–7901 or 800/695–4946.* ◔ *Apr.–Dec., daily 11:30–5; rest of yr by appointment.*

Girardet Wine Cellars has won gold medals for its Bacot Noir and other wines—its Pinot Noir and rare Maréchal Foch are two standouts. ⊠ *895 Reston Rd., Tenmile (from I–5's Exit 119 head south on Hwy. 99 to the town of Winston, west on Hwy. 42, and north on Reston),* ☏ *541/679–7252.* ◔ *Mar.–Aug., daily 11–5; Sept.–Feb., Sat. 11–5.*

Henry Estate Winery, north of Roseburg along the Umpqua River, produces Pinot Noir, Chardonnay, Gewürtztraminer, and Riesling wines. The vineyard's flower garden is perfect for summer picnics. ⊠ *678 Hubbard Creek Rd., Umpqua (from I–5's Exit 136 head west ¼ mi on Hwy. 138 and take the 1st left onto Fort McKay Rd.—on some maps the Sutherlin–Umpqua Rd. or County Rd. 9—which runs into Hubbard Creek),* ☏ *541/459–5120.* ◔ *Daily 11–5.*

An early (1960s) entrant in the Oregon wine-making industry, **Hillcrest Vineyard** specializes in dry Riesling and Cabernet Sauvignon wines but also produces Zinfandels, unusual for these parts. The panoramic views of the countryside from here are splendid. ⊠ *240 Vineyard La., Roseburg (from I–5's Exit 125, head west on Garden Valley Rd. to Melrose Rd. to Doerner Rd. and north on Elgarose Loop Rd.),* ☏ *800/736–3709.* ◔ *Daily 11–5.*

La Garza Cellars, which is known for its Cabernet Sauvignon and Chardonnay wines, has a covered deck for picnics and a shop that sells many regional wines. A restaurant, La Garza Gourmet, is open during the summer Wednesday–Sunday 11–4. ⊠ *491 S.W. Winery La., Roseburg (head southwest from I–5's Exit 119 to Winery La. and turn left),* ☏ *541/679–9654.* ◔ *June–Sept., daily 11–5; Oct.–May, Wed.–Sun. noon–4.*

Dining and Lodging

$–$$ ✕ **Tolly's.** You can go formal or informal at this restaurant in Oakland, 18 mi north of Roseburg. Have an old-fashioned soda or malt downstairs in the Victorian ice cream parlor, or head upstairs to the oak- and antiques-filled dining room for expertly prepared beef, chicken, seafood, and lamb. Try the grilled salmon or the grilled flank steak marinated and served with fiery chipotle chilies. ⊠ *115 Locust St. (take I–5's Exit 138 and follow the road north from the exit for 4 mi, cross the railroad tracks, and turn west on Locust),* ☏ *541/459–3796.* AE, D, MC, V.

$$–$$$ ✕▥ **The Steamboat Inn.** Oregon's most famous fishing lodge was first
★ brought to the world's attention in the 1930s in travel articles by the western writer Zane Grey. Every fall a Who's Who of the world's top fly fishermen converges here, high in the Cascades above the emerald North Umpqua River, in search of the 20-pound steelhead that haunt these waters. (Guide services are available, as are equipment rentals and sales.) Others come simply to relax in the reading nooks or on the broad decks of the riverside guest cabins. Another renowned attraction is the nightly Fisherman's Dinner, a multicourse feast served around a massive 50-year-old sugar-pine dinner table. Lodging choices include riverside cabins, forest bungalows, and riverside suites; the bun-

galows and suites have kitchens. Make reservations well in advance, especially for a stay between July and October, the prime fishing months. Smoking is not permitted. The inn is closed in January and February. ✉ 42705 N. Umpqua Hwy. (38 mi east of Roseburg on Hwy. 138, near Steamboat Creek), Steamboat 97447, ☎ 541/498–2230, FAX 541/498–2411. 8 cabins, 5 bungalows, 2 suites. Restaurant, library, meeting room. MC, V.

$$ ✕🏨 **Seven Feathers Hotel and Casino Resort.** Located just south of Roseburg, about halfway between Medford and Eugene, is a hotel and a casino owned by the Cow Creek Tribe. It features 500 slots, blackjack, roulette, poker, craps, keno, and bingo. Big-name entertainers perform in the showroom, and for the kids, there's an arcade and an ice cream parlor. Guests of the hotel receive a complimentary Continental breakfast. There's also a 32-space RV park. ✉ 146 Chief Miwaleta La., Canyonville 97417, ☎ 800/548–8461. 154 rooms. 2 restaurants, lounge, in-room data ports, indoor pool, hot tubs, steam room, exercise room, concierge. AE, MC, V.

OFF THE
BEATEN PATH

ROGUE RIVER VIEWS – Nature lovers who want a glimpse of the Rogue River's loveliest angle can take a side trip to the Avenue of the Boulders, Mill Creek Falls, and Barr Creek Falls, off Highway 62, near Prospect. Here the wild waters of the upper Rogue foam through volcanic boulders and the dense greenery of the Rogue River National Forest.

Crater Lake National Park

★ ❷ 85 mi east of Roseburg on Hwy. 138; 71 mi northeast of Medford on Hwy. 62.

Oregon's only national park got its start 7,700 years ago, when Mount Mazama erupted in a volcanic explosion that spewed hot ash and pumice for hundreds of miles. Rain and snowmelt eventually filled the resulting caldera, creating a sapphire-blue lake so clear that sunlight penetrates to a depth of 400 ft. In 1902 this geological curiosity, the crown jewel of the Cascades and Oregon's most famous tourist attraction, was established as **Crater Lake National Park.** The park is closed most of the year because of heavy snows, but the north and south entrance roads are generally clear by early June. Peak visiting times are July and August, but even then you'll rarely encounter a traffic jam. Drive, bicycle, or hike Crater Lake's 25-mi rim; watch the chipmunks along either **Godfrey Glen Nature Trail** or the 4-mi **Castle Crest Wildflower Trail;** or take a boat ride out to **Wizard Island,** a perfect miniature cinder cone protruding 760 ft above the surface of the lake. Private boats are not allowed on Crater Lake, so these tours provide a unique surface-level view of the caldera. Several times a day from June to early September, boat tours leave from Cleetwood Cove on the lake's north side. ✉ Steel Information Center: Munson Valley Rd. on south side of park (follow signs from entrances), ☎ 541/594–2211. 🎟 Day use $10 per vehicle, campsites $10–$15. ☉ Visitor center daily 9–5. Rim Dr. closed mid-Sept.–mid-May.

Dining and Lodging

$$–$$$ ✕ **Dining Room at Crater Lake Lodge.** Open for breakfast, lunch, and dinner, this restaurant serves ambitious fare in decidedly upscale surroundings. The room itself is magnificent, with a large stone fireplace and views out over the clear blue waters of Crater Lake. This is virtually the only place to dine well once you're in the park. The evening menu usually includes fresh Pacific Northwest seafood, a pasta dish, pork medallions, and steak Oscar. The wines are from Oregon and Wash-

Crater Lake National Park

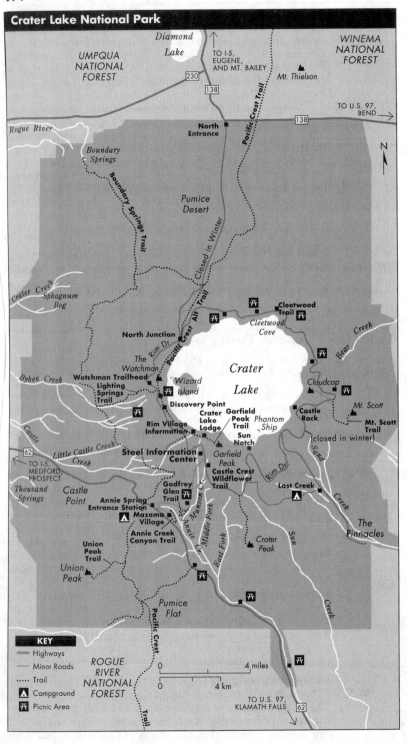

UMPQUA
NATIONAL
FOREST

Diamond
Lake

WINEMA
NATIONAL
FOREST

TO I-5,
EUGENE,
AND MT. BAILEY

[230]
[138]

Mt. Thielson

Pacific Crest Trail

TO U.S. 97,
BEND →

[138]

Rogue River

Boundary
Springs

North
Entrance

N

Pumice
Desert

Boundary Springs Trail

Closed in Winter

Crater Creek

Sphagnum
Bog

Cleetwood
Trail

Cleetwood
Cove

Bear
Creek

North Junction

Rim Dr.

Pacific Crest Alt Trail

Crater
Lake

Claudcap

The Watchman

Bybee Creek

Watchman Trailhead

Wizard
Island

Mt. Scott

Lighting
Springs
Trail

Discovery Point

Castle
Rock

Mt. Scott
Trail

Phantom
Ship

Sand
Creek

(closed in winter)

Castle

Rim Village
Information

Crater
Lake
Lodge

Garfield
Peak
Trail

Sun
Notch

[62]

Little Castle Creek

Steel Information
Center

Garfield Peak

Castle Crest
Wildflower
Trail

Rim Dr.

Lost Creek

TO I-5,
MEDFORD,
PROSPECT

Creek

Thousand
Springs

Castle
Point

Godfrey
Glen Trail

Annie Creek

Middle Fork

The
Pinnacles

Annie Spring
Entrance Station

Mazama
Village

Sun

Annie Creek
Canyon Trail

East Fork

Crater
Peak

Union
Peak
Trail

Union
Peak

Creek

Pacific Crest

Pumice
Flat

KEY

Highways

Minor Roads

Trail

Campground

Picnic Area

ROGUE
RIVER
NATIONAL
FOREST

0   4 miles

0   4 km

Trail

TO U.S. 97,
KLAMATH FALLS

[62]

ington. ⊠ *Crater Lake Lodge, Rim Village,* ☎ *541/594–2255. Reservations essential for dinner. MC, V. Closed mid-Oct.–mid-May.*

$$–$$$ 🏨 **Crater Lake Lodge.** The historic 1915 lodge on the rim of the caldera was renovated in the mid-1990s yet retains a period ambience. Lodgepole pine columns, gleaming wood floors, and stone fireplaces grace the common areas, and the newer furnishings blend in perfectly. The lodge has only two telephones, in the lobby area, and there are no televisions or electronic diversions of any kind. ⊠ *1211 Ave. C, White City 97503,* ☎ *541/830–8700,* ℻ *541/830–8514. 71 rooms. Restaurant, no-smoking rooms. MC, V. Closed mid-Oct.–mid-May.*

$$ 🏨 **Mazama Village Motor Inn.** This 40-room Forest Service complex south of the lake provides basic accommodations in 10 A-frame buildings. ⊠ *Box 128, Crater Lake, Rim Village 97604,* ☎ *541/594–2255,* ℻ *541/594–2622. 40 rooms. MC, V.*

🛆 **Mazama Campground.** All the sites here, along with 900 more in the surrounding national forests, are available on a first-come, first-served basis. ⊠ *Mazama Village near Annie Springs entrance station,* ☎ *541/594–2255. 198 sites.* 🎫 *$13. Flush toilets, potable water, showers, laundry facilities.* ☉ *Mid-June–mid-Oct.*

OUTDOOR ACTIVITIES AND SPORTS

If you're an advanced-intermediate or expert downhill skier and crave solitude, **Mount Bailey Snocat Skiing** (☎ 541/793–3348 or 800/446–4555) is the ski-guide service for you. Heated Sno-Cats deliver you to the summit of Mount Bailey, an 8,300-ft peak not far from Crater Lake, where you can attack the virgin powder on 4 mi of runs, with a vertical drop of 3,000 ft. The excursions are limited to 12 skiers a day. Tours leave Diamond Lake Resort (⊠ Hwy. 138, 76 mi east of Roseburg and 25 mi north of Crater Lake) daily at 7 AM. The resort's facilities include three restaurants, a bar, lodging, Nordic trails, and downhill and Nordic ski rentals.

Klamath Falls

㉕ *60 mi south of Crater Lake National Park on U.S. 97.*

Often overlooked because of its proximity to the more popular travel destination of Ashland, the Klamath Falls area is nonetheless one of the most beautiful parts of Oregon. The city of Klamath Falls stands at an elevation of 4,100 ft, on the southern shore of Upper Klamath Lake. The highest elevation in Klamath County is the peak of Mount Scott, at 8,926 ft. The Klamath Basin, with its six national wildlife refuges, hosts the largest wintering concentration of bald eagles in the contiguous United States, sometimes as many as 1,000 birds. Each February nature enthusiasts from around the world flock to Klamath Falls for the Bald Eagle Conference, the nation's oldest birding festival. There are more than 82 lakes and streams in Klamath County, including Upper Klamath Lake, which covers 133 square mi.

Many species of migratory birds congregate in the Klamath Basin, including the largest concentration of migratory waterfowl on the continent. The Nature Conservancy has called the basin a western Everglades because it is the largest wetland area west of the Mississippi. But humans have significantly damaged the ecosystem through farming and development, and the waters have become polluted. More than 25% of vertebrate species in the area are now endangered or threatened. Where 30 years ago about 6 million birds use the area every year, today that number is down to 2 to 3 million. Environmental organizations are working to reverse some of the damage.

Sights to See

Lower Klamath National Wildlife Refuge. Almost 1 million waterfowl use this area during fall migration. In summer white pelicans, cormorants, herons, egrets, terns, white-faced ibis, grebes, and gulls congregate here. But the area's star is the bald eagle: During winter, Lower Klamath is home to the largest concentration of bald eagles (an estimated 1,000) in the lower 48 states. ⊠ *8 mi south of Klamath Falls on U.S. 97.,* ☎ *916/667–2231.*

Fort Klamath Museum and Park. A frontier military post was established in 1863 at this site to protect pioneers from Indian attack. In 1973, 8 acres of the original post, including the original buildings, were dedicated as Klamath County Park. ⊠ *44 mi north of Klamath Falls on Hwy. 62.,* ☎ *541/381–2230.* 🎫 *Donation requested.* ☉ *June–Labor Day.*

Klamath County Museum. The museum features the anthropology, history, geology, and wildlife of the Klamath Basin. ⊠ *1451 Main St., 97601,* ☎ *541/883–4208.* 🎫 *$2.* ☉ *Labor Day–Memorial Day, Tues.– Sat. 8–4:30; Memorial Day–Labor Day, Tues.–Sat. 9–5:30.*

Kla-Mo-Ya Casino. Located on 9 acres along the Williamson River, this casino 22 mi north of Klamath Falls has 300 slot machines, poker, black-jack, and a buffet restaurant. There are no hotel accommodations. The casino is owned by the Klamath, Modoc, and Yahooskin tribes. ⊠ *22 mi north of Klamath Falls on Hwy. 97 at Crater Lake Junction, Chiloquin 97417,* ☎ *888/552–6692.*

Dining and Lodging

$$ 🏨 **Shilo Inn Suites Hotel–Klamath Falls.** This all-suites hotel overlooks the Cascades and Upper Klamath Lake. The large, comfy suites have microwaves, refrigerators, wet bars, coffeemakers, and irons. Continental breakfast is complimentary. ⊠ *2500 Almond St., 97601,* ☎ *541/885–7980 or 800/222–2244,* ℻ *541/885–7959. 143 suites. Restaurant, lounge, refrigerators, in-room data ports, in-room VCRs, indoor pool, sauna, spa, steam room, exercise room, coin laundry, meeting rooms, business services, Amtrak/airport shuttle, car rental. AE, D, DC, MC, V.*

$–$$ 🏨 **Red Lion Inn.** The rooms in this motel are nothing fancy, but they're bright and comfortable and have irons and coffeemakers. ⊠ *3612 S. 6th St., 97603,* ☎ *541/882–8864,* ℻ *541/884–2046. 108 rooms. Restaurant, in-room data ports, lounge, pool, hot tub, meeting rooms. AE, D, DC, MC, V.*

Outdoor Activities and Sports

Meridian Sail Center (⊠ 531 S. 8th St., ☎ 541/884–5869) rents boats and schedules charters.

The **Klamath Basin Audubon Society** (⊠ Box 354, Klamath Falls 97601, ☎ 541/884–0666 or 800/445–6728) has information on birds and other wildlife in the Klamath Falls Basin.

For information on national wildlife refuges in the Klamath Falls area, contact the **Klamath Basin National Wildlife Refuge Complex** (⊠ Rte. 1, Box 74, Tulelake, CA 96134, ☎ 530/667–2231).

Medford

71 mi southwest of Crater Lake on Hwy. 62; 88 mi south of Roseburg on I–5.

Strip malls surround Medford, the commercial center of southern Oregon, though in recent years the town has restored most of its old downtown core.

Dining and Lodging

$–$$ ✕ **Chevy's.** This popular chain serves good Mexican dishes, including burritos, tamales, nachos, and fajitas, at reasonable prices. It's a kid-friendly place, but you can dine sans kids in the lounge, which specializes in margaritas. The chips and salsa are made fresh daily. ⊠ *3125 Crater Lake Hwy.,* ☎ *541/774–8844. AE, MC, V.*

$$$ 🏠 **Under the Greenwood Tree.** Regular guests at this B&B between Med-
★ ford and Ashland find themselves hard-pressed to decide what they like most: the luxurious and romantic rooms, the stunning 10-acre gardens, or the breakfasts cooked by the owner, a Cordon Bleu–trained chef. Gigantic old oaks hung with hammocks shade the inn, a 130-year-old farmhouse exuding genteel charm. There's a manicured 2-acre lawn and a creaky three-story barn for exploring; an outbuilding holds the buckboard wagon that brought the property's original homesteaders westward on the Oregon Trail. The interior is decorated in Renaissance splendor and all rooms have private baths. Afternoon tea is served. ⊠ *3045 Bellinger La., 97501 (head west from I–5's Exit 27 on Barnett Rd., south briefly on Hwy. 99, west on Stewart Ave., south briefly on Hull Rd., and west on Bellinger),* ☎ *541/776–0000. 5 rooms. MC, V.*

$ 🏠 **Motel 6.** It's not the Savoy, but it's clean, cheap, and close to the Shakespeare Festival, the Mount Ashland ski area, and Crater Lake. ⊠ *950 Alba Dr. (Exit 27 off I–5), 97504,* ☎ *541/773–4290 or 800/ 466–8356 (central reservations),* 📠 *541/857–9574. 101 units. Pool. AE, D, DC, MC, V.*

Nightlife and the Arts

The **Ginger Rogers Theatre** (⊠ 23 S. Central Ave., ☎ 541/779–8195), a restored vaudeville house named for the late Hollywood star, who became an area resident after her retirement, presents concerts, theater works, and touring shows.

Outdoor Activities and Sports

GOLF

Cedar Links Golf Club (⊠ 3155 Cedar Links Dr., ☎ 541/773–4373 or 800/853–2754), an 18-hole, par-70 public golf course, charges $20– $22, plus $9 per rider for an optional cart.

JET-BOAT EXCURSIONS

Hellgate Jetboat Excursions (⊠ 966 S.W. 6th, Grants Pass, ☎ 800/648– 4874) operates jet-boat trips down the Rogue River's Hellgate Canyon from May to September.

Shopping

Harry and David's/Jackson & Perkins (⊠ 2518 S. Pacific Hwy., ☎ 800/ 547–3033 or 800/872–7673) are two of the largest mail-order companies in the world: Harry and David's for fruit and gift packs, Jackson & Perkins for roses. Harry and David's Country Store in the complex is a retail outlet for its products, most of which are grown in the Bear Creek Orchards.

Jacksonville

5 mi west of Medford on Hwy. 238.

In many ways southern Oregon has become as important to the cultural life of the state as are Portland and Eugene. Tiny Jacksonville, once a stagecoach stop, hosts the Britt Festivals (☞ Nightlife and the Arts, *below*) of music and theater each summer. All of Jacksonville is on the National Register of Historic Places. Several of the 80 privately owned landmark buildings date from the town's gold-rush heyday of 1853. For free maps and guides to Jacksonville's many historic structures, stop by the **Jacksonville Visitors Information Center** (✉ 185 N. Oregon St., ☎ 541/899–8118).

The **Jacksonville Museum,** inside the old Jackson County Courthouse, houses intriguing gold-rush-era artifacts. The "Jacksonville! Boomtown to Home Town" exhibit lays out the area's history. The **Children's Museum,** occupying the 80-year-old Jackson County Jail, contains hands-on exhibits about pioneer life and has a splendid collection of antique toys. ✉ 206 N. 5th St., ☎ 541/773–6536. ☞ *$3 for each museum, $7 pass for both.* ☉ *Memorial Day–Sept., daily 11–5; Oct.–Memorial Day, Tues.–Sun. 11–5.*

Dining and Lodging

$–$$ ✕ **Bella Union.** The menu is downright sophisticated at this unpretentious restaurant in an 1870s saloon. Fresh fish—familiar species and more exotic ones like Hawaiian opah and mako shark—is flown in daily, and the pastas are handmade on the premises. ✉ *170 California St.,* ☎ *541/899–1770. AE, D, MC, V.*

$$–$$$$ ✕🖼 **Jacksonville Inn.** The spotless period antiques and the host of well-
★   chosen amenities at this 1863-vintage inn evoke what the Wild West might have been had Martha Stewart been in charge. A block away are three larger and more luxurious cottages with fireplaces and saunas. The Continental fare and 600-label wine cellar in the basement dining room (reservations essential; no lunch Mon.) are among the best in southern Oregon—fresh razor clams and veal dishes are the house specialties. Book well in advance, particularly between late June and August, when the Britt Festivals draw thousands of visitors. The room rates include a full breakfast. ✉ *175 E. California St., 97530,* ☎ *541/ 899–1900 or 800/321–9344,* 𝔽𝔸𝕏 *541/899–1373. 8 rooms, 3 cottages. Restaurant, refrigerator. AE, D, DC, MC, V.*

$$ ✕🖼 **The McCully House Inn.** One of Jacksonville's six original homes, a gleaming white Gothic Revival mansion built in 1860, McCully House sits amid a fragrant rose garden. The period-decorated rooms, one with a fireplace and all of them filled with antiques, are on the second floor and they have private baths. One of the town's best restaurants (reservations essential; no lunch), on the ground level, specializes in seafood and has a Sunday brunch. The room rates include a full breakfast. ✉ *240 E. California St., 97530,* ☎ *541/899–1942 or 800/367–1942,* 𝔽𝔸𝕏 *541/899–1560. 3 rooms. Restaurant. AE, MC, V.*

Nightlife and the Arts

Every summer some of the finest musicians in the world gather for the **Britt Festivals** (☎ 541/773–6077 or 800/882–7488), outdoor concerts and theater presentations lasting from mid-June to early September. Contemporary and classical performances are staged in an outdoor amphitheater on the estate of 19th-century photographer and painter Peter Britt.

Oregon Caves National Monument

🕸 *90 mi from Jacksonville, west on Hwy. 238, south on U.S. 199, and east on Hwy 46.*

The town of **Cave Junction** is the turn-off point for the Oregon Caves National Monument. The Marble Halls of Oregon, high in the verdant Siskiyou Mountains, have enchanted visitors since local hunter Elijah Davidson chased a bear into them in 1874. Huge stalagmites and stalactites, the Ghost Room, Paradise Lost, and the River Styx are part of a ½-mi subterranean tour that lasts about 75 minutes. The tour includes more than 200 stairs and is not recommended for anyone who experiences difficulty in walking or has respiratory or coronary problems. Children over six must be at least 42 inches tall and pass a safety and ability test, because they cannot be carried. ⊠ *Hwy. 46, 20 mi southeast of Cave Junction,* ☎ *541/592–3400.* ☜ *$7.* ☉ *May–mid-June, daily 9–5; mid-June–Sept., daily 9–7; Oct.–Apr., daily 8:30–4.*

Dining and Lodging

$$　✕🏨 **Oregon Caves Lodge.** If you're looking for a quiet retreat in an unusual setting, consider this lodge on the grounds of the national monument. Virtually unchanged since it was built in 1934, it has a rustic authenticity you'll find nowhere else in the state. Rooms, all with their original furnishings, have canyon or waterfall views. The dining room serves the best regional fare in the vicinity. ⊠ *20000 Caves Hwy., Cave Junction 97523,* ☎ *541/592–3400,* 🅵🅰🆇 *541/592–6654. 22 rooms, 3 suites. Restaurant, coffee shop, hiking. No smoking. MC, V.*

Ashland

㉗　*20 mi from Jacksonville, east on Hwy. 238 and southeast on I–5; 90 mi from Oregon Caves National Monument, west on Hwy. 46, northeast on U.S. 199, and southeast on I–5; 180 mi south of Eugene on I–5.*

★　Ashland, the home of the **Oregon Shakespeare Festival** (☞ Nightlife and the Arts, *below*), attracts hundreds of thousands of theater lovers to the Rogue Valley every year. The greatest influx is between June and September.

At the Oregon Shakespeare Festival's **Exhibit Center** in the festival complex, theater fans can try on costumes and view displays that outline the history of the festival. A fascinating guided backstage tour includes peeks at production shops and the Angus Bowmer Theatre and a walk to the very heavens above the Elizabethan stage. ⊠ *S. Pioneer and Main Sts.,* ☎ *541/482–4331,* 🅵🅰🆇 *541/482–8045.* ☜ *Backstage tour $11 early June–early-Oct., $9 Feb.–early June, mid-late Oct. (under 5 not admitted); exhibit center $2.* ☉ *Tues.–Sun. 10–11:45.*

The Elizabethan Theatre overlooks **Lithia Park,** a 99-acre swath of green in the center of the town. An old-fashioned band shell, a duck pond, a children's playground, nature trails, and Ashland Creek make this a perfect spot for a pretheater picnic. Each June the festival opens its outdoor season by hosting the Feast of Will in the park, complete with music, dancing, bagpipes, and food. Tickets (about $16) are available through the festival box office (☞ Nightlife and the Arts, *below*).

The **Pacific Northwest Museum of Natural History** emphasizes hands-on exploration of the natural world through "multisensory" exhibits that visitors can touch and manipulate. ⊠ *1500 E. Main St. (1 mi east of downtown),* ☎ *541/488–1084.* ☜ *$6.* ☉ *May–Oct., daily 9–5; Nov.–Apr., daily 10–4.*

Dining and Lodging

The Oregon Shakespeare Festival has stimulated one of the most extensive networks of B&Bs in the country—more than 50 in all. High season for Ashland-area B&Bs is between June and October. Expect to pay $90–$150 per night, which includes breakfast for two; during the off-season the rates are between $60 and $100. The **Ashland B&B Clearinghouse** (☎ 541/488–0338 or 800/588–0338) and the **Ashland & Jacksonville B&B Guild** (☎ 541/482–2133) provide lodging referrals.

$$$　✕ **Chateaulin.** One of southern Oregon's most romantic restaurants
★　occupies an ivy-covered storefront a block from the Oregon Shakespeare Festival center, where it dispenses French food, local wine, and impeccable service with equal facility. Try the pan-roasted rack of lamb with a white-wine demi-glace sauce of roasted garlic, fresh basil, black olives, and sun-dried tomatoes, accompanied by a bottle of Ken Wright Cellars

Pinot Noir. ⊠ *50 E. Main St.,* ☎ *541/482–2264. AE, D, MC, V. No lunch.*

\$\$\$ ✕ **Winchester Country Inn.** The menu is small but imaginative at the restaurant inside this inn built in 1886. High-windowed dining rooms, set among manicured gardens, radiate a feeling of casual elegance. Menu items are seasonal but sometimes include an ambrosial roast duck in a sauce of caramel, brandy, and fresh fruit; the homemade scones, crab Benedict, and duck hash with orange hollandaise, served for Sunday brunch, are equally memorable. The restaurant (no lunch) is closed on Monday between November and May. ⊠ *35 S. 2nd St.,* ☎ *541/488–1113 or 800/972–4991,* FAX *541/488–4604. AE, D, MC, V.*

\$\$–\$\$\$ ✕ **Il Giardino.** An orange Vespa parked in the front entrance sets the casually chic tone at this Italian-run restaurant with great food and a warm atmosphere. The dozen or so pasta dishes are based on traditional recipes but incorporate local ingredients; the remainder of the menu is divided between meat and fresh fish. ⊠ *5 Granite St.,* ☎ *541/488–0816. MC, V.*

\$\$ ✕ **Thai Pepper.** Spicy Thai-style curries and stir-fries are the specialties at this restaurant above Ashland Creek. With an interior filled with local art, rattan, linen, and crystal, the restaurant feels like a French café in downtown Bangkok. Try the coconut prawns or the Thai beef-salad appetizers, followed by the house curry. ⊠ *84 N. Main St.,* ☎ *541/482–8058. AE, DC, MC, V. No lunch Sat.–Thurs.*

\$–\$\$ ✕ **Gepetto's.** Kids love this unpretentious eatery, open daily for breakfast, lunch, and dinner. The friendly and fast-moving staff serves pasta dishes and delicious and unusual sandwiches, salads, and soups. Try the fresh-grilled marinated turkey served on crispy cheese bread. ⊠ *345 E. Main St.,* ☎ *541/482–1138. MC, V.*

\$\$–\$\$\$\$ 🏨 **Mt. Ashland Inn.** Close to the summit ski area on Mount Ashland, ★ 15 mi south of Ashland, this 5,500-square-ft lodge, hand built of cedar logs, has magnificent views of Mount Shasta and the rest of the Siskiyou Mountains; the Pacific Crest Trail runs through the parking lot. A large stone fireplace, antiques, hand-stitched quilts, and natural wood provide welcoming warmth, and a sauna and outdoor hot tub overlooking the mountains add to the alpine splendor. The room rates include a three-course breakfast that's wonderfully prepared and gracefully served, and the owners plan bike trips and provide snowshoes for guests. ⊠ *550 Mt. Ashland Rd., 97520 (take Exit 6 from I–5 and follow signs west toward ski area to just beyond milepost 5),* ☎ FAX *541/482–8707 or* ☎ *800/830–8707. 5 rooms. Hiking, mountain bikes, cross-country skiing. D, MC, V.*

\$\$–\$\$\$ 🏨 **Best Western Bard's Inn.** Original local art hangs on the walls of this property close to the theaters. The rooms, decorated with oak and knotty-pine furniture, are small but have Rogue Valley views. ⊠ *132 N. Main St., 97520,* ☎ *541/482–0049 or 800/528–1234,* FAX *541/488–3259. 91 units. Refrigerators, outdoor pool, outdoor hot tub. AE, D, DC, MC, V.*

Nightlife and the Arts

From February to October, more than 100,000 Bard-loving fanatics descend on Ashland for the **Oregon Shakespeare Festival** (⊠ 15 S. Pioneer St., 97520, ☎ 541/482–4331, FAX 541/482–8045), presented in three theaters. Its accomplished repertory company mounts some of the finest Shakespearean productions you're likely to see on this side of Stratford-upon-Avon—plus works by Ibsen, Williams, and contemporary playwrights. Between June and October, plays are staged in the 1,200-seat Elizabethan Theatre, an atmospheric re-creation of the Fortune Theatre in London. The festival generally operates close to capacity, so it's important to book ahead.

Ashland's after-theater crowd (including many of the actors) congregates in the bar at **Chateaulin** (⊠ 50 E. Main St., ☎ 541/482–2264).

Outdoor Activities and Sports

Siskiyou Adventures, Inc. (⊠ 37 3rd St., ☎ 888/747–5496) provides guides and basic equipment for all manner of outdoor recreational sports, including white-water rafting, kayaking, fishing, and skiing.

SKIING

Mount Ashland (⊠ Mt. Ashland Access Rd., 18 mi southwest of downtown Ashland; follow signs 9 mi from I–5's Exit 6, ☎ 541/482–2897 or 888/747–5496), a cone-shape 7,523-ft Siskiyou peak, has some of the steepest runs in the state. Two triple and two double chairlifts accommodate a vertical drop of 1,150 ft; the longest of the 22 runs is 1 mi. Facilities include rentals, repairs, instruction, a ski shop, a restaurant, and a bar.

The Willamette Valley and Wine Country Essentials

Arriving and Departing

BY BUS

Greyhound (☎ 800/231–2222) serves Eugene and many other towns along the I–5 corridor.

BY CAR

I–5 runs north–south the length of the Willamette, Umpqua, and Rogue River valleys.

BY PLANE

Eugene Airport (☎ 541/687–5430) is served by **Horizon, Skywest, and United/United Express.** Horizon and United Express serve the **Rogue Valley Airport** (☎ 541/772–8068) in Medford. *See* Air Travel *in* Smart Travel Tips A to Z for airline phone numbers.

BY TRAIN

The **Amtrak** *Coast Starlight,* which runs daily between Seattle and Los Angeles, stops in Albany (near Corvallis), Salem, and Eugene. *Cascades* trains run daily between Seattle, Portland, and Eugene.

Getting Around

BY CAR

Many Willamette, Umpqua, and Rogue River valley attractions lie not too far east or west of I–5. **Highway 22** travels west from the Willamette National Forest through Salem to the coast. **Highway 99** travels parallel to I–5 through much of the Willamette Valley. **Highway 34** leaves I–5 just south of Albany and heads west, past Corvallis and into the Coast Range, where it follows the Alsea River. **Highway 138** winds along the Umpqua River, east of Roseburg to the back door of Crater Lake National Park. **Highway 126** heads east from Eugene toward the Willamette National Forest; it travels west from town to the coast.

Visitor Information

Ashland Chamber of Commerce and Visitors Information Center (⊠ 110 E. Main St., 97520, ☎ 541/482–3486). **Corvallis Convention and Visitors Bureau** (⊠ 420 N.W. 2nd St., 97330, ☎ 541/757–1544 or 800/334–8118). **Eugene Convention & Visitors Bureau** (⊠ 115 W. 8th St., Suite 190, 97440, ☎ 541/484–5307 or 800/452–3670). **Grant's Pass Visitors & Convention Bureau** (⊠ 1501 N.E. 6th St., 97526, ☎ 541/476–7717 or 800/547–5927). **McMinnville Chamber of Commerce** (⊠ 417 N.W. Adams St., 97128, ☎ 503/472–6196). **Roseburg Visitors & Convention Bureau** (⊠ 410 S.E. Spruce St., 97470, ☎ 541/672–9731 or 800/444–9584). **Salem Convention & Visitors Center** (⊠ 1313 Mill St. SE, 97301, ☎ 503/581–4325 or 800/874–7012).

THE COLUMBIA RIVER GORGE AND THE OREGON CASCADES

There are two reasons to drive to the Columbia River Gorge and the Oregon Cascades: recreation and beauty. Sightseers, hikers, skiers, and waterfall lovers all find contentment in this rugged region east of Portland. The highlights of the Columbia River Gorge, where the mighty waterway slashes through the Cascade Range, include, from west to east, Multnomah Falls, Bonneville Dam, and the windsurfing hub and rich orchard land of Hood River. To the south of Hood River lie the skiing and other alpine attractions of the 11,245-ft-high Mount Hood.

From Portland, the **Columbia Gorge–Mount Hood Loop** is the easiest way to see the gorge and the mountain. Take I–84 east to Troutdale and follow U.S. 26 to Bennett Pass (near Timberline), where Highway 35 heads north to Hood River; then follow I–84 back to Portland. Or make the loop in reverse.

Winter weather in the Columbia Gorge and the Mount Hood area is much more severe than that in Portland and western Oregon. Even I–84 may be closed because of snow and ice. If you're planning a winter visit, be sure your car has chains and carry plenty of warm clothes. At any time of year, if you stop to explore, take your valuables with you—in spite of the idyllic surroundings, car prowlers are not unknown in the gorge.

Numbers in the margin correspond to points of interest on the Columbia River Gorge, the Cascades, and Central Oregon map.

Troutdale Area

13 mi east of Portland on I–84.

★ The town of Troutdale is the gateway to the **Columbia River Gorge.** Here, the 22-mi-long **Historic Columbia River Highway** (U.S. 30, also known as the Columbia River Scenic Highway and the Scenic Gorge Highway) leaves I–84 and begins its climb to the forested riverside bluffs high above the interstate. Completed in 1915, the serpentine highway was the first paved road in the gorge built expressly for automotive sightseers.

28 East of Troutdale a few miles on U.S. 30 is **Crown Point State Park,** a 730-ft-high bluff with an unparalleled 30-mi view down the Columbia River Gorge. **Vista House,** the two-tier octagonal structure on the side of the cliff, opened its doors to visitors in 1918; the rotunda contains displays about the gorge and the highway. ⊠ *U.S. 30,* ☎ *503/695–2240.* ▣ *Free.* ⊙ *Mid-Apr.–mid-Oct., daily 8:30–6.*

Rooster Rock State Park, the most famous beach lining the Columbia River, is below Crown Point; access is from the interstate only. Nudists and conventional bathers soak up the sun here. ⊠ *I–84, 7 mi east of Troutdale,* ☎ *503/695–2261.* ▣ *Day use $3 per vehicle.* ⊙ *Daily 7 AM–dusk.*

Shopping
Columbia Gorge Factory Stores. Save a bundle on your favorite brand-name products at this outlet mall in suburban Portland, near the entrance to the gorge. Columbia Gorge Factory Stores has more than 40 shops, including Mikasa, Adidas, Harry and David, G.H. Bass, Levi Strauss, Carter's Childrenswear, Big Dog Sportswear, Great Outdoor Clothing Co., and Norm Thompson. Take I–84 east to Exit 17. ⊠ *450*

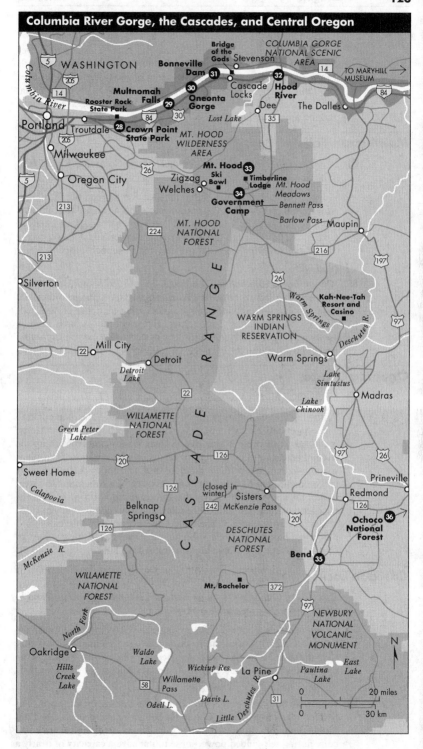

Columbia River Gorge, the Cascades, and Central Oregon

N.W. 257th Ave., Troutdale 97060, ☎ 503/669–8060. ☉ Mon.–Sat.
10–8, Sun. 10–7.

En Route   From Crown Point, the Columbia River Highway heads downhill over
graceful stone bridges built by Italian immigrant masons and winds
through quiet forest glades. More than a dozen waterfalls pour over
fern- and lichen-covered cliffs in a 10-mi stretch. Latourell, Bridal
Veil, Wahkeena, and Horsetail falls are the most impressive. All have
parking areas and hiking trails.

Multnomah Falls

㉙   20 mi east of Troutdale on I–84 or Historic Columbia River Hwy.
(U.S. 30).

Multnomah Falls, a 620-ft-high double-decker torrent, the fifth-highest waterfall in the nation, is by far the most spectacular of the cataracts
east of Troutdale. The scenic highway leads down to a parking lot; from
there, a paved path winds to a bridge over the lower falls. A much steeper
trail climbs to a viewing point overlooking the upper falls.

Dining

$–$$ ✕ **Multnomah Falls Lodge.** The lodge, built in 1925 and listed on the
National Register of Historic Places, has vaulted ceilings and classic
stone fireplaces. Freshwater trout, salmon, and a platter of prawns, halibut, and scallops are the specialties. The restaurant is justly famous
for its wild-huckleberry daiquiris and desserts. ✉ Historic Columbia
River Hwy. (or Exit 31 off I–84), ☎ 503/695–2376. AE, D, MC, V.

Oneonta Gorge

㉚   2 mi east of Multnomah Falls on Historic Columbia River Hwy.

Following the old highway east from Multnomah Falls, you come to
a narrow, mossy cleft with walls hundreds of feet high. Oneonta Gorge
is the most enjoyable during the summer, when you can walk up the
streambed through the cool green canyon, where hundreds of plant
species—some found nowhere else—flourish under the perennially
moist conditions. At other times of year, take the trail along the west
side of the canyon. The clearly marked trailhead is 100 yards west of
the gorge, on the south side of the road. The trail ends at Oneonta Falls,
about ½ mi up the stream. You'll need boots or submersible sneakers—
plus a strong pair of ankles—because the rocks are slippery. East of
Oneonta Gorge, the scenic highway returns to I–84.

Cascade Locks

7 mi east of Oneonta Gorge on Historic Columbia River Hwy. and I–
84; 30 mi east of Troutdale on I–84.

In pioneer days, boats needing to pass the bedeviling rapids near the
town of Cascade Locks had to portage around them. The locks that
gave the town its name were completed in 1896, allowing waterborne
passage for the first time. Native Americans still use the locks for their
traditional dip-net fishing.

㉛   **Bonneville Dam** is Oregon's most impressive man-made attraction. The
first federal dam to span the Columbia, Bonneville was dedicated by President Franklin D. Roosevelt in 1937. Its generators (visible from a balcony during self-guided powerhouse tours) have a capacity of nearly a
million kilowatts, enough to supply power to more than 200,000 sin-
gle-family homes. There is a modern visitor center on Bradford Island,
complete with underwater windows for viewing migrating salmon as they

struggle up fish ladders. The best viewing times are between April and October. In recent years the dwindling runs of wild Columbia salmon have made the dam a subject of much environmental controversy. ⊠ *From I–84 take Exit 40, head northeast, and follow signs 1 mi to visitor center,* ☎ *541/374–8820.* ☜ *Free.* ☉ *Visitor center daily 9–5.*

Below the dam, the ponds at the **Bonneville Fish Hatchery** teem with fingerling salmon, fat rainbow trout, and 6-ft-long sturgeon. The hatchery raises chinook and coho salmon; from mid-October to late November, you can watch as staff members spawn the fish, beginning a new hatching cycle, or feed the trout with food pellets from a coin-operated machine. ⊠ *From I–84 take Exit 40 and follow signs northeast 1 mi to hatchery,* ☎ *541/374–8393.* ☜ *Free.* ☉ *Hatchery grounds daily dawn–dusk, spawning room daily 7:30–4:30.*

Cascade Locks is the home port of the 600-passenger stern-wheeler *Columbia Gorge.* Between mid-June and early October the commodious ship churns its way upriver, then back again, on two-hour excursions through some of the gorge's most awesome scenery. ⊠ *Cruises leave from Marine Park in Cascade Locks,* ☎ *541/374–8427. Reservations essential for any cruise with meal.* ☜ *2-hr cruises (no meal) $12.95, longer cruises with meals $26–$36.* ☉ *2-hr cruises (no meal) June–Sept., daily at 10, 12:30, and 3; dinner cruise Fri. 7 PM, Sat. 6 PM; brunch cruise weekends 12:30 PM. AE, MC, V.*

Dining and Lodging

$ ✕ **Char Burger Restaurant.** Arrowheads, rifles, and wagon-wheel chandeliers carry out the western motif of this dining room overlooking the Columbia River. Hamburgers, salmon, seafood, steaks, and breakfast favorites are served cafeteria-style. ⊠ *745 S.W. Wanapa St.,* ☎ *541/ 374–8477. Reservations essential for Sun brunch. AE, MC, V.*

$–$$$ ☷ **Best Western Columbia River Inn.** Most rooms in this comfortable inn have wonderful river views. Pale-blue carpeting, upholstered sofas and chairs, and oak tables decorate the rooms, all of which have microwave ovens. Here's the downside: The inn sits above railroad tracks plied by numerous freight trains. Upper-floor rooms are a bit quieter than lower ones. ⊠ *735 Wanapa St., 97014,* ☎ *541/374—8777 or 800/ 595–7108,* ℻ *541/374–2279. 62 rooms. Refrigerators, indoor pool, hot tub. AE, D, DC, MC, V.*

Stevenson, Washington

Across the river from Cascade Locks via the Bridge of the Gods and 4 mi east on Washington State Hwy. 14.

For a magnificent vista from high above the Columbia, pay the 75¢ toll and take the truss bridge, called the **Bridge of the Gods,** above Cascade Locks over to the Washington side.

The **Columbia Gorge Interpretive Center,** below the dramatic basaltic cliffs on the north bank of the Columbia River Gorge, contains exhibits that explain the volcanic forces that shaped the gorge landscape and the cultural history of the area. On display are a huge fish wheel and native dip nets used for salmon fishing, a Native American pit house, and artifacts pertaining to the explorers, missionaries, fur trappers, and soldiers who came through the gorge. ⊠ *990 S.W. Rock Creek Dr., Stevenson, WA (1 mi east of Bridge of the Gods on Hwy. 14),* ☎ *509/ 427–8211.* ☜ *$6.* ☉ *Daily 10–5.*

Dining and Lodging

$$$–$$$$ ✕ **Dining Room at Skamania Lodge.** Windows in this cavernous dining room overlook the Columbia River Gorge. Fresh oysters, crab

cakes, plank-roasted salmon, and succulent rack of lamb, all cooked in a wood-burning oven, are worth trying. The Friday-night Gorge Harvest Seafood Buffet and the Sunday brunch draw patrons from miles around. The dining room is open for breakfast daily. ✉ *Skamania Lodge Way north of Hwy. 14, 2 mi east of the Bridge of the Gods,* ☎ *509/ 427–2508. Reservations essential for dinner. AE, D, DC, MC, V.*

$ ✕ **Big River Grill.** The fare at this appealing storefront grill on Stevenson's main street is simple—chili, soup, sandwiches, and burgers. High-back wooden booths line one side; photos and memorabilia provide insight into the local past. ✉ *192 S.W. 2nd St.,* ☎ *509/427–4888. Reservations not accepted. MC, V.*

$$–$$$$ ✕🏨 **Skamania Lodge.** The great Work Projects Administration lodges of the 1930s inspired this full-service resort built in the 1990s, high on a knoll overlooking the Columbia River. The Georgian pine floors, fir walls, and stone fireplace of the Gorge Room set a tone of rustic grandeur. The rooms, decorated with framed rubbings of petroglyphs and furnished with lodge-style furniture covered with handwoven fabrics, have views of the river and the surrounding gorge landscape. A restaurant (☞ *above*) and outstanding recreational facilities make this the premier resort on the Washington side of the Columbia. ✉ *Skamania Lodge Way north of Hwy. 14, 2 mi east of the Bridge of the Gods, 98648,* ☎ *509/ 427–7700 or 800/221–7117,* 🖷 *509/427–2548. 195 rooms. Restaurant, bar, indoor pool, indoor and outdoor hot tubs, massage, sauna, 18-hole golf course, 2 tennis courts, exercise room, hiking, volleyball, bicycles, cross-country skiing, library, business center. AE, D, DC, MC, V.*

$–$$ 🏨 **Carson Mineral Hot Springs Resort.** People have been coming to this funky place for decades to soak in the hot mineral-laden water pumped up to the two bathhouses (virtually unchanged since they opened in 1923) from the Wind River. After a soak in an old claw-foot tub, you're wrapped in sheets and blankets for a blissful snooze. The bathhouses are open daily 8:45 AM–7 PM. Call ahead if you want a massage; baths ($10) are available to nonguests on a first-come, first-served basis. The hotel, dating from 1897, is clean, if charmless, with spartan rooms and cabins. The restaurant, open for breakfast, lunch, and dinner, serves decent if generally uninspired old-fashioned cooking. ✉ *372 St. Martin's Springs Rd., Carson, WA 98610 (4 mi east of Stevenson on Hwy. 14),* ☎ *509/427–8292 or 800/607–3678,* 🖷 *509/427–7242. 9 rooms share 4 baths; 1 suite; 14 cabins with ½ bath; 2 cabins with full bath and kitchen. Restaurant, golf course. AE, MC, V.*

Hood River

㉜ *17 mi east of Cascade Locks on I–84.*

For years the incessant easterly winds at the town of Hood River, where the Columbia Gorge widens and the scenery changes to tawny, wheat-covered hills, were nothing but a nuisance. Then somebody bolted a sail to a surfboard, and a new recreational craze was born. A fortuitous combination of factors—mainly the reliable gale-force winds blowing against the current—has made Hood River the self-proclaimed board-sailing capital of the world. Especially in the summer, this once-somnolent fruit-growing town swarms with colorful "boardheads," many of whom have journeyed from as far away as Europe and Australia.

🔄 **Mount Hood Railroad,** established in 1906 as a passenger and freight line, is a delightful way to take in the changing seasons and scenery of the Hood River valley. In operation from April to October, the train chugs alongside the Hood River through vast fruit orchards before climbing up steep forested canyons, providing views of Mount Hood along the way. Excursions include brunch, dinner, or no meal. ✉ *Depot: 110*

Railroad Ave., ☎ *800/872–4661.* ☜ *$22.95–$68.50.* ⊙ *July–Aug., Tues.–Sun. 10 AM, weekends 3 PM, Sat. 5:30 PM (dinner), Sun. 10:30 AM (brunch); Apr.–June and Sept.–Oct., Wed.–Sun. 10 AM, weekends 3 PM, Sat. 5:30 PM (dinner), Sun. 10:30 AM (brunch); Nov.–Dec., weekends 10 AM. AE, D, MC, V.*

Columbia Gorge Sailpark (⊠ Port Marina, Exit 64 off I–84, ☎ 541/386–1645), on the river downtown, has a boat basin, a swimming beach, jogging trails, picnic tables, and rest rooms.

Dining and Lodging

$$ ✕ **6th Street Bistro and Loft.** The menu here changes weekly but concentrates on Pacific Northwest flavors, right down to the coffees and salads. Try the grilled fresh fish and chicken or, in season, local fresh steamer clams and wild coral mushrooms. ⊠ *6th and Cascade Sts.,* ☎ *541/386–5737. MC, V.*

$–$$ ✕ **The Mesquitery.** Fresh herbs and tangy marinades supply added flavor to the fish, beef, chicken, and pork grilled over aromatic mesquite at this sunny restaurant. ⊠ *1219 12th St. (atop the hill south of downtown),* ☎ *541/386–2002. MC, V.*

$ ✕ **Full Sail Tasting Room and Pub.** This glass-walled microbrewery with a windswept deck overlooking the Columbia has won major awards at the Great American Beer Festival. Savory snack foods complement the fresh ales. ⊠ *506 Columbia St. (in the old Diamond cannery overlooking downtown Hood River),* ☎ *541/386–2247. Reservations not accepted. AE, MC, V.*

$$$ ✕🏨 **Columbia Gorge Hotel.** The ambience at the grande dame of gorge hotels is a bit florid, but the view of a 208-ft-high waterfall is magnificent. Rooms with plenty of wood, brass, and antiques overlook the formal gardens. The rates include a seven-course breakfast dubbed the World Famous Farm Breakfast (nonguests pay $24.95). While watching the sun set on the Columbia River, you can dine on breast of pheasant with pear wine, hazelnuts, and cream; grilled venison; breast of duck; Columbia River salmon; or sturgeon. ⊠ *4000 Westcliff Dr., 97031, off I–84's Exit 62,* ☎ *541/386–5566 or 800/345–1921,* ℻ *541/387–5414. 46 rooms. Restaurant, bar. AE, D, DC, MC, V.*

$$ 🏨 **Hood River Hotel.** Public areas at this 1913 landmark are rich in beveled glass, warm wood, and tasteful jade-and-cream-color fabrics. Rooms have fir floors, Oriental carpets, four-poster beds, and skylights. The suites, all with kitchens, can sleep five. There's a lively lobby bar and a Mediterranean-inspired restaurant, plus—a thoughtful touch—plenty of locked storage for boardsailors. ⊠ *102 Oak St., 97031,* ☎ *541/386–1900,* ℻ *541/386–6090. 33 rooms, 9 suites. Restaurant, bar, café, hot tub, sauna, exercise room. AE, D, DC, MC, V.*

$$ 🏨 **Lakecliff Estate.** Architect A. E. Doyle, who designed the Multnomah Falls Lodge and the Classic Revival public library and U.S. Bank Building in Portland, also designed the summer home that holds this small bed-and-breakfast inn. The 1908 house, built on a cliff overlooking the river, is beautifully maintained and exceptionally comfortable. A deck at the back of the house and wood-burning fireplaces in three of the rooms ensure a relaxing stay. ⊠ *3820 Westcliff Dr., 97031 (head east from I–84's Exit 62),* ☎ *541/386–7000,* ℻ *541/386–1803. 4 rooms. No smoking. No credit cards. Closed Labor Day–Apr.*

$–$$ 🏨 **Best Western-Hood River Inn.** This modern hotel on the river within paddling distance of the Columbia Gorge Sailpark is the address of choice for visiting windsurfers. There's nothing fancy about the rooms, but they are clean. Ask for a room with a river view. ⊠ *1108 E. Marina Way, 97031,* ☎ *541/386–2200 or 800/828–7873,* ℻ *541/386–8905. 149 rooms. Restaurant, bar, outdoor pool, hot tub. AE, D, DC, MC, V.*

OFF THE
BEATEN PATH

LOST LAKE – The waters of one of the most photographed sights in the Pacific Northwest reflect towering Mount Hood and the thick forests that line the lakeshore. Cabins are available for overnight stays, and because no motorboats are allowed on Lost Lake, the area is blissfully quiet. ⊠ *Lost Lake Rd. (take Hood River Hwy. south from Hood River to town of Dee and follow signs),* ☎ *541/386–6366 for cabin reservations.* 🖼 *$5 day use fee.*

The Dalles

20 mi east of Hood River on I–84.

The Dalles has a small-town, Old West feel, possibly because it's the traditional end of the **Oregon Trail,** where the wagons were loaded onto barges for the final leg of their 2,000-mi journey from western Missouri.

Outstanding exhibits at the 130-year-old **Wasco County Courthouse** illustrate the trials and tribulations of those who traveled the Oregon Trail. ⊠ *410 W. 2nd Pl.,* ☎ *541/296–4798.* 🖼 *Free (donation suggested).* ⊙ *Mon.–Tues. and Fri.–Sat. 11–3.*

The 1856-vintage Fort Dalles Surgeon's Quarters houses the **Fort Dalles Museum.** On display are the personal effects of some of the region's settlers and a collection of early automobiles. The entrance fee gains you admission to the **Anderson House museum** across the street, which also has pioneer artifacts. ⊠ *15th and Garrison Sts.,* ☎ *541/296–4547.* 🖼 *$3.* ⊙ *Daily 10–5.*

Dining and Lodging

$$ ✕ **Ole's Supper Club.** The fine western-style food at this restaurant with friendly, competent service has a Continental twist. It's hard to go wrong when choosing an entrée—try a thick slab of prime rib or the veal Oscar—especially when it's accompanied by a selection from the well-conceived wine list. ⊠ *2620 W. 2nd St.,* ☎ *541/296–6708. AE, MC, V. Closed Sun.–Mon. No lunch.*

$$ 🏨 **Columbia House.** A period feel lingers at this enormous late-1930s house on a cliff overlooking the Columbia. The rooms have king-size beds; two have river views. On a quiet wooded acre three blocks from downtown, the B&B has three decks out back, perfect for relaxing or, in good weather, enjoying the breakfast served up by the owner. ⊠ *525 E. 7th St., 97058,* ☎ *541/298–4686 or 800/807–2668. 4 rooms, 1 with shared bath. Airport shuttle. MC, V.*

OFF THE
BEATEN PATH

MARYHILL MUSEUM OF ART – One of the Columbia Gorge's most unusual cultural attractions, this museum in a castlelike mansion perches high on a cliff on the Washington side of the river. Built by a colorful character named Sam Hill as a private residence, the house was dedicated as a museum by Queen Marie of Romania in 1923. It contains the largest collection of Rodin sculptures and watercolors west of the Mississippi; prehistoric Native American tools and baskets; and the charming "Théâtre de la Mode," a miniature fashion show devised by French couturiers after World War II. Queen Marie's coronation gown and personal artifacts are also on display. Three miles east of the museum, just off Washington State Highway 14, is an even stranger landmark in this unpopulated high-desert country: a replica of Stonehenge, built by Sam Hill as a memorial to soldiers killed in World War I. ⊠ *35 Maryhill Museum Dr., Goldendale, WA (20 mi east of The Dalles on I–84, 2 mi north of Biggs on U.S. 97, about 1 mi west on Hwy. 14),* ☎ *509/773–3733.* 🖼 *$6.50.* ⊙ *Mid-Mar.–mid-Nov., daily 9–5.*

Mount Hood

★ ㉝ *About 60 mi east of Portland on I–84 and U.S. 26; 65 mi from The Dalles, west on I–84 and south on Hwy. 35 and U.S. 26.*

Regal, snow-covered Mount Hood is currently dormant, but it is capable of the same violence that decapitated nearby Mount St. Helens in 1980. The mountain is just one feature of the 1.1-million-acre **Mount Hood National Forest,** an all-season playground that attracts more than 7 million visitors annually. Within the forest are 95 campgrounds and 50 lakes stocked with brown, rainbow, cutthroat, brook, and steelhead trout. The Sandy, Salmon, and other rivers are known for their fishing, rafting, canoeing, and swimming. Both forest and mountain are crossed by an extensive trail system for hikers, cyclists, and horseback riders. The **Pacific Crest Trail,** which begins in British Columbia and ends in Mexico, crosses here at the 4,157-ft-high Barlow Pass, the highest point on the highway. ⊠ *Information center 3 mi west of town of Zigzag on the north side of U.S. 26,* ☏ *503/622–7674.* ⊡ *Day use varies from free to $5, campsites $12–$14.* ⊙ *Information center daily 8–6; most campgrounds open year-round.*

Dining and Lodging

$$–$$$ ×⛺ **Timberline Lodge.** This National Historic Landmark has withstood howling winter storms on an exposed flank of the mountain for more than 50 years—not to mention the maniacal behavior of Jack Nicholson (in *The Shining,* one of a number of films shot here). Everything at this Work Projects Administration structure has a handcrafted, rustic feel, from the wrought-iron chairs with rawhide seats to the massive hand-hewn beams. The expert cuisine at the Cascade Dining Room incorporates the freshest Oregon products. ⊠ *Timberline Rd., Timberline 97028 (north from U.S. 26; follow signs),* ☏ *503/231–5400 or 800/547–1406,* ℻ *503/727–3710. 60 rooms. Restaurant, bar, pool, outdoor hot tub, sauna, downhill and cross-country skiing. AE, D, MC, V.*

Outdoor Activities and Sports

Timberline Lodge Ski Area. The U.S. ski team conducts summer training at this full-service ski area, which welcomes snowboarders. Timberline is famous for its Palmer chairlift, which takes skiers to a high glacier for summer skiing. There are five double chairs and two high-speed quad chairs. The top elevation is 8,500 ft, with a 3,600-ft vertical drop, and the longest run is 3 mi. Facilities include a day lodge with fast food and a ski shop; lessons and equipment rental and repair are available. ⊠ *Off U.S. 26, Timberline,* ☏ *503/272–3311.* ⊡ *Lift tickets weekdays $31, weekends $34.* ⊙ *Sun.–Tues. 9–5, Wed.–Sat. 9 AM–10 PM; lift 7 AM–1:30 PM June–Aug.*

Government Camp

㉞ *45 mi from The Dalles, south on Hwy. 35 and west on U.S. 26; 54 mi east of Portland on I–84 and U.S. 26.*

Government Camp, an alpine resort village, holds an abundance of lodging and restaurants. It's a convenient drive from here to Mount Hood's five ski resorts or to Welches, which has restaurants and a resort. A road from U.S. 26 (follow signs) leads south to **Trillium Lake** (☏ 503/666–1771), a fine spot for picnicking, overnight camping, and fishing for brown and rainbow trout.

Dining and Lodging

$$–$$$ ×⛺ **Falcon's Crest Inn.** The three common areas at this sophisticated cedar-and-glass chalet have different moods and styles, and the theme-oriented rooms run the gamut from safari to French provincial. A

nightly six-course gourmet dinner (open to nonguests; reservations essential) includes entrées like chicken stuffed with shrimp in a sauce of champagne and Pernod. The room rates include a full breakfast. ⌧ 87287 *Government Camp Loop Hwy., 97028,* ☎ *503/272–3403 or 800/624–7384,* FAX *503/272–3454. 5 rooms. Restaurant. AE, D, DC, MC, V.*

$$$ 🍽 **Mount Hood Inn.** The Mount Hood National Forest is right outside the east windows of this comfortable contemporary inn; rooms facing the southwest have a remarkable view of Ski Bowl, which is across the street. Accommodations come in various sizes, from spacious standards to king-size suites with refrigerators and hot tubs. Among the amenities are complimentary ski lockers and a ski tuning room; the rates include a Continental breakfast. ⌧ *87450 Government Camp Loop Hwy., 97028,* ☎ *503/272–3205 or 800/443–7777,* FAX *503/272–3307. 55 rooms. No-smoking rooms, hot tub, coin laundry. AE, D, DC, MC, V.*

Outdoor Activities and Sports

CROSS-COUNTRY SKIING

Nearly 120 mi of cross-country ski trails lace the **Mount Hood National Forest**; try the trailheads at Government Camp, Trillium Lake, or the Cooper Spur Ski Area, on the mountain's northeast flank.

DOWNHILL SKIING

Cooper Spur Ski and Recreation Area. This ski area on the eastern slope of Mount Hood caters to families and has two rope tows and a T-bar. The longest run is ⅔ mi, with a 500-ft vertical drop. Facilities and services include rentals, instruction, repairs, and a ski shop, day lodge, snack bar, and restaurant. ⌧ *Follow signs from Hwy. 35 for 3½ mi to ski area,* ☎ *541/352–7803.* ☉ *Call for hrs.*

Mount Hood Meadows Ski Resort. The resort, Mount Hood's largest, has more than 2,000 skiable acres, dozens of runs, seven double chairs, one triple chair, one quad chair, a top elevation of 7,300 ft, a vertical drop of 2,777 ft, and a longest run of 3 mi. Facilities include a day lodge, seven restaurants, two lounges, a ski school, and a ski shop; equipment rental and repair are also available. ⌧ *10 mi east of Government Camp on Hwy. 35,* ☎ *503/337–2222 or 800/754–4663.* ☉ *Mon.–Tues. 9–4, Wed.–Sat. 9 AM–10 PM, Sun. 9–7.*

Mount Hood Ski Bowl. The ski area closest to Portland has 63 trails serviced by four double chairs and five surface tows, a top elevation of 5,050 ft, a vertical drop of 1,500 ft, and a longest run of 3½ mi. Night skiing is a major activity here. Visitors can take advantage of two day lodges, a mid-mountain warming hut, three restaurants, and two lounges. Sleigh rides are conducted, weather permitting. ⌧ *53 mi east of Portland, across U.S. 26 from Government Camp,* ☎ *503/272–3206.* ☉ *Mon.–Thurs. 9 AM–10 PM, Fri. 9 AM–11 PM, Sat. 8:30 AM–11 PM, Sun. 8:30 AM–10 PM.*

Summit Ski Area. The longest run at Summit is ½ mi, with a 400-ft vertical drop; there's one chairlift and one rope-tow. Facilities include instruction, a ski shop, a cafeteria, and a day lodge. Bike rentals are available in summer. ⌧ *Government Camp Loop Hwy., east end, Government Camp,* ☎ *503/272–0256.* ☉ *Nov.–Apr., daily 9–5.*

SUMMER SPORTS

🍃 During the summer months, **Ski Bowl** has go-carts, mountain- and alpine-bike rentals, and pony rides. The **Alpine Slide** gives the intrepid a chance to whiz down the slopes on a European-style toboggan run. This is heady stuff, with a marvelous view. **Eastside Action Park,** ½ mi to the east, has more than 20 kids-oriented attractions, including something called the Rapid Riser, a sort of reverse bungee-jumping device that catapults riders 80 ft in the air. ⌧ *87000 E. Hwy. 26 (at milepost*

53), ☎ *503/222–2695.* 🎟 *Day pass $25.* ⊙ *June–Sept., weekdays 11– 6, weekends 10–7 (weather permitting).*

Welches and Zigzag

14 mi west of Government Camp on U.S. 26; 40 mi east of Portland, I–84 to U.S. 26.

These two small towns at the base of Mount Hood have restaurants and other services. Drop by the **Mount Hood Visitors Center** (✉ 65000 E. Hwy. 26, ☎ 503/622–3017) in Welches for detailed information on all the area attractions.

Dining and Lodging

$–$$ ✕🏨 **Resort at the Mountain.** This sprawling golf and ski resort in the burly Cascade foothills is the Mount Hood area's most complete resort. Outdoor activities are plentiful, including fly-fishing on the Salmon River, horseback riding, white-water rafting, and croquet. Accommodations run from double rooms to two-bedroom condos. Each of the tastefully decorated rooms has a deck or patio overlooking the forest, courtyard, or a fairway. The Pacific Northwest cuisine at the Highlands restaurant includes fillet of salmon with fresh herbs and red wine, venison with black-currant sauce, and quail sautéed with mustard. They also serve a Sunday brunch. The resort is about a one-hour drive east of Portland. ✉ *68010 E. Fairway Ave. (follow signs south from U.S. 26 in Welches), 97067,* ☎ *503/622–3101 or 800/669–7666,* 📠 *503/622–2222. 160 rooms. 2 restaurants, 2 bars, pool, indoor and outdoor hot tubs, 9- and 18-hole golf courses, 6 tennis courts, health club, bicycles, meeting rooms. AE, D, DC, MC, V.*

The Columbia River Gorge and the Oregon Cascades Essentials

Arriving and Departing

BY BUS

Greyhound (☎ 800/231–2222) provides service from Portland to Troutdale, Hood River, The Dalles, and Government Camp.

BY CAR

I–84 is the main east–west route into the Columbia River Gorge. **U.S. 26** heading east from Portland and northwest from Prineville is the main route into the Mount Hood area. The portions of I–84 and U.S. 26 that pass through the mountains can be difficult to maneuver in winter, though the state plows them regularly. The gorge is closed frequently during harsh winters due to ice and mudslides. It can also get extremely windy here. **U.S. 97** heads north from Weed, California, to Klamath Falls, then north to Bend.

BY PLANE

Klamath Falls International Airport (☎ 541/883–5372) is served by Horizon Air.

BY TRAIN

The daily **Amtrak** (☎ 800/872–7245) *Coast Starlight,* which runs between Seattle, Portland, Oakland, and Los Angeles, stops in Klamath Falls.

Getting Around

BY CAR

The **Historic Columbia River Highway** (U.S. 30) from Troutdale to just east of Oneonta Gorge passes Crown Point State Park and Multnomah Falls. **I–84/U.S. 30** continues on to The Dalles. **Highway 35** heads south from The Dalles to the Mount Hood area, intersecting with U.S. 26 at Government Camp.

Visitor Information

Hood River County Chamber of Commerce (⊠ Port Marina Park, 97031, ☎ 541/386–2000 or 800/366–3530). **Klamath County Tourism Dept.** (⊠ Box 1867, Klamath Falls 97601, ☎ 541/884–0666). **Mount Hood National Forest Ranger Stations** (⊠ 6780 Hwy. 35, Mount Hood, 97041, ☎ 541/352–6002; ⊠ Superintendent, 16400 Champion Way off Hwy. 26, Sandy 97055, ☎ 503/668–1771; ⊠ Mount Hood Information Center, 65000 E. Hwy. 26, Welches 97067, ☎ 503/622–7674; ⊠ 70220 W. Hwy. 26, Zigzag 97049, ☎ 503/662–3191). **Mount Hood Recreation Association** (⊠ 65000 E. Hwy. 26, Welches 97067, ☎ 503/622–3162 or 503/622–4822).

CENTRAL OREGON

The arid landscape east of the Cascades differs dramatically from that on the lush, wet western side. Crossing the mountains, you enter a high-desert plateau with scrubby buttes, forests of ponderosa pine, and mile after mile of sun-bleached earth. The booming resort town of Bend is the most prominent playground in central Oregon, but within the region are dozens of other outdoor recreational hubs, many of them blissfully uncrowded.

Numbers in the margin correspond to numbers on the Columbia River Gorge, the Cascades, and Central Oregon map.

Warm Springs

115 mi southeast of Portland on U.S. 26.

Warm Springs, in the southeastern corner of the 640,000-acre Warm Springs Indian Reservation, is not so much a town as a place to refuel, stretch your legs, and take a deep breath of the juniper-scented high-desert air.

The Confederated Tribes of the Warm Springs Reservation created the **Museum at Warm Springs** just south of town to preserve their traditions and keep their legacy alive. On display are tribal heirlooms, beaded artifacts, baskets, historic photographs, ceramics, and traditional dwellings. The museum's gift shop sells Native American crafts. ⊠ 2189 U.S. 26, ☎ 541/553–3331. ⊡ $6. ☉ Daily 10–5.

Dining and Lodging

$$$ ✕⊡ **Kah-Nee-Tah Resort and Casino.** Located in a remote desert spot in the middle of the Warm Springs Reservation, Kah-Nee-Ta is perfect for a quick getaway from Portland. The culture of the native Wasco, Warm Springs, and Paiute tribes permeates the luxurious resort, where traditional Indian salmon bakes, festivals, arts events, and dances enliven an austerely beautiful setting. In addition to the hotel and casino (300 slots, blackjack, and poker), there is an RV park and Spa Wanapine, which has aromatherapy, massage, reflexology, facials, and manicure. Mineral hot springs bubbling up from the desert floor fill baths and pools. If you like to rough it and don't mind bringing your own bedroll, check into one of the wood-frame, canvas-covered tepees. The Warm Springs, Wasco, and Paiute suites, which cost a little extra, have tile fireplaces and hot tubs, big-screen TVs, king-size beds, and grand desert views. The resort sets aside kayaks for guests to use. ⊠ 6823 Hwy. 8 (11 mi north of Warm Springs), Hwy. 3 north of U.S. 26 (follow signs), 97761, ☎ 541/553–6123 or 800/831–0100, ℻ 541/553–6119. 139 rooms, 21 tepees. 2 restaurants, bar, 2 pools, hot tubs, *sauna, 18-hole golf course, tennis court, exercise room, hiking, horseback riding, water slide, fishing, mountain bikes, casino, convention center. AE, D, DC, MC, V.*

Bend

35 *58 mi south of Warm Springs, U.S. 26 to U.S. 97; 160 mi from Portland, east and south on U.S. 26 and south on U.S. 97.*

Bend, a city of 30,000 that very nearly sits in the center of Oregon, occupies a high-desert plateau perfumed with juniper and surrounded by 10,000-ft Cascade peaks. Called Bend because it was built on Farewell Bend in the Deschutes River—an easy-flowing river that becomes a roaring cataract a few miles downstream—the city holds restaurants, dance bars, equipment-rental places, and reasonably priced hostelries. Because Bend is among Oregon's fastest-growing cities, its stretch of U.S. 20 has become one enormous strip mall and is frequently snarled with traffic. To see old Bend, turn off the highway and head downtown.

The intricately crafted walk-through dioramas at the **High Desert Museum** include a stone-age Indian campsite, a pioneer wagon camp, a mine, and an Old West boardwalk. The displays capture the sights and even the smells of various historical periods. There are outstanding exhibits on local Native American cultures as well. In the 150-acre outdoor section, fat porcupines, baleful birds of prey, and crowd-pleasing river otters play aboveground and underwater. ⊠ *59800 S. Hwy. 97, 3 ½ mi south of Bend,* ☎ *541/382–4754.* ⊠ *$6.25.* ⊙ *Daily 9–5.*

OFF THE BEATEN PATH

NEWBERRY VOLCANIC NATIONAL MONUMENT – The last time Newberry Volcano blew its top was about 13 centuries ago. Paulina Peak, up an unpaved road at the south end of the national monument, has the best view into the crater and its two lakes (Paulina and East). Lava Butte and Lava River Cave are at the north end of the monument near the visitor center. ⊠ *Visitor center: U.S. 97, 10 mi south of Bend,* ☎ *541/388–2715.* ⊠ *$5 per vehicle.* ⊙ *Memorial Day–Labor Day, daily 9:30–5; Labor Day–Memorial Day, Wed.–Sun. 9:30–5.*

Dining and Lodging

$$ ✕ **Coho Grill.** Innovative Pacific Northwest dishes, geared to the season, are the hallmarks of this well-respected restaurant. Asparagus, fresh fish, and Cascade morels are on the spring menu; in the fall expect Oregon crab and fruits from the Hood River valley and in winter American classics like pot roast and braised lamb shanks. ⊠ *61535 Fargo La.,* ☎ *541/388–3909. AE, MC, V.*

$$ ✕ **Giuseppe's Ristorante.** This downtown restaurant has won awards for its ethnic Italian food—homemade pastas, chicken, seafood, veal, steak, and vegetarian dishes. ⊠ *932 N.W. Bond St.,* ☎ *541/389–8899. AE, DC, MC, V. Closed Mon. No lunch.*

$ ✕ **Deschutes Brewery & Public House.** Try the admirable Black Butte Porter, a local ale, at this brew pub, which serves upscale Pacific Northwest cuisine. Gourmet burgers and sandwiches, such as smoked salmon sandwich, brewery-cured pastrami reuben, or chicken enchiladas, dominate the menu. Vegetarians can choose the smoked vegetable sandwich or the vegetarian black bean chili. Dinner specials vary daily (check the blackboard) and frequently include smoked prime rib or grilled marlin. Portions are large. ⊠ *1044 N.W. Bond St.,* ☎ *541/382–9242. Reservations not accepted. MC, V.*

$$ ✕🏠 **Inn of the Seventh Mountain.** This resort nestled in ponderosa pines in the Deschutes National Forest has been offering year-round outdoor

activities and relaxation for 25 years. It's on the banks of the Deschutes River, so white-water rafting and fishing are right at your doorstep in summer. On the property are a host of recreational facilities, including a 65-ft water slide, canoeing, and an outdoor ice-skating rink. Five golf courses are within 15 minutes, and Mount Bachelor, with great downhill skiing, is only 14 mi away. The inn is child-friendly: Kids Camp 7 offers activities for children ages 4 to 11. Accommodations include standard bedrooms with a queen-size bed, deluxe bedrooms with an additional Murphy bed and private deck, and studios with fireplaces and full kitchens. There are also suites and lofts with extra amenities. Dining options include Josiah's restaurant, which serves pasta, seafood, and steak; and a café off the lobby. This is a very good value. ⊠ *18575 S.W. Century Dr., Bend 97702,* ☎ *800/452–6810,* FAX *541/382–3517. 300 rooms. 2 restaurants, bar, deli, grocery, 2 pools, hot tub, 4 tennis courts, horseback riding, jogging, water slide, fishing, ice-skating, children's programs, meeting rooms. AE, D, DC, MC, V.*

\$\$\$–\$\$\$\$ 🖬 **Sunriver Resort.** One of Oregon's premier outdoor resort destinations, Sunriver provides a slew of facilities and is convenient to skiing at Mount Bachelor; Class 4 white-water rafting on the Deschutes River (which flows right through the complex); and high-desert hiking and mountain biking. A former army base, the self-contained community has stores, restaurants, contemporary homes, condominiums, and even a private airstrip—all in a pine-scented desert landscape. Visitors can rent condos, hotel rooms, or houses; shops rent a host of outdoorsy paraphernalia. ⊠ *Box 3609, Sunriver 97707 (west of U.S. 97, 15 mi south of Bend),* ☎ *541/593–1000 or 800/547–3922,* FAX *541/593–5458. 510 units. 6 restaurants, 2 pools, no-smoking rooms, hot tubs, saunas, three 18-hole golf courses, 28 tennis courts, horseback riding, boating, fishing, bicycles. AE, D, DC, MC, V.*

\$–\$\$\$ 🖬 **Lara House Bed & Breakfast Inn.** This restored 1910 Craftsman house sits on a huge sloping lot in a residential district overlooking Drake Park and Mirror Pond, a five-minute walk from downtown. The rooms, all on the second floor, have seating areas and private bathrooms, and the public areas are sunny and inviting. Breakfast is included. Smoking is not permitted. ⊠ *640 N.W. Congress St., 97701 (west 1 mi on Franklin St. from U.S. 97),* ☎ FAX *541/388–4064 or* ☎ *800/766–4064. 6 rooms. Outdoor hot tub. D, MC, V.*

\$\$ 🖬 **The Riverhouse.** A cut or two above what you'd expect given its very reasonable rates, this hotel within earshot of the rushing Deschutes River contains large rooms with contemporary oak furniture. Many have river views—well worth the extra \$5 charge. ⊠ *3075 N. Hwy. 97, 97701,* ☎ *541/389–3111 or 800/547–3928,* FAX *541/389–0870. 220 units. 3 restaurants, bar, indoor and outdoor pools, hot tub, sauna, 18-hole golf course, 2 tennis courts, exercise room, jogging. AE, D, DC, MC, V.*

\$\$ 🖬 **Sather House Bed & Breakfast.** The Colonial Revival Sather House, built in 1911, occupies a prominent spot in Bend's oldest residential neighborhood. The exterior, glistening white with green trim, has a wraparound veranda and overhanging eaves; period furnishings and original Douglas-fir woodwork fill the interior. Breakfast, included in the room rates and served in the formal dining room, typically consists of French toast with raspberries and almonds, or pecan pancakes; fireside teas are served in the winter, and lemonade and cookies are on the veranda in the summer. Rooms are bright with large windows and have private baths. Smoking and pets are not allowed at the inn. ⊠ *7 N.W. Tumalo, 97701,* ☎ *541/388–1065.* FAX *541/* · *4 rooms. D, MC, V.*

Outdoor Activities and Sports

BICYCLING

U.S. 97 north to the Crooked River Gorge and the Smith Rocks provides bikers with memorable scenery and a good workout. **Sunriver** (☞ Dining and Lodging, *above*) has 26 mi of paved bike paths.

CANOEING AND RAFTING

The **Deschutes River** flows north from the Cascades west of Bend, gaining volume and momentum as it nears its rendezvous with the Columbia River at The Dalles. Its upper stretches, particularly those near Sunriver and Bend, are placid and suitable for leisurely canoeing. Whitewater rafters flock to the stretch of the Deschutes between Madras and Maupin. You need a state marine boater pass to participate. For details contact the **Bureau of Land Management** (☎ 541/416–6700) in Prineville.

Rafting Guides: The following businesses offer white-water rafting trips on the Deschutes River near Bend: **River Trails Deschutes** (⊠ Box 309, Maupin 97037, ☎ 541/395–2545 or 888/324–8837); **Portland River Co.** (⊠ 0315 S.W. Montgomery St., Portland 97201, ☎ 503/229–0551); **Sun Country Tours** (531 S.W. 13th St., Bend 97702, ☎ 800/770–2161); and **Inn of the Seventh Mountain Whitewater Rafting** (18575 S.W. Century Dr., Bend 97702, ☎ 541/382–8711).

GOLF

The semi-private **Awbrey Glen Golf Club** (⊠ 2500 N.W. Awbrey Glen Dr., ☎ 541/388–8526 or 800/697–0052), an 18-hole, par-72 course, is open to the public daily between 11 and 4. The greens fee is $30–$62; an optional cart costs $14. **Rivers Edge Golf Course** (⊠ 400 Pro Shop Dr., ☎ 541/389–2828) is an 18-hole, par-72 course. The greens fee ranges $32–$42; an optional cart costs $13.

SKIING

Mount Bachelor Resort (⊠ 22 mi southwest of Bend off U.S. 97, ☎ 541/382–7888 or 800/829–2442), the Northwest's largest facility, is one of the best in the United States—60% of the downhill runs are rated expert. One of the 11 lifts takes skiers all the way to the mountain's 9,065-ft summit. The vertical drop is 3,265 ft; the longest of the 70 runs is 2 mi. Facilities and services include equipment rental and repair, a ski school, ski shop, Nordic skiing, weekly races, and day care; visitors can enjoy restaurants, bars, and six lodges. The 36 mi of trails at the **Mount Bachelor Nordic Center,** most of them near the base of the mountain, are by and large intermediate.

Many Nordic trails—more than 165 mi of them—wind through the **Deschutes National Forest.** For information about conditions call ☎ 541/388–2715.

Sisters

18 mi northwest of Bend on U.S. 20.

Sisters, with a population of about 3,000, provides an alternative to the frenetic pace and traffic tie-ups that plague Bend. The town was named for and sits in the lap of the stunning mountain peaks known as the "Sisters." To lure tourists, it has adopted a western look.

Dining and Lodging

$–$$ ✕ **Hotel Sisters Restaurant.** The most popular restaurant in Sisters first opened as a hotel in 1912. Broiled steaks, barbecued chicken and ribs, and Mexican dishes form the backbone of the extensive menu. ⊠ *105 W. Cascade St.,* ☎ *541/549–7427. AE, MC, V.*

$ ✕ **Seasons.** Gourmet quiches, salads, and sandwiches are among the fare at this small café and wine shop with a streamside picnic area in the back. ⊠ *411 E. Hood St.,* ☎ *541/549–8911. MC, V. No dinner.*

$$$ 🏨 **Metolius River Resort.** The wood-shake cabins in this upscale resort 14 mi from Sisters have fully equipped kitchens, river-rock fireplaces laid with firewood, and large riverside decks. The atmosphere resembles that of a 1930s alpine fishing village. All units are no-smoking and set up for at least four guests. From late spring to fall, there's dining at the adjacent Kokanee Cafe. ⊠ *Forest Service Rd. 1419, Camp Sherman 97730 (take U.S. 20 northeast 10 mi from Sisters, turn north on Camp Sherman Rd. and east on Forest Service Rd. 1419),* ☎ *541/595– 6281 or 800/595–6290,* 🖷 *541/595–6281. 11 cabins. In-room VCRs, refrigerators, fishing. MC, V.*

Prineville

52 mi east of Sisters on Hwy. 126; 35 mi northeast of Bend on Hwy. 126 and U.S. 97; 146 mi southeast of Portland on U.S. 26.

Despite its rough-hewn reputation, Prineville, the oldest town in Oregon and the state's unofficial "cowboy capital," was once the most genteel place in central Oregon. Nearby Bend now takes the honors in the trendy department, but low-key Prineville still makes a good base for exploring the **Crooked River** and the **Ochoco National Forest.** The town is a worldwide mecca for rock hounds, who come seeking agate, obsidian, and other rocks.

Exhibits and artifacts at the **Bowman Museum** document Prineville's history as the booming cattle and logging center of Crook County. ⊠ *246 N. Main St.,* ☎ *541/447–3715.* 🖭 *$1 suggested donation.* ☉ *Mar.– Dec., weekdays 10–5, Sat. 11–4.*

Dining and Lodging

$$ ✕ **Crooked River Railroad Company Dinner Train.** Dine aboard this excursion train as it winds through the rimrock-lined Crooked River valley between Redmond and Prineville. The ride and show are the draw here; the food is nothing special. Murder mysteries are played out on Saturday nights year-round and on Friday nights from June to September, while a simulated Jesse James train robbery keeps the Sunday champagne brunch hopping with live entertainment. Call for reservations and departure times. ⊠ *525 S.W. 6th St., Redmond,* ☎ *541/548– 8630. AE, D, MC, V.*

$ ✕ **Dad's Place.** A typical American diner, Dad's dishes out no-nonsense breakfasts and lunches at no-nonsense prices. If you're not afraid of fat and cholesterol, try the sandwich of ham, bacon, cheese, and egg on a toasted biscuit. ⊠ *229 N. Main St.,* ☎ *541/447–7059. MC, V. Closed Sun. No dinner.*

$–$$ 🏨 **Rustler's Roost.** From the old-style covered walkways to the large, antiques-furnished rooms, this motel is Old West all the way. Each room is decorated differently—if you call in advance, the managers will attempt to match your sleeping decor to your personality. Some rooms have kitchenettes. ⊠ *960 W. 3rd St./U.S. 26, 97754,* ☎ *541/447–4185. 20 rooms. AE, D, DC, MC, V.*

$ 🏨 **Elliott House.** With its thick green lawns, wraparound porch, Tuscan columns, and bay windows, this B&B stands out like a wellgroomed dowager in an otherwise undistinguished neighborhood. Century-old furnishings and accessories fill the house. One of the two rooms contains a double cast-iron bed and an embroidered quilt, and the large shared bathroom has original brass fixtures and a marbletop sink. Breakfast is served on antique china. ⊠ *305 W. 1st St.,*

97754, ☎ 541/416–0423, ℻ 541/416–9368. *2 rooms share bath. No-smoking rooms. No credit cards.*

Ochoco National Forest

36 *25 mi east of Prineville off U.S. 26.*

East of the flat juniper-dotted countryside around Prineville the landscape changes to forested ridges covered with tall ponderosa pines and Douglas firs. Sheltered by the diminutive Ochoco Mountains and with only about a foot of rain each year, the **Ochoco National Forest** manages to lay a blanket of green across the dry high desert of central Oregon. This arid landscape—marked by deep canyons, towering volcanic plugs, and sharp ridges—goes largely unnoticed except for the annual influx of hunters during the fall. The Ochoco is a great place for camping, hiking, biking, and fishing in relative solitude. In its three wilderness areas—Mill Creek, Bridge Creek, and Black Canyon—where cars, roads, and even bicycles are not allowed, it's possible to see elk, wild horses, eagles, and even cougars. ⊠ *Ochoco National Forest Headquarters/Prineville Ranger Station, 3160 N.E. 3rd St. (U.S. 26),* ☎ *541/ 416–6500.* ☼ *Forest year-round (some sections closed during bad weather), ranger station weekdays 7:30–4:30.*

The **Ochoco Ranger Station** has trail maps and other information. ⊠ *County Rd. 23 (25 mi east of Prineville off U.S. 26),* ☎ *541/416–6645.* ☼ *Daily 7–4:30.*

OFF THE
BEATEN PATH
BIG SUMMIT PRAIRIE LOOP – This 43-mi scenic route starts at the Ochoco Ranger Station (☞ *above*) and winds past Lookout Mountain, Round Mountain, Walton Lake, and Big Summit Prairie. The prairie abounds with trout-filled creeks and has one of the finest stands of ponderosa pines in the state; wild mustangs roam the area. The prairie can be glorious between late May and June, when wildflowers with evocative names like mules ear, wyethia, biscuit root, and yellow bells burst into bloom. ⊠ *Forest Service Rd. 22 east to Forest Service Rd. 30 (which turns into Forest Service Rd. 3010) south, to Forest Service Rd. 42 heading west, which loops back to Forest Service Rd. 22.*

Camping

Most of the area's developed campsites are open between May and September. All operate on a first-come, first-served basis. Phone 541/ 416–6500 for campground information.

⚠ **Ochoco Forest Camp.** Elk, wild horses, and mule deer thrive at this campground adjacent to the Ochoco Ranger Station and the trailhead for the Lookout Mountain Trail. The tent sites are along Ochoco Creek. ⊠ *Forest Service Rd. 2610, 25 mi east of Prineville. 6 sites.* 🍴 *$8. Pit toilets, potable water.*

⚠ **Walton Lake Campground.** This developed setting on Walton Lake is a great place for an afternoon swim or a trek along the nearby Round Mountain Trail. The sites fill up early on weekends and holidays. ⊠ *Forest Service Rd. 22; from Prineville head northeast on U.S. 26 for 15 mi, east on County Rd. 23 for 8 mi, and northeast on Forest Service Rd. 22 for 7 mi. 30 sites.* 🍴 *$8. Pit toilets, potable water.*

⚠ **Wildcat Campground.** On the edge of the Mill Creek Wilderness amid ponderosa pines, Wildcat is the trailhead for the Twin Pillars Trail. ⊠ *Mill Creek Rd./Forest Service Rd. 33; from Prineville head northeast on U.S. 26 for 10 mi and north on Mill Creek Rd. for 10 mi. 17 sites.* 🍴 *$10. Pit toilets, potable water. Closed Nov.–Mar., depending on weather.*

Outdoor Activities and Sports

BIKING

The Ochoco National Forest contains hundreds of miles of dirt roads and multiuse trails. The forest headquarters (☞ *above*) has a guide to 10 trails in the forest. Cougar Trail and the more harrowing Lone Mountain Trail, both about 25 mi east of Prineville, are two worthy options.

FISHING

Steelhead and rainbow trout pack the forest's rivers and streams, but serious fly fishers should head south of Prineville on Highway 27, which parallels Crooked River. Along the way are the bankside Bureau of Land Management campgrounds, where you can pull off and troll for fish. Walton Lake (☞ Camping, *above*) also has fishing. Most large supermarkets sell permits, as does **Prineville Sporting Goods** (⌂ 346 N. Deer St., off U.S. 26, ☎ 541/447–6883).

HIKING

Pick up maps at the Prineville or Ochoco ranger station (☞ *above*) for the trails through the 5,400-acre **Bridge Creek Wilderness** and the demanding **Black Canyon Trail** (24 mi round-trip) in the Black Canyon Wilderness. The 1½-mi **Ponderosa Loop Trail** follows an old logging road through ponderosa pines growing on rolling hills. In early summer, wildflowers take over the open meadows. The trailhead begins at Bandit Springs Rest Area, 22 mi east of Prineville on U.S. 26. A 2½-mi, one-way trail winds through old-growth forest and mountain meadows to **Steins Pillar,** a giant lava column with panoramic views; be prepared for a workout on the trail's poorly maintained second half, and allow at least three hours for the hike. To get to the trailhead drive east 9 mi from Prineville on U.S. 26, head north (to the left) for 6½ mi on Mill Creek Road (also signed as Forest Service Road 33), and head east (to the right) on Forest Service Road 500.

ROCKHOUNDING

Stones in the area include agate, obsidian, fire obsidian, petrified wood, and red and green jasper. A free brochure from forest headquarters and the informative "Rockhound's Handbook," available from the Prineville/Crook County Chamber of Commerce (☞ Visitor Information, *below*), map out the best locations for prospecting.

Thunder eggs—egg-shape rocks with crystalline interiors—can be found at **White Fir Springs** (⌂ Forest Service Rd. 3350; from Prineville head east on U.S. 26 to milepost 41, turn left, and continue for about 5 mi).

SKIING

Two loops for cross-country skiers start at Bandit Springs Rest Area, 29 mi east of Prineville on U.S. 26. One loop is designed for beginners and the other for intermediate to advanced skiers. Both traverse the area near the Ochoco Divide and have great views. The forest headquarters (☞ *above*) has a handout on the trails and can provide the required Sno-Park permits, which are also available from the **Department of Motor Vehicles** (⌂ Ochoco Plaza, 1595 E. 3rd St., Suite A-3, Prineville, ☎ 541/447–7855).

Central Oregon Essentials

Arriving and Departing

BY BUS

Greyhound (☎ 800/231–2222) serves Bend and Sisters from Portland.

BY CAR

U.S. 20 heads west from Idaho and east from the coastal town of Newport into central Oregon. **U.S. 26** travels southeast from Portland to

Prineville, where it heads northeast into the Ochoco National Forest. **U.S. 97** heads north from California and south from Washington to Bend. **Highway 126** travels east from Eugene to Prineville; it connects with U.S. 20 heading south (to Bend) at Sisters.

BY PLANE

Bend-Redmond Municipal Airport (☎ 541/548–6059) is served by **Horizon** (☎ 800/547–9308) and **United Express** (☎ 800/241–6522).

Getting Around

BY BUS

See Getting Around *in* Oregon A to Z, *below.*

BY CAR

Roads throughout central Oregon (☞ Arriving and Departing, *above*) are well maintained and open throughout the winter season, though it's always advisable to carry chains.

Guided Tours

Oregon Llamas (☎ 541/595–2088 or 888/722–5262), north of Sisters in Camp Sherman, operates fully catered three- to five-day llama treks in the Sisters, Mount Jefferson, and Cascade wilderness areas.

Visitor Information

Central Oregon Visitors Association (✉ 63085 N. Hwy. 97, Suite 104, Bend 97701, ☎ 541/389–8799 or 800/800–8334). **Confederated Tribes of Warm Springs** (✉ Warm Springs 97761, ☎ 541/553–1161). **Deschutes National Forest** (✉ 1645 Hwy. 20 E, Bend 97701, ☎ 541/388–2715). **Ochoco National Forest Headquarters and Prineville Ranger Station** (✉ 3160 N.E. 3rd St., Prineville 07754, ☎ 541/416–6500). **Prineville/Crook County Chamber of Commerce** (✉ 390 N. Fairview St., 97754, ☎ 541/447–6304). **Sisters Chamber of Commerce** (✉ 222 Hood Ave., 97759, ☎ 541/549–0251).

EASTERN OREGON

Travel east from The Dalles, Bend, or any of the foothill communities blossoming in the shade of the Cascades, and a very different side of Oregon makes its appearance. The air is drier, clearer, and often pungent with the smell of juniper. The vast landscape of sharply folded hills, wheat fields, and mountains shimmering in the distance evokes the Old West. There is a lonely grandeur in eastern Oregon, a plain-spoken, independent spirit that can startle, surprise, and entrance.

Much of eastern Oregon consists of national forest and wilderness, and the people who live here lead very real, very rural lives. This is a world of ranches and rodeos, pickup trucks and country-western music. Some of the most important moments in Oregon's history took place in the towns of northeastern Oregon. The Oregon Trail passed through this corner of the state, winding through the Grande Ronde Valley between the Wallowa and Blue mountain ranges. The discovery of gold in the region in the 1860s sparked a second invasion of settlers and eventually led to the displacement of the Native American Nez Perce and Paiute tribes. Pendleton, La Grande, and Baker City were all beneficiaries of the gold fever that swept through the area.

Numbers in the margin correspond to points of interest on the Eastern Oregon map.

Eastern Oregon

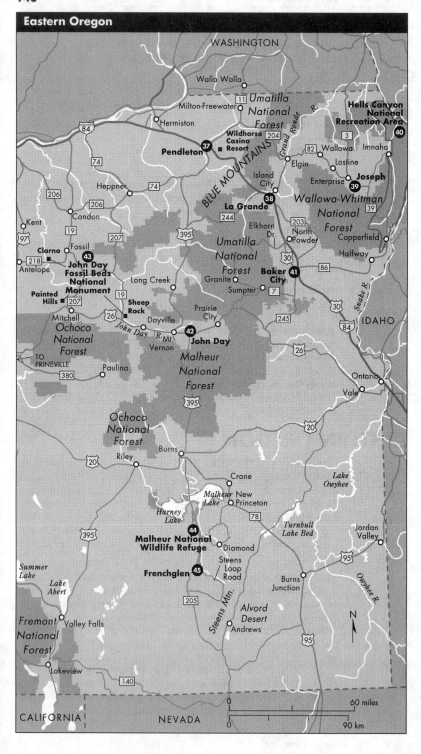

WASHINGTON

Walla Walla

Milton-Freewater

11

Hermiston

Umatilla
National
Forest

Hells Canyon
National
Recreation Area

84

74

Pendleton

37

Wildhorse
Casino
Resort

204

3

82

Wallowa

Lostine

Imnaha

40

Grand Ronde R.

Heppner

74

Island
City

Elgin

Enterprise

Joseph

39

206

206

La Grande

38

244

Wallowa-Whitman
National
Forest

39

Kent

97

Condon

19

207

Umatilla
National
Forest

395

Elkhorn
Dr.

North
Powder

203

30

Copperfield

Halfway

Clarno

43

Fossil

John Day
Fossil Beds
National
Monument

218

Antelope

Long Creek

Granite

Baker
City

41

7

86

Snake R.

Painted
Hills

207

19

Sheep
Rock

26

Dayville

245

30

Mitchell

John Day R.

R. Mi.
Vernon

John Day

42

84

IDAHO

Ochoco
National
Forest

Prairie
City

Malheur
National
Forest

26

TO
PRINEVILLE

380

Paulina

395

Ontario

Vale

Ochoco
National
Forest

Burns

20

20

Riley

Crane

Lake
Owyhee

Malheur
Lake

New
Princeton

Harney
Lake

78

Turnbull
Lake Bed

Jordan
Valley

Summer
Lake

395

Malheur National
Wildlife Refuge

44

Diamond

Steens
Loop
Road

95

Owyhee R.

Lake
Abert

Frenchglen

45

205

Burns
Junction

Fremont
National
Forest

Valley Falls

Steens Mtn.

Alvord
Desert

Andrews

95

N

Lakeview

140

0   60 miles

CALIFORNIA

NEVADA

0   90 km

Pendleton

37 *211 mi east of Portland; 129 mi east of The Dalles on I–84.*

At the foot of the Blue Mountains amid vast wheat fields and cattle ranches, Pendleton is a quintessential western town with a rip-snorting history. The huge herds of wild horses that once thundered across this rolling landscape were at the center of the area's early Native American cultures. Later, Pendleton became an important pioneer junction and home to a sizable Chinese community. Lacking a sheriff until 1912, Pendleton was a raw and wild frontier town filled with cowboys, cattle rustlers, saloons, and bordellos. The many century-old homes still standing range in style from simple farmhouses to stately Queen Annes.

Given its raucous past, Pendleton, the largest city in eastern Oregon (population 15,900), looks unusually sedate. But all that changes in September when the **Pendleton Round-Up** (☞ Outdoor Activities and Sports, *below*) draws thousands for a rodeo and related events. Motels fill up, schools close down, and everybody goes hog-wild for a few days.

The **Pendleton Woolen Mills** produce superb Indian blankets and Pendleton shirts and sportswear. In days past the clothing of choice for cowboys, the western and Indian-inspired threads have gained popularity among urbanites for their colors, warmth, and durability. A free tour that lasts about 20 minutes describes the weaving process from start to finish. The mill's retail store stocks blankets and men's clothing; there are good bargains on factory seconds. ⊠ *1307 S.E. Court Pl.,* ☎ *541/ 276–6911.* ⊙ *Mon.–Sat. 8–5; tours weekdays at 9, 11, 1:30, 3.*

The collection at the **Round-Up Hall of Fame Museum** spans the rodeo's history since 1910 with photographs—including some great ones of Rodeo Queens and the Happy Canyon Princesses (all Native American)—as well as saddles, guns, costumes, and even a stuffed championship bronco named War Paint. ⊠ *Round-Up Grounds, 1205 S.W. Court Ave., near S.W. 12th St.,* ☎ *541/278–0815.* ⊠ *Free.* ⊙ *May–Oct., daily 10–5; other times, call for appointment.*

The **Underground,** a 90-minute vividly guided tour, yields clues about life in Pendleton a century ago, when the town held 32 saloons and 18 brothels. The first half of the tour heads into a subterranean labyrinth that hid gambling rooms, an opium den, and other illegal businesses. Chinese laborers lived in a chilly jumble of underground rooms. The second half focuses on the life of Madame Stella Darby, the town's best-known madam, and includes a visit to her bordello. Tours operate year-round and leave at various times during the day. Call for information; reservations are strongly recommended. ⊠ *37 S.W. Emigrant Ave.,* ☎ *541/276–0730 or 800/226–6398.* ⊠ *$10.*

The **Tamástslikt Cultural Institute** (⊠ *72777 Hwy. 331,* ☎ *541/966–9748*) at the Wildhorse Casino Resort (☞ Dining and Lodging, *below*) opened in 1998. The $18 million, 45,000-square-ft building has exhibits depicting history from the perspective of the Cayuse, Umatilla, and Walla Walla tribes. An art gallery showcases art of local and regional tribal artists. There's also a museum gift shop, a theater, and a café. Tamástslikt means "interpret" in the Walla Walla native language. The institute is operated by the Confederated Tribes of the Umatilla Indian Reservation. ⊠ *72789 Hwy. 331, north of I–84 at Exit 216, 97801,* ☎ *541/966–9748.* ⊠ *$6.* ⊙ *Daily 9–5.*

Displays and photographs at the **Umatilla County Historical Society Museum** outline Pendleton's story. The town's old railway depot houses the museum. ⊠ *108 S.W. Frazer Ave.,* ☎ *541/276–0012.* ⊠ *$2.* ⊙ *Tues.–Sat. 10–4.*

The **Pendleton Chamber of Commerce** (⊠ 501 S. Main St., ☎ 541/276–7411 or 800/547–8911), open on weekdays between 8 and 5, has information about the town and surrounding area, including the Umatilla National Forest and the Blue Mountains.

Dining and Lodging

$$ ✗ **Cimmiyotti's.** Eat here just to enjoy the Old West decor, complete with chandeliers and flocked wallpaper. Well-prepared steaks and Italian food are the main fare. ⊠ 137 S. Main St., ☎ 541/276–4314. AE, DC, MC, V. Closed Sun. No lunch.

$$ ✗ **Raphael's.** Chef Raphael Hoffman serves traditional steaks, seafood, and fettuccine dishes, but she also specializes in adventurous seasonal cuisine—venison, elk, rattlesnake, blackened Cajun alligator, and Indian salmon topped with huckleberries. This may be the only place in eastern Oregon to get a huckleberry daiquiri. A garden out back is perfect for alfresco dining. ⊠ 233 S.E. 4th St., ☎ 541/276–8500. AE, D, DC, MC, V. Closed Sun.–Mon. No lunch.

$ ✗ **Great Pacific Wine and Coffee Company.** Yes, it is possible to get a decent cup of coffee—even a latte—in Pendleton. This downtown café, open until 6 PM, also serves bagels, muffins, and good deli sandwiches; dozens of gourmet beers and wines are available. ⊠ 403 S. Main St., ☎ 541/276–1350. AE, MC, V. Closed Sun.

$ ✗ **Rainbow Cafe.** Even if you don't eat, drink, or pass out here, you owe it to yourself to step through the swinging door and into the past: The Rainbow is a glimpse of how the West was fun. Take a seat at the counter surrounded by crusty locals eating fried-egg sandwiches, tall stacks of hotcakes, and fried chicken. ⊠ 209 S. Main St., ☎ 541/276–4120. No credit cards.

$$ ▥ **Parker House.** Virtually unchanged since it was built in 1917, this
★   handsome pink stucco home in Pendleton's North Hill neighborhood is a very grand reminder that the Old West had its share of wealth and worldly sophistication. A hybrid blend of French neoclassical and Italianate styles, Parker House is a rarity among B&Bs: It still has its original Chinese wallpaper, custom fittings, and woodwork, which is nothing less than astonishing. The rooms, furnished with period furniture, are quiet and comfortable. Four of the rooms share one bathroom, but once you see it you'll understand why the owner has chosen to preserve everything as it was rather than adding modern "improvements." Breakfasts are delicious and filling. ⊠ 311 N. Main St., 97801, ☎ 541/276–8581 or 800/700–8581. 5 rooms, 1 with bath. AE, MC, V.

$–$$ ▥ **Wildhorse Casino Resort.** Owned and operated by the Cayuse, Umatilla, and Walla Walla tribes, this gaming resort is about 6 mi east of downtown Pendleton, making it Oregon's easternmost casino. Gamblers can hunker down at 400 slot machines, poker, blackjack tables, keno, bingo, and off-track betting, while golfers can play the 18-hole championship golf course (greens fee range $21–$26, carts $22). The entertainment highlight of the year is the July 4–6 Pow-Wow, which draws up to 1,000 Native American dancers. The motel-style rooms, many of which have whirlpools, are large and comfortable, if not particularly luxurious. Guests receive a Continental breakfast and there are coffeemakers in the rooms. There's a buffet restaurant and snack bar, as well as a 100-space RV park. ⊠ 72777 Hwy. 331 (head north from I–84's Exit 216), 97801, ☎ 541/276–0355 or 800/654–9453, FAX 541/276–0297. 100 rooms. 2 restaurants, lounge, indoor pool, hot tub, sauna, steam room, golf, exercise room. AE, D, DC, MC, V.

$ ▥ **Working Girls Hotel.** This 1890s building in downtown Pendleton served time as a boardinghouse and a bordello—hence its name—before it became a B&B. The rooms are individually furnished with antiques dating from the early 1900s to the 1950s; ceilings are 18 ft high. ⊠ *17 S.W. Emigrant Ave., 97801,* ☎ *541/276–0730 or 800/226–6398,* ℻ *541/276–0665. 5 rooms share 2 baths. D, MC, V.*

⚠ **Emigrant Springs State Heritage Area.** At this historic site that was part of the Oregon Trail, campers can stay in covered wagons or rustic totem cabins, pitch a tent, or hook up an RV. The full-service facility has exhibits, a nature trail, a horse camp, and a free day-use area. ⊠ *I–84 (Exit 234 W), 26 mi east of Pendleton,* ☎ *541/983–2277; 800/452–5687 for reservations only. 33 tent campsites, 18 trailer hookups, 2 covered camper wagons, 7 cabins.* 🍴 *$25 covered wagons, $20–$35 cabins, $17 RV sites, $13 tent sites. Flush toilets, potable water, showers.* ☉ *Mid-Apr.–mid-Oct.*

Outdoor Activities and Sports

The Blue Mountains may be the area's largest attraction, but the **Pendleton Round-Up** is certainly the biggest; more than 50,000 people roll into town for this overwhelming event. Held on the second full week of September, it attracts rodeo performers and fans for four days of rodeo events, wild-horse races, barbecues, parades, and milking contests. Vendors line the length of Court Avenue and Main Street, selling beadwork and western-style curios while country bands twang in the background. Tickets for the various events—which include the Happy Canyon Pageant and Dance—cost between $6 and $12; make your reservations far in advance. ⊠ *Rodeo Grounds and ticket office: 1205 S.W. Court Ave., at S.W. 12th St. (mailing address for tickets: Box 609, Pendleton 97801),* ☎ *541/276–2553 or 800/457–6336.*

Shopping

Court Avenue downtown contains several antiques stores. The Chamber of Commerce (☞ *above*) has a detailed list.

Hamley & Co. Western Store & Custom Saddlery (⊠ 30 S.E. Court Ave., ☎ 541/276–2321) carries authentic cowboy or cowgirl gear and quality leather products. On-site craftspeople fashion hand-tooled saddles that are considered the best in the world.

Murphy House (⊠ 1112 S.E. Emigrant Ave., ☎ 541/276–7020) is the only store in town that sells the women's line of Pendleton fashions.

La Grande

㊳ *56 mi southeast of Pendleton on I–84 at Hwy. 82.*

La Grande started life in the late 1800s as a farming community. It grew slowly while most towns along the Blue Mountains were booming or busting in the violent throes of gold-fueled stampedes. When the railroad companies were deciding where to lay their tracks through the valley, a clever local farmer donated 150 acres to ensure that the iron horse would run through La Grande. With the power of steam fueling a new boom, the town quickly outgrew its neighbors, claimed the title of county seat from fading Union City, and now sits at the urban center of the valley.

With a population of 12,000, La Grande isn't exactly a bustling metropolis, but the presence of Eastern Oregon State College—the only four-year college in the region—lends it some sophistication. La Grande is a convenient stop if you're heading to the nearby Wallowa Mountains. Stop by the **La Grande Chamber of Commerce** (⊠ 1912 4th St., Suite 200, ☎ 541/963–8588 or 800/848–9969) for information and brochures.

The **Wallowa Mountains** form a rugged U-shape fortress between Hells Canyon on the Idaho border and the Blue Mountains, west of the Grande Ronde Valley. Sometimes called the American Alps or Little Switzerland, the granite peaks in this range are between 5,000 and 9,000 ft in height. Dotted with crystalline alpine lakes and meadows, rushing rivers, and thickly forested valleys that fall between the mountain ridges, the Wallowas have a grandeur that can take your breath away. Bighorn sheep, elk, deer, and mountain goats populate the entire area.

The 358,441-acre **Eagle Cap Wilderness,** the largest in Oregon, encompasses most of the Wallowa range. Many of the more remote areas are accessible only to hard-core backpackers or horseback riders. From La Grande, the most scenic route through the area is Highway 82.

Dining and Lodging

$ ✕ **Mamacita's.** This Mexican restaurant with hand-painted murals serves the best food in town. Daily lunch specials include enchiladas, tacos, tostadas, burritos, and salads. ⊠ *110 Depot St.,* ☎ *541/963–6223. No credit cards. Closed Mon. No lunch on weekends.*

$ ✕ **Smokehouse.** This family-style restaurant serves steaks, seafood, and sandwiches. There's a salad bar, and breakfast is served any time. ⊠ *2208 E. Adams Ave.,* ☎ *541/963–9692. D, MC, V.*

$$ 🏠 **Best Western Rama Inn and Suites.** This motel is two blocks from the Grande Ronde shopping center. Rooms have basic motel decor, with refrigerators and microwaves. A Continental breakfast is included in the room rate. ⊠ *1711 21st St., 96850,* ☎ *541/963–3100,* 🖷 *541/ 963–8621. 65 rooms. In-room data ports, no-smoking rooms, pool, exercise room, coin laundry, business services, meeting room. AE, D, DC, MC, V.*

$$ 🏠 **Stang Manor Bed and Breakfast.** You'll get a feel for the luxury of
★   a bygone era at this 10,000-square-ft Georgian Revival mansion built in 1926 by a timber baron. Extraordinary features are found in every room of the house, which has remained unmodified except for its wallcoverings. Breakfast, included in the room rates, is a lavish affair served in the formal dining room by the charming and witty hosts. ⊠ *1612 Walnut St., 97850,* ☎ *541/963–2400,* 🖷 *888/286–9463. 3 rooms, 1 suite. MC, V.*

Outdoor Activities and Sports

BICYCLING

Cyclers should check in with La Grande's Chamber of Commerce (☞ *above*), which actively touts the region's paths. Two short trails leave from **Spring Creek,** about 16 mi west of La Grande. Eight pairs of great gray owls—the largest concentration of the species in the world—live along the routes. To reach the trailhead from La Grande, take I–84 west 13 mi to the Spring Creek Exit and head south on Spring Creek Road/Forest Service Road 21 for 3 mi.

En Route   Heading north from La Grande, Highway 82 passes through the small towns of Elgin and Minam before looping south toward Wallowa, Lostine, Enterprise, and Joseph en route to Wallowa Lake, where it dead-ends. Packed with RVs and cars during the summer, the road sprouts diners, motels, and plenty of antiques shops in every town it passes. If you have only limited time for browsing, save it for Joseph.

For information about the Eagle Cap Wilderness, stop in at the **Wallowa Mountains Visitors Center** outside Enterprise. It has videos of the area, pamphlets, and topographical maps. ⊠ *Hwy. 82, 1 mi west of Enterprise,* ☎ *541/426–5546.* ☉ *Memorial Day–Labor Day, Mon.– Sat. 8–5; Labor Day–Memorial Day, weekdays 8–5.*

Joseph

㊴ *80 mi east of La Grande on Hwy. 82.*

The area around Wallowa Lake was the traditional home of the Nez Perce Indians—the town of Joseph is named for Chief Joseph, their famous leader. The peaks of the Wallowa Mountains, snow covered until July, tower 5,000 ft above the town and lake, which are the regional tourist hubs. Handicraft and antiques shops line Main Street; galleries exhibit the works of area artists and bronze castings from local metal foundries. Tours of the **Valley Bronze of Oregon** (⊠ 18 Main St., ☎ 541/432–7551) foundry facility leave from its showroom.

The **David and Lee Manuel Museum** displays a superb collection of Nez Perce clothing and artifacts. The museum, which also contains pioneer wagons, is one of the town's leading bronze foundries, with 14,000 square ft of facilities in separate buildings. There's also a children's museum and an exhibit of bronze sculptures. ⊠ *400 N. Main St.,* ☎ *541/432–7235.* ☞ *$6.* ☉ *June–Oct., daily 8–5; Nov.–May, Mon.–Sat. 10–4; tours at 10:15 and 2:15.*

The **Wallowa County Museum** in Joseph has a small but poignant collection of artifacts and photographs chronicling the Nez Perce Wars, a series of battles against the U.S. Army that took place in the late 1870s. The building, originally built as a bank in 1888, was robbed in 1896, an event that is reenacted with full pageantry every Wednesday at 1 PM in the summer, complete with music, dancing girls, gunshots, and yelping. ⊠ *110 S. Main St.,* ☎ *541/432–6095.* ☞ *Free.* ☉ *Memorial Day–Sept., daily 10–5.*

Magnoni's Market Place, across from the David and Lee Manuel Museum (☞ *above*), has an Italian restaurant that serves pasta and salads, plus a beauty salon, an espresso café, and gift shops. ⊠ *403 N. Main St.,* ☎ *541/432–3663.*

From Joseph, Highway 82 continues south and ends at sparkling, blue-green **Wallowa Lake** (⊠ Wallowa Lake Hwy.), the highest body of water in eastern Oregon (elevation 5,000 ft). Call the **Joseph Chamber of Commerce** (⊠ 102 E. 1st St., 97846, ☎ 541/32–1015) for information about Wallowa Lake and its facilities.

The **Wallowa Lake Tramway,** the steepest gondola in North America, rises to the top of 8,150-ft Mount Howard in 15 minutes. Vistas of mountain peaks, forest, and Wallowa Lake far below will dazzle you on the way up and at the summit. ⊠ *59919 Wallowa Lake Hwy.,* ☎ *541/432–5331.* ☞ *$14.95.* ☉ *May, June, and Sept., daily 10–4; July–Aug., daily 10–5.*

Dining and Lodging

$$–$$$ ✕🏨 **Wallowa Lake Lodge.** The rustic atmosphere at this fine and friendly 1920s lodge is tasteful and true to the period. Handmade replicas of the structure's original furniture fill a large common area that contains a massive fireplace. The lodge's rooms are simple yet appealing; the grandest have balconies facing the lake. The cabins, all with fireplaces and some with lake views, are small, old-fashioned havens of knotty pine. The on-site restaurant serves standard American fare for breakfast, lunch, and dinner. ⊠ *60060 Wallowa Lake Hwy., Wallowa Lake 97846,* ☎ *541/432–9821,* ﬁ *541/432–4885. 22 rooms, 8 cabins. Restaurant. No smoking. D, MC, V.*

$–$$ 🏨 **Chandler's Bed, Bread & Trail Inn.** An extensive deck surrounds this lodgelike modern house between Joseph and Wallowa Lake. The rooms have high, sloping, beamed ceilings and are furnished in an eclectic suburban style. All have private baths. The "bread" in the inn's name refers to Ethel Chandler's homemade loaves, a staple of the breakfasts (included in the room rates) she prepares daily. As for the "trail" part, Ethel and her husband, Jim, advise guests on the best places to hike or backpack and provide a shuttle service to nearby trailheads. Pets and smoking are not permitted at the inn. ⊠ *700 S. Main St., 97846,* ☎ *541/432–9765 or 800/452–3781. 5 rooms. Outdoor hot tub. MC, V.*

Outdoor Activities and Sports

BOATING AND FISHING

Rainbow trout, kokanee, and mackinaw are among the species of fish in 300-ft-deep, 4½-mi-long Wallowa Lake. You can picnic on the water at several moored docks. **Wallowa Lake Marina Inc.** (⊠ Wallowa Lake, south end, ☎ 541/432–9115) rents paddleboats, motorboats, rowboats, and canoes by the hour or the day.

HORSEBACK RIDING

Eagle Cap Wilderness Pack Station (⊠ 59761 Wallowa Lake Hwy., ☎ 541/432–4145 or 800/681–6222), at the south end of Wallowa Lake, conducts guided rides and leads summer pack trips into the Eagle Cap Wilderness.

En Route The **Wallowa Mountain Loop** is a relatively easy way to take in the natural splendor of the Eagle Cap Wilderness and reach Baker City without backtracking to La Grande. The 3½-hour trip from Joseph to Baker City winds through the national forest and part of Hells Canyon Recreation Area, passing over forested mountains, creeks, and rivers. Before you travel the loop, check with the Joseph Chamber of Commerce (☞ *above*) about road conditions; in winter always carry chains. ⊠ *From Joseph take Little Sheep Creek Hwy. east for 8 mi, turn south onto Forest Service Rd. 39, and continue until it meets Hwy. 86, which winds past the town of Halfway to Baker City.*

Hells Canyon

 30 mi northeast of Joseph on Wallowa Mountain Loop.

This remote place along the **Snake River** is the world's deepest river-carved gorge (7,800 ft) and home to many rare and endangered animal species. Most travelers take a scenic peek from the overlook on the **Wallowa Mountain Loop** (☞ *above*). The more adventurous experience this dramatic and formidable landscape by following the Snake River segment of the Wallowa Mountain Loop. Following Highway 86 north from Copperfield, the 60-mi round-trip route winds along the edge of Hells Canyon Reservoir, crosses the Snake River to Hells Canyon Dam on the border of Oregon and Idaho, and continues on to the 700,000-acre Hells Canyon National Recreation Area. At places the canyon is 10 mi in width. The trip is a memorable one, but be certain you have plenty of gas before starting out.

The **Hells Canyon National Recreation Area** is home to one of the largest elk herds in the United States, plus 422 other species, including bald eagles, bighorn sheep, mule deer, white-tailed deer, black bears, bobcats, cougars, beavers, otters, and rattlesnakes. The peregrine falcon has also been reintroduced here. Part of the area was designated as Hells Canyon Wilderness, in parts of Oregon and Idaho, with the establishment of the Hells Canyon National Recreation Area in 1975. Additional acres were added as part of the Oregon Wilderness Act of 1984. There are now 219,006 acres and about 360 mi of trails in the wilderness area and are thus closed to all mechanized travel. If you want to visit the wilderness it must be on foot or horseback. Environmental groups have proposed the creation of Hells Canyon National Park to better manage the area's critical habitat. ⊠ *88401 Hwy. 82, Enterprise, OR 97828,* ☎ *541/426–4978. Wildlife viewing guide available from Idaho Department of Fish and Game,* ⊠ *Box 25, Boise, ID 83707.*

The **Wild and Scenic Snake River Corridor** consists of 67½ mi of river federally designated as part of the National Wild and Scenic Rivers System. Extending ¼ mi back from the high-water mark on each shore, the corridor is available for managed public use. Since the corridor itself is not designated wilderness and wilderness area regulations do not apply, you'll find developed campsites and man-made structures here, and some motorized equipment is allowed. In season, both powerboaters and rafters must make reservations and obtain permits for access to the river corridor. ☎ *509/758–1957 float reservations; 509/758–0270 powerboat reservations.* ☉ *Memorial Day weekend–early Sept.*

Camping
⚠ **Imnaha River.** Hells Canyon National Scenic Byway runs through the Imnaha corridor, a critical habitat for the chinook salmon and bull trout. Access to the camping areas is via dirt and gravel roads that are generally not suitable for passenger cars. Some of the areas have toilets, RV hookups, picnic areas, swimming, and boat launches. Forest Road No. 46, or the Wellamotkin Drive area, has two developed camp sites located along the rim area within timbered groves north and west of Enterprise, permitting spectacular views of Hells Canyon. The Hat Point area begins at the Imnaha River and ends at Hat Point Lookout. Duck Lake and Twin Lakes campgrounds are in an alpine zone near the lakes for which they are named. ⊠ *Wallowa-Whitman National Forest, Box 907, Baker City 97814,* ☎ *541/523–4476.*

Halfway

63 mi south of Joseph on Wallowa Mountain Loop.

Halfway, the closest town to Hells Canyon, got its name because it was midway between the town of Pine and the gold mines of Cornucopia. On the southern flanks of the Wallowas, it's a straightforward, unpretentious community with a Main Street and a quiet rural flavor.

Dining and Lodging
$$ ✕🏠 **Pine Valley Lodge and Halfway Supper Club.** From the outside, this house on Main Street in "downtown" Halfway is styled like many others built in eastern Oregon during the timber boom of the late 1920s. Inside, the common area is artfully cluttered with a mixture of antique fishing gear, Native American artifacts, and paintings. The rates include a full breakfast prepared by the inn's owner, Babette Beatty, a gourmet cook who runs the very fine Halfway Supper Club (closed Tuesday and Wednesday; no lunch) and bakery across the street. ⊠ *163 N. Main St., 97834,* ☎ *541/742–2027. 4 rooms, 2 suites. Restaurant, bicycles. No credit cards.*

$$ 🏠 **Clear Creek Farm Bed and Breakfast.** Set amid 160 acres of orchards, woods, and fields on the southeastern flank of the Wallowa Mountains, this 1880s Craftsman farmhouse is a simple but comfortable rural retreat. The main house has four rooms. Two bunkhouses with ceilings but no windows are available May–October. Lakeview, with a balcony overlooking a small pond, is the better of the two. Breakfast, served in an outdoor kitchen in warm weather, includes eggs, buffalo sausage, Dutch babies, and home-grown raspberries and peaches in season. The Hells Canyon Bison Ranch, with 60 head, is located nearby. ⊠ *Fish Lake Rd., 5½ mi north of Halfway, 97834,* ☎ *541/742–2238 or 800/742–4992,* FAX *541/742–5175. 4 rooms share 1 bath, two 2-room bunkhouses share 3 baths. Outdoor hot tub. MC, V.*

Outdoor Activities and Sports

Wallowa Llamas (⊠ Rte. 1, Box 84, 97834, ☎ 541/742–4930) conducts guided tours into the Eagle Cap Wilderness. The company's llamas can be easily led by those with no previous experience, including children. The company provides tents, eating utensils, and all meals on three- to seven-day pack trips.

Baker City

❹ *53 mi west of Halfway on Hwy. 86; 44 mi south of La Grande on U.S. 30 off I–84.*

You'd never guess that quiet Baker City, positioned between the Wallowa Mountains and the Elkhorn Range of the Blue Mountains, was once bigger than Spokane and Boise. During the gold-rush era in the late 19th century, the town profited from the money that poured in from nearby mining towns. With the end of the gold rush, the city transformed itself into the logging and ranching town it is today. Remnants of its opulence are still visible in the many restored Victorian houses and downtown shops, but all this history seems minor when you consider the region's fascinating geography. The **Baker County Visitors and Convention Bureau** (⊠ 490 Campbell St., ☎ 541/523–3356 or 800/523–1235) operates a small pioneer museum and has information on area attractions.

The highlight of the gold display at the **U.S. Bank** (⊠ Washington and Main Sts.) is the 6¾-pound Armstrong Nugget, found in 1913.

★ The **National Historic Oregon Trail Interpretive Center,** a few miles outside Baker City, does a superb job of re-creating pioneer life in the mid-1800s. From 1841 to 1861 about 300,000 people made the 2,000-mi journey from western Missouri to the Columbia River and the Oregon coast, looking for agricultural land in the west. A simulated section of the Oregon Trail will give you a feel for camp life, the toll the trip took on marriages and families, and the settlers' impact on Native Americans; an indoor theater presents movies and plays. A 4-mi round-trip trail winds from the center to the actual ruts left by the wagons. ⊠ *Hwy. 86 E, east of I–84,* ☎ *541/523–1843.* ≤ *$10 per vehicle.* ☉ *Apr.–Oct., daily 9–6; Nov.–Mar., daily 9–4.*

The **Oregon Trail Regional Museum** seems rather staid after the interpretive center. A covered wagon, an old fire-fighting wagon, and pioneer tools fill the back room. The museum has an enormous butterfly collection and one of the most impressive rock collections in the west, including thunder eggs, glowing phosphorescent rocks, and a 950-pound hunk of quartz. ⊠ *2490 Grove St., at Campbell St.,* ☎ *541/523–9308.* ≤ *$2.50.* ☉ *Mid-Apr.–Oct., daily 9–5; Nov.–mid-Apr., by appointment.*

Dining and Lodging

$ ✕ **Baker City Cafe–Pizza à Fetta.** The gourmet pizzas here are made from hand-thrown dough; the pesto and three-tomato pies are particularly good. Also on the menu are pastas, salads, Italian sodas, and espresso. ⊠ *1915 Washington Ave., 1 block from Main St.,* ☎ *541/523–6099. MC, V. Closed Sun. No dinner Sat.*

$$–$$$$ ✕▥ **Geiser Grand Hotel.** Considered for many years the finest hotel
★ between Portland and Salt Lake City, the Geiser Grand was built in 1889 during the height of the gold rush. The Italian Renaissance Revival gem reopened in 1997 after a meticulous restoration. The rooms, filled with period furnishings and every modern amenity, have 18-ft ceilings, enormous windows (many overlooking the nearby moun-

tains), and large bathrooms. The striking Palm Court, with a suspended stained-glass ceiling, dominates the first floor. The hotel's Swan dining room, serving steaks, prime rib, fresh fish, and pasta dishes, is Baker City's finest restaurant. A breakfast coupon is provided upon check-in. ☒ *1996 Main St., 97814,* ☎ *541/523–1889 or 888/434–7374,* FAX *541/523–1800. 30 rooms. Restaurant, bar, no-smoking floors, room service, beauty salon, exercise room, concierge, meeting rooms. AE, D, MC, V.*

$$ 🏨 **Best Western Sunridge Inn.** The inn's five well-maintained buildings surround a swimming pool. Rooms are large and decorated with pine and upholstered furniture. Poolside rooms are preferable—the mountain-view rooms overlook the parking lot. There's a good restaurant on the premises. ☒ *1 Sunridge La., 97814 (off I–84's City Center exit),* ☎ *541/523–6444 or 800/233–2368,* FAX *541/523–6446. 156 rooms. 3 restaurants, bar, no-smoking rooms, outdoor pool, hot tub, coin laundry, business services, meeting rooms. AE, D, DC, MC, V.*

🏕 **Anthony Lake.** The premier camping spots near Baker City are the three campgrounds at Anthony Lake. These sites, which usually fill up early during summer weekends, are available on a first-come, first-served basis. ☒ *Anthony Lakes Hwy., 20 mi west of North Powder off I–84; from Baker City take U.S. 30 (when it splits off from I–84) north 10 mi to the Haines exit, turn west on County Rd. 1146, and follow the Elkhorn Drive Scenic Byway signs about 24 mi to the lake,* ☎ *541/ 523–4476. 37 campsites.* 🔳 *$3–$5. Pit toilets, potable water.* ☺ *Late June–Sept.*

John Day

㊷ *80 mi west of Baker City on U.S. 26.*

From Baker City, Highway 7 and then U.S. 26 wind west past mountain, high-desert, and forest terrain to the town of John Day, a central location for trips to the John Day Fossil Beds National Monument to the west or the Malheur National Wildlife Refuge and the towns of Burns, Frenchglen, and Diamond to the south.

★ The small restored building that houses the **Kam Wah Chung & Co. Museum** was a trading post on The Dalles Military Road in 1866 and 1867. It later served as a general store, a Chinese labor exchange for the area's mines, a Chinese doctor's shop, and an opium den. The museum contains a completely stocked Chinese pharmacy, items that would have been sold at the general store, and re-created living quarters. Adjacent to the City Park, the museum is an extraordinary testament to the early Chinese community in Oregon. ☒ *Ing-Hay Way off Canton St.,* ☎ *541/ 575–0028.* 🔳 *$3.* ☺ *May–Oct., Mon.–Thurs. 9–noon and 1–5, weekends 1–5.*

As you drive west through the dry, shimmering heat of the John Day Valley on U.S. 26, it may be hard to imagine this area as a humid subtropical forest filled with lumbering 50-ton brontosauruses and 50-ft-long crocodiles. But so it was, and the eroded hills and sharp, barren-looking ridges contain the richest concentration of prehistoric plant and animal fossils in the world.

★ **㊸** Formed as a result of volcanic activity during the Cenozoic era 5 to 50 million years ago, the geological formations that make up the **John Day Fossil Beds National Monument** cover hundreds of square miles but are divided into three "units"—**Sheep Rock, Painted Hills,** and **Clarno** (☞ *below*). If your time is limited, skip Clarno: It's the farthest from John Day and the least interesting. The park's headquarters is at the Sheep Rock unit. ☎ *541/987–2333.* 🔳 *Free.* ☺ *Year-round.*

Sheep Rock

40 mi from John Day, west 38 mi on U.S. 26 and north 2 mi on Hwy. 19.

Exhibits, a video, and handouts at the **Sheep Rock visitor center** outline the significance of the John Day Fossil Beds. Two miles north of the visitor center on Highway 19 lies the impressive **Blue Basin,** a badlands canyon with sinuous blue-green spires. Winding through this basin is the ½-mi **Island in Time Trail,** where trailside exhibits explain the area's 28 million-year-old fossils. The 3-mi **Blue Basin Overlook Trail** loops around the rim of the canyon, yielding some splendid views. ⊠ *Visitor center: Hwy. 19,* ☎ *541/987–2333.* ☉ *Memorial Day–Labor Day, daily 9–6; Labor Day–Memorial Day, weekdays 9–5; off-season hrs sometimes vary.*

Lodging

$ ⊞ **Fish House Inn.** The Piscean decor at this B&B 9 mi east of the Sheep Rock fossil beds includes fishing gear, nets, and framed prints of fish. The main house holds three rooms, and behind it is a cottage with two. The friendly hosts serve a huge country breakfast (on the lawn in good weather). Low-fat and vegetarian options are available as well. While you're in town, stop by the Dayville Mercantile, a century-old general store on U.S. 26. ⊠ *110 Franklin St., Dayville 97825,* ☎ *541/987–2124 or 888/286–3474. 5 rooms, 3 with bath. MC, V.*

Mitchell

37 mi from Sheep Rock, south 2 mi on Hwy. 19 and west 35 mi on U.S. 26; 70 mi east of John Day on U.S. 26.

Mitchell, an authentic homey desert town, has a small business district with food and basic services. From Mitchell, U.S. 26 continues southwest for 48 mi through the Ochoco National Forest to Prineville (☞ *Central Oregon, above*).

Dining and Lodging

$ ✕ **Bridgecreek Cafe.** A friendly glow envelops this sunny roadside café serving old standards: pancakes for breakfast, sandwiches for lunch, burgers and fried chicken with all the fixings for dinner. ⊠ *218 U.S. 26,* ☎ *541/462–3434. No credit cards.*

$ ⊞ **Sky Hook Motel.** This carefully tended inn surrounded by flower and vegetable gardens is a welcome haven after a day's hike in the fossil beds. The owners are friendly and the rooms, two with kitchenettes, are homey and comfortably furnished. ⊠ *101 U.S. 26, 97750,* ☎ *541/462–3569. 6 rooms. MC, V.*

Painted Hills

9 mi from Mitchell; head west on U.S. 26 and follow signs north.

The fossils at Painted Hills date back about 33 million years and reveal a climate that had become noticeably drier than that of Sheep Rock's era. The eroded buff-color hills reveal striking red and green striations created by minerals in the clay. Come at dusk or just after it rains, when the colors are most vivid. Take the steep ¾-mi **Carroll Rim Trail** for a commanding view of the hills or sneak a peek from the parking lot at the trailhead, about 2 mi beyond the picnic area.

Clarno

67 mi from Mitchell, north 25 mi on Hwy. 207, north 21 mi on Hwy. 19 (to Fossil), and west 20 mi on Hwy. 218.

The 48-million-year-old fossil beds in this small section have yielded the oldest remains in the national monument. The drive to the beds traverses forests of ponderosa pines and sparsely populated valleys along the John Day River before turning through a landscape filled with spires and outcroppings that attest to the region's volcanic past. A short trail that runs between the two parking lots contains fossilized evidence of an ancient subtropical forest. Another trail climbs ¼ mi from the second parking lot to the base of the **Palisades,** a series of abrupt, irregular cliffs created by ancient volcanic mud flows.

Burns Area

76 mi south of the town of John Day on U.S. 395.

The stretch of U.S. 395 between John Day and Burns cuts a winding swath through the **Malheur National Forest** in the Blue Mountains. Black bears, bighorn sheep, elk, and wolverines inhabit thickly wooded stands of pine, fir, and cedar. Near Burns the trees dwindle in number and the landscape changes from mountainous forest to open areas covered with sagebrush and dotted with junipers.

Burns is the only place in Harney County—10,185 square mi of sagebrush, rimrock, and grassy plains—that has basic tourist amenities. Think of it as a rest stop or a jumping-off point for exploring the real poetry of the Malheur National Wildlife Refuge, Steens Mountain, and the Alvord Desert.

The Harney County Chamber of Commerce and the Bureau of Land Management office in Hines (☞ Visitor Information *in* Eastern Oregon Essentials, *below*) are good places to obtain information about the area.

Dining and Lodging

$ ✕ **Hilander Restaurant.** In 1997 the wood-panel Hilander began serving Chinese food in addition to its usual American dishes. Daily specials might include pork chops with apple sauce or roast beef with brown gravy, but spicy Szechuan chicken, curry beef, and various foo yungs and chow meins are also on the menu. ⊠ *195 N. Broadway,* ☎ *541/573–2111. MC, V. Closed Mon.*

$ ✕ **Mazatlan.** Part of a Northwest chain, this place on the main drag in Burns serves large portions of reliable Mexican food—enchiladas, tacos, tostadas, chilies rellenos, chimichangas, and tamales. ⊠ *293 N. Broadway,* ☎ *541/573–1829. MC, V.*

$ 🏨 **Bontemps Motel.** The Bontemps is a throwback to the days when motels had personalities. The rooms, decorated with a funky mixture of old and new furnishings, still retain a 1930s charm. With old-fashioned tile showers, mirrored alcoves, cable TV, and coffeemakers, you can't beat this motel for the price. Everything in Burns is within walking distance. ⊠ *74 Monroe St., 97220,* ☎ *541/573–2037 or 800/229–1394,* 🖷 *541/573–2577. 15 units. Refrigerators. AE, D, DC, MC, V.*

Outdoor Activities and Sports

GOLF

Valley Golf Club (⊠ 345 Burns–Hines Hwy., ☎ 541/573–6251) has a challenging 9-hole, par-36 course open to the public; the clubhouse facilities are reserved for members. The greens fee is $17; a cart costs $20.

ROCKHOUNDING

Rockhounding enthusiasts flock to Harney County to collect fossils, jasper, obsidian, agates, and thunder eggs. The Stinkingwater Mountains, 30 mi east of Burns, contain petrified wood and gemstones. Warm Spring Reservoir, just east of the mountains, is a good source for agates. At Charlie Creek, west of Burns, and at Radar, to the north, black, banded, and brown obsidians can be found. It is illegal to remove arrowheads and other artifacts from public lands. Check with the Harney County Chamber of Commerce (⊠ 75 E. Washington St., ☎ 541/573–2636) for more information.

Malheur National Wildlife Refuge

④④   *32 mi southeast of Burns on Hwy. 205.*

Highway 205 slices south from Burns through one of the most unusual desert environments in the West. The squat snow-covered summit of Steens Mountain is the only landmark in this area of alkali playas, buttes, scrubby meadows, and, most surprising of all, marshy lakes. The **Malheur National Wildlife Refuge,** bounded on the north by Malheur and Harney lakes, covers 193,000 acres. It's arid and scorchingly hot in the summer, but in the spring and early summer more than 320 species of migrating birds descend on the refuge's wetlands for their annual nesting and mating rituals. Following an ancient migratory flyway, they've been coming here for nearly a million years. The species include sandhill cranes, snowy white egrets, trumpeter swans, numerous hawks, golden and bald eagles, and white-faced ibis. The number of bird-watchers who turn up for this annual display sometimes rivals the number of birds.

The 30-mi Central Patrol Road, which runs through the heart of the refuge, is your best bet for viewing birds. But first stop at the **Malheur National Wildlife Refuge Headquarters,** where you can pick up leaflets and a free map. The staff will tell you where you're most likely to see the refuge's winged inhabitants. The refuge is a short way from local petroglyphs (ask at the headquarters); a remarkable pioneer structure called the **Round Barn** (head east from the headquarters on Narrows-Princeton Road for 9 mi; road turns to gravel and then runs into Diamond Highway, a paved road that leads south 12 mi to the barn); and **Diamond Craters,** a series of volcanic domes, craters, and lava tubes (continue south from the barn 6 mi on Diamond Highway). ⊠ *Malheur National Wildlife Refuge Headquarters: 32 mi southeast of Burns on Hwy. 205 (follow signs 26 mi south of Burns),* ☎ *541/493–2612.* ☞ *Free.* ☉ *Park dawn–dusk; headquarters Mon.–Thurs. 7–4:30, Fri. 7–3:30, also 8–3 weekends mid-Mar.–Oct.*

Diamond

54 mi from Burns, south on Hwy. 205 and east on Diamond–Grand Camp Rd.

The tiny town of Diamond has a few lodgings. It's not far from the **Kiger Mustang Lookout,** a wild-horse viewing area run by the Bureau of Land Management. With their dun-color coats, zebra stripes on knees and hocks, and hooked ear tips, the Kiger Mustangs are thought to be one of the purest herds of wild Spanish mustangs in the world today. They may even be the descendants of Barb horses brought by the Spanish to North America in the 16th century. The viewing area is accessible to high-clearance vehicles only and is passable only in dry weather. The road to it descends from Happy Valley Road 6 mi north of Diamond. ⊠ *11 mi from Happy Valley Rd.,* ☎ *541/573–4400.* ☞ *Free.* ☉ *Dry season (generally May–Oct.) dawn–dusk.*

Lodging

$–$$ 🏨 **Hotel Diamond.** A hundred years ago the Hotel Diamond served the local population of ranchers, Basque sheepherders, and cowhands. Now it caters to the birders, naturalists, and high-desert lovers who flock to the Malheur refuge. The air-conditioned rooms are clean, comfortable, and pleasantly furnished with a mix of old-fashioned furniture. Family-style meals are served (to hotel guests only) downstairs. Adjacent to the hotel are a deli, a general store, and a post office. ⊠ *10 Main St., Diamond–Grand Camp Rd., 10 mi east of Hwy. 205, 97722,* ☎ *541/493–1898,* 𝔽𝔸𝕏 *541/493–2084. 3 rooms with bath, 3 rooms share 1 bath. Dining room, no-smoking rooms. AE, MC, V.*

$–$$ 🏨 **McCoy Creek Inn.** Peaceful and well maintained, this B&B is on the grounds of a working ranch that was established in 1918. You can sit on the porch and watch cows grazing and peacocks strutting. Reproduction Victorian-style furnishings decorate the house. Prix-fixe dinners are available by reservation only; no smoking is permitted at the inn. ⊠ *HC 72, Box 11, Diamond 97722 (off Diamond–Grand Camp Rd., 10 mi east of Hwy. 205, 2 mi south down a gravel road),* ☎ 𝔽𝔸𝕏 *541/493–2131. 3 rooms with bath, 1 cabin. Restaurant, hot tub, hiking, swimming. No smoking. MC, V.*

Frenchglen

㊺ *61 mi south of Burns on Hwy. 205.*

Frenchglen is the gateway to **Steens Mountain.** Amid the flat landscape of eastern Oregon, the mountain is hard to miss, but the sight of its 9,700-ft summit is more remarkable from the east, where its sheer face rises from the flat basin of the Alvord Desert. On the western side, Steens Mountain slopes gently upward over a space of about 20 mi and is less astonishing. Steens is not your average mountain—it's a huge fault block created when the ancient lava that covered this area fractured. Except for groves of aspen, juniper, and a few mountain mahogany, Steens is almost entirely devoid of trees and resembles alpine tundra. But starting in June, the wildflower displays are nothing short of breathtaking, as are the views: On Steens you'll encounter some of the grandest scenery in the West.

The mountain is a great spot for hiking over untrammeled and un-populated ground, but you can also see it by car (preferably one with four-wheel drive) on the rough but passable 52-mi **Steens Loop Road,** open mid-July–October. You need to take reasonable precautions; storms can whip up out of the blue, creating hazardous conditions.

On the drive up you might spot golden eagles, bighorn sheep, and deer. The view out over **Kiger Gorge,** on the southeastern rim of the mountain, includes a dramatic U-shape path carved out by a glacier. A few miles farther along the loop road, the equally stunning **East Rim viewpoint** is more than 5,000 ft above the valley floor. The view on a clear day takes in desolate Alvord Desert, which stretches into Idaho and Nevada. *Northern entrance to Steens Loop Rd. leaves Hwy. 205 at the south end of Frenchglen and returns to Hwy. 205 about 9 mi south of Frenchglen.*

Frenchglen Mercantile (⊠ Hwy. 205, ☎ 541/493–2738), Frenchglen's only store, is packed with intriguing high-quality western merchandise, including Stetson hats, horsehair belts, antique housewares and horse bits, fossilized shark's teeth, silver and turquoise Native American jewelry, Navajo rugs, books, postcards, and maps. Cold drinks, film, sunscreen, good coffee, snacks, and canned goods are also for sale.

Dining and Lodging

$$ ✕ **Buckaroo Room.** In a region where the food is pretty basic, this tiny
★   restaurant adjoining the Frenchglen Mercantile serves sophisticated fare.
The rustic but carefully furnished dining room has a sloping ceiling,
rough-hewn timber walls, deer heads, period memorabilia, and kerosene
lamps. Sandwiches only are served for lunch. Dinner entrées are few
but expertly prepared: Basque chicken coated with olive oil and mar-
inated in herbs and Greek wine, a succulent filet mignon, pasta, and
(a rarity in meat-and-potato land) a vegetarian dish. There's a good
selection of beer and wine, and the only full bar for miles around. ⊠
Hwy. 205, ☎ *541/493–2738. Reservations essential for dinner. AE,
D, MC, V. Closed mid-Nov.–Mar.*

$$ ▦ **Steens Mountain Resort.** Missy and Lance Litchy, the owners of this
★   small, sophisticated inn, combined and transformed two buildings—
the home of Frenchglen's first schoolteacher and a two-story dance hall
moved from a nearby ghost town—into a bright haven of handsome
western furniture, art, and artifacts. From the starched sheets on the
beds to the white-tile bathrooms with oversize towels, the attention to
detail sets this place apart. The two second-floor bedrooms open out
onto a large cedar deck with sweeping views eastward across the broad
Blitzen Valley and up the sloping shoulders of Steens Mountain. Missy
and Lance also operate the only full-scale guide service in the area—
a perfect opportunity for eco-minded visitors to find out more about
this fascinating region's natural history and archaeology. ⊠ *Hwy. 205,
97736,* ☎ *541/493–2738,* ℻ *541/493–2835. 2 rooms with bath.
Room service, laundry service. AE, D, MC, V.*

$ ▦ **Frenchglen Hotel.** The ambience is simple and rustic at this state-
owned hotel built in 1920. Every evening a family-style dinner (reservations essential) is prepared for guests and the public in the combination
lobby-dining room; breakfast and lunch are also served. The smallish
rooms are upstairs off a single hallway; pets and smoking are not permitted. ⊠ *Hwy. 205, 97736,* ☎ ℻ *541/493–2825. 8 rooms share 2
baths. Restaurant. MC, V. Closed mid-Nov.–mid-Mar.*

⚠ Page Springs. A profusion of birds greets you as you set up camp
at this idyllic oasis—easily the best campsite in the desert—next to the
Blitzen River. ⊠ *4 mi east of Frenchglen on N. Steens Loop Rd. 30
sites.* ▤ *$4. Pit toilets, potable water.* ☾ *Apr.–Oct.*

OFF THE   **ALVORD DESERT –** With the eastern face of Steens Mountain in the back-
BEATEN PATH   ground, the Alvord Desert conjures up western-movie scenes of parched
cowboys riding through the desert—though today you're more likely to
see wind sailors scooting across these hard-packed alkali flats and
glider pilots using the basin as a runway. But once the wind jockeys and
flyboys go home, this desert is deserted. Snowmelt from Steens Mountain can turn it into a shallow lake until as late as mid-July. *From Frenchglen take Hwy. 205 south for about 33 mi until the road ends at a
T-junction near the town of Fields; go left (north) to the Alvord Desert and
the tiny settlement of Andrews.*

Eastern Oregon Essentials

Arriving and Departing

BY BUS

Greyhound (☎ 800/231–2222) buses traveling between Portland and
Boise, Idaho, stop in Pendleton, Baker City, and La Grande.

BY CAR

I-84 runs east along the Columbia River and dips down to Pendleton,
La Grande, and Baker City. **U.S. 26** heads east from Prineville through

the Ochoco National Forest, passing the three units of the John Day Fossil Beds. **U.S. 20** travels southeast from Bend in central Oregon to Burns. U.S. 20 and U.S. 26 both head west into Oregon from Idaho.

BY PLANE

Eastern Oregon Regional Airport (☎ 541/276–7754) in Pendleton is served by **Horizon Air** (☎ 800/547–9308).

Getting Around

BY BUS

Wallowa Valley Stage Line (⊠ La Grande Station, 2108 Cove Ave., ☎ 541/963–5165) operates buses between La Grande and Joseph. *See also* Getting Around *in* Oregon A to Z, *below.*

BY CAR

To reach Joseph take **Highway 82** east from La Grande. **Highway 86** loops down from Joseph to Baker City. From Baker City, **Highway 7** heading west connects to **U.S. 26** and leads to John Day. **U.S. 395** runs south from John Day to Burns. **Highway 205** heads south from Burns through the Malheur National Wildlife Refuge to Frenchglen, Steens Mountain, and the Alvord Desert (all accessed by local roads). In all these areas, equip yourself with chains for winter driving.

Guided Tours

Eagle Cap Fishing Guides (⊠ 110 S. River St., Enterprise 97828, ☎ 541/426–3493 or 541/432–9685) operates guided fishing trips on the Grande Ronde, Wallowa, and Imnaha rivers. The company's customized tours ($80–$325) in air-conditioned vans explore the wildlife, wildflowers, and geology of Hells Canyon and the Eagle Cap Wilderness.

A trip by raft or jet boat on the Snake River is an exciting and unforgettable way to see Hells Canyon. **Hells Canyon Adventures** (⊠ Box 159, Oxbow 97840, ☎ 800/422–3568) operates jet-boat and other trips of varying lengths.

Visitor Information

Baker County Visitors and Convention Bureau (⊠ 490 Campbell St., Baker City 97814, ☎ 541/523–3356 or 800/523–1235). **Bureau of Land Management** (⊠ Hwy. 20 W, Burns 97220, ☎ 541/573–5241). **Harney County Chamber of Commerce** (⊠ 18 W. D St., Burns 97720, ☎ 541/573–2636). **La Grande Chamber of Commerce** (⊠ 1912 4th St., Suite 200, La Grande 97850, ☎ 541/963–8588 or 800/848–9969). **Pendleton Chamber of Commerce** (⊠ 501 S. Main St., 97801, ☎ 541/276–7411 or 800/547–8911).

OREGON A TO Z

Arriving and Departing

By Bus

Greyhound (☎ 800/231–2222) services the state with routes from elsewhere on the West Coast and from points east.

People Mover (⊠ 229 N.E. Dayton St., John Day, ☎ 541/575–2370 or 800/527–2370) travels on U.S. 26 between Bend and John Day.

By Car

I–5 and **U.S. 101** enter Oregon heading north from California and south from Washington. **I–84** and **U.S. 26** head west from the Idaho border to Portland.

By Plane

Portland International Airport (☞ Portland A to Z *in* Chapter 2) is Oregon's main airport.

By Train

The **Amtrak** (☎ 800/872–7245) *Coast Starlight,* which runs between Seattle and Los Angeles, passes through the Willamette Valley, serving Portland, Salem, Albany (near Corvallis), Eugene, and Klamath Falls. *Cascades* trains operate daily between Seattle, Portland, and Eugene.

Contacts and Resources

Emergencies

In most parts of the state, calling 911 will summon **police, fire,** or **ambulance** services. In some rural areas, it may be necessary to dial the **Oregon State Police** (☎ 800/452–7888).

Guided Tours

ORIENTATION TOURS

Gray Line Sightseeing Tours (☎ 503/285–9845) conducts guided tours of Oregon. Regular destinations include the Mount Hood Loop and the Oregon coast.

WINERY

"Discover Oregon Wineries," the free map and guide published by the **Oregon Wine Winegrowers Association** (☎ 503/228–8403 or 800/242–2363), provides profiles and service information about many Oregon wineries. It's available at many wine shops in the state.

Outdoor Activities and Sports

BIKING

The **Oregon Bikeway Program** (✉ Room 210, Transportation Bldg., 355 Capitol St. NE, Salem 97310, ☎ 503/986–3200 or 503/986–3555) has information about biking throughout the state. Call 503/986–3556 for a free bicycle map of the Coast/U.S. 101 route.

BOATING AND RAFTING

Boating and rafting permits are required for the Rogue and lower Deschutes rivers. Recreational access to the Rogue is limited; a lottery for permits is held each February. For more information, contact the **Rand Visitors Center** (☎ 541/479–3735) in Galice. Permits for the Deschutes can be obtained at the **Bureau of Land Management** (☎ 541/416–6700) office in Prineville.

FISHING

To fish in most areas of Oregon, out-of-state visitors need a yearly (about $41), seven-day ($31), or daily ($7) nonresident angler's license. Additional tags are required for those fishing for salmon or steelhead ($11), sturgeon ($6), or halibut ($6); these tags are available from any local sporting-goods store. For more information, contact the **Sport Fishing Information Line** (☎ 800/275–3474).

SKIING

Sno-Park permits, distributed by the Oregon Department of Transportation (☎ 503/986–3006), are required for parking at winter recreation areas from mid-November to April. The permits may be purchased for one day ($2), three days ($3.50), or a full season ($10) at DMV offices and retail agents—sporting-goods stores, markets and gas stations, usually near the areas—which sometimes charge slightly more than the listed price. Permits can often be purchased upon arrival at a ski area, but it's best to call ahead.

Road Conditions
Road Conditions hot line (☎ 503/588–2941; 800/977–6368 in OR).

State Parks
The **Oregon State Park Information Center** (☎ 800/551–6949) has information about campsite availability, rental rates, and recreational activities at 225 state parks. Its operators take calls on weekdays 8 AM–5 PM.

Visitor Information
National Park Service Pacific Northwest Regional Office (☎ 206/470–4060). **Oregon Economic Development Tourism Division** (✉ 595 Cottage St. NE, Salem 97310, ☎ 800/547–7842). **Oregon State Parks Information Line** (☎ 800/551–6949). **Portland/Oregon Visitors Association** (✉ 28 World Trade Center, 26 S.W. Salmon St., 97204, ☎ 503/222–2223 or 800/962–3700). **Oregon Tourism Commission** (✉ 775 Summer St. NE, Salem 97310, ☎ 800/547–7842, www.traveloregon.com).

4 SEATTLE

Coffeehouses, brew pubs, independent music, and lots of rain—these are what many people associate with the hippest city in the Pacific Northwest. But Seattle has more to offer than steaming lattes and garage bands. You can wander historic neighborhoods, browse amid the sights and smells of Pike Place Market, explore lakes and islands, or just eat, eat, eat. Seattle restaurants are among the nation's most innovative and diverse.

By Wier
Harman

Updated by
Julie Fay

SEATTLE IS DEFINED BY WATER. There's no use deny-
ing the city's damp weather, or the fact that its skies
are cloudy for much of the year. Seattleites don't tan,
goes the joke, they rust. But Seattle is also defined by the rivers, lakes,
and canals that bisect its steep green hills, creating a series of distinctive areas along the water's edge. Funky fishing boats, floating homes,
swank yacht clubs, and waterfront restaurants exist side by side.

A city is defined by its people as well as by its geography, and the people of Seattle—a half million within the city proper, another 2.5 million
in the surrounding Puget Sound region—are a diversified bunch. Seattle has long had a vibrant Asian and Asian-American population, and
well-established communities of Scandinavians, African-Americans,
Jews, Native Americans, and Latinos live here, too. It's impossible to gen-
eralize about such a varied group, but the prototypical Seattleite was once
pithily summed up by a *New Yorker* cartoon in which one arch-eyebrowed
East Coast matron says to another, "They're backpacky, but nice."

Seattle's climate fosters an easygoing indoor lifestyle. Overcast days
and long winter nights have made the city a haven for moviegoers
and book readers. Hollywood often tests new films here, and residents' per-capita book purchases are among North America's highest. Seattle has all the trappings of a metropolitan hub—two daily
newspapers, a state-of-the-art convention center, professional sports
teams, a diverse music-club scene, and top-notch ballet, opera, symphony, and theater companies. A major seaport, the city is a vital link
in Pacific Rim trade.

Seattle's expansion has led to the usual big-city problems—increases
in crime, drug abuse, homelessness, poverty, and traffic congestion, along
with a decline in the quality of the public schools. Many residents have
fled to the nearby suburb of Bellevue, which has swollen from a quiet
farming community to become Washington's fifth-largest city. But despite the growing pains they've endured, Seattleites have a great love
for their city and a firm commitment to maintaining its reputation as
one of the most livable areas in the country.

Pleasures and Pastimes

Dining
The best Seattle restaurants build their menus around local ingredients.
The city has an invaluable resource in Pike Place Market, which warehouses bountiful supplies of seafood and produce. A quick scan of the
stalls will tell you what to expect on restaurant plates in any given season: strawberries in June; Walla Walla sweets—a mild softball-size
onion—in July; wild blackberries in August; and Washington's renowned
apples during autumn. All year long you'll find Washington wines and
beer at Seattle restaurants. The locally produced ingredients and the
synthesis of European and Asian cooking techniques (with a touch of
irreverence) are the basis for what has come to be known as Pacific
Northwest cuisine.

Nightlife and the Arts
A mid-1990s restaurant boom in Seattle has resulted in a livelier nightlife
that lasts later into the evening than before. Seattle achieved fleeting notoriety in the early 1990s as the birthplace of grunge rock. Nirvana, Pearl
Jam, and Soundgarden were among the bands to emerge from the local
music scene. But jazz, blues, and R&B have been perennial favorites,
and you'll find clubs that showcase everything from tinny garage bands
to subtle stylists. Beyond music, you can catch a comedian or a movie—

Greater Seattle

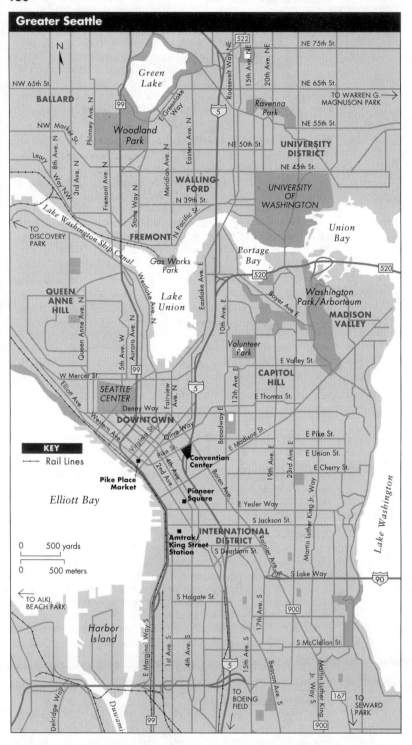

N

NW 65th St.

Green Lake

NE 75th St.

522

BALLARD

15th Ave. NE

20th Ave. NE

NE 65th St.

TO WARREN G. MAGNUSON PARK

Roosevelt Way NE

99

Phinney Ave. N

E Greenlake Way N

Ravenna Park

NE 55th St.

NW Market St.

Woodland Park

5

NE 50th St.

UNIVERSITY DISTRICT

8th Ave. N

3rd Ave. N

Fremont Ave. N

Meridian Ave. N

Eastern Ave. N

NE 45th St.

Leary Way NW

WALLING-FORD

UNIVERSITY OF WASHINGTON

TO DISCOVERY PARK

Stone Way N

N 39th St.

Lake Washington Ship Canal

FREMONT

N Pacific St.

Union Bay

Gas Works Park

Portage Bay

520

Westlake Ave. N

Lake Union

Eastlake Ave. E

520

Washington Park/Arboretum

QUEEN ANNE HILL

Boyer Ave. E

MADISON VALLEY

Queen Anne Ave. N

5th Ave. W

Aurora Ave. N

Fairview Ave. N

10th Ave. E

Volunteer Park

99

W Mercer St.

5

12th Ave. E

E Valley St.

CAPITOL HILL

SEATTLE CENTER

Denny Way

DOWNTOWN

Broadway

E Thomas St.

Elliott Ave.

Western Ave.

Virginia St.

Olive Way

E Madison St.

E Pike St.

KEY

Pike St.

4th Ave.

2nd Ave.

Boren Ave.

19th Ave. E

23rd Ave. E

E Union St.

E Cherry St.

Rail Lines

Convention Center

Pike Place Market

Pioneer Square

Lake Washington

Elliott Bay

E Yesler Way

S Jackson St.

0   500 yards

Amtrak/ King Street Station

INTERNATIONAL DISTRICT

Martin Luther King Jr. Way

0   500 meters

S Dearborn St.

Rainier Ave. S

90

TO ALKI BEACH PARK

S Lake Way

Harbor Island

S Holgate St.

17th Ave. S

900

E Marginal Way S

1st Ave. S

4th Ave. S

5

15th Ave. S

S McClellan St.

Beacon Ave. S

Martin Luther King Jr. Way S

TO SEWARD PARK

Delridge Way

Duwamish

99

TO BOEING FIELD

167

900

or have a drink while watching the lights flicker on the water. On any given night there are usually several worthwhile dance or theater offerings. Seattle's galleries support an active community of painters, sculptors, woodworkers, and glass artists. The annual Northwest Folklife Festival on Memorial Day weekend celebrates their creativity.

Parks and Gardens

"Seattle possesses extraordinary landscape advantages. . . . In designing a system of parks and parkways the primary aim should be to secure and preserve for the use of the people as much as possible of these advantages of water and mountain views and of woodlands . . . as well as some fairly level land for field sports and the enjoyment of scenery." These words appeared in a surveyors report prepared in 1903 for Seattle's fledgling parks commission and established the foundation for an ambitious master plan, the spirit of which has been maintained to this day. Seattle's extensive parks system retains that delicate balance between the fanciful and functional—the primeval growth of Schmitz Park, the manicured ball fields around Green Lake, the sprawl of the Washington Park Arboretum, and Parson's Garden, a prim urban oasis.

EXPLORING SEATTLE

Seattle, like Rome, is built on seven hills. As a visitor, you're likely to spend much of your time on only two of them (Capitol Hill and Queen Anne Hill), but the seven knobs are indeed the most definitive element of the city's natural and spiritual landscape. Years of largely thoughtful zoning practices have kept tall buildings from obscuring the lines of sight, maintaining vistas in most directions and around most every turn. The hills are lofty, privileged perches from which residents are constantly reminded of the beauty of the forests, mountains, and water lying just beyond the city—that is, when it stops misting long enough to see your hand in front of your face.

To know Seattle is to know its distinctive neighborhoods. Because of the hills, comfortable walking shoes are a must.

Ballard, home to Seattle's fishing industry and fun-to-tour locks, is at the mouth of Salmon Bay, northwest of downtown.

Capitol Hill, northeast of downtown on Pine Street, east of Interstate 5 (I–5), is the center of youth culture in this very young city.

Downtown is bounded on the west by **Elliott Bay,** on the south by **Pioneer Square** (the city's oldest neighborhood) and the **International District,** on the north by the attractive residences lining the slopes of **Queen Anne Hill,** and by I–5 to the east. You can reach most points of interest by foot, bus, trolley, or the monorail that runs between the Seattle and Westlake centers.

Fremont, Seattle's eccentric and artsy hamlet, is north of **Lake Union** and the **Lake Washington Ship Canal,** east of Ballard, west of **Wallingford,** and south of **Woodland Park.**

Magnolia, dotted with expensive (and precariously perched) homes, is at the northwestern edge of Elliott Bay, west of Queen Anne Hill.

University District, the area around the University of Washington, is north of Capitol Hill and Union Bay.

Great Itineraries

If you're planning to visit all or most of Seattle's top tourist destinations, pick up a **Citypass** ticket book for $26.50 and you'll get 50%

off admission to the Space Needle, the Seattle Art Museum, the Seattle Aquarium, the Pacific Science Center, the Woodland Park Zoo, and the Museum of Flight. The Citypass booklet, which is available at any of the six attractions, is valid for nine consecutive days.

IF YOU HAVE 1 DAY

If you've come to Seattle on business or for another reason only have a day for sightseeing, focus your energy on downtown. Weather permitting, an after-dinner ferry ride to Bainbridge Island (☞ Chapter 5) and back is a perfect way to conclude your day.

IF YOU HAVE 3 DAYS

Get a feel for what makes Seattle special at Pike Place Market and then explore more of downtown and the waterfront. Start your second day at the Ballard Locks, heading east to Fremont in time for lunch there. After a stroll through the neighborhood's galleries and shops, grab a beer at the Redhook Brewery before heading to the Space Needle, where the views are the most spectacular as sunset approaches. Venture outside the city on I–90 to Snoqualmie Falls (☞ Chapter 5) on day three. Hike to the falls and lunch at Salish Lodge. To get a true sense of the pace of life in the Northwest, on your return to Seattle, detour north from I–90 on Highway 203 and stop in tiny Duvall, home to antiques shops, boutiques, and cafés. You can easily make it back to Seattle in time for dinner or a night on the town.

IF YOU HAVE 5 TO 7 DAYS

Follow the three-day itinerary above. Take a morning bay cruise on day four and spend the afternoon at the Washington Park Arboretum before heading to Capitol Hill for dinner and some nightclubbing. If you're only staying in the Seattle area one more day, take the ferry to Port Townsend on day five. If you have a few days, take the ferry to one or more of the San Juan Islands.

Pike Place Market, the Waterfront, and Seattle Center

Numbers in the text correspond to numbers in the margin and on the Downtown Seattle map.

A Good Tour

Spend some time at **Pike Place Market** ① before walking south a block on 1st Avenue to the **Seattle Art Museum** ②, whose postmodern exterior is worth a look even if you're not going inside. From the museum, walk west across 1st Avenue and descend the **Harbor Steps.** Carry on straight ahead one block from the bottom of the steps to the waterfront. Head north (to the right). At Pier 59 you'll find the **Seattle Aquarium** ③ and the **Omnidome Film Experience** ④. You can walk out on Piers 62 and 63 for a good view of Elliott Bay. The newly refurbished **Bell Street Pier** (Pier 66) contains a marina, several restaurants, and **Odyssey: The Maritime Discovery Center** ⑤.

Continue up the waterfront to **Myrtle Edwards Park,** past Pier 70. It's a good place to rest a moment before making the several-block walk up **Broad Street** through the northern part of the Belltown neighborhood (be forewarned: the first three blocks are a tad steep) to the **Seattle Center** and the **Space Needle** ⑥. Especially if you've got kids in tow, you'll want to arrive here before the **Pacific Science Center** ⑦ and **Seattle Children's Museum** ⑧ close. Music fans won't want to miss the **Experience Music Project** ⑨, an interactive museum celebrating American popular music slated to open in mid-2000. Take the **Seattle Center Monorail** to return to downtown. The monorail stops at **Westlake Center** ⑩, at 5th Avenue and Pine Street. To get to the **Washington State Convention and Trade Center** ⑪, walk one block southeast to Pike Street and east to 8th Avenue. Seattle's main **Visitor Information Center** is inside the street-level mall at Convention Place.

TIMING

It would take about half the day to complete the above route stopping only a little, but you'll need to devote the whole day or more to fully appreciate the various sights. A visit to Pike Place Market can easily fill two hours. Plan on an hour for the art museum. The aquarium is a two-hour stop at most. You could spend half a day or more in Seattle Center. Most sights listed below are open daily; the Frye Art Museum and the Seattle Art Museum are closed on Monday and open until 9 PM on Thursday.

Sights to See

⑨ Experience Music Project. This 140,000-square-ft interactive museum celebrating American popular music is slated to open in mid-2000. The nonprofit EMP is funded by Microsoft cofounder Paul Allen and designed by Frank Gehry. The exhibits will include a Jimi Hendrix gallery containing the world's largest collection of Hendrix artifacts. There will also be a gallery featuring guitars owned by Bob Dylan, Hank Williams, Kurt Cobain, and the bands Pearl Jam, Soundgarden, and the Kingsmen. An interactive Sound Lab will let visitors experiment with various instruments and recording equipment. At press time, admission fees and opening hours had not been announced. ⊠ *5th Ave., between Broad St. and Thomas St.,* ☎ *425/990–0575.*

Frye Art Museum. Among the pivotal late-19th- and early 20th-century American and European realist works at this gallery east of downtown are German artist Franz von Stuck's *Sin,* a painting with Impressionist leanings that predates the movement, and Alexander Koester's *Ducks,* an example of the Academy school of German painting. The Frye, which opened in 1952, has an outdoor garden courtyard and a reflecting pool. ⊠ *704 Terry Ave.,* ☎ *206/622–9250.* 🖾 *Free.* ☉ *Tues.–Sat. 10–5 (Thurs. until 9), Sun. noon–5.*

Myrtle Edwards Park. Sandwiched between the Burlington Northern Railroad to the east and the gently lapping waters of Elliott Bay to the west, this sliver of a park north of Pier 70 is popular for jogging, walking, and picnicking. As a place to catch the sunset, it's rivaled only by the deck of a westbound Bainbridge Island ferry. ⊠ *Alaskan Way between W. Bay and W. Thomas Sts.*

⑤ Odyssey: The Maritime Discovery Center. Cultural and educational maritime exhibits on Puget Sound and ocean trade are the focus of this new waterfront attraction. Also here are a conference center, a short-stay boat basin, fish-processing terminals, a fish market, and a restaurant. ⊠ *Pier 66 off Alaskan Way,* ☎ *206/374–4001.* 🖾 *$6.50.* ☉ *Daily 10–5, extended hrs in July and Aug.*

④ Omnidome Film Experience. The theater next to the aquarium shows 30- to 45-minute films on a large, curved screen. Recent topics have included Alaska and whales; the eruption of Mount St. Helens is a mainstay. ⊠ *Pier 59 off Alaskan Way,* ☎ *206/622–1868.* 🖾 *$6.95; combination tickets including aquarium admission $13.50.* ☉ *Daily 10–5.*

⑦ Pacific Science Center. An excellent stop for children and adults, the Pacific Science Center has 200 hands-on exhibits. The large, brightly colored machines of Body Works amusingly analyze human physiology, while Tech Zones has robots and virtual-reality diversions that participants can control. The dinosaurs exhibit is wildly popular. IMAX screenings and laser light shows take place daily. A *Jetsons*-style outdoor plaza, with fountains and concrete towers, dates from the 1962

164

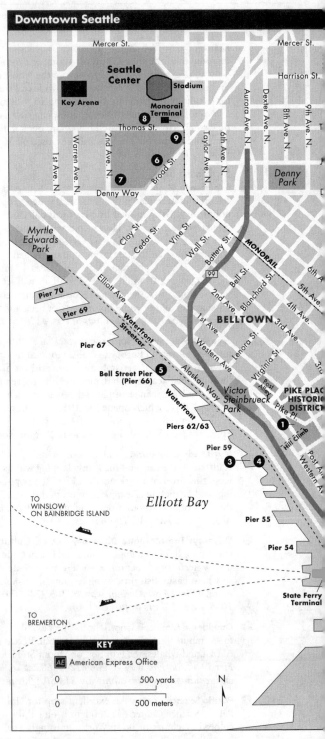

Downtown Seattle

KEY

AE American Express Office

0 ——— 500 yards

0 ——— 500 meters

N

World's Fair. ⊠ *200 2nd Ave. N,* ☏ *206/443–2001.* ☏ *$7.50.* ☉ *Week-days 10–5, weekends 10–6.*

★ ❶ **Pike Place Market.** The heart of the Pike Place Historical District, this Seattle institution began in 1907 when the city issued permits to farmers allowing them to sell produce from their wagons parked at Pike Place. Later the city built stalls for the farmers. At one time the market was a madhouse of vendors hawking their produce and haggling with customers over prices. Some of the fishmongers still carry on this kind of frenzied banter, but chances are you won't get them to waver on their prices.

Urban renewal almost killed the market, but city voters, led by the late architect Victor Steinbrueck, rallied and voted it an historical asset in 1973. Many buildings have been restored, and the project is connected to the waterfront by stairs and elevators. Besides a number of restaurants, you'll find booths selling fresh seafood—which can be packed in dry ice for your flight home—produce, cheese, Pacific Northwest wines, bulk spices, tea, coffee, and arts and crafts.

If the weather is nice, gather a picnic—fresh fruit and smoked salmon, of course, but soups, sandwiches, pastries, and various ethnic snacks are also available in the market or from the small shops facing it along Pike Place. Carry your bounty north, past the market buildings, to **Victor Steinbrueck Park,** a small green gem named for Pike Place's savior. To learn more about the history of the market, stop south of the park at the **Heritage Center** (⊠ 1531 Western Avenue), which has interactive displays on the people and businesses that have made the market such an essential part of Seattle. The center is open 10–6 daily. You can reach it directly from the market via the entertaining **Heritage Trail,** which leads you through the hubbub while teaching you interesting facts about the market. The trail starts at Rachel, the big bronze pig. ⊠ *Pike Pl. at Pike St., west of 1st Ave.,* ☏ *206/682–7453.* ☉ *Mon.–Sat. 9–6, Sun. 11–5.*

NEED A   **Three Girls Bakery** (⊠ Pike Pl. Market, 1514 Pike Pl., ☏ 206/622–
BREAK?   1045), a 13-seat glassed-in lunch counter that's tucked behind a bakery outlet, serves sandwiches, soups, and pastries. Go for the chili and a hunk of Sicilian sourdough, or buy a loaf at the take-out counter, pick up some smoked salmon at the fish place next door, and head for a picnic table in Steinbrueck Park.

🖐 ❸ **Seattle Aquarium.** Pacific Northwest marine life is the emphasis at this waterfront facility. At the Discovery Lab you'll see baby barnacles, minute jellyfish, and other "invisible" creatures through high-resolution video microscopes. The Tide Pool exhibit re-creates Washington's rocky coast and sandy beaches at low tide. There's even a 6,000-gallon wave that sweeps in over the underwater life. Sea otters and seals swim and dive in their pools, and the "State of the Sound" exhibit shows the aquatic life and ecology of Puget Sound. ⊠ *Pier 59 off Alaskan Way,* ☏ *206/386–4320.* ☏ *$8.* ☉ *Memorial Day–Labor Day, daily 10–8, Labor Day–Memorial Day, daily 10–6.*

❷ **Seattle Art Museum.** Postmodern architect Robert Venturi designed this five-story museum, which is a work of art in itself. The 1991 building has a limestone exterior with large-scale vertical fluting accented by terra-cotta, cut granite, and marble. Sculptor Jonathan Borofsky's several-stories-high *Hammering Man* pounds away outside the front door. The extensive collection inside surveys Asian, Native American, African, Oceanic, and pre-Columbian art. Among the highlights are the anonymous 14th-century

Buddhist masterwork *Monk at the Moment of Enlightenment* and Jackson Pollock's *Sea Change*. A ticket to the museum is valid for admission to the Seattle Asian Art Museum (☞ *below*) in Volunteer Park if used within one week. ⊠ *100 University St.,* ☎ *206/654–3100.* ☜ *$7; free 1st Thurs. of month.* ☉ *Tues.–Sun. 10–5 (Thurs. until 9).*

Seattle Center. The 74-acre Seattle Center complex was built for the 1962 World's Fair. A rolling green campus organized around the massive International Fountain, the center includes an amusement park, theaters, exhibition halls, museums, shops, restaurants, a skateboard park, Key Arena, the Pacific Science Center (☞ *above*), and the Space Needle (☞ *below*). Among the arts groups headquartered here are the Seattle Repertory Theatre, Intiman Theatre, the Seattle Opera, and the Pacific Northwest Ballet. The center hosts several professional sports teams: the Seattle Supersonics (NBA basketball), Sounders (soccer), Seadogs (indoor soccer), and Thunderbirds (hockey). It's a bit cramped, and parking can be a nightmare, but the Seattle Center is the undisputed hub of the city's leisure life. It's also the site of three of the area's largest summer festivals: the Northwest Folklife Festival, Bite of Seattle, and Bumbershoot. *See* Festivals and Seasonal Events *in* Chapter 1 for details about these. The **Seattle Center Monorail** (☞ Getting Around *in* Seattle A to Z, *below*) travels between the center and Westlake Center. ⊠ *Between 1st and 5th Aves. N and Denny Way and Mercer St.,* ☎ *206/684–8582.*

☝ ❽ **Seattle Children's Museum.** The global village at this colorful and spacious facility introduces children to everyday life in Ghana, the Philippines, and other lands. A mountain wilderness area (including a slide and waterfall) educates kids about climbing and camping and highlights the Northwest environment. Cog City is a giant maze of pipes and pulleys. A pretend neighborhood contains a post office, café, fire station, and grocery store. An area for infants and toddlers is well padded for climbing and sliding. Arts-and-crafts activities, special exhibits, and workshops are also offered. ⊠ *Seattle Center House, fountain level, 305 Harrison St.,* ☎ *206/441–1768.* ☜ *$4.* ☉ *Weekdays 10–5, weekends 10–6.*

★ ❻ **Space Needle.** The distinctive exterior of the 520-ft-high Space Needle can be seen from almost any spot in the downtown area. The view (especially at sunset) from the inside out is even better. The observation deck, a 42-second elevator ride from street level, yields vistas of the entire region. Have a drink at the Space Needle Lounge or a latte at the adjacent coffee bar and take in Elliott Bay, Queen Anne Hill, and on a clear day the peaks of the Cascade Range. (If it's stormy, have no fear: 25 lightning rods protect the tower.) The needle's rotating restaurants, one family style and the other more formal, are not known for innovative cuisine. ⊠ *5th Ave. and Broad St.,* ☎ *206/443–2111.* ☜ *Observation deck $9.* ☉ *Daily 8 AM–11 PM.*

❶❶ **Washington State Convention and Trade Center.** Seattle's vine-covered exhibition hall straddles I–5. The design of verdant **Freeway Park** south of here is intended to convey the spirit and flavor of the Pacific Northwest, which it does fairly well, considering the urban location. The street-level **Visitor Information Center** has maps, brochures, and event listings. ⊠ *Visitor center: 800 Convention Pl., at 8th Ave. and Pike St.,* ☎ *206/461–5840.* ☉ *Memorial Day–Labor Day, daily 10–4; Labor Day–Memorial Day, weekdays 8:30–5, Sat. 10–4.*

❶⓪ **Westlake Center.** This three-story mall (☞ Shopping, *below*) is also a major terminus for buses and the Seattle Center Monorail, which was built for the 1962 World's Fair and connects downtown to Seattle Center. The ground-level Made in Washington store showcases the state's products. ✉ *1601 5th Ave.,* ☎ *206/467–1600.* ☉ *Mon.–Sat. 9:30–8, Sun. 11–6.*

Pioneer Square and the International District

A walk through Seattle's Pioneer Square and International District provides a glimpse into the city's days as a logging and shipping center and a haven for immigrants from Asia and the Pacific Islands.

Numbers in the text correspond to numbers in the margin and on the Downtown Seattle map.

A Good Walk

Begin at **Pioneer Place,** at 1st Avenue and Yesler Way in the **Pioneer Square District.** Explore the shops and historic buildings along 1st Avenue before heading to the **Klondike Gold Rush National Historical Park** ⑫, on Main Street two blocks south and one block east of Pioneer Place. A restful stop along Main Street heading east to the **International District** is **Waterfall Garden** park, designed by Masao Kinoshita on the site where the messenger service that became United Parcel Service began operations.

Head south (right) on 2nd Avenue South and east (left) at South Jackson Street. You'll see the **Kingdome** sports stadium and Amtrak's **King Street Station** on your right as you head up South Jackson to 7th Avenue, where the **Wing Luke Museum** ⑬ surveys the past and present of immigrants from Asia and the Pacific Islands and their descendants. The museum has walking-tour maps of historic buildings and businesses. One intriguing stop is the **Uwajimaya** store at 6th Avenue South and South King Street (head south one block on 7th Avenue South and turn right on South King Street). You can return to the harbor in one of the vintage **Waterfront Streetcar** trolleys—the southern terminus is at 5th Avenue South and Jackson Street. You can also catch a bus to downtown at the same corner.

TIMING

You can explore Pioneer Square and the International District in one to two hours unless you stop for lunch or like to shop. The Wing Luke Museum is closed on Monday.

Sights to See

International District. The 40-block "I.D.," as the International District is locally known, began as a haven for Chinese workers who came to the United States to work on the transcontinental railroad. The community has remained largely intact despite anti-Chinese riots and the forcible eviction of Chinese residents during the 1880s, and the internment of Japanese-Americans during World War II. About one third of the I.D.'s residents are Chinese, one third are Filipino, and another third come from elsewhere in Asia or the Pacific Islands. The district, which includes many Chinese, Japanese, and Korean restaurants, also contains herbalists, acupuncturists, antiques shops, and private clubs for gambling and socializing. Among the many great markets is the huge **Uwajimaya** Japanese supermarket and department store (☞ *Shopping, below*). ✉ *Between Main and S. Lane Sts. and 4th and 8th Aves.*

⑫ **Klondike Gold Rush National Historical Park.** Film presentations, exhibits, and gold-panning demonstrations are among the ways this indoor center illustrates Seattle's role in the 1897–98 gold rush in northwestern Canada's Klondike region. ✉ *117 S. Main St.,* ☎ *206/553–7220.* ☜ *Free.* ☉ *Daily 9–5.*

Pioneer Square District. The ornate iron-and-glass pergola at **Pioneer Place**, at 1st Avenue and Yesler Way, marks the site of the pier and sawmill owned by Henry Yesler, one of Seattle's first businessmen. Timber logged off the hills was sent to the sawmill on a "skid road"—now Yesler Way—made of small logs laid crossways and greased so that the freshly cut trees would slide down to the mill. The area grew into Seattle's first business center; in 1889 a fire destroyed many of the district's wood-frame buildings, but the industrious residents and businesspeople rebuilt them with brick and mortar.

With the 1897 Klondike gold rush, however, this area became populated with saloons and brothels. Businesses gradually moved north, and the old pioneering area deteriorated. Eventually, only drunks and bums hung out in the neighborhood that had become known as Skid Row, and the name became synonymous with "down and out." The Pioneer Square District encompasses about 18 blocks and includes restaurants, bars, shops, and the city's largest concentration of art galleries. It is once again a hangout for those down on their luck. Incidents of crime in the neighborhood have increased lately, especially after dark, but few find it intimidating during the day.

⓭ **Wing Luke Museum.** The small but well-organized museum named for the first Asian-American elected official in the Northwest surveys the history and cultures of people from Asia and the Pacific Islands who have settled in the Pacific Northwest. The emphasis is on how immigrants and their descendants have transformed and been transformed by American culture. The permanent collection includes costumes, fabrics, crafts, basketry, photographs, and Chinese traditional medicines. ✉ *407 7th Ave. S,* ☏ *206/623–5124.* ✆ *$2.50.* ☉ *Tues.–Fri. 11–4:30, weekends noon–4.*

Capitol Hill Area

With its mix of theaters and churches, coffeehouses and nightclubs, stately homes and student apartments, Capitol Hill demonstrates Seattle's diversity better than any other neighborhood. There aren't many sights in the traditional sense, but you can while away an enjoyable day here and perhaps an even more pleasurable evening.

Numbers in the text correspond to numbers in the margin and on the Downtown Seattle and North Seattle maps.

A Good Walk

If you're prepared for some hills, this walk will give you a great overview of the area. From downtown, walk up Pine Street to Melrose Avenue, where you can fortify yourself with a jolt of java at the **Bauhaus** coffeehouse. This section of the hill is called the **Pike–Pine corridor** ⑭. Continue east on Pine Street to Broadway and turn left (but don't miss the Art Deco Egyptian Theater to the right). Passing Seattle Central Community College you'll cross Denny Way, the unofficial threshold of the **Broadway shopping district** ⑮. After six blocks, the road bears to the right, becoming 10th Avenue East.

You'll notice many beautiful homes on the side streets off 10th Avenue East in either direction as you continue north to Prospect Street. Turn right at Prospect and gird yourself for another hill. Continue on to 14th Avenue East and turn left (north) to enter **Volunteer Park** ⑯. After walking around a picturesque water tower (with a good view from the top), you'll see the **Volunteer Park Conservatory** straight ahead, the **reservoir** to your left, and the **Seattle Asian Art Museum** to your right. Leave the park to the east via Galer Street. At 15th Avenue East, you can turn left (north) to visit **Lakeview Cemetery** (where Bruce Lee lies in repose),

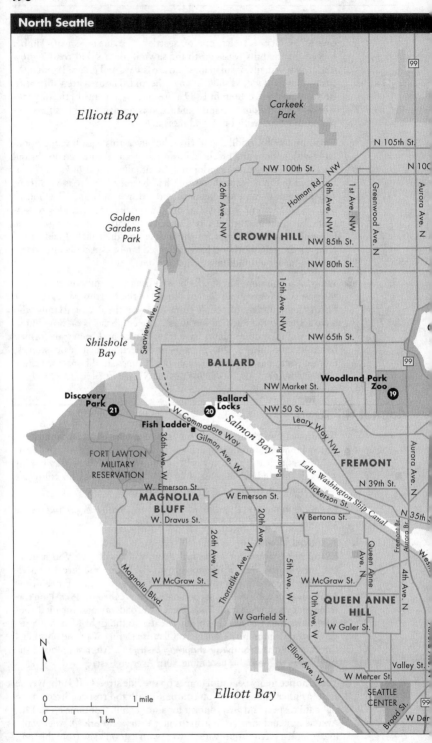

Elliott Bay

Carkeek Park

N 105th St.

99

NW 100th St.

N 100

Golden Gardens Park

Holman Rd. NW

26th Ave. NW

8th Ave. NW

1st Ave. NW

Greenwood Ave. N

Aurora Ave. N

CROWN HILL NW 85th St.

15th Ave. NW

NW 80th St.

Shilshole Bay

Seaview Ave. NW

NW 65th St.

BALLARD

99

NW Market St.

Woodland Park Zoo 19

Discovery Park 21

Ballard Locks 20

NW 50 St.

Leary Way NW

Fish Ladder

W Commodore Way

Salmon Bay

Gilman Ave. W

36th Ave. W

Ballard Br.

Lake Washington Ship Canal

FREMONT

Aurora Ave. N

FORT LAWTON MILITARY RESERVATION

N 39th St.

W. Emerson St.

Nickerson St.

N 35th

MAGNOLIA BLUFF

W Emerson St.

20th Ave.

W Bertona St.

Fremont Br.

Aurora Br.

4th Ave. N

West

W. Dravus St.

26th Ave. W

Thorndike Ave. W

5th Ave. W

Queen Anne Ave. N

Magnolia Blvd

W McGraw St.

10th Ave. W

W McGraw St.

QUEEN ANNE HILL

W Garfield St.

W Galer St.

N

Elliott Ave. W

Valley St.

0   1 mile

0   1 km

Elliott Bay

W Mercer St.

SEATTLE CENTER

Broad St.

99

W Der

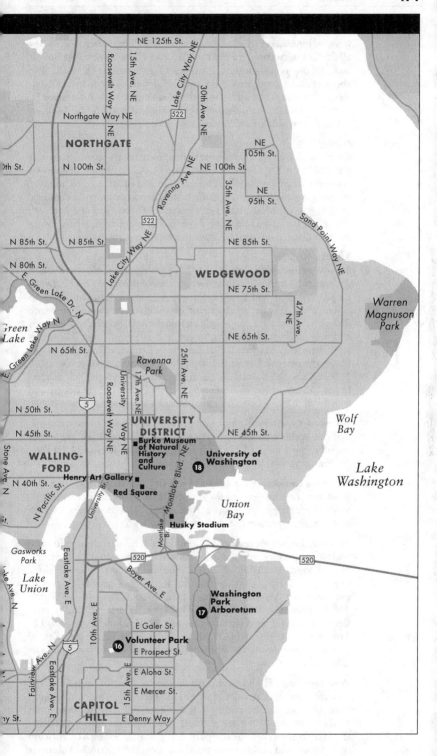

NE 125th St.

Roosevelt Way NE

15th Ave. NE

Lake City Way NE

30th Ave. NE

Northgate Way NE

NE

522

NORTHGATE

NE
105th St.

0th St.

N 100th St.

NE 100th St.

Ravenna Ave NE

35th Ave. NE

NE
95th St.

Sand Point Way NE

522

N 85th St.

N 85th St.

Lake City Way NE

NE 85th St.

N 80th St.

WEDGEWOOD

E. Green Lake Dr. N

NE 75th St.

*Warren
Magnuson
Park*

*Green
Lake*

47th Ave.
NE

E. Green Lake Way N

N 65th St.

NE 65th St.

*Ravenna
Park*

25th Ave. NE

University

17th Ave. NE

Roosevelt Way NE

N 50th St.

5

*Wolf
Bay*

N 45th St.

**UNIVERSITY
DISTRICT**

Way NE

NE 45th St.

Stone Ave. N

**WALLING-
FORD**

**Burke Museum
of Natural
History
and
Culture**

Montlake Blvd. NE

**University of
Washington**

18

*Lake
Washington*

N 40th St.

Henry Art Gallery ■

N Pacific St.

University Br.

Red Square ■

*Union
Bay*

St.

Montlake — Montlake Br.

■ **Husky Stadium**

*Gasworks
Park*

Eastlake Ave. E

520

520

ke Ave. N

*Lake
Union*

Boyer Ave. E

10th Ave. E

**Washington
Park
Arboretum**

17

Fairview Ave. N

Eastlake Ave. E

5

E Galer St.

Volunteer Park

16

E Prospect St.

15th Ave. E

E Aloha St.

E Mercer St.

ny St.

**CAPITOL
HILL**

E Denny Way

or turn right (south) and walk four blocks to shops and cafés. To return to downtown, continue walking south on 15th Avenue East and west on Pine Street (if you've had enough walking, catch Metro Bus 10 at this intersection; it heads toward Pike Place Market). At Broadway, cut one block south to Pike Street for the rest of the walk. The above tour is a good survey of Capitol Hill, but it's by no means complete. The area's best attraction, the **Washington Park Arboretum** ⑰, is too far to walk. You'll need to take the bus (catch Metro Bus 11 heading northeast along East Madison Street) or drive.

TIMING

Simply walking this tour requires about four hours—two if you start and end in the Broadway shopping district. Allow at least one to two hours for shopping the Pike–Pine corridor and Broadway, an hour for the Asian Art Museum, and a half hour for the conservatory. The amount of time you spend at Bruce Lee's grave is between you and Mr. Lee. Plan on at least two hours for a visit to the arboretum, where losing track of time, and yourself, is pretty much the point.

Sights to See

⓰ **Broadway shopping district.** Seattle's youth-culture, old-money, and gay scenes all converge on the lively stretch of Broadway East between East Denny Way and East Roy Street. A great place to stroll and sip coffee or have a brew, the strip contains the obligatory art-house movie theater (☞ Harvard Exit *in* Nightlife and the Arts, *below*), record shops and new and vintage clothing stores, and plenty of cafés. The three-story **Broadway Market** (⊠ 401 Broadway E) has the Gap, Urban Outfitters, and other slick merchandisers, along with some smaller boutiques. You won't be able to miss the glaring sign for the open-air **Dick's Drive-In** (⊠ 115 Broadway E). Dropping in for a Dick's Deluxe Burger and a shake at 1 AM is a quintessential Seattle experience.

Lakeview Cemetery. Kung-fu star **Bruce Lee's grave** is the most-visited site at this cemetery directly north of Volunteer Park. Inquire at the office for a map. ⊠ 1554 15th Ave. E, ☎ 206/322–1582. ⊡ Free. ☉ Weekdays 9–4:30.

⓮ **Pike–Pine corridor.** A hip center of activity, this strip between downtown and the south end of the Broadway shopping district holds galleries, thrift shops, music stores, restaurants, and rock clubs. ⊠ Pike and Pine Sts. between 6th Ave. and Broadway.

Seattle Asian Art Museum. This facility holds thousands of paintings, sculptures, pottery, and textiles from China, Japan, India, Korea, and several southeast Asian countries. You can sip any of nearly three dozen distinctive teas at the tranquil **Kado Tea Garden.** A ticket to the Asian Art Museum is good for $3 off admission to the Seattle Art Museum (☞ Pike Place Market, the Waterfront, and Seattle Center, *above*) if used within one week. ⊠ Volunteer Park, 1400 E. Prospect St., ☎ 206/654–3100. ⊡ $3; free 1st Thurs. and Sat. of month. ☉ Tues.–Sun. 10–5 (Thurs. until 9) and some Mon. holidays; call for tour schedule.

⓰ **Volunteer Park.** High above the mansions of North Capitol Hill sits 45-acre Volunteer Park, a grassy affair perfect for picnicking, sunbathing, reading, and strolling. It's a mere 108 steps to some great views at the top of the water tower near the main entrance. Beside the lake in the center of the park is the **Seattle Asian Art Museum** (☞ *above*), and across from the museum is the romantic **Volunteer Park Conservatory** (☎ 206/684–4743). The greenhouse, which was completed in 1912, has accumulated its inhabitants largely by donation, including an extensive collection of orchids begun in 1919.

Rooms here are dedicated to ferns, palms, cacti, and exotic flowers. Admission is free; hours are seasonal, so call ahead. ⊠ *Park entrance: 14th Ave. E at Prospect St.*

⑰ Washington Park Arboretum. The 200-acre arboretum's Rhododendron Glen and Azalea Way are in full bloom from March through June. During the rest of the year other plants and wildlife flourish. From March through October visit the peaceful **Japanese Garden,** a compressed world of mountains, forests, rivers, lakes, and tablelands. The **Graham Visitors Center** at the north end provides explanations of the arboretum's flora and fauna and has brochures with self-guided walking tours. Or you can dispense with maps and follow your bliss. ⊠ *2300 Arboretum Dr. E,* ☎ *206/325–4510.* 🎟 *Free.* ☉ *Park daily 7 AM–sunset, visitor center daily 10–4.*

University District

The U District, as the University District is called locally, is bounded by Ravenna Boulevard to the north, the Montlake Cut waterway (connecting Lake Union and Lake Washington) to the south, 25th Avenue Northeast to the east, and I–5 to the west. A stroll through the University of Washington campus can include stops at its museums and other cultural attractions. To get a whiff of the slightly anarchic energy that fuels this part of town, head off campus to "The Ave," the student-oriented shopping area along University Way Northeast.

Numbers in the text correspond to numbers in the margin and on the North Seattle map.

A Good Walk

Start at Northeast 45th Street and University Way Northeast. Proceed south on University Way ("The Ave") through the heart of the district's many shopping and dining options. Turn left at Northeast Campus Parkway, stopping by the visitor center at the **University of Washington** ⑱. Straight ahead at the end of the block is the **Henry Art Gallery.** Continue east to Central Plaza, better known as **Red Square.** On clear days you'll be rewarded with views of Mount Rainier to the southeast. Walk down Rainier Vista (past the Frosh Pond and fountain) to Stevens Way, turning left into **Sylvan Grove,** a gorgeous outdoor theater. Return via Rainier Vista to Red Square and strike out due north. A walk along shady Memorial Way past the commuter lot deposits you at the **Burke Museum of Natural History.** From the Burke step out onto Northeast 45th Street, walking two longish blocks to the left to return to University Way Northeast.

TIMING

The route above should only take about two hours, but factor in an hour or so each for the Henry gallery and Burke museum and an additional hour if you want to shop along the Ave.

Sights to See

The Ave. University Way Northeast, the hub of University of Washington social life, has all the activities (and the grungy edge) one expects in a student-oriented district—great coffeehouses, cinemas (☞ the Grand Illusion and Varsity theaters *in* Nightlife and the Arts, *below*), clothing stores, and cheap restaurants, along with panhandlers and pockets of grime. The major action along the Ave is between 42nd and 50th streets, though there are more shops and restaurants as University Way continues north to 58th Street and the entrance to Ravenna Park. Stop in the **Big Time Brewery** (☞ Brew Pubs *in* Nightlife and the Arts, *below*) for a pint of ale and a gallon of local color.

Burke Museum of Natural History and Culture. Exhibits at this facility on the northwest edge of the University of Washington campus survey the cultures of the Pacific Northwest and Washington State's 35 Native American tribes. The museum's permanent collection focuses on anthropological, geological, and zoological specimens. ⊠ *17th Ave. NE and N.E. 45th St.,* ☎ *206/543–5590* ☑ *$5.50.* ☉ *Daily 10–5 (Thurs. until 8).*

Henry Art Gallery. The many works by Northwest artists at this gallery on the west side of the University of Washington campus include photography, 19th- and 20th-century paintings, and textiles; the facility often presents important touring exhibitions. ⊠ *15th Ave. NE and N.E. 41st St.,* ☎ *206/543–2280.* ☑ *$5.* ☉ *Tues.–Sun. 11–5 (Thurs. until 8).*

☾ **Museum of History and Industry.** An 1880s-era room and a Seattle time line at this museum depict the city's earlier days. Other displays from the permanent collection are shown on a rotating basis—a recent one surveyed Pacific Coast League baseball teams—along with traveling exhibits. ⊠ *2700 24th Ave. E,* ☎ *206/324–1125.* ☑ *$5.50.* ☉ *Weekdays 11–5, weekends 10–5.*

⓲ **University of Washington.** Locals know this university with 35,000 students as "U-Dub." Founded in 1861 downtown, the university moved in 1895 to Denny Hall, the first building on the present campus. The Alaska-Yukon-Pacific Exposition, which the school hosted in 1909, brought the Northwest national attention. The University of Washington is respected for its research and graduate programs in medicine, nursing, oceanography, drama, physiology, and social work, among many others. Its athletic teams—particularly football and women's basketball—have strong regional followings, and the **Henry Art Gallery** and **Burke Museum of Natural History and Culture** (☞ *above*) are both worth a look. **Red Square** is the nerve center for student activity and politics. The "red" refers to its brick paving, not students' political inclinations. This is a decidedly nonactivist campus, though it's in the square that you'll see animal-rights, environmental, and other advocates attempting to rouse the masses. On sunny days the steps are filled with students sunbathing, studying, or hanging out. ⊠ *Visitor Information Center, 4014 University Way NE,* ☎ *206/543–9198.* ☉ *Daily 8–5.*

OFF THE   **WARREN MAGNUSON PARK –** Jutting into Lake Washington northeast of
BEATEN PATH   the University District, "Sand Point" (as it's called by locals) is one of the
              best beaches in the city for quiet sunbathing. The Soundgarden, a
              grassy area filled with metal sculptures that emit tones when the wind
              blows, is in the northern part of the park, through the turnstile and
              across *Moby Dick* Bridge (embedded with quotes from Melville's novel).
              ⊠ *Park entrance: Sand Point Way NE at 65th St.*

Fremont and Environs

Around Seattle, the word "Fremont" is invariably preceded by the words "funky," "artsy," or "eclectic." And why not? The neighborhood's residents—largely artists—do little to challenge the image. "The Artists' Republic of Fremont," as many prefer to call it, brims with sass and self-confidence. Signs on the outskirts proclaim it THE CENTER OF THE UNIVERSE and instruct visitors to set their watches back five minutes, or to throw them away entirely. Given the area's many assets—galleries, restaurants, coffeehouses, brew pubs, antiques shops, and the like—dispensing with time can be a very good idea. To the east of Fremont is Wallingford, an inviting neighborhood of bungalow homes and boutique shopping. You'll find Phinney Ridge and the Woodland Park Zoo to the north of Fremont. Ballard, a neighborhood with a strong Scandinavian flavor, and the center of Seattle's fishing industry, lies to the west.

Numbers in the text correspond to numbers in the margin and on the North Seattle map.

A Good Tour

Coming from downtown, you'll probably enter Fremont via the **Fremont Bridge,** one of the busiest drawbridges in the world. Central Fremont is tiny and can easily be explored by intuition. Here's one strategy: Proceed north on Fremont Avenue North, turning right at North 35th Street. Walk two blocks to the **Aurora Bridge** (you'll be standing underneath it). Turn left and walk one block, but approach with care. The "Fremont troll"—a whimsical concrete monster that lurks beneath the bridge—jealously guards his Volkswagen Beetle. Head back along North 36th Street, making a hard left at the **statue of Lenin** (seriously) at Fremont Place, the first street after you cross Fremont Avenue North. Walk a half block southeast, go right at the crosswalk, and then make a right on North 35th Street. At the end of the block is the 53-ft **Fremont Rocket,** officially designating the center of the universe. Walk straight ahead one long block to Phinney Avenue to **Redhook Brewery** (tours are conducted daily) and the **Trolleyman** (☞ Brew Pubs *in* Nightlife and the Arts, *below*). Turn left and continue one block to the **Ship Canal.** On the right is **Canal Park.** Linger there, or turn left on North 34th Street and return to the Fremont Bridge. On the way you'll pass a parking lot that hosts two important Fremont traditions—the Sunday Flea and Crafts Market (from spring to fall, weather permitting) and the Outdoor Cinema (bring a chair on Saturday after dusk in the summer).

The major Fremont-area attractions are best reached by car, bus, or bike. The **Woodland Park Zoo** ⑲ is due north of Fremont via Fremont Avenue North (catch Bus 5 heading north from the northeast corner of Fremont Avenue North and North 39th Street). The **Ballard Locks** ⑳ are west of Fremont (take Bus 28 from Fremont Avenue North and North 35th Street to Northwest Market Street and 8th Avenue North and transfer to Bus 44 or, on weekdays only, Bus 46, heading west). **Discovery Park** ㉑ is a walk of less than a mile from the south entrance to the Ballard Locks. Head west (right) on Commodore Way and south (left) on 40th Street.

TIMING

The walk around Fremont takes an hour at most, but the neighborhood is meant for strolling, browsing, sipping, and shopping. Plan to spend a full morning or a good part of an afternoon. You could easily spend two hours at the Ballard Locks and several hours at Discovery Park or the zoo.

Sights to See

★ ☾ ⑳ **Ballard Locks.** Officially the Hiram M. Chittenden Locks, this part of the 8-mi Lake Washington Ship Canal connects Lake Washington and Lake Union with the salt water of Shilshole Bay and Puget Sound. The locks, which were completed in 1917, service 100,000 boats yearly by raising and lowering water levels anywhere from 6 to 26 ft. On the north side of the locks is a 7-acre **ornamental garden** of native and exotic plants, shrubs, and trees. Also on the north side are a staffed visitor center with displays on the history and operation of the locks as well as several fanciful sculptures by local artists. Along the south side is a 1,200-ft promenade with a footbridge, a fishing pier, and an observation deck.

Take some time to watch the progress of fishing boats and pleasure craft passing through the locks. Observe how the marine population makes the same journey from saltwater to fresh on the **fish ladder,** whose 21 levels form a gradual incline that allows an estimated half-million salmon and trout each year to swim upstream. Several windows at the waterline afford views of the fish struggling against the current as they migrate to their spawning grounds. Most of the migration takes place between June and October. (The fish ladder, by the way, is where various attempts are being carried out to prevent sea lions, including the locally notorious Herschel, from depleting the salmon population.) If you're coming via bus from downtown, take Bus 15 or 18 to the stop at Northwest Market Street and 15th Avenue Northwest and transfer to Bus 44 or (weekdays only) 46 heading west on Market. ⊠ *3015 N.W. 54th St.; from Fremont, head north on Leary Way NW, west on N.W. Market St., and south on 54th St.,* ☎ *206/783–7059.* 🖾 *Free.* ☺ *Locks daily 7 AM–9 PM, visitor center June–Sept., daily 10–7; Oct.– May, Thurs.–Mon. 11–5; call for tour information.*

Center for Wooden Boats. Though slightly off the main drag at the south end of Lake Union, the center is a great place to launch your expedition if you're interested in exploring the water (or just the waterfront). You can check out the 1897 schooner *Wawona* and the other historic vessels on display, watch the staff at work on a restoration, rent a boat at the Oarhouse for a sail around the lake, or have a picnic. ⊠ *1010 Valley St.,* ☎ *206/382–2628.* 🖾 *Free.* ☺ *Memorial Day–Labor Day, Wed.–Mon. 11–6 (boat rentals until 7); Labor Day–Memorial Day, Wed.–Mon. 11–5 (museum and rentals).*

㉑ **Discovery Park.** At Seattle's largest park (520 acres), a former military base converted into a wildlife sanctuary, you can hike through cool forests, explore saltwater beaches, or take in views of Puget Sound and Mount Rainier. A 2¾-mi trail traverses this urban wilderness. From Fremont, take Leary Way Northwest to 15th Avenue Northwest, turn left, and head south on 15th Avenue over the Ballard Bridge. Turn right on West Emerson Street, right on Gilman Avenue West, left on West Fort Street, and right on East Government Way. From downtown, take Elliott Avenue north until it becomes 15th Avenue Northwest, turn left on West Emerson, and follow the previous directions the rest of the way. ⊠ *3801 E. Government Way,* ☎ *206/386–4236.* 🖾 *Free.* ☺ *Park daily 6 AM–11 PM, visitor center daily 8:30–5.*

Fremont Center. The self-styled Republic of Fremont is one of Seattle's most distinctive neighborhoods. The center is an eclectic strip of Fremont Avenue stretching from the Ship Canal at the south end to North 36th Street, with shops and cafés two blocks to either side. The area also contains many lighthearted attractions, including a statue of Lenin, a 53-ft rocket, and the Fremont troll.

Gasworks Park. Colorful kites soar in the air and bright-hued spinnakers bob offshore in Lake Union on summer days at this park. Get a glimpse of your future (and downtown Seattle) from the zodiac sculpture at the top of the hill, or feed the ducks on the lake. Outdoor concerts take place at Gasworks in summer. On Independence Day there's a fireworks display and a performance by the Seattle Symphony. ⊠ *North end of Lake Union, N. Northlake Way and Meridian Ave. N.*

Green Lake. Across Highway 99 (Aurora Avenue North) from the Woodland Park Zoo (☞ *below*), Green Lake is the recreational hub of the city's park system. A 3-mi jogging and bicycling trail rings the lake, and there are facilities for basketball, tennis, baseball, and soccer. The park is generally packed (and the facilities overbooked) on weekday evenings, which has made this the best time for active Seattleites to see and be seen (it's something of a young-singles' scene). ⊠ *E. Green Lake Dr. N and W. Green Lake Dr. N.*

(🖐 ⑲ **Woodland Park Zoo.** Many of the 300 species of animals in this 92-acre botanical garden roam freely in habitat areas that have won several design awards. The African Savanna, the Asian Elephant Forest, and the Northern Trail, which shelters brown bears, wolves, mountain goats, and otters, are of particular interest. Wheelchairs and strollers can be rented. A memorial to musician Jimi Hendrix, a Seattle native, overlooks the African Savanna exhibit; appropriately, it's a big rock. ⊠ *5500 Phinney Ave. N,* ☎ *206/684–4800.* ⌑ *$8.50.* ☉ *Mid-Mar.–mid-Oct., daily 9:30–6; mid-Oct.–mid-Mar., daily 9:30–4.*

On Seattle's Outskirts and Beyond

Chateau Ste. Michelle Winery. One of the oldest wineries in the state is 15 mi northeast of Seattle on 87 wooded acres that were once part of the estate of lumber baron Fred Stimson. Trout ponds, a carriage house, a caretaker's cottage, formal gardens, and the 1912 family manor house—which is on the National Register of Historic Places—are part of the original estate. Visitors are invited to picnic and explore the grounds; the wine shop sells delicatessen items. During the summer Chateau Ste. Michelle hosts nationally known performers and arts events in its amphitheater. ⊠ *14111 N.E. 145th St., Woodinville,* ☎ *425/488–1133. From downtown Seattle take I–90 east to north I–405. Take Exit 23 east (S.R. 522) to the Woodinville exit.* ☉ *Complimentary wine tastings and cellar tours daily 10–4:30.*

Columbia Winery. Founded in 1962 by a group of University of Washington professors, this is the oldest winery in the state. Using only European vinifera-style grapes grown in Eastern Washington, the founders' aim was to take advantage of the fact that the vineyards share the same latitude as the best wine-producing areas of France. The gift shop is open year-round and offers the wines themselves and a variety of wine-related merchandise. Columbia hosts special events throughout the year that focus on food and wine pairings and is the final destination of the Spirit of Washington Dinner Train (see Guided Tours, *below*). ⊠ *14030 N.E. 145th St., Woodinville,* ☎ *425/488–2776 or 800/488–2347. From downtown Seattle take I–90 east to north I–405. Take Exit 23 east (S.R. 522) to the Woodinville exit, go right. Go right again on 175th St., and left on Hwy. 202.* ☉ *Complimentary wine tastings daily 10–7, cellar tours available on weekends.*

Jimi Hendrix Grave Site. The famed guitarist's grave is in Greenwood Cemetery in Renton. From Seattle take I–5 south to the Renton exit, then I–405 past Southcenter to Exit 4B. Bear right under the freeway. Take a right on Sunset Boulevard and another right one block later at 3rd Street. Continue 1 mi, turning right at the third light. ⊠ *3rd and Monroe Sts.,* ☎ *425/255–1511.* ☉ *Daily dawn–dusk. Inquire at the office; a counselor will direct you to the site.*

★ 🖐 **Museum of Flight.** Boeing, the world's largest builder of aircraft, is based in Seattle, so it's not surprising that this facility at Boeing Field is one of the city's best museums. The Red Barn, Boeing's original airplane factory, houses an exhibit on the history of human flight. The Great Gallery, a dramatic structure designed by Ibsen Nelson, contains more than 20 vintage airplanes. ⊠ *9404 E. Marginal Way S (take I–5 south to Exit 158; turn right on Marginal),* ☎ *206/764–5720.* ⌑ *$8.* ☉ *Daily 10–5 (Thurs. until 9).*

DINING

See the Downtown Seattle and Capitol Hill Dining map to locate restaurants in those areas and the North of Downtown Seattle Dining map for all other establishments.

CATEGORY	COST*
$$$$	over $35
$$$	$25–$35
$$	$15–$25
$	under $15

per person for a three-course meal, excluding drinks, service, and sales tax (about 9.1%, varies slightly by community)

Downtown Seattle and Capitol Hill

Chinese

$$–$$$ ✕ **Chef Wang.** Striving for a balance between the hipness of its Belltown neighbors and the unintentional kitsch of the "classic" American Chinese restaurant, Chef Wang is generally on target. The decor benefits from clean lines, rich colors, and low-voltage lighting but suffers from a feeling of incompleteness, as if the budget ran out sooner than expected. Ingredients are above-average in quality and freshness and cooked with a more delicate touch and presentation than one might expect from the typical Chinese restaurant. The menu contains familiar dishes, such as Peking duck and mu shu pork, executed with a welcome piquancy, depth, and textural subtlety. You can also create your own combination dish from the 22-item list of meats, vegetables, and sauces. ⊠ *2230 1st Ave.,* ☎ *206/448–5407. MC, V. No lunch weekends.*

Contemporary

$$$$ ✕ **Hunt Club.** Dark wood and plush seating provide a traditional setting for chef Brian Scheehser's interpretations of Pacific Northwest meat and seafood. The house-made squash ravioli and the saffron mussel bisque are excellent starters. Entrées on the seasonal menu include succulent jumbo prawns, pan-roasted sea scallops served with truffle risotto, and steak with garlic mashed potatoes and paper-thin onion rings. ⊠ *Sorrento, 900 E. Madison St.,* ☎ *206/622–6400. AE, DC, MC, V.*

$$$–$$$$ ✕ **El Gaucho.** Dress to impress here—you don't want to be outclassed
★   by the waistcoated wait staff coolly navigating the packed floor of this retro steak house. El Gaucho serves up some of the city's most basic, most satisfying fare in a swanky, expansive room. For the complete show, order the items prepared table-side. From the flaming lamb shish kebab to the cool Caesar salad (the best in the city), everything tastes better—or at least it seems that way—with the virtuosic presentation. ⊠ *2505 1st Ave.,* ☎ *206/728–1337. Reservations essential. AE, MC, V. No lunch.*

$$$–$$$$ ✕ **Fullers.** Consistently ranked at or near the top of Seattle's restaurants in local and national publications, Fullers delivers a rare commodity: a dining experience of exceptional poise and restraint born of unconventional risk-taking. Chef Tom Black, who trained as a line cook under Monique Barbeau, shows his unique sensibilities in menu offerings such as pan-seared king salmon with braised fennel ravioli, haricot verts, and caviar–dill beurre blanc; five-spice duck with savory bread pudding; artichoke and baby Italian onion salad with port reduction; and New York strip steak with potato cake and escarole. Works by Pacific Northwest artists adorn an otherwise austere dining room. ⊠ *Seattle Sheraton Hotel and Towers, 1400 6th Ave.,* ☎ *206/447–5544. Reservations essential. AE, D, DC, MC, V. Closed Sun. No lunch Sat.*

$$$–$$$$ ✕ **Lampreia.** The beige-and-gold interior of this Belltown restaurant
★   is the perfect backdrop for chef-owner Scott Carsberg's sophisticated cuisine. After an appetizer of cream of polenta with shiitake mushrooms, try one of the seasonal menu's intermezzo or light main courses—per-

haps squid and cannelloni filled with salmon—or a full entrée such as pheasant with apple-champagne sauerkraut or lamb with pesto and whipped potatoes. The clear flavors of desserts like lemon mousse with strawberry sauce bring a soothing conclusion to an exciting experience. ⊠ 2400 1st Ave., ☎ 206/443–3301. Reservations essential. AE, MC, V. Closed Sun.–Mon. No lunch.

\$\$\$–\$\$\$\$
★ ✕ **Metropolitan Grill.** Meals at this favorite lunching spot of the white-collar crowd are not for timid eaters: custom-aged mesquite-broiled steaks—the best in Seattle—are huge and come with baked potatoes or pasta. Even the veal chop is extra thick. Lamb, chicken, and seafood entrées are also on the menu. Among the accompaniments, the onion rings and the sautéed mushrooms are tops. ⊠ 818 2nd Ave., ☎ 206/624–3287. AE, D, DC, MC, V. No lunch weekends.

\$\$\$–\$\$\$\$ ✕ **Painted Table.** Chef Tim Kelly selects the freshest regional ingredients for dishes that are served on hand-painted plates. His seasonal menu might include spicy rock-shrimp linguine, wild-mushroom risotto, or herb-crusted lamb with grilled Japanese eggplant, fennel, and polenta. Desserts include a frozen-banana soufflé and a jasmine-rice custard made with coconut milk. ⊠ Alexis Hotel, 1007 1st Ave., ☎ 206/624–3646. Reservations essential. AE, D, DC, MC, V. No lunch weekends.

\$\$\$–\$\$\$\$ ✕ **Place Pigalle.** Large windows look out on Elliott Bay from this restaurant tucked behind a meat vendor in Pike Place Market's main arcade; in nice weather, they're left ajar to admit the fresh salt breeze. Bright flowers lighten up the café tables, and the friendly staff makes you feel right at home. Despite its French name, this is a very American restaurant. Go for the rich oyster stew, the Dungeness crab (available only when it is truly fresh), or the fish of the day baked in hazelnuts. ⊠ 81 Pike Pl. Market, ☎ 206/624–1756. AE, MC, V. Closed Sun.

\$\$\$–\$\$\$\$ ✕ **Stars.** After a bumpy start, San Francisco chef Jeremiah Tower seems to have worked out the kinks at this Seattle location opened in 1998. He has transplanted some of the menu items, along with adding new creations featuring local ingredients, such as grilled spiced duck with pear, Washington apple, and fresh fig compote. The space is dramatic and fun, with 25-ft-high ceilings, equally tall windows, an enormous circular fireplace in the bar with a grand stainless-steel flue, and a smart seating arrangement from which to view the proceedings. There is an ever-so-slight tendency toward style over substance, but the staff helps to keep things from getting too pretentious. ⊠ 600 Pine St., ☎ 206/264–1112. AE, DC, MC, V.

\$\$–\$\$\$\$
★ ✕ **Dahlia Lounge.** Romantic Dahlia worked its magic on Tom Hanks and Meg Ryan in Sleepless in Seattle. With valentine-red walls lighted so dimly you can't see much farther than your dinner companion's eyes, this place is cozy and then some. But the food plays its part, too. Crab cakes, served as an entrée or an appetizer, lead an ever-changing regionally oriented menu. Other standouts are seared ahi tuna, near-perfect gnocchi, and desserts like coconut-cream pie and fresh fruit cobblers. Chef-owner Tom Douglas is Seattle's most energetic restaurateur. He also owns Etta's Seafood in Pike Place Market, and the excellent Palace Kitchen on 5th Avenue, but Dahlia is the one to make your heart go pitter-pat. ⊠ 1904 4th Ave., ☎ 206/682–4142. Reservations essential. AE, D, DC, MC, V. No lunch weekends.

\$\$–\$\$\$\$ ✕ **Sazerac.** The spunky restaurant at the Hotel Monaco gleefully thumbs its nose at the traveler's fallback, the hotel dining room. "Big dawg" Jan Birnbaum presides over a whimsical (if not downright goofy) patchwork of Pacific Northwest and American favorites with a quirky Southern accent. The cedar-plank smoked salmon sits comfortably alongside collard greens, the braised pork shoulder hosts

Downtown Seattle and Capitol Hill Dining

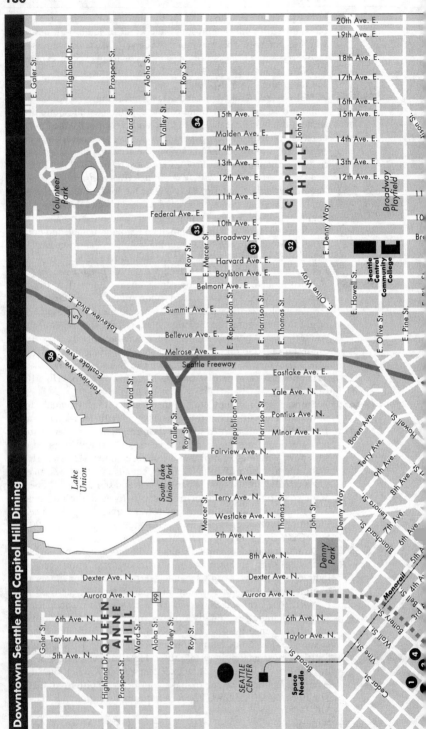

20th Ave. E.
19th Ave. E.
18th Ave. E.
17th Ave. E.
16th Ave. E.
15th Ave. E.
14th Ave. E.
13th Ave. E.
12th Ave. E.
11

E. Galer St.
E. Highland Dr.
E. Prospect St.
E. Aloha St.
E. Roy St.

E. Ward St.
E. Valley St.

Volunteer Park

15th Ave. E.
Malden Ave. E.
14th Ave. E.
13th Ave. E.
12th Ave. E.
11th Ave. E.

CAPITOL HILL

John St.

Broadway Playfield

Federal Ave. E.
10th Ave. E.
Broadway E.
Harvard Ave. E.
Boylston Ave. E.
Belmont Ave. E.

E. Roy St.
E. Mercer St.

E. Denny Way

Seattle Central Community College

Bro

Summit Ave. E.

E. Republican St.
E. Harrison St.
E. Thomas St.

E. Howell St.

E. Olive St.

E. Pine St.

Bellevue Ave. E.
Melrose Ave. E.
Seattle Freeway

Lakeview Blvd. E.
5

E. Olive Way

Fairview Ave. E.
Eastlake Ave. E.

Eastlake Ave. E.
Yale Ave. N.
Pontius Ave. N.
Minor Ave. N.

Ward St.
Aloha St.

Republican St.
Harrison St.

Boren Ave.
Terry Ave.
9th Ave.
8th Ave.
7th Ave.

Howell St.

Lake Union

Valley St.
Roy St.

Fairview Ave. N.

South Lake Union Park

Boren Ave. N.
Terry Ave. N.
Westlake Ave. N.
9th Ave. N.

Mercer St.

Thomas St.

John St.

Denny Way

Lenora St.

8th Ave. N.

Denny Park

Dexter Ave. N.
Aurora Ave. N.

Dexter Ave. N.
Aurora Ave. N.

Blanchard St.

6th Ave.
5th Ave.

Monorail

Galer St.
Taylor Ave. N.
5th Ave. N.

QUEEN ANNE HILL

6th Ave. N.

Highland Dr.
Prospect St.
Ward St.
Aloha St.
Valley St.
Roy St.

99

6th Ave. N.
Taylor Ave. N.

Bell St.
Battery St.
Wall St.

4th A

Cedar St.
Vine St.
Broad St.

SEATTLE CENTER

Space Needle

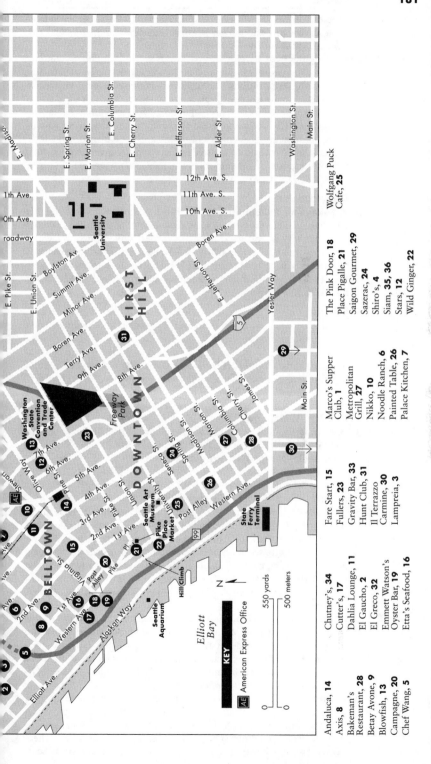

"apple-cider luv sauce" and "soft sexy grits." A great bar (with late-night service) and an indulgent dessert list round out the fun. ☒ *1101 4th Ave.,* ☎ *206/624–7755. AE, D, DC, MC, V.*

$$–$$$$ ✕ **Wolfgang Puck Café.** A laid-back staff serves postmodern comfort food—barbecued-duck quesadillas, jerk-chicken Caesar salads, linguine with seared jumbo sea scallops—at this vivacious enterprise across 1st Avenue from the Seattle Art Museum. You can slurp down some oyster shooters or "sip" a jumbo gulf-shrimp "martini" at the seafood bar. This is one of the kid-friendliest of the downtown restaurants; children are given pieces of dough at their tables to make little pizzas. Their creations are cooked in the wood-fire ovens and returned for consumption by the junior chefs. ☒ *1225 1st Ave.,* ☎ *206/621–9653. AE, D, DC, MC, V.*

Delicatessen

$ ✕ **Bakeman's Restaurant.** Low on frills but high on atmosphere, this well-lighted lunchery attracts a steady stream of business suits with its signature turkey and meat-loaf sandwiches, served on fluffy white bread. Bakeman's, open weekdays 10–3, is within easy striking distance of Pioneer Square, but the feel here is far from touristy. ☒ *122 Cherry St.,* ☎ *206/622–3375. Reservations not accepted. No credit cards. Closed weekends. No dinner.*

Eclectic

$$$–$$$$ ✕ **Andaluca.** A synthesis of fresh local ingredients and Mediterranean techniques, the food at this secluded spot downstairs at the Mayflower Park Hotel includes small plates that can act as starters or be combined to make a satisfying meal. A Dungeness crab tower with avocado, hearts of palm, and gazpacho salsa is cool and light, while the beef tenderloin with pears and blue cheese is a glorious trip to the opposite end of the sensory spectrum. ☒ *407 Olive Way,* ☎ *206/382–6999. AE, D, DC, MC, V.*

$$–$$$$ ✕ **Axis.** Restaurant as theater is the angle at this Belltown spot with a wood-fire grill. Diners can view the kitchen from almost every seat in the house. The food is worthy of the show, with appetizers like crispy eggplant wonton and an entrée of oven-roasted Dungeness crab with Cajun seasonings. ☒ *2214 1st Ave.,* ☎ *206/441–9600. Reservations essential. AE, DC, MC, V. No lunch.*

$$–$$$$ ✕ **Palace Kitchen.** The star of this chic yet convivial Tom Douglas eatery may be the 45-ft bar, but the real show takes place within the giant open kitchen at the back. Sausages, sweet-pea ravioli, salmon carpaccio, and a nightly selection of exotic cheeses vie for your attention on an ever-changing menu of small plates, a few entrées, and 10 fantastic desserts. There's always a rotisserie special from the apple-wood grill as well. ☒ *2030 5th Ave.,* ☎ *206/448–2001. AE, D, DC, MC, V. No lunch.*

$$–$$$ ✕ **Marco's Supper Club.** Multiregional cuisine is the specialty of this
★ casual restaurant with shrimp-color walls and mismatched flatware. Start with the fried sage-leaf appetizer with garlic aioli and salsa, then move on to sesame-crusted ahi tuna, Jamaican jerk chicken, or a pork porterhouse in an almond mole sauce. ☒ *2510 1st Ave.,* ☎ *206/441–7801. AE, MC, V. No lunch weekends.*

$ ✕ **Fare Start.** The homeless men and women who operate this café, a project of FareStart, a job-training program, prepare a simple lunch buffet during the week. On Thursday night a guest chef from a restaurant like Ray's Boathouse or the Metropolitan Grill runs the kitchen. You're assured a great meal for a great cause and a real taste of Seattle's community spirit. ☒ *1902 2nd Ave.,* ☎ *206/443–1233, ext. 28. Reservations essential for Thurs. dinner. D, MC, V. No lunch weekends, no dinner Fri.–Wed..*

French

$$$$ ✕ **Campagne.** The white walls, picture windows, snowy linens, candles, and fresh flowers at this urbane restaurant evoke Provence, as does the menu. French cuisine here means the robust flavors of the countryside, not the more polished tastes of Paris. To start, try the seafood sausage or the calamari fillets with ground almonds. Main plates include panfried scallops with a green-peppercorn and tarragon sauce, cinnamon-roasted quail served with carrot and orange essence, and Oregon rabbit accompanied by an apricot-cider and green-peppercorn sauce. Campagne, which overlooks Pike Place Market and Elliott Bay, is open only for dinner, but the adjacent Café Campagne serves breakfast, lunch, and dinner daily. ⊠ *Inn at the Market, 86 Pine St.,* ☎ *206/ 728–2800. Reservations essential. AE, DC, MC, V. No lunch.*

Indian

$$ ✕ **Chutney's.** The local chain (☞ Indian *in* North of Downtown Seattle Dining, *below*) has a Capitol Hill branch. The outstanding dishes include tandoori halibut and prawns, chicken kebabs, five curries, and rack of lamb. ⊠ *605 15th Ave. E,* ☎ *206/726–1000. AE, D, DC, MC, V.*

Italian

$$$–$$$$ ✕ **Il Terrazzo Carmine.** On the ground floor of a Pioneer Square office building, this restaurant owes its refined ambience to ceiling-to-floor draperies, genteel service, and quiet music. Chef-owner Carmine Smeraldo prepares flavorful chicken dishes with prosciutto and fontina, and his veal baked with spinach and scallops is excellent. The pasta dishes are superb. In the summer you can eat outdoors on a patio that faces a large fountain. ⊠ *411 1st Ave. S,* ☎ *206/467–7797. AE, D, DC, MC, V. Closed Sun. No lunch Sat.*

$$–$$$ ✕ **The Pink Door.** This restaurant with a "secret" entrance off Post Alley dishes up a generous portion of atmosphere along with solid Italian food. The roasted garlic and *tapenada* (a caper, anchovy, and black-olive spread) are eminently sharable appetizers; spaghetti *alla puttanesca* (with anchovies, capers, and tomatoes) and cioppino are the standout entrées. The quirky bar is often crowded with young people, and cabaret acts regularly perform on a small stage in the corner. But the real draw here is the outdoor deck, rimmed in flowers, topped with a canopy of colored lights, and perched perfectly over Pike Place Market, with a terrific view of the water beyond. ⊠ *1919 Post Alley,* ☎ *206/443–3241. AE, MC, V. Closed Sun.–Mon.*

Japanese

$$$–$$$$ ✕ **Nikko.** The ultrachic sushi bar is the architectural centerpiece at sophisticated Nikko, where the talented chefs prepare some of the best sushi and sashimi in Seattle. On the regular menu, the Kasu sake–marinated cod and teriyaki salmon are consistent winners. ⊠ *Westin Hotel, 1900 5th Ave.,* ☎ *206/322–4641. AE, D, DC, MC, V. Closed Sun. No lunch Sat.*

$$–$$$ ✕ **Shiro's.** Willfully unconcerned with atmosphere, this simple spot is a real curiosity amid Belltown's chic establishments. The focus is entirely on the exceptional menu of authentic Japanese fare. Indulge your curiosity in the more exotic offerings; a sure hand guides this sushi bar. ⊠ *2401 2nd Ave.,* ☎ *206/443–9844. AE, MC, V. Closed Sun.*

Mediterranean

$$–$$$ ✕ **Betay Avone.** The Mediterranean-inspired dishes at this restaurant inside an unassuming Belltown storefront are administered under rabbinical supervision. Moroccan *bysteeyas* (braised chicken with scallions, cinnamon, cayenne, and cumin wrapped in phyllo) are a fantastic starter, and the salmon fillet with caramelized onions and tahini over

couscous is an imaginative spin on a Pacific Northwest staple. ⊠ *113 Blanchard St.,* ☎ *206/448–5597. AE, MC, V. Closed Fri.–Sat. No lunch.*

$$–$$$ ✕ **El Greco.** Long on entertainment and shopping, the stretch of Broadway through Capitol Hill is curiously short on interesting dining options. El Greco's fresh, unadorned Mediterranean fare is your best bet. A Moroccan vegetable stew and rosemary grilled lamb are standouts on a sturdy menu, and there's a satisfying Sunday brunch. ⊠ *219 Broadway E,* ☎ *206/328–4604. AE, MC, V. Closed Mon. No dinner Sun.*

Pan-Asian

$$–$$$ ✕ **Blowfish.** From the pachinko machines around the bar to the colorful origami and rattan fans on the ceiling, kid-friendly Blowfish is a festive, freewheeling place that takes advantage of the yen of Seattleites for Pan-Asian cuisine. The seafood and noodle specialties are worth investigating, but the small plates from the grill are the real stars on the flashy menu. Try the Korean *bulgogi* skirt steak (marinated in a tangy sauce of soy, mirin, and ginger) or the chicken wings in a caramel ginger sauce. Top it all off with a lime leaf and lemongrass "limontini." ⊠ *722 Pine St.,* ☎ *206/467–7777. AE, D, DC, MC, V.*

$$–$$$ ✕ **Wild Ginger.** The seafood and Southeast Asian fare at this restaurant near Pike Place Market ranges from mild Cantonese to spicier Vietnamese, Thai, and Korean dishes. House specialties include *satay* (chunks of beef, chicken, or vegetables skewered and grilled, and usually served with a spicy peanut sauce), live crab cooked to order, sweetly flavored duck, wonderful soups, and some fine vegetarian options. The satay bar, where you can sip local brews and eat skewered tidbits until 2 AM, is a local hangout. The clubby, old-fashioned dining room has high ceilings and lots of mahogany and Asian art. ⊠ *1400 Western Ave.,* ☎ *206/623–4450. AE, D, DC, MC, V. No lunch Sun.*

$–$$ ✕ **Noodle Ranch.** Tongue planted firmly in cheek, Noodle Ranch bills itself as Belltown's purveyor of "Pan-Asian vittles." Standouts on chef Nga Bui's inexpensive menu include sugar-cane shrimp, Japanese eggplant in ginger, and a spicy basil stir-fry. The gentle sense of humor evident in the name is borne out in the dressed-down decor. ⊠ *2228 2nd Ave.,* ☎ *206/728–0463. AE, MC, V. Closed Sun.*

Seafood

$$–$$$$ ✕ **Cutter's.** Enthusiastic service and a harbor view go a long way to recommend Cutter's, but its allure doesn't stop there. Fresh fish is prepared on an apple-wood grill in a variety of creative ways. Fish-and-chips receive traditional treatment, but Asian accents can be discerned in a dish like the Penn Cove mussels in a coconut-curry broth, and European and South American influences are at work as well. ⊠ *2001 Western Ave.,* ☎ *206/448–4884. AE, D, DC, MC, V.*

$$–$$$$ ✕ **Etta's Seafood.** Tom Douglas's restaurant near Pike Place Market has a sleek and slightly whimsical design and views of Victor Steinbrueck Park. In season try the Dungeness crab cakes or the various Washington oysters on the half shell. Brunch, served on weekends, always includes zesty seafood omelets, but the chef also does justice to French toast, eggs and bacon, and Mexican-influenced breakfast dishes. ⊠ *2020 Western Ave.,* ☎ *206/443–6000. AE, D, DC, MC, V.*

$ ✕ **Emmett Watson's Oyster Bar.** This unpretentious spot can be hard to find—it's in the back of Pike Place Market's Soames-Dunn Building, facing a small flower-bedecked courtyard—but for Seattleites and visitors who know their oysters, it's worth the special effort. Not only are the oysters very fresh and the beer icy cold, but both are inexpensive and available in any number of varieties. If you don't like oysters, try the salmon soup or the fish-and-chips—flaky pieces of fish with very little grease. ⊠ *1916 Pike Pl.,* ☎ *206/448–7721. Reservations not accepted. No credit cards. No dinner Sun.*

Thai

$–$$ ✕ **Siam.** Thai cooking is ubiquitous in Seattle—it can almost be considered a mainstream cuisine. Start your meal at popular Siam with a satay skewer or the city's best *tom kah gai,* a soup of coconut, lemongrass, chicken, and mushrooms. Entrées include curries, noodle dishes, and many prawn, chicken, and fish preparations. You can specify one to five stars according to your tolerance for heat. The location on Fairview Avenue near Lake Union has a more relaxed atmosphere than the energetic Capitol Hill original on Broadway. ⊠ *616 Broadway,* ☎ *206/ 324–0892;* ⊠ *1880 Fairview Ave. E,* ☎ *206/323–8101. AE, MC, V. No lunch weekends.*

Vegetarian

$ ✕ **Gravity Bar.** Sprouty sandwiches and other "modern food," all healthful and then some, are dished up at this congenial juice bar with a sci-fi–industrial ambience. The juices—from any number of fruits and vegetables, solo or in combo—are often zippier than the solid food. ⊠ *415 Broadway E,* ☎ *206/325–7186. No credit cards.*

Vietnamese

$ ✕ **Saigon Gourmet.** This small café in the International District is
★ about as plain as they get, but the food is superb and incredibly inexpensive. Aficionados make special trips for the Cambodian soup and the shrimp rolls, but also consider the unusual papaya with beef jerky. Parking can be a problem, but the food rewards your patience. ⊠ *502 S. King St.,* ☎ *206/624–2611. Reservations not accepted. MC, V. Closed Mon.*

North of Downtown Seattle

American

$$$$ ✕ **Canlis.** Little has changed at this Seattle institution since the '50s, when steak served by kimono-clad waitresses represented the pinnacle of high living. Renovations in the mid-'90s made for a less old-boys'-club feel than before, but the restaurant is still very expensive and very popular. The view across Lake Union is almost as good as ever, though it now includes a forest of high-rises. Besides the famous steaks, there are equally famous oysters from Quilcene Bay and fresh fish in season. In 1998, *Wine Spectator* magazine bestowed a Grand Award on Canlis for its wine list and service. ⊠ *2576 Aurora Ave. N,* ☎ *206/283–3313. Reservations essential. AE, DC, MC, V. Closed Sun. No lunch.*

$$$ ✕ **Kaspar's.** A decidedly unglamorous atmosphere and its location amid lower Queen Anne Hill's low-rise office buildings and light-industrial warehouses focus the attention at this restaurant where it belongs— on chef-owner Kaspar Donier's finely wrought contemporary cuisine. Seafood, steak, and poultry options abound. The Muscovy duck with Bosc pears and Hanoi-style sea bass with fennel and green onions are especially striking. The five-course Pacific Northwest seafood dinner is a lifeline for the indecisive. Its proximity to Seattle Center makes Kaspar's a natural destination before or after your evening's entertainment, but the food insists that you take your time. ⊠ *19 W. Harrison St., west of Queen Anne Ave. N,* ☎ *206/298–0123. AE, MC, V. Closed Sun.–Mon. No lunch.*

$$–$$$ ✕ **Five Spot.** Up the hill from Seattle Center, the unpretentious Five Spot has a regional American menu that makes a new stop every four months or so—Little Italy, New Orleans, and Florida have been previous ones. The Five Spot is also popular for Sunday brunch. At the

North of Downtown Seattle Dining

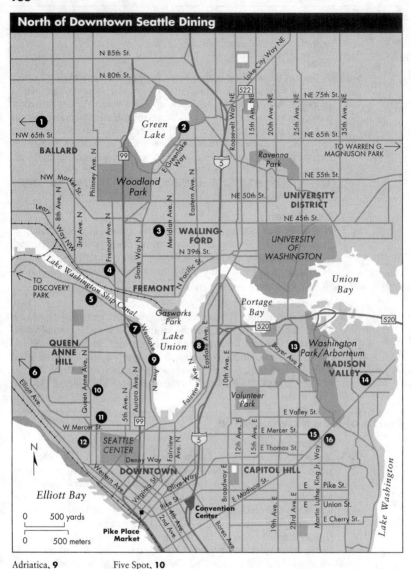

restaurant's kitchen cousins, Jitterbug in Wallingford and the Coastal Kitchen in Capitol Hill, the same rotating menu strategy, with more international flavor but equally satisfying results, applies. ⊠ *1502 Queen Anne Ave. N,* ☎ *206/285–7768. MC, V. Jitterbug:* ⊠ *2114 N. 45th St.,* ☎ *206/547–6313. MC, V. Coastal Kitchen:* ⊠ *429 15th Ave. E,* ☎ *206/322–1145. MC, V.*

Eclectic

$$–$$$ ✗ **Bandoleone.** Here's a place that leads a double life. The dining room is simple and austere, even rustic, but the deck out back is festive and fun, decorated with colorful Mexican paper cutouts. Both spaces are perfect for a romantic dinner. The atmosphere here is decidedly unpretentious, and the sophisticated menu of large and small plates roams Spain, the Caribbean, and Central and South America. A sweet and clean grilled ahi tuna entrée comes with papaya black-bean salsa; the eggplant *relleno* is a swampy blend of squash, summer corn, sweet onions, and goat cheese. Tequila-cured salmon gravlax and a banana-macadamia empanada with a tamarind dipping sauce are two of several outstanding tapas. The gravlax also appears on the imaginative and inexpensive menu for Saturday and Sunday brunch (served between 9 and 2). ⊠ *2241 Eastlake Ave. E,* ☎ *206/329–7559. MC, V. No lunch.*

French

$$$$ ✗ **Rover's.** The restaurant of Thierry Rautereau, one of the Pacific North-
★ west's most imaginative chefs, is an essential destination on any culinary tour of Seattle. Sea scallops, venison, squab, lobster, and rabbit are frequent offerings (vegetarian items are also available) on the restaurant's prix-fixe menu. The incomparable sauce work and reliance on delicacies such as foie gras and truffles pay homage to Rautereau's French roots, but bold combinations of ingredients are evidence of his wanderlust. The service at Rover's is excellent—friendly but unobtrusive—the setting romantic, and the presentation stunning. ⊠ *2808 E. Madison St.,* ☎ *206/325–7442. Reservations essential. AE, MC, V. Closed Sun.–Mon. No lunch.*

Indian

$$ ✗ **Chutney's.** The aromas of cardamom, cumin, and jasmine wafting through the air may make you feel like you've been transported to another continent. The outstanding dishes include tandoori halibut and prawns, chicken kebabs, five different curries, and rack of lamb. Consistently rated as one of Seattle's top restaurants, Chutney's has a flagship location in Queen Anne, a branch in Wallingford, and another in Capitol Hill (☞ Downtown Seattle and Capitol Hill Dining, *above*). ⊠ *Queen Anne: 519 1st Ave. N,* ☎ *206/284–6799.* ⊠ *Wallingford: 1815 N. 45th St.,* ☎ *206/634–1000. AE, D, DC, MC, V.*

Italian

$$$ ✗ **Saleh Al Lago.** Some of the best Italian and Mediterranean food in the city can be found north of downtown. The well-lighted dining room here is done in soft colors and, with its view of Green Lake, invites slow-paced dining. The traditional dishes are excellent, as are more exotic offerings like beet ravioli with Dungeness crab and caviar, and pan-seared tenderloin in a balsamic vinegar and peppercorn glaze. ⊠ *6804 E. Greenlake Way N,* ☎ *206/522–7943. AE, DC, MC, V. Closed Sun.–Mon. No lunch Sat.*

$$–$$$$ ✗ **Cafe Lago.** Hugely popular with locals, Cafe Lago specializes in wood-fired pizzas and light handmade pastas. The lasagna—ricotta, béchamel, and cherry-tomato sauce amid paper-thin pasta sheets—perfectly represents the menu's inclination toward the simply satisfying. Spare table settings, high ceilings, and a friendly atmosphere make the restaurant suitable for a night out with friends or a romantic getaway. ✉ *2305 24th Ave. E,* ☎ *206/329–8005. D, DC, MC, V. Closed Mon. No lunch.*

Mediterranean

$$$–$$$$ ✕ **Adriatica.** The dining room and upstairs bar in this hillside Craftsman-style house have terrific views of Lake Union. The food could best be described as Pacific Northwest–influenced Greek and Italian cuisine. Regular offerings include fresh fish, pastas, risotto, and seafood souvlaki. ✉ *1107 Dexter Ave. N,* ☎ *206/285–5000. Reservations essential. AE, DC, MC, V. No lunch.*

Mexican

$$–$$$ ✕ **El Camino.** The atmosphere at this loose, loud, and funky Fremont storefront perfectly mirrors El Camino's irreverent Pacific Northwest interpretation of Mexican cuisine. Rock-shrimp quesadillas, chipotle-pepper and garlic sea bass, and duck with a spicy green sauce are typical of the kitchen's gentle spin. Even a green salad becomes transformed with toasted pumpkin seeds on crispy romaine with a cool dressing of garlic, lime juice, and cilantro. As for cool, there's no better place to chill on a summer afternoon than El Camino's deck. A tart margarita, served in a pint glass, makes the perfect accessory. ✉ *607 N. 35th St.,* ☎ *206/632–7303. AE, DC, MC, V. No lunch weekdays.*

Seafood

$$$–$$$$ ✕ **Palisade.** The short ride to the Magnolia neighborhood yields a stunning view back across Elliott Bay to the lights of downtown. And there's no better place to take in the vista than this restaurant at the Elliott Bay Marina. Palisade scores points for its playfully exotic ambience—complete with a gurgling indoor stream. As for the food, the simpler preparations, especially the signature plank-broiled salmon, are most satisfying. Maggie Bluffs, an informal café downstairs, is a great spot for lunch on a breezy summer afternoon. ✉ *2601 W. Marina Pl.; from downtown, take Elliott Ave. northwest across Magnolia Bridge to Elliott Bay Marina exit,* ☎ *206/285–1000. AE, D, DC, MC, V.*

$$$–$$$$ ✕ **Ray's Boathouse.** The view of Puget Sound may be the big draw here,
★   but the seafood is impeccably fresh and well prepared. Perennial favorites include broiled salmon, Kasu sake–marinated cod, Dungeness crab, and regional oysters on the half shell. Ray's has a split personality: there's a fancy dining room downstairs and a casual café and bar upstairs. In warm weather you can sit on the deck outside the café and watch the parade of fishing boats, tugs, and pleasure craft floating past, almost right below your table. ✉ *6049 Seaview Ave. NW,* ☎ *206/789–3770. Reservations essential for dining room; reservations not accepted for café. AE, DC, MC, V.*

$$–$$$$ ✕ **Ponti.** Working in a placid, canal-side villa-like location a stone's throw from the Fremont and Aurora Bridges, chef Alvin Binuya builds culinary bridges between Pacific Northwest ingredients and Mediterranean and Asian techniques. Alaskan king crab legs with a Chardonnay butter and herb mayonnaise manifest the kitchen's classic restraint; the grilled mahimahi with satsuma potato gratin and shallot jus walks on the wilder side. ✉ *3014 3rd Ave. N,* ☎ *206/284–3000. AE, DC, MC, V.*

Southwestern

$$ ✕ **Cactus.** It's worth the drive to Madison Park to experience the rich flavors and colorful atmosphere of Cactus. The food, which displays Native American, Spanish, and Mexican influences, will satisfy wide-ranging palates, from the vegetarian to the carnivorous. From the tapas bar, sample the marinated eggplant, the garlic shrimp, or the tuna *escabeche* (spicy cold marinade). Larger plates include the vegetarian chili relleno, the grilled pork with orange and chipotle peppers, and a

flavorful ancho-chili and cinnamon roasted chicken. ⊠ *4220 E. Madison St.,* ☎ *206/324–4140. D, DC, MC, V.*

Vegetarian

$$–$$$ ✕ **Cafe Flora.** This sophisticated Madison Valley café attracts vegetarians and meat eaters for artistically presented full-flavored meals. An adventurous menu includes Portobello mushroom Wellington, fajitas, and polenta topped with onion, rosemary, and mushrooms. Sunday brunch draws a crowd. ⊠ *2901 E. Madison St.,* ☎ *206/325–9100. MC, V. Closed Mon. No dinner Sun.*

LODGING

Seattle has lodgings to suit most budgets. Though the city has many rooms, you need to book as far in advance as possible if you're coming between May and September. The most elegant properties are downtown; less expensive but still tasteful options, usually smaller in size (and with more of a Seattle feel), can be found in the University District. Many of the lower-price motels along Aurora Avenue North (Highway 99) were built for the 1962 World's Fair. Air travelers often stay along Pacific Highway South (also Highway 99), near Seattle-Tacoma International Airport. Always inquire about special rates based on occupancy or weekend stays.

CATEGORY	COST*
$$$$	over $170
$$$	$110–$170
$$	$60–$110
$	under $60

All prices are for a standard double room, excluding 15.6% combined hotel and state sales tax.

Downtown

$$$$ ⊞ **Alexis Hotel.** The European-style Alexis occupies two restored build-
★ ings near the waterfront. Complimentary sherry awaits you in the lobby bar upon your arrival, a prelude to the attentive service you'll receive during your stay. Rooms are decorated in subdued colors and with imported Italian and French fabrics, with at least one piece of antique furniture. Some suites have whirlpool tubs or wood-burning fireplaces, and some have marble fixtures. Unfortunately, views are limited and rooms facing 1st Avenue can be noisy. Amenities include shoe shines, the morning newspaper, and access to workout facilities. Pets are welcome. ⊠ *1007 1st Ave., 98104,* ☎ *206/624–4844 or 800/426–7033,* 📠 *206/621–9009. 65 rooms, 44 suites. Restaurant, bar, in-room data ports, minibars, room service, spa, steam room, exercise room, laundry service, meeting rooms, parking (fee). Continental breakfast. AE, D, DC, MC, V.*

$$$$ ⊞ **Four Seasons Olympic Hotel.** The 1920s Renaissance Revival–
★ style Olympic is the grande dame of Seattle hotels. Marble, wood paneling, potted plants, thick rugs, and plush armchairs adorn the public spaces. Palms and skylights in the Garden Court provide a relaxing background for lunch, afternoon tea, or dancing to a live swing band on the weekends. The Georgian Room, the hotel's premier dining room, exudes Italian Renaissance elegance. The Shuckers oyster bar is more casual. Guest rooms, decorated with period reproductions and floral print fabrics, are less luxurious than the public areas but have a homey feel. All have sofas, comfortable reading chairs, and desks. Amenities include valet parking, chocolates on your pillow, complimentary shoe shines, the morning newspaper, and a bathrobe. ⊠ *411*

190

Seattle Lodging

Mercer St.

Mercer St.

Harrison St.

Seattle Center

Stadium

Key Arena

Monorail Terminal

Aurora Ave. N.

Dexter Ave. N.

8th Ave. N.

9th Ave. N.

Thomas St.

2nd Ave. N.

6th Ave. N.

Taylor Ave. N.

Space Needle

Broad St.

Denny Park

1st Ave. N.

Warren Ave. N.

Denny Way

Clay St.

Cedar St.

Vine St.

Wall St.

Battery St.

MONORAIL

Myrtle Edwards Park

Elliott Ave.

99

Bell St.

6th Av

5th Av

18

Pier 70

2nd Ave.

Blanchard St.

4th Ave.

1st Ave.

BELLTOWN

3rd Ave.

Pier 69

Waterfront Streetcar

Lenora St.

Western Ave.

3rd A

Pier 67

19

Bell Street Pier (Pier 66)

Alaskan Way

Virginia St.

Post Alley

20

21 PIKE PLA HISTOR DISTRI

Pike Pl.

Waterfront

Piers 62/63

Hill Climb

Post Alley

22

Pier 59

Western Ave

TO WINSLOW ON BAINBRIDGE ISLAND

Elliott Bay

Pier 55

Pier 54

State Ferry Terminal

TO BREMERTON

KEY

AE American Express Office

0   500 yards

0   500 meters

N

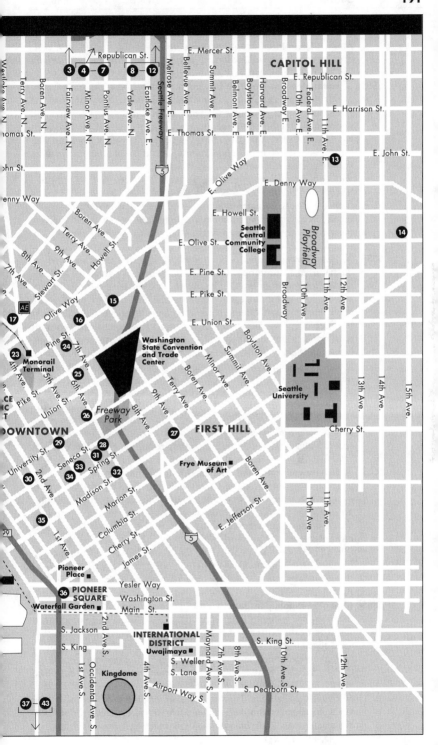

Republican St.

③ ④ ⑦ ⑧ ⑫

Melrose Ave. E.
Seattle Freeway

E. Mercer St.

CAPITOL HILL

E. Republican St.

Westlake Ave. N.
Terry Ave. N.
Boren Ave. N.
Fairview Ave. N.
Minor Ave. N.
Pontius Ave. N.
Yale Ave. N.
Eastlake Ave. E.
Bellevue Ave. E.
Summit Ave. E.
Belmont Ave. E.
Boylston Ave. E.
Harvard Ave. E.
Broadway E.
10th Ave. E.
Federal Ave. E.
11th Ave. E.

E. Harrison St.

homas St.

E. Thomas St.

ohn St.

E. Olive Way

E. John St.

⑬

enny Way

E. Denny Way

⑭

Boren Ave.

E. Howell St.

8th Ave.
9th Ave.
Terry Ave.
Howell St.

E. Olive St.

Seattle Central Community College

Broadway Playfield

7th Ave.

Stewart St.

Olive Way

E. Pine St.

E. Pike St.

Broadway
10th Ave.
11th Ave.
12th Ave.

AE

⑮

⑯

E. Union St.

15th Ave.

⑰

Pine St.

⑯

7th Ave.

⑮

Washington State Convention and Trade Center

Boylston Ave.
Summit Ave.
Minor Ave.

13th Ave.
14th Ave.

⑳

⑳

Monorail Terminal

5th Ave.
6th Ave.

⑳

Terry Ave.
Boren Ave.
9th Ave.

Seattle University

CE
CT

Pike St.
Union St.

⑳

Freeway Park

8th Ave.

⑳

FIRST HILL

Cherry St.

OWNTOWN

⑳

University St.

⑳

⑳

⑳

Seneca St.

⑳

Spring St.

⑳

⑳

Madison St.

Frye Museum of Art ■

Boren Ave.

11th Ave.
10th Ave.

2nd Ave.

⑳

⑳

Marion St.

E. Jefferson St.

⑳

1st Ave.

Columbia St.

Cherry St.

James St.

Pioneer Place ■

Yesler Way

⑳ **PIONEER SQUARE**

Waterfall Garden ■

Washington St.

Main St.

S. Jackson

INTERNATIONAL DISTRICT

Uwajimaya ■

2nd Ave. S.

Maynard Ave. S.
7th Ave. S.
8th Ave.
10th Ave. S.

S. King St.

12th Ave.

S. King

S. Weller St.

S. Lane

1st Ave. S.

Kingdome

Occidental Ave. S.

4th Ave. S.

Airport Way S.

S. Dearborn St.

⑳ ⑤

University St., 98101, ☎ *206/621–1700 or 800/223–8772,* FAX *206/ 682–9633. 450 rooms. 3 restaurants, lounge, in-room data ports, in-room safes, minibars, room service, indoor pool, health club, children's programs, laundry service, concierge, meeting rooms, parking (fee). AE, D, DC, MC, V.*

$$$$ 🏨 **Hotel Monaco.** Goldfish in your room are among the fun touches
★ at this luxury hotel inside a former office building in the heart of the Financial District. The light and whimsical lobby has high ceilings and hand-painted nautical murals inspired by the fresco at the Palace of Knossos in Crete. A pleasing blend of bold and bright colors and patterns graces the spacious guest rooms. The in-room amenities include voice mail, fax machines, irons, hair dryers, coffeemakers, and stereos with compact-disc players. The hotel welcomes pets. ⊠ *1101 4th Ave., 98101,* ☎ *206/621–1770 or 800/945–2240,* FAX *206/621–7779. 144 rooms, 45 suites. Restaurant, bar, in-room data ports, no-smoking rooms, room service, exercise room, dry cleaning, laundry service, concierge, business services, meeting rooms, airport shuttle, parking (fee). AE, D, DC, MC, V.*

$$$$ 🏨 **Hotel Vintage Park.** As a tribute to the state's growing wine industry, each accommodation in this small hotel is named for a Washington winery or vineyard. The theme is extended to complimentary servings of local wines each evening in the lobby, where patrons can relax on richly upholstered sofas and chairs arranged around a marble fireplace. The rooms, which are decorated in color schemes of dark green, plum, deep red, taupe, and gold, are furnished with custom-made cherry-wood pieces and original works by San Francisco artist Chris Kidd. For literary-minded guests, hotel staff will check out and deliver your choice of titles from the nearby Seattle Public Library. The more athletically inclined can have exercise equipment brought to their rooms. ⊠ *1100 5th Ave., 98101,* ☎ *206/624–8000 or 800/624–4433,* FAX *206/623–0568. 126 rooms. Restaurant, in-room data ports, minibars, no-smoking floors, refrigerators, room service, spa, laundry service, concierge, meeting rooms, parking (fee). AE, D, DC, MC, V.*

$$$$ 🏨 **Mayflower Park Hotel.** The brass fixtures and antiques at this older property near the Westlake Center lend its public and private spaces a muted Asian feel. The service here is unobtrusive and smooth. Rooms are on the small side, but the Mayflower Park is so sturdily constructed that it is much quieter than many modern downtown hotels. Guests have privileges at a nearby health club. ⊠ *405 Olive Way, 98101,* ☎ *206/623–8700 or 800/426–5100,* FAX *206/382–6997. 159 rooms, 13 suites. Restaurant, bar, no-smoking rooms, room service, exercise room, laundry service, business services, meeting rooms, parking (fee). AE, D, DC, MC, V.*

$$$$ 🏨 **Seattle Hilton.** This hotel west of I–5 hosts many conventions and meetings. The tastefully nondescript rooms have soothing color schemes. The Top of the Hilton serves well-prepared salmon dishes and other local specialties and has excellent views of the city. An underground passage connects the Hilton with the Rainier Square shopping concourse, the 5th Avenue Theater, and the convention center. ⊠ *1301 6th Ave., 98101,* ☎ *206/624–0500, 800/542–7700, or 800/426–0535,* FAX *206/ 682–9029. 237 rooms, 3 suites. 2 restaurants, piano bar, in-room data ports, minibars, no-smoking floors, room service, exercise room, laundry service, concierge, business services, meeting rooms, parking (fee). AE, D, DC, MC, V.*

$$$$ 🏨 **Sorrento.** The Sorrento, built in 1909, was designed to look like an Italian villa. The dramatic entrance is along a circular driveway around a fountain ringed with palms. Sitting high on First Hill, the hotel has views overlooking downtown and Elliott Bay. The rooms, some of them quite small, are quiet and comfortable. The largest are the corner suites, which have some antiques and spacious baths. The Hunt Club (☞ Dining, *above*) serves Pacific Northwest dishes. The dark-paneled Fireside Lounge in the lobby is an inviting spot for coffee, tea, or cocktails. Other amenities include complimentary limousine service within the downtown area and privileges at a nearby athletic club. ✉ *900 Madison St., 98104,* ☎ *206/622–6400 or 800/426–1265,* 𝔽𝔸𝕏 *206/343–6155. 76 rooms, 42 suites. Restaurant, bar, in-room data ports, minibars, room service, laundry service, concierge, meeting rooms, parking (fee). AE, D, DC, MC, V.*

$$$$ 🏨 **Warwick Hotel.** Despite its size, the Warwick has an intimate feel. Service is friendly and leisurely (but not slow), and the rooms are understated without being bland. Most have small balconies with views of downtown. There is live entertainment in the Liaison restaurant and lounge, and 24-hour courtesy transportation within downtown. ✉ *401 Lenora St., 98121,* ☎ *206/443–4300 or 800/426–9280,* 𝔽𝔸𝕏 *206/448–1662. 225 rooms, 4 suites. Restaurant, bar, in-room data ports, no-smoking rooms, room service, indoor pool, hot tub, sauna, exercise room, concierge, parking (fee). AE, D, DC, MC, V.*

$$$$ 🏨 **WestCoast Roosevelt Hotel.** An older hotel near the convention center and the shopping district, the Roosevelt has an elegant lobby with a grand piano, a fireplace, a Chinese lacquered screen, and walls of windows—a great place to relax and watch the foot traffic outside. Smallish rooms are furnished with period reproduction furniture upholstered in mellow pinks and greens. Thanks to the insulated windows you can enjoy city views without hearing street noise. Some bathrooms have their original tile work, though there isn't much counter space. ✉ *1531 7th Ave.,* ☎ *206/621–1200 or 800/426–0670,* 𝔽𝔸𝕏 *206/233–0335. 138 rooms, 13 suites. Restaurant, bar, in-room data ports, no-smoking rooms, room service, exercise room, laundry service, meeting rooms, parking (fee). AE, D, DC, MC, V.*

$$$$ 🏨 **Westin Hotel.** The flagship of the Westin chain often hosts visiting dignitaries, including U.S. presidents. Northeast of Pike Place Market, the hotel is easily recognizable by its twin cylindrical towers. With this design, all rooms have terrific views of Puget Sound, Lake Union, the Space Needle, or the city. Airy rooms are furnished in a plain but high-quality style. A number have been turned into guest office rooms equipped with fax machines, speakerphones, and modem hookups. ✉ *1900 5th Ave., 98101,* ☎ *206/728–1000 or 800/228–3000,* 𝔽𝔸𝕏 *206/ 727–5896. 822 rooms, 43 suites. 3 restaurants, 2 bars, in-room data ports, in-room safes, minibars, no-smoking floors, room service, indoor pool, beauty salon, massage, exercise room, children's programs, laundry service, concierge, business services, convention center, car rental, parking (fee). AE, D, DC, MC, V.*

$$$–$$$$ 🏨 **Edgewater.** The spacious accommodations on the waterfront side of the only hotel on Elliott Bay have views of ferries, barges, and the Olympic Mountains. Rooms are decorated in rustic plaids and pale unfinished wood furniture. From the lobby's comfortable sofas and chairs, you can sometimes see sea lions frolicking in the bay. A courtesy van shuttles patrons to the downtown area on a first-come, first-served basis. ✉ *Pier 67, 2411 Alaskan Way, 98121,* ☎ *206/728–7000 or 800/624–0670,* 𝔽𝔸𝕏 *206/441–4119. 237 rooms. Restaurant, bar, in-room data ports, minibars, no-smoking rooms, room service, exercise room, bicycles, laundry service, concierge, meeting rooms, parking (fee). AE, D, DC, MC, V.*

$$$–$$$$ 🏨 **Inn at Harbor Steps.** On the lower floors of a high-rise residential
★ building, this lodging is a departure for Four Sisters Inns, whose collection of small hotels focuses on country getaways. Although the en-

trance and corridors have something of a yuppie-dormitory feel to them, the rooms are commodious, with high ceilings, gas fireplaces, and tidy kitchenettes. The bathrooms accommodate large tubs (some of them whirlpools) and oversize glass-enclosed shower stalls. A tempting breakfast buffet is served in the dining room; afternoon tea, poured in the library, provides a welcome respite from the bustle of the city outside. A full breakfast is included. ⊠ *1221 First Ave., 98101,* ☎ *206/748–0973 or 888/728–8910,* ₣ₐₓ *206/682–6045. 20 rooms. In-room data ports, refrigerators, indoor pool, sauna, basketball court, exercise room, coin laundry, laundry service, concierge, meeting room, parking (fee). AE, MC, V.*

$$$–$$$$ ⊞ **Inn at the Market.** This sophisticated yet unpretentious property
★   up the street from Pike Place Market is perfect for travelers who prefer originality, personality, and coziness. The good-size rooms are decorated with comfortable modern furniture and small touches such as fresh flowers and ceramic sculptures. Ask for a room with views of the market and Elliott Bay. Coffee and the morning newspaper are complimentary each morning. An added plus is the fifth-floor deck, furnished with Adirondack chairs and overlooking the water and market. Guests have access to a health club and spa. The restaurants here include Campagne (☞ Dining, *above*), its less formal yet equally romantic café spin-off, and Bacco, which serves tasty variations on breakfast classics. ⊠ *86 Pine St., 98101,* ☎ *206/443–3600 or 800/446–4484,* ₣ₐₓ *206/448–0631. 60 rooms, 10 suites. 3 restaurants, in-room data ports, no-smoking rooms, refrigerators, room service, laundry service, concierge, meeting room, parking (fee). AE, D, DC, MC, V.*

$$$–$$$$ ⊞ **Madison.** Rooms at this high-rise between downtown and I–5 are decorated in deep green, burgundy, and brown, with metal accents and dark-wood furniture. Good views of downtown, Elliott Bay, and the Cascades can be had from above the 10th floor—above the 20th they're excellent. Guests on club-level floors (25, 26, and 27) receive complimentary Continental breakfast and have their own concierge. Amenities on other floors include complimentary coffee, the morning newspaper, and shoe shines. The health club has a 40-ft rooftop pool and a hot tub. ⊠ *515 Madison St., 98104,* ☎ *206/583–0300 or 800/278–4159,* ₣ₐₓ *206/622–8635. 466 rooms, 88 suites. 2 restaurants, bar, in-room data ports, minibars, room service, laundry service, concierge, meeting rooms, parking (fee). AE, D, DC, MC, V.*

$$$–$$$$ ⊞ **Marqueen Hotel.** This elegant 1918 brick apartment building at the foot of Queen Anne Hill was converted into a hotel in 1998. Just blocks away from the Seattle Center, this location is ideal for patrons of the opera, ballet, theater, or events at the Key Arena. The dark lobby has marble floors, original wainscoting, box beam ceilings, overstuffed furniture, Asian-style lacquered screens and a grand staircase looking out at a garden mural painted on the facing building. All of the guest rooms are spacious with kitchens and sitting areas. The beds have down comforter covers in green, gold, pink, and burgundy that coordinate with the window coverings. The rooms are furnished with antique replicas. A complimentary paper is left outside the door each morning. ⊠ *600 Queen Ave. N., 98109,* ☎ *206/282–7407,* ₣ₐₓ *206/283–1499. 47 rooms, 4 suites. Kitchens, in-room data ports, room service, laundry service, valet parking (fee). AE, D, DC, MC, V.*

$$$–$$$$ ⊞ **Paramount Hotel.** The château-style Paramount opened in 1996 as a companion to the high-tech entertainment sites one block away, including Planet Hollywood, GameWorks, NikeTown, and a 16-screen Cineplex Odeon multiplex. Neither the Paramount nor these facilities have a particularly Seattle feel, but the hotel's comfortable

lobby has a fireplace, bookshelves, and period reproductions lending it the feel of a country gentleman's smoking parlor. Rooms, quiet but small, are decorated in hunter green and beige with gray accents. All have work areas, lounge chairs, large bathrooms, and movie and game systems. ⊠ *724 Pine St., 98101,* ☎ *206/292–9500 or 800/426–0670,* FAX *206/292–8610. 146 rooms, 2 suites. Restaurant, in-room data ports, no-smoking rooms, room service, exercise room, laundry service, concierge, meeting rooms, parking (fee). AE, D, DC, MC, V.*

$$$–$$$$ ☷ **Pioneer Square Hotel.** A mid-1990s renovation trimmed this 1914 workmen's hotel down to 75 generously sized rooms and three suites. Furnishings are standard issue; the color scheme is predominantly pink. Rooms at the back of the hotel face an air shaft, creating a dark but peaceful refuge. Guests have access to a nearby health club. ⊠ *77 Yesler Way, 98104,* ☎ *206/340–1234,* FAX *206/467–0707. 75 rooms, 3 suites. Coffee shop, pub, in-room data ports, no-smoking rooms, room service, laundry service, concierge, business services, meeting rooms, parking (fee). Continental breakfast. AE, D, DC, MC, V.*

$$$–$$$$ ☷ **Seattle Sheraton Hotel and Towers.** Business travelers are the primary patrons of this large hotel near the convention center. Rooms on the top five floors, larger and more elegant than those on lower floors, include concierge service and complimentary Continental breakfast. Dining options within the complex include Fullers (☞ Dining, *above*), one of Seattle's best restaurants. The Pike Street Cafe serves all-American cuisine in a casual atmosphere. The lobby features an art-glass collection by well-known Pacific Northwest artist Dale Chihuly. ⊠ *1400 6th Ave., 98101,* ☎ *206/621–9000 or 800/325–3535,* FAX *206/621–8441. 800 rooms, 40 suites. 4 restaurants, 2 bars, in-room data ports, in-room safes, minibars, room service, indoor pool, health club, laundry service, concierge, meeting rooms, parking (fee). AE, D, DC, MC, V.*

$$$ ☷ **Crowne Plaza.** This favorite of business travelers is directly off I–5, midway between First Hill and the Financial District. The lobby is small and plainly appointed in teal and cream with brass accents and houseplants. Rooms are quiet and spacious, with views of the Kingdome and Harbor Island to the south and Elliott Bay and the Space Needle to the north; all have lounge chairs and work areas. The relaxed and friendly staff is very attentive. ⊠ *1113 6th Ave., 98101,* ☎ *206/464–1980 or 800/521–2762,* FAX *206/340–1617. 415 rooms, 28 suites. Restaurant, bar, in-room data ports, no-smoking rooms, room service, sauna, health club, laundry service, concierge, business services, meeting rooms, parking (fee). AE, D, DC, MC, V.*

$$–$$$ ☷ **Pacific Plaza.** This 1929 property, which retains a '20s–'30s feel, is a good bargain for singles or couples; families may find the nondescript rooms too small to accommodate them. ⊠ *400 Spring St., 98104,* ☎ *206/623–3900 or 800/426–1165,* FAX *206/623–2059. 159 rooms. Restaurant, coffee shop, pizzeria, no-smoking rooms, concierge, parking (fee). Continental breakfast. AE, D, DC, MC, V.*

$$–$$$ ☷ **WestCoast Camlin Hotel.** The lobby of this 1926 apartment-hotel on the edge of downtown but near the convention center has Oriental carpets, large mirrors, and lots of marble. Rooms ending with the number 10 are the best; they have windows on three sides. All rooms have work spaces with a chair and a table, and a cushioned chair to relax in. One drawback here is the noisy heating, air-conditioning, and ventilation system, but these (along with the rest of the hotel) are slated to be upgraded in 2000. ⊠ *1619 9th Ave., 98101,* ☎ *206/682–0100 or 800/426–0670,* FAX *206/682–7415. 132 rooms, 4 suites. Restaurant, bar, in-room data ports, room service, pool, dry cleaning, concierge, meeting rooms. AE, D, DC, MC, V.*

$$ ⊞ **Pensione Nichols.** One block from Pike Place Market, the location of this B&B can't be beat. Suites on the second floor have enclosed balconies, full-size kitchens, private baths, separate bedrooms, and large open living rooms. Most rooms on the third floor have skylights rather than windows and are decorated in light colors with antique and contemporary furnishings. ⊠ *1923 1st Ave., 98101,* ☎ *206/441–7125 or 800/440–7125. 10 rooms share 4 baths, 2 suites. Continental breakfast. AE, D, DC, MC, V.*

$ ⊞ **Youth Hostel: Seattle International.** You can bed down in dormitory style for about $20 a night at this hostel near Pike Place Market. Guests have kitchen and dining-room access. ⊠ *84 Union St., 98101,* ☎ *206/622–5443. 3 rooms, 191 dormitory beds share baths. Library, coin laundry. AE, MC, V.*

Capitol Hill

$$–$$$ ⊞ **Gaslight Inn.** The rooms at this B&B range from a crow's nest with ★ peeled-log furniture and Navajo-print fabrics to suites with gas fireplaces and antique carved beds. There's also an apartment with a blown-glass chandelier and views of downtown and Elliott Bay. The large common areas have a masculine feel, with oak wainscoting, animal statuary, high ceilings, and hunter-green carpeting. One owner's past career as a professional painter is evident in the impeccable custom-mixed finishes throughout the inn. All patrons have the use of a laundry room; those staying in the suites receive free off-street parking. A Continental breakfast is offered. ⊠ *1527 15th Ave., 98122,* ☎ *206/325–3654,* ℻ *206/328–4803. 9 rooms, 7 suites. No-smoking rooms, pool. AE, MC, V.*

$$–$$$ ⊞ **Hill House.** Inside an impeccably restored 1903 Victorian, this B&B contains richly colored rooms with a mix of antique and contemporary furnishings. Two suites have phones and televisions. That the rates here include a filling breakfast and free off-street parking makes this one of the city's best bargains. Book well in advance for summer weekends. Full breakfast is included. ⊠ *1113 E. John St.,* ☎ *206/720–7161 or 800/720–7161,* ℻ *206/323–0772. 7 rooms, 5 with bath. Free parking. AE, D, DC, MC, V.*

Lake Union and Fremont

$$$$ ⊞ **Marriott Residence Inn.** An extended-stay hotel on scenic Lake Union, the Marriott is a perfect choice for families. All rooms are either one- or two-bedroom suites, each with a living room and a fully equipped kitchen. Decorated in greens and blues, the comfortable suites get plenty of natural light. The lobby is within a seven-story atrium with a waterfall and many areas to relax, watch TV, play games, or look up recipes in cookbooks displayed on bookshelves. Room rates include complimentary shuttle service within a 2½-mi radius of the hotel and a Continental breakfast. ⊠ *800 Fairview Ave. N, 98109,* ☎ *206/624–6000, 800/331–3131 central reservations,* ℻ *206/223–8160. 234 suites. Room service, no-smoking rooms, indoor pool, sauna, spa, exercise room, children's programs, parking (fee). AE, D, DC, MC, V.*

$$–$$$ ⊞ **Chelsea Station.** The feel is very Seattle at this B&B across the street from the Woodland Park Zoo. The parlor and breakfast rooms are decorated in sage green with mission-oak furniture, brocade upholstery, lace curtains, and works by local artists. Spacious guest rooms, each with a phone and a writing desk, have antique and contemporary furnishings. The accommodations in front have views of the Cascades. One suite has a piano, another a kitchen. Several rooms have adjoining doors, useful for families or larger groups. Breakfast will be tailored to your special dietary needs upon request and is included in the room rates. ⊠ *4915 Linden Ave. N, 98103,* ☎ *206/547–6077 or 800/400–6077,* ℻ *206/632–5107. 2 rooms, 7 suites. In-room data ports. AE, D, DC, MC, V.*

University District

$$$$ 🖭 **Edmond Meany Tower Hotel.** This 1931 property within blocks of the University of Washington contains rooms bathed in soothing shades of white, with bright-red lounge chairs providing a bold contrast. The rooms, whose amenities include hair dryers and irons, have unparalleled views of the university, Mount Rainier, Green Lake, or Lake Union. ⊠ *4507 Brooklyn Ave. NE, 98105,* ☎ *206/634–2000 or 800/899–0251,* ℻ *206/547–6029. 155 rooms. Restaurant, bar, in-room data ports, no-smoking rooms, room service, exercise room, laundry service, concierge, meeting rooms, free parking. AE, DC, MC, V.*

$$–$$$$ 🖭 **University Plaza Hotel.** Families and business travelers like this full-service motor hotel across I–5 from the University of Washington. The mock-Tudor decor gives the place a dated feel, but the service is cheerful and the rooms are spacious and pleasantly decorated in teak furniture. Ask for a room away from the freeway. ⊠ *400 N.E. 45th St., 98105,* ☎ *206/634–0100 or 800/343–7040,* ℻ *206/633–2743. 135 rooms. Restaurant, bar, no-smoking rooms, room service, pool, beauty salon, exercise room, meeting rooms, free parking. AE, D, DC, MC, V.*

$$$ 🖭 **University Inn.** The no-nonsense accommodations at this modern hotel have writing desks and are decorated in light wood and floral patterns. Some rooms have decks. Units in back are quieter. Enjoy the hot tub year-round and the outdoor pool in season as well as the complimentary Continental breakfast. ⊠ *4140 Roosevelt Way NE, 98105,* ☎ *206/632–5055 or 800/733–3855,* ℻ *206/547–4937. 102 rooms. Restaurant, in-room data ports, in-room safes, no-smoking floors, outdoor pool, hot tub, exercise room, coin laundry, dry cleaning, meeting rooms, free parking. AE, D, DC, MC, V.*

$$–$$$ 🖭 **Chambered Nautilus.** A resident teddy bear will keep you company at this Georgian Colonial B&B, which was built in 1915 by a professor of Asian studies at the University of Washington. Rooms all have private baths, some with antique dressers converted to serve as sinks and counters. Most rooms have private porches, one has a fireplace, and all come with robes and well-stocked bookshelves. Breakfast, included in the room rates, might include French toast with orange syrup or a breakfast pie made with salmon, dill, and Swiss cheese. ⊠ *5005 22nd Ave. NE, 98105,* ☎ *206/522–2536,* ℻ *206/528–0898. 6 rooms. AE, MC, V.*

Seattle-Tacoma International Airport

$$$–$$$$ 🖭 **Doubletree Inn, Doubletree Suites.** These two hotels across the street from each other are adjacent to the Southcenter shopping mall and convenient to business-park offices. The Inn is a classic Pacific Northwest-style lodge; its rooms are smaller and less lavish than those at the Suites, but they're perfectly fine and cost at least $25 less. Accommodations at the Suites all have sofas, tables and chairs, and wet bars. ⊠ *Doubletree Inn: 205 Strander Blvd., 98188,* ☎ *206/575–8220 or 800/325–8733,* ℻ *206/575–4743. 193 rooms, 5 suites. Bar, coffee shop, dining room, 1 indoor and 1 outdoor pool, meeting rooms, airport shuttle, free parking. Doubletree Suites:* ⊠ *16500 Southcenter Pkwy., 98188,* ☎ *206/575–8220 or 800/325–8733,* ℻ *206/575–4743. 221 suites. Restaurant, bar, refrigerators, indoor pool, hot tub, sauna,* health club, racquetball, meeting rooms, airport shuttle, free parking. AE, D, DC, MC, V.

$$$–$$$$ ⊞ **Marriott Sea-Tac.** The luxurious Marriott has a five-story, 21,000-
★ square-ft tropical atrium that's complete with a waterfall, a dining area, an indoor pool, and a lounge. Rooms are decorated in greens and mauve with dark-wood and brass furnishings. ⊠ *3201 S. 176th St., 98188,* ☎ *206/241–2000 or 800/643–5479,* 🖷 *206/248–0789. 459 rooms. Restaurant, lobby lounge, in-room data ports, no-smoking rooms, room service, indoor pool, hot tubs, sauna, health club, video games, laundry service, concierge, meeting rooms, airport shuttle, free parking. AE, D, DC, MC, V.*

$$$–$$$$ ⊞ **Wyndham Garden Hotel.** This hotel has convenient airport access. The elegant lobby has a fireplace, a marble floor, and comfortable furniture. Rooms have large desks, overstuffed chairs, irons and boards, coffeemakers, and hair dryers. ⊠ *18118 Pacific Hwy. S, 98188,* ☎ *206/244–6666,* 🖷 *206/244–6679. 180 rooms, 24 suites. Restaurant, lobby lounge, in-room data ports, no-smoking floors, room service, indoor pool, exercise room, coin laundry, laundry service, meeting rooms, airport shuttle, free parking. AE, D, DC, MC, V.*

$$$ ⊞ **Doubletree Hotel Seattle Airport.** The Doubletree is a full-service convention hotel. The large and bright rooms all have balconies—corner "king rooms" have wraparound ones with great views. Furnishings include comfortable chairs, a dining table, and a desk. ⊠ *18740 Pacific Hwy. S, 98188,* ☎ *206/246–8600,* 🖷 *206/431–8687. 837 rooms, 13 suites. 3 restaurants, 2 bars, in-room data ports, room service, pool, beauty salon, exercise room, laundry service, meeting rooms, airport shuttle, parking (fee). AE, D, DC, MC, V.*

$$$ ⊞ **Seattle Airport Hilton.** With its lobby fireplace and paintings of Pacific Northwest scenery, this hotel, only a half-hour drive from downtown, has a surprisingly cozy feel. Large rooms are bright and decorated in pastel colors. ⊠ *17620 Pacific Hwy. S, 98188,* ☎ *206/244–4800,* 🖷 *206/248–4499. 175 rooms, 3 suites. Restaurant, bar, in-room data ports, pool, exercise room, coin laundry, laundry service, concierge, business services, meeting rooms, airport shuttle, free parking. AE, D, DC, MC, V.*

$$–$$$ ⊞ **WestCoast Gateway Hotel.** Perfect for the traveler catching an early flight, this hotel contains quiet rooms in shades of burgundy and gray. All have coffeemakers, and Continental breakfast is included. ⊠ *18415 Pacific Hwy. S, 98188,* ☎ *206/248–8200 or 800/426–0670,* 🖷 *206/244–1198. 145 rooms. Breakfast room, in-room data ports, no-smoking floors, room service, exercise room, dry cleaning, meeting room, airport shuttle, free parking. AE, D, DC, MC, V.*

$$–$$$ ⊞ **WestCoast Sea-Tac Hotel.** The enthusiastic and helpful staff at this conveniently located property make it attractive to the business or leisure traveler. Guests are welcome to play the baby grand piano in the small but comfortable lobby. All rooms come equipped with Nintendo systems. Rooms in the rear have views of Bow Lake. ⊠ *18220 International Blvd., 98188,* ☎ *206/246–5535 or 800/426–0670,* 🖷 *206/246–9733. 146 rooms. Restaurant, bar, room service, pool, hot tub, sauna, exercise room, business services, meeting rooms, airport shuttle, free parking. AE, D, DC, MC, V.*

Bellevue/Kirkland

$$$$ ⊞ **Bellevue Club Hotel.** The locally produced fine, decorative, and applied artwork that adorns its public and private spaces are among the
★ standout features of this boutique hotel, which has won numerous awards for its design. The warm earth tones incorporated into the decidedly modern setting, coupled with the clever use of lighting, create an illu-

In case you want to see the world.

At American Express, we're here to make your journey a smooth one. So we have over 1,700 travel service locations in over 130 countries ready to help. What else would you expect from the world's largest travel agency?

do more

Travel

Call 1 800 AXP-3429 or visit
www.americanexpress.com/travel

In case you want to be welcomed there.

We're here to see that you're always welcomed at establishments everywhere. That's why millions of people carry the American Express® Card – for peace of mind, confidence, and security, around the world or just around the corner.

do more **AMERICAN EXPRESS**

Cards

To apply, call 1 800 THE-CARD
or visit www.americanexpress.com

In case you're running low.

We're here to help with more than 190,000 Express Cash
locations around the world. In order to enroll, just call
American Express at 1 800 CASH-NOW before you start
your vacation.

do more AMERICAN EXPRESS

Express
Cash

And in case you'd rather be safe than sorry.

We're here with American Express® Travelers Cheques. They're the safe way to carry money on your vacation, because if they're ever lost or stolen you can get a refund, practically anywhere or anytime. To find the nearest place to buy Travelers Cheques, call 1 800 495-1153. Another way we help you do more.

do more

Travelers Cheques

sion of sunlight even when it's raining outside. Original oil paintings by Pacific Northwest artist Mark Rediske hang in each room. Pillows made from African Kuba textiles, Turkish area rugs, and raku pottery offset cherry-wood furniture. All the rooms have sumptuous armchairs and large spa-inspired, limestone-tiled bathrooms with separate tubs and glass-enclosed showers. ⊠ *11200 S.E. 6th St., Bellevue 98004,* ☎ *425/454–4424 or 800/579–1110,* FAX *425/688–3101. 64 rooms, 3 suites. 2 restaurants, lounge, in-room data ports, in-room safes, minibars, refrigerators, room service, pool, spa, tennis, basketball, health club, laundry service, concierge, business services, meeting rooms, parking (fee). AE, DC, MC, V.*

$$$$ 🏨 **Doubletree Hotel Bellevue.** The 10-story Doubletree has an airy atrium filled with trees, shrubs, and flowering plants. The property also has a formal dining room, a lounge with two dance floors, and oversize guest rooms decorated in hunter green, burgundy, and beige. Rooms have either king- or queen-size beds. Two-room suites contain wet bars and whirlpool tubs. ⊠ *300 112th Ave. SE, Bellevue 98004,* ☎ *425/ 455–1300 or 800/733–5466,* FAX *425/455–0466. 348 rooms, 5 suites. 2 restaurants, bar, in-room data ports, room service, pool, exercise room, laundry service, concierge, business services, meeting rooms, free parking. AE, D, DC, MC, V.*

$$$$ 🏨 **Hyatt Regency Bellevue.** Near Bellevue Square and other downtown shopping centers, the Hyatt has an exterior much like that of any other sleek high-rise, but its interior has Asian touches like antique Japanese chests and huge displays of fresh flowers. The rooms are decorated in similarly understated ways, with dark wood and earth tones predominating. Deluxe suites include two bedrooms, bar facilities, and meeting rooms with desks and full-length tables; business-plan rooms have modem lines. Guests have access to a health club and pool. The restaurant serves excellent and reasonably priced breakfast, lunch, and dinner; an English-style pub and sports bar serves lunch and dinner. ⊠ *900 Bellevue Way NE, 98004,* ☎ *425/462–2626,* FAX *425/646–7567. 353 rooms, 29 suites. Restaurant, sports bar, no-smoking rooms, room service, concierge, meeting rooms, parking (fee). AE, D, DC, MC, V.*

$$$$ 🏨 **Woodmark Hotel.** Only steps away from downtown Kirkland, 7
★ mi east of Seattle, this hotel is the only one on the shores of Lake Washington. Its contemporary-style rooms, which face the water, a courtyard, or the street, are done in exquisite shades of café au lait, taupe, and ecru. The numerous amenities include terry-cloth bathrobes, coffeemakers, irons, hair dryers, complimentary shoe shines, and the morning paper. Guests have privileges at the health club in the hotel complex. A circular staircase descends from the lobby to the Library Lounge, passing a huge bay window with a vast view of Lake Washington. Waters Bistro serves Pacific Rim cuisine, with dishes such as lemongrass steamed clams and grilled halibut with roasted onion–ginger relish. ⊠ *1200 Carillon Pt., Kirkland 98033,* ☎ *425/822–3700 or 800/822–3700,* FAX *425/822–3699. 79 rooms, 21 suites. Restaurant, bar, in-room data ports, in-room safes, minibars, refrigerators, room service, exercise room, laundry service, concierge, business services, meeting rooms, parking (fee). AE, DC, MC, V.*

$$ 🏨 **WestCoast Bellevue Hotel.** This hotel–motor inn has a number of town-house suites, suitable for two to four people, with sleeping lofts and wood-burning fireplaces. Rooms are clean. Those facing the courtyard are larger and quieter than the others. The hotel is a 20-minute walk from Bellevue Square. A substantial, complimentary appetizer buffet, served in the lounge weekdays between 5 and 7, includes seafood and roast beef. ⊠ *625 116th Ave. NE, Bellevue*

98004, ☎ *425/455–9444,* FAX *425/455–2154. 160 rooms, 16 suites. Restaurant, bar, room service, pool, exercise room, laundry service, business services, meeting rooms, free parking. AE, D, DC, MC, V.*

NIGHTLIFE AND THE ARTS

The Thursday edition of the *Seattle Times* and the Friday *Seattle Post-Intelligencer* include pullout weekend sections that detail upcoming arts and entertainment events. *Seattle Weekly,* which hits most newsstands on Wednesday, has even more detailed coverage and reviews. The *Stranger,* a provocative free weekly, provides broad, though not necessarily deep, coverage of the city's cultural activities and is the unofficial bible of the music and club scenes.

Ticketmaster (☎ 206/628–0888) sells tickets to most arts, entertainment, and sports events in the Seattle area; for a steep fee, you can charge by phone. The two locations of **Ticket/Ticket** (✉ Broadway Market, 401 Broadway E, 2nd floor, ☎ 206/324–2744; ✉ Pike Pl. Market Information Booth, 1st Ave. and Pike St., ☎ 206/682–7453, ext. 226) sell half-price tickets to many events on the day of the performance (or previous day for matinees). Sales are cash and in-person only.

Nightlife

Neighborhoods with high concentrations of clubs and bars include **Ballard, Pioneer Square, Capitol Hill,** and **Belltown** (also known as the Denny Regrade, north of Pike Place Market).

Amusement Centers/Theme Entertainment

The amusements at **GameWorks** (✉ 7th Ave. and Pike St., ☎ 206/521–0952) a Steven Spielberg–Sega collaboration, run the gamut from old-style arcade games to high-tech road-racing and other electronic games. In the same block with Gameworks is **NikeTown** (✉ 6th Ave. and Pike St., ☎ 206/447–6453), where the line between shopping and being entertained has been all but blurred. The Seattle edition of **Planet Hollywood** (✉ 6th Ave. and Pike St., ☎ 206/287–0001) is the same scene it is elsewhere around the world.

For a uniquely Seattle entertainment experience, venture out to South Lake Union, where **Entros** (✉ 823 Yale Ave. N, ☎ 206/624–0057) bills itself as "an intelligent amusement park." This hip spot is an adult playground of interactive games and installations set around a first-rate bar and restaurant, the World Grill. Some people come just to eat or to play, but those adventurous enough to try the Segovian prawns in cayenne-lime butter or the tamarind chicken with Thai chilies tend to stick around for Interface (a high-tech trust walk using closed-circuit TV and two-way radios) and Perfect Burger (a conveyor-belt game reminiscent of the famous candy-factory episode from *I Love Lucy*).

Bars and Lounges

Bars with waterfront views are plentiful—you just have to pick your body of water. **Anthony's Home Port** (✉ 6135 Seaview Ave. NW, ☎ 206/783–0780) overlooks Shilshole Bay. **Arnie's** (✉ 1900 N. Northlake Way, ☎ 206/547–3242) has a great view of downtown from north Lake Union. **Duke's at Chandler's Cove** (✉ 901 Fairview Ave. N, 206/382–9963) surveys south Lake Union. **Ernie's Bar & Grill** (✉ Edgewater, 2411 Alaskan Way, Pier 67, ☎ 206/728–7000) has great views of Elliott Bay and the Olympic Mountains. The deck at **Ponti** (✉ 3014 3rd Ave. N, ☎ 206/284–3000) overlooks the Ship Canal.

If the view's not important, check out three of Seattle's hipper venues, all near Pike Place Market. The **Alibi Room** (✉ 85 Post Alley, ☎ 206/623–3180) is the unofficial watering hole of the city's film community. The romantic **Il Bistro** (✉ 93A Pike St., ☎ 206/682–3049) has low lights, low ceilings, and stiff drinks. Installations by local artists adorn the **Virginia Inn** (✉ 1937 1st Ave., ☎ 206/728–1937).

The **Bungalow** (✉ 2412 N. 45th St., ☎ 206/632–0254) is an intimate spot to sip fine wines from around the world. The **Garden Court** (✉ Four Seasons Hotel, 411 University St., ☎ 206/621–1700) is downtown's most elegant lounge. **Palomino** (✉ 1420 5th Ave., ☎ 206/623–1300) is a sophisticated spot patronized by the after-work crowd.

In Pioneer Square check out **F. X. McRory's** (✉ 419 Occidental Ave. S, ☎ 206/623–4800), near the Kingdome; the bar is famous for its single-malt whiskeys and fresh oysters. **Pioneer Square Saloon** (✉ 77 Yesler Way, ☎ 206/340–1234) is a great, easygoing, no-frills tavern.

Brew Pubs

Seattle brew pubs churn out many high-quality beers made for local distribution. All the pubs listed below serve food and nonalcoholic beverages. If live music is performed, a cover charge may be required; otherwise admission is free. Unless noted, the establishments listed below are open daily from at least noon to 11 PM; call ahead if you're planning a visit at other hours.

Big Time Brewery (✉ 4133 University Way NE, ☎ 206/545–4509) caters to the U District crowd and resembles an archetypal college-town pub, with the obligatory moose head on the wall and vintage memorabilia scattered about. Pale ale, amber, and porter are always on tap; the imaginative specialty brews change monthly.

The taps at the **Elysian Brewing Company** (✉ 1221 E. Pike St., ☎ 206/860–1920) flow with Golden Fleece Ale, Zephyrus Pilsner, the Immortal India Pale Ale, and other brews. If the cute mythological names don't appeal, the dependable pub fare and eccentric Capitol Hill clientele will win you over.

Hales Ales Brewery and Pub (✉ 4301 Leary Way NW, ☎ 206/782–0737) serves up nine regular and seasonal offerings in a cheerful Fremont setting. The pub's signature brews are its Honey Wheat and Moss Bay Amber ales; order a taster's "flight" to test the rest as well.

Pike Pub and Brewery (✉ 1415 1st Ave., ☎ 206/622–6044), a dandy downtown establishment, is operated by the brewers of the award-winning Pike Place Pale Ale. Proudly proclaiming itself Beer Central, the Pike also houses the Seattle Microbrewery Museum and an excellent shop with supplies for home brewing.

Pyramid Alehouse (✉ 91 S. Royal Brougham Way, at 1st Ave. S, ☎ 206/682–3377), south of the Kingdome, brews the varied Pyramid Line—including a top-notch Hefeweizen and an Apricot Ale that tastes much better than it sounds—and Thomas Kemper Lagers. A loud, festive atmosphere makes Pyramid the perfect place to gather after a Mariners baseball game.

Redhook Brewery has an in-town location (☞ The Trolleyman, *below*) and a larger complex—with a pub, a beer garden, and a gift shop in addition to brewing facilities ($1 tours available daily; call for hours and directions)—in Woodinville (✉ 14300 N.E. 145th St., ☎ 425/483–3232).

Six Arms (✉ 300 E. Pike St., ☎ 206/223–1698) features the same comfortably eccentric decor that has become the trademark of the chain of pubs operated by the McMenamin family of Portland, Oregon. The beer is equally memorable, especially the challenging Terminator Stout. The Six Arms displays considerably more charm than her Seattle cousins, **McMenamin's** (⊠ 200 Roy St., ☎ 206/285–4722) and **Dad Watson's** (⊠ 3601 Fremont Ave., ☎ 206/632–6505), though the beer at all three tastes the same.

The **Trolleyman** (⊠ 3400 Phinney Ave. N, ☎ 206/548–8000), near the north end of the Fremont Bridge, is the birthplace of local favorites Ballard Bitter and Redhook Ale. The pub mixes Pacific Northwest style (whitewashed walls and a no-smoking policy) with a relaxed atmosphere that includes a fireplace and ample armchairs. The original Redhook Brewery is right next door—take a 45-minute tour before you pop in for a pint. The pub opens at 11 AM except Sunday, when it opens at noon (and closes at 7). Call for tour times.

Coffeehouses

Unlike the city's brew pubs, Seattle's coffeehouses are defined as much by the people they serve as the beverages they pour. Most cafés serve the same drinks, but though some Seattleites will linger for hours over their latte, others prefer a cup to go from a drive-through espresso stand. Every neighborhood has its own distinctive coffee culture—usually three or four, actually. Below are a few of the options on Capitol Hill and downtown.

CAPITOL HILL

Local favorite **B&O Espresso** (⊠ 204 Belmont Ave. E, ☎ 206/322–5028) lures Capitol Hill hipsters and solitary types. The on-site bakery turns out gorgeous wedding cakes. A youngish crowd browses through the art and architecture books on the shelves of **Bauhaus** (⊠ 301 E. Pine St., ☎ 206/625–1600). Scribble and brood with the poetry set at **Café Vita** (⊠ 1005 E. Pike St., ☎ 206/325–2647). Take a trip to Paris when you enter **Septième** (⊠ 214 Broadway E, ☎ 206/860–8858), which, despite its white-linen tablecloths, has a calculatedly seedy feel. In back is an open patio, where during the summer you can listen to rhumba and salsa music and sip by the light of tiki torches. The friendly **Habitat Espresso** (⊠ 202 Broadway E, ☎ 206/329–3087) is a coffee collective that donates a significant portion of its profits to local and national charities. Exceptional, no-nonsense **Vivace Roasteria** (⊠ 901 E. Denny Way, ☎ 206/860–5869) roasts its own coffee and sells to other coffeehouses.

DOWNTOWN

The rich smell of the roaster as you step through the door of tiny **Caffé Vita** (⊠ 2621 5th Ave., ☎ 206/441–4351) is intoxicating. **Lux** (⊠ 2226 1st Ave., ☎ 206/443–0962) has a thrift-store opulence that's right at home among the boutiques of 1st Avenue and the Belltown arts scene. The **Sit & Spin** (⊠ 2219 4th Ave., ☎ 206/441–9484) café has a full-service laundry on one side. Sit & Spin's rival for the award for the coffeehouse most likely to improve your time management is **Speakeasy** (⊠ 2304 2nd Ave., ☎ 206/728–9770), where you can download your E-mail along with your caffeine. Both cafés also double—or is it triple?—as performance spaces in the evening.

Comedy Clubs

Comedy Underground (⊠ 222 S. Main St., ☎ 206/628–0303), a Pioneer Square club that's literally underground, beneath Swannie's bar and restaurant, presents stand-up comedy nightly. **Giggles** (⊠ 5220 Roosevelt Way NE, ☎ 206/526–5653) in the University District books local and nationally known comedians from Thursday through Sunday, with late shows on Friday and Saturday.

Music

For $8 you can purchase the Pioneer Square joint cover charge, which will admit you to up to 10 area clubs; contact the New Orleans Restaurant (☞ Jazz, *below*) for details.

BLUES AND R&B

Ballard Firehouse (⊠ 5429 Russell St. NW, ☎ 206/784–3516), Ballard's music mecca, books local and national blues acts. **Larry's** (⊠ 209 1st Ave. S, ☎ 206/624–7665) presents live blues and rhythm and blues nightly in an unpretentious, friendly, and usually jam-packed tavern-restaurant in Pioneer Square. **Old Timer's Cafe** (⊠ 620 1st Ave., ☎ 206/623–9800), a popular Pioneer Square restaurant and bar, has live music—mostly rhythm and blues—nightly. **Scarlet Tree** (⊠ 6521 Roosevelt Way NE, ☎ 206/523–7153), a neighborhood institution north of the University District, serves up great burgers and live rhythm and blues most nights.

DANCE CLUBS

The local chapter of the **U.S. Amateur Ballroom Dancing Association** (☎ 425/822–6686) holds regular classes and dances throughout the year at the **Avalon Ballroom** (⊠ 1017 Stewart St.). The **Century Ballroom** (⊠ 915 E. Pine St., ☎ 206/324–7263) holds regular classes and dances throughout the year. The **Washington Dance Club** (⊠ 1017 Stewart St., ☎ 206/628–8939) sponsors nightly workshops and dances in various styles.

Several Seattle clubs celebrate cocktail culture. **700 Club** (⊠ 700 Virginia Ave., ☎ 206/343–1255) presents live and recorded swing music. The chic **Baltic Room** (⊠ 1207 Pine St., ☎ 206/625–4444) hosts retro and contemporary dance nights and the occasional film screening. **Pampas Room** (⊠ 90 Wall St., ☎ 206/728–1140) presents jazz on Friday and Saturday evenings.

For more contemporary sounds, **Downunder** (⊠ 2407 1st Ave., ☎ 206/728–4053) is an old-school disco with a packed floor. The moody **Romper Room** (⊠ 106 1st Ave. N, ☎ 206/284–5003) specializes in '70s soul. **Re-Bar** (⊠ 1114 Howell St., ☎ 206/233–9873) presents an eclectic mix of music nightly, including acid jazz, rock, and soul. The **Vogue** (⊠ 2018 1st Ave., ☎ 206/443–0673) hosts reggae, industrial, and gothic dance nights. Several rock clubs (☞ *below*) have dance floors.

FOLK

The cheerful **Hopvine Pub** (⊠ 507 15th Ave. E, ☎ 206/328–3120) hosts local folk musicians. **Kells** (⊠ 1916 Post Alley, ☎ 206/728–1916), a snug Irish-style pub near Pike Place Market, books Celtic-music artists from Wednesday through Saturday. **Murphy's Pub** (⊠ 2110 45th St. NE, ☎ 206/634–2110), a neighborhood bar, has Irish and other folk music on Friday and Saturday.

JAZZ

Dimitriou's Jazz Alley (⊠ 2037 6th Ave., ☎ 206/441–9729), a downtown club, books nationally known, consistently high-quality performers every night but Sunday. Excellent dinners are served before the first show. **Latona Pub** (⊠ 6423 Latona Ave. NE, ☎ 206/525–2238) is a funky, friendly neighborhood bar at the south end of Green Lake that presents local folk, blues, or jazz musicians nightly. **New Orleans Restaurant** (⊠ 114 1st Ave. S, ☎ 206/622–2563), a popular Pioneer Square restaurant, has good food and jazz nightly—mostly top local performers, with occasional national acts.

ROCK

The **Moore Theater** (⊠ 1932 2nd Ave., ☎ 206/443–1744) and the **Paramount** (⊠ 907 Pine St., ☎ 206/682–1414 or 206/628–0888 or

☎ 206/682–1414 or 206/628–0888) are elegant structures from the early 20th century that host visiting big-name acts.

Crocodile Café (✉ 2200 2nd Ave., ☎ 206/441–5611), one of Seattle's most successful rock clubs, books alternative music acts nightly except Monday. The **Fenix** (✉ 315 2nd Ave. S, ☎ 206/467–1111) is a crowded Pioneer Square venue with an ever-changing roster of local and national acts. **O.K. Hotel** (✉ 212 Alaskan Way S, ☎ 206/621–7903) hosts rock, folk, and jazz nightly in a small venue near Pioneer Square. **Showbox** (✉ 1426 1st Ave., ☎ 206/628–3151) presents locally and nationally acclaimed artists near Pike Place Market.

The Arts

The Arts for Free
Seattle's summer concerts, the **Out to Lunch Series** (☎ 206/623–0340), happen every weekday at noon from mid-June to early September in various parks, plazas, and atriums downtown. Concerts showcase local and national musicians and dancers.

First Thursday Gallery Walk (☎ 206/587–0260), an open house hosted by Seattle's art galleries, visits new local exhibits on the first Thursday of every month from 6 to 9 PM.

Dance
Meany Hall for the Performing Arts (✉ University of Washington campus, ☎ 206/543–4880) hosts important national and international companies, from September through May, with an emphasis on modern and jazz dance.

On the Boards (✉ 100 W. Roy St., ☎ 206/217–9888) presents and produces contemporary dance performances and also theater, music, and multimedia events. The main subscription series runs October–May, but events are scheduled nearly every weekend year-round.

Pacific Northwest Ballet (✉ Opera House at Seattle Center, Mercer St. at 3rd Ave., ☎ 206/441–2424) is a resident company and school. Attending its Christmastime production of *The Nutcracker,* with choreography by Kent Stowell and sets by Maurice Sendak, is a Seattle tradition.

Film
The strongest evidence of Seattle's passion for the movies is the wildly popular **Seattle International Film Festival** (☎ 206/324–9996), held each May and June. For show times and theater locations of current releases, call the **Seattle Times InfoLine** (☎ 206/464–2000, ext. 3456).

The **Egyptian Theater** (✉ 801 E. Pine St., at Broadway, ☎ 206/323–4978), an Art Deco movie palace that was formerly a Masonic temple, screens first-run films and is the prime venue of Seattle's film festival. **Grand Illusion Cinema** (✉ 1403 N.E. 50th St., at University Way, ☎ 206/523–3935), in the U District, was a tiny screening room for exhibitors in the '30s. A venue for independent and art films, it has a terrific espresso bar. **Harvard Exit** (✉ 807 E. Roy St., ☎ 206/323–8986), a first-run and art-film house, has Seattle's most inviting theater lobby—complete with couches and a piano. **Varsity Theater** (✉ 4329 University Way NE, ☎ 206/632–3131), in the U District, usually dedicates two of its three screens to classic films.

Music
Northwest Chamber Orchestra (✉ 1305 4th Ave., ☎ 206/343–0445) presents a full spectrum of music, from baroque to modern, at the University of Washington's Kane Hall. The subscription series, generally from September through May, includes a baroque-music festival every

fall. **Seattle Symphony** (⊠ Benaroya Hall, 1203 2nd Ave., at University St., ☎ 206/215–4747) performs under the direction of Gerard Schwartz from September through June in the Benaroya Hall.

Opera

Seattle Opera (⊠ Opera House at Seattle Center, Mercer St. at 3rd Ave., ☎ 206/389–7676), considered among the top operas in the United States, presents five productions during its season, which runs August–May.

Performance Venues

Broadway Performance Hall (⊠ Seattle Central Community College, 1625 Broadway, ☎ 206/325–3113), small but acoustically outstanding, often hosts dance and music concerts.

Cornish College of the Arts (⊠ 710 E. Roy St., ☎ 206/323–1400) serves as headquarters for distinguished jazz, dance, and other groups.

Fifth Avenue Theater (⊠ 1308 5th Ave., ☎ 206/625–1900) is the home of the Fifth Avenue Musical Theater Company (☞ Theater Companies, *below*). When the company is on hiatus, this chinoiserie-style historic landmark, carefully restored to its original 1926 condition, hosts traveling musical and theatrical performances.

Moore Theater (⊠ 1932 2nd Ave., ☎ 206/443–1744), a 1908 music hall, presents dance concerts and rock shows.

Paramount Theatre (⊠ 907 Pine St., ☎ 206/682–1414), a 3,000-seat building from 1929 that has seen duty as a music hall and a movie palace, hosts Best of Broadway touring shows and national pop-music acts.

Seattle Center (⊠ 305 Harrison St., ☎ 206/684–8582) contains several halls that present theater, opera, dance, music, and performance art.

Theater Companies

Annex Theatre (⊠ 1916 4th Ave., ☎ 206/728–0933), run by a collective of artists, presents avant-garde works year-round. **A Contemporary Theater** (⊠ Eagles Auditorium, 700 Union St., ☎ 206/292–7676) specializes in regional premieres of new works by established playwrights. Every December the theater revives its popular production of *A Christmas Carol*. **Crêpe de Paris** (⊠ 1333 5th Ave., ☎ 206/623–4111), a restaurant in the Rainier Tower building downtown, books sidesplitting cabaret theater and musical revues.

Empty Space Theater (⊠ 3509 Fremont Ave., ☎ 206/547–7500) has a reputation for introducing Seattle to new playwrights. Its season generally runs from November through June, with five or six main-stage productions and several smaller shows. **Fifth Avenue Musical Theater Company** (⊠ Fifth Avenue Theater, 1308 5th Ave., ☎ 206/625–1900) is a resident professional troupe that mounts four lavish musicals from October to May. **Intiman Theater** (⊠ Playhouse at Seattle Center, 2nd Ave. N and Mercer St., ☎ 206/269–1901) presents important contemporary works and classics of the world stage. The season generally runs May–November.

New City Theater and Arts Center (⊠ 1634 11th Ave., ☎ 206/323–6800) hosts experimental performances by local, national, and international artists. **Seattle Children's Theatre** (⊠ Charlotte Martin Theatre at Seattle Center, 2nd Ave. N and Thomas St., ☎ 206/441–3322), the second-largest resident professional children's theater company in the United States, has commissioned several dozen new plays, adaptations, and musicals. The theater's six-play season runs September–June. **Seattle Repertory Theater** (⊠ Bagley Wright Theater at Seattle Center, 155 Mercer St., ☎ 206/443–2222) performs six new or classic plays on its main stage from October through May, along with three developmental shows at an adjoining smaller venue. **Village Theater** (⊠ 303 Front St. N, Issaquah, ☎ 425/392–2202) produces high-quality family musicals, comedies, and dramas from September through May in Issaquah, a town east of Seattle. The main stage is at 303 Front Street; the theater's original venue, at 120 Front Street, is known as First Stage.

OUTDOOR ACTIVITIES AND SPORTS

Beaches

If you happen to be in town on a sunny day, catch those precious rays at **Golden Gardens** (⊠ Seaview Ave. NW, ☎ 206/684–4075), a bit north of the Ballard Locks, or at **Alki Beach** (⊠ Alki Ave. SW; from downtown, take Hwy. 99 west, then head north on Harbor Ave. SW, ☎ 206/684–4075) in West Seattle. Another option is **Warren Magnuson Park** (☞ University District, *in* Exploring Seattle, *above*).

There are several public beaches on the western shores of Lake Washington. Where eastbound Madison Street runs into the lake you'll find **Madison Beach** (⊠ 2300 43rd Ave. E). This spot offers a playground, sandy beach, and easy access to the water. Heading south along Lake Washington Boulevard East is **Denny Blaine,** with a grassy park under towering shady trees and difficult access to the water. A mile farther south lies **Madrona Beach** (⊠ 853 Lake Washington Blvd.), which has a sculpted sand garden for the kids. **Mt. Baker Beach** (⊠ 2521 Lake Park Dr. S) has a dock and anchored raft with diving boards. **Seward Park** (⊠ 5898 Lake Washington Blvd. S), which offers a large playfield, has many covered picnic spots and a playground.

All of these locations are operated and maintained by the Seattle Parks Department (☎ 206/684–4075). With the exception of Denny Blaine, all of the beaches have lifeguards on duty during the summer months. The water stays pretty cold in Seattle year-round, with the best swimming temperatures in July and August.

Participant Sports

Seattle Parks and Recreation (☎ 206/684–4075) has information about participant sports and facilities.

Bicycling

The Burke-Gilman Trail and the trail that circles Green Lake are popular among recreational bicyclists and children, but at Green Lake joggers and walkers tend to impede fast travel. The city-maintained Burke-Gilman Trail extends 12 mi along Seattle's waterfront from Lake Washington nearly to Salmon Bay along an abandoned railroad line; it is a much less congested path. Myrtle Edwards Park, north of Pier 70, has a two-lane path for jogging and bicycling.

Gregg's Greenlake Cycle (⊠ 7007 Woodlawn Ave. NE, ☎ 206/523–1822) in North Seattle rents mountain bikes, standard touring or racing bikes, and equipment.

Billiards

Rack 'em up and run the table at the **211 Club** (⊠ 2304 2nd Ave., ☎ 206/443–1211). For billiards with a Vegas feel and a hibachi grill there's **Jillian's Billiard Cafe** (⊠ 731 Westlake Ave. N, ☎ 206/223–0300). **Temple Billiards** (⊠ 126 S. Jackson St., ☎ 206/682–3242), in Pioneer Square, caters to the hip crowd.

Boating and Sailboarding

Wind Works Rentals (✉ 7001 Seaview Ave. NW, ☎ 206/784–9386), on Shilshole Bay, rents sailboats with or without skippers by the half day, day, or week. **Yarrow Bay Marina** (✉ 5207 Lake Washington Blvd. NE, ☎ 425/822–6066 or 800/336–3834), in Kirkland, rents 17- and 20-ft runabouts by the day or week.

Lake Union and Green Lake are Seattle's prime sailboarding spots. Sailboards can be rented year-round at **Urban Surf** (✉ 2100 N. Northlake Way, ☎ 206/545–9463) on Lake Union.

Fishing

There are plenty of good spots for fishing on Lake Washington, Green Lake, and Lake Union, and there are several fishing piers along the Elliott Bay waterfront. Companies operating from Shilshole Bay operate charter trips for catching salmon, rock cod, flounder, and sea bass. **Ballard Salmon Charter** (☎ 206/789–6202) is a recommended local firm. Like most companies, **Pier 54 Adventures** (☎ 206/623–6364) includes the cost of a two-day fishing license ($3.50) in its fee.

Golf

The city-run **Jackson Park** (✉ 1000 N.E. 135th St., ☎ 206/363–4747), **Jefferson Park** (✉ 4101 Beacon Ave. S, ☎ 206/762–4513), and **West Seattle Golf Course** (✉ 4470 35th Ave. SW, ☎ 206/935–5187) golf facilities each have an 18-hole course (greens fee: $18.50, plus $20 for optional cart) and a 9-hole executive course ($8, plus $13 for optional cart). Closer to downtown, the **Interbay Family Golf Center** (✉ 2501 15th Ave W, ☎ 206/285–2200) has a driving range and 9-hole executive and miniature golf courses.

Jogging, Skating, and Walking

Green Lake is far and away Seattle's most popular spot for jogging, and the 3-mi circumference of this picturesque lake is custom-made for it. Walking, bicycling, rollerblading, fishing, lounging on the grass, and feeding the plentiful waterfowl are other possibilities. Several outlets clustered along the east side of the lake have skate and cycle rentals. Seward Park has a much more secluded and less used 3-mi loop where the park juts out into Lake Washington in Southeast Seattle.

Other good jogging locales are along the Burke-Gilman Trail (☞ Bicycling, *above*), around the reservoir at Volunteer Park (☞ Capitol Hill Area *in* Exploring Seattle, *above*), and at Myrtle Edwards Park, north of Pier 70 downtown.

Kayaking

Kayaking—around the inner waterways (Lake Union, Lake Washington, the Ship Canal) and open water (Elliott Bay)—affords some singular views of Seattle. The **Northwest Outdoor Center** (✉ 2100 Westlake Ave. N, ☎ 206/281–9694), on the west side of Lake Union, rents one- or two-person kayaks and equipment by the hour or week and provides both basic and advanced instruction.

Skiing

There's fine downhill skiing in and around Snoqualmie (☞ Chapter 5). For Snoqualmie ski reports and news about conditions in the more distant White Pass, Crystal Mountain, and Stevens Pass, call 206/634–0200 or 206/634–2754. For recorded messages about road conditions in the passes, call 888/766–4636.

Tennis

There are public tennis courts in parks around the Seattle area. Many courts are in the U District, and several are near Capitol Hill. For information, contact the athletics office of the **King County Parks and Recreation Department** (☎ 206/684–7093).

Spectator Sports

Ticketmaster (☎ 206/622–4487) sells tickets to many local sporting events.

Baseball

The **Seattle Mariners** (☎ 206/346–4000) in the West Division of the American League play at a new retractable-roof stadium, opened in the summer of 1999, called **Safeco Field** (⊠ 1st Ave. S. and Atlantic St.).

Basketball

The **Seattle SuperSonics** (☎ 206/283–3865) of the National Basketball Association play at **Key Arena** (⊠ 1st Ave. N and Mercer St.) in the Seattle Center.

Boat Racing

The **unlimited hydroplane races** (☎ 206/628–0888) are a highlight of Seattle's Seafair festivities from mid-July to the first Sunday in August. The races are held on Lake Washington near Seward Park. Tickets cost $10–$20. Weekly sailing regattas are held in the summer on Lakes Union and Washington. Call the **Seattle Yacht Club** (☎ 206/325–1000) for schedules.

Football

Seattle Seahawks (☎ 425/827–9777) National Football League games take place in the **Kingdome** (⊠ 201 S. King St.). The **University of Washington Huskies** (☎ 206/543–2200), every bit as popular as the Seahawks, play out their fall slate at Husky Stadium, off Montlake Boulevard Northeast on the UW campus.

Horse Racing

Take in Thoroughbred racing from April through September at **Emerald Downs** (⊠ 2300 Emerald Downs Dr., Auburn, ☎ 253/288–7000), a 166-acre track about 15 mi south of downtown, east of I–5.

Soccer

For outdoor soccer, catch the A-League **Seattle Sounders** at Memorial Stadium (⊠ Seattle Center, 5th Ave. N and Harrison St., ☎ 800/796–5425).

SHOPPING

Most Seattle stores are open daily. Mall hours are generally from 9:30 to 9 except Sunday, when stores usually stay open 11–6. Some specialty shops keep shorter evening and Sunday hours.

Shopping Districts

Broadway in the Capitol Hill neighborhood is lined with clothing stores selling new and vintage threads and high-design housewares shops.

Fremont Avenue contains a funky mix of galleries, thrift stores, and boutiques around its intersection with North 35th Street, above the Fremont Bridge.

The **International District,** bordered roughly by South Main and South Lane streets and 4th and 8th avenues, contains many Asian herb shops and groceries. **Uwajimaya** (✉ 519 6th Ave. S, ☎ 206/624–6248), one of the largest Japanese stores on the West Coast, sells Asian foods and affordable china, gifts, fabrics, and housewares. Okazuya, the snack bar in Uwajimaya, prepares noodle dishes, sushi, tempura, and other Asian dishes to take out or to eat in.

University Way Northeast, in the University District between Northeast 41st and Northeast 50th streets, has a few upscale shops, many bookstores, and businesses that carry such student-oriented imports as ethnic jewelry and South American sweaters.

Shopping Centers and Malls

Bellevue Square (✉ N.E. 8th St. and Bellevue Way, ☎ 425/454–8096), an upscale shopping center about 8 mi east of Seattle, is home to more than 200 shops and includes a children's play area, the Bellevue Art Museum, and covered parking.

Northgate Mall (✉ I–5 and Northgate Way, ☎ 206/362–4777), 10 mi north of downtown, houses 118 stores, including Nordstrom, the Bon Marché, Lamonts, and JCPenney.

Pacific Place (✉ 6th and Pine Sts.), a chichi glass-ceiling complex opened in 1998, has Tiffany & Co., J. Crew, Barnes & Noble, Restoration Hardware, Stars restaurant, and other mostly chain operations.

Southcenter Mall (✉ I–5 and I–405 in Tukwila, ☎ 206/246–7400) contains 140 shops and department stores.

University Village (✉ NE 45th St. and 25th Ave. NE, ☎ 206/523–0622) is an upscale open-air mall with more than 80 national and locally owned shops and restaurants, including the Pottery Barn, the Gap, Sundance, and Restoration Hardware.

Westlake Center (✉ 1601 5th Ave., ☎ 206/467–1600), in downtown Seattle, has 80 upscale shops and covered walkways to Seattle's two major department stores, Nordstrom and the Bon Marché.

Specialty Shops

Antiques

Antique Importers (✉ Alaskan Way between Columbia and Yesler, ☎ 206/628–8905), a large warehouselike structure, carries mostly English oak and Victorian pine antiques.

Art Galleries

Foster/White Gallery (✉ 311 Occidental Ave. S, ☎ 206/622–2833) represents many Pacific Northwest painters and sculptors, as well as glass artists of the Pilchuck School, which is outside Seattle. **Frank & Dunya** (✉ 3418 Fremont Ave. N, ☎ 206/547–6760) carries unique art pieces, from furniture to jewelry. The **Glass House** (✉ 311 Occidental Ave. S, ☎ 206/682–9939) has one of the largest displays of glass artwork in the city. **Stonington Gallery** (✉ 2030 1st Ave., ☎ 206/405–4040) specializes in contemporary Native American and other Pacific Northwest works.

Books

The University District is home to a large concentration of general-interest stores. Elsewhere in the city, **Arundel Books** (✉ 944 3rd Ave., ☎ 206/624–4442), across from the Seattle Art Museum, carries used art and architecture titles. **Bailey/Coy Books** (✉ 414 Broadway, ☎ 206/323–8842), on Capitol Hill, stocks contemporary and classic fiction and nonfiction and has a magazine section. **Bowie and Company** (✉

314 1st Ave. S, ☎ 206/624–4100) sells antiquarian books and **David Ishii Books** (✉ 212 1st Ave. S, ☎ 206/622–4719) specializes in books on baseball and fly-fishing.

Elliott Bay Book Company (✉ 101 S. Main St., ☎ 206/624–6600), a mammoth general independent bookstore in Pioneer Square, hosts lectures and readings by local and international authors. **Flora and Fauna Books** (✉ 121 1st Ave. S, ☎ 206/623–4727) offers nature-oriented titles. The specialties at **Left Bank Books** (✉ 92 Pike St., ☎ 206/622–0195) include progressive politics, gender issues, and poetry. **M. Coy Books** (✉ 117 Pine St., ☎ 206/623–5354), in the heart of downtown, carries a large selection of contemporary literature and has a small espresso bar.

The **Mountaineers Bookstore** (✉ 300 3rd Ave. W, ☎ 206/284–6310) sells expert guides to the great outdoors. **Peter Miller** (✉ 1930 1st Ave., ☎ 206/441–4114) stocks excellent new architecture and design books. **Seattle Mystery Bookshop** (✉ 117 Cherry St., ☎ 206/587–5737) straddles downtown and Pioneer Square. The large Capitol Hill location of **Twice Sold Tales** (✉ 905 E. John St., ☎ 206/324–2421) is open 24 hours on Friday and Saturday for restless sleepers.

University of Washington Bookstore (✉ 4326 University Way NE, ☎ 206/634–3403), which carries textbooks and general-interest titles, is one of Seattle's best bookshops. **Wide World Books and Maps** (✉ 1911 N. 45th St., ☎ 206/634–3453), north of downtown in the Wallingford neighborhood, carries travel books and maps.

Barnes & Noble (✉ 2700 Northeast University Village, ☎ 206/517–4107; ✉ 626 106th Ave. NE, Bellevue, ☎ 425/451–8463) has 11 stores in Seattle and environs. **Borders Books & Music** (✉ 1501 4th Ave., ☎ 206/622–4599; ✉ 16549 Northeast 74th St., Redmond, ☎ 425/869–1907; ✉ 17501 Southcenter Pkwy., Suite 200, Tukwila, ☎ 206/575–4506) is also conveniently located throughout the area. **Tower Books** (✉ 20 Mercer St., ☎ 206/283–6333) is another large chain store.

Clothing

Baby and Co. (✉ 1936 1st Ave., ☎ 206/448–4077) sells contemporary fashions and accessories for women. **Butch Blum** (✉ 1408 5th Ave., ☎ 206/622–5760) carries contemporary menswear. **C. C. Filson** (✉ 2700 4th Ave. S, ☎ 206/622–3147) is a renowned outdoor outfitter. **Ebbets Field Flannels** (✉ 406 Occidental Ave. S, ☎ 206/623–0724) specializes in replicas of vintage athletic apparel. **Helen's Of Course** (✉ 1302 5th Ave., ☎ 206/624–4000) stocks classic fashions for women.

Isadora's Antique Clothing (✉ 1915 1st Ave., ☎ 206/441–7711) specializes in women's antique clothing and jewelry. **Local Brilliance** (✉ 1535 1st Ave., ☎ 206/343–5864) is a showcase for fashions from local designers. **Opus 204** (✉ 2004 1st Ave., ☎ 206/728–7707) carries its own private label of clothing constructed from fabrics chosen for their longevity and ease of care, as well as their unique look. **Passport** (✉ 112 Pine St., ☎ 206/628–9799) specializes in natural fiber clothing. **Rudy's Vintage Clothing** (✉ 1424 1st Ave., ☎ 206/682–6586) stocks vintage men's and women's clothing and antiques.

Crafts

Dusty Strings (✉ 3406 Fremont Ave. N, ☎ 206/634–1656) is the place to pick up hammered dulcimers. **Hands of the World** (✉ 1501 Pike Pl., ☎ 206/622–1696) carries textiles, jewelry, and art from around the world. **Ragazzi's Flying Shuttle** (✉ 607 1st Ave., ☎ 206/343–9762) displays handcrafted jewelry, whimsical folk art, and hand-knit items.

Gifts

At **Armadillo & Co.** (✉ 3510 Fremont Pl. N, ☎ 206/633–4241), you'll find jewelry, T-shirts, and other armadillo-theme accessories and gifts. **Ruby Montana's Pinto Pony** (✉ 1623 2nd Ave., ☎ 206/443–9363) is kitsch heaven. You'll find furniture, housewares, T-shirts, books, and other postmodern accessories here.

Jewelry

Fireworks Gallery (✉ 210 1st Ave. S, ☎ 206/682–8707; ✉ 400 Pine St., ☎ 206/682–6462) sells handmade gifts.

Newspapers and Magazines

Read All About It (✉ 93 Pike Pl., ☎ 206/624–0140) serves downtown. **Steve's Broadway News** (✉ 204 Broadway E, ☎ 206/324–7323) covers Capitol Hill. **Steve's Fremont News** (✉ 3416 Fremont Ave. N, ☎ 206/633–0731) is north of the bridge in Fremont Center.

Outdoor Wear and Equipment

Recreational Equipment, Inc. (✉ 222 Yale Ave. N, ☎ 206/223–1944)—which everybody calls REI—has Seattle's most comprehensive selection of gear for the great outdoors at its state-of-the-art downtown facility. The nearly 80,000-square-ft store contains a mountain-bike test trail, a simulated rain booth for testing outerwear, and the REI Pinnacle, an enormous freestanding indoor climbing structure. It's unbelievable, but there's room left over for a wildlife art gallery, a café, and a 250-seat meeting room for how-to clinics.

Toys

Archie McPhee (✉ 3510 Stone Way N, ☎ 206/545–8344), Seattle's self-proclaimed "outfitters of popular culture," specializes in bizarre toys and novelties. **Magic Mouse Toys** (✉ 603 1st Ave., ☎ 206/682–8097) has two floors of toys, from small windups to giant stuffed animals.

Wine

Delaurenti Wine Shop (✉ 1435 1st Ave., ☎ 206/622–0141) has a knowledgeable staff and a large selection of Pacific Northwest Italian–style wines. **Pike & Western Wine Merchants** (✉ Pike Pl. and Virginia St., ☎ 206/441–1307 or 206/441–1308) carries Pacific Northwest wines from small wineries.

SEATTLE A TO Z

Arriving and Departing

By Bus

Greyhound Lines (☎ 800/231–2222 or 206/628–5526) serves Seattle at 8th Avenue and Stewart Street.

By Car

Seattle is accessible by I–5 and Highway 99 from Vancouver (three hours north) and Portland (three hours south), and by I–90 from Spokane (six hours east).

By Plane

Among the carriers serving **Seattle–Tacoma International Airport** (☎ 206/431–4444), also known as Sea-Tac, are Air Canada, Alaska, America West, American, British Airways, Continental, Delta, EVA Airways, Hawaiian, Horizon, Japan, Northwest, Southwest, Thai, TWA, United, United Express, and US Airways. *See* Air Travel *in* Smart Travel Tips A to Z for airline phone numbers.

Between the Airport and the City: Sea-Tac is about 15 mi south of downtown on I–5; a taxi costs about $30. **Gray Line Airport Express** (☎ 206/626–6088) service to downtown hotels costs $7.50. **Shuttle Express** (☎ 206/622–1424; 800/487–7433 in WA only) has 24-hour door-to-door service from $18 to $25, depending on the location of your pickup. **Metro Transit** (☎ 206/553–3000) city buses (Express Tunnel Bus 194 and regular Buses 174 and 184) pick up passengers outside the baggage claim areas.

By Train

Amtrak (☎ 800/872–7245) trains serve Seattle from the north, south, and east. The *Mt. Baker International* operates between Seattle and Vancouver, there is daily service between Portland and Seattle, the *Empire Builder* comes into Seattle from Chicago, and the *Coast Starlight* heads north from Los Angeles. All the trains stop at **King Street Station** (✉ 303 S. Jackson St., ☎ 206/382–4125). In 1999, Amtrak began its *Cascades* high-speed train service between Vancouver, British Columbia, and Eugene, Oregon, with stops in Seattle.

Getting Around

By Bus and Streetcar

Metropolitan Transit (✉ 821 2nd Ave., ☎ 206/553–3000) is convenient, inexpensive, and fairly comprehensive. For questions about specific destinations, call the Automated Schedule Line (206/287–8463). Most buses run until around midnight or 1 AM; some run all night. Most buses are wheelchair accessible. The visitor center at the Washington State Convention and Trade Center has maps and schedules.

Between 6 AM and 7 PM, all public transportation is free within the **Metro Bus Ride Free Area,** bounded by Battery Street to the north, 6th Avenue to the east (and over to 9th Avenue near the convention center), South Jackson Street to the south, and the waterfront to the west; you'll pay as you disembark if you ride out of this area. At other times (or in other places), fares range $1–$1.75, depending on how far you travel and at what time of day. Onboard fare collection boxes have prices posted on them. On weekends and holidays you can purchase a **Day Pass** from bus drivers for $1.70, a bargain if you're doing a lot of touring.

The **Waterfront Streetcar** line of vintage 1920s-era Australian trolleys runs south along Alaska Way from Pier 70, past the Washington State Ferries terminal at Piers 50 and 52, turning inland on Main Street, and passing through Pioneer Square before ending in the International District. It runs at about 20-minute intervals daily 7 AM to 9 or 10 PM (less often and for fewer hours in the winter). The fare is $1. The stations and streetcars are wheelchair accessible.

By Car

Parking downtown is scarce and expensive. Metered parking is free after 6 PM and on Sunday. Be vigilant during the day. Parking enforcement officers are notoriously efficient.

If you plan to be downtown longer than two hours (the maximum parking time allowed on the street), you may find parking in a garage easier. The Bon Marché garage (entrance on 3rd Avenue between Stewart and Pine streets) is centrally located. Many downtown retailers participate in the Easy Streets discount parking program. Tokens are good for $1 off parking in selected locations, and you receive more substantial reductions at the Shopper's Quick Park garages at 2nd Avenue and Union Street and at Rainier Square on Union Street between 4th and 5th avenues.

Right turns are allowed on most red lights after you've come to a full stop, and left turns are allowed on adjoining one-way streets.

By Ferry

Washington State Ferries (☎ 206/464–6400; 800/843–3779 in WA only) serves the Puget Sound and San Juan Islands area. For more information about the ferry system, *see* Ferry Travel *in* Smart Travel Tips A to Z.

By Monorail

The **Seattle Center Monorail** (☎ 206/441–6038), built for the 1962 World's Fair, shuttles between its terminals in Westlake Center and the Seattle Center daily weekdays 7:30 AM–11 PM, and weekends 9 AM–11 PM; the trip takes less than three minutes. The adult fare is $1.25.

By Taxi

It's difficult but not impossible to flag a taxi on the street, though it's usually easier to call for a ride. **Orange Cab** (☎ 206/522–8800) is Seattle's friendliest company. **Graytop Cab** (☎ 206/282–8222) is the oldest. Taxis are readily available at most downtown hotels, and the stand at the **Westin Hotel** (⊠ 1900 5th Ave., ☎ 206/728–1000) is generally attended all night.

Contacts and Resources

B&B Reservation Agencies
Bed & Breakfast Association of Seattle (☎ 206/547–1020).

Car Rental
Most major rental agencies have offices downtown as well as at Sea-Tac Airport, including **Avis** (⊠ 1919 5th Ave., ☎ 800/831–2847), **Enterprise** (⊠ 2116 Westlake Ave., ☎ 800/736–8222), **Hertz** (⊠ 722 Pike St., ☎ 800/654–3131), and **National** (⊠ 1942 Westlake Ave. N, ☎ 206/448–7368).

Consulates
Canadian Consulate (⊠ Plaza 600 Bldg., 6th Ave. and Stewart St., 4th floor, ☎ 206/443–1777). **U.K. Consulate** (⊠ First Interstate Center, 999 3rd Ave., Suite 820, ☎ 206/622–9255).

Emergencies
Ambulance (☎ 911). **Fire** (☎ 911). **Police** (☎ 911).

Doctors, Inc. (⊠ 1215 4th Ave., ☎ 206/622–9933) gives referrals of physicians and dentists in the Seattle area.

Guided Tours
Three companies offer orientation tours of Seattle. The price of most tours is between $18 and $29, depending on the tour's length and mode of transportation. Custom packages cost more.

Gray Line of Seattle (☎ 206/626–5208 or 800/426–7505) operates bus and boat tours, including a six-hour Grand City Tour ($33) that includes many sights, lunch in Pike Place Market, and admission to the Space Needle observation deck. **Show Me Seattle** (☎ 206/633–2489) surveys the major Seattle sights and also operates a tour that takes in the *Sleepless in Seattle* floating home, the Fremont Troll, and other offbeat stops. **Seattle Tours** (☎ 206/768–1234) conducts tours in customized vans. The tours cover about 50 mi with stops for picture-taking.

BALLOON

Over the Rainbow (☎ 206/364–0995) operates balloon tours in Woodinville in the spring and summer, weather permitting. They cost between $135 and $165.

BICYCLING

Terrene Tours (☎ 206/325–5569) operates day and overnight bicycling and other tours of Seattle, the wine country surrounding the city, and points farther afield. The prices vary, depending on the destination and length of the tour.

BOAT

Argosy Cruises (☎ 206/623–4252) sail around Elliott Bay (one hour, from Pier 55, $13.40), the Ballard Locks (2½ hours, from Pier 57, $21.70), and other area waterways. **Pier 54 Adventures** (☎ 206/623–6364) arranges speedboat rides, and sailboat excursions on Elliott Bay. Salmon-fishing packages are also available; rates vary.

CARRIAGE

Sealth Horse Carriages (☎ 425/277–8282) offers narrated tours ($60 per hour) that trot away from the waterfront and Westlake Center.

PLANE

Galvin Flying Service (☎ 206/763–9706) departs from Boeing Field in southern Seattle on excursions over downtown, Vashon and Bainbridge Islands, and Snoqualmie Falls. Prices begin at $89 ($10 for a second person). **Seattle Seaplanes** (☎ 800/637–5553) operates a 20-minute scenic flight that takes in views of the Woodland Park Zoo, downtown Seattle, and the Microsoft "campus." Custom tours are also available. Prices begin at $42.50. **Sound Flight** (☎ 425/255–6500) runs a 30-minute scenic flight for $79, custom sightseeing packages, and flights to secluded fishing spots.

SAILING

Let's Go Sailing (☎ 206/624–3931) permits passengers to take the helm, trim the sails, or simply enjoy the ride aboard the *Obsession,* a 70-ft ocean racer. Three 1½-hour excursions ($22) depart daily from Pier 56. A 2½-hour sunset cruise ($38) is also available. Passengers can bring their own food on board. Private charters can also be arranged.

TRAIN

The *Spirit of Washington* **Dinner Train** (☎ 800/876–7245) departs from Renton for a three-hour trip ($47–$69) along the eastern shores of Lake Washington up to the Columbia Winery in Woodinville. Sights include the Boeing Renton Plant, the Wilburton Trestle, and the Sammamish River valley.

WALKING

Chinatown Discovery Tours (☎ 206/236–0657) include four culinary excursions—from a light sampler to an eight-course banquet. The rates run between $9.95 and $34.95, based on a minimum of four participants.

Seattle Walking Tours (☎ 425/885–3173) through the city's historic areas, which give special attention to Pioneer Square, cost $15.

Underground Seattle (☎ 206/682–4646) tours ($6.50) of the now-buried original storefronts and sidewalks of Pioneer Square are extremely popular. They offer an effective primer on early Seattle history, and it may be a good place to take cover if your aboveground tour starts to get soggy.

Late-Night Pharmacies

Bartell Drugs (✉ 600 1st Ave. N, at Mercer St., ☎ 206/284–1353) is a 24-hour pharmacy.

Travel Agencies

AAA Travel (✉ 330 6th Ave. N, ☎ 206/448–5353). **American Express Travel Office** (✉ 600 Stewart St., ☎ 206/441–8622). **Doug Fox Travel** (✉ 1321 4th Ave., ☎ 206/628–6171).

Visitor Information

Seattle/King County Convention and Visitors Bureau (✉ 520 Pike St., Suite 1300, 98101, ☎ 206/461–5800). **Seattle Visitor Center** (✉ 800 Convention Pl., ☎ 206/461–5840). **Washington State Convention & Trade Center** (✉ 800 Convention Pl., ☎ 206/447–5000). **Washington Tourism Development Division** (✉ Box 42500, Olympia, WA 98504, ☎ 360/753–5600).

5 WASHINGTON

Long before outdoor adventures became popular in the rest of the country, they were a way of life for Washington residents, but the yearning to join with the mighty and majestic forces of nature has ever been tempered by an appreciation for the civilized aspects of life. Washington is thus a place where people not only search out raw nature in the wilderness but celebrate its presence in the city.

Revised by
John Doerper

WASHINGTON'S NATURAL ATTRACTIONS, its saltwater sounds and alpine peaks, its windswept beaches and purling rivers, its majestic canyons and rolling hills, are never far from the city. On the coast, the sandy strands and calm bays of the southern shore contrast with the rugged sea cliffs of the Olympic Peninsula. The tall trees of coastal rain forests and the moist slopes of the western Cascade Mountains are robed in moss and bedecked with ferns; the music of waterfalls and songbirds enlivens the deepest woods. East of the Cascades, mighty rivers flow through steep-walled coulees, below grasslands and wheat fields where the cries of eagles and curlews drift above the wildflowers and sagebrush. Here ponds and lakes attract vast flocks of ducks, geese, and sandpipers; sandhill cranes stalk through irrigated fields bordering dry steppe.

The Salish Sea, a much-branched saltwater inlet, meanders far inland, south to the state capital of Olympia and north to the Canadian waters of the Inland Passage. Large cities and busy ports—Seattle, Bellingham, Tacoma, and Everett—border these inland waters. The islands of southern Puget Sound, the Kitsap Peninsula, the central lowlands, and the San Juan archipelago divide the Salish Sea into many inlets and tidal passages, whose labyrinthine shores today harbor small villages with sheltered moorage for pleasure boats. Mount Rainier, the Olympic Mountains, Mount Baker, and the jagged peaks of the North Cascades tower above the waters. In spring and early summer, flowering plums and cherries, dogwoods, rhododendrons, azaleas, and peonies light up the sea-green landscape with the bright colors of an impressionist palette.

The North Cascades put on the region's most spectacular display of wildflowers in spring and summer; in winter, with the highest snowfalls in North America, they attract skiers to slopes from Mount Baker in the north to White Pass in the south. Winthrop, Leavenworth, and the other small, friendly towns of the glaciated valleys east of the mountains are popular with cross-country skiers. Two mighty rivers, the Columbia and the Snake, flow through the arid steppes of the Columbia Plateau, greening a patchwork quilt of irrigated fields and fruit orchards. Along the way their flow is interrupted by many dams, of which Grand Coulee Dam is the mightiest. The warm beaches of Lake Chelan, a deep inland fjord, draw Seattleites pining for the sun. Bathed in constant radiance, vegetables and fruits thrive in the deep, fertile soils of the Yakima and Walla Walla valleys, beneath slopes covered with vineyards. Vast fields of wheat and barley gild the flanks of the Palouse and Horse Heaven Hills. Spokane, Washington's second-largest city, rules as the "Capital of the Inland Empire," a mountainous region of pastures and forests, as well as gold and silver mines.

Pleasures and Pastimes

Boating

The saltwater bays, channels, and inlets of the Salish Sea, as well as Washington's rivers and inland lakes, make boating the state's most popular sport. The coastal waterways are rated among the best in the world for sea kayaking, an appealing way to explore the scenic shores. But keep in mind that this is not one of the world's best regions for sailing—especially in summer, when strong tidal currents counteract the season's limp winds. For charters and outfitters, *see* the Outdoor Activities and Sports sections within each town or area's listings.

Washington

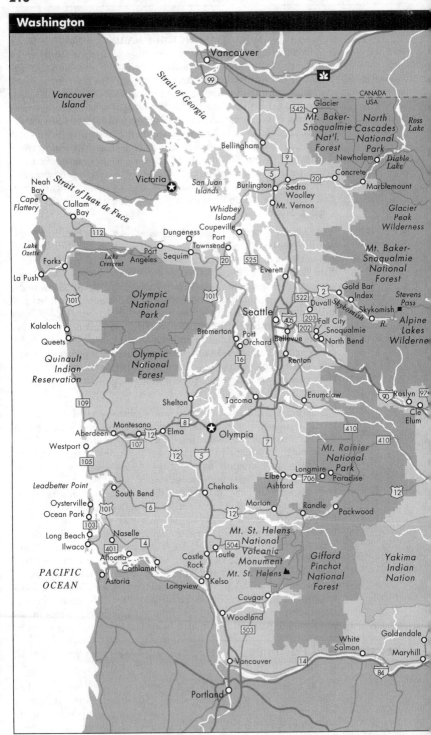

Vancouver Island

Strait of Georgia

Vancouver

99

CANADA
USA

542

Glacier

Mt. Baker-Snoqualmie Nat'l. Forest

North Cascades National Park

Ross Lake

Bellingham

9

5

Newhalem

Diablo Lake

Concrete

20

Marblemount

Neah Bay

Strait of Juan de Fuca

Cape Flattery

Clallam Bay

Victoria

San Juan Islands

Burlington

Sedro Woolley

Mt. Vernon

Glacier Peak Wilderness

112

Lake Ozette

Lake Crescent

Whidbey Island

Coupeville

Port Townsend

20

525

Dungeness

Port Angeles

Sequim

Mt. Baker-Snoqualmie National Forest

Forks

101

Everett

Gold Bar

Index

2

Stevens Pass

La Push

Olympic National Park

101

Seattle

522

Duvall

Skykomish

Skykomish

R.

Alpine Lakes Wilderne

Kalaloch

Queets

405

203

Fall City

202

Snoqualmie

North Bend

Bremerton

Port Orchard

Bellevue

Quinault Indian Reservation

Olympic National Forest

Renton

16

109

Shelton

Tacoma

Enumclaw

Roslyn

97

90

Cle Elum

Montesano

Elma

12

410

Aberdeen

107

8

Olympia

410

Westport

105

12

5

7

Mt. Rainier National Park

Leadbetter Point

South Bend

6

Chehalis

Elbe

Ashford

Longmire

706

Paradise

12

Oysterville

Ocean Park

101

Morton

Randle

Packwood

103

12

Long Beach

Naselle

Ilwaco

401

4

Castle Rock

Toutle

504

Mt. St. Helens National Volcanic Monument

Gifford Pinchot National Forest

Yakima Indian Nation

Attoona

Cathlamet

Mt. St. Helens

PACIFIC OCEAN

Astoria

Longview

Kelso

Cougar

Woodland

503

White Salmon

Goldendale

Maryhill

Vancouver

14

84

Portland

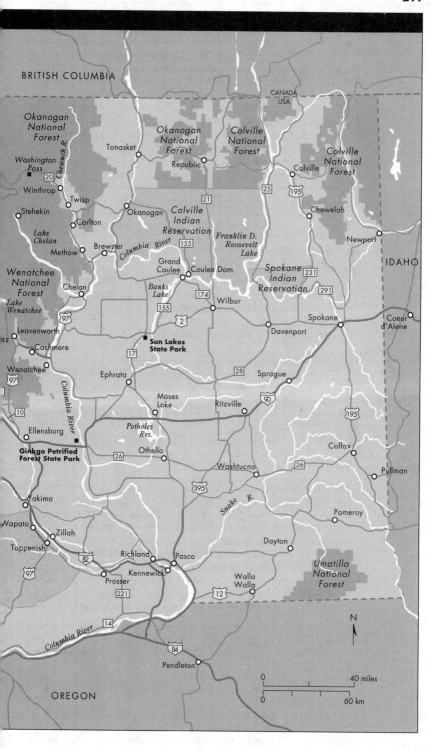

BRITISH COLUMBIA

CANADA
USA

Okanogan National Forest

Washington Pass ■

20

Winthrop

Twisp

Stehekin

Carlton

Methow

Brewster

Tonasket

Okanogan

Okanogan National Forest

Republic

21

Colville National Forest

25

195

Colville

Colville National Forest

Chewelah

Newport

IDAHO

Colville Indian Reservation

155

Franklin D. Roosevelt Lake

Spokane Indian Reservation

231

291

Grand Coulee

Coulee Dam

Banks Lake

174

Wilbur

Davenport

Spokane

Coeur d'Alene

Lake Chelan

Wenatchee National Forest

Chelan

Lake Wenatchee

97

155

2

■ **Sun Lakes State Park**

Leavenworth

Cashmere

Wenatchee

97

17

Ephrata

28

Sprague

90

195

10

Ellensburg

Ginkgo Petrified Forest State Park

26

Othello

Potholes Res.

Moses Lake

Ritzville

Washtucna

26

Colfax

Pullman

Columbia River

395

Snake R.

Pomeroy

Yakima

Wapato

Zillah

Toppenish

82

97

Richland

Prosser

221

Kennewick

Pasco

Dayton

Walla Walla

12

Umatilla National Forest

14

Columbia River

84

Pendleton

OREGON

N

0   40 miles

0   60 km

Dining

Washington's abundant seafood shows up on menus throughout the state, and spicy yet subtle flavorings testify to the strong Asian influences on local cooking. Tender halibut, sweet Dungeness crab, plump oysters, and delicate mussels are as popular as the ubiquitous salmon. Moist coastal forests are rich in wild mushrooms, and the inland valleys are famed for their beef and lamb, as well as for their wines. Almost every region of the state grows great vegetables, berries, and apples. In autumn, the mountains produce a bountiful harvest of wild berries. This bounty translates, in the hands of the state's many skilled chefs, into some of the finest cuisine in the West.

CATEGORY	COST*
$$$$	over $35
$$$	$25–$35
$$	$15–$25
$	under $15

per person for a three-course meal, excluding drinks, service, and sales tax (about 8.1%, varies slightly by community)

Lodging

First-rate hotels and moderately priced lodgings can be found throughout the state. Most of Washington's small inns make up with the breathtaking beauty of their surroundings for any lack of long history. They're often equipped with hot tubs and in-room fireplaces that take the edge off the crisp coastal or wintry inland air.

CATEGORY	COST*
$$$$	over $170
$$$	$110–$170
$$	$60–$110
$	under $60

All prices are for a standard double room, excluding 14.1% combined hotel and state sales tax.

Exploring Washington

The Cascade Range divides Washington into a western and an eastern half, which differ considerably in climate and topography. Western ecosystems vary from tidewater to moist forests; eastern ecosystems range from pine woods to dry grass-and-brush steppes, from deep river valleys to lakes and marshes. Curiously, the hot-summer "dry" east side has more wetlands and marshes than the cool-summer "wet" west side of the state. Both sections have alpine fells, which on the eastside have two timberlines: one on the upper slopes (where forests are restricted by the heavy snows and frosts of an alpine climate); another on the lower slopes (where tree growth is limited by lack of moisture).

Numbers in the text correspond to numbers in the margin and on the Puget Sound, Tacoma, Olympic Peninsula, Long Beach Peninsula, San Juan Islands, Whatcom and Skagit Counties, and Crossing the Cascades maps.

Great Itineraries

IF YOU HAVE 4 DAYS

In four days, you can tour the northern section of the Olympic Peninsula, visit one of the coastal islands, and roam through a bit of the Cascade Range. **Port Townsend** ㉔ is an ideal base for exploring the **Olympic Peninsula**'s crowning jewel—**Hurricane Ridge** ㉓. Depart for the **San Juan Islands** the next day. Take the ferry to **Whidbey Island** ①, where you can have lunch in Coupeville and visit **Deception Pass State**

Park on the way up to **Anacortes,** on **Fidalgo Island** ②, the point of departure for the three largest San Juan Islands. Choose between ☷ **Orcas Island** ④ and ☷ **San Juan Island** ⑤; for either you'll need two full days to experience the beauty of the scenery. On the fourth day, head back to the mainland early and, from Anacortes, via Everett and U.S. 2, take a loop through the North Cascades, with their towering peaks, alpine meadows, and walking trails. Plan to have lunch in **Leavenworth** ㉝ and return to Seattle across **Snoqualmie** ㉚ summit via U.S. 97 and I–90 (you could stop in **Cle Elum** for dinner—from here it's less than two hours of leisurely driving back to Seattle).

IF YOU HAVE 10 DAYS

From Seattle, drive south on I–5 to ☷ **Tacoma** ⑪–⑱ and explore downtown and Point Defiance Park. Your exact itinerary will depend on when you leave Seattle, but give yourself two or three extra hours to continue south and visit the Capitol Campus in **Olympia** ⑲—you can have dinner in Olympia and spend the night here, or you could plan ahead and reserve lodging near ☷ **Mount Rainier.** Spend much of day two exploring the mountain, and then head west on U.S. 12 to **Grays Harbor,** at the foot of the **Olympic Peninsula.** As you drive west toward the Pacific Ocean, pause along the northern shore of Grays Harbor to watch the many shorebirds. Stay in the seaside town of ☷ **Copalis Beach** or in ☷ **Moclips.** On the third day, drive up U.S. 101 through the old-growth forests of **Olympic National Park** (hiking to the beaches takes extra time; most are not accessible by car). Spend some time walking beneath the enormous, and incredibly tall, moss-covered trees and plants in the rain forest on either the Hoh or Quinault Indian Reservation. Stay overnight in ☷ **Port Angeles** ㉒, to be near your day-four destination: 5,200-ft-high **Hurricane Ridge** ㉓. The ridge, part of the Olympic Range, has unparalleled views into the heart of the national park. In the late afternoon, head to ☷ **Port Townsend** ㉔. Explore the waterfront shops, dine, and spend the night (reservations are essential here). The next morning, explore Fort Worden State Park before taking the ferry for **Whidbey Island** ①. When you get to Whidbey, ignore the direction signs and turn left (instead of right). Explore Fort Casey and the old Admiralty Head lighthouse, before continuing to **Ebey's Landing National Historic Reserve,** and ☷ **Coupeville,** where you can shop, eat, and spend the night. On the morning of day six, head up to Anacortes and catch the ferry to the San Juan Islands, where you'll stay for two days. Choose between quiet ☷ **Orcas Island** ④ and the more compact and lively village of Friday Harbor, on ☷ **San Juan Island** ⑤, for your base of operations. Interisland day trips (without taking your car) are easy. On the seventh day head north from Anacortes to ☷ **Bellingham** ⑥ via scenic Chuckanut Drive (WA 11). Explore the historic Fairhaven neighborhood in south Bellingham and drive to nearby **Mount Baker** ⑦ for the next day and a half. Bellingham is the gateway to the North Cascades Range, which you can sample on day nine. A scenic highway (WA 542) starts on I–5 in north Bellingham and winds east to the mountains (no outlet for the last 30-plus mi). Dine and stay the night in ☷ **Glacier,** below **Mount Baker** ⑦. Return to Seattle via Highways 9, 20, and I–5.

When to Tour Washington

Summer is the best time for hiking mountain trails and enjoying coastal beaches. Skies are often clear and the temperatures mild; July and August can be outright hot. Spring is often overcast or even wet, but it is the time to catch the tulips in the Skagit Valley. Leavenworth and other mountain towns can be as busy in summer with hikers as they are with skiers in winter. On the coast, some inns and restaurants are closed from late fall through winter into spring (call ahead). But Washington's cities stay lively year-round; in Seattle and Spokane winter is the height of the entertainment, theater, opera, and concert seasons.

BAINBRIDGE ISLAND

From the Seattle waterfront take the half-hour ride on the **Bainbridge Island ferry** (☞ *below*) for great views of the city skyline and the surrounding hills. The ferry trip itself lures most of the island's visitors—this is the least expensive way to cruise Puget Sound—along with Bainbridge's small-town atmosphere and scenic countryside. From the Bainbridge Island terminal, continue north up a short hill on Olympic Drive to Winslow Way. If you turn west (left), you'll find yourself in **Winslow,** where there are several blocks of antiques shops, clothing boutiques, galleries, bookstores, and restaurants.

Pass the Winslow Way turnoff and head about ¼ mi farther north on Olympic to the **Bainbridge Island Vineyard and Winery** (⊠ 682 Hwy. 305, ☎ 206/842–9463), which is open for tastings and tours Wednesday–Sunday noon–5.

★ You'll need a car to get to the **Bloedel Reserve,** whose grounds, the 150-acre estate of Prentice and Virginia Bloedel, contain a Japanese garden, a bird refuge, a moss garden, and a number of other "garden rooms" designed to blend man-made gardens into the natural, untamed look of the island's native (second-growth) vegetation. Within the park are ponds with ducks and trumpeter swans, Bloedel's French Renaissance–style grand mansion, and 2 mi of trails. Dazzling displays of rhododendrons and azaleas bloom in spring, and the leaves of Japanese maples and other trees colorfully signal the arrival of autumn. Reservations are essential, and picnicking is not permitted. No pets are allowed. ⊠ *7571 N.E. Dolphin Dr. (from ferry follow signs on Hwy. 305),* ☎ *206/842–7631.* ⊡ *$6.* ⊘ *Wed.–Sun. 10–4.*

Bainbridge Island Essentials

Getting Around
The **Bainbridge Island ferry** (☎ 206/464–6400), which takes cars and walk-on passengers, leaves Seattle and Bainbridge every 20 minutes during the day from Pier 52 (Colman Dock), south of the Pike Place Market, and stops at Winslow. Highway 305 is the main road through the island.

Visitor Information
The **Bainbridge Island Chamber of Commerce** (⊠ 590 Winslow Way, ☎ 206/842–3700), two blocks from the ferry dock, has maps and tourist information.

WHIDBEY ISLAND AND FIDALGO ISLAND

On a nice day a pleasant excursion from Seattle is a ferry trip across Possession Sound to **Whidbey Island,** 30 mi northwest of Seattle. It's a great way to watch seagulls, terns, sailboats, and the occasional orca or bald eagle—not to mention the surrounding scenery, which takes in Camano Island and the North Cascades. When the weather is blustery, travelers can stay snug inside the ferry, have a snack, and listen to folk musicians. Some passengers are commuters who work in Everett and live on south Whidbey.

From the air, Whidbey Island looks like a languid dragon, with Fidalgo Island to the north as its head. The island is a blend of low pastoral

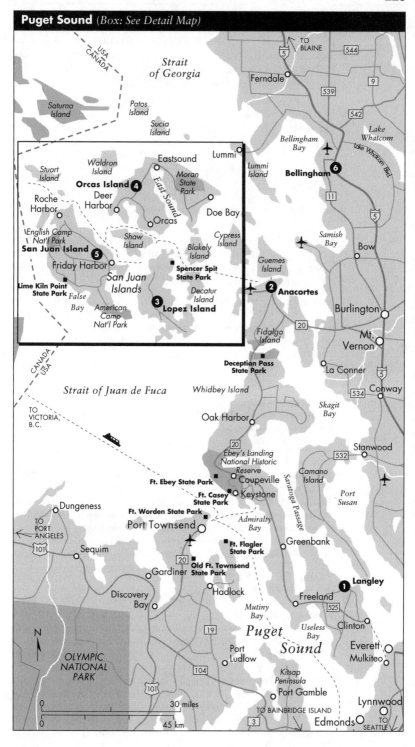

hills, evergreen and oak forests, wildflower meadows (some species thriving here do not occur on the mainland), sandy beaches, and dramatic (though unstable) bluffs. It's a great place for taking slow drives or bicycle rides down country lanes, for viewing sunsets over the water, and for boating or kayaking along the protected shorelines of Saratoga Passage, Holmes Harbor, Penn Cove, and Skagit Bay.

The best beaches are on the west side, where wooded and wildflower-bedecked bluffs drop steeply to sand or surf (which can cover the beaches at high tide and can be unexpectedly rough on this exposed shore). Both beaches and bluffs have great views of the shipping lanes and the Olympic Mountains. If you're lucky, a big freighter or aircraft carrier will cruise by. **Maxwelton Beach** (⊠ Maxwelton Beach Rd.) is popular with the locals. **Possession Point** (⊠ Off Cultus Bay Rd.) includes a park, a beach, and a boat launch. Fort Ebey in Coupeville has a sandy spread, and West Beach is a stormy patch north of the fort with mounds of driftwood.

Whidbey is easily accessible via the Washington State Ferry from Mukilteo (pronounced "Muck-ill-*tee*-oh") to Clinton on the southern part of the island. Or you can drive across from the mainland on Highway 20 at the northern end of the island.

Sixty miles long and 8 mi wide, Whidbey is the second-longest island in the contiguous United States; only Long Island in New York stretches farther. The tour below begins at the island's southern tip, which has a mostly rural landscape of undulating hills, gentle beaches, and little coves.

Langley

❶ *From Seattle, take I–5 north 21 mi to Exit 189 (Whidbey Island–Mukilteo Ferry) and follow signs 7 mi to ferry landing; from Clinton (Whidbey Island ferry terminal), take Hwy. 525 north 2 mi to Langley Rd., turn right, and follow road 5 mi.*

The village of Langley rises above a 50-ft-high bluff overlooking Saratoga Passage, which separates Whidbey from Camano Island. A grassy terrace just above the beach is a great place for viewing birds on the water or in the air. On a clear day, you can see Mount Baker in the distance. Upscale boutiques selling art, glass, jewelry, and clothing line 1st and 2nd streets in the heart of town. The **South Whidbey Historical Museum** (⊠ 312 2nd St., ☎ 360/579–4696), open on weekends 1–4 in a former one-room schoolhouse, displays old Victrolas, farm tools, kitchen utensils, and antique toys. A donation is requested.

Dining and Lodging

$$$ ✕ **Country Kitchen.** Tables for two unobtrusively line the walls of this
★   intimate restaurant. On the other side of the fireplace is the "great table," which seats 10. The prix-fixe, five-course seasonal menu highlights local produce. Dinners might include locally gathered mussels in a black-bean sauce, breast of duck in a loganberry sauce, or rich Columbia River salmon. ⊠ *Inn at Langley, 400 1st St., ☎ 360/221–3033. Reservations essential. MC, V.*

$$ ✕ **Garibyan Brothers Café Langley.** Terra-cotta tile floors, antique oak tables, and the aroma of garlic, basil, and oregano set the mood at this Greek restaurant. The menu includes eggplant moussaka, Dungeness crab cakes, Mediterranean seafood stew, and lamb kabobs. Greek salads accompany all entrées. ⊠ *113 1st St., ☎ 360/221–3090. MC, V. Closed Tues. in winter. No lunch Tues.*

$$ ✕ **Star Bistro.** This slick 1980s-vintage bistro atop the Star Store serves Caesar salads, shrimp-and-scallop linguine, and gourmet burgers. Popular for lunch, it remains crowded well into the late afternoon. ⊠ *201½*

1st St., ☎ 360/221–2627. *Reservations not accepted. AE, MC, V. No dinner Mon.*

$ ✕ **Dog House Backdoor Restaurant.** Friendly and relaxed, this waterfront tavern and family restaurant, on the National Register of Historic Places, is filled with collectibles that include a 1923 nickelodeon. Juicy burgers, homemade chili, and vegetarian entrées are made from lowsalt recipes. The restaurant has a fine view of Saratoga Passage. ⊠ *230 1st St., ☎ 360/221–9996. Reservations not accepted. No credit cards.*

$$$$ ⊡ **Inn at Langley.** Langley's most elegant and comfortable inn, a con-
★ crete-and-wood Frank Lloyd Wright–inspired structure, perches on the side of a bluff that descends to the beach. The Asian-style guest rooms have dramatic views of the Saratoga Passage and the Cascade Range. All have whirlpool tubs, fireplaces, outdoor balconies, and TVs. Meals are served in the inn's restaurant, the Country Kitchen (☞ *above*). ⊠ *400 1st St., 98260, ☎ 360/221–3033. 24 rooms. Restaurant. MC, V.*

$–$$ ⊡ **Drake's Landing.** Langley's most affordable lodging has humble but clean rooms with quilts on the beds and fine views. It's at the edge of town, across the street from the harbor off 1st Street. ⊠ *203 Wharf St., 98260, ☎ 360/221–3999. 3 rooms. MC, V.*

Outdoor Activities and Sports

BICYCLING

In the Bayview area of Whidbey Island, off Highway 525 near Langley, the **Pedaler** (⊠ 5603½ S. Bayview Rd., ☎ 360/321–5040) rents bikes year-round.

BOATING AND FISHING

Langley's small **boat harbor** (☎ 360/221–6765) provides moorage for 35 boats, plus utilities and a 160-ft fishing pier, all protected by a timber-pile breakwater. You can catch sea perch, lingcod (a kind of greenling), sculpin, and perhaps a rockfish from the Langley pier. Supplies are available from the **Langley Marina** (⊠ 202 Wharf St., ☎ 360/221–1771).

Shopping

Childers/Proctor Gallery (⊠ 302 1st St., ☎ 360/221–2978) exhibits and sells paintings, jewelry, pottery, and sculpture. The **Cottage** stocks vintage and imported women's clothing (⊠ 210 1st St., ☎ 360/221–4747). You can meet glass and jewelry artist Gwenn Knight at her shop, the **Glass Knight** (⊠ 214 1st St., ☎ 360/221–6283). The **Museo Piccolo** (⊠ 215 1st St., ☎ 360/221–7737), a gallery and gift shop, carries contemporary art by recognized and emerging artists.

Outside Langley at the **Blackfish Studio** (⊠ 5075 S. Langley Rd., ☎ 360/221–1274), you can see works-in-progress and finished pieces by Kathleen Miller, who produces enamel jewelry and hand-painted clothing and accessories; and Donald Miller, whose photographs depict the land and people of the Northwest.

Freeland

7 mi north of Langley on Hwy. 525.

The sprawling, unincorporated village of Freeland is home to two parks. You'll find picnic spots and a sandy beach at **Freeland Park** on Holmes Harbor. **Bush Point Lighthouse** and the beach are the main attractions at **South Whidbey State Park,** which has hiking, camping, and swimming.

Lodging

$$$–$$$$ ⊡ **Cliff House.** A winding drive through the woods leads to this secluded three-story house overlooking Admiralty Inlet. The award-winning

architectural design is uncompromisingly modern; one side is nearly all glass and provides sweeping views. The comfortable, well-appointed rooms lie off a 30-ft-high atrium with a wood-burning fireplace. An adjacent cottage also has sea views. Guests in both buildings are pampered with fresh flowers, every modern amenity, and miles of driftwood beach. You'll have the house or cottage to yourself, since each is rented to only one couple at a time. ⊠ *5440 Windmill Rd., 98249,* ☎ *360/ 221–1566. 2 rooms. No credit cards.*

Greenbank

11 mi north of Freeland on Hwy. 525.

About halfway up Whidbey is the town of Greenbank, home to the 125-acre **Greenbank Farm Winery,** which Island County purchased in late 1997. The vineyard here produces a small portion of the loganberries used for production of the island's unique spirit, Whidbey's Liqueur (available at the gift shop). Picnic tables are scattered throughout the farm. ⊠ *657 Wonn Rd.,* ☎ *360/678–7700.* 🎟 *Free.* ☉ *Gift shop 10–5.*

The 53-acre **Meerkerk Rhododendron Gardens** contain 1,500 native and hybrid species of rhododendrons, numerous walking trails, and ponds. The flowers are in full bloom in April and May. ⊠ *Resort Rd.,* ☎ *360/678–1912.* 🎟 *$2.* ☉ *Daily 9–4.*

Lodging

$$$ 🏠 **Guest House Cottages.** The very private log cabins here, surrounded
★ by 25 forested acres, have feather beds, VCRs, whirlpool tubs, country antiques, and fireplaces. Fresh flowers, robes, and a fine Continental breakfast are among the other draws, along with an enormous two-story lodge filled with collectibles that include a working pump organ. ⊠ *835 E. Christianson Rd., 98253,* ☎ *360/678–3115. 6 units. Pool, exercise room. No credit cards.*

Coupeville

On the south shore of Penn Cove, 15 mi north of Greenbank, Hwy. 525 to Hwy. 20.

Restored Victorian houses grace many of the streets in quiet Coupeville, which has one of the largest national historic districts in Washington and often stands in for 19th-century New England villages in movies. Stores above the waterfront have maintained their second-story false fronts and old-fashioned character. Captain Thomas Coupe founded the town in 1852; his house, built in 1853, is one of the state's oldest. Other houses and commercial buildings were built in the late 1800s.

☾ The **Island County Historical Museum** has exhibits on the history of the island's fishing, timber, and agricultural industries and conducts tours and walks. The squared-timber blockhouse outside dates from the Puget Sound Indian War of 1855. ⊠ *908 N.W. Alexander St.,* ☎ *360/678–3310.* 🎟 *$2.* ☉ *May–Oct., daily 10–5; Nov.–Apr., Fri.–Mon. 11–4.*

☾ **Ebey's Landing National Historic Reserve** encompasses a sand and cobble beach, bluffs with dramatic views down the Strait of Juan de Fuca, two state parks, and several (privately held) pioneer farms homesteaded in the early 1850s. The reserve, the first and largest of its kind, holds nearly 100 nationally registered historic structures, most of them from the 19th century. A 22-acre beach area is the highlight of **Fort Ebey State Park,** which blazes with native rhododendrons in late May. The best view over Ebey's prairie can be had from the park's Sunnyside Cemetery. **Fort Casey State Park,** set on a bluff overlooking the Strait of Juan de Fuca and the Port Townsend ferry landing, was one of three forts

built in 1890 to protect the entrance to Admiralty Inlet. The park has
a small interpretive center in an 1890s lighthouse, old gun batteries, grassy
picnic sites, rocky fishing spots, and a boat launch. ⊠ *Fort Ebey State
Park: 2 mi west of Hwy. 20,* ☎ *360/678–4636.* ⊠ *Fort Casey State Park:
3 mi west of Hwy. 20,* ☎ *360/678–4519. Follow signs from Hwy. 20
to each park.* 🕮 *Day use free, campsites $11–$16.* ☉ 8 AM–dusk.

Dining and Lodging

$$–$$$ ✕ **Rosi's.** Deceptively simple-looking Rosi's is inside the Victorian
home of its chef-owners, who serve outstanding Italian and Pacific Northwest cuisine. Chicken mascarpone, osso buco, scallops pesto, prime
rib, and Penn Cove mussels are among the entrées. ⊠ *606 N. Main
St.,* ☎ *360/678–3989. AE, MC, V. No lunch.*

$$ ✕ **Christopher's.** The ambience is warm and casual at this eclectically
furnished restaurant whose tables are set with linens, fresh flowers, and
candles. The New American menu features local oysters and mussels,
and such standard fare as lamb stew and grilled ahi tuna—all prepared
with a light touch. The wine list here is extensive. ⊠ *23 Front St.,* ☎
360/678–5480. AE, MC, V.

🏨 **The Captain Whidbey Inn.** Almost a century old, this venerable
madrona lodge on a wooded promontory offers a special kind of hos-
pitality and charm now rarely found. The lodge rooms, furnished with
antiques, tend to be small, but they are well appointed with modern
amenities and those on the north side have splendid views of Penn Cove,
a lake-like saltwater inlet. Gracefully aged, surrounded by native
shrubs and trees, the Captain Whidbey is the perfect hideout for those
who wish to escape from the worry and stress of the modern age. The
cozy bar is the perfect place for relaxing on a stormy winter night. Ad-
ditional rooms in a separate modern motel building overlook a quiet
saltwater lagoon. ⊠ *2073 Captain Whidbey Inn Rd. (off Madrona Way),
98239,* ☎ *360/678–4097; 800/366–4097. 12 rooms in the lodge, 13
in the motel. Restaurant, bar, library. AE, MC, V,.*

$$ 🏨 **Fort Casey Inn.** The inn comprises nine Georgian Revival duplexes
built in 1907 to house U.S. Army artillery officers and their families.
Stationed here until the 1940s, the officers manned coastal batteries
designed to defend Puget Sound and the U.S. naval base at Bremerton
from possible attack by enemy navies. Their former quarters, a row
of houses split into two two-story units each, stand on a hillside overlooking the former parade grounds. Each duplex has a fireplace, two
bedrooms, a living room, and a full country kitchen (with breakfast
fixings on hand). Owners Gordon and Victoria Hoenig restored the
duplexes's tin ceilings and decorated the units with rag rugs, old quilts,
hand-painted furniture, and sundry Colonial touches. Children are welcome here. ⊠ *1124 S. Engle Rd., 98239,* ☎ *360/678–8792. 9 units.
Bicycles. AE, MC, V.*

Oak Harbor

10 mi north of Coupeville on Hwy. 20.

Oak Harbor gets its name from the majestic Oregon oaks that grow
above the bay. Dutch and Irish immigrants settled the town in the mid-
1800s; several windmills were recently built by descendants of the Dutch
as symbols of their heritage. Unfortunately, suburban sprawl has over-
taken Whidbey Island's largest city in the form of multiple strips of
fast-food restaurants and service stations.

★ ☉ **Deception Pass State Park,** the state's most popular, has 19 mi of rocky
shore and beaches, three freshwater lakes, and more than 38 mi of
forest and meadow trails. The park occupies the northernmost point
of Whidbey Island and the southernmost tip of Fidalgo Island, on

both sides of the Deception Pass Bridge. Park on Canoe Island and walk across the bridge for views of two dramatic saltwater gorges, whose tidal whirlpools have been known to swallow large logs. ⊠ *Hwy. 20, 7 mi north of Oak Harbor,* ☎ *360/675–2417.* ⚑ *Park free, campsite fees vary.* ☉ *Apr.–Sept., daily 6:30* AM*–dusk; Oct.–Mar., daily 8* AM*–dusk.*

Anacortes

➋ *15 mi north of Oak Harbor on Hwy. 20; 76 mi from Seattle, north on I–5 (to Exit 230) and west on Hwy. 20.*

Deception Pass Bridge links Whidbey to **Fidalgo Island.** From the bridge it's just a short drive to Anacortes, Fidalgo's main town and the terminus for ferries to the San Juan Islands. Anacortes has some well-preserved brick buildings along the waterfront, several old business structures downtown (like the Majestic Hotel), and many beautiful older homes off the main drag. The frequently changing exhibits at the **Anacortes Historical Museum** (⊠ 1305 8th St., ☎ 360/293–1915) focus on the cultural heritage of Fidalgo and nearby Guemes Island.

Lodging

$$$–$$$$ ⊞ **Majestic Hotel.** One of the finest small hotels in the Northwest
★ began life in 1889 as a mercantile building. From the Victorian-style two-story lobby, you can enter the Rose & Crown pub and the banquet rooms or ascend a sweeping staircase to your room or the English-style library. The top-floor gazebo has views of the marina, Mount Baker, and the Cascades. The rooms are decorated with European antiques and down comforters; several contain whirlpool tubs. A complimentary Continental breakfast is served in the dining room. ⊠ *419 Commercial Ave., 98221,* ☎ *360/293–3355,* FAX *360/293–5214. 23 rooms. Restaurant, pub, library. MC, V.*

Whidbey Island and Fidalgo Island Essentials

Getting Around

BY CAR

Whidbey Island can be reached by heading north from Seattle or south from the Canadian border on **I–5,** west on **Highway 20** onto Fidalgo Island, and south across Deception Pass Bridge.

BY FERRY

Washington State Ferries (☎ 206/464–6400) operates a ferry to Whidbey Island that leaves from Mukilteo, off I–5's Exit 189, 20 mi north of Seattle. Walk-on passengers pay only for the westward leg of the trip. Ferries leave roughly every half hour, more erratically off-season. To reach Mukilteo from Seattle, take I–5 north to Exit 189. Ferries also run from Port Townsend to Keystone (at Whidbey's midpoint). The ride is 20 minutes one-way.

BY PLANE

Harbor Airlines (☎ 800/359–3220) flies to Whidbey Island from Friday Harbor and Sea-Tac Airport. **Kenmore Air** (☎ 206/486–1257 or 800/543–9595) can arrange charter floatplane flights to Whidbey Island.

Visitor Information

Anacortes Chamber of Commerce (⊠ 819 Commercial Ave., Suite G, 98221, ☎ 360/293–7911). **Central Whidbey Chamber of Commerce** (⊠ 5 S. Main St., Coupeville 98239, ☎ 360/678–5434). **Langley Chamber of Commerce** (⊠ 124½ 2nd St., 98260, ☎ 360/221–6765).

THE SAN JUAN ISLANDS

The San Juans, the loveliest of the Pacific Northwest's islands, are separated from the mainland (and from each other) by miles of saltwater and deep, swift-running tidal channels or saltwater straits. This small archipelago of rock and glacial till derives its singular beauty from dramatic cliffs where eagles soar and from lush seaside meadows, gnarled trees, and multicolored wildflowers clinging to seemingly barren rock. The islands have valleys and mountains, forests filled with bird song, and leafy glens where the tiny island deer browse. Even a species of prickly pear cactus (*Opuntia fragilis*) grows here. Beaches can be of sand or shingle, but all are scenic and invite beachcombers and kayakers to explore their (often hidden) charms. The islands are visited by ducks and swans, herons and hawks, humans and whales. Offshore, seals haul out on sandbanks and orcas patrol the deep channels. Since the late 1990s, gray whales have begun to summer here, instead of heading north to their arctic breeding grounds; an occasional minke or humpback whale might also be seen frolicking in the kelp.

There are 176 named islands in the San Juan archipelago, although the islands and large rocks amount to 743 at low tide and 428 at high tide. Sixty are populated (though most have only a house or two) and 10 are state marine parks. Ferries stop at the four largest: Lopez, Shaw, Orcas, and San Juan; other islands, many privately owned, can be reached by commuter ferry from Bellingham, or by private plane or boat. The San Juans average more than 250 days of sunshine a year, but they stay cool in summer (temperatures hover around 70°F) and can get outright cold in winter, when temperatures average between 30 and 40°F (and can drop into the single digits when the dreaded northeasters blow).

San Juans residents are generally highly educated and quite well-to-do, though they also include a few folk seeking alternative lifestyles in a rustic saltwater setting. The larger islands support a little fishing and farming, but tourism generates by far the largest revenues. Serene, well-appointed inns cater to visitors, and creative chefs operate small restaurants on Lopez, Orcas, and San Juan, serving food as contemporary as anything in Seattle. Despite recent changes, each of the islands still maintains a distinct character, though all share in the islands' blessings of serene farmlands, unspoiled coves, blue-green or gray tidal waters embroidered by the lacy edges of tide rips, and a uniquely radiant light.

Lopez Island

❸ *45 mins by ferry from Anacortes.*

Quiet and relatively flat Lopez, the island closest to the mainland, is a favorite of bicyclists because of its gentle slopes. But Lopez has a lot to offer anyone, from breezy beaches to peaceful trails through the woods. Of the three San Juan islands that accommodate visitors, Lopez has the smallest population (approximately 1,800), and with its old orchards, weathered barns, and pastures of sheep and cows it's the most rustic, and in many ways the most subdued. There is only one settlement, Lopez Village, which has a few shops, a good restaurant, galleries exhibiting local artists' works, and the post office.

The **Lopez Island Historical Museum,** across the street from the island's only bank, has some impressive ship and small-boat models. The museum also has maps of local landmarks. ⊠ *Weeks and Washburn Rds.,* ☎ *360/468–2049.* ⊡ *Donations accepted.* ⊘ *July–Aug., Wed.–Sun. noon–4; May, June, and Sept., Fri.–Sun. noon–4.*

The San Juan Islands

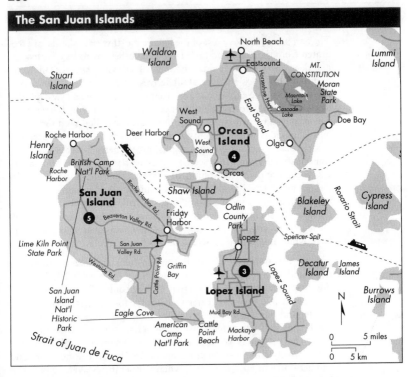

🖐 Beaches, trails, and wildlife are the draws at 130-acre **Spencer Spit State Park** (⊠ Rte. 2, ☎ 360/468–2251), on the northeast shore about 2 mi from Lopez Village. Popular **Odlin County Park** (⊠ Off Ferry Rd., ☎ 360/ 468–2496) is 1 mi from the ferry landing. You'll probably spot marine life—sea anemones; pink, yellow, or white nudibranchs (sea slugs); bright orange sea cucumbers; purple sea stars; blue-green shore crabs; and small sculpins—in the tide pools, and perhaps seals and herons at the water's edge. You might even see river otters frolic among the sea lettuce and limpets at craggy, isolated **Shark Reef.** Park in the lot south of Lopez Village on Shark Reef Road and follow the unmarked trail (it begins next to the out-house) for about 15 minutes through a thick forest to the water's edge.

The **Lopez Island Vineyard** (⊠ Fisherman Bay Rd. north of Cross Rd., ☎ 360/468–3644), the only vineyard in the San Juans, has a tasting room that is open between Memorial Day and Labor Day, from Wednesday to Sunday between noon and 5 (call for the hours during rest of the year).

Dining and Lodging

$$ ✕ **Bay Café.** Both locals and visitors hang out at this colorful restaurant; many customers dock their boats right at the restaurant. Menu highlights include seafood tapas: basil- and goat-cheese-stuffed prawns with saffron rice, sea scallops with sun-dried tomatoes. All entrées come with soup and salad. Homemade sorbet and a fine crème caramel are among the desserts. ⊠ *Lopez Village,* ☎ *360/468–3700. MC, V. Closed Mon.–Thurs. in winter. No lunch.*

$$$ 🏠 **Edenwild.** This large, gray Victorian-style farmhouse surrounded by gardens and framed by Fisherman's Bay looks as if it has been restored, but it dates from 1990, not 1890. The rooms are airy, each painted in a bold color; some have fireplaces, and all are furnished with simple antiques. Tiny roses fill the trellis on the wraparound ground-floor ve-

randa. Rates include a full breakfast. The inn welcomes children. ✉ *Eades La. at Lopez Village Rd., 98261, ☎ 360/468–3238, FAX 360/468–4080. 8 rooms. AE, D, MC, V.*

$$–$$$ 🖭 **Inn at Swifts Bay.** This Tudor-style house has eclectic furnishings, a fascinating collection of books, and an exhaustive video library. Bay windows in the living and dining areas overlook well-kept gardens, and a crackling fire warms the living room on winter evenings. Downstairs rooms have heavy floral drapes and elaborate bedding but are small and share baths. The downstairs suite has more space and a private entrance, but even nicer are the two upstairs suites, which are roomier and have private baths. Gourmet breakfasts include exotic creations like pumpkin eggnog muffins. ✉ *Rte. 2, Box 3402, 98261, ☎ 360/468–3636, FAX 360/468–3637. 2 rooms, 3 suites. Hot tub, beach. AE, D, MC, V.*

$$ 🖭 **Mackaye Harbor Inn.** This two-story inn, a 1920s sea captain's frame house with ½ mi of beach, rises above the rocks at the southern end of Lopez Island. Rooms have golden-oak and brass details and wicker furniture; three have views of Mackaye Harbor. Breakfast often includes Finnish pancakes and other Scandinavian specialties. Three rooms share 2½ baths; two suites have private baths, small decks, and fireplaces. The carriage house has a two-bedroom suite with a steam room and a full kitchen; a small studio here also has a kitchen. Breakfast is not included for guests in the carriage house. Boats and mountain bikes are available for rent. ✉ *Rte. 1, Box 1940, 98261, ☎ 360/468–2253, FAX 360/468–3293. 5 rooms, 2 suites. Beach. MC, V.*

Outdoor Activities and Sports
BICYCLING

Cycle San Juans Tours and Rentals (✉ Rte. 1, ☎ 360/468–3251) advertises this tour: "Cycle with bald Lopezian to discover island curiosities." **Lopez Bicycle Works** (✉ Fisherman Bay Rd., ☎ 360/468–2847) provides free bicycle delivery all year.

MARINAS

Islands Marine Center (✉ Fisherman Bay Rd. north of Hummel Lake Rd., ☎ 360/468–3377), near Lopez Village, has standard marina amenities, repair facilities, and transient moorage.

Shopping
The **Chimera Gallery** (✉ Lopez Village, ☎ 360/468–3265), a local artists' cooperative, exhibits crafts, jewelry, and fine art. **Grayling Gallery** (✉ 3630 Hummel Lake Rd., ☎ 360/468–2779) displays the paintings, prints, sculptures, and pottery of nearly a dozen artists from Lopez Island, some of whom live and work on the gallery's premises. The gallery is open on Friday and weekends from 10 to 5.

Shaw Island

20 mins on ferry from Lopez; 65 mins from Anacortes.

At tiny Shaw Island, local nuns wear their traditional habits while running the ferry dock. Few ferry passengers get off here, because there are no visitor facilities on this residential island. **King Salmon Charters** (☎ 360/468–2314) operates saltwater fishing excursions.

Orcas Island

❹ *10 mins from Shaw Island by ferry; 75 mins from Anacortes.*

The roads on saddlebag-shape Orcas Island sweep through wide valleys and rise to pretty hilltop views. Farmers, fishermen, and wealthy landowners on the largest island of the San Juans are balanced by a somewhat countercultural artists' community. Public access to the waterfront is limited to parks and public beaches.

Eastsound Village, the island's business and social center, lies at the top of East Sound, which almost cuts the island in half. Shops here sell jewelry, pottery, and other crafts made by local artisans. Along Prune Alley you'll find a handful of small shops and restaurants. Pick up free maps and brochures at the unstaffed **Travel Infocenter** (✉ Main St., ☎ 360/ 376–2273), next to the **Orcas Island Museum** (worth a stop if you're a history buff). Nearby is the simple yet stately **Emmanuel Church,** built in 1886 to resemble an English countryside chapel. The church's **Brown Bag Concerts** (☎ 360/376–2352)—you'll hear anything from a piano sonata to the vocalizing of a barbershop quartet—take place on summer Thursdays at noon.

★ **Moran State Park** has 151 campsites, 14 hiking trails, some sparkling lakes, 5,000 acres of old-growth forests, and **Mount Constitution,** the tallest peak in the San Juans. Drive to the mountain's 2,400-ft summit for exhilarating views of the San Juan Islands, the Cascades, the Olympics, and Vancouver Island. ✉ *Star Rte. 22; from Eastsound, head northeast on Horseshoe Hwy. and follow signs (mailing address: Box 22, Eastsound 98245),* ☎ *360/376–2326; 800/452–5678 for reservations.* ▨ *Camping $11 fee, plus $6 per night.*

Dining and Lodging

$$$ ✕ **Christina's.** The modern decor at the premier Orcas restaurant in-
★ cludes original works of art and copper-top tables. The seasonal menu changes daily but generally emphasizes local fish and seafood prepared with fresh herbs and served with seasonal vegetables. Sauces are light but flavorful. Expect a wait in-season at this very popular spot, which has fine views from its rooftop terrace and enclosed porch. ✉ *N. Beach Rd. and Horseshoe Hwy., Eastsound,* ☎ *360/376–4904. AE, DC, MC, V. Closed Tues. Oct.–mid-June. No lunch.*

$–$$ ✕ **Bilbo's Festivo.** Stucco walls, Mexican tiles, wood benches, and weavings from New Mexico betray this restaurant's culinary inclinations. Munch on burritos, enchiladas, and other Mexican favorites. In warm weather, it's pleasant to sip lime margaritas in the courtyard. ✉ *N. Beach Rd. and A St., Eastsound,* ☎ *360/376–4728. Reservations not accepted. AE, MC, V. No lunch Oct.–May.*

$$$–$$$$ ▥ **Rosario Spa & Resort.** Shipbuilding magnate Robert Moran built this Mediterranean-style mansion on Cascade Bay in 1906. Told he had six months to live, Moran pulled out all the stops on his last extravagance—then lived another 30 years. Now his mansion is on the National Register of Historic Places. The original Mission-style furniture, displayed for the public, is worth a look even if you're not staying here. The house's centerpiece, an Aeolian pipe organ with 1,972 pipes, is used for summer music concerts. The resort is renovating the villas and hotel units that were added in 1960 when Rosario was converted from a private residence. The rooms completed so far are comfortable, with gas fireplaces and other modern amenities. The spa offers everything from aerobic instruction to herbal wraps and massage. A shuttle meets every ferry and provides transportation into Eastsound. ✉ *Horseshoe Hwy., Eastsound 98245,* ☎ *360/376–2222 or 800/562–8820. 131 rooms. Dining room, 1 indoor and 2 outdoor pools, hot tub, sauna, spa, 2 tennis courts, hiking, dock, boating, fishing. AE, DC, MC, V.*

$$$–$$$$ ▥ **Spring Bay Inn.** Sandy Playa and Carl Burger, former park rangers,
★ run this bed-and-breakfast on acres of woodland surrounding private Spring Bay. All rooms have bay views (this is the only Orcas B&B actually on the water), wood-burning fireplaces, feather beds, and private sitting areas; one room has an outdoor hot tub. Walking trails mean-

der through the property, and you can kayak on the bay. Mornings begin with coffee, fresh muffins, and croissants outside your door—fortification for a two-hour kayaking experience, should you care to partake. While one of your hosts is out on the water—expect to see bald eagles, herons, or other wildlife—the other is preparing a full breakfast that includes fresh-squeezed orange juice and smoothies. ⊠ *Obstruction Pass Trailhead Rd. off Obstruction Pass Rd., Olga 98279,* ☏ *360/376–5531,* ℻ *360/376–2193. 5 rooms. Refrigerators, hot tub. D, MC, V.*

$$$ 🏠 **Deer Harbor Inn.** The original 1915 log lodge here, on a knoll overlooking Deer Harbor, was the island's first resort. The lodge is now the inn's dining room. A log cabin built later holds eight rooms with peeled-log furniture and meadow views from balconies. Three newer cottages have whirlpool tubs and propane fireplaces. A complimentary Continental breakfast is delivered to your door in a picnic basket. The large but cozy dining room, which serves seafood, has an adjoining deck for outdoor eating. ⊠ *Box 142, Deer Harbor 98243,* ☏ *360/376–4110,* ℻ *360/376–2237. 11 units. Restaurant. AE, MC, V.*

$$–$$$ 🏠 **Orcas Hotel.** Construction began in 1900 on this three-story red-roof Victorian hotel on a hill across from the Orcas ferry landing. The building, complete with a wraparound porch and a white picket fence, is on the National Register of Historic Places. Guest rooms have feather beds, down comforters, and wicker, brass, and antique furnishings; many rooms have water views. All second-floor rooms share baths. Two suites have whirlpool tubs. The dining room—open in season (from June to Oct.) to guests and nonguests—overlooks gardens and the ferry landing. In-season room rates include a full breakfast; lower off-season rates do not, but you can grab an espresso or baked goods at the on-site café. ⊠ *Horseshoe Hwy., Box 155, Orcas 98280,* ☏ *360/376–4300,* ℻ *360/376–4399. 12 rooms, 2 with bath, 3 with ½ bath. Restaurant, bar, café. AE, D, MC, V.*

$$–$$$ 🏠 **Turtleback Farm Inn.** Eighty acres of meadow, forest, and farmland in the shadow of Turtleback Mountain surround this forest-green inn, which dates from the late 1800s. The rooms have easy chairs, good beds with woolen comforters made from the fleece of resident sheep, some antiques, and views of meadows and forest. Breakfast can be taken in the dining room or on the deck overlooking the valley. ⊠ *R.R. 1, Box 650, Eastsound 98245,* ☏ *360/376–3914 or 800/376–4914. 7 rooms. Dining room. MC, V.*

$–$$ 🏠 **Doe Bay Village Resort.** A haven for neohippies and outdoorsy families, this property at the eastern tip of Orcas morphed from a nudist colony into a commune, a youth hostel, and finally a resort. Prices for the patchwork of accommodations—campsites, yurts, a hostel, and cabins tucked between two forested hills—start as low as $12, and there's a mostly vegetarian café on site. The resort's small beach is perfect for kayak launches. Guests staying in the cabins may also use the resort's mineral baths and sauna for free ($3 fee for hostel guests and campers). ⊠ *Star Rte. 86 off Pt. Lawrence Rd. near Olga, 98279,* ☏ *360/376–2291,* ℻ *360/376–4755. 30 cabins and structures, 24 campsites. Café, hot tubs, massage, mineral baths, sauna, volleyball, beach. AE, MC, V.*

Outdoor Activities and Sports

BICYCLING

Dolphin Bay Bicycles (☏ 360/376–3093) is at the ferry landing. **Key Moped Rental** (⊠ Eastsound, ☏ 360/376–2474) rents mopeds during the summer. **Wildlife Cycles** (⊠ Eastsound, ☏ 360/376–4708) also has bikes for rent.

FISHING

Three lakes at **Moran State Park** (☞ *above*) are open for fishing from late April to October.

MARINAS

Deer Harbor Resort & Marina (☎ 360/376–3037) and **West Sound Marina** (☎ 360/376–2240) have standard marina facilities. **Island Petroleum** (⊠ Orcas, ☎ 360/376–3883) has gas and diesel at the ferry landing. **Rosario Resort** (⊠ Eastsound, ☎ 360/376–2222) has boat slips.

Shopping

Darvill's Rare Print Shop (⊠ Eastsound, ☎ 360/376–2351) specializes in maps and bird and floral prints that are difficult to find elsewhere.

San Juan Island

❺ *45 mins by ferry from Orcas; 75 mins from Anacortes on express ferries.*

From the 1880s Friday Harbor and its newspaper were controlled by lime company owner and Republican big wig John S. McMillin, who virtually ran San Juan Island as a personal fiefdom from 1886 until his death in 1936. The town's main street, rising from the harbor and ferry landing up the slopes of a modest hill, hasn't changed much in decades, though the cafés and shops are snazzier now than they were in the 1960s and '70s. The Island County seat is the most convenient San Juans destination for visitors without cars or bicycles, since it's easy to spend an entire vacation in town, or to explore the island by public transportation. Some folks have even been known to hitch rides.

☉ You'll recognize the **Whale Museum** by the whale mural painted on its exterior. To reach the entrance, walk up Spring Street and turn right on 1st Street. Models of whales and whale skeletons, recordings of whale sounds, and videos of whales are the attractions. Workshops survey marine-mammal life and San Juan ecology. ⊠ *62 1st St. N,* ☎ *360/ 378–4710.* ☐ *$3.* ☉ *June–Sept., daily 10–5; Oct.–May, daily 11–4.*

★ To watch whales cavorting in Haro Strait, head to **Lime Kiln Point State Park,** on San Juan's west side just 6 mi from Friday Harbor. The best months for sighting whales are from the end of April through August. A resident pod of orcas regularly cruises past the point. ⊠ *6158 Lighthouse Rd.,* ☎ *360/378–2044.* ☐ *Free.* ☉ *Daily 8 AM–10 PM.*

☉ **San Juan Island National Historic Park** (☎ 360/468–3663) is a remnant of the "Pig War," an *opera buffa* of a scuffle between American settlers and British troops. It began with a Yank killing a Brit's pig in 1859, but it really concerned British claims to the islands, which were not settled until 1872 (in the Americans' favor, with Emperor William I of Germany as arbitrator). A joint military occupation did not lead to hostilities but to much partying among soldiers from both sides, prefiguring the way disputes are settled in the islands to this day.

The park encompasses two separate areas: **British Camp,** in a sheltered cove on the northwest side of the island (follow Roche Harbor Rd. north from Friday Harbor), has a blockhouse, a commissary, and barracks; **American Camp,** near the island's southern end (follow Cattle Point Rd. south from Friday Harbor), has a visitor center and remnants of fortifications. From June to August, the park conducts hikes and reenacts 1860s-era military life.

It seems hard to believe now that fashionable **Roche Harbor** at the northern end of San Juan Island was once the most important producer of builder's lime on the West Coast, shipping its product as far as Hawaii and South America. In 1882 John S. McMillin gained control of the lime company and put the kilns to work. But even in its heyday as a limestone quarrying village, Roche Harbor was known for abundant flowers and welcoming accommodations. McMillin transformed a bunkhouse into private lodgings for his invited guests, who included such notables as Teddy Roosevelt. The guest house is now the **Hotel de Haro** (☞ Roche Harbor Resort, *below*), which displays period photographs and artifacts in its lobby. If you're interested, ask the staff for a map of the old quarry, kilns, and the **Mausoleum,** an eerie Greek-inspired memorial to McMillin.

McMillin's heirs continued to operate the quarries and plant until 1956, when they sold out to the Tarte family. Although the old lime kilns still stand below the bluff, the company town has become a resort. Locals say it took two years for the limestone dust to wash off the trees around the harbor, but McMillin's former home is now a restaurant, and workers' cottages have been transformed into comfortable visitors' lodgings. With its rose gardens, cobblestone waterfront, and well-manicured lawns, Roche Harbor retains the flavor of its days as a hangout for McMillin's powerful friends—especially since the sheltered harbor is very popular with well-to-do pleasure boaters.

Dining and Lodging

$$$ ✕ **Duck Soup Inn.** Everything the Duck Soup Inn serves is made from
★ scratch daily—including fresh bread, vegetarian dishes, and delicious ice cream. Mediterranean-inspired entrées range from grilled fresh fish seasoned with local herbs to applewood-smoked Westcott Bay oysters to local prawns with wild blackberry sauce. Northwest, California, and European wines are on the list here. ⊠ *3090 Roche Harbor Rd., near town of Roche Harbor,* ☎ *360/378–4878. MC, V. Closed Mon.–Tues. Apr.–Oct.; closed entirely Nov.–Mar. No lunch.*

$$–$$$ ✕ **Springtree Café.** Chef James Boyle devises his daily menu around
★ fresh seafood and Waldron Island organic produce and herbs, creating savory dishes that you won't soon forget. Dungeness crab cakes are made with fresh local shellfish and herbs, and locally caught salmon, rockfish, and flounder are lightly sauced to highlight the freshness of the fish. Vegetarian options abound, and there's a full bar and an extensive wine selection. ⊠ *310 Spring St., Friday Harbor,* ☎ *360/ 378–4848. MC, V. Closed Sun.–Mon. mid-Oct.–Apr.*

$ ✕ **Front Street Ale House.** The English-style ale house serves sandwiches, salads, and traditional pub fare—lamb stew, meat pasties, steak-and-kidney pie, and the like. On-tap brews from the San Juan Brewing Company carry such locally inspired names as Pig War Stout. ⊠ *1 Front St., Friday Harbor,* ☎ *360/378–2337. Reservations not accepted. MC, V.*

$$$–$$$$ ✕⌸ **Mariella Inn & Cottages.** This impeccably maintained property sits on 8 acres on a cove just outside Friday Harbor. Rooms inside a 100-year-old country house have English antique furniture. Each room has a private bath and a view of either the water or the exquisite gardens, but some are small. Some of the private cottages and waterfront suites scattered throughout the grounds have modern amenities such as VCRs and kitchenettes. Especially romantic are the contemporary solarium suites with private whirlpool tubs inside glass-enclosed atriums. Breakfast and the newspaper are delivered to the cottages each morning. ⊠ *630 Turn Point Rd., Friday Harbor 98250,* ☎ *360/378–6868 or 800/ 700–7668,* ℻ *360/378–6822. 8 rooms, 3 suites, 12 cottages. Restaurant, bicycles. AE, MC, V.*

$$$ ✕⌸ **Friday Harbor House.** The ceiling-to-floor windows of this contemporary bluff-top hotel take advantage of its views of the marina, ferry landing, and San Juan Channel—as do the whirlpool tubs in the center of each room. Slate tiles, fireplaces, cable TV, and sleek, modern wood wall units all contribute to the casually upscale atmosphere. Guests take their elaborate complimentary Continental breakfasts in the intimate harbor-view dining room. ⊠ *130 West St., Friday Harbor 98250,* ☎ *360/378–8455,* ℻ *360/378–8453. 20 rooms. Restaurant, refrigerators. MC, V.*

$$–$$$ ☒ **Hillside House.** This split-level house less than a mile from Friday Harbor has views of the waterfront and Mount Baker from a large deck, where breakfast is often served. Some of the modern, well-furnished guest rooms with private baths have window seats overlooking the inn's private 10,000-square-ft, two-story full-flight aviary filled with exotic birds. On the deck, a pair of mounted 200-mm binoculars allows guests to observe local birds, including bald and golden eagles. The inn's penthouse is a popular honeymoon retreat. ☒ *365 Carter Ave., Friday Harbor 98250,* ☏ *360/378–4730 or 800/232–4730,* FAX *360/378–4715. 6 rooms, 1 suite. AE, D, MC, V.*

$$–$$$ ☒ **Roche Harbor Resort.** The choice here is between plain but comfortable cottages and condominiums or rooms in the 1886 restored Hotel de Haro. The old hotel building has small, rustic, but comfortable rooms. The harbor has slips for several hundred boats, plus a full-service marina; a 4,000-ft airstrip is just to the south. Whale-watching and day cruises, plus kayaking tours, are available. ☒ *4950 Tarte Memorial Dr., Roche Harbor 98250, 10 mi northwest of Friday Harbor off Roche Harbor Rd.* ☏ *360/378–2155 or 800/451–8910,* FAX *360/378–6809. 59 rooms, 5 with bath. Restaurant, grocery, pool, tennis court, boating, motorbikes. AE, MC, V.*

$$ ☒ **San Juan Inn.** Rooms in this restored 1873 main-street property less than a block from the ferry landing are small but serviceable; the real charm here is that the place has been operated as an inn for more than 100 years. A breakfast of muffins, coffee, and juice is served each morning in a parlor overlooking the harbor. The garden suite behind the inn has a TV and VCR, a full kitchen, and a fireplace. ☒ *50 Spring St., Box 776, Friday Harbor 98250,* ☏ *360/378–2070 or 800/742–8210,* FAX *360/378–6437. 9 rooms, 4 with bath; 1 suite. Outdoor hot tub, car rental. MC, V.*

Outdoor Activities and Sports

BEACHES

American Camp (☞ San Juan Island National Park, *above*) has 6 mi of public beach. You'll find 10 acres of beachfront at **San Juan County Park** (☒ 380 Westside Rd. N, Friday Harbor, ☏ 360/378–2992).

BICYCLING

San Juan Island Bicycles (☒ 380 Argyle St., Friday Harbor, ☏ 360/378–4941) has a reputation for good service and equipment. **Susie's Mopeds** (☒ Friday Harbor, ☏ 360/378–5244 or 800/532–0087), at the top of the hill behind the line to board the ferry, rents mopeds.

BOATING

Port of Friday Harbor (☏ 360/378–2688), **Roche Harbor Resort** (☏ 360/378–2155), and **Snug Harbor Resort Marina** (☏ 360/378–4762) have standard marina facilities.

FISHING

You can fish year-round for bass and trout at Egg and Sportsman lakes, both north of Friday Harbor off Roche Harbor Road. **Buffalo Works** (☏ 360/378–4612) arranges saltwater fishing trips. Licenses are required.

WHALE-WATCHING

San Juan Excursions (☏ 360/378–6636 or 800/809–4253) cruises the waters around the islands. **Western Prince Cruises** (☏ 360/378–5315 or 800/757–6722) operates a four-hour narrated tour.

Shopping

Boardwalk Bookstore (☒ 5 Spring St., Friday Harbor, ☏ 360/378–2787) is strong in the classics and has a good collection of popular literature. **Dan Levin** (☒ 50 1st St., ☏ 360/378–2051) stocks original jewelry. **Island Wools & Weaving** (☒ 30 1st St. S, Friday Harbor, ☏ 360/378–2148) carries yarns, imaginative buttons, quilting supplies, and some hand-knit items. **Napier Sculpture Gallery** (⊠ 232 A St., ☎ 360/378–2221) exhibits many bronze and steel sculptures. **Waterworks Gallery** (⊠ 315 Argyle St., Friday Harbor, ☎ 360/378–3060) represents eclectic contemporary artists.

San Juan Islands Essentials

Arriving and Departing

BY CAR

To reach the San Juan Islands from Seattle, drive north on **I–5** to Burlington; at Exit 230 head west on **Highway 20** and follow signs to Anacortes, the mainland terminal for the Washington State Ferry to the islands (☞ *below*). Taking your car with you usually means waiting in long lines at the ferry terminals. With prior arrangement, most B&B owners will pick up guests without cars at the ferry terminals.

BY FERRY

The vessels of the **Washington State Ferries** (☎ 206/464–6400; 800/843–3779 in WA) range from one that holds 40 cars to jumbo craft capable of carrying more than 200 cars and 2,000 passengers each. Ferries depart from Anacortes, about 76 mi north of Seattle, to the San Juan Islands.

Sunny weekends in the off-season and just about every day during the summer travel season are heavy traffic times all around the San Juan Islands. Since no reservations are accepted on Washington State Ferries (except for the Sidney–Anacortes run during the summer), arriving at least a half hour before a scheduled departure—even more at peak times—is always advised. Prior to boarding, lower your antenna. Only parking lights should be used at night, and it is considered bad form to start your engine before the ferry docks. Passengers and bicycles always load first unless otherwise instructed. In an effort to run on time, ferries stop loading cars and foot passengers two minutes before sailing time.

San Juan Islands Shuttle Express (⊠ Bellingham Cruise Terminal [aka Alaska Ferry Terminal], 355 Harris Ave., No. 105, Bellingham 98225, ☎ 360/671–1137) takes passengers from Bellingham to Orcas Island and Friday Harbor.

San Juan Island Commuter (⊠ Bellingham Cruise Terminal, 355 Harris Ave., No. 104, Bellingham 98225, ☎ 888/734–8180, 360/734–8180) has daily scheduled service to 16 different islands in the San Juans, including four islands that are state parks. The boat will also carry kayaks, bicycles, and camping equipment (a front-loading ramp allows it to load and unload passengers and gear on beaches).

BY PLANE

West Isle Air (☎ 800/874–4434) flies to Friday Harbor on San Juan Island from Sea-Tac and Bellingham airports. **Kenmore Air** (☎ 206/486–1257 or 800/543–9595) flies floatplanes from Lake Union in Seattle to the San Juan Islands.

Contacts and Resources

CAMPING

Marine State Parks (☎ 360/753–2027) are accessible by private boat, floatplane, and by San Juan Island Commuter ferry from Bellingham (☞ *above*). No moorage or camping reservations are available, and fees are charged at some parks from May through Labor Day. Fresh water, where available, is limited. Island parks are Blind, Clark, Doe, James, Jones, Matia, Patos, Posey, Stuart, Sucia, and Turn. All have a few campsites; there are no docks at Blind, Clark, Patos, Posey, or Turn islands.

Amante Sail Tours (☎ 360/376–4231). **Charters Northwest** (☎ 360/378–7196). **Harmony Sailing Charters** (☎ 360/468–3310). **Kismet Sailing Charters** (☎ 360/468–2435). **Nor'wester Sailing Charters** (☎ 360/378–5478).

KAYAKING

If you are kayaking on your own, beware of the ever-changing conditions, ferry and shipping lanes and landings, and the strong tides and currents. Go ashore only on known public property. **Shearwater Sea Kayak Tours** (☎ 360/376–4699), **Doe Bay Resort** (☎ 360/376–2291), **San Juan Kayak Expeditions** (☎ 360/378–4436), and **Seaquest** (☎ 360/378–5767) conduct day trips and longer expeditions.

VISITOR INFORMATION

San Juan Island Chamber of Commerce (✉ Friday Harbor 98250, ☎ 360/378–5240). **San Juan Islands Tourism Cooperative and Visitors Information Service** (✉ Lopez 98261, ☎ 360/468–3663).

WHATCOM AND SKAGIT COUNTIES

North of the Seattle metropolitan area, I–5 crosses the the Skagit River valley, the Chuckanut Range, and the Nooksack Flats below the Canadian border. To the west spread the channels and islands of the Salish Sea, and to the east loom the tall, jagged peaks of the North Cascades. Where the foothills meet the river, the highway passes through the Skagit County seat of Mount Vernon, with its riverfront downtown (where steamers once docked) enlivened by small cafés, shops, and a microbrewery. The city is surrounded by dairy pastures; tulip, iris, and daffodil fields; and apple orchards. It is famous for its annual Tulip Festival in April, when thousands of people visit to admire the floral exuberance. The hills bordering the valley are often veiled in mist, their wooded ridges flowing from the haze like the brush strokes of a Japanese landscape painting. Bayview and La Conner, west of Mount Vernon, have attractive waterfronts. Sedro Woolley, to the east, is the gateway to North Cascades National Park. From Sedro Woolley you can take Highway 9 north to Highway 542, which leads to the Mount Baker National Recreation Area (and makes for a less urban drive than the main approach from Bellingham).

Bellingham, the Whatcom County seat, is the region's metropolis. But unlike Mount Vernon, which looks south to Seattle for inspiration, Bellingham looks north to Vancouver, British Columbia. Lummi Island, to the west across the bay, is a suburban community reached by a ferry ride. Ferndale (on the Nooksack River) and Blaine (on Georgia Strait) are a few miles north.

Bellingham

❻ *90 mi north of Seattle on I–5.*

The fishing port, mill town, and college community of Bellingham is transforming itself from a grungy blue-collar area to the arts, retirement, and pleasure-boating capital of Washington's northwest corner. Downtown has cafés, specialty shops, and galleries, and the waterfront, once dominated by lumber mills and shipyards, is slowly being converted into a string of parks with connecting trails. College students and professors from Western Washington University make up a sizable part of the town's population and contribute to its laid-back intellectual climate. The lushly green bayfront, creeks meandering through town, and Lakes Whatcom and Padden attract wildlife like deer, raccoons, river otters, beavers, ducks, geese, herons, bald eagles, and the occasional cougar.

Whatcom and Skagit Counties

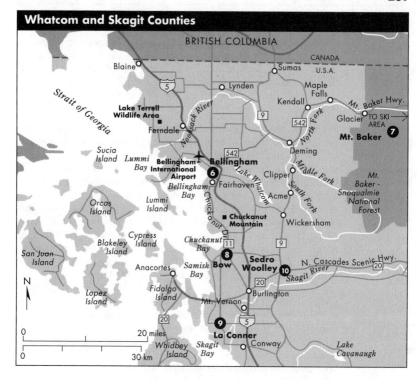

🕑 The impressive four-building **Whatcom Museum of History and Art** has as its centerpiece Bellingham's 1892 former city hall, a redbrick structure converted into a museum in 1940. Victorian clothing, toys, games, and clocks are on display, and there are art exhibits as well. The other buildings in the complex include a natural-history gallery (with a stuffed-bird collection) and a children's museum. ⊠ *121 Prospect St.,* ☎ *360/ 676–6981.* 🎟 *Free; children's museum $2.* ☉ *Tues.–Sun. noon–5.*

🕑 Stairs behind the museum lead down into **Maritime Heritage Park,** which pays tribute to Bellingham's fishing industry. On self-guided tours at the **Marine Heritage Center,** you can learn about hatcheries and salmon life cycles, see salmon-rearing tanks and fish ladders, and watch salmon spawning. You can go fishing for sea-run trout at Whatcom Creek within the park. A pretty waterfall is just upstream, below the post office. Bellingham was founded in 1852 at the foot of these falls. ⊠ *1600 C St.,* ☎ *360/676–6806.* 🎟 *Free.* ☉ *Weekdays 9–5.*

Boulevard Park (⊠ S. State St. and Bayview Dr.), south of downtown, has 14 acres of lawns and woods, and ½ mi of shoreline. You can play volleyball or Frisbee, or search for starfish and other sea creatures.

🕑 A good place to fish, lounge, picnic, or walk is the **Squalicum Harbor Marina** (⊠ Roeder Ave. and Coho Way), which holds more than 1,900 commercial and pleasure boats. **Pete Zuanich Park,** at the end of the spit, has a telescope for close-up views of the water, and there's a marine-life center with touch tanks.

On Railroad Avenue between Chestnut and Magnolia streets, you'll find cafés, vintage clothing and consignment shops, a batik boutique, and the narrow but engaging **Bellingham Antique Radio Museum** (⊠ 1515 Railroad Ave., ☎ no phone). A statue of the RCA dog keeps watch on the museum, whose friendly operator has been collecting radios for half a century.

Western Washington University, high up on tree-clad Sehome Hill, overlooks the waterfront, Bellingham Bay, and Lummi Island. The visitor center has maps and an audio tour of the nearly two dozen outdoor sculptures scattered about campus, including works by Mark DiSuvero, Isamu Noguchi, Richard Serra, and George Rickey. Take Garden Street to get to the university from the north, and Bill McDonald Parkway if you're coming from the south (Samish Way Exit from I–5). ⊠ *Visitor Center: S. College Dr. off Bill McDonald Pkwy.,* ☎ *360/650–3000.*

Fairhaven, the historic district to the south of Bellingham, at the beginning of Chuckanut Drive (Highway 11), was an independent city until 1903 and still retains its distinct identity as an intellectual and artistic center. The beautifully restored 1890s redbrick buildings of the **Old Fairhaven District,** especially on Harris Avenue between 10th and 12th streets, house restaurants, galleries, and specialty boutiques. In the early 1900s, the American Rose Society developed **Fairhaven Park** (⊠ 107 Chuckanut Dr., ☎ 360/671–1570) as a testing site. Unfortunately, the city parks department pulled up the roses in 1999. But the park, which is open daily from 10 to 5, still has beautiful trails along **Padden Creek** (where chum and silver salmon spawn every year just before Thanksgiving), picnic tables, a playground, tennis courts, playing fields, and a wading pool. Nearby, on Harris Avenue, **Padden Lagoon** is home to Canada geese and kingfishers. There's public access to the waterfront at the foot of the hill at the **Bellingham Cruise terminal** (⊠ 355 Harris Ave., ☎ 360/676–2500), where passengers leave for the San Juan Islands and Victoria, British Columbia, daily, and where an Alaska ferry docks every Friday. The ferry dock and adjacent shore are a great place to spot wildlife, from Dungeness crabs, sea lions, and an occasional gray whale to great blue herons, cormorants, and harlequin ducks. A couple of blocks south, at the foot of Harris Street, **Marine Park**'s small, sandy beach is a great place for launching sea kayaks. An unmarked (and unofficial) trail runs south from the park along the railroad tracks to shingle beaches and rocky headlands. Here you'll find clams and blackberries in season and splendid views of Lummi Island and spectacular sunsets year-round.

Dining and Lodging

$$–$$$ ✕ **Pacific Café.** The understated decor at this restaurant next door to the Mount Baker Theatre (☞ Nightlife and the Arts, *below*) is Asian inspired: white walls, rice-paper screens, and wood shutters. The Asian influence extends to dishes like Alaska spot prawns in a garlicky black-bean sauce and grilled king salmon in hoisin sauce. The portions are large, but save room for wickedly good desserts like the chocolate éclairs. ⊠ *100 N. Commercial St.,* ☎ *360/647–0800. AE, MC, V. Closed Sun. No lunch Mon.*

$$–$$$ ✕ **Wild Garlic.** Serving American food with a touch of the sun, this small, elegant restaurant is tucked into a tiny space across the street from the Whatcom Museum of History and Art (☞ *above*). Walls are painted in subdued colors, and the restaurant's narrow dining room with booths on one side offers the kind of intimate setting all too rare in Bellingham. It seems almost too sophisticated for fusty downtown, but it has a very loyal local clientele. Garlic reigns supreme in the kitchen, handled with finesse and used with such a sure touch that even those who dread this pungent herb need have no fear to taste a dish called "Swimming Garlic," a delicate version of an Italian *bagna cauda.* Other dishes include garlic shrimp linguine, roast garlic fettuccine, roast chicken, and sautéed fresh fish and prawns. The service is friendly and very professional; the wine list is respectable. ⊠ *114 Prospect St.,* ☎ *360/671–1955. MC, V. Closed Sun. No lunch Sat.*

$$ ✕ **Orchard Street Brewery.** The purple floor, orangish walls, and red tables of this upscale contemporary restaurant complement the industrial

ambience—it's in a former manufacturing complex. Among the menu highlights are a crab turnover appetizer and a salmon entrée with shiitake and oyster mushrooms in puff pastry. You can also order pizza baked in a wood oven. ⊠ *709 W. Orchard Dr., No. 1,* ☎ *360/647–1614. Reservations not accepted. AE, MC, V. Closed Sun.*

$ ✕ **Colophon Café.** The restaurant inside the Village Bookstore serves African peanut soup, quiches, deli sandwiches, and other hearty fare. Homemade desserts and ice cream are also on the menu. ⊠ *1208 11th St., Old Fairhaven* ☎ *360/647–0092. Reservations not accepted. MC, V.*

$ ✕ **Stanello's.** This Fairhaven restaurant sits high up on the hill, with distant views of the waterfront, Bellingham Bay, and the Lummi Peninsula. The fare is simple but tasty, ranging from a superbly flavorful minestrone and a very clammy clam chowder to pastas, pizzas (white and Greek pizzas are tops), chicken dishes, and steak. Highlights include the spinach salad, the Greek *salata kota* (chicken salad), and the vegetarian lasagna. The pizza here has several times been voted the best in Bellingham and Whatcom County. ⊠ *1514 12th St.,* ☎ *360/676–1304. AE, D, DC, MC, V. No lunch Mon.–Thurs.*

$$$–$$$$ ⌂ **Schnauzer Crossing.** Meticulously maintained gardens surround this contemporary B&B in a peaceful residential neighborhood overlooking Lake Whatcom. The original 1920s house was extended in the 1970s; the modern living room has extremely high ceilings. One of the two rooms in the house has a lake view; the other, a large suite, has a glass-enclosed atrium, a fireplace, and a whirlpool tub. A cottage unit, whose cost may leave you expecting something more lavish, has a kitchen, a gas fireplace, and a whirlpool tub. Friendly owners Donna and Vermont McAllister serve ample, unusual breakfasts like triple-sec French toast. ⊠ *4421 Lakeway Dr. 98226,* ☎ *360/733–0055 or 800/562–2808,* FAX *360/734–2808. 1 room, 1 suite, 1 cottage. Outdoor hot tub, boating. MC, V.*

$$ ⌂ **Best Western Lakeway Inn.** The bustling Lakeway is just off the interstate in downtown Bellingham. Its four floors surround an open-air courtyard with a clover-shape indoor pool and a hot tub. Rooms are functional; the rates include a hot breakfast. Children under 12 stay for free when sharing a room with their parents. ⊠ *714 Lakeway Dr., east of I–5's Exit 253, 98225,* ☎ *360/671–1011,* FAX *360/676–8519. 132 rooms. Restaurant, bar, indoor pool, hot tub, sauna, exercise room, airport and ferry shuttle. AE, D, DC, MC, V.*

$$ ⌂ **North Garden Inn.** This B&B in a noteworthy Queen Anne–style mansion near Western Washington University is on the National Register of Historic Places. Some rooms have views of Bellingham Bay; all have antique furnishings and plenty of character. The Steinway grand piano in the entryway is occasionally used for concerts; guests may play it, too. ⊠ *1014 N. Garden St., 98225,* ☎ *360/671–7828 or 800/922–6414. 10 rooms. MC, V.*

Nightlife and the Arts

Boundary Bay Brewery & Bistro (⊠ 1107 Railroad Ave., ☎ 360/647–5593), a warehouse turned classy brewery, pours five beers, serves some of Bellingham's best food, and displays eclectic local art. The mellowest place in Bellingham for a beer is the **Up and Up** (⊠ 1234 N. State St., ☎ 360/733–9739).

In late August and early September, the **Bellingham Festival of Music** (☎ 360/676–5997) presents nearly 20 orchestral, chamber-music, and jazz concerts at Western Washington University and other nearby locations. Informative talks are given an hour prior to the chamber and symphony performances.

The **Mount Baker Theatre** (⊠ 104 N. Commercial St., ☎ 360/734–6080), a restored theater from the vaudeville era, has a 110-ft Moorish tower and a lobby fashioned after a Spanish galleon. The theater, home to the Whatcom Symphony Orchestra, presents movies and touring performances. **Western Washington University** (✉ 516 High St., ☎ 360/650–6146) presents classical music concerts and theatrical productions. The **Whatcom Museum of History and Art** (✉ 121 Prospect St., ☎ 360/676–6981) sponsors downtown gallery walks several times a year; call for information.

Outdoor Activities and Sports

CLIMBING

The **American Alpine Institute** (✉ 1515 12th St., ☎ 360/671–1505) is a prestigious mountain- and rock-climbing school.

GOLF

Lake Padden Golf Course (✉ 4882 Samish Way, ☎ 360/738–7400), an 18-hole, par-72 municipal course, is carved out of second-growth forest. The greens fee runs from $15 to $20; an optional cart costs $22.

KAYAKING

Elakah! Expeditions (☎ 360/734–7270 or 800/434–7270) is dedicated to environmentally sensitive low-impact travel. **Moondance Kayak Tours and Sales** (✉ 2448 Yew Street Rd., ☎ 360/738–7664) conducts tours that range in length from a half day to five.

WHALE-WATCHING

Island Mariner Cruises (✉ 5 Harbor Esplanade, ☎ 360/734–8866) conducts whale-watching and nature cruises to the Queen Charlotte Islands and Alaska and sunset cruises around Bellingham Bay. **San Juan Islands Shuttle Express** (✉ Alaska Ferry Terminal, 355 Harris Ave. at railroad tracks, ☎ 360/671–1137) operates summer whale-watching trips from Bellingham to the San Juan Islands.

Shopping

Along lower Holly Street in Bellingham's Old Town, you'll find antiques shops, secondhand stores, and suppliers of outdoor-recreation equipment. Try the **Old Town Antique Mall** (✉ 427 W. Holly St., ☎ 360/671–3301) for antiques and collectibles.

The glossy **Bellis Fair** (✉ I–5, Exit 256B, ☎ 360/734–5022), a regional shopping mall a few miles north of downtown, has major department stores, several restaurants, shops, and a multiplex movie theater.

Ferndale

10 mi north of Bellingham on I–5.

The country town of Ferndale lies on the Nooksack River north of Bellingham. In **Pioneer Park** you can wander through log buildings from the 1870s—including Whatcom County's first church—that have been restored and converted into museums. Note the beautifully "squared" cedar logs, a Western Washington pioneer building technique. ✉ *1st and Cherry Sts. (2 blocks south of Main St.), ☎ 360/384–6461. ⚍ Free. ☉ May–Sept., Tues.–Sun. 11:30–4:30.*

⌕ **Hovander Homestead Park,** a pioneer farm, is now a national historic site complete with a Victorian-era farmhouse, barnyard animals, a water tower, vegetable gardens, and antique farm equipment. Surrounding it are 60 acres of walking trails, picnic grounds, and access to fishing in the Nooksack. ✉ *5299 Nielsen Rd., ☎ 360/384–3444. ⚍ Free. ☉ Daily dawn–dusk.*

The **Tennant Lake Natural History Interpretive Center,** within the Nielsen House, an early homestead, has exhibits and information about nature walks. A new observation tower makes for great bird-watching from an eagle's perspective. The lake is part of a 200-acre marshy habitat where bald eagles, ducks, beavers, muskrats, and other wildlife can be seen. The unusual **Fragrance Garden**—with herbs and flowers—is designed for the visually impaired and can be explored by following Braille signs. ⊠ *5236 Nielsen Rd.,* ☎ *360/384–3444.* 🖅 *Free.* ⊙ *Daily dawn–dusk.*

Many species of waterfowl live within the 11,000-acre **Lake Terrell Wildlife Preserve.** This is a great place for watching birds, but stay away in fall, when the reserve is open to hunting. You can try to catch perch, catfish, bass, and cutthroat year-round. ⊠ *5975 Lake Terrell Rd.,* ☎ *360/384–4723.* 🖅 *Free.* ⊙ *Weekdays 8–5.*

Blaine

16 mi north of Ferndale on I–5.

This small town has a busy fishing port and yacht moorage on Drayton Harbor, a bay protected from the storm waters of Georgia Strait by sandy Semiahmoo Spit. Blaine also has Washington's busiest border crossing into Canada, where a white "Peace Arch" straddles the border line at the I–5/BC 99 crossing in **Peace Park.** The arch was built in 1921 to celebrate the peaceful nature of this undefended border. "Semiahmoo" is the Salish word for "clam eaters," and indeed, the miles of shoreline along the spit are good for clamming and fishing as well as swimming, beachcombing, and strolling.

Dining and Lodging

$ ✕ **Harbor Cafe.** The dining room of this portside tavern and family restaurant overlooks the fishing fleet moored in Drayton Harbor. Local and out-of-town diners flock here for the fish-and-chips, which are the best served anywhere in the county—and have been considered so for at least two decades. ⊠ *295 Marine Dr., 98230,* ☎ *360/332–5176. MC, V.*

$$$ 🏨 **Inn at Semi-ah-moo.** A dramatic waterside location and many outdoor activities are the chief lures of the hostelry inside the old Semiahmoo Salmon Cannery building. The rooms range from motel-like accommodations to suites with fireplaces, balconies, and expansive views. You can join a fishing charter or sightseeing cruise, play golf on a course designed by Arnold Palmer, work out at the health club or indoor track, swim in heated pools indoors or out, and bike, jog, or hike around the nearby nature trails. ⊠ *9565 Semiahmoo Pkwy., 98230,* ☎ *360/371–2000 or 800/770–7992,* FAX *360/371–5490. 188 rooms, 12 suites. 2 restaurants, bar, 1 indoor and 1 outdoor pool, golf course, tennis court, health club, jogging, racquetball, squash, dock, boating, bicycles. AE, MC, V.*

Glacier

30 mi east of Bellingham on Hwy. 542.

The canyon village of Glacier, just outside the Mount Baker–Snoqualmie National Forest boundary, has a few shops, cafés, and lodgings.

Lodging

$$ 🏨 **Mount Baker Lodging & Travel.** Cabins nestled in a wooded setting range from snug hideaways suitable for couples to larger chalets for families or groups. All the rooms are clean and charming, if rustic, with wood-burning stoves or fireplaces. Some units are equipped with VCRs. ⊠ *7500 Mt. Baker Hwy., 98244,* ☎ *360/599–2453 or 800/709–7669. 19 units. Hot tub, sauna. AE, MC, V.*

$–$$$ 🏨 **Mount Baker Chalet.** The privately owned units here are available for one-night or longer rentals. Smallish two-person cabins are more in the rustic vein, but you can opt for upscale condominiums—some with several bedrooms—that have access to a hot tub, a sauna, and tennis, squash, and racquetball courts. All the units are in secluded wooded locations and have wood-burning stoves or fireplaces. Jogging and walking trails are right outside the door. Weekly rates are quite reasonable. ⊠ *9857 Mt. Baker Hwy., 98244,* ☎ *360/599–2405 or 800/258–2405,* FAX *360/599–2255. 25 units. 1 indoor and 1 outdoor pool. MC, V.*

En Route Highway 542 winds east from Glacier into the Mount Baker–Snoqualmie National Forest through an increasingly steep-walled canyon. It passes 170-ft-high **Nooksack Falls,** about 5 mi east of Glacier, and travels up the north fork of the Nooksack River and the slopes of Mount Baker to a ski area, which is bright with huckleberry patches and wildflowers in summer.

Mount Baker

❼ *25 mi east of Glacier on Hwy. 542.*

The 10,778-ft-high, snow-covered volcanic dome of Mount Baker is visible from much of Whatcom County and from as far north as Vancouver and as far south as Seattle. It's particularly exciting to watch when it smokes, which it does occasionally. The surrounding **Mount Baker National Recreation Area** attracts hikers, mountain bikers, and skiers. Craggy and glacier-bedecked Mount Shuksan, just to the northeast in North Cascades National Park, is nonvolcanic and reaches a height of 9,038 ft.

Skiing

You can snowboard and ski downhill or cross-country at the **Mount Baker Ski Area** (⊠ Mount Baker Hwy. 542, ☎ 360/734–6771), 17 mi east of Glacier. The facility has the longest season in the state, lasting from roughly November to the end of April. Call 360/671–0211 for snow reports.

Bow

❽ *18 mi south of Bellingham on Chuckanut Dr. (Hwy. 11) or west of I–5 via Bow Hill Road, Exit 236.*

Highway 11, also known as **Chuckanut Drive,** was once the only highway heading south from Bellingham and Fairhaven. For a dozen miles this 23-mi road winds along the cliffs above beautiful Chuckanut Bay and Samish Bay. On one side rises steep and heavily wooded Chuckanut Mountain; on the other you get stunning views across saltwater to the San Juan Islands. Many attractive houses have been built along this stretch of road.

The drive begins in Fairhaven (☞ *above*), reaches the flat farm lands of the Samish Valley near Bow, and joins up with I–5 at Burlington, in Skagit County; the full loop can be made in a couple of hours. Along the way, you'll pass **Larrabee State Park** south of Chuckanut Bay. The park, which lies on the Whatcom-Skagit county line, is one of the state's most scenic and popular. It straddles a rocky shore with quiet, sandy coves and runs high up along the slopes of **Chuckanut Mountain**. Even though the mountain has been logged repeatedly, some of it is still a virtual wilderness. Miles of trails lead through ferny fir and maple forests to hidden lakes, caves, and clifftop lookouts, from which you can look all the way to the San Juan Islands. At the shore there is a sheltered boat launch; you can go crabbing here or watch the birds—and the occasional harbor seal—that perch on the offshore rocks. The area west of Chuckanut Drive has picnic tables as well as tent and RV sites with hook-ups, which are open all year. ⊠ *245 Chuckanut Dr.,* ☎ *360/676–2093.*

At the southern end of Chuckanut Drive lies Bow, just east of Samish Bay, where oysters and clams are farmed on the tidelands. Bow is not a "town" in the traditional sense, not even a hamlet, but consists of a post office and a couple of shops at a crossroads, and a few scattered houses and barns. It does, however, have several good restaurants lined up along the highway.

Dining

$$–$$$ ✗ **Chuckanut Manor.** The old-fashioned, glassed-in dining room and bar overlook the mouth of the Samish River, the adjacent mudflats, Samish Bay, and a few of the more easterly San Juan Islands. Come here for traditional American-Continental fare with an emphasis on steak and fried seafood. ⊠ *302 Chuckanut Dr.,* ☎ *360/766–6191. Closed Mon. AE, DC, MC, V.*

$$–$$$ ✗ **Oyster Bar.** Poised above the shore on a steep, wooded bluff, this intimate restaurant has probably the best marine view of any Washington restaurant and is regionally famous for it. People come here to dine and watch the sun set over the islands to the west or to watch the full moon reflect off the waters of Samish Bay. The dining room has two levels, so every table has a view. The menu has changed so often in recent years it's hard to predict what you might find, but the seafood dishes are always good. The selection of wines is very good. ⊠ *240 Chuckanut Dr.,* ☎ *360/766–6185. AE, MC, V.*

$$–$$$ ✗ **Oyster Creek Inn.** Window tables at this small restaurant overlook
★ the tumbling waters of the creek below, where you might be able to watch otters probe for salmon ascending the cascades to spawn. Oysters (from the oyster farm at the bottom of the hill) prepared in traditional and imaginative ways are the menu highlights; other seafood dishes are also excellent. The wine list is limited to bottlings from Northwest wineries and has the best selection of regional wines anywhere in the Northwest, including some very rare and hard-to-find vintages (and at reasonable prices, too). ⊠ *190 Chuckanut Dr.,* ☎ *360/766–6179. AE, MC, V.*

La Conner

❾ *39 mi from Bellingham, south on I–5 and west on WA 20, Exit 230 to the traffic light at LaConner/Whitney Road, then south to La Conner; 65 mi from Seattle, north on I–5 to Conway, and west on Fir Island Road (Exit 221); follow signs to La Conner.*

Morris Graves, Kenneth Callahan, Guy Anderson, Mark Tobey, and other painters set up shop in La Conner in the 1940s, and the village on the Swinomish Channel (Slough) has been a haven for artists ever since. In recent years La Conner has become increasingly popular as a weekend escape for Seattle residents, because it can be reached after a short drive but seems far away. The number of good shops and restaurants has increased, but so has the traffic—in summer the village becomes congested with people and cars, and parking can be very hard to find.

The flat land around La Conner makes for easy bicycling along levees and through the tulip fields.

Roozengaarde (⊠ 1587 Beaver Marsh Rd., ☎ 360/424–8531) is one of the largest growers of tulips, daffodils, and irises in the United States—200 or so varieties in all. It's open daily from 9 to 5 during the blooming season (from March to May) and is closed on Sunday the rest of the year.

La Conner has several historic buildings near the waterfront or a short walk up the hill (make use of the stairs leading up the bluff, or go around and walk up one of the sloping streets).

The **Volunteer Fireman's Museum** (✉ 611 S. 1st St., ☎ no phone) contains turn-of-the-century equipment that you can see from the street through the building's large windows. Historic furnishings are on display at the Victorian **Gaches Mansion** (✉ 2nd and Calhoun Sts., ☎ 360/466–4288). Admission is $3; the house is open on Friday, Saturday, and Sunday from 1 to 4 (and until 5 in summer).

The **Museum of Northwest Art** (✉ 121 S. 1st St. ☎ 360/466–4446) presents the works of regional artists past and present. Admission is $3; the museum is open daily except Monday between 10 and 5. The **Skagit County Historical Museum** (✉ 501 4th St., ☎ 360/466–3365) surveys domestic life in early Skagit County and Northwest Coastal Indian history. Admission is $2; the museum is open daily except Monday between 11 and 5.

Dining and Lodging

$$$–$$$$ ✕ **Palmer's Restaurant and Pub.** There's a distinctly French influence to the seasonally changing menu at this restaurant on the bluff a block from the channel. The chef's signature dish is a braised lamb shank, but you'll find salads, pastas, and other lighter fare as well. The adjacent pub (with much stained glass) serves bistro fare. ✉ 205 E. Washington St., ☎ 360/466–4261. AE, MC, V. No lunch Mon.–Thurs. Sept.–Mar.

$$$–$$$$ ☰ **La Conner Channel Lodge.** La Conner's only waterfront hotel is an
★   understated modern facility overlooking the narrow Swinomish Channel. Each room has a private balcony and a gas fireplace and is decorated in subdued gray tones with wooden trim; 12 rooms have whirlpool baths. Room rates include a Continental breakfast. ✉ 205 N. 1st St., 98257, ☎ 360/466–1500, ℻ 360/466–5902. 29 rooms, 12 suites. Business services, meeting rooms. AE, D, DC, MC, V.

$$ ☰ **Hotel Planter.** This renovated hotel, the oldest in La Conner, is on the National Register of Historic Places. The rooms, which have fine views of the hill or the waterfront, are furnished with handmade country style furniture. The rooms are quite homey, and the TVs are hidden in armoires. No smoking is allowed in the hotel. ✉ 715 1st St., 98257, ☎ 360/466–4710 or 800/488–5409, ℻ 360/466–1320. 12 rooms. Hot tub. AE, MC, V.

$$ ☰ **Rainbow Inn.** A white picket fence surrounds this stately three-story, century-old country house outside town. The large rooms are furnished with antiques; one room has a whirlpool tub. All guests have access to the hot tub in the gazebo behind the house, from which Mount Baker can be seen. Breakfast, included in the room rates, is served in an enclosed porch with views of farmland. Smoking is not permitted at the inn. ✉ 1075 Chilberg Rd., 98257, ☎ 360/466–4578 or 800/888–8879, ℻ 360/466–3844. 5 rooms with bath, 3 rooms share 1 bath. Hot tub. MC, V.

Sedro Woolley

🔟 9 mi northeast of Mount Vernon; follow signs from I–5's Exit 232.

On its way east from I–5, Highway 20 skirts Burlington, the Skagit Valley's Hispanic capital, and Sedro Woolley, a former mill and logging town. Look for the headquarters of **North Cascades National Park** to the left as you approach the town. Public murals and carved log statues outside shops along the main streets give testament to the town's logging past, as does the **Sedro Woolley Museum** (✉ 725 Murdock St., ☎ 360/855–2390), open on Saturday from 9 to 4 and Sunday from 1:30 to 4:30.

OFF THE   **NORTH CASCADES SCENIC HIGHWAY** – From Sedro Woolley, Highway 20
BEATEN PATH   winds through the green pastures and woods of the slowly narrowing

upper Skagit Valley, passing Lyman and Hamilton and other "Tarheel" villages. The Tarheels (as they still proudly call themselves) migrated here from the mountains of North Carolina during the last century and still maintain their clannish, tight-knit community, with traditional customs and crafts. Tarheel country stretches up the Skagit and south along the Sauk to Darrington, which is famous for its annual Bluegrass Festival (held the third weekend in July). Look for roadside signs advertising impromptu fiddle contests.

As the mountains close in on the river and the highway they grow in height, but the road climbs only imperceptibly. That's because the Skagit Valley, like other valleys of the North Cascades, was cut below sea level by the glaciers of the last ice age, some 15,000 years ago. Close to sea level, the largely flat valley floor was created when the gash was filled in with alluvial deposit carried down from the mountains by the rivers. Beyond Concrete, a former cement-manufacturing town, the road begins to climb into the mountains, to Ross and Diablo dams.

A tugboat operated from June to September by **Seattle City Light** takes passengers from Diablo Dam to the base of Ross Dam. Four-hour tours operated by Seattle City Light's Skagit Tours include a ride up an antique incline lift, a boat cruise on Diablo Lake, a tour of the Ross Power House, and a meal of chicken and spaghetti with vegetarian sauce. Ninety-minute tours include a ride on the lift, a walk to Diablo Dam, and a tour of Diablo Power House. ⊠ *Seattle City Light, 500 Newhalem St., Rockport, WA 98283,* ☎ *206/684–3030.* ☞ *$25 plus tax for 4-hr tour, $5 plus tax for 90-min tour, $2.50 each way for tugboat ride.* ☉ *Tours June–Sept. (hrs vary). Tugboat ride leaves Diablo Dam at 8:30 and 3.*

Beyond Ross Lake the highway runs toward Washington Pass through a very picturesque region of craggy peaks and subalpine wildflower meadows (this stretch of the North Cascades Highway is closed in winter). It then continues down into the Methow Valley, whose wooded, surprisingly flat valley floor, surrounded by towering cliffs, is covered with wildflowers in spring. The road next crosses the Okanogan Valley and River and passes over the northeastern mountains to Idaho.

HIGHWAY 9 – From Sedro Woolley, Highway 9 travels north past the hamlets of Wickersham, Acme, and Clipper, through a pretty green valley to Highway 542, which leads to Mount Baker (☞ *above*). At Wickersham, a detour northwest to Lake Whatcom makes for a short but splendid drive. On Saturday in July and August at 11 AM and 1 PM, you can ride through the woods on the vintage **Lake Whatcom Steam Train** (⊠ Lake Whatcom, south end, ☎ 360/595–2218). **Everybody's Store** (⊠ Hwy. 9, Van Zandt, ☎ 360/592–2297) in the town of Van Zandt is a good place to stock up on sandwiches and exotic foods. You can picnic on the store's grounds on tables beneath fruit trees.

Whatcom and Skagit Counties Essentials

Arriving and Departing

BY BUS

Greyhound (☎ 360/733–5251 or 800/231–2222) serves Fairhaven Station daily from downtown Seattle and Vancouver.

BY CAR

The entire region is easily accessible by driving north from Seattle on **I-5.**

BY PLANE

Horizon Air and United Express service **Bellingham International Airport** (⊠ 4255 Mitchell Way, Bakerview Exit off I-5, ☎ 360/676–

2500). *See* Air Travel *in* Smart Travel Tips A to Z for airline phone numbers.

BY TRAIN

Amtrak (☎ 800/872–7245) connects Seattle, Bellingham, and Vancouver.

Getting Around

BY CAR

Interstate 5 is the main north–south route through western Whatcom and Skagit counties. **Highway 542** winds east from Bellingham to Mount Baker. **Highway 20** heads east from Burlington to Sedro Woolley and continues on through the North Cascades to the Methow and Okanogan Valleys, and across the northeastern mountains to the Idaho state line near Newport.

Visitor Information

BABS (✉ Bed and Breakfast Service, ☎ 360/733–8642). **Bellingham/Whatcom County Convention and Visitors Bureau** (✉ 904 Potter St., Bellingham 98227, ☎ 360/671–3990 or 800/487–2032). **La Conner Chamber of Commerce** (✉ Lime Dock, 109 N. 1st St., 98257, ☎ 360/466–4778). **North Cascades National Park** (✉ 2105 Hwy. 20, Sedro Woolley 98264, ☎ 360/856–5700).

TACOMA AND VICINITY

Tacoma's history, unlike that of many other towns in the Northwest, is not linked inextricably to lumber and fishing but to the railroad (Tacoma was the first port on Puget Sound connected to the East by rail), to mining, and to the shipping of wheat to countries as far away as England. Old Tacoma photos show tall-masted windjammers loading at the City Waterway, whose storage sheds were promoted by local boosters as the "longest warehouse under one continuous roof in the world." Today, Tacoma is the largest container port in the Northwest. With a vibrant downtown, beautiful residential neighborhoods, and glorious parks, it is little wonder the self-proclaimed "City of Destiny" frequently appears on most-livable-cities lists.

This city of nearly 200,000 has many handsome brick buildings, fine views of Commencement Bay, a world-class state-history museum, and an impressive zoo. Tacoma is a convenient jumping-off point for exploring southern Washington, particularly Mount Rainier and Mount St. Helens and, across the Tacoma Narrows Bridge, the small waterfront towns of the Kitsap Peninsula.

Tacoma

36 mi south of Seattle on I–5.

A Good Walk

Begin your tour in the Waterfront District at **Union Station** ⑪, on Pacific Avenue between East 18th and 19th streets. Next door is the state-of-the-art **Washington State History Museum** ⑫. After lunch at one of the district's funky eateries, head north on Pacific to the **Tacoma Art Museum** ⑬. From the museum, head west on 11th Street to Broadway. Walk north on Broadway past the **Broadway Center for the Performing Arts** ⑭ and the **Children's Museum of Tacoma** ⑮. At 9th Street begins **Antique Row,** a collection of shops that are fun to browse through. Continue north along Tacoma Avenue to **Wright Park** ⑯ and the **Stadium Historic District** ⑰. No tour of Tacoma is complete without a visit to **Point Defiance Park** ⑱, which is at the far northwestern end of the city and is reached by car or bus.

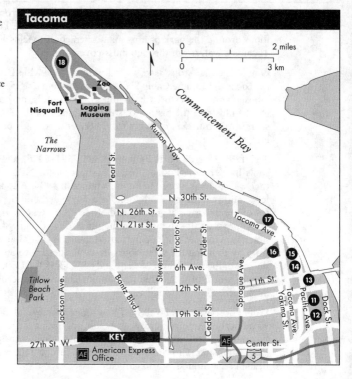

Tacoma

TIMING

Take at least an hour to look at the art at Union Station, but plan to spend half a day or more in the Washington State History Museum. The Tacoma Art Museum and Children's Museum each require about an hour. Antique Row and Wright Park are half-hour stops at most. A full day is necessary to take in all the attractions at Point Defiance Park, but the highlights can be visited in a few hours.

Sights to See

⑭ Broadway Center for the Performing Arts. Cultural activity in Tacoma centers on this complex of historic and new theaters. The famous theater architect B. Marcus Pritica designed the **Pantages** at 901 Broadway, a 1918 Greco-Roman–influenced music hall with classical figures, ornate columns, arches, and reliefs. W. C. Fields, Mae West, Charlie Chaplin, Bob Hope, and Stan Laurel all performed here. The Tacoma Symphony and BalleTacoma perform at the Pantages, which also presents touring musicals and other shows. Adjacent to the Pantages, the very contemporary **Theatre on the Square** (⊠ Broadway between 10th and 11th Sts.) is the home of the Tacoma Actors Guild, one of Washington's largest professional theater companies. In its early days, the **Rialto Theater** (⊠ 301 S. 9th St.), up Broadway a few blocks, presented vaudeville performances and silent films. The Tacoma Youth Symphony performs in the 1918 structure. ☎ 253/591–5890 for all theaters.

☼ ⑮ Children's Museum of Tacoma. Many of the hip and fun cultural, historical, and science exhibits at this facility are interactive, but you'll also find displays such as old board games and the artifacts of civilizations past and present. ⊠ 936 Broadway, ☎ 253/627–6031. ☞ $3.75. ☺ Tues.–Sat. 10–5, Sun. noon–5.

★ ☼ ⑱ Point Defiance Park. This 698-acre park, which juts into Commencement Bay, contains several museums and historical sites, extensive footpaths and hiking trails, picnic areas, a wide beachfront, and rose, dahlia, rhododendron, and other gardens. **Five Mile Drive,** which loops around the park past its major attractions, yields fine views of Tacoma's waterfront through moss-covered trees.

One of the first stops as you head west on Five Mile Drive south of the zoo is the 15-acre **Camp Six Logging Museum** (☎ 253/752–0047), whose exhibits—restored bunkhouses, hand tools, and other equipment—illustrate the history of steam logging from 1880 to 1950. A steam-train ride ($2) operates from here on weekends between noon and 4.

A bit farther west is **Fort Nisqually** (☎ 253/591–5339), a restored Hudson's Bay Trading Post. A British outpost on the Nisqually Delta in the 1830s, it was moved to Point Defiance in 1935. A spiked wooden fence and two fun-to-climb lookout towers surround the compound. Inside are the original granary and officers' quarters. Within the main house are a small exhibition on the fur trade and a gift shop. Admission to the fort is $1; it's open from Memorial Day to Labor Day daily from 11 to 4 and the same hours from Wednesday to Sunday during the rest of the year. **Never Never Land** (☎ 253/591–6117), a children's fantasy world of sculptured storybook characters, is across the parking lot from Fort Nisqually.

From Fort Nisqually, Five Mile Drive loops past several lookouts with views of the Narrows waterway. As it heads back toward the park entrance the drive passes viewing points that look onto lower Puget Sound and later onto Commencement Bay. Just past the road to Owen Beach is the rhododendron garden.

The natural habitats at the **Point Defiance Zoo and Aquarium** (☎ 253/591–5335) bring you close to beluga whales, walruses, sharks, apes, reptiles, and birds and other animals of the Pacific Rim. The zoo and the aquarium have gained an international reputation for their expert caretakers who treat injured wildlife.

Near the zoo are bus stops, several gardens, a marina, the ferry landing, and other facilities. ⊠ *Point Defiance Park: 5400 N. Pearl St.,* ☎ *253/305–1000.* ⌨ *Park free, zoo $6.75.* ☉ *Park daily dawn–dusk; zoo June–Aug., daily 10–7; Sept.–May, weekdays 10–4, weekends 10–5.*

⑰ Stadium Historic District. Several of the Victorian homes in this charming neighborhood, high on a hill overlooking Commencement Bay, have been converted to bed-and-breakfast inns. **Stadium High School** at 111 North E Street is in an elaborate château-style structure that was built in 1891 as a luxury hotel for the Northern Pacific Railroad. The building was converted into a high school after a 1906 fire.

⑬ Tacoma Art Museum. Among the highlights of this museum are works by artists of the Northwest and collections of Impressionist and 20th-century European paintings. Also on exhibit are many glass sculptures by Tacoma native Dale Chihuly. ⊠ *12th St. at Pacific Ave.,* ☎ *253/272–4258.* ⌨ *$3.* ☉ *Tues.–Sat. 10–5, Sun. noon–5.*

⑪ Union Station. This heirloom from the golden age of railroads dates from Tacoma's days as the western terminus of the Northern Pacific Railroad. Built by Reed and Stem, the architects of New York City's Grand Central Station, the copper-domed, Beaux Arts–style depot, which opened in 1911, shows the influence of the Roman Pantheon and 16th-century Italian Baroque building design. The station houses federal district courts; its rotunda (open to the public on weekdays from 10 to 4) contains what's billed as the largest single exhibit of glass sculptures by Dale Chihuly.

The area around the station is known as the **Waterfront District.** Many formerly run-down redbrick buildings have been renovated and opened as shops and businesses; the atmosphere here has been getting hipper by the minute. The first section of the Tacoma branch of the **University of Washington** opened in 1997 across from Union Station. ⊠ *1717 Pacific Ave.,* ☏ *253/931–7884.*

★ ⑫ **Washington State History Museum.** Adjacent to Union Station inside a 1996 building with the same opulent architecture and mammoth arches, Washington's official history museum presents interactive exhibits and multimedia installations about the exploration and settlement of the state. Indian, Eskimo, pioneer, and other artifacts are also on display. ⊠ *1911 Pacific Ave.,* ☏ *253/272–3500.* 🎟 *$7.* ☉ *Tues.–Wed. and Fri. 10–5, Thurs. 10–8, Sun. 1–5.*

⑯ **Wright Park.** The chief attraction at this 28-acre park, all of which is on the National Register of Historic Places, is the glass-domed **W. W. Seymour Botanical Conservatory** (⊠ 4th and S. G Sts., ☏ 253/591–5330), a Victorian-style greenhouse (one of only three such structures on the West Coast) with exotic flora. Across the street is the **Karpeles Manuscript Library Museum** (⊠ 407 S. G St., ☏ 253/383–2575), which preserves and exhibits letters and documents by individuals who have shaped history. ⊠ *Between 6th and Division Sts., Yakima and Tacoma Aves.,* ☏ *253/591–5331.* 🎟 *Free.* ☉ *Park daily dawn–dusk, conservatory daily 8:30–4:20, museum daily 10–4.*

Dining and Lodging

$$–$$$ ✕ **E. R. Rogers Restaurant.** One of the best restaurants in the Tacoma area is 10 mi south of town in Steilacoom, the oldest incorporated town in Washington. Housed in an 1891 mansion with views of the Tacoma Narrows Bridge, it is decorated in Victorian style, with lace valances, brass fixtures, and antiques. The place is most famous for its prime rib and for its extensive Sunday brunch buffet, consisting of local favorites such as fresh oysters, poached or smoked salmon, cracked Dungeness crab, steamed clams, and pickled herring. ⊠ *1702 Commercial St., Steilacoom,* ☏ *253/582–0280. MC, V. No lunch.*

$$–$$$ ✕ **Harbor Lights.** This waterfront institution adorned with glass floats, stuffed fish, life preservers, and other nautical furnishings hasn't changed since the 1950s. Many of the seafood and other preparations are also classic—the steamed clams (in season) and the fish-and-chips (light and not greasy) are particularly good. The view of Commencement Bay is splendid, so try to snag a window seat. ⊠ *2761 Ruston Way,* ☏ *253/752–8600. AE, DC, MC, V. No lunch Sun.*

$$ ✕ **Lobster Shop.** Of this traditional seafood restaurant's two locations, the older one, on Dash Point, is cozier than its sister on Ruston Way. But both have fine views of Commencement Bay and simply prepared seafood, with salmon the perennial favorite. There's a cocktail lounge on Ruston Way; beer and wine are available on Dash Point. ⊠ *6912 Soundview Dr. NE (off Dash Point Rd.),* ☏ *253/927–1513;* ⊠ *4013 Ruston Way,* ☏ *253/759–2165. AE, DC, MC, V.*

$$ ✕ **Luciano's.** Chef Alfredo Russo and his staff prepare southern Italian cuisine with a neapolitan influence. The decor takes advantage of the waterfront setting, with three-story-high skylights and black or red exposed beams against forest-green walls. ⊠ *3327 Ruston Way,* ☏ *253/ 756–5611. MC, V.*

$$ ✕ **Old House Café.** Its location in the heart of the Proctor District shopping area makes this upstairs café an especially convenient place for lunch. The café's interior incorporates many antique fixtures, including a stained-glass window from a Yakima building and light fixtures from a turn-of-the-century Seattle bank. The kitchen specializes in the

eclectic fare known as new American; culinary highlights include a warm scallop salad, and king salmon baked in phyllo dough. ⊠ *2717 N. Proctor St.,* ☎ *253/759–7336. AE, MC, V. Closed Sun. No dinner Mon.*

$–$$ ✕ **The Swiss.** The former Swiss Hall holds this extremely popular Waterfront District eatery, which serves creative fare. At lunch, try one of the hot sandwiches, which are huge by local standards; at dinner the menu turns to pasta dishes and fresh local seafood. A high, pressed-tin ceiling covers the main dining and bar area. Rooms in the back have pool tables and a stage where jazz is played on the weekends. ⊠ *1904 S. Jefferson Ave.,* ☎ *253/572–2821. No credit cards.*

$ ✕ **Antique Sandwich Company.** You can get breakfast, lunch, or dinner at this deli-style café, which specializes in hearty soups, classic children's food like waffles and peanut butter and jelly sandwiches, and well-prepared espresso drinks. Old posters on the walls, plastic bears for serving honey, and a toy-covered children's play area help set a cheerful mood. On weekends come hear live folk and classical music; Tuesday is open-mike night. ⊠ *5102 N. Pearl St.,* ☎ *253/752–4069. Reservations not accepted. AE, MC, V.*

$$$ 🛏 **Chinaberry Hill.** Original fixtures and stained-glass windows are among the grace notes in this B&B in a 1889 Queen Anne–style home in the Stadium Historic District. Former Coloradans Cecil and Yarrow Wayman have furnished each room with an antique feather bed, robes, and fine-quality linens; three rooms have whirlpool tubs. The carriage house in back, which sleeps six, contains memorabilia from its "horse and buggy" days. Room rates include a breakfast of a seasonal fruit cup followed by an enormous hot entrée. ⊠ *302 N. Tacoma Ave., 98403,* ☎ *253/272–1282,* 🖷 *253/272–1335. 5 rooms. AE, D, MC, V.*

$$$ 🛏 **Sheraton Tacoma Hotel.** The only high-quality alternative to the Victorian B&Bs in the city is adjacent to the convention center. Most rooms in the 26-story hotel are smallish but have tasteful but, unobtrusive corporate decor, and views of Commencement Bay, Mount Rainier, or both. Guests in the executive suites have a concierge and receive a complimentary Continental breakfast. ⊠ *1320 Broadway Plaza, 98402,* ☎ *253/572–3200 or 800/845–9466,* 🖷 *253/591–4105. 319 rooms. 2 restaurants, 3 bars, in-room data ports, room service, hot tub, sauna, dry cleaning, concierge, business services, meeting rooms, parking (fee). AE, DC, MC, V.*

$$–$$$ 🛏 **The Villa.** Friendly hosts Becky and Greg Anglemyer operate this Stadium Historic District B&B. The focal point of the grand entrance to their Mediterranean-style mansion is a curved wooden staircase leading to the guest suites. The Bay View suite has a fireplace and views of Commencement Bay and the Olympic Mountains. You can lounge in several downstairs rooms, one of them a glassed-in sunporch teeming with plants and flowers. The room rates include a full gourmet breakfast. ⊠ *705 N. 5th St., 98403,* ☎ *253/572–1157,* 🖷 *253/572–1805. 4 rooms. Business services. AE, MC, V.*

$$ 🛏 **Commencement Bay Bed & Breakfast.** This home in north Tacoma contains three individually decorated rooms. Myrtle's Room has a four-poster queen bed and a view of the bay, the Cascade Range, and Mount Rainier. All rooms have telephones and voice mail, and two have TVs with VCRs. Hosts Sharon and Bill Kaufmann supply a full breakfast (included in the room rates) and plenty of information about the area. ⊠ *3312 N. Union Ave., 98407,* ☎ *253/752–8175,* 🖷 *253/759–4025. 3 rooms. Hot tub, business services. MC, V.*

Nightlife and the Arts

BARS AND LOUNGES

Head to **McCabe's** (⊠ 2611 Pacific Ave., ☎ 253/272–5403) for country music and dancing (lessons provided most nights). On weekends, live jazz and blues heighten the Cajun atmosphere at **Roof-n-Doof's New Orleans Cafe** (⊠ 754 Pacific Ave., ☎ 253/572–5113). The **Swiss** (⊠ 1904 S. Jefferson Ave., ☎ 253/572–2821) has microbrews on tap, pool tables, and weekend jazz. The music varies from night to night at the **Vault** (⊠ 1025 Pacific Ave., ☎ 253/572–3145), a dance club.

THEATER

The theaters of the **Broadway Center for the Performing Arts** (☎ 253/591–5890) present concerts and musicals and other theatrical productions (☞ Sights to See, *above*).

Outdoor Activities and Sports

GOLF

The **Elks-Allenmore Public Golf Course** (⊠ 2125 S. Cedar St., ☎ 253/627–7211) is an 18-hole, par-71 course; the greens fee is $20, plus $20 for a cart. **North Shore Golf and Country Club** (⊠ 4101 North Shore Blvd., ☎ 253/927–1375) is an 18-hole, par-71 course; the greens fee is $20 on weekdays and $30 on weekends, plus $20 for a cart. Call seven days in advance to obtain a tee time.

SPECTATOR SPORTS

The **Tacoma Rainiers,** the Class AAA affiliate of the Seattle Mariners baseball team, play at Cheney Stadium (⊠ 2502 S. Tyler St., ☎ 253/752–7707). The **Tacoma Rockets** (☎ 360/627–3653) of the Western Hockey League play their games at the Tacoma Dome (⊠ 2727 E. D St., ☎ 253/272–3663).

Spanaway Speedway (⊠ 16413 22nd Ave. E, Spanaway, ☎ 253/537–7551), 7 mi south of Tacoma, hosts auto racing. Midweek competition features amateurs racing their "street legal" automobiles.

Shopping

Antique Row (⊠ Broadway and St. Helen's St. between 7th and 9th Sts.) contains a few upscale antiques stores and boutiques selling collectibles and 1950s paraphernalia. A farmers' market is held here during the summer on Thursday.

Freighthouse Square Public Market (⊠ Corner of 25th and D streets) is a former railroad warehouse that's been converted into several small gift shops, offbeat boutiques, and ethnic food stalls.

The **Proctor District** in Tacoma's north end has several dozen businesses of all types. The district's **Pacific Northwest Shop** (⊠ 2702 N. Proctor St., ☎ 253/752–2242) sells apparel, books, pottery, food, and wine from the region. Neon lights in the shape of little blue mice adorn the marquee of the **Blue Mouse Theater** (⊠ 2611 N. Proctor St., ☎ 253/752–9500) screening room.

Tacoma Mall (⊠ Tacoma Mall Blvd. off I–5, ☎ 253/475–4565), 1½ mi south of the Tacoma Dome, contains department stores, specialty shops, and restaurants.

Tacoma Essentials

Arriving and Departing

BY BOAT

Argosy Cruises (⊠ Pier 55, Seattle, ☎ 206/623–4252) operates daily tour-boat service to Tacoma.

BY BUS

Pierce Transit (☎ 253/581–8000) runs a shuttle between Seattle and Tacoma. **Shuttle Express** (☎ 425/487–7433) provides service between Sea-Tac Airport and Tacoma. Rides can be arranged in advance or upon arrival.

BY CAR
Interstate 5 is the main north–south route into Tacoma.

BY PLANE
Sea-Tac International Airport (☞ Seattle A to Z *in* Chapter 4) is 18 mi from Tacoma.

Getting Around
BY BUS
Pierce Transit (☎ 253/581–8000) provides local bus service.

BY CAR
Pearl Street and Broadway are two of the main north–south streets through downtown Tacoma. Ruston Way winds to the northwest along the Commencement Bay waterfront.

Contacts and Resources
GUIDED TOURS
Tacoma Architectural Foundation (☎ 253/594–7839) conducts Saturday walking tours ($5) of Tacoma that begin at the Washington State History Museum (✉ 1911 Pacific Ave.).

VISITOR INFORMATION
Tacoma–Pierce County Visitor and Convention Bureau (✉ Box 1754, Tacoma 98401, ☎ 253/627–2836 or 800/272–2662).

THE OLYMPIC PENINSULA

Wilderness covers much of the rugged Olympic Peninsula, the westernmost corner of the lower 48 United States. Its heart of craggy mountains and a large section of its ocean shore are safeguarded in Olympic National Park and several Indian reservations. Olympic National Forest encircles the park like a protective shield. This is a landscape of almost incredible variety, from the wild Pacific coast to the sheltered waters of the Hood Canal, from the semi-dry bluffs of the Strait of Juan de Fuca to the gushing rivers of the Olympic Rain Forest, from smoothly glaciated valleys to the razor edges of the Olympic Mountain ridges.

The Olympic Peninsula's deeply glaciated and heavily forested terrain—large portions of which are almost inaccessible—and the exceptionally wet climate create an otherworldly air, helping to define the peninsula as a land apart. The rain forest of the western river valleys may get more than 160 inches of rain per year; the dry slopes of the northeastern peninsula, in the rain shadow of the mountains, may receive less than 16 inches. As a result, the peninsula has some of the wettest and driest climates in the coastal Pacific Northwest, which in turn supports a greater than usual diversity of plants and animals.

Another reason the peninsula has sustained its lush vegetation and great variety of wildlife is that all plants and animals within Olympic National Park are strictly protected—all hunting, firearms, and off-road vehicles are prohibited, as is any disturbance to plants or wildlife. Many areas of the national forest are maintained as untrafficked wilderness. Furthermore, Native American tribal regulations restrict access to, and activity within, certain parts of reservations; check with local authorities for details.

Because of the rugged terrain and because no roads cross the heart of the peninsula's mountains, much of the region is accessible only to backpackers, but the 300-mi loop made by U.S. 101 provides glimpses of ocean, rain forest, and mountains. Several side roads offer excellent (if sometimes unpaved) opportunities for exploring remote villages,

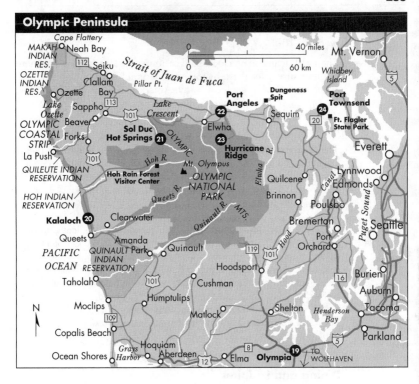

beaches, and valleys. This section describes a journey clockwise, primarily via U.S. 101 (although jaunts from the main drag are suggested), beginning and ending in Olympia.

Sea-run cutthroat trout and steelhead are abundant in several coastal rivers. In Aberdeen and Hoquiam, Dungeness crabs and rockfish are the primary catches. For more information about fishing in the region, contact the **North Olympic Peninsula Visitor and Convention Bureau** (☞ The Olympic Peninsula Essentials, *below*).

Olympia

⑲ *28 mi south of Tacoma on I–5.*

Olympia, Washington's state capital, was first settled in 1846, the year the Oregon Territory was established by the United States. The town itself was founded in 1850, and it has served as capital since Washington split off from Oregon in 1853. Olympia retains a relaxed small-town air even when the state legislature is in session. When the legislators are away, the mood can be downright drowsy.

★ Olympia's main attractions are the buildings grouped together on the **Capitol Campus** on a bluff high above Capitol Lake. The handsome neo-Roman-style **Legislative Building** was finished in 1928. Its 287-ft dome is patterned on that of the Capitol Building in Washington, D.C. Visitors' galleries provide glimpses of state senators and representatives in action. The grounds surrounding the Legislative Building contain memorials, monuments, rose gardens (at their best in summer), and Japanese cherry trees (usually in glorious bloom by March). The 1920s **Conservatory** is open year-round on weekdays from 8 to 3 and also on weekends in summer. Directly behind the Legislative Building is the modern **State Library**, which has exhibits devoted to Washington's history. Murals by Washington artists Mark

Tobey and Kenneth Callahan hang here. ⊠ *Legislative Bldg., Capitol Way between 10th and 14th Aves.,* ☎ *360/586–8687.* 🎟 *Free.* ⊙ *Tours daily on the hr 10–3.*

The 1920s mansion of a local banker houses the **State Capitol Museum.** Exhibits survey local art, history, and natural history. The permanent collection includes rare local Native American baskets. ⊠ *211 W. 21st St., off Capitol Way, 7 blocks south of the Legislative Bldg.,* ☎ *360/753–2580.* 🎟 *Free; donations accepted.* ⊙ *Tues.–Fri. 10–4, weekends noon–4.*

The **Japanese Garden,** a symbol of the sister-city relationship between Olympia and Yashiro, Japan, opened in 1989. Within the garden are a waterfall, a bamboo grove, a koi pond, and stone lanterns. ⊠ *Union and Plum Sts. east of the Capitol Campus,* ☎ *no phone.* 🎟 *Free.* ⊙ *Daily dawn–dusk.*

OFF THE BEATEN PATH
WOLFHAVEN INTERNATIONAL – This 80-acre sanctuary dedicated to wolf conservation is 15 mi south of Olympia. You can take walk-through guided tours year-round. On Friday and Saturday evenings in the summer, the facility opens for a public Howl-in (reservations essential), with tours, musicians performing around a campfire, and howling with the wolves. ⊠ *3111 Offut Lake Rd., Tenino (from Olympia, take I–5 south to Exit 99 and follow brown-and-white signs east for 7 mi),* ☎ *800/448–9653.* 🎟 *Daily tours $5, Howl-ins $6.* ⊙ *Guided walking tours May–Sept., Wed.–Mon. 10–4; Oct.–Apr., Wed.–Mon. 10–3. Howl-ins May–Labor Day, Fri.–Sat. 6:30–9:30.*

Dining and Lodging

$$$ ✕ **La Petite Maison.** The chefs at Olympia's premier fine-dining establishment prepare imaginative French food inside a converted 1890s farmhouse. Classical music, unobtrusive service, and crisp linens create a quietly elegant ambience. An eclectic wine list and excellent desserts, among them a Grand Marnier torte, complete the picture. ⊠ *101 Division St.,* ☎ *360/943–8812. MC, V. Closed Sun. No lunch Mon. or Sat.*

$$ ✕ **Alice's Restaurant.** A rural farmhouse adjacent to the Johnson Creek
★ Winery in the Skookumchuck Valley, 15 mi southeast of Olympia, holds this restaurant, whose ambience is right out of a Norman Rockwell illustration. The winery's vintages accompany six-course meals that are sophisticated variations on classical American cuisine. ⊠ *19248 Johnson Creek Rd. E (from Olympia, follow Capitol Blvd. south, head east at Hwy. 507 in Tenino for 5 mi, and turn right onto Johnson Creek Rd. for 5 mi),* ☎ *360/264–2887. Reservations essential. AE, MC, V. Closed Mon.–Tues. No lunch.*

$–$$ ✕ **Ben Moore's Cafe.** This old-fashioned café serves homey South Sound fare like oyster and geoduck (a huge, tasty northwestern clam) tempura, plus hamburgers and microbrews. ⊠ *112 4th Ave.,* ☎ *360/357–7527. MC, V.*

$–$$ ✕ **Mondo Shrimp.** The younger crowd hangs out at this spunky storefront cafe to partake of variations on a theme. Shrimp is served in a spicy red sauce, as a salad, wrapped in tortillas, and more. ⊠ *415 Water St.,* ☎ *360/352–5759. AE, D, DC, MC, V.*

$ ✕ **The Fish Bowl Pub and Cafe.** In a very "fishy" setting, great beer and great nibbles (such as whole-wheat-crust pizzas from the wood-fired ovens) are to be had at this brew pub in downtown Olympia. ⊠ *515 Jefferson Ave.,* ☎ *360/943–3650. MC, V.*

$ ✕ **Wagner's.** A local landmark, this bakery and deli serves sumptuous pastries and delectable sandwiches. ⊠ *1013 Capitol Way,* ☎ *360/357–7268. MC, V.*

$$ 🏨 **Holiday Inn Select.** Large but friendly, this hotel close to downtown has views of Capitol Lake, the capitol dome, and the surrounding hills. The rooms are spacious and comfortable; those facing the water are especially appealing. The rates include breakfast. ⊠ *2300 Evergreen Park Dr., 98502,* ☎ *360/943–4000,* FAX *360/357–6604. 177 rooms. 2 restaurants, bar, no-smoking rooms, pool, hot tub. AE, D, MC, V.*

Nightlife
The **Fourth Avenue Tavern** (⊠ 210 E. 4th Ave., ☎ 360/786–1444), a beer-and-wine joint with pool tables and assorted games, serves up 26 brews on tap, homemade pizza, and, on weekends, live rock music.

Grays Harbor

50 mi west of Olympia on Hwy 109.

This large bay and marine estuary at the mouth of the Chehalis River is separated from the fury of the North Pacific by long, forested sand spits. Local marshes support an oyster industry and cranberries are raised commercially in the bogs to the south. The second-growth rain forest here is the densest in the state, in part because Grays Harbor has one of the highest rainfalls in the state. When it doesn't rain, fogs usually hide the sun.

The bay's two major towns, **Aberdeen** and **Hoquiam,** once lived off the logging, pulp, and fishing industries, but the tall trees have been cut down and the salmon are almost extinct. Today, the towns still maintain much of their historic character, and now that the industrial noise and stink are gone, increasing numbers of visitors flock here year-round to enjoy the region's natural beauty. In fall and spring, Grays Harbor is home to thousands of migrating sea and shorebirds. So many visitors arrive at those times that shuttle buses from Hoquiam high school to the most popular bird-watching sites on the Bowerman Basin, west of town (in the northeastern corner of the harbor).

En Route From Grays Harbor, Highway 109 runs north along the coast to Ocean City and Moclips. In spring and autumn, follow signs to the **Bowerman Basin** west of Hoquiam to look at the thousands of migratory shorebirds that pause here during their annual migration. A few stay here year-round. Keep a lookout for bald eagles, harriers, red-tailed hawks, merlins, and peregrine falcons.

Copalis Beach

5 mi north of Grays Harbor, 21 mi from Hoquiam on Hwy. 109.

Copalis Beach is a pleasant huddle of roadside stores and motels that serves visitors to the easily accessible beach and picnic areas.

Lodging
$$ 🏨 **Iron Springs Resort.** The cottages here accommodate from 2 to 10 people. Each has its own fireplace and kitchen; dimly lit older cabins are decorated with a fun hodgepodge of furniture from the 1950s to the 1970s; newer ones (Nos. 22 to 25) are brighter and more comfortable, with wide ocean views. Cottage No. 6 has no view, but all the others have unobstructed beach, river, or forest views. ⊠ *3707 Hwy. 109 (3 mi north of Copalis Beach), 98535,* ☎ *360/276–4230,* FAX *360/276–4365. 25 units. Pool. AE, MC, V.*

Moclips

8 mi north of Copalis Beach on Hwy. 109.

The homes in unpretentious Moclips are scattered among the woods hugging the main road high above the ocean.

Dining and Lodging

$$ ✕⊡ **Ocean Crest Resort.** Casual and alluringly sea worn, the Ocean
★   Crest rests high on a bluff above a stunning stretch of the Pacific. The
accommodations vary from single studios with no views or fireplaces
to large studios with both; there are well-situated family cottages as
well. The resort has direct access to the beach down a maze of steps.
Moss-covered woods frame the restaurant's ocean views. Though it's
not included in the room rate, the breakfast served in the resort's no-
table dining room is especially famous. ⊠ *4651 Hwy. 109, 98562,* ☎
360/276–4465, 🄵🄰🄷 *360/276–4149. 45 rooms. Restaurant, bar, pool,
hot tub, health club. AE, D, MC, V.*

En Route   Though they are closed to nontribal visitors, the beaches along High-
way 109 north of Moclips are magnificent. Surf-tossed driftwood piles
up dramatically on the strand, particularly where the highway ends,
8 mi north of Moclips at **Taholah.** Taholah, the central village of the
Quinault Indian Reservation, has a gas station, a seafood store, and
an excellent museum where you can learn about tribal culture and
history. The Quinault Pride Fish House sells fresh, canned, and
smoked salmon and steelhead, as well as Quinault arts and crafts.

Quinault

38 mi north of Hoquiam on U.S. 101.

U.S. 101 heads north from Hoquiam along the west fork of the Ho-
quiam River but soon follows the Humptulips River until it crosses the
divide to **Quinault Lake.** Part of this beautiful lake lies in Olympic Na-
tional Park, part in Olympic National Forest, and part on the Quin-
ault reservation. The town of Quinault has the Lake Quinault Lodge
and a general store.

Dining and Lodging

$$$ ✕⊡ **Lake Quinault Lodge.** The lodge is set on a perfect glacial lake amid
★   the Olympic National Forest. Old-growth forests are an easy hike
away, and there is good trout fishing. The main lodge, built in 1926
of cedar shingles, has antiques-filled public rooms and a large stone
fireplace. Most of the sparsely furnished guest rooms have views of the
landscaped lawns that frame the perfectly serene lake. The lodge has
a very fine restaurant; the old-fashioned bar is lively and inviting. ⊠
S. Shore Rd. (Box 7), 98575, ☎ *360/288–2900 or 800/562–6672,* 🄵🄰🄷
*360/288–2901. 92 rooms. Restaurant, bar, indoor pool, hot tub, sauna,
putting green. MC, V.*

Kalaloch

⓴   *32 mi west of Quinault on U.S. 101.*

Many well-marked trails lead from the coastal highway north of
Kalaloch (pronounced "*Kway*-lock")—each ¼ mi or less in length—
to spectacular Pacific beaches.

Dining and Lodging

$$–$$$ ✕⊡ **Kalaloch Lodge.** An older lodge and cabins plus a newer hotel
and log cabins make up this facility within the Olympic National Forest. Lodge rooms are unadorned, rustic, and clean; most have ocean
views and fireplaces. A few larger cabins have private outdoor picnic areas near the beach. The old cabins can be drafty in winter and
have minimal kitchens and other amenities, though they are atmospheric. The informal lodge offers few resort-type amenities. The upstairs cocktail lounge, like the restaurant, has unobstructed ocean views.
⊠ *157151 U.S. 101 (HC 80, Box 1100), Forks-Kalaloch 98331,* ☎

360/962–2271, FAX 360/962–3391. 58 rooms and cabins. Restaurant. AE, MC, V.

OFF THE BEATEN PATH

HOH RAIN FOREST – An 18-mi spur road winds from U.S. 101 to the Hoh River Rain Forest, where spruce and hemlock trees soar to heights of more than 200 ft. Alders and big-leaf maples are so densely covered with mosses they look more like shaggy prehistoric animals than trees. A visitor center explains how the forest functions and has short trails leading among the trees. Look for elk browsing in shaded glens. The average rainfall here is 150 inches a year. The Hoh Visitor Center, at the campground and ranger center at road's end, has information about the nature trails. The Hall of Mosses trail is a well-maintained ¾-mi path; the 1¼-mi Spruce Trail follows the Hoh River. Naturalist-led campfire programs and walks are conducted daily in July and August. The 18-mi Hoh River Trail follows the Hoh River to the base of Mount Olympus, which rises 7,965 ft above the forest floor. The climb requires experience and equipment, but the views from the base are spectacular. ✉ *From U.S. 101 (about 20 mi north of Kalaloch) take Upper Hoh Rd. 18 mi east to Hoh Rain Forest Visitor Center,* ☎ *360/374–6925.* 🎫 *Park $10.* ⏲ *Visitor center year-round but often unstaffed Sept.–May.*

Forks

35 mi north of Kalaloch on U.S. 101.

The small town of Forks is a friendly former logging town that takes its name from its proximity to the junction of the Bogachiel and Calawah rivers; they merge with the Soleduck River to form the Quillayute, which empties into the Pacific at the Indian village of La Push. Since the decline of logging due to a shortage of trees, Forks has been marketing the beauty of the neighboring rain forests and rivers. The countryside surrounding Forks is exceptionally green, since the town receives more than 100 inches of rain in an average year.

La Push

15 mi west of Forks on Hwy. 106 (La Push Rd.).

La Push is the tribal center of the Quileute Indians. One theory about the town's name is that it is a variation on the French *la bouche,* "the mouth"; this makes sense, since it's at the mouth of the Quileute River. The coast here is dotted with offshore rock spires known as seastacks, and you may catch a glimpse of bald eagles nesting in the nearby cliffs. During low tide, the tide pools on nearby **Second and Third beaches** brim with life, and you can walk out to some seastacks. Gray whales play offshore during their annual migrations, and most of the year the waves are great for surfing and kayaking (if you bring a wet suit).

OFF THE BEATEN PATH

THE NORTHWESTERN COAST – From Forks, U.S. 101 continues north and east through the Soleduck River valley, which is known for its great steelhead fishing. At Sappho, Burnt Mountain Road (Highway 113) heads north to Highway 112. If you head west on Highway 112, you'll eventually end up at Neah Bay and Cape Flattery. The **Makah Indian Reservation** is at Neah Bay; 500-year-old artifacts are carefully preserved and displayed in the truly splendid Makah Museum. If you head southwest on Hoko-Ozette Road at Hoko, 18 mi east of Neah Bay, you'll end up at beautiful **Ozette Lake,** where a 3-mi planked trail leads to pristine beaches and campsites (☎ 360/963–2725 to reserve a space). The 57-mi Olympic Coastal Strip between the edge of the Quinault Indian Reservation and Cape Flattery is accessible from here.

En Route U.S. 101 at Sappho leads east through the Olympic National Forest toward Lake Crescent. The Washington State Department of Fisheries operates the **Soleduck Hatchery,** 8 mi east of Sappho. Interpretive displays describe the nuances of fish breeding. ⊠ *1420 Pavel Rd., ☎ 360/327–3246.* 🎫 *Free.* ⊙ *Daily 8–4:30.*

Lake Crescent

28 mi east of Forks on U.S. 101.

The appearance of deep-azure Lake Crescent, a mountain lake in an enormous crescent shape, changes depending on your perspective. In the evening, low bands of clouds often linger over its reflective surface, caught between the surrounding mountains. Along the lake's 12-mi perimeter are campgrounds, resorts, trails, and places to canoe and fish. Among Lake Crescent's famous guests was Franklin D. Roosevelt, whose negotiations with U.S. senators and Parks Department officials at the Lake Crescent Lodge in 1937 (for which the cabins were built) led to the creation of the Olympic National Forest. The original lodge buildings of 1915 are still in use, well worn but still comfortable.

Dining and Lodging

$$–$$$ ✕🏨 **Lake Crescent Lodge.** The big main lodge and small cabins at this facility 20 mi west of downtown Port Angeles overlook Lake Crescent. Units in the lodge are minimal—bathrooms down the hall, dimly lit rooms. Standard motel-style units are available with private baths and lake views but no TVs or phones. Trout fishing, hiking, and boating are among the daily activities, and you can also take part in evening nature programs. The food in the restaurant is nothing special, but the service is cheerful and efficient. ⊠ *416 Lake Crescent Rd., Port Angeles 98363, ☎ 360/928–3211. 52 units. Restaurant, boating, fishing. AE, DC, MC, V. Closed Nov.–Apr.*

Sol Duc Hot Springs

㉑ *12 mi from Lake Crescent on Soleduck Rd., south from U.S. 101 at Fairholm.*

Native Americans have known about the soothing waters of Sol Duc Hot Springs for generations, and the springs been popular with non-natives since pioneer days. There are three hot sulfur pools, ranging in temperature from 98°F to 104°F. The **Sol Duc Hot Springs Resort** (☞ *below*), which dates from 1910, has cabins, a restaurant, and a hamburger stand. It is not necessary to stay at the resort to use the hot springs. ⊠ *Soleduck Rd., ☎ 360/327–3583.* 🎫 *Springs $6.* ⊙ *Mid-May–Sept., daily 9–9; Apr.–mid-May and Oct., daily 9–5.*

Dining and Lodging

$$ ✕🏨 **Sol Duc Hot Springs Resort.** The 32 cheery, if minimally outfitted, cabins at this century-old resort all have separate bathrooms, and some have kitchens. The attractive dining room serves unpretentious meals (breakfast, lunch, and dinner). ⊠ *Soleduck Rd. (Box 2168), 98362, ☎ 360/327–3583, FAX 360/327–3398. 32 units and camping and RV facilities. Restaurant, pool, hot springs. MC, V. Closed mid-Oct.–mid-May.*

Port Angeles

㉒ *27 mi east of Lake Crescent on U.S. 101.*

Port Angeles is a former mill town and commercial fishing port directly across the Strait of Juan de Fuca from Victoria, British Columbia. The town has several natural and historical points of interest.

Ediz Hook, at the western end of Port Angeles, is a long natural sand spit that protects the harbor from big waves and storms. The Hook is a fine place to take a walk along the water and watch shore and sea birds, and to spot the occasional seal, orca, or gray whale. From downtown, take Front Street west and follow it as it meanders past the shuttered lumber mill.

The **Clallam County Historical Museum** is a handsome 1914 Georgian Revival building that was a courthouse. You can explore the original courtroom, which is still intact, and sit in the judge's chair. An engaging exhibition details the lifestyles and history of Port Angeles's Native American and Anglo communities. The museum is scheduled to relocate to the nearby Lincoln School at 8th and C streets, probably sometime in 2000. ⊠ 223 E. 4th St., ☎ 360/417–2364. ☜ Free; donations accepted. ☉ June–Aug., Mon.–Sat. 10–4; Sept.–May, weekdays 10–4.

The **Port Angeles Fine Arts Center,** a small but surprisingly sophisticated museum, is inside the former home of artist and publisher Esther Barrows Webster, one of Port Angeles's most energetic and cultured citizens. Outdoor sculpture and trees surround the center, which has panoramic views of the city and the harbor. Exhibitions emphasize the works of emerging and well-established Pacific Northwest artists in various media. ⊠ 1203 W. Lauridsen Blvd., ☎ 360/457–3532. ☜ Free. ☉ Thurs.–Sun. 11–5, and by appointment.

☾ The city of Port Angeles and Peninsula College operate the modest **aquarium** of the Arthur D. Feiro Marine Laboratory. Many kinds of local sea life, including octopuses, scallops, rockfish, and anemones, are on display, and there are a few touch tanks. The tour is self-guided, but volunteers are on hand to answer questions. ⊠ Port Angeles City Pier, ☎ 360/452–9277, ext. 264. ☜ $3. ☉ June–Aug., daily 10–8; Sept.–May, weekends noon–4.

★ ㉓ The view from 5,200-ft-high **Hurricane Ridge,** 17 mi south of Port Angeles, includes the Olympics, the Strait of Juan de Fuca, and Vancouver Island. The winding road leading to the ridge is easily negotiated by car. In the summer, rangers lead hikes and give talks about local geology and flora and fauna. Paved walkways that are accessible to users of wheelchairs, and trails for advanced climbers provide an opportunity to see wildflowers like glacier lilies and lupine, as well as deer, marmots, and mountain goats (though the last are not native but were introduced). Do *not* feed the deer, even though they're quite tame. In winter, the area has miles of cross-country ski routes and a modest downhill ski operation, which is open on weekends when the snow is not too deep. ⊠ National Park Visitor Center, 600 E. Park Ave., Port Angeles 98362, ☎ 360/452–0330. ☉ Daily 9–4.

Dining and Lodging

$$$–$$$$ ✕ **C'est Si Bon.** More formal and more French than is typical on the decidedly informal, very northwestern Olympic Peninsula, this spot stands out for its ambience. Ornate lighting fixtures illuminate large European oil paintings hanging against bold red walls. French expatriates Norbert and Michele Juhasz prepare good dishes that reflect the influence of their homeland. The wine list is superb, as are the desserts (especially the chocolate mousse). ⊠ 2300 Hwy. 10 1E (4 mi east of Port Angeles), ☎ 360/452–8888. Reservations essential. AE, DC, MC, V. Closed Mon. No lunch.

$ ✕ **First Street Haven.** Small and informal, this storefront restaurant serves high-quality breakfasts and lunches, plus good espresso drinks and desserts. Breakfast is served all day on Sunday. All the muffins, coffee cakes, and scones are baked on the premises. ⊠ *107 E. 1st St.,* ☎ *360/ 457–0352. Reservations not accepted. No credit cards. No dinner.*

$$$–$$$$ 🏠 **Domaine Madeleine.** The owners of this luxury B&B on a bluff above
★ the Strait of Juan de Fuca love to pamper their guests. Each of the four rooms, decorated with either impressionist or Asian accents, has a view of the water set against impeccably landscaped grounds. Gas fireplaces, whirlpool tubs, VCRs (you can borrow videos from an extensive collection), and CD/tape players are other pluses. The living room has a 14-ft basalt fireplace, antique Asian furnishings, and a harpsichord. For breakfast (included in the room rates) expect a five-course gourmet affair with fresh baguettes and entrées like chicken crepes and seafood omelets. ⊠ *146 Wildflower La., 8 mi east of Port Angeles, 98362,* ☎ *360/457–4174,* ℻ *360/457–3037. 4 rooms. AE, D, DC, MC, V.*

$$–$$$ 🏠 **Tudor Inn.** This B&B in a 1910 Tudor-style house in a residential neighborhood is about 12 blocks from the dock for the Victoria-bound ferry. The largest room has a private balcony, a fireplace, and an English garden painted on the wall; the smaller rooms have just enough space for the bed and a dresser. Breakfast and afternoon tea are included in the room rates. No smoking is permitted at the inn. ⊠ *1108 S. Oak St., 98362,* ☎ *360/452–3138. 5 rooms. MC, V.*

$ 🏠 **Flagstone Motel.** Many of the small but immaculate rooms here have views of the harbor or Mount Olympus. Fresh coffee and sweet rolls will get you started again in the morning. ⊠ *415 E. 1st St., 98362,* ☎ *360/457–9494,* ℻ *360/457–9494. 45 rooms. Pool, sauna. AE, D, DC, MC, V.*

Outdoor Activities and Sports

Hurricane Ridge (☞ *above*) has a modest downhill skiing operation, with two rope tows and a lift, as well as miles of cross-country ski trails.

Sequim

17 mi east of Port Angeles on U.S. 101.

There's not much to Sequim, as seen from U.S. 101, since most of the homes are tucked away on bluffs or under trees, but a few miles north is the beautiful and fertile Dungeness region. This shallow valley, framed to the south by the majestic Olympic Mountains, has some of
★ the lowest rainfall in western Washington. At its northern tip is **Dungeness Spit,** a finger of sand sheltering the bay from the crashing surf. The 8-mi spit (one of the longest in the world) extends to the **Dungeness Lighthouse,** in operation since 1867. A temporary home to at least 30,000 migratory waterfowl each year (spring and fall are the best viewing times, but many species live here in summer), the entire spit has been protected within the **Dungeness National Wildlife Refuge** since 1915. ⊠ *Kitchen Rd., 3 mi north from U.S. 101, 4 mi west of Sequim,* ☎ *360/ 457–8451 for wildlife refuge, 360/683–5847 for campground.* 🎫 *Refuge $2 per family, campsites $10.* ☉ *Wildlife refuge daily dawn– dusk, campground Feb.–Sept.*

Ↄ The **Olympic Game Farm**—part petting zoo, part safari—is unique among exotic-animal habitats. For years the farm's exclusive client was Walt Disney Studios, and many of the bears and tigers here are former movie stars. The more than 200 acres include a studio barn with movie sets, a snack bar, and a gift shop. Guided lecture tours take place at 2 PM in the summer. ⊠ *1423 Ward Rd.,* ☎ *360/683–4295 or 800/778– 4295.* 🎫 *$6.* ☉ *Weekdays 9–5, weekends 9–6.*

In 1977, 12,000-year-old mastodon remains were discovered near Sequim. You can view these ice-age creatures at the **Sequim-Dungeness**

Museum, along with exhibits about Captain Vancouver, the early Klallam Indians, and the area's pioneer towns. ⊠ *175 W. Cedar St.,* ☎ *360/683–8110.* 🖾 *Free.* ☉ *May–Sept., Wed.–Sun. noon–4; Oct.–Nov. and mid-Feb.–Apr., weekends noon–4.*

Dining and Lodging

$$–$$$ ✕ **Marina Restaurant.** This large family restaurant has a great view, overlooking John Wayne Marina and Sequim Bay. There's seafood on the menu, as well as pastas, salads, and sandwiches, but the emphasis is placed on red meat—especially prime rib, which is served every Saturday night. ⊠ *2577 W. Sequim Bay Rd.,* ☎ *360/681–0577. AE, D, MC, V.*

$$–$$$ 🏨 **Greywolf Inn.** Peggy and Bill Melang, from North Carolina and still brimming with Southern hospitality, had fun turning their family home into a B&B. Because the furnishings include some antiques, the decor and the mood varies from room to room. But all have private baths, hair dryers, robes, and either king or queen beds. "Nancy's Room" has a view across the meadows all the way to Mount Baker. The glass-enclosed dining room and deck also overlook a meadow, and a woodland trail winds through the property's 5 acres. ⊠ *395 Keeler Rd., 98392,* ☎ *360/683–5889 or 800/914–9055,* 🖾 *360/683–1487. 5 rooms. Outdoor hot tub, business services. AE, D, MC, V.*

Nightlife and the Arts

The Jamestown S'Klallam tribe's enormous yet oddly subdued **7 Cedars Casino** (⊠ 270756 Hwy. 101, east of Sequim, ☎ 360/683–7777) has blackjack, roulette, and slots. One end of the casino is devoted to bingo. The tribe also runs an excellent art gallery and gift shop.

Port Townsend

㉔ *31 mi from Sequim, 13 mi east on U.S. 101 and 18 mi north on Hwy. 20.*

Many writers, musicians, painters, and other artists live in Port Townsend, a Victorian-era city on the northern tip of the Olympic Peninsula. The city was originally laid out as two totally separate urban quarters with separate shopping districts: "Watertown" on the waterfront catered to sailors and their needs, while "uptown" on the plateau above the bluffs was where watertown merchants lived and raised their families. The distinction has been blurred by Port Townsend's resuscitation, which made the waterfront respectable, but both areas still support shops and other businesses. Handsome restored brick buildings from the 1888–1890 railroad boom, with shops and restaurants inside, are lined up in two parallel blocks near the waterfront; the many impressive yachts docked here attest to the area's status as one of the Salish Sea's premier sailing spots.

The "Genuine Bull Durham Smoking Tobacco" ad on the **Lewis Building** (⊠ Madison and Water Sts.) is among the many relics of Port Townsend's glory days as a customs port. The **bell tower** on Jefferson Street, at the top of the Tyler Street stairs, is the last of its kind in the country. Built in 1890, it was used to call volunteer firemen to duty; it houses artifacts from the city museum, including a 19th-century horse-drawn hearse that you can peek at through the windows.

The 1892 City Hall building—Jack London languished briefly in the jail here on his way to the Klondike—contains the **Jefferson County Historical Museum,** four floors of Native American artifacts, photos of the Olympic Peninsula, and exhibits chronicling Port Townsend's past. ⊠ *210 Madison St.,* ☎ *360/385–1003.* 🖾 *$2 suggested donation.* ☉ *Mon.–Sat. 11–4, Sun. 1–4.*

⌛ The neatly manicured grounds of 443-acre **Fort Worden State Park** include a row of restored Victorian officers' houses, a World War II balloon hangar, and a sandy beach that leads to the **Point Wilson Lighthouse.** The fort, which was built on Point Wilson in 1896, 17 years after the lighthouse, hosts art events sponsored by Centrum (☞ Nightlife and the Arts, *below*). The **Marine Science Center** has aquariums and touch tanks where you can reach in and feel sea creatures like crabs and anemones. ⊠ *200 Battery Way,* ☎ *360/385–4730.* 🖾 *Park day use free, Marine Science Center $2.* ☉ *Park daily dawn–dusk, Marine Science Center Tues.–Sun. noon–6.*

A 15- to 20-minute drive from town leads to the tip of Marrowstone Island and **Fort Flagler State Park.** The fort's century-old gun placements overlook beaches. The park has campgrounds and 7 mi of wooded and oceanfront hiking trails—the nameless remnants of old army roads that radiated from a perimeter road. The inlets of the island are great for paddling around, and you can rent canoes, kayaks, and pedal boats from the **Nordland General Store** (☎ 360/385–0777), near the park entrance. ⊠ *10341 Flagler Rd. (from Port Townsend take Hwy. 20 and Hwy. 19 south to Hwy. 116 east and north), Nordland,* ☎ *360/385–1259.* 🖾 *Day use free, campground $10–$16.* ☉ *Daily dawn–dusk.*

Guided Historical Tours (⊠ 820 Tyler St., ☎ 360/385–1967) conducts several tours of Port Townsend, the most popular of which is a one-hour walking tour of the waterfront and downtown, focusing on the town's architecture, history, and humor.

Dining and Lodging

$$$ ✕ **Lonny's.** Chef-owner Lonny Ritter aims to provide a sensual din-
★ ing experience at this spot featuring contemporary American cuisine with an Italian touch. The handsome wooden furnishings and the texture of the ocher-color walls at his restaurant are as carefully selected as the professional staff and the extensive wine collection. Entrées change with the seasons, focusing on fresh local seafood—such as Dungeness crabs or Dabob Bay oyster stew richly laced with butter— and seasonal vegetarian dishes like grilled eggplant with fresh mozzarella and basil. ⊠ *2330 Washington St.,* ☎ *360/385–0700. MC, V. Closed Tues. in winter.*

$$ ✕ **Fountain Café.** This funky, art- and knickknack-filled café is a local favorite. Locals come here for the vegetarian dishes and salads as well as for the unabashedly sumptuous desserts. Expect the occasional wait; it's a good idea to call ahead to get your name on the list for tables. ⊠ *920 Washington St.,* ☎ *360/385–1364. Reservations not accepted. MC, V. Closed Tues. in winter.*

$–$$ ✕ **Salal Café.** Informal and bright, this restaurant is especially beloved for its ample, all-day Sunday breakfasts (you can also get breakfast the rest of the week). The lunch menu mixes standard American fare with vegetarian options. Try to get a table in the glassed-in back room, which faces a plant-filled courtyard. ⊠ *634 Water St.,* ☎ *360/385–6532. Reservations not accepted. No credit cards. No dinner Tues.–Wed.*

$$–$$$ 🏠 **James House.** This antiques-filled Victorian-era inn sits on the bluff
★ overlooking Port Townsend's waterfront district. Some guest rooms are spacious and have waterfront views, whereas others are small and share baths. Breakfasts are served in the formal dining room, as is complimentary sherry in the evening. The gardener's cottage next door has a wood-burning fireplace, a whirlpool tub, and other modern amenities. ⊠ *1238 Washington St., 98368,* ☎ *360/385–1238 or 800/385–1238,* 𝖥𝖠𝖷 *360/379–5551. 12 rooms, 10 with bath. Dining room. MC, V.*

$$ ☷ **Palace Hotel.** The decor of this spacious hotel reflects the building's history as a bordello: You can easily imagine the exposed-brick-wall lobby filled with music and men waiting for the ladies whose names now grace hallway plaques. The large rooms have 14-ft ceilings and worn antiques. The outstanding corner suite—Miss Marie's—has full views of the bay and the original working fireplace from Marie's days as a madam. ⊠ *1004 Water St., 98368,* ☎ *360/385–0773 or 800/962–0741,* FAX *360/946–5287. 15 rooms, 12 with bath. AE, D, MC, V.*

$$ ☷ **Tides Inn.** Comfortable and unfancy, the Tides has an old-fashioned seaside-motel atmosphere. Some rooms have small private decks that extend over the water's edge. All the rooms have TVs and phones; some have kitchens, decks, hot tubs, or all three. A Continental breakfast (muffins and juice) is served each morning. ⊠ *1807 Water St., 98368,* ☎ *360/385–0595 or 800/822–8696,* FAX *360/385–7370. 21 rooms. AE, D, DC, MC, V.*

Nightlife and the Arts

NIGHTLIFE

Back Alley (⊠ 923 Washington St., ☎ 360/385–2914), a favorite with locals, hosts rock-and-roll musicians on weekends. Secluded **Sirens** (⊠ 832 Water St., 3rd floor, ☎ 360/379–0776) overlooks the water and books a variety of musical acts on weekends. The large old **Town Tavern** (⊠ 639 Water St., ☎ 360/385–4706) has live music—from jazz to blues to rock—on weekends.

THE ARTS

Centrum (⊠ Box 1158, 98368, ☎ 800/733–3608), Port Townsend's well-respected performing-arts organization, presents performances, workshops, and conferences throughout the year at Fort Worden State Park. The **Centrum Summer Arts Festival** runs from June to September.

Outdoor Activities and Sports

BICYCLING

P. T. Cyclery (⊠ 100 Tyler St., south of Water St., ☎ 360/385–6470) rents mountain bikes year-round. The nearest place to go riding is Fort Worden, but you can range as far afield as Fort Flagler, the lower Dungeness trails (no bikes are allowed on the spit itself), or across the water to Whidbey Island.

BOAT CRUISE

P. S. Express (⊠ 431 Water St., ☎ 360/385–5288) operates narrated passenger tours to San Juan Island from April to October for $49 round-trip.

KAYAK TOURS

Kayak Port Townsend (⊠ 435 Water St., ☎ 360/385–6240) conducts guided kayak tours from April to September ($40 for about 3 hrs or $70 for a full day with lunch).

Shopping

The best shopping in Port Townsend is found near the waterfront; many of the boutiques and stores here carry Northwest arts and crafts. **North by Northwest Gallery** (⊠ 18 Water St., ☎ 360/385–0955) specializes in Eskimo and Native American art, artifacts, jewelry, and clothing. **Russell Jaqua Gallery** (⊠ 21 Taylor St., ☎ 360/385–5262) exhibits blacksmith and other iron-work creations. **William James Bookseller** (⊠ 829 Water St., ☎ 360/385–7313) stocks used and out-of-print books in all fields, with an emphasis on nautical, regional history, and theology titles.

Three dozen dealers at the two-story **Port Townsend Antique Mall** (⊠ 802 Washington St., ☎ 360/385–2590) flea market sell merchandise ranging from pricey Victorian collectors' items to cheap, funky junk.

More shops are uptown on **Lawrence Street** near an enclave of Victorian houses.

En Route U.S. 101 travels south along the west side of Hood Canal past oyster-picking and clam-digging areas. The retail store of the **Hama Hama Oyster Company** (✉ N. 35959 Hwy. 101, ☎ 360/877–5811), south of the town of Eldon, sells fresh salmon, mussels, crab, shrimp, and other seafood; you purchase these plus pickled and smoked items and then dine on the picnic tables outside. The store is open daily from 9:30 to 5:30, but it's closed on Wednesday in winter.

Hoodsport

66 mi south of Port Townsend, Hwy. 20 to U.S. 101.

Near the southern bend of Hood Canal and the town of Hoodsport is the **Hoodsport Winery,** whose wines include Chardonnays, Rieslings, and even gooseberry and rhubarb. The staff gives tours and tastings on an informal basis as requested. ✉ N. 23501 Hwy. 101, ☎ 360/877–9894. ⌦ Free. ◷ Daily 10–6.

OFF THE BEATEN PATH **LAKE CUSHMAN –** An important source of water for Tacoma's powerhouse on Hood Canal, the lake is the trailhead to numerous hiking paths, including one to the very scenic and impressive Staircase Rapids on the Skokomish River. Here the steep country gives rise to rushing cataracts and boulder-strewn rapids, broken up by deep pools where Dolly Varden trout rest. ✉ *11 mi west of Hoodsport on Staircase Rd. (Rte. 119).*

En Route If you continue south on U.S. 101, you'll pass the sawmill town of **Shelton** before arriving back in Olympia.

The Olympic Peninsula Essentials

Arriving and Departing

BY BUS
Jefferson Transit (☎ 800/436–3950) services Port Angeles from Seattle and Olympia. **Olympic Bus Lines** (☎ 800/550–3858) offers service twice daily to Port Angeles from downtown Seattle and Sea-Tac Airport. Reservations are recommended.

BY CAR
Interstate 5 skirts the southeastern edge of the Olympic Peninsula.

BY FERRY
Washington State Ferries (☎ 206/464–6400) travel from Seattle to Bainbridge Island; from the ferry terminal, drive west on Highway 305, north on Route 3, and west on Highway 104 over the Hood Canal bridge to Discovery Bay, until you reach U.S. 101.

BY PLANE
Fairchild International Airport (✉ 1404 Fairchild International Airport Rd., ☎ 360/457–1138) is west of Port Angeles off U.S. 101 (take Airport Rd. north from 101). **Jefferson County International Airport** (✉ 310 Airport Rd., ☎ 360/385–0656) is south of Port Townsend off Highway 19. **Port Townsend Airways** (☎ 800/385–6554) flies charter planes between Sea-Tac Airport and Port Townsend.

Harbor Air has scheduled service to Port Angeles from Seattle, the San Juan Islands, and elsewhere. **Horizon Air** has scheduled service between Seattle and Port Angeles. *See* Air Travel *in* Smart Travel Tips A to Z for airline phone numbers.

Getting Around

BY BUS

Traveling by bus is slow going on the Olympic Peninsula. **Clallam Transit** (☎ 360/452–4511 or 800/858–3747) , **Jefferson Transit** (☎ 800/ 436–3950), and **West Jefferson Transit** (☎ 360/452–1397 or 800/ 436–3950) service the area.

BY CAR

U.S. 101 loops around the Olympic Peninsula. **Highway 112** heads west from U.S. 101 at Port Angeles to Neah Bay. **Highway 113** winds north from U.S. 101 at Sappho to Highway 112. **Highway 110** travels west from U.S. 101 at Forks to La Push. **Highway 109** leads west from U.S. 101 at Hoquiam to Copalis Beach, Moclips, and Taholah. **Highway 8** heads west from U.S. 101 at Olympia. At Elma, Highway 8 connects with **U.S. 12,** which travels west to Aberdeen.

Guided Tours

Olympic Raft and Guide (☎ 360/452–1443) conducts white-water and scenic float trips on the Hoh and Elwha rivers. **Peak Six Tours** (⊠ 4883 Upper Hoh Rd., Forks, ☎ 360/374–5254) provides gear and information for hiking, biking, camping, climbing, and sightseeing on the Olympic Peninsula.

Visitor Information

North Olympic Peninsula Visitor and Convention Bureau (⊠ Box 670, Port Angeles 98362, ☎ 360/452–8552 or 800/942–4042). **Olympic National Forest** (⊠ 1835 Blacklake Blvd., Olympia 98512, ☎ 360/956– 2400). **Olympic National Park** (⊠ 1835 Blacklake Blvd., Olympia 98512, ☎ 360/956–4501). **Port Angeles Chamber of Commerce** (⊠ 121 E. Railroad Ave., 98362, ☎ 360/452–2363). **Port Townsend Chamber of Commerce** (⊠ 2437 E. Sims Way, 98368, ☎ 360/385–2722). **Sequim-Dungeness Valley Chamber of Commerce** (⊠ Box 907, Sequim 98382, ☎ 360/683–6197 or 800/737–8462).

LONG BEACH PENINSULA

The seas are so turbulent beneath the cliffs of Cape Disappointment, where the mighty Columbia River meets the stormy waters of the Pacific Ocean, that several explorers, from James Cook to George Vancouver, mistook the river's mouth for surf breaking on a wild shore. Many ships have crossed (and many have come to grief) here since American sea captain Robert Gray sailed into the river on May 11, 1792, and named it after his ship.

When the Hudson's Bay Company opened the area's first commercial salmon packing operations in the 1830s, the lower river became a major salmon fishing area. The river's shores bristled with canneries from 1866 onward, even after fish traps were outlawed in the 1930s. The last large canneries closed after World War II, when the salmon runs collapsed following the construction of Grand Coulee, Bonneville, and other dams on the river. Today, there's still a lot of ship traffic on the Columbia. Huge tankers and freighters moor at Astoria or head upriver to Longview, Kalama, or Portland to unload oil or automobiles and to load logs or wheat. The Pacific coast north of the Columbia River up to the mouth of the Willapa now makes a living catering to visitors (many from Portland, Oregon, only a two-hour drive away) rather than to industry.

A long, sandy spit known as the Long Beach Peninsula stretches north from the rocky knobs at Cape Disappointment, shielding Willapa Bay from the ocean's fury. It has vast stretches of sand dunes, friendly beach towns, dank cranberry bogs, and verdant forests and meadows. Willapa Bay was originally known as Shoalwater Bay, because it runs almost dry at low tide. It is prime oyster habitat and has been called the cleanest estuary in North America. Oyster farms raise the Pacific Oyster, once imported from Japan but now spawning freely in Washington waters. The bay currently produces more oysters than any other estuary in the country (indeed, Washington is America's leading oyster-producing state), and local oysters are now shipped (live, in the shell) all over the country.

Great for hiking, biking, bird-watching, and beachcombing, the peninsula is also the perfect place for cuddling up in front of a crackling fire and reading a good book, or bundling up and venturing out to watch winter storms, of which there are plenty. Don't even think about swimming in the ocean. The water is too cold and the surf too rough; hypothermia, shifting sands underfoot, and tremendous undertows account for several drownings each year.

The ocean shore of the Long Beach Peninsula has North America's longest uninterrupted stretch (28 mi) of sandy beach. Unfortunately, cars, trucks, recreational vehicles, and motorcycles drive up and down the strand, despite the trauma this practice may wreak on the clamming beds or the psyche of beachgoers. (From April to Labor Day, 40% of the beach is off-limits to motor vehicles, so it is possible to find quiet.) Lakes and marshes on the peninsula attract migrating birds, among them trumpeter swans. Long Island, in southeastern Willapa bay, has a stand of old-growth red-cedar trees, home to spotted owls, marbled murrelets (a western sea bird), elks, and black bears. The island is accessible only by private boat (the boat ramp is on the eastern shore of the bay).

Chinook

118 mi from Olympia, west on U.S. 101 and Hwy. 8, southwest on Hwy. 107, south on U.S. 101 and Hwy. 4, and west on Hwy. 401.

The pleasant Columbia River fishing village of Chinook takes its name from the local tribe that once controlled the Columbia River from its mouth to Celilo Falls. The group encountered William Clark and Meriwether Lewis during their stay on the Pacific coast. Chinook has a boat basin and is a great place for starting an aquatic exploration of the lower Columbia River.

The **Sea Resources Hatchery Complex** (⊠ Houtchen Rd., ☎ 360/777–8229) conducts free tours of its hatchery and fish-rearing ponds. Phone ahead to arrange a tour.

★ ☉ ㉕ **Fort Columbia State Park and Interpretive Center** blends so well into a rocky knob above the river that it is all but invisible from land or water (U.S. 101 passes underneath, via tunnel). But the 1902 bastions offer great views of the river's mouth that their guns once targeted and of the river flowing past the foot of the cliff. In spring the slopes are fragrant with wildflowers. Watch for bald eagles soaring by *below* you, as they patrol the shore. The interpretive center has displays on barracks life and Chinook Indian culture. A hike behind the fort up Scarborough Hill yields a breathtaking view of the Long Beach Peninsula and the Columbia River. ⊠ U.S. 101, 2 mi east of Chinook, ☎ 360/777–8221. ☞ Free. ☉ Memorial Day–Sept., Wed.–Sun. 10–5.

Dining

$$–$$$ ✕ **The Sanctuary.** The soft lighting, stained-glass windows, and fine Pacific Rim cuisine at the Sanctuary make this a very popular restau-

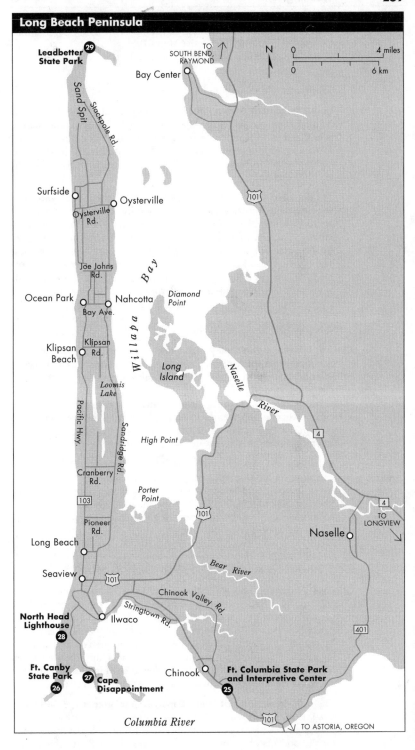

Long Beach Peninsula

Leadbetter State Park 29

TO SOUTH BEND, RAYMOND

Bay Center

N

0   1   4 miles
0   6 km

Sand Spit

Stackpole Rd.

Surfside   Oysterville

Oysterville Rd.

Willapa Bay

Joe Johns Rd.

Ocean Park   Nahcotta

Diamond Point

Bay Ave.

Klipsan Beach

Klipsan Rd.

Long Island

Naselle River

Loomis Lake

Pacific Hwy.

Sandridge Rd.

High Point

Cranberry Rd.

Porter Point

103

101

Pioneer Rd.

Naselle

4

TO LONGVIEW

Long Beach

Seaview

101

Bear River

Chinook Valley Rd.

North Head Lighthouse 28

Ilwaco

Stringtown Rd.

401

Ft. Canby State Park 26

Cape Disappointment 27

Chinook

Ft. Columbia State Park and Interpretive Center 25

Columbia River

101

TO ASTORIA, OREGON

rant. Local labels and a few foreign vintages are represented on the wine list. ⊠ *U.S. 101 and Hazel St.,* ☎ *360/777–8380. Reservations essential. AE, D, MC, V. Closed Mon.–Tues. No lunch.*

Ilwaco

13 mi west of Chinook on Hwy. 401.

Until a decade ago, Ilwaco was a bustling fishing port. But salmon stocks (and those of some other fish) have declined, and the port community of 600 is now a friendly riverfront town where visitors love to linger. A 3-mi scenic loop winds past Fort Canby State Park to North Head Lighthouse and through the town. The harbor is a great place for watching gulls and boats.

The dioramas and miniatures of Long Beach towns at the **Ilwaco Heritage Museum** illustrate the history of southwestern Washington, beginning with the Native Americans; moving on to the influx of traders, missionaries, and pioneers; and concluding with the contemporary workers and owners of the fishing, agriculture, and forest industries. The museum also houses a model of the peninsula's "clamshell railroad," a narrow-gauge train that transported passengers and mail along the beach. Ground-up clam and oyster shells formed the rail bed on which the tracks were laid. ⊠ *115 S.E. Lake St., off U.S. 101 N,* ☎ *360/642–3446.* ☞ *$3.* ☉ *May–Aug., Mon.–Sat. 9–5, Sun. noon–4; Sept.–Apr., Mon.–Sat. 10–4.*

❷❻ The 1,700-acre **Fort Canby State Park** was an active military installation until 1957, when it became a state park. Emplacements for the guns that once guarded the mouth of the Columbia remain, some of them hidden by the dense vegetation. The park attracts beachcombers, hikers, ornithologists, and fishermen; during winter storms it's fun to watch the huge waves crashing over the Columbia River bar. Look for deer on the trails and for eagles on the cliffs. All of the park's 250 campsites have stoves and tables; some sites have water, sewer, and electric hookups.

Exhibits at the park's **Lewis & Clark Interpretive Center** describe the famous duo's 8,000-mi round-trip journey of discovery, which left Wood River, Illinois, in 1803 and arrived at Cape Disappointment in 1805 (they got back to Illinois in 1807). Artwork, photographs, and the journal entries of volunteers are arranged along ramps that lead to a view of the spot where the Columbia empties into the Pacific. ⊠ *Robert Gray Dr., 2½ mi southwest of Ilwaco off U.S. 101,* ☎ *360/642–3029 or 360/642–3078.* ☞ *Park and interpretive center free, campsites $11–$16.* ☉ *Park daily dawn–dusk, interpretive center daily 10–5.*

❷❼ **Cape Disappointment** was named in 1788 by Captain John Meares, an English fur trader who had been unable to find the Northwest Passage. This rocky cape and treacherous sandbar—known as "the graveyard of the Pacific"—has been the scourge of sailors since the 1800s: More than 250 ships have sunk after running aground on its ever-shifting sands. A ½-mi path from the Lewis & Clark Interpretive Center (☞ *above*) leads to the **Cape Disappointment Lighthouse.** Built in 1856, it's the oldest lighthouse on the West Coast still in use.

The **U.S. Coast Guard Station Cape Disappointment** (☎ 360/642–2384) is the largest search-and-rescue station on the Northwest coast. The rough conditions of the Columbia River bar provide plenty of lessons for the students of the on-site **National Motor Life Boat School.** The only institution of its kind, the school teaches elite rescue crews from around the world advanced skills in navigation, mechanics, fire fighting, and lifesaving. The observation platform on the North Jetty at Fort

Canby State Park is a good viewing spot for watching the motor lifeboats. Informal tours are possible if you call ahead.

★ ㉘ **North Head Lighthouse** was built in 1899 to help skippers sailing from the north who could not see the Cape Disappointment Lighthouse. Stand high on a bluff above the pounding surf here, amid the windswept trees, for superb views of the Long Beach Peninsula. ⊠ *From Cape Disappointment follow the Spur 100 road for 2 mi,* ☎ *360/642–3078.* ⊠ *$1.* ☉ *Apr.–Sept., daily 10–5; Oct.–Mar., weekends only, hrs subject to volunteer availability.*

Lodging

$$–$$$ ⊞ **Chick-a-dee Inn.** This B&B inside a 1928 New England–style church sits on a knoll overlooking the port of Ilwaco. All but two of the guest rooms are upstairs in the old Sunday school, and all are cozily furnished with antiques. A full American breakfast, included in the room rate, is served on the altar stage in the sanctuary. ⊠ *120 Williams St. NE, 98624,* ☎ *360/642–8686,* ⨳ *360/642–8686. 10 rooms, 7 with bath. MC, V.*

Outdoor Activities and Sports

FISHING

The fish that swim in the waters near Ilwaco include salmon, rock cod, lingcod, flounder, perch, sea bass, and sturgeon. A free fishing guide is available from the **Port of Ilwaco** (⊠ Box 307, 98624, ☎ 360/642–3145).

WHALE-WATCHING

Gray whales pass by the Long Beach Peninsula twice a year: December–February, on their migration from the Arctic to their winter breeding grounds in Californian and Mexican waters; and March–May, on the return trip north. The view from the **North Head Lighthouse** (☞ *above*) is particularly spectacular. The best conditions exist in the mornings, when the water is calm and overcast conditions reduce the glare. Look on the horizon for a whale blow—the vapor, water, or condensation that spouts into the air when the whale exhales. If you spot one blow, you're likely to see others: Whales often make several shorter, shallow dives before a longer dive that can last as long as 10 minutes.

Seaview

2 mi north of Cape Disappointment on Hwy. 103.

Seaview, an unincorporated town, contains several homes dating from the 1800s. The **Shelburne Inn,** built in 1896, is on the National Register of Historic Places. In 1892 U.S. Senator Henry Winslow Corbett built what's now the **Sou'wester Lodge.**

Dining and Lodging

$$–$$$ ✕ **Shoalwater Restaurant.** The Shoalwater Restaurant at the Shelburne Inn has a dark wooden interior and a comforting atmosphere. The contemporary American menu emphasizes fresh local seafood such as steamed Willapa Bay manila clams piccata; Shoalwater seafood pasta with scallops, mussels, clams; and fresh seasonal fish. Ann Kischner, a master pastry chef, creates some exquisite desserts. Lunch is served daily in the Heron & Beaver Pub; the restaurant offers a Sunday brunch during summer. ⊠ *Pacific Hwy. and N. 45th St.,* ☎ *360/ 642–4142. AE, D, DC, MC, V. No lunch in restaurant.*

$$ ✕ **42nd Street Cafe.** Chef Cheri Walker spent more than a decade honing her skills at the Shoalwater Restaurant (☞ *above*) before opening her own place, which is now by far the best restaurant on the peninsula. Her fare is inspired, original, and reasonably priced. Local oysters are baked with spinach, Parmesan cheese, cream, bacon, brandy, fresh fennel, and cracker crumbs; charbroiled local albacore tuna is served

with hoisin sauce and sesame guacamole; and baked spice-rubbed sturgeon comes with a salad of wild rice, dried cranberries, apples, and carrots, topped with a bacon vinaigrette. In 1999, Walker was nominated for a James Beard Award. ⊠ *Hwy. 103 and 42nd Pl.,* ☎ *360/642–2323. MC, V. No lunch Mon.–Tues.*

$$–$$$ 🏨 **Shelburne Inn.** Sitting along the peninsula's main thoroughfare, be-
★   hind a white picket fence enclosing rose and other gardens, is a wood-frame Craftsman-style building that is the oldest continuously run hotel in Washington. Fresh flowers, original works of art, antiques, and fine-art prints adorn the guest rooms, a few of which have decks or balconies. The Shelburne's major drawback is that it is right on the highway and can be very noisy. ⊠ *Hwy. 103 and N. 45th St., 98644,* ☎ *360/642–2442,* 🖷 *360/642–8904. 15 rooms. Restaurant, pub. AE, MC, V.*

$–$$ 🏨 **Sou'wester Lodge.** A stay at the Sou'wester is a bohemian experience. Proprietors Len and Miriam Atkins came to Seaview from South Africa, by way of Israel and Chicago, where they worked with the late psychologist Bruno Bettelheim, and they are always up for a stimulating conversation. The lodge was built in 1892 as the summer retreat for Henry Winslow Corbett, a Portland banker, timber baron, shipping and railroad magnate, and U.S. senator. Soirees and chamber-music concerts sometimes occur in the parlor. Rooms are funky and eclectic in decor. Beach cottages and the classic mobile-home units just behind the beach have cooking facilities; guests are also welcome to make breakfast in the Atkinses' homey kitchen. ⊠ *Beach Access Rd. (Box 102), 98644,* ☎ *360/642–2542. 3 rooms share 1 bath; 6 suites; 4 cottages; 10 trailers. Beach. D, MC, V.*

Long Beach

½ mi north of Seaview on Hwy. 103.

Tourist-oriented Long Beach bears a striking resemblance to Coney Island in the 1950s. Along its main drag, which stretches southwest from 10th Street to Bolstadt Street, you'll find everything from cotton candy and hot dogs to go-carts and bumper cars. A new boardwalk runs through the dunes parallel to the beach and is a great place for strolling, bird-watching, or just sitting and listening to the wind and the roar of the surf. Each August the community of 1,400 hosts the **Washington State International Kite Festival** (☎ 800/451–2542), which bills itself as the largest and most popular event of its kind in the Western Hemisphere.

At the interesting **World Kite Museum and Hall of Fame,** you can view an array of kites and learn about kite making, kite history, and international kiting celebrities. ⊠ *N. Pacific Hwy. (Hwy. 103) at 3rd St. N,* ☎ *360/642–4020.* ⌨ *$1.50.* ☉ *June–Aug., daily 11–5; May and Sept.–Oct., Fri.–Mon. 11–5; Nov.–Apr., weekends 11–5.*

Dining and Lodging

$$ ✗ **Doogers.** Locals will urge you to eat here—listen to them. The place serves seafood all day long. The ample portions come with potatoes and shrimp-topped garlic toast. ⊠ *900 S. Pacific Hwy. (Hwy. 103),* ☎ *360/642–4224. AE, D, MC, V.*

$ ✗ **My Mom's Pie Kitchen.** Small and frilly, this lunch spot serves a limited selection of comfort food. It's worth dropping by just for the pies—banana whipped cream, chocolate almond, pecan, sour-cream raisin, fresh raspberry, and more. ⊠ *4316 S. Pacific Hwy. (Hwy. 103),* ☎ *360/642–2342. Reservations not accepted. MC, V. Closed Sun.–Tues. No dinner.*

$$ 🏨 **Edgewater Inn Motel.** The Edgewater's two boxy buildings sit behind the sand dunes at the main entrance to the public beach. The motel-style rooms have heavy nylon curtains that peel back to expose an expansive parking lot and, beyond that, the dunes and beach. ⊠ *409 10th St. SW, 98631,* ☎ *360/642–2311 or 800/561–2456,* FAX *360/ 642–8018. 84 rooms. Restaurant, bar. AE, D, DC, MC, V.*

$–$$$ 🏨 **Breakers Motel and Condominiums.** Four identical buildings on the beach (they look like a public housing project) have contemporary one- and two-bedroom rental condominiums. Most are comfortable, "beachy," and clean; many have wood-burning fireplaces, TVs, VCRs, and private balconies with exceptional views of the dunes and the surf. Some units have kitchenettes. ⊠ *26th St. and Hwy. 103, 98631,* ☎ *360/642–4414 or 800/288–8890,* FAX *360/642–8772. 114 rooms. Indoor pool, spa, playground. AE, D, DC, MC, V.*

Outdoor Activities and Sports

BICYCLING

Long Beach Bike Shop (⊠ 1st Place Shopping Center, 811 S. Pacific Hwy., ☎ 360/642–7000) rents bikes.

GOLF

The **Peninsula Golf Course** (⊠ 9604 Pacific Hwy., ☎ 360/642–2828), a nine-hole, par-33 course, is on the northern edge of Long Beach. The greens fee is $9; an optional cart costs $9.

HORSEBACK RIDING

Back Country Horse Rides (⊠ 10th St. next to Edgewater Inn, ☎ 360/ 642–2576) rents horses. Horses are also available for rent at **Skippers** (⊠ S. 10th St. and Beach Access Rd., ☎ 360/642–3676).

Shopping

Gray Whale Gallery & Gifts (⊠ 105 N. Pacific Hwy., ☎ 360/642–2889) carries Northwest art, cards, jewelry, and cranberry products. **Long Beach Kites** (⊠ 104 N. Pacific Hwy., ☎ 360/642–2202) stocks box, dragon, and many other kites. **North Head Gallery** (⊠ 600 S. Pacific Hwy., ☎ 360/642–8884) sells the works of Elton Bennett and other Northwest artists.

Ocean Park

9 mi north of Long Beach on Hwy. 103.

Ocean Park is the commercial center of the peninsula's quieter north end. It was founded as a camp for the Methodist Episcopal Church of Portland in 1883, but the law that prohibited the establishment of saloons and gambling houses no longer exists. The deeds of some homes still state that the property will be forfeited if alcohol is bought on the premises, though today no one would think of enforcing them. The **Taylor Hotel,** built in 1892 on Bay Avenue and N Place, houses retail businesses and is the only structure from the early days that is open to the public.

Lodging

$$–$$$ 🏨 **Caswell's on the Bay B&B.** From the outside, this B&B with a
★ wraparound porch looks like an old Victorian house. But inside it's clearly a modern creation (Caswell's was built in 1995), with high ceilings and enormous windows looking onto Willapa Bay and the isolated Long Island wildlife sanctuary. The innkeepers go to great lengths to indulge their guests. The antiques-furnished rooms have sitting areas and waterside or garden views. The rates include a full breakfast. ⊠ *25204 Sandridge Rd., 98640,* ☎ *360/665–6535,* FAX *360/665– 6500. 5 rooms. MC, V.*

Outdoor Activities and Sports

The **Surfside Golf and Country Club** (⊠ 31508 Jay Pl., behind the Surfside Inn, ☎ 360/665–4148), 2 mi north of Ocean Park, is a nine-hole, par-36 course. The greens fee is $12; an optional cart costs $12.

Nahcotta

3 mi from Ocean Park, east on Bay Ave. to Hwy. 103 (Sandridge Rd.).

Nahcotta, on the bay side of the Long Beach Peninsula, supports an active oyster industry—oysters are shucked and canned on the Willapa Bay docks. Named for a Native American chief who invited oystermen to settle on the peninsula, Nahcotta was the northernmost point on the peninsula's defunct narrow-gauge railway; the schedule is still posted in the Nahcotta Post Office. The town's waterfront is a good place from which to view the bay and Long Island.

Dining

$$$ ✕ **The Ark.** At this rambling nautical shack, the creation of Jimella Lucas
 ★ and Nanci Main, seafood reigns supreme—the house specialty is oysters, which are raised in beds behind the restaurant. Less-expensive lighter fare, including soup and sandwiches, is available at the bar. ⊠ *273 Sandridge Rd.,* ☎ *360/665–4133. AE, MC, V. Closed Mon.*

Outdoor Activities and Sports

Clamming is a popular pastime here; the season varies depending on the supply. For details, call 360/665–4166 or 360/902–2250.

Oysterville

6 mi north of Nahcotta on Hwy. 103 (Sandridge Rd.).

Oysterville is a delightful, beautifully maintained 19th-century waterfront village, with houses set in gardens or surrounded by greenswards. Signs posted on the fence of each building tell when the home or business was built and who lived in it. You can tour the restored Oysterville Church (pick up a free historical map of Oysterville here), the schoolhouse, the late-19th-century tannery, and the home of the mayor. The town, established in 1854, got out of the oyster business after the native oyster industry's decline in the late 1800s. But while the native shellfish were harvested to extinction, they were successfully replaced with the Pacific Oyster, a Japanese native that has become thoroughly naturalized. The modern oyster industry is based in Nahcotta and east of the bay in Bay Center and South Bend.

Leadbetter State Park

 ㉙ *3 mi north of Oysterville; take Sandridge Rd. to the left and follow the signs.*

 ★ **Leadbetter State Park,** at the northernmost tip of Long Beach Peninsula, is a wildlife refuge and a great spot for bird-watching. The dune area at the very tip of the point is closed from April to August to protect the nesting snowy plover. Black brants, sandpipers, turnstones, yellowlegs, sanderlings, knots, and plovers are among the 100 species biologists have recorded at the point. From the parking lot, a ½-mi paved wheelchair-accessible path leads to the ocean and a 2½-mi loop trail winds through the dunes along the ocean and Willapa Bay. Several trails along the loop lead to isolated patches of coast. These trails flood in winter and may become impassable swamps. (Pay attention to the warning signs. They tell the truth!) ⊠ *Off Stackpole Rd.,* ☎ *360/642–3078.* ◻ *Free.* ☉ *Apr.–mid-Oct., daily 6:30 AM–dusk; mid-Oct.–Mar., daily 8 AM–dusk.*

Long Beach Peninsula Essentials

Arriving and Departing

BY CAR

From I–5 north of Kelso, take **Highway 4** west through Longview to **Highway 401.** Turn south if you're going to Chinook or Ilwaco; or continue on Highway 4 to **U.S. 101** if you're going to Seaview, Long Beach, and points north. The stretch of U.S. 101 along the rocky eastern shore of Willapa Bay, south of the Naselle River estuary, is one of the most scenic stretches of highway in Washington. From Olympia, take **U.S. 101** west; continue west on **Highway 8** and **U.S. 12.** At Montesano turn south onto **Highway 107,** which will take you to U.S. 101; turn left (south) onto U.S. 101 at the junction.

Getting Around

U.S. 101 curves around the southern part of the peninsula. **Highway 103** travels north through the peninsula.

Visitor Information

Long Beach Peninsula Visitors Bureau (⊠ U.S. 101 and Hwy. 103, Box 562, 98631, ☎ 360/642–2400 or 800/451–2542).

MOUNT ST. HELENS

In recent years, Mount St. Helens has regained the popularity it lost after the 1980 eruption blew off its top and denuded its forested slopes. The 8,365-ft-high mountain, formerly 9,665 ft high, is one of a string of volcanic Cascade Range peaks that runs from British Columbia's Mount Garibaldi south to California's Mount Lassen (including such notable peaks as Mount Baker and Mount Rainier to the north, Mount Adams to the east, Mount Hood in Oregon, and Mount Shasta in California). The mountain is most easily reached via the Spirit Lake Memorial Highway (Highway 504), whose predecessor was destroyed in a matter of minutes on May 18, 1980. This highway has unparalleled views of the mountain and the surrounding Toutle River Valley.

Mount St. Helens National Volcanic Monument

151 mi from Seattle, south on I–5 and east on Hwy. 504.

★ ♺ The U.S. Forest Service operates the **Mount St. Helens National Volcanic Monument.** The $8-per-person user fee (children under 15 are admitted free) is good for three days.

The three visitor centers along Highway 504 on the west side of the forest are open daily from 9 to 6. The **Mount St. Helens Visitor Center** (⊠ Hwy. 504, 5 mi east of I–5, Silver Lake, ☎ 360/274–2100) does not have great views of the mountain, but it has exhibits documenting the eruption and a walk-through volcano. Exhibits at the **Coldwater Ridge Visitor Center** (⊠ Hwy. 504, 43 mi east of I–5, ☎ 360/274–2131), a multimillion-dollar facility, document the great blast and its effects on the surrounding 150,000 acres—which were devastated but are in the process of a remarkable recovery. A ¼-mi trail leads from the visitor center to Coldwater Lake, which has a recreation area. The **Johnston Ridge Observatory** (⊠ Hwy. 504, 53 mi east of I–5, ☎ 360/274–2140) has the most spectacular views of the crater and lava dome. Exhibits here interpret the geology of the mountain and explain how scientists monitor an active volcano.

On the east side of the mountain are two bare-bones visitor centers, **Windy Ridge** and **Ape Cave.** On the south side of the mountain there's a center at **Lava Canyon.**

The dining options at Mount St. Helens are limited. Coldwater Ridge Visitor Center (☞ *above*) has a small concession area. **Weyerhauser/Hoffstadt Bluff Visitor Center** (⊠ Hwy. 504, 27 mi east of I–5, ☎ 360/274–7750), run by Cowlitz County, contains the only full-service restaurant along Highway 504.

The Eruption of Mount St. Helens, a 30-minute giant-screen film, plays every 45 minutes from 9 AM to 6 PM at the **Cinedome theater** (⊠ I–5's Castle Rock Exit 49, ☎ 360/274–9844). Admission is $5.

Climbing

Climbing is restricted to the south side of the mountain. Permits (☎ 360/247–3900 or 360/247–3961) are required; the fee is $15 per person.

Mount St. Helens Essentials

Arriving and Departing

BY CAR

The Castle Rock Exit (No. 49) of **I–5** is just outside the western entrance to the monument. Follow **Highway 504** into the park. You can access the park from the north by taking **Forest Service Road 25** south from U.S. 12 at the town of Randle. Forest Service Road 25 connects with **Forest Service Road 90,** which heads north from the town of Cougar. The two forest-service roads are closed by snow in winter.

Getting Around

BY CAR

Highway 504 is the main road through the monument.

Visitor Information

Mount St. Helens National Volcanic Monument (☎ 360/247–3900).

MOUNT RAINIER NATIONAL PARK

Magnificent 14,411-ft-high Mount Rainier—the fifth-highest mountain in the lower 48 states—is the centerpiece of Mount Rainier National Park, about 60 mi southeast of Tacoma. The mountain is so big it creates its own weather system. The local Native Americans called the mountain Tahoma, "white mountain," and avoided its higher slopes for fear of evil skookums (spirits). In 1792 the first European traveler to visit the region, British explorer George Vancouver, named the mountain after his friend Rear Admiral Peter Rainier and described its beauties in glowing terms, noting in his journal that "the whole produced a most grand, picturesque effect."

Mount Rainier National Park encompasses nearly 400 square mi of wilderness. Three hundred miles of hiking trails, from easy to advanced, crisscross the park, which contains lakes, rivers, glaciers, isolated cross-country-skiing spots, and ample camping facilities. Bears, mountain goats, deer, elk, eagles, beavers, and mountain lions live within the park; the dense vegetation includes old-growth Douglas fir, hemlock, cedar, ferns, and wildflowers.Admission is $10 per vehicle, $5 for those who arrive by any other means. It is possible to sample Rainier's main attractions—Longmire, Paradise, the Grove of Patriarchs, and Sunrise—in a single day by car, but you'll need to stay longer to stop more than just briefly elsewhere in the park or hike the forest, meadow, and high-mountain trails. Be forewarned: A narrow and winding paved road links Rainier's main sights; during the peak months of July and August, traffic can be slow and heavy.

Finding a decent meal around Mount Rainier isn't difficult, but lodging can be a problem; book in advance if possible. The park contains five drive-in campgrounds—Cougar Rock, Ipsut Creek, Ohanapecosh, Sunshine Point, and White River—which have almost 700 campsites for tents and RVs. All are first-come, first-served and have parking spaces, drinking water, garbage cans, fire grates, and picnic tables with benches;

most have flush or pit toilets, but none have hot water. In the winter, chains are often required to reach Paradise.

Ashford

53 mi southeast of Tacoma; from I–5's Exit 127 follow Hwy. 512 east to Rte. 7 south to Hwy. 706 east.

Founded as a railroad and lumber mill town, Ashford now serves the 2 million annual visitors to Mount Rainier National Park. Stores, restaurants, and lodgings are strung out along Highway 706.

Dining and Lodging

$ ✕ **Wild Berry Restaurant.** The ski-and-hot-tub crowd refuels after a long day in the woods at this ramshackle eatery. Salads, pizzas, crepes, sandwiches, and home-baked desserts are served in relaxed surroundings. ⊠ *37720 Hwy. 706 E, 4 mi east of Ashford,* ☎ *360/569–2628. MC, V.*

$$–$$$ ✕🏨 **Alexander's Country Inn.** The rooms in this well-maintained 1912 inn sparkle with fresh paint, carpeting, antiques, and marble-top pine bedside tables, but the walls in the main house are thin. Room rates include a hearty breakfast and evening wine. The inn's cozy restaurant (closed on weekdays in winter), the best place in town for lunch or dinner, serves fresh fish and pasta dishes; the bread and the desserts are baked on the premises. ⊠ *37515 Hwy. 706 E (4 mi east of Ashford), Ashford 98304,* ☎ *360/569–2300 or 800/654–7615,* 🇫🇦🇽 *360/569–2323. 12 rooms, two 3-bedroom houses. Restaurant, hot tub. MC, V.*

$–$$ 🏨 **The Bunkhouse.** "The place to stop on the way to the top" was built in 1908 to house loggers and was originally located a few miles down the road, in the long-gone town of National. The accommodations at this old-style motel range from inexpensive bunks in a large dormitory-style room to private suites. ⊠ *30205 Hwy. 706 E, 98304,* ☎ *360/569–2439,* 🇫🇦🇽 *360/569–2436. 18 private rooms, 1 bunk room. Hot tub. MC, V.*

Longmire

12 mi east of Ashford on Hwy. 706.

☾ Glass cases at the **Longmire Museum** display samples of preserved plants and stuffed animals from Mount Rainier National Park, including a friendly-looking cougar. Photos and geographical displays give an overview of the park's history. ⊠ *Hwy. 706, 6 mi east of Nisqually entrance,* ☎ *360/569–2211, ext. 3314.* 🎫 *Free with park admission.* ☽ *July–Labor Day, daily 9–5; Labor Day–June, daily 9–4:15.*

The ½-mi **Trail of Shadows,** which begins just across the road from the National Park Inn (☞ Dining and Lodging, *below*), passes colorful soda springs, James Longmire's old homestead cabin, and the foundation of the old Longmire Springs Hotel, which was destroyed around the turn of the century.

Dining and Lodging

$$–$$$ ✕🏨 **National Park Inn.** An early 1990s renovation robbed the only year-round lodging in the park of much of its charm, but the old stone fireplaces are still here. The small rooms mix functionality with backwoods touches like wrought-iron lamps and antique bentwood headboards. A large restaurant serves decent American food. ⊠ *Hwy. 706, 6 mi east of Nisqually entrance, 98304,* ☎ *360/569–2275. 25 rooms, 18 with bath. Restaurant, shop. MC, V.*

Outdoor Activities and Sports

The **Longmire Ski Touring Center** (☎ *360/569–2411*), adjacent to the National Park Inn, rents cross-country ski equipment and provides lessons from mid-December to early April.

Mount Rainier National Park

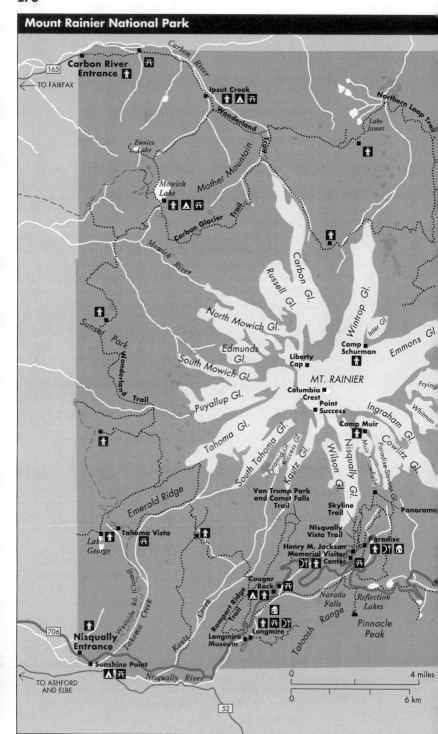

TO FAIRFAX

Carbon River
Entrance

Ipsut Creek

Carbon River

Wonderland

Northern Loop Trail

Lake
James

Eunice
Lake

Mother Mountain

Mowich
Lake

Carbon Glacier

Trail

Mowich River

Carbon Gl.

Wintrop Gl.

Inter Gl.

Sunset Park

North Mowich Gl.

Russell Gl.

Emmons Gl

Wonderland

Edmunds
Gl.

South Mowich Gl.

Liberty
Cap

Camp
Schurman

Trail

Puyallup Gl.

MT. RAINIER

Frying

Columbia
Crest

Tahoma Gl.

South Tahoma Gl.

Point
Success

Ingraham Gl.

Whitman

Camp Muir

Cowlitz Gl.

Emerold Ridge

Pyramid Gl.
Success Gl.

Kautz Gl.

Wilson Gl.

Nisqually Gl.

Muir Snowfield

Paradise-Stevens Gl.

Van Trump Park
and Comet Falls
Trail

Skyline
Trail

Panorama

Nisqually
Vista Trail

Lake
George

Tahoma Vista

Paradise

Henry M. Jackson
Memorial Visitor Center

Cougar
Rock

Narada
Falls

Reflection
Lakes

Pinnacle
Peak

Rampart Ridge
Trail

Longmire

Westside Rd. (Closed)

Tahoma Creek

Kautz Creek

Longmire
Museum

Tatoosh Range

Nisqually
Entrance

Sunshine Point

TO ASHFORD
AND ELBE

Nisqually River

| 0 | | | 4 miles |
| 0 | | | 6 km |

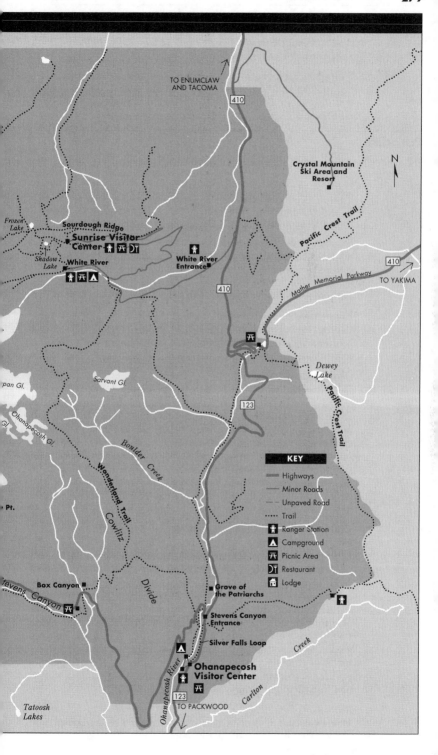

TO ENUMCLAW
AND TACOMA

410

N

Crystal Mountain
Ski Area and
Resort

*Frozen
Lake*

Pacific Crest Trail

Sourdough Ridge
**Sunrise Visitor
Center**

*Shadow
Lake*
White River

**White River
Entrance**

410

410

TO YAKIMA

Mather Memorial Parkway

*Dewey
Lake*

pan Gl.

Sarvant Gl.

Ohanapecosh Gl.

Gl.

123

Pacific Crest Trail

Pt.

Boulder Creek

Wonderland Trail

Cowlitz

KEY

	Highways
	Minor Roads
	Unpaved Road
	Trail
	Ranger Station
	Campground
	Picnic Area
	Restaurant
	Lodge

Box Canyon

Stevens Canyon

Divide

**Grove of
the Patriarchs**

**Stevens Canyon
Entrance**

Silver Falls Loop

Carlton

Creek

**Ohanapecosh
Visitor Center**

123

TO PACKWOOD

*Tatoosh
Lakes*

Ohanapecosh River

Mount Rainier Guest Services (✉ National Park Inn, Hwy. 706, ☎ 360/569–2411) rents cross-country ski equipment, snowshoes, and hiking gear from mid-December to early April. **Ed Strauss** (☎ 360/569–2271), a ski instructor, is also a tour guide.

En Route   From Longmire, Highway 706 climbs northeast into the mountains toward Paradise. Both the gorgeous **Christine Falls,** north of the highway 1½ mi past Cougar Rock Campground, and **Narada Falls,** 3 mi farther on, are spanned by graceful stone footbridges.

Paradise

9 mi east of Longmire on Hwy. 706.

Fantastic mountain views, alpine meadows crisscrossed by nature trails, a welcoming lodge and restaurant, and an excellent visitor center combine to make Paradise the first stop for most visitors to Mount Rainier National Park.

Exhibits at the **Henry M. Jackson Visitor Center** focus on geology, mountaineering, glaciology, winter storms, and alpine ecology. Two worthwhile 20-minute multimedia programs repeat at half-hour intervals. ✉ *Hwy. 706, 20 mi east of Nisqually entrance,* ☎ *360/569–2211.* ☉ *Early May–mid-Oct., daily 9–6; mid-Oct.–Apr., weekends 10–5.*

Hiking trails to various points begin at the Henry M. Jackson Visitor Center. One outstanding, if grueling, way to explore the high country is to hike the 5-mi **Skyline Trail** to Panorama Point, which has stunning 360-degree views.

Dining and Lodging

$$–$$$ ✕▥ **Paradise Inn.** With its hand-carved cedar logs, burnished parquet
★   floors, stone fireplaces, Indian rugs, and glorious mountain views, this 75-year-old inn is loaded with atmosphere. Its small, sparsely furnished rooms have no TVs or telephones, the walls are thin, and showers can run cold, but it's hard to beat the inn's alpine setting. The full-service dining room serves leisurely Sunday brunches in summer; the lodge also has a small snack bar and a snug lounge. ✉ *Hwy. 706 (mailing address: c/o Mount Rainier Guest Services, Box 108, Star Rte., Ashford 98304),* ☎ *360/569–2275,* ﷽ *360/569–2770. 127 rooms, 96 with bath. Restaurant, bar. MC, V. Closed Nov.–mid-May.*

Outdoor Activities and Sports

MOUNTAIN CLIMBING

Highly regarded **Rainier Mountaineering** (✉ Paradise 98398, ☎ 360/627–6242 in winter, 360/569–2227 in summer) teaches the fundamentals of mountaineering at one-day classes held during the climbing season, which lasts from late May through early September. Participants are evaluated for their fitness for the climb; they must be able to withstand a 16-mi round-trip with a 9,000-ft gain in elevation. Those who meet the fitness requirement may choose between guided two- and four-day summit climbs, the latter via the more demanding Emmons Glacier. Experienced climbers can fill out a climbing card at the Paradise, White River, or Carbon River ranger station and lead their own groups of two or more.

SKIING

Mount Rainier is a major cross-country ski center. The ungroomed trails around Paradise are particularly popular.

SNOWSHOEING

Snowshoe rentals are available at the **Longmire Ski Touring Center** (☞ *above*). From December through April, park rangers lead free twice-daily snowshoe walks that start at the visitor center at Paradise and cover 1¼ mi in about two hours.

Eastern Side of Mount Rainier National Park

21 mi east of Paradise on Hwy. 706.

★ The **Grove of the Patriarchs,** a small island of 1,000-year-old trees protected from the fires that afflicted surrounding areas, is one of Mount Rainier National Park's most stunning features. A 2-mi loop trail that begins just west of the Stevens Canyon entrance heads over a small bridge through lush old-growth forest of Douglas fir, cedar, and hemlock.

As you head north from the Grove of the Patriarchs you'll reach the White River and the **Sunrise Visitor Center,** from which you can watch the alpenglow fade from Mount Rainier's domed summit. The visitor center has exhibits on this region's alpine and subalpine ecology. ✉ 70002 S.R. 410 E, Enumclaw, ☎ 360/569–2211, ext. 2357. ☯ July 4–Oct. 1, daily 9–6.

Outdoor Activities and Sports

SKIING

If you want to cross-country ski with fewer people, try the trails in and around the **Ohanapecosh–Stevens Canyon area,** which are just as beautiful as those at Paradise. Never ski on the plowed main roads—the snowplow operator can't see you.

SNOWMOBILING AND SNOWSHOEING

Snowmobiling is allowed on the east side of the park on sections of **Highway 123** and **Stevens Canyon Road**—between the ranger station at Ohanapecosh Visitor Center and Box Canyon—and on Highway 410, which is accessible from the north entrance. **Highway 410** is unplowed after its junction with the road to the Crystal Mountain Ski Area. A State of Washington **Sno-Park** permit (☞ Outdoor Activities and Sports *in* Washington A to Z, *below*), available at stores and gas stations throughout the area, is required to park in the area near the north park-entrance arch. Highways 123 and 410 are good places to snowshoe.

Mount Rainier National Park Essentials

Getting Around

BY BUS

Gray Line of Seattle (☎ 206/624–5813) operates daily tours to Longmire and Paradise in the summer.

BY CAR

Most visitors arrive at the park's Nisqually entrance, the closest entrance to I–5, via **Highway 706. Highway 410** enters the park from the east. **Highway 123** enters from the southeast. Highways 410 and 123 are usually closed in winter. **Highway 165** leads to Ipsut Creek Campground through the Carbon River entrance to Mowich Lake, in the park's northwest corner.

Visitor Information

Superintendent, Mount Rainier National Park (✉ Tahoma Woods, Star Rte., Ashford 98304, ☎ 360/569–2211).

CROSSING THE CASCADES

East of Seattle, Interstate 90 crosses a floating bridge and an island and passes through suburbs before escaping to the bucolic farmlands east of Issaquah. Soon snowcapped peaks crowd in upon the road, but the highway rises only slowly at first: the Snoqualmie Valley through which it passes is heavily glaciated and its floor is only a few hundred feet above sea level. A short side trip takes you to Snoqualmie Falls, one of the area's most popular attractions. Soon, beyond North Bend, forests and mountains without end dominate the landscape. The freeway rises steeply as you approach Snoqualmie Summit but descends more gently on the eastern slopes as it winds past Lake Kecheelus and the old coal-mining towns of Roslyn and Cle Elum, down onto the Kittitas Valley. As you descend from the mountains, the air becomes warmer (colder in winter), the forests open up into woodlands, and in spring and early summer, wildflowers paint the meadows golden, white, pink, red, and blue. Ellensburg, a pleasant college town on the upper Yakima River, makes for a refreshing stop on the way to the Yakima Valley wineries. If you have time, be sure to take the scenic canyon road (Exit 3 off WA 821, south of the I–90/I–82 junction) to Yakima.

Snoqualmie

③⓪ *28 mi east of Seattle on I–90.*

★ ℭ   Spring and summer snowmelt turns the Snoqualmie River into a thundering torrent at **Snoqualmie Falls,** where the river pours over a 268-ft rock ledge (100 ft higher than Niagara Falls) to a 65-ft-deep pool below. The falls, which were considered sacred by the native people who lived along the riverbank, are Snoqualmie's biggest attraction. A 2-acre park, including an observation platform 300 ft above the Snoqualmie River, offers a view of Snoqualmie Falls and the surrounding area. You can hike the **River Trail,** a 3-mi round-trip route through trees and open slopes that ends at the base of the falls. Be prepared for an uphill workout on the return to the trailhead.

ℭ   The vintage cars of the **Snoqualmie Valley Railroad,** built in the mid-1910s for the Spokane, Portland, and Seattle Railroad, travel between the landmark **Snoqualmie Depot** and a depot in North Bend. The 50-minute (round-trip) excursion passes through woods and farmland. The **Northwest Railway Museum** within Snoqualmie's depot displays memorabilia and has a bookstore. ✉ *Snoqualmie Depot: 38625 S.E. King St., at Hwy. 202,* ☎ *206/746–4025 in Seattle; 425/888–0373 in Snoqualmie.* ➲ *$6.* ☉ *Trains May–Sept., weekends; Oct., Sun. only; on the hr 11–4 from Snoqualmie and on the ½ hr 11:30–3:30 from North Bend. Museum, depot, and bookstore Thurs.–Mon. 10–5.*

The **Herbfarm** is famous for its herb gardens (its once-renowned restaurant burned down) and offers a selection of unusual plants and other items for sale. ✉ *32804 Issaquah–Fall City Rd., Fall City (from I–90 Exit 22 head left, then take 1st right onto Preston–Fall City Rd.; follow this 3 mi to Y in road, then go left over the bridge and another ½ mi),* ☎ *425/784–2222.* ☉ *Apr.–Sept., daily 9–6; Oct.–Mar., daily 10–5.*

Winding north through heavy forest from Snoqualmie, Highway 203 becomes plain old Main Street when it reaches the unassuming town of **Duvall,** a good place to stop for peeks in antiques or bookshops, a glimpse of the Snoqualmie River, or a mid-afternoon latte. To return to Seattle you can backtrack to Snoqualmie or head west on the Woodinville–Duvall Road.

Dining and Lodging

$$$$ ╳▥ **Salish Lodge.** Eight of the 91 rooms at this lodge look out over
★   Snoqualmie Falls, and others have a view upriver. All have an airy feeling, wood furniture, whirlpool baths, and window seats or balconies. The restaurant's elaborate Saturday and Sunday brunches include eggs, bacon, fish, fresh fruit, pancakes, and the Salish's renowned oatmeal. Jacket and tie are required for dinner; reservations are essential.

Crossing the Cascades

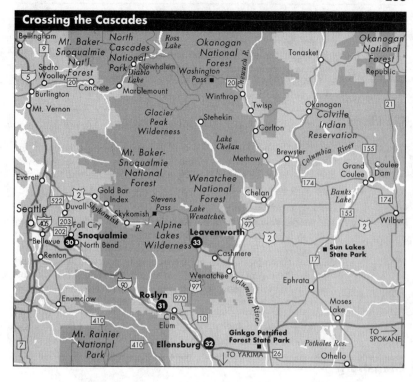

Breakfast is served on weekdays. ✉ *6501 Railroad Ave. SE, 98065,* ☎ *206/888–2556 or 800/826–6124,* FAX *425/888–2420. 91 rooms. 2 restaurants, bar, spa, health club, laundry service, concierge, business services, meeting rooms. AE, D, DC, MC, V.*

Nightlife and the Arts

Snoqualmie Falls Forest Theater (☎ 425/222–7044) presents two or three plays, usually melodramas performed by acting students and community performers, in a 250-seat outdoor amphitheater near Fall City—from I-90 take Exit 22 and go 4 mi; take a right on David Powell Road, follow signs, and continue through the gate to the parking area. Tickets are $13. For another $12, you can enjoy a salmon or steak barbecue after the matinee or before the evening performance. Reservations are required for dinner.

Outdoor Activities and Sports

Snoqualmie Pass has three downhill and cross-country ski areas—**Alpental, Ski Acres,** and **Snoqualmie** Summit(✉ Mailing address for all three: 3010 77th St. SE, Mercer Island 98040, ☎ 206/232–8182). Each area rents equipment and has a full restaurant and lodge facilities.

Roslyn

③① *58 mi from Snoqualmie; 83 mi from Seattle, east on I–90 and north on Hwy. 903.*

Roslyn, a former coal-mining town, gained notoriety as the real-life stand-in for the Alaskan town of Cicely on the mid-1990s TV program *Northern Exposure*. The **Brick Tavern** (✉ 1 Pennsylvania Ave., ☎ 509/649–2643), which opened in 1889, is the oldest operating bar in Washington. Roslyn is also notable for its two dozen ethnic cemeteries, established by communities of miners in the late 1800s and early 1900s.

Dining

$–$$ ✕ **Roslyn Café.** High ceilings and neon in the window add a touch of nostalgia to this funky café. The hamburgers are delicious (try the one with spinach and onions), and entrées include fresh halibut in dill sauce. Save room for the decadent desserts. ⊠ *28 Pennsylvania Ave.,* ☎ *509/649–2763. Reservations not accepted. MC, V.* ⊙ *Breakfast and lunch daily, call ahead for dinner days and hrs.*

Cle Elum

3 mi east of Roslyn; 86 mi east of Seattle on I–90.

Cle Elum (pronounced "Klee *ell*-um"), another former coal-mining town, doesn't have many sights, but because it's right off I–90 it's a convenient stop for lunch or gas.

Dining and Lodging

$$ ✕☂ **Mama Vallone's Steakhouse and Inn.** The pasta dishes, the pasta and *fagioli* soup (a tomato-based soup with vegetables and beans), and the *bagna calda* (a bath of olive oil, garlic, anchovies, and butter for dredging vegetables and meat) are worthy favorites at this cozy and informal restaurant (closed Mon., no lunch). For Sunday brunch, you might find ravioli or tortellini along with a standard eggs-and-ham buffet. The inn upstairs was built in 1906 as a boardinghouse for unmarried miners; today there are three moderately priced rooms with antique-style furnishings. ⊠ *302 W. 1st St., 98922,* ☎ *509/674–5174. 3 rooms. Restaurant. AE, DC, MC, V.*

Ellensburg

③② *110 mi east of Seattle on I–90.*

Modern Ellensburg had its origin in a Fourth of July fire that engulfed the original city in 1889. Almost overnight, Victorian brick buildings rose from the ashes; many of still them stand today, though their functions have changed to fit the times. Stroll through Ellensburg's historic downtown district and you'll pass art galleries, used-book stores, an old-time hardware store, and one antiques shop after another.

♻ Ellensburg is home to the 7,000-student Central Washington University. Every weekend the university hosts hour-long **Chimposiums,** at which you can see chimpanzees using sign language. ⊠ *D St. and Nicholson Blvd.,* ☎ *509/963–2244.* ⊡ *$10.* ⊙ *Sat. 9:15 AM and 10:45 AM, Sun. 12:15 PM and 2 PM.*

The promoters of the **Ellensburg Rodeo** (☎ 800/637–2444) tout the four-day event during Labor Day weekend as "the greatest show on dirt."

OFF THE   **DICK AND JANE'S SPOT –** Hidden in suburbia near downtown Ellensburg
BEATEN PATH   is the area's most peculiar attraction. The home of artists Dick Elliott and Jane Orleman is a continuously growing whimsical sculpture, a collage of 20,000 bottle caps, 1,500 bicycle reflectors, bicycle pinwheels, and bizarre statues, all thrown together haphazardly on the outside of the house. Their masterpiece stands on private property, so don't cross the fence, but try to view the recycled creation from all angles. ⊠ *101 N. Pearl St.,* ☎ *509/925–3224.*

Dining

$–$$ ✕ **Valley Cafe.** Lunch at this Art Deco eatery in a late-1930s structure includes a chicken Dijon sandwich, Mediterranean tortellini salad, and the café plate—a cup of soup with an open-face sandwich. Lamb, salmon, chicken tortellini, and pasta primavera are among the dinner highlights. ⊠ *105 W. 3rd Ave.,* ☎ *509/925–3050. AE, D, DC, MC, V.*

Crossing the Cascades Essentials

Arriving and Departing

BY BUS

Metro Bus 210 originates in downtown Seattle (☞ Seattle A to Z *in* Chapter 4) and travels to Snoqualmie and North Bend. **Greyhound Lines** (☎ 800/231–2222) or its affiliate, Northwest Trailways, travels from Seattle to Snoqualmie, Cle Elum, and Ellensburg.

BY CAR

To reach the towns east of the Cascades, you must go over Snoqualmie Pass—a winding, four-lane stretch of road. As far as western mountain passes go, **Interstate 90** east of Seattle is among the easiest to drive, since the crossing is at a relatively low 3,000 ft. Snow tires or chains are often required in winter; call 888/866–4636 for pass conditions.

Getting Around

BY CAR

U.S. 12 crosses the southern Cascades south of Mount Rainier, via White Pass. Farther north, **Interstate 90** skirts the southern edge of the North Cascades. **U.S. 2** crosses the mountains parallel to I–90, 25 to 65 mi north of I–90, from Everett to Wenatchee, Spokane, and beyond. **Highway 203** runs north from I–90 at North Bend through Snoqualmie and Duvall before connecting with U.S. 2 at Monroe. **U.S. 97** heads north from I–90 near Ellensburg and meets with U.S. 2 east of Leavenworth before running north along the Columbia and Okanogan rivers to Canada. At the top of the state, **WA 20,** the North Cascades Highway, runs between I–5 at Burlington and the Methow Valley, crossing the Cascades via Washington Pass.

Visitor Information

Ellensburg Chamber of Commerce and Forest Service Office (⊠ 436 N. Sprague St., 98926, ☎ 509/925–3137). **Upper Snoqualmie Valley Chamber of Commerce** (⊠ Box 356, North Bend 8045, ☎ 425/888–4440).

YAKIMA VALLEY WINE COUNTRY

The Yakima River flows southeast from its source in the Cascade Mountains, cutting steep canyons through serried basalt ridges east of Ellensburg and between the Kittitas Valley and Yakima. After merging with the Naches River in Yakima, the Yakima crosses the Ahtanum Valley and breaks through Union Gap to enter the long valley bearing its name. Throughout its course, the Yakima is a rocky river with many rapids. Before the ridges of the Cascades rose in its path, the river meandered across the once flat region; later it gashed its way through the new mountains. It was once a major salmon stream, and few salmon, undeterred by dams and fishermen, still ascend the river to spawn. Grass-covered hills, dun at harvesttime, rise above fields, orchards, and vineyards. Here, with their vast herds of horses, the Yakama people roamed widely more than a century ago. Horses still run wild in the Horse Heaven Hills on the Yakama Reservation.

The Yakima Valley is Washington's produce basket and wine vat. Apples and other fruits came to the valley in the 1890s, with the first irrigation schemes. Grapes came much later: Concord grapes were planted first (during the 1960s, the valley supplied Gallo and New York State wineries with Concord grape juice), and they still take up large tracts of land. They helped make Washington the nation's number two grape-growing state. But *vinifera* grapes, the noble grapes of Europe, now domi-

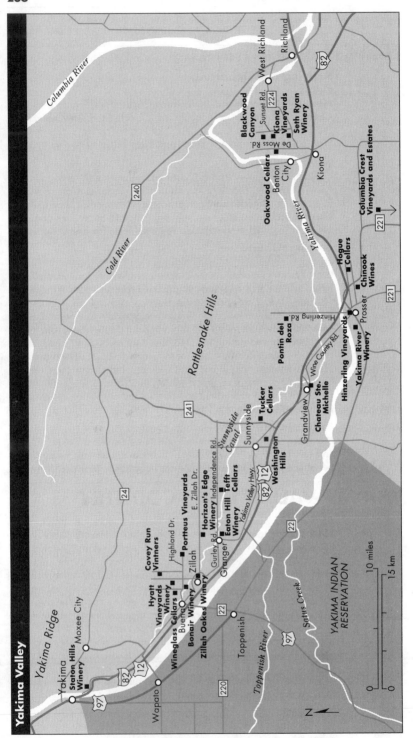

Yakima Valley

Columbia River

Yakima Ridge

Cold River

Rattlesnake Hills

Richland
West Richland
82
Sunset Rd.
224
Blackwood Canyon
Kiona Vineyards
De Moss Rd.
Seth Ryan Winery
Oakwood Cellars
Benton City
Kiona
Yakima River
Columbia Crest Vineyards and Estates
221
Hogue Cellars
Chinook Wines
Prosser
221
Hinzerling Rd.
Hinzerling Vineyards
Yakima River Winery
Pontin del Roza
Wine Country Rd.
Grandview
Chateau Ste. Michelle
Tucker Cellars
Sunnyside Canal
Sunnyside
240
241
24
Horizon's Edge Winery
Tefft Cellars
Eaton Hill Winery
Washington Hills
82 12
Yakima Valley Hwy.
Independence Rd.
Portteus Vineyards
E. Zillah Dr.
Highland Dr.
Covey Run Vintners
Gurley Rd.
Granger
Hyatt Vineyards Winery
Wineglass Cellars
Bonair Winery
Zillah
Zillah Oakes Winery
Bueno
Station Hills Winery
Yakima
Moxee City
82 12
97
Wapato
220
22
Toppenish
97
Toppenish River
Satus Creek
YAKIMA INDIAN RESERVATION

10 miles
15 km

N

nate the local wine industry. Familiar varieties include Cabernet Sauvignon, white Riesling, Chardonnay, Sauvignon Blanc, Chenin Blanc, Grenache, Merlot, Sémillon, Muscat, and Gewürztraminer. There are even plantings of Syrah, Nebbiolo, and Lemberger (a German red wine grape).

Yakima Valley wineries range in size from small backyard cellars to large commercial operations. Barrels are tapped and the main wine-tasting season begins about the last week of April and runs to the end of the fall harvest in November. Most wineries are easily reached from I–82. Winter hours are spotty—call ahead to be sure an establishment is open. The **Yakima Valley Wine Grower Association** (⊠ Box 39, Grandview 98930) publishes a map-brochure that lists local wineries with tasting-room tours. Here you'll find a welcoming informality—the wineries are managed by unpretentious enthusiasts, and their cellar masters are often on hand to answer questions.

But Yakima is more than just another wine valley. Other harvests begin in April, with asparagus and cherries. The soft fruits—cherries, apricots, and peaches—ripen from late spring to early autumn. Hops are ready by late August, and the apple harvest runs from August to October.

Yakima

38 mi southeast of Ellensburg on U.S. 97/I–82.

Yakima is a pleasant but sprawling agricultural metropolis with a busy modern downtown, a quaint old town, tree-shaded residential neighborhoods, a lovely arboretum, and cottonwood- and willow-lined trails along the river. With several malls, Yakima is *the* major regional shopping center. It holds the **Central Washington Fair** each fall and has a horse-racing track. Yakima has more than its share of resort motels, because Puget Sounders, chilled by their region's often cool summer climate, flock here to lie in the sun and soak up the warmth, which is why the city bills itself as the "Palm Springs of Washington." By the way, you will not find any "Yakima Valley" wineries in Yakima. Officially, the city of Yakima is in the Ahtanum Valley, not in the Yakima Valley, which begins east of Union Gap.

★ ☾ The **Yakima Valley Museum and Historical Association** (⊠ 2105 Tieton Dr., ☎ 509/248–0747) has a comprehensive collection of horse-drawn vehicles, and a model of Yakima native and Supreme Court Justice William O. Douglas's office in Washington, D.C. The **Yakima Electronic Railway Museum** (⊠ 3rd Ave. and W. Pine St., ☎ 509/575–1700) is a good option for railroad buffs.

Dining and Lodging

$ ✕ **Grant's Brewery Pub.** America's oldest brew pub is a Yakima institution. The usual pub grub—burgers, salads, sandwiches—complements the suds daily and there's live jazz on weekends. ⊠ *32 N. Front St.,* ☎ *509/575–2922. MC, V.*

$$–$$$ ✕🖭 **Birchfield Manor.** The only true luxury accommodation in the val-★ ley sits on a perfectly flat plateau in Moxee City, 2 mi outside Yakima, surrounded by fields and grazing cattle. The Old Manor House contains an award-winning restaurant and four upstairs rooms. A newer cottage house maintains the country ambience while providing every modern convenience; its rooms, each with a whirlpool tub, a steam-sauna shower, a TV with VCR, and a gas fireplace, have been designed for maximum privacy. Owner Wil Masset, a European-trained chef, oversees the restaurant (reservations essential), whose menu changes seasonally. The downstairs wine cellar has an excellent selection of local and imported vintages. ⊠ *2018 Birchfield Rd., 98901,* ☎ *509/452–1960,* 🖷 *509/452–2334. 11 rooms. Restaurant, pool. AE, DC, MC, V.*

Outdoor Activities and Sports

The popular **Apple Tree Golf Course** (⌧ 8804 Occidental Ave., ☎ 509/966–5877) is an 18-hole, par-72 course. The greens fee ranges from $35 to $50; an optional cart costs $24.

Wapato

7 mi east of Yakima, I–82 to Exit 40.

Staton Hills Winery, just east of Union Gap, produces bubblies, Cabernet Sauvignon, Merlot, Pinot Noir, and Chardonnay. The main building has a huge stone fireplace and a commanding view of the upper valley. ⌧ *71 Gangl Rd., off Thorpe–Parker Rd.,* ☎ *509/877–2112.* ⊙ *Mar.–Oct., daily 11–5:30; Nov.–Feb., daily noon–5.*

Toppenish

9 mi southeast of Wapato on U.S. 97.

The Toppenish Mural Association began commissioning murals in 1989 to draw commerce to the small town. The resulting 40-plus colorful paintings, in a variety of styles by artists from around the region, commemorate the town's history and western spirit. You can wander ★ ⊙ through shops that sell crafts and antiques, or stop by the **Hops Museum** (⌧ 22 S. B St., ☎ 509/865–4677) or the **Yakama Nation Cultural Center** (⌧ U.S. 97, ☎ 509/865–2800), which has a fascinating tribal museum, plus a gift shop, a restaurant, and a longhouse where traditional dances and other cultural events are performed.

Zillah

10 mi east of Wapato; 17 mi east of Yakima on I–82.

The slopes above Zillah, a town named after the daughter of a railroad manager, are covered with orchards and vineyards. Seven wineries are in or near the town.

Zillah Oakes Winery, now owned by Corus Brands, produces Muscat, Chardonnay, Riesling, and other wines. ⌧ *Vintage Valley Pkwy. off I–82,* ☎ *509/829–6990.* ⊙ *Apr.–Nov., daily 10–5; Dec.–Mar., daily 11–4:40.*

Bonair Winery is run by the Puryear family, who after years of amateur wine making in California began commercial production of Chardonnay, Cabernet, and Riesling wines in their native Yakima Valley. ⌧ *500 S. Bonair Rd. (head north from I–82's Exit 52 on Cheyne Rd., turn left on Highland Dr., and left on Bonair),* ☎ *509/829–6027.* ⊙ *Apr.–Nov., daily 10–5; Dec.–Mar., weekends and most weekdays 10–4:30.*

You'll find an unusual collection of wine glasses at **Wineglass Cellars,** which produces Merlot, Cabernet Sauvignon, Pinot Noir, and Chardonnay wines. ⌧ *206 N. Bonair Rd. (head north from I–82's Exit 52),* ☎ *509/829–3011.* ⊙ *Presidents' Day–Nov., Fri.–Sun. 10:30–5.*

Hyatt Vineyards Winery specializes in barrel-fermented Chardonnay, Merlot, Sauvignon Blanc, late-harvest Riesling, and dessert wines. ⌧ *2020 Gilbert Rd., off Bonair Rd.,* ☎ *509/829–6333.* ⊙ *Apr.–Nov., daily 11–5; Dec. and Feb.–Mar., daily 11–4:30.*

Covey Run Vintners, one of the valley's largest wineries, has expansive decks and grounds with commanding views of the surrounding vineyards and orchards. Through large windows off the tasting room you can watch the wine—Cabernet Sauvignon, Chardonnay, Riesling, Merlot, and Chenin Blanc—being made. ⌧ *1500 Vintage Rd. (head north* *from I–82's Exit 52, turn east on Highland Dr., and north on Vintage),* ☎ *509/829–6235.* ⊙ *Apr.–Oct., daily 10–5; Nov.–Mar., daily 11–4:30.*

Portteus Vineyards, a favorite among Washington residents, limits its production mainly to Cabernet Sauvignon and Chardonnay wines from grapes grown at a 1,440-ft elevation on 47 acres above Zillah. ⊠ *5201 Highland Dr. (head north from I–82's Exit 52),* ☎ *509/829–6970.* ⊙ *Mid-Feb.–Nov., daily noon–5; Dec.–mid-Feb. by appointment.*

Horizon's Edge Winery takes its name from its tasting room's view of the Yakima Valley, Mount Adams, and Mount Rainier. The winery produces sparkling wines, barrel-fermented Chardonnays, and Pinot Noir, Cabernet Sauvignon, and Muscat Canelli wines. ⊠ *4530 E. Zillah Dr., east of Yakima Valley Hwy.,* ☎ *509/829–6401.* ⊙ *May–Nov., weekdays 11–5, weekends 10–5; Dec.–Feb. by appointment.; Mar.–Apr., weekends 11–5.*

Dining

$$ ✕ **Squeeze Inn Restaurant.** A family-operated establishment (since 1932), the Squeeze Inn looks as timeworn as the surrounding structures on Zillah's main street. Prime rib and steaks are the big draws, but you'll also find seafood on the menu. Come here for hearty breakfasts, too. ⊠ *611 E. 1st Ave.,* ☎ *509/829–6226. MC, V. Closed Sun.*

$ ✕ **El Ranchito.** The food—for breakfast, lunch, or dinner—is tasty and inexpensive at this large, authentic, cafeteria-style Mexican restaurant, tortilla factory, deli, and import shop. ⊠ *1319 E. 1st Ave.,* ☎ *509/829–5880. Reservations not accepted. No credit cards.*

Granger

6 mi east of Zillah on I–82.

Eaton Hill Winery, in the restored Rinehold Cannery building, produces Riesling and Semillon wines. ⊠ *530 Gurley Rd., off Yakima Valley Hwy.,* ☎ *509/854–2220.* ⊙ *Apr.–Nov., Fri.–Wed. 10–5; Dec.–Mar., usually Fri.–Wed. noon–4.*

Tefft Cellars sells limited editions of its wines. The tasting room is behind the home of owners Joe and Pam Tefft. ⊠ *1320 Independence Rd., Outlook (take Gurley Rd. east from Yakima Valley Hwy.; it becomes Independence Rd.),* ☎ *509/837–7651.* ⊙ *Apr.–Nov., daily noon–5 or by appointment.*

Sunnyside

7 mi east of Granger on I–82.

At **Washington Hills,** Brian Carter, one of Washington's most respected wine makers, crafts Washington Hills, Apex, and W. B. Bridgman wines—several whites, a red, and a blush. You can picnic in the winery's English gardens. ⊠ *111 E. Lincoln Ave., off Yakima Valley Hwy.,* ☎ *509/839–9463.* ⊙ *Daily 11–5:30.*

Tucker Cellars makes 20,000 gallons of wine—Cabernet Sauvignon, Chardonnay, Riesling, Gewürztraminer, and Muscat Canelli—each year. The Tucker family market, a roadside farm stand east of Sunnyside on U.S. 12, sells splendid homegrown fruits and vegetables. ⊠ *70 Ray Rd., off Yakima Valley Hwy.,* ☎ *509/837–8701.* ⊙ *Apr.–Oct., daily 9–5; Nov.–Mar., daily 9–4.*

Dining and Lodging

$ ✕ **El Conquistador.** The broad menu at this Mexican restaurant includes everything from burritos and fajitas to shrimp sautéed with green peppers and onions and served with a tangy salsa. ⊠ *612 E. Edison Ave.,* ☎ *509/839–2880. MC, V. No lunch.*

$-$$ ⬚ **Sunnyside Inn Bed & Breakfast.** Each clean and comfortable room in this 1910 house on the main road in Sunnyside comes with cable TV and a private phone line. Seven rooms have whirlpool baths. The rates include a breakfast of breads, pastries, meats, and a griddle entrée. Families are welcome. ⊠ *800 E. Edison Ave., 98944, ☎ 509/839–5557 or 800/221–4195, ⛶ 509/839–5350. 8 rooms. AE, MC, V.*

Grandview

7 mi east of Sunnyside on I–82.

Chateau Ste. Michelle no longer makes wine in a local building dating from the 1930s (the winery now operates out of Woodinville; *see* On Seattle's Outskirts and Beyond *in* Chapter 4). But you can sample the company's wines here and view European-style open-top fermentors and a collection of wood aging tanks. ⊠ *W. 5th St. and Ave. B off Wine Country Rd., ☎ 509/882–3928. ⊙ Daily 10–4:30.*

Prosser

7 mi east of Grandview on I–82.

The **Yakima River Winery,** specializing in barrel-aged red wines and dessert wines, is southwest of town. ⊠ *143302 N. River Rd., off Wine Country Rd., ☎ 509/786–2805. ⊙ Mar.–Nov., daily 10–5; Dec.–Feb., generally noon–4 (call ahead).*

Pontin del Roza is named for its owners, the Pontin family, and the grape-friendly southern slopes of the Yakima Valley, known as the Roza. The winery produces Rieslings, Chenin Blancs, Chardonnays, Sauvignon Blancs, and Cabernet Sauvignons. ⊠ *Rte. 4, off Hinzerling Rd., ☎ 509/786–4449. ⊙ Daily 10–5.*

Hinzerling Vineyards specializes in estate-grown Cabernet and late-harvest Gewürztraminer and Riesling wines. ⊠ *1520 Sheridan Rd., off Wine Country Rd., ☎ 509/786–2163. ⊙ Mar.–Dec. 24, Mon.–Sat. 11–5, Sun. 11–4.*

East of Prosser is **Chinook Wines,** a small family winery run by Kay Simon and Clay Mackey, vintners regionally renowned for splendid Merlot, Chardonnay, and Sauvignon Blanc wines. ⊠ *Wine Country Rd. east of I–82, ☎ 509/786–2725. ⊙ Presidents' Day–Dec. 24, Fri.–Sun. noon–5.*

Hogue Cellars, which has won numerous awards, is a few blocks east of Chinook. There's a tasting room here and a gift shop that carries Hogue wines—Cabernet Sauvignon, Merlot, and Fumé Blanc among them—and the family's famous pickled beans and asparagus. ⊠ *Wine Country Rd. at I–82's Exit 82, ☎ 509/786–4557. ⊙ Daily 10–5.*

Dining

$-$$ ✕ **Wine Country Inn.** This restaurant alongside the Yakima River serves lunch, dinner, and Sunday brunch in a pretty spot overlooking the grass- and tree-lined banks of the Yakima River. In warm weather you can dine on an old-fashioned porch. Choose from classic American soups and salads, as well as meat and vegetable dishes. The inn, a B&B, has four rooms available. ⊠ *1106 Wine Country Rd., ☎ 509/786–2855. AE, MC, V. No dinner Mon.–Tues.*

Benton City

16 mi east of Prosser on I–82.

Seth Ryan Winery is a boutique winery producing German-style Gewürztraminer and Riesling wines, plus Cabernet Sauvignons, Caber-

net Francs, and Merlots. ✉ *Sunset Rd. (Rte. 2) off Hwy. 224,* ☎ *509/
588–6780.* ⊘ *Weekends 11–6 (noon–5 in winter).*

Almost all the work is done by hand at **Oakwood Cellars,** a tiny winery on the slopes of Red Mountain that produces Lembergers, Merlots, Cabernet Sauvignons, and Semillons. ✉ *40504 N. Demoss Rd.,
off Hwy. 224,* ☎ *509/588–5332.* ⊘ *Mar.–Nov., weekends noon–6; Dec.–
Feb., call ahead.*

Kiona Vineyards, one of Washington's best wineries, produced the first
commercial Lemberger wine released in this country. The small family winery also makes superbly fruity Riesling, elegant Chenin Blanc,
complex Cabernet Sauvignon, deeply flavored Merlot, and a crisp, barrel-fermented Chardonnay. ✉ *Sunset Rd. (Rte. 2) off Hwy. 224,* ☎
509/588–6716. ⊘ *Daily noon–5.*

Meticulously crafting wines by hand, the workers at **Blackwood Canyon**
use as few modern filters, pumps, and other gadgets as possible. The
winery specializes in Chardonnays, Semillons, Merlots, Cabernets,
and late-harvest wines. ✉ *Red Mountain Rd. off Sunset Rd. north of
Hwy. 224,* ☎ *509/588–6249.* ⊘ *Daily 10–6.*

Yakima Valley Wine Country Essentials

Arriving and Departing

BY BUS

Greyhound (✉ Depot: 801 Okanogan St., ☎ 509/925–1177 or 800/
231–2222) has daily bus service from Seattle (2½ hrs) and elsewhere.

BY CAR

Interstate 82 and **U.S. 12** are the main routes to and through the
Yakima Valley.

BY PLANE

Horizon Air and United Express serve the **Yakima Air Terminal** (✉ W.
Washington Ave., ☎ 509/575–6149). *See* Air Travel *in* Smart Travel
Tips A to Z for airline phone numbers.

Getting Around

BY CAR

As you travel up or down the valley, it is best to stick to **I-82,** since
many of the country roads (even U.S. 12) make unexpected sharp
turns around land sections. Most wineries are within a mile or two of
the freeway. Pick up a free valley guide with maps at the first winery
you visit, and you should not get lost. If you're confused, don't hesi-
tate to call a winery and ask for directions. And should you get lost,
don't be afraid to ask someone to point you in the right direction—
the locals are very friendly.

Guided Tours

Accent! Tours & Charters (✉ 3701 River Rd., Yakima, ☎ 509/575–3949)
operates informative tours of Yakima-area wineries. **Moonlit Rides** (✉
3908 River Rd., Yakima, ☎ 509/575–6846) also conducts tours of the
Yakima area.

Visitor Information

Yakima Valley Visitors & Convention Bureau (✉ 10 N. 8th St., Yakima
98901, ☎ 509/575–3010 or 800/221–0751).

LEAVENWORTH

U.S. 2 is one of the main routes crossing the Cascades. It connects the
Seattle metropolitan area ("Pugetopolis") to eastern Washington and

Spokane. Small towns and villages cater to visitors between Snohomish and Stevens Pass; east of the Cascade Crest, the road traverses the spectacular Tumwater Canyon of the Wenatchee River before emerging into the fertile fruit-growing valley that stretches from Leavenworth to Wenatchee. The scenery is particularly splendid in spring, when the snowy peaks are offset by the white blossoms of apricot and apple trees and by the pink blossoms of peach trees. In winter, Stevens Pass may be closed temporarily (usually for not more than an hour or two) for snow removal and avalanche control.

Leavenworth

★ ③③ *116 mi east of Seattle on U.S. 2.*

Leavenworth is one of Seattle's favorite weekend getaways and it's easy to see why: The charming (if occasionally *too* cute) Bavarian-style village, home to good restaurants and attractive lodgings, is a hub for some of the Northwest's best skiing, hiking, rock climbing, rafting, canoeing, and snowshoeing. To get here, take WA 520 from Seattle to Bellevue and go north on I–405 to Hwy 522; then take Hwy 522 north to U.S. 2 and follow U.S. 2 east across Stevens Pass.

Leavenworth was a railroad and mining center for many years, but by the 1960s it had fallen on hard times. Civic leaders, looking for ways to capitalize on the town's setting in the heart of the Central Cascade Range, convinced shopkeepers and other businesspeople to maintain a gingerbread-Bavarian architectural style in their buildings—even the Safeway supermarket and the Chevron gas station carry out the theme. Restaurants prepare Bavarian-influenced dishes, candy shops sell gourmet Swiss-style chocolates, and stores and boutiques stock music boxes, dollhouses, and other Bavarian items.

The **Marlin Handbell Ringers** (☎ 509/548–5807) keep alive an 18th-century English tradition that evolved into a musical form. Twelve ringers play 107 bells covering 5½ chromatic octaves. The bells are rung as part of the town's Christmas festivities and also in early May. Also noteworthy is the **Nutcracker Museum** (⊠ 735 Front St., ☎ 509/548–4708), which contains more than 2,500 different kinds of antique and present-day nutcrackers. The museum is open May to October, daily from 2 to 5.

Dining and Lodging

$$$–$$$$ ✕ **Restaurant Osterreich.** Chef Leopold Haas, who hails from Austria,
★ prepares authentic German cuisine, such as Wiener schnitzel, pork chops with apple sauce, crawfish strudel, venison topped with chanterelle mushrooms, red cabbage salad, potato salad, and apple strudel. The menu changes daily. The atmosphere is infinitely more casual than the food. ⊠ *Tyrolean Ritz Hotel, 633A Front St., ☎ 509/548–4031. MC, V. Closed Mon.*

$$$ ✕ **Lorraine's Edel House.** The candlelit rooms at this understated
★ restaurant, a rare Leavenworth eatery that doesn't focus on German food, are quiet and cozy. The menu of expertly prepared Continental and contemporary dishes changes monthly, but typical offerings include game, seafood, and pasta (try the putanesca if it's available). Openers might be Portobello mushrooms with a goat cheese topping seasoned with fresh herbs and garlic, or apple-beet polenta with Gorgonzola cheese. ⊠ *320 9th St., ☎ 509/548–4412. D, DC, MC, V.*

$$ ✕ **Cougar Inn.** This family restaurant, established in 1890, is on the shores of Lake Wenatchee, about 25 mi from Leavenworth. Locals often come by boat and tie up at the restaurant's dock. Great views of the lake can be had, especially in summer from the big outdoor deck. Breakfast, lunch, and dinner are served daily from a menu built around thick

steaks, grilled and baked fish, burgers, and pastas. The hearty Sunday brunch is especially popular. ⊠ *23379 Hwy. 207, Lake Wenatchee,* ☎ *509/763–3354. AE, MC, V.*

$$ ✕ **Pewter Pot.** This intimate restaurant with lace curtains and fresh flowers is worth the 10-mi drive from Leavenworth to the town of Cashmere. The tasty, well-prepared traditional American fare—a turkey dinner, a New England boiled dinner, a roasted chicken, etc.—incorporates fresh local ingredients. Desserts, which include a deep-dish marionberry pie, are memorable. ⊠ *124½ Cottage Ave., Cashmere,* ☎ *509/782–2036. Reservations essential. MC, V. Closed Sun.–Mon.*

$ ✕ **Baren Haus.** The cuisine at this spacious, noisy, and often crowded beer-hall-style room may not be haute, or even particularly interesting, but the generous servings and low prices will appeal to those traveling on a budget. Fill up on generous servings of basic American fare, like burgers and fries, sandwiches, and salads. ⊠ *208 9th St.,* ☎ *509/548–4535. MC, V.*

$ ✕ **Danish Bakery.** Come to this small shop for tasty homemade pastries, strong espresso drinks, and friendly service. ⊠ *731 Front St.,* ☎ *509/548–7514. Reservations not accepted. No credit cards.*

$ ✕ **Leavenworth Brewery.** The only brewery in Leavenworth pours 8 to 10 fresh brews—the selection changes every two to three weeks. The highly trained brew masters provide detailed descriptions of their beers (daily brewery tours are given at 2 PM). Sandwiches and bar food are available. ⊠ *636 Front St.,* ☎ *509/548–4545. Reservations not accepted. MC, V.*

$$–$$$ ⊡ **Pension Anna.** Rooms and suites at this family-run Austrian-style pension in the heart of the village are decorated with sturdy antique pine furniture; added touches include fresh flowers and comforters on the beds. Two of the suites have whirlpool baths. A solid breakfast of coffee, fruit, cereal, and rich pastries is served in a room decorated in traditional European style, with crisp linens, pine decor, dark-green curtains, and a cuckoo clock. ⊠ *926 Commercial St., 98826,* ☎ *509/548–6273 or 800/509–2662,* 𝐅𝐀𝐗 *509/548–4656. 12 rooms, 3 suites. AE, D, MC, V.*

$$–$$$ ⊡ **Pine River Ranch.** Mountains completely surround this B&B on 32 acres, 16 mi outside Leavenworth. Two extremely private suites have kitchens, gas fireplaces, whirlpool tubs, stereos, televisions with VCRs, and decks. Four rooms in the farmhouse in front are significantly less spacious and private but still quite nice. A full breakfast is served in the dining room, but guests staying in the suites can have it delivered to them. ⊠ *19668 Hwy. 207, 98826,* ☎ *509/763–3959,* 𝐅𝐀𝐗 *509/763–2073. 6 rooms. AE, D, MC, V.*

$$–$$$ ⊡ **Run of the River.** This intimate, relaxed mountain inn stands on the ★ banks of the Icicle River near Leavenworth, placing the modern rooms close to nature. The largest of them, the Tumwater Suite, has two wood stoves, a loft, and a private deck overlooking the river's cascading torrents. Other rooms have views of the Pinnacles (a dramatic rock formation), an aspen grove, meadows (where deer browse), or Icicle and Tumwater canyons. Cushy bathrobes, toothpaste and toothbrushes, and private whirlpool tubs are among the amenities at this luxury accommodation. Breakfast is served in an enormous dining room on the main floor. ⊠ *9308 E. Leavenworth Rd., 98826,* ☎ *509/548–7171 or 800/288–6491,* 𝐅𝐀𝐗 *509/548–7547. 6 rooms. Dining room, refrigerators. AE, D, MC, V.*

$$ ⊡ **Evergreen Inn.** Popular with hikers and skiers, the Evergreen was built in the 1930s, and it still has much of the charm of the roadside inn it once was. Furnished in typical motel style, some of the rooms have king beds, gas fireplaces, wet bars, and Jacuzzis. Room rates include a Continental breakfast served by the very friendly staff. ⊠ *1117 Front St., 98826,* ☎ *509/548–5515 or 800/327–7212,* 𝐅𝐀𝐗 *509/548–6556. 39 rooms. AE, D, DC, MC, V.*

$$ ☷ **Haus Rohrbach.** This alpine-style B&B sits on the side of a hill with an unobstructed view of the village and the entire surrounding valley. Some of its comfortable rooms have king beds, balconies with valley views, and separate sitting areas. Two suites also feature whirlpool tubs, microwave ovens, refrigerators, coffeemakers, and private decks. The full breakfast served here typically includes Dutch babies (a sweet, fluffy omelet) or sourdough pancakes and sausage. ✉ *12882 Ranger Rd., 98826,* ☎ *509/548–7024 or 800/548–4477,* ℻ *509/548–5038. 7 rooms, 5 with bath; 3 suites. Pool, hot tub. AE, D, DC, MC, V.*

$$ ☷ **Linderhof Motor Inn.** This motel at the west end of Leavenworth is one of the best values in town. Although basic, the rooms are modern and comfortable, with a bit of chintz added for character and all of the usual amenities. You can have your complimentary Continental breakfast—fresh fruit juice, muffins, and Danish pastries—in your room or outside on the inn's balcony. ✉ *690 Hwy. 2, 98826,* ☎ *509/548–5283 or 800/828–5680,* ℻ *509/548–6705. 34 rooms. Pool, hot tub. AE, D, DC, MC, V.*

Outdoor Activities and Sports

FISHING

Trout are plentiful in many streams and lakes around Lake Wenatchee. **Leavenworth Ranger Station** (☎ 509/782–1413) issues permits for the Enchantment Lakes and Alpine Lake Wilderness area.

GOLF

Leavenworth Golf Club (✉ 9101 Icicle Rd., ☎ 509/548–7267) has an 18-hole, par-71 course. The greens fee is $20, plus $20 for an optional cart.

HIKING

The Leavenworth Ranger District has more than 320 mi of scenic trails, among them Hatchery Creek, Icicle Ridge, the Enchantments, Tumwater Canyon, Fourth of July Creek, Snow Lake, Stuart Lake, and Chatter Creek. Contact the **Leavenworth Ranger District** (✉ 600 Sherburne St., 98826, ☎ 509/782–1413) or the **Lake Wenatchee Ranger Station** (✉ 22976 Hwy. 207, ☎ 509/763–3101) for more information.

HORSEBACK RIDING

Hourly and daily horseback rides and pack trips are available at **Eagle Creek Ranch** (✉ 7951 Eagle Creek Rd., ☎ 509/548–7798).

SKIING

More than 20 mi of cross-country ski trails lace the Leavenworth area. **Mission Ridge** (☎ 800/374–1693) has 35 major downhill runs and night skiing from late December to early March. **Stevens Pass** (☎ 360/973–2441 or 360/634–1645) has 36 major downhill runs and slopes and lifts for skiers of every level. Several shops in Leavenworth rent and sell ski equipment. For more information, contact the **Leavenworth Winter Sports Club** (☎ 509/548–5115).

WHITE-WATER RAFTING

Rafting is a popular sport from March to July; the prime high-country runoff occurs in May and June. The Wenatchee River, which runs through Leavenworth, is considered one of the best white-water rivers in the state—a Class 3 on the International Canoeing Association scale.

Rafting outfitters and guides in the area include **All Rivers Adventures/Wenatchee Whitewater** (☎ 509/782–2254 or 800/743–5628), **Alpine Adventures** (☎ 509/548–4159 or 800/926–7238), **Leavenworth Outfitters** (☎ 509/763–3733 or 800/347–7934), and **Northern Wilderness River Riders** (☎ 509/548–4583).

Leavenworth Essentials

Arriving and Departing

BY BUS

Greyhound Lines (☎ 800/231–2222) and its affiliate, Northwest Trailways, travel from Seattle to Leavenworth.

BY CAR

Getting to Leavenworth via **U.S. 2** over Stevens Pass can be a bit difficult in winter, since the two-lane highway crosses at above 4,000 ft and is often closed for avalanche control. The drive to Leavenworth from Seattle (WA 520, I–405, WA 522, U.S. 2 east) usually takes a little more than 2½ hours in good weather.

BY TRAIN

Amtrak (☎ 800/872–7245) travels from Seattle to Wenatchee, which is 20 minutes from Leavenworth; a free county bus travels between Wenatchee and Leavenworth.

Visitor Information

Leavenworth Chamber of Commerce (✉ 894 U.S. 2, Box 327, 98826, ☎ 509/548–5807).

EASTERN WASHINGTON

A few miles south of its confluence with the Spokane River, the Columbia River (backed up behind Grand Coulee Dam as Lake Roosevelt) turns west as it skirts the vast basalt mass of the Columbia Plateau. The river turns south again at the mouth of the Okanogan River, squeezing its waters through steep-walled gorges that mark the geologic boundary between the rocky edge of the plateau and the craggy peaks of the North Cascade Mountains. Cliffs drop more than a thousand feet off the plateau's western edge down to the river, and the eastern rims of the gorges give way to a gentle landscape of plains, uplands, and rolling hills cut by steep-walled and generally dry coulees.

This is eastern Washington, a wide-open, big-sky country. Fields of dryland wheat stretch from coulee to coulee. Now and then the bucolic landscape bristles with wild, brushy creek beds and with the water towers, grain silos, and clumps of trees around the region's isolated farms, villages, and towns. Hawks and eagles circle overhead, the cry of the curlew and the trill of meadowlarks drift over the sea of grain and bunchgrass, and the creek bottoms are filled with the songs of sparrows, buntings, and warblers.

Eastern Washington is bisected by the Grand Coulee, an ancient flood channel stretching from Grand Coulee Dam at the northern edge of the plateau south to Soap Lake. Its towering basalt cliffs shield a string of natural and artificial lakes, whose marshes are home to beavers and muskrats, rabbits and otters, ducks, geese, and great blue herons. Deer rest in the moist dells; coyotes and bobcats skulk through the dry brush of the uplands. In spring and early summer the land not tamed by agriculture is blanketed with wildflowers. West of Spokane, the hills become higher and the wheat fields flow into meadows studded with pine trees. Beyond the broad valley of Crab Creek lie the softly contoured slopes of the Palouse Hills.

The main artery to and through eastern Washington is I–90, but to see the region at its best, approach via U.S. 2 from Leavenworth. Wending through orchards, the highway follows the Wenatchee River to the city of Wenatchee and crosses the Columbia River. It then runs up the Columbia for a stretch before climbing a bluff and passing through a dramatic gap to emerge in the wheat fields of the Waterville Plateau, a sweeping countryside of seemingly unlimited vistas. But you're in for a surprise. The highway suddenly drops down into Moses Coulee, a straight-walled canyon with 1,000-ft-high walls. In spring and early summer, the level coulee floor is awash with the reds, purples, and yellows of wildflowers. Then road rises back to the top, where you soon come to the Grand Coulee, which isn't as deep as Moses Coulee to the west but is a lot broader.

From Dry Falls Junction (look for the very conspicuous yellow-headed blackbirds in the marsh here), take WA 17 south to Dry Falls and Sun Lakes State Park. Or continue east on U.S. 2 and, after crossing the low dam that holds Banks Lake in place, take WA 155 from Coulee City north along the lake for one of Washington's most beautiful drives. At the top of the lake is Grand Coulee Dam, a genuine technological wonder. The aptly named Electric City, near the dam and Coulee City to the south serve as launching points for recreational activities on and around the 151-mi-long Lake Roosevelt, the lake backed up behind Coulee Dam.

Coulee Dam National Recreation Area

87 mi from Spokane, west on U.S. 2 and northwest on Hwy. 174.

Grand Coulee Dam, the largest concrete structure in the world—it's almost a mile long—is an engineering marvel that has justly earned its status as the Eighth Technological Wonder of the World. Beginning in 1932, 9,000 men excavated 45 million cubic yards of rock and soil and dammed the Grand Coulee, a gorge created by the Columbia River, with 12 million cubic yards of concrete—enough to build a sidewalk the length of the equator. By the time the dam was completed in 1941, 77 men had perished and 11 towns were submerged under the newly formed Roosevelt Lake. The waters backed up behind the dam turned eastern Washington's arid soil into fertile farming land, but not without consequence: Salmon fishing stations that were a source of food and spiritual identity for Native Americans were destroyed. Half the dam was built on the Colville Indian Reservation on the north shore of the Columbia; the Colville tribes later received restitution in excess of $75 million from the U.S. Government.

In 1946 most of Roosevelt Lake and the grassy and pine woodland hills surrounding it were designated the **Coulee Dam National Recreation Area.** Crown Point Vista, about 5 mi west of Grand Coulee on Highway 174, may have the best vantage for photographs of the dam, Roosevelt Lake, Rufus Woods Lake (below the dam), and the town of Coulee Dam.

After nightfall from Memorial Day through September, the dam is transformed into an unlikely entertainment complex by an extravagant, free **laser light show.** With 300-ft eagles flying across the white water that flows over the dam, the show is spectacular, if sometimes hokey. The audio portion is broadcast on KEYG 1490 AM and 98.5 FM. Show up early to get a good seat.

Ⓒ The **Visitor's Arrival Center** has colorful displays about the dam, a 13-minute film on the site's geology and the dam's construction, and information about the laser light show. The U.S. Bureau of Reclamation, which oversees operation and maintenance of the dam, conducts tours year-round, weather and maintenance schedules permitting. ⊠ *U.S. 155 north of Grand Coulee,* ☎ *509/633–9265.* ⊙ *Late May–July, daily 8:30 AM–11 PM; Aug., daily 8:30 AM–10:30 PM; Sept., daily 8:30 AM–9:30 PM; Oct.–late May, weekdays 9–5.*

Highway 155 passes through the **Colville Indian Reservation,** one of the largest reservations in Washington, with about 7,700 enrolled members in the Colville Confederated Tribes. This was the final home for Chief Joseph and the Nez Perce, who fought a series of fierce battles with the U.S. Army in the 1870s after the U.S. Government enforced a treaty that many present-day historians agree was fraudulent. Chief Joseph lived on the Colville reservation until his death in 1904. There's a memorial to him off Highway 155 east of the town of Nespelem, 17 mi north of the dam; four blocks away (two east and two north) is his grave. You can drive through the reservation's undeveloped landscape, and except for a few highway signs you'll feel like you've time-traveled to pioneer days. For a better understanding of frontier history, visit the **Colville Confederated Tribes Museum and Gift Shop** (⊠ 512 Mead Way, ☎ 509/633–0751), ½ mi north of Grand Coulee Dam via Highway 155.

Sun Lakes State Park, 20 mi south of the Grand Coulee Dam on Highway 17 (south of U.S. 2), reminds us of the enormous power of nature. During the last ice age, a lake *covering* most of western Montana burst (several times) through an ice dam holding it back; the resulting floods raged toward the sea with 10 times the combined flow of all the world's rivers, altering the landscape so drastically that ripple marks are visible from outer space. Presentations at the park's Interpretive Center at Dry Falls survey the area's geology, and an excellent film describes the great floods. ⊠ *From Grand Coulee Dam take Hwy. 155 south, U.S. 2 east, and Hwy. 17 south,* ☎ *509/632–5214.* ⎁ *Free.* ☉ *May–Sept., daily 10–6.*

Dining and Lodging

$ ✕ **Flo's Place.** One mile south of the dam, this diner dishes up heaps of local color along with loggers' food: biscuits and gravy, corned-beef hash, hamburgers, chicken-fried steak, and chef's salads. Flo's closes at 2 PM daily. ⊠ *316 Spokane Way, Grand Coulee,* ☎ *509/633–3216. No credit cards. No dinner.*

$ ✕ **Melody Restaurant.** This casual, family-friendly spot with excellent views of Grand Coulee Dam prepares sandwiches, steaks, seafood, and pasta and is open for breakfast. ⊠ *512 River Dr., Coulee Dam,* ☎ *509/ 633–1151. AE, D, MC, V.*

$ ✕ **Siam Palace.** Locals love this informal restaurant, which serves delicious and moderately priced Chinese and Thai food along with hamburgers, fries, salads, and sandwiches. ⊠ *213 Main St., Grand Coulee,* ☎ *509/633–2921. D, MC, V.*

$–$$ ☷ **Coulee House Motel.** This motel with "the best dam view in town" (someone had to say it) has modern rooms decorated in earth tones. Some rooms have kitchenettes. ⊠ *110 Roosevelt Way, Coulee Dam 99116,* ☎ *509/633–1101 or 800/715–7767,* ℻ *509/633–1416. 61 rooms. Pool, 2 hot tubs, coin laundry. AE, D, DC, MC, V.*

$ ☷ **Gold House Inn.** Some of the rooms at this big, golden-colored contemporary B&B on a hilltop have breathtaking views of Grand Coulee Dam. The guest rooms have double beds; several of them have TV sets. ⊠ *411 Partello Park, Grand Coulee 99133,* ☎ *509/633–3276 or 800/ 835–9369,* ℻ *509/633–1298. 7 rooms, 5 with private bath. AE, D, MC, V.*

△ **Spring Canyon.** The National Park Service runs the closest public campground to the dam. It's a good place to set your tent if you plan to catch the laser show. For $10 you get a site with a view of the lake but no privacy. On the grounds are rest rooms, swimming areas, and a playground. ⊠ *Hwy. 174, 13 mi west of Grand Coulee,* ☎ *509/725– 2715. 87 sites. No credit cards.*

Outdoor Activities and Sports

There is year-round fishing in Banks Lake, Roosevelt Lake, and Rufus Woods Lake. Roosevelt Lake, a haven for bald eagles, is a popular spot to rent or launch motorboats and houseboats or engage in swimming, waterskiing, and other water sports.

Spokane

282 mi east of Seattle on I–90; 200 mi from Yakima, north on I–82 and east on I–90.

Spokane (pronounced Spo-*can*) bills itself as the "Capital of the Inland Empire." Its Indian name translates as "children of the sun," a fitting designation for this beautiful city basking in seemingly eternal sunshine. Spokane combines the modernity of Seattle with the idealism and friendly charm of a small town. It is the largest city between Seattle and Minneapolis, but the feel is more family oriented than cosmopolitan. Nonetheless, it is undoubtedly a cosmopolis.

The Spokane River has been the lifeblood of far eastern Washington since time immemorial. Several Native American villages stood near the falls, which were a favorite fishing station. It was here that white settlers built the first sawmill and the first electric plant west of the Mississippi. Most of the city's major civic and cultural facilities cluster near the river's banks.

The dry, hot summers of Spokane make it easy to plan golf, fishing, and hiking excursions, and long, snowy winters provide nearly six months to enjoy skiing, snowboarding, and sledding.

A Good Tour

Numbers in the margin correspond to points of interest on the Spokane map.

Begin your tour of Spokane west of downtown (about 1 mi east of the airport) at the **Finch Arboretum,** on Woodland Boulevard off Sunset Boulevard. From the arboretum, head east on Sunset Boulevard, north (left) on Chestnut Street, and west (left) on 1st Avenue to get to the **Cheney Cowles Memorial Museum** ㉞. Riverside Avenue, a block north of 1st Avenue, leads east to **Riverfront Park** ㉟. Two miles south of Riverfront Park on Grand Boulevard is pleasant **Manito Park and Gardens** ㊱. To get to the **Arbor Crest Winery Cliff House,** take I–90 east 6 mi to Exit 287. Head north on Argonne Road across the Spokane River, east on Upriver Drive, and north on Fruithill Road.

TIMING

You could easily drive this route in an hour. Plan to spend a half day at Riverfront Park, with at least half- to one-hour stops at the other sights.

Sights to See

Arbor Crest Winery Cliff House. The eclectic mansion of Royal Riblet, the inventor of a square-wheel tractor and the poles that hold up ski lifts, was built in 1924. Sample complimentary Arbor Crest wines, enjoy the striking view of the Spokane River below, or meander through the impeccably kept grounds (the house is not open for touring). ⊠ *4705 N. Fruithill Rd.,* ☎ *509/927–9894.* ⊞ *Free.* ☉ *Daily noon–5.*

㉞ **Cheney Cowles Memorial Museum.** An audiovisual display and the artifacts at this museum trace Spokane's history; works by area artists are also on exhibit. The museum's Native American collection—one of the country's finest—includes baskets and beadwork of the Plateau Indians. The adjacent **Campbell House** surveys Spokane's mining-era past. Guided tours of the three-story Victorian begin every 45 minutes.

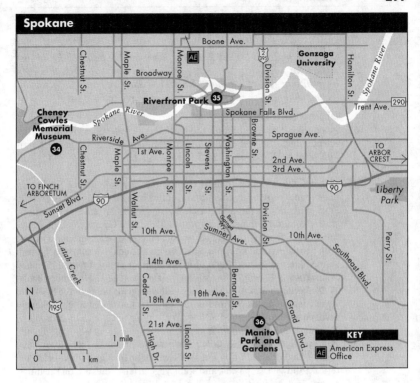

Spokane

⊠ *2316 W. 1st Ave., between Hemlock and Coeur d'Alene Sts.,* ☎ *509/ 456–3931.* ☞ *$4, half price Wed. 10–5.* ☉ *Tues. and Thurs.–Sat. 10– 5, Wed. 10–9, Sun. 1–5.*

Finch Arboretum. This mile-long patch of green along Garden Springs Creek has an extensive botanical garden with 2,000 labeled trees, shrubs, and flowers. You can stroll beside the creek on the well-man- icured paths outlined in the walking tour (the map is available in the brown box at the parking lot), or follow your whim—depending on the season—through flowering rhododendrons, hibiscus, magnolias, dogwoods, hydrangeas, and more. ⊠ *3404 W. Woodland Blvd., off Sunset Blvd. (from downtown, head west on 2nd Ave. and Sunset),* ☎ *509/625–6657.* ☞ *Free.* ☉ *Daily dawn–dusk.*

❸❻ Manito Park and Gardens. The 90-acre tract, a pleasant place to stroll in summer, holds a formal Renaissance-style garden, a conservatory, rose and perennial gardens, a Japanese garden (complete with koi-stocked pools), and a duck pond. ⊠ *S. Grand Blvd. between 17th and 25th Aves.,* ☎ *509/625–6622.* ☞ *Free.* ☉ *Daily 8–7.*

★ ☝ ❸❺ Riverfront Park. The 100-acre park is what remains of the Expo '74 world's fair in Spokane. It is one of the city's main attractions. Sprawl- ing across several islands in the Spokane River, near the falls, the park was developed from old downtown railroad yards. One of the mod- ernist buildings from Expo '74 houses an IMAX theater, a skating rink, and an exhibition space. The Opera House occupies the former Wash- ington State pavilion. The stone clock tower of the former **Great Northern Railroad Station** (⊠ *516 N. Tower Rd.*), which was built in 1902, stands in sharp architectural contrast to the Expo '74 building.

A children's train chugs around the park in the summertime. At the south edge of the park, a 1909 **carousel,** hand carved by master builder

Charles I. D. Looff, is a local landmark. Another icon here is the giant red sled shaped like a Radio Flyer wagon. A small farmers' market takes place from Wednesday to Sunday. ⊠ *Riverfront Park, 507 N. Howard St.,* ☎ *509/625–6600. ⊟ Park free, summer day pass good for most attractions $9.95. ☉ Park 4 AM–midnight, rides Apr.–Oct. (hrs vary by month or day of wk but at least 11–5 daily and until as late as 10 during summer); skating rink Oct.–Mar. (days and hrs vary).*

Dining and Lodging

$$$ ✕ **Paprika.** Stuffed ahi tuna and stuffed poblano chilies are among the eclectic dishes served at this formal, intimate restaurant in the South Hill neighborhood. ⊠ *1228 S. Grand Blvd.,* ☎ *509/455–7545. AE, D, DC, MC, V.*

$$$ ✕ **Patsy Clark's.** The chefs at the restaurant inside one of Spokane's finest mansions serve up eclectic fare for lunch, dinner, and Sunday brunch. Start with hot garlic and artichoke dip or Asian crab-and-shrimp-stuffed tomatoes; then try a light dish like Cajun Caesar salad or a Portobello mushroom "burger," or go for something heartier, such as steak with prosciutto and Gorgonzola or breast of duck à l'orange. A Tiffany stained-glass window is one of many opulent appointments. ⊠ *2208 W. 2nd Ave.,* ☎ *509/838–8300. AE, D, DC, MC, V. No lunch Sat.*

$$ ✕ **Clinkerdagger's.** A former flour mill with great views of the Spokane River houses Clink's (as this fine restaurant is known locally), Spokane's favorite seafood house. ⊠ *621 W. Mallon Ave.,* ☎ *509/328–5965. AE, D, DC, MC, V. No lunch Sun.*

$$ ✕ **Fugazzi Bakery and Cafe.** The aroma of rosemary, olives, and freshly baked breads fills Fugazzi's wrought-iron and glass-brick interior. Sandwiches, pastas, and some vegetarian dishes are on the lunch menu. ⊠ *1 N. Post St.,* ☎ *509/624–1133. AE, MC, V. Closed Sun.–Mon.*

$$ ✕ **Luna.** You'll find pasta, seafood, and gourmet pizza baked in wood-fired ovens at this neighborhood Italian restaurant with more than 400 vintages on its wine list. ⊠ *5620 S. Perry St.,* ☎ *509/448–2383. AE, DC, MC, V.*

$ ✕ **Elk Café.** West of downtown in the laid-back Browne's Addition neighborhood is the self-proclaimed home of the oldest soda fountain in Spokane. Breakfast is served daily—don't miss the potatoes. Sandwiches and pesto pizzas are the favorites for lunch and dinner. Singers often serenade patio guests. ⊠ *1931 W. Pacific Ave.,* ☎ *509/456–0454. D, MC, V.*

$ ✕ **Rock City Grill.** Upbeat and close to Riverfront Park, the Grill prepares excellent pastas and gourmet pizzas baked in wood-fired ovens. ⊠ *505 W. Riverside Ave.,* ☎ *509/455–4400. AE, D, DC, MC, V.*

$$–$$$ ⊞ **Cavanaugh's Inn at the Park.** Offering modern rooms with all the standard amenities, this hotel has the added asset of a location adjacent to Riverfront Park and a two-block walk from the downtown shopping district. All floors in the main building open onto an atrium lobby; more guest rooms are in two newer wings. ⊠ *303 W. North River Dr., 99201,* ☎ *509/326–8000 or 800/843–4667,* ℻ *509/325–7329. 402 rooms. Restaurant, bar. AE, D, DC, MC, V.*

$$–$$$ ⊞ **Doubletree Hotel Spokane City Center.** This link in a chain is convenient to downtown cultural facilities. The comfortable rooms feature chain-hotel decor and amenities. ⊠ *322 N. Spokane Falls Ct., 99201,* ☎ *509/455–9600 or 800/848–9600,* ℻ *509/455–6285. 379 rooms. 2 restaurants, bar, indoor pool, sauna, exercise room. AE, D, DC, MC, V.*

$$–$$$ ⊞ **Ridpath Hotel.** Business and leisure travelers like the downtown Ridpath. Towering above the city, this older hotel has spacious, well-appointed rooms. All guests have access to a nearby full-service health club. Ankeny's Restaurant atop the hotel has a panoramic view of

Spokane. ⊠ *515 W. Sprague Ave., 99201,* ☎ *509/838–2711 or 800/ 426–0670,* FAX *509/747–6970. 350 rooms. 2 restaurants, 2 bars, pool, exercise room. AE, D, DC, MC, V.*

$$ 🛏 **Mariana Stolz House.** Jim and Phyllis Maguire's B&B across from Gonzaga University has something of a split personality: Leaded- glass china cabinets, Renaissance Revival armchairs, and the original dark- fir woodwork compete with run-of-the-mill lamps and fake-flower ar- rangements you might expect at a chain motel. ⊠ *427 E. Indiana Ave., 99207,* ☎ *509/483–4316 or 800/978–6587,* FAX *509/483–6773. 4 rooms, 2 with bath. AE, D, DC, MC, V.*

$$ 🛏 **Waverly Place.** Mother-and-daughter team Marge and Tammy Arndt have created a bed-and-breakfast inn whose distinctive late-Vic- torian furnishings seem truly at home amid the graceful architecture of their turreted Queen Anne home. Menus for breakfast (included in the room rates) and dinner reflect the innkeepers' Swedish heritage. ⊠ *709 W. Waverly Pl., 99205,* ☎ *509/328–1856. 4 rooms, 1 with bath. Pool. AE, D, MC, V.*

Nightlife and the Arts

NIGHTLIFE

The downtown area, especially along Division Street near Riverside Avenue, abounds with small local taverns. **Fort Spokane Brewery** (⊠ 401 W. Spokane Falls Blvd., ☎ 509/838–3809) is an upscale bar across from Riverfront Park. The atmosphere is friendly and the microbrews are excellent—the Border Run, a sweet, smooth ale, is not to be missed. Musicians perform on Friday and Saturday night. You can tour the brew- ery on weekdays from 11 to 5.

Dempsey's Brass Rail (⊠ 909 W. 1st St., ☎ 509/747–5362) is actu- ally two establishments in one: Downstairs it's Spokane's most popu- lar gay bar and restaurant; upstairs it's a dance club popular with the local college crowd, gay and straight. On Friday and Saturday, there's a cover charge.

THE ARTS

Interplayers Ensemble (⊠ 174 S. Howard St., ☎ 509/455–7529) is a professional theater company whose season runs October–June. The 200-seat **Spokane Civic Theatre** (⊠ 1020 N. Howard St., ☎ 509/325– 2507) presents musicals and dramas. The **Spokane Symphony** plays a season of classical and pops concerts from September to May in the Opera House (⊠ 601 W. Riverside Ave., ☎ 509/624–1200). The **The- atre Ballet of Spokane** and various entertainers perform in the Metropoli- tan Performing Arts Center (⊠ 901 W. Sprague St., ☎ 509/455–6500), a restored neoclassical structure built in 1915.

Outdoor Activities and Sports

BASEBALL

The **Spokane Indians** baseball team, the Northwest League's Class A affiliate of the Kansas City Royals, plays at Seafirst Stadium (⊠ 602 N. Havana St., ☎ 509/535–2922).

BICYCLING

Rent a bike at **Quinn's** (⊠ Riverfront Park, on the Howard Street Bridge, ☎ 509/456–6545) for as little as $4 per hour and get out on the miles of trails along the Spokane River. The shop is open daily from June to September and on weekends the rest of the year.

CLIMBING

You can get a taste of rock climbing on the indoor wall at **Mountain Gear** (⊠ 2002 N. Division St., ☎ 509/325–9000 or 800/829–2009). A three-hour class costs $20. Climbing shoes cost $6 a day.

GOLF

Hangman Valley Golf Course (⊠ 2210 E. Hangman Valley Rd., ☎ 509/
448–1212), an 18-hole, par-72 course, has a greens fee of $14.50; a
cart (optional) costs $22.

HIKING

The hills around Spokane are laced with trails, almost all of which connect with the 41-mi **Centennial Trail,** which winds along the Spokane
River. The well-marked trail begins in Nine Mile Falls, northwest of
Spokane, and ends in Idaho; maps are available at the visitor center at
201 West Main Avenue. Northwest of downtown at **Riverside State
Park** (⊠ Hwy. 291; from downtown head north on Division St. and
west on Mission Rd., ☎ 509/456–3964), a paved trail leads through
a 17-million-year-old fossil forest in Deep Creek Canyon. From here
it's easy to get to the western end of the Centennial Trail by crossing
the suspension bridge at the day-use parking lot; trails heading both
left and right will lead to the Centennial.

HOCKEY

The **Spokane Chiefs** of the Western Hockey League play at Veterans
Memorial Arena (⊠ 720 W. Mallon Ave., ☎ 509/328–0450).

SKIING

49° North (⊠ U.S. 395, ☎ 509/935–6649), an hour north of Spokane
in the Kaniksu National Forest, is an 800-acre family-oriented resort.
Lift tickets and snowboards cost about $25, ski rentals $16. **Mount
Spokane** (⊠ Hwy. 206, ☎ 509/238–6281), 31 mi northeast of Spokane,
is a modest downhill resort with 10 mi of groomed cross-country ski
trails. A state Sno-Park permit (☞ Outdoor Activities and Sports *in*
Washington A to Z, *below*), available at the resort, is required here.

The Palouse and South

*158 mi from Spokane to Walla Walla south on U.S. 195, west on Hwy.
26, and south on Hwy. 127 and U.S. 12; 62 mi from Spokane to Colfax and 76 mi to Pullman, south on U.S. 195.*

Those interested in Northwest history will find the Palouse, south of
Spokane and north of the Snake River, particularly rich. The Lewis and
Clark expedition passed through in 1805, and the U.S. Cavalry lost
an important battle to the Indians on the site of the **Steptoe Battlefield.**
The battlefield is north of **Pullman** on U.S. 195 near Rosalia.

On U.S. 12 between Colfax and Walla Walla, **Dayton** is worth a stop
just to see the 88 Victorian buildings listed on the National Register
of Historic Places. A brochure with two self-guided walking tours of
Dayton is available from the **Dayton Chamber of Commerce** (⊠ 166
E. Main St., ☎ 509/382–4825).

In 1836 missionary Marcus Whitman built a medical mission 7 mi west
of present-day **Walla Walla.** A band of Cayuse Indians massacred
Whitman and more than a dozen other settlers in 1847; a **visitor center** (⊠ Off U.S. 12, 7 mi west of Walla Walla, ☎ 509/529–2761)
marks the site. Nearby **Fort Walla Walla Park** (⊠ 755 Myra Rd., ☎
509/525–7703) has 14 historic buildings and a pioneer museum.

History buffs can take a walking or bicycle tour of Walla Walla, one
of the earliest settlements in the Inland Northwest. Maps are available
from the Chamber of Commerce (☞ Visitor Information, *below*). **Pioneer Park** (⊠ E. Alder St.), which has a fine aviary, was landscaped
by sons of Frederick Law Olmsted, who designed New York City's Central Park.

Just north of its confluence with the Snake River, the Palouse River gushes over a basalt cliff higher than Niagara Falls and drops 198 ft into a steep-walled basin. Those who are sure-footed can hike to an ★ overlook above the falls, part of **Palouse Falls State Park,** which are at their fastest during spring runoff in March. Just downstream from the falls is the **Marmes Rock Shelter,** where remains of the earliest-known inhabitants of North America, dating back 10,000 years, were discovered by archaeologists. The park has 10 primitive campsites. ⊠ *Hwy. 261, 65 mi north of Walla Walla (U.S. 12 north to Hwy. 261 west),* ☎ *509/ 646–3252.* ⊠ *$5 per vehicle, $7 for campsites.* ☉ *Park daily dawn–dusk, campsites mid-Mar.–Sept.*

Eastern Washington Essentials

Arriving and Departing

BY BUS

Greyhound Lines (⊠ W. 221 1st Ave., in the Amtrak station, ☎ 509/ 624–5251) runs daily buses to Spokane from Seattle (5–6½ hrs) and Portland (8–13 hrs). Greyhound buses stop in Pullman and Walla Walla.

BY CAR

Spokane can be reached by **I–90** from the east or west. **U.S. 195** passes north–south through the city. The Grand Coulee Dam is 20 mi north of **U.S. 2** on **Highway 174.** To get to the Palouse from Spokane, drive south on **U.S. 195** to Pullman. Or, when U.S. 195 reaches Colfax, take **Highways 26 and 127,** and then **U.S. 12** to Walla Walla.

BY PLANE

Spokane Airport (⊠ 9000 W. Airport Dr., ☎ 509/455–6455) is served by Horizon, Northwest, and United. *See* Air Travel *in* Smart Travel Tips A to Z for airline numbers. Pullman has a small airport that it shares with Moscow, Idaho, 8 mi to the east.

BY TRAIN

Amtrak (⊠ W. 221 1st Ave., ☎ 509/624–5144 or 800/872–7245) serves Spokane from Seattle and Portland four times a week. There is no train service to the Palouse.

Getting Around

BY BUS

Spokane has an extensive local bus system. The fare is 75¢; exact change or a token is required. You can pick up schedules, route maps, and tokens at the **bus depot** (⊠ 1229 W. Boone Ave., ☎ 509/328–7433) or the **Plaza** (⊠ 510 W. Riverside Ave., between Wall and Post Sts.), the major downtown transfer point.

BY CAR

Downtown Spokane is laid out along a true grid: Streets run north–south, avenues east–west, and many of them are one-way. A good way to explore the city is to follow the **City Loop Drive,** which takes you out of the city and into the residential hills of greater Spokane; start at Stevens and Riverside streets and follow the arrowhead signs. **Yellow Cab** (☎ 509/624–4321) serves the greater Spokane area. The north–south-running **Highway 155** is the main road through the Grand Coulee Dam area.

Contacts and Resources

VISITOR INFORMATION

Grand Coulee Chamber of Commerce (⊠ Box 760, 99133, ☎ 509/633–3074). **Pullman Chamber of Commerce** (⊠ 415 N. Grande Ave., 99163, ☎ 509/334–3565). **Spokane Area Visitors Information** (⊠ 201 W. Main Ave., 99202, ☎ 509/747–3230 or 800/248–3230). **Walla Walla Chamber of Commerce** (⊠ 29 E. Sumach St., 99362, ☎ 509/525–0850).

WASHINGTON A TO Z

Arriving and Departing

By Bus

Greyhound Lines (☎ 800/231–2222) connects Washington with adjoining states and Canada.

By Car

Interstate 5 is the main north–south route through the state. **Interstate 90** enters Washington from the east and runs across the Cascades to Seattle.

By Ferry

A number of ferries carry cars and passengers between ports in Washington and Canada. In Anacortes, about 90 minutes north of Seattle, the **Washington State Ferries** (☎ 206/464–6400) depart for Vancouver Island, British Columbia. Bellingham is the southern terminus of the **Alaska Marine Highway System** (☎ 800/642–0066), providing transportation between Bellingham and Alaska's Inside Passage. **Victoria San Juan Cruises** (☎ 800/443–4552) operates passenger-only service between Bellingham and Victoria, British Columbia, in the summer.

By Plane

Seattle-Tacoma International Airport (☞ Seattle A to Z *in* Chapter 4) is served by most major airlines. *See* Air Travel *in* Smart Travel Tips A to Z for airline numbers.

By Train

Amtrak (☎ 800/872–7245) serves major cities and towns throughout the state.

Contacts and Resources

Emergencies

Throughout Washington State, except on Orcas Island and Long Beach Peninsula, dial 911 for **police, ambulance,** or other emergencies. On Orcas dial 0 or 360/468–3663; on Long Beach dial 360/642–2911 for police and 360/642–4200 for fire.

Guided Tours

CRUISES AND WHALE-WATCHING

San Juan Islands Shuttle Express (⊠ Alaska Ferry Terminal, 355 Harris Ave., Bellingham, ☎ 360/671–1137) operates whale-watching trips. **Victoria San Juan Cruises** (⊠ Alaska Ferry Terminal, 355 Harris Ave., Bellingham, ☎ 800/443–4552) operates all-day nature cruises through the San Juan Islands to Victoria. **Western Prince Cruises** (⊠ Friday Harbor, San Juan Island, ☎ 360/378–5315) charters boats for half-day whale-watching cruises during the summer; in the spring and fall, bird-watching and scuba-diving tours are offered.

ORIENTATION

Hesselerave International (⊠ 1268 Mount Baker Hwy., Bellingham, ☎ 360/734–3570) operates a variety of tours and trips in the Northwest. **Sunshine Ventures** (⊠ 909 Alder St., Sumner, ☎ 800/377–4970) operates walking and general tours of Tacoma and the entire Northwest region.

Outdoor Activities and Sports

FISHING LICENSES

You can pick up a fishing license at any sporting-goods store in the state. A three-day license costs about $5 for nonresidents. For more information, call the **Department of Fish and Wildlife** (☎ 360/902–2700).

SKIING

Skiers with motor vehicles are required to purchase Sno-Park permits ($7 for a one-day pass or $20 for a season pass); you can pick them up at ski resorts and sporting-goods stores. For more information, call the state parks department's **Office of Winter Recreation** (☎ 360/902–8552). For information about snow conditions, call 888/766–4636.

Visitor Information

National Park Service (☎ 206/470–4060). **Washington State Parks Department** (☎ 800/233–0321 for campsite and other park information). **Washington State Tourism** (✉ 101 General Administration Bldg., Olympia 98504, ☎ 800/544–1800).

6 VANCOUVER

The spectacular setting of cosmopolitan Vancouver, British Columbia, has drawn people from around the world to settle here. The ocean and mountains form a dramatic backdrop to downtown's gleaming towers of commerce and make it easy to pursue all kinds of outdoor pleasures. You can trace the city's history in Gastown and Chinatown, savor the wilderness only blocks from the city center in Stanley Park, or dine on superb ethnic or Pacific Northwest cuisine before you sample the city's nightlife.

VANCOUVER IS A YOUNG CITY, even by North American standards. It was not yet a town when British Columbia became part of the Canadian confederation in 1871. The city's history, such as it is, remains visible to the naked eye: eras are stacked east to west along the waterfront, from cobblestone late-Victorian Gastown to shiny postmodern glass cathedrals of commerce.

By Sue
Kernaghan

The Chinese, among the first to recognize the possibilities of Vancouver's setting, came to British Columbia during the 1850s seeking the gold that inspired them to name the province Gum-shan, or Gold Mountain. As laborers they built the Canadian Pacific Railway, giving Vancouver a purpose—one beyond the natural splendor that Royal Navy captain George Vancouver admired during his lunchtime cruise around its harbor on June 13, 1792. The Canadian transcontinental railway, along with the city's Great White Fleet of clipper ships, gave Vancouver a full week's edge over the California ports in shipping tea and silk to New York at the end of the 19th century.

For its original inhabitants, the Coast Salish peoples, Vancouver was the sacred spot where the mythical Thunderbird and Killer Whale flung wind and rain all about the heavens during their epic battles. How else to explain the coast's fits of meteorological temper? Devotees of a later religious tradition might worship in the groves of Stanley Park or in the fir and cedar interior of Christ Church Cathedral, the city's oldest church.

Vancouver, with a metropolitan-area population of 1.9 million, is booming. Many Asians have migrated here, mainly from Hong Kong, but other regions are represented as well. The mild climate, exquisite natural scenery, and relaxed, outdoor lifestyle is attracting new residents to British Columbia's business center, and the number of visitors is increasing for the same reasons. Many people get their first glimpse of Vancouver when catching an Alaskan cruise, and many return at some point to spend more time here.

Pleasures and Pastimes

Dining
Downtown bistros, creek-side seafood palaces, and upscale pan-Asian restaurants are among Vancouver's diverse gastronomical offerings. Several cutting-edge establishments are perfecting and defining Pacific Northwest fare, which incorporates regional salmon and oysters and locally grown produce, often accompanied by wines from British Columbia, Oregon, or Washington.

The Great Outdoors
Nature has truly blessed this city, surrounding it with verdant forests, towering mountains, coves, inlets, rivers, and the wide sea. Biking, hiking, skiing, snowboarding, and sailing are among the many outdoor activities possible in or near the city. Whether you prefer to relax on a beach by yourself or join a kayaking tour with an outfitter, Vancouver has plenty to offer.

Nightlife and the Arts
Vancouver residents support the arts enthusiastically, especially during the city's film, performing arts, and other cultural festivals, most of which take place between June and October. Year-round, there's a complete range of live music, from jazz and blues to heavy metal. The city's opera, ballet, and symphonic companies are thriving. Peculiar

liquor laws have created a shortage of pubs and bars. Many pubs operate with a restaurant license, which requires patrons to order food with their drink.

EXPLORING VANCOUVER

The heart of Vancouver—which includes downtown, Stanley Park, Yaletown, and the West End—sits on a peninsula bordered by English Bay and the Pacific Ocean to the west; by False Creek, the inlet home to Granville Island, to the south; and by Burrard Inlet, the working port of the city, to the north, past which loom the North Shore mountains. The oldest parts of the city—Gastown and Chinatown—lie at the edge of Burrard Inlet, around Main Street, which runs north–south and is roughly the dividing line between the east side and the west side. All the avenues, which are numbered, have east and west designations. One note about printed Vancouver street addresses: Suite numbers often appear *before* the street number, followed by a hyphen.

Great Itineraries

IF YOU HAVE 1 OR 2 DAYS

If you have only one day in Vancouver, start with an early morning walk, bike, or shuttle ride through Stanley Park to see the Vancouver Aquarium and Second Beach on English Bay. Head northeast from the park on Denman Street to Robson Street to lunch and meander on foot through the trendy shops between Denman and Burrard, and then walk northeast on Burrard Street to view the many buildings of architectural interest. Stop along the way at the Vancouver Art Gallery and the Canadian Craft Museum. On day two take a leisurely walking tour of the shops, eateries, and cobblestone streets of Gastown, Chinatown, and Yaletown. There are plenty of places to eat and shop in these districts.

IF YOU HAVE 3 OR 4 DAYS

If you have another day to tour Vancouver after you've followed the itinerary above, head to the south side of False Creek and English Bay on day three to delve into the many boutiques, dining outlets, theaters, and the public market of Granville Island. Buses and ferries provide easy transit. Parking is available, but traffic getting onto the island can be congested, especially on weekends. Touring Granville Island is best accomplished on foot.

On day four, tour the sights beyond downtown Vancouver. Make time for the Museum of Anthropology on the campus of the University of British Columbia. Also visit the Vancouver Museum, the Pacific Space Centre, and the Vancouver Maritime Museum, all south of downtown in the Kitsilano area.

Robson to the Waterfront

Numbers in the text correspond to numbers in the margin and on the Downtown Vancouver map.

Museums and buildings of architectural and historical significance are the primary draw in downtown Vancouver, but there's also plenty of fine shopping.

A Good Walk

Begin at the northwest end of **Robson Street** ①, at Bute or Thurlow Street. Follow Robson southeast to Hornby to reach landscaped **Robson Square** ② and the **Vancouver Art Gallery** ③. On the north side of the gallery across Hornby Street sits the **Hotel Vancouver** ④, a city landmark. The **Cathedral Place** office tower stands across the street at

Hornby Street and Georgia Street. The three large sculptures of nurses at the corners of the building are replicas of the statues that adorned the Georgia Medical-Dental Building, the Art Deco structure that previously occupied this site.

To the west of Cathedral Place is a walkway that leads to a peaceful green courtyard, off which is the **Canadian Craft Museum** ⑤. Farther to the west of Cathedral Place is the Gothic-style **Christ Church Cathedral** ⑥. North down Burrard Street, toward the water on the opposite side of the street, is the Art Deco **Marine Building** ⑦.

Cross Burrard and follow Hastings Street to the east for a look at the outside of the exclusive **Vancouver Club** ⑧. The club marks the start of the old financial district, which runs southeast along Hastings. The district's older temple-style banks, investment houses, and business-people's clubs are the surviving legacy of the city's sophisticated pre–World War I architecture. **Sinclair Centre** ⑨, at Hastings and Howe streets, is a magnificently restored complex of government buildings that houses offices and retail shops. Near Granville Street at 698 West Hastings, a jewelry store now occupies the Roman-influenced former headquarters of the **Canadian Imperial Bank of Commerce.** The equally striking **Royal Bank** building stands directly across the street. Southeast of here at Hastings and Seymour streets is the elevator to the **Lookout at Harbour Centre** ⑩.

Head northeast up Seymour toward Burrard Inlet to the **Waterfront Station** ⑪. Take a peek at the murals inside the 19th-century structure, and then take the west staircase (to your left) up to Granville Square Plaza. Wander across the plaza to the SkyTrain station, and you'll face the soaring canopies of **Canada Place** ⑫, where you can stop for a snack in one of the dining outlets on the water or catch a film at the IMAX theater. Across Canada Place Way (next door to the Waterfront Centre Hotel) is the **Vancouver Tourist Info Centre.**

TIMING

This tour takes about an hour to walk, not counting stops along the way. The Canadian Craft Museum and the Vancouver Art Gallery each warrant an hour or more, depending on the exhibits.

Sights to See

⑫ **Canada Place.** When Vancouver hosted the Expo '86 world's fair, a former cargo pier was transformed into the off-site Canadian pavilion. Following the fair, Canada Place was transformed yet again, into Vancouver's trade and convention center, below which cruise ships dock. The roof, shaped like 10 sails, that covers the convention space has become a landmark of Vancouver's skyline. The luxurious **Pan Pacific Hotel** (☞ Lodging, *below*) dominates the shoreline edge of Canada Place. At the north end are an IMAX theater, a restaurant, and an outdoor performance space. A promenade around the pier affords views of Burrard Inlet and Stanley Park. At press time, plans were in place to build a bigger adjacent convention center. ⊠ *999 Canada Pl.,* ☎ *604/775–8687.*

⑤ **Canadian Craft Museum.** One of Vancouver's most interesting cultural facilities, the craft museum displays functional and decorative modern and historical crafts. Exhibits change throughout the year, so there's always something new to see. The courtyard is a quiet place to take a break. ⊠ *Cathedral Place Courtyard, 639 Hornby St. (also accessible from 925 W. Georgia St.),* ☎ *604/687–8266.* ⊡ *$5; Thurs. 5 PM–9 PM by donation.* ☉ *May–Aug., Mon.–Wed. and Fri.–Sat. 10–5, Thurs. 10–9, Sun. noon–5; Sept.–Apr., Mon. and Wed. and Fri.–Sat. 10–5, Thurs. 10–9, Sun. noon–5.*

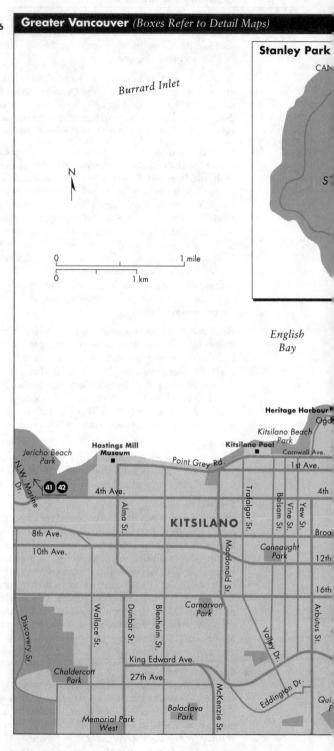

Greater Vancouver *(Boxes Refer to Detail Maps)*

Stanley Park

CAN

S

Burrard Inlet

N

0   1 mile

0   1 km

*English
Bay*

Heritage Harbour
Ogd

*Kitsilano Beach
Park*

Kitsilano Pool

Cornwall Ave.

*Jericho Beach
Park*

**Hastings Mill
Museum**

Point Grey Rd.

1st Ave.

N.W. Marine Dr.

41 42

4th Ave.

4th

Alma St.

KITSILANO

Trafalgar St.

Balsam St.

Vine St.

Yew St.

Broa

8th Ave.

Macdonald St.

*Connaught
Park*

12th

10th Ave.

16th

*Carnarvon
Park*

Arbutus St.

Wallace St.

Dunbar St.

Blenheim St.

Valley Dr.

Discovery St.

King Edward Ave.

McKenzie St.

*Chaldercott
Park*

27th Ave.

Eddington Dr.

Qui
P

*Memorial Park
West*

*Balaclava
Park*

Downtown Vancouver

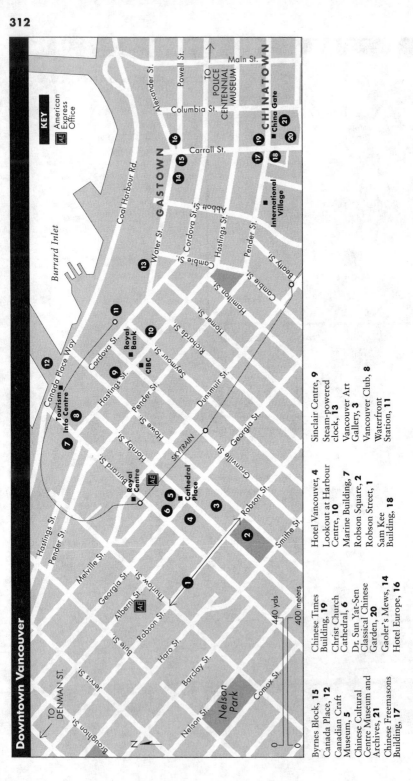

KEY

AE American Express Office

Burrard Inlet

GASTOWN

CHINATOWN

China Gate

TO POLICE CENTENNIAL MUSEUM

International Village

Tourism Info Centre

Royal Bank

CIBC

Royal Centre

Cathedral Place

SKYTRAIN

Nelson Park

TO DENMAN ST.

N

440 yds

400 meters

Byrnes Block, **15**
Canada Place, **12**
Canadian Craft Museum, **5**
Chinese Cultural Centre Museum and Archives, **21**
Chinese Freemasons Building, **17**

Chinese Times Building, **19**
Christ Church Cathedral, **6**
Dr. Sun Yat-Sen Classical Chinese Garden, **20**
Gaoler's Mews, **14**
Hotel Europe, **16**

Hotel Vancouver, **4**
Lookout at Harbour Centre, **10**
Marine Building, **7**
Robson Square, **2**
Robson Street, **1**
Sam Kee Building, **18**

Sinclair Centre, **9**
Steam-powered clock, **13**
Vancouver Art Gallery, **3**
Vancouver Club, **8**
Waterfront Station, **11**

⑥ Christ Church Cathedral. The oldest church in Vancouver was built in 1889. Constructed in the Gothic style with buttresses and pointed-arch windows, the tiny cathedral looks like the parish church of an English village from the outside, but the Douglas fir and cedar interior is thoroughly Canadian. The stained-glass windows show Vancouver landmarks (one shows St. Christopher presiding over the Lions Gate Bridge), and the building's excellent acoustics enhance the choral evensong, carols, and Gregorian chants frequently sung here. ⊠ *690 Burrard St.,* ☎ *604/682–3848.* ⊙ *Weekdays 10–4.*

④ Hotel Vancouver. One of the last railway-built hotels in Canada, the Hotel Vancouver was designed in the château style, its architectural details reminiscent of a medieval French castle. Construction began in 1928. The hotel was barely finished in time for the visit of King George VI of England in 1939. The exterior of the building, one of the most recognizable on Vancouver's skyline, has carvings of malevolent-looking gargoyles at the corners, native chiefs on the Hornby Street side, and an assortment of grotesque mythological figures. ⊠ *900 W. Georgia St.,* ☎ *604/684–3131.*

⑩ Lookout at Harbour Centre. The lookout looks like a flying saucer stuck on top of a high-rise. At 553 f) high, it affords one of the best views of Vancouver. A glass elevator whizzes you up 50 stories to the circular observation deck, where knowledgeable guides point out the sights. On a clear day you can see Vancouver Island. Tickets are good all day, so you can come during daylight hours and return for another peek after dark. The top-floor restaurant makes one complete revolution per hour; the ride up in the elevator is free for diners. ⊠ *555 W. Hastings St.,* ☎ *604/689–0421.* 🖾 *$8.* ⊙ *May–Aug., daily 8:30–10:30; Sept.– Apr., daily 9–9.*

⑦ Marine Building. Terra-cotta bas-reliefs depicting the history of transportation—airships, steamships, locomotives, and submarines—adorn this Art Deco structure erected in 1930. Because most architects still applied classical or Gothic ornamentation, these motifs were considered radical at the time. From the east, the Marine Building is reflected in bronze by 999 West Hastings, and from the southeast it is mirrored in silver by the Canadian Imperial Bank of Commerce. Step inside for a look at the beautifully restored interior, and then walk to the corner of Hastings and Hornby streets for the best view of the building. ⊠ *355 Burrard St.*

② Robson Square. Architect Arthur Erickson designed this plaza, which was completed in 1979, to be *the* gathering place of downtown Vancouver. Landscaped walkways connect the **Vancouver Art Gallery** (☞ *below*), government offices, a convention center, and law courts. An ice-skating rink (used for ballroom dancing in summer) and restaurants occupy the level below the street. Political protests and impromptu rants take place on the gallery stairs, a tradition that dates from the days when the building that houses the gallery was a courthouse. ⊠ *Bordered by Howe, Hornby, Robson, and Smithe Sts.*

① Robson Street. Ultrachic Robson Street is often called Vancouver's Rodeo Drive because of the many see-and-be-seen sidewalk cafés and high-end boutiques. The street, which links downtown and the West End, is particularly lively between Jervis and Burrard streets. The shops (☞ Shopping, *below*) are like those you'll find anywhere. It's the people-watching, café-lounging, and window-shopping scene that draw the crowds day and night.

⑨ Sinclair Centre. The outstanding Vancouver architect Richard Henriquez knitted four government office buildings into Sinclair Centre, an office-retail complex. The two Hastings Street buildings—the 1905 **Post Office,** which has an elegant clock tower, and the 1911 **Winch Building**—are linked with the **Post Office Extension** and **Customs Examining Warehouse** to the north. Painstaking and costly restoration involved finding master masons and uncovering and refurbishing the pressed-metal ceilings. ⊠ *757 W. Hastings St.*

③ Vancouver Art Gallery. Painter Emily Carr's haunting evocations of the British Columbian hinterland are the biggest attraction at the city's main art gallery. Carr, who lived from 1871 to 1945, was a grocer's daughter from Victoria. She fell in love with the wilderness around her and shocked middle-class society by running off to paint it. Her work accentuates the mysticism and the danger of B.C.'s wilderness—no pretty landscapes here—and records the passing of native cultures. The gallery, which also hosts touring exhibits of varying quality, is inside a 1911 courthouse that Arthur Erickson redesigned in the early-1980s. Lions guard the majestic front steps, and columns and domes are among the original classical architectural elements. The Gallery Café has a fine terrace, and the gallery's shop has a noteworthy selection of prints and cards. You can visit the café and the shop without an admission ticket. ⊠ *750 Hornby St.,* ☎ *604/662–4719.* ☜ *June–Sept. $10; Oct.–May $8; Thurs. 5–9 by donation.* ☾ *June–Sept., Mon.–Wed. and Fri. 10–6, Thurs. 10–9, Sat. 10–5, Sun. noon–5; Oct.–May, Tues., Wed., and Fri.–Sun. 10–5:30, Thurs. 10–9.*

⑧ Vancouver Club. George Lister, Thornton Sharp, and Charles Joseph Thompson, the brains behind many city landmarks including the galleries of the Burrard Bridge and the original University of British Columbia, built this elite private club between 1912 and 1914. Its architecture evokes that of private clubs in England inspired by Italian Renaissance palaces. The Vancouver Club is still the private haunt of city businesspeople, so it's not possible to view the interior. ⊠ *915 W. Hastings St.*

Vancouver Tourist Info Centre. Here you'll find brochures and personnel to answer questions—and a nice view to boot. ⊠ *200 Burrard St.,* ☎ *604/683–2000.* ☾ *Sept.–late May, weekdays 8:30–5, Sat. 9–5; Late May–Aug., daily 8–6.*

⑪ Waterfront Station. This former Canadian Pacific Railway passenger terminal was built between 1912 and 1914 as the western terminus for Canada's transcontinental railway. After Canada's railways merged, the station became obsolete, but a 1978 renovation turned it into an office-retail complex and depot for SkyTrain, SeaBus, and West Coast Express passengers. Murals in the waiting rooms show the scenery travelers once saw on journeys across Canada. Here you can catch a 13-minute SeaBus trip across the harbor to the waterfront public market at Lonsdale Quay in North Vancouver. During 2000, SeaBuses may leave from a temporary station just to the east while a new waterfront development is under construction. ⊠ *601 W. Cordova St.,* ☎ *604/521–0400 for SeaBus and SkyTrain; 604/683–7245 for West Coast Express.*

Gastown and Chinatown

Gastown is where Vancouver originated after "Gassy" Jack Deighton arrived at Burrard Inlet in 1867 with his wife, some whiskey, and a few amenities. The smooth-talking Deighton convinced local loggers and trappers into building him a saloon for a barrel of whiskey. (It didn't take much convincing. His saloon was on the edge of lumber company land, where alcohol was forbidden.) When the transcontinental train arrived in 1887, Gastown became the transfer point for trade with the Far East and was soon crowded with hotels and warehouses. The Klondike gold rush encouraged further development that lasted until 1912, when the so-called Golden Years ended. From the 1930s to the 1950s hotels were converted into rooming houses, and the warehouse district shifted elsewhere. The neglected area gradually became run down. Gastown and Chinatown were declared historic districts in the late 1970s, though, and have been revitalized. Gastown contains boutiques, cafés, loft apartments, and souvenir shops.

Some of the oldest buildings in the city are in Chinatown, the third-largest such area in North America. There was already a sizable Chinese community here because of the 1858 Cariboo gold rush in central British Columbia, but the greatest influx from China came in the 1880s during construction of the Canadian Pacific Railway when more than 10,000 laborers were recruited. Though they were performing the valuable and hazardous task of blasting the rail bed through the Rocky Mountains, the Chinese were discriminated against. The Anti-Asiatic Riots of 1907 stopped growth in Chinatown for 50 years, and immigration from China was discouraged by increasingly restrictive policies that climaxed in a $500-per-head tax during the 1920s. In the 1960s the city council planned bulldozer urban renewal for Strathcona, the residential part of Chinatown, as well as freeway connections through the most historic blocks of the district. Fortunately, the project was halted, and today Chinatown is an expanding, vital neighborhood fueled by the investments of immigrants from Hong Kong and elsewhere. The style of architecture in Vancouver's Chinatown is patterned on that of Guangzhou (Canton).

Numbers in the text correspond to numbers in the margin and on the Downtown Vancouver map.

A Good Walk

Pick up Water Street at Richards Street in downtown Vancouver and head east into Gastown. At the corner of Water and Cambie streets you can see and hear the world's first **steam-powered clock** ⑬. About a block east on the other side of the street, tucked behind 12 Water Street, is **Gaoler's Mews** ⑭. Two buildings of historical and architectural note are the **Byrnes Block** ⑮, on the corner of Water and Carrall streets, and the **Hotel Europe** ⑯, at Powell and Alexander streets. A statue of Gassy Jack Deighton stands on the west side of Maple Tree Square, at the intersection of Water, Powell, Alexander, and Carrall streets, where he built his first saloon.

From Maple Tree Square it's only three blocks south on Carrall Street to Pender Street, where Chinatown begins. This route passes through a rough part of town. It's safer to backtrack two blocks on Water Street through Gastown to Cambie Street, then head south to Pender and east to Carrall.

If you come along Pender Street, you'll pass **International Village**, a new Asian-oriented shopping and cinema development. Old Chinatown starts at the corner of Carrall and Pender streets. The **Chinese Freemasons Building** ⑰ and the **Sam Kee Building** ⑱ are here, and directly across Carrall Street is the **Chinese Times Building** ⑲. About a half block east and across Pender, tucked into a courtyard behind the brightly painted China Gate, is the **Dr. Sun Yat-Sen Classical Chinese Garden** ⑳. Next to the garden is the free, public **Dr. Sun Yat-Sen Park**. A short path through the park will take you out to Columbia Street, where, to your left, you'll find the entrance to the **Chinese Cultural Centre Museum and Archives** ㉑ (not to be confused with the Chinese Cultural Centre, which fronts Pender Street). Finish up your tour of Chinatown by poking around in the open-front markets and import shops that line several blocks of Pender and Keefer running east. **Ten Ren Tea and Ginseng Company,** at 550 Main, and **Ten Lee Hong Tea and Ginseng,** at 500 Main, carry every kind of tea imaginable. For art, ceramics, and rosewood furniture have a look at **Yeu Hua Handicraft Ltd.,** at 173 East Pender. If you're in the area in summer on a Friday, Saturday, or Sunday, check out the bustling **Night Market,** for which the 200 blocks of Keefer and East Pender are closed to traffic from 6:30 to 11.

TIMING

The walk described above takes about an hour. Allow extra time for the guided tour of the Dr. Sun Yat-Sen Classical Chinese Garden. This tour is best done by day, though shops and restaurants are open into the night in both areas.

Sights to See

❶⑤ Byrnes Block. This building was constructed on the site of Gassy Jack Deighton's second saloon after the 1886 Great Fire, which wiped out most of the fledgling settlement of Vancouver. The date is visible at the top of the building above the door where it says "Herman Block," which was its name for a short time. The site of Deighton's original saloon, just east of the Byrnes block where his statue now stands, is the zero point from which all Vancouver street addresses start. ⊠ *2 Water St.*

㉑ Chinese Cultural Centre Museum and Archives. The first museum in Canada dedicated to preserving and promoting Chinese-Canadian history and culture opened in 1998. The art gallery on the main floor exhibits the works of Chinese and Chinese-Canadian artists. The museum on the second floor has an intriguing collection of historical photos. ⊠ *555 Columbia St.,* ☎ *604/687–0282.* ⊡ *$3.* ☉ *Tues.–Sun. 11–5.*

⑰ Chinese Freemasons Building. Two completely different facades distinguish this structure on the northwest corner of Pender and Carrall streets. The side facing Pender represents a fine example of Cantonese recessed balconies. The Carrall Street side displays the standard Victorian style common throughout the British Empire. Dr. Sun Yat-Sen hid for months in this building from agents of the Manchu dynasty while he raised funds for its overthrow, which he accomplished in 1911. ⊠ *3 W. Pender St.*

⑲ Chinese Times Building. Police officers during the early 20th century could hear the clicking sounds of clandestine mah-jongg games played after sunset on the hidden mezzanine floor of this 1902 structure. But attempts by vice squads to enforce restrictive policies against the Chinese gamblers proved fruitless because police were unable to find the players. ⊠ *1 E. Pender St.*

★ **⑳ Dr. Sun Yat-Sen Classical Chinese Garden.** The first authentic Ming Dynasty–style garden outside of China, this garden was built in 1986 by 52 artisans from Suzhou, the Garden City of the People's Republic. It incorporates design elements and traditional materials from several of that city's centuries-old private gardens. No power tools, screws, or nails were used in the construction. Forty-five-minute guided tours, included in the ticket price, are offered throughout the day. Call ahead for times. On Friday evenings between mid-June and September, musicians perform traditional Chinese music in the garden. The free public park next door is also designed as a traditional Chinese garden. ⊠ *578 Carrall St.,* ☎ *604/689–7133.* ⊡ *$6.50.* ☉ *Mid-June–mid-Sept., daily 9:30–7:30; call for winter hrs.*

⓮ **Gaoler's Mews.** Once the site of the city's first civic buildings—the constable's cabin and customs house, and a two-cell log jail—today this atmospheric cobblestone courtyard is home to cafés and architectural offices. ⊠ *Behind 12 Water St.*

⓰ **Hotel Europe.** Once billed as the best hotel in the city, this 1908 flatiron building is one of the world's best examples of this style of triangular architecture. Now used for government-subsidized housing and not open to the public, the hotel still has its original Italian tile work and leaded-glass windows. The glass tiles in the sidewalk on Alexander Street once provided light for an underground saloon. ⊠ *43 Powell St.*

⓲ **Sam Kee Building.** *Ripley's Believe It or Not!* recognizes this structure as the narrowest office building in the world. In 1913, when the city confiscated most of Chang Toy's land to widen Pender Street, he built on what he had left—just 6 ft—in protest. These days the building houses an insurance agency, whose employees make do within the 4-ft-10-inch–wide interior. ⊠ *8 W. Pender St.*

⓭ **Steam-powered clock.** An underground steam system, which also heats many local buildings, powers the world's first steam clock. Every quarter hour the whistle blows, and on the hour a huge cloud of steam spews from the apparatus, which was built by Ray Saunders of Landmark Clocks (⊠ 123 Cambie St.). ⊠ *Water and Cambie Sts.*

Stanley Park

A 1,000-acre wilderness park only blocks from the downtown section of a major city is both a rarity and a treasure. In the 1860s, because of a threat of American invasion, the area that is now Stanley Park was designated a military reserve—though it was never needed. When the city of Vancouver was incorporated in 1886, the council's first act was to request that the land be set aside as a park. In 1888 permission was granted and the grounds were named Stanley Park after Lord Stanley, then governor general of Canada.

If you're driving to Stanley Park, head northwest on Georgia Street from downtown and stay in the right lane or you'll end up going over the Lions Gate Bridge. If you're taking public transit, catch any bus labeled Stanley Park at the corner of Hastings and Granville streets downtown. You can also catch North Vancouver buses 240 or 246 from anywhere on West Georgia Street to the park entrance at Georgia and Chilco streets, or a Robson bus 5 to Robson and Denman Streets, where you'll find a number of bicycle rental outlets.

To reach Stanley Park's main attractions, you can bike, walk, drive, or take the park shuttle. The seawall path, a 9-km (5½-mi) paved shoreline route popular with walkers, cyclists, and rollerbladers, is one of several car-free zones within the park. If you have the time (about a half day) and the energy, strolling the entire seawall is an exhilarating experience. Cyclists (☞ Biking, *below,* for information about rentals) must ride in a counterclockwise direction and stay on their side of the path.

The **Stanley Park Shuttle** (☎ 604/257–8400) operates between mid-May and mid-September, providing frequent (15 minute intervals) transportation between 14 major park sites. You can pick it up on Pipeline Road, near the Georgia Street park entrance, or at any of the stops in the park. At press time the shuttle was expected to remain free of charge and run 9:30 to 6 daily, though a small fare may be introduced.

Between mid-September and mid-May the traffic in Stanley Park is lighter and there's little competition for parking. There are lots at or near all the major attractions. A $5 ticket allows you to park all day, and to move between lots. Another way to see the park is on one of the **Stanley Park Horse Drawn Tours** (☞ Guided Tours *in* Vancouver A to Z, *below*).

Numbers in the text correspond to numbers in the margin and on the Stanley Park map.

A Good Tour

If you're walking or cycling, start at the foot of Alberni Street beside Lost Lagoon. Go through the underpass and veer right, following the cycle path markings, to the seawall. If you're driving, enter the park at the foot of Georgia Street. Keep to your right, and you'll go beneath an underpass. This will put you on scenic Stanley Park Drive, which circles the park.

Whether you're on the seawall or Stanley Park Drive, the old wooden structure that you pass on your right is home of the Vancouver Rowing Club, a private athletic club established in 1903. On your left are an **Information Booth** (staffed daily from April through October) and the turnoff to the **Vancouver Aquarium** ㉒ and the **Miniature Railway and Children's Farmyard.**

Continuing on Stanley Park Drive or the seawall, you'll next pass the Royal Vancouver Yacht Club. About ½ km (⅓ mi) farther is the causeway to **Deadman's Island** ㉓. The **totem poles** ㉕, which are a bit farther down Stanley Park Drive and slightly inland on your left, are a popular photo stop. Ahead at the water's edge is the **Nine O'Clock Gun** ㉔. To the north is Brockton Point and its small lighthouse and foghorn. At kilometer 3 (mile 2) of the drive is **Lumbermen's Arch** ㉖, a log archway. The **Children's Water Park** across the road is well attended throughout the summer. Cyclists and walkers can turn off here for a shortcut back to the aquarium, the Miniature Railway and Children's Farmyard, and the park entrance.

About 2 km (1 mi) farther along the seawall or Stanley Park Drive is the Lions Gate Bridge. Here drivers and cyclists part company. Cyclists ride under the bridge and past the cormorants' nests tucked beneath **Prospect Point** ㉗. Drivers pass over the bridge and reach a viewpoint and café at the top of Prospect Point. Both routes then continue around to the English Bay side of the park and the beginning of sandy beaches. The imposing monolith offshore is **Siwash Rock** ㉘, the focus of a native legend.

The next attraction along the seawall is the large heated pool at **Second Beach** ㉙. If you're walking or cycling, you can take a shortcut from here back to Lost Lagoon by walking along the perpendicular pathway behind the pool, which cuts into the park. The wood footbridge that's ahead will lead you to a path along the south side of the lagoon to your starting point at the foot of Alberni or Georgia Street. If you continue along the seawall, you will emerge from the park into a high-rise residential neighborhood, the West End. You can walk back to Alberni Street along Denman Street, where there are places to stop for coffee, a drink, or ice cream. **Mum's Gelato,** at 855 Denman Street, serves delicious ice cream.

TIMING

The driving tour takes about an hour. You'll find parking near most of the sights in the park. Your biking time will depend on your speed, but with stops to see the sights, expect the ride to take several hours. It takes at least two hours to see the aquarium thoroughly. If you're going to walk the park and take in most of the sights, plan on spend-

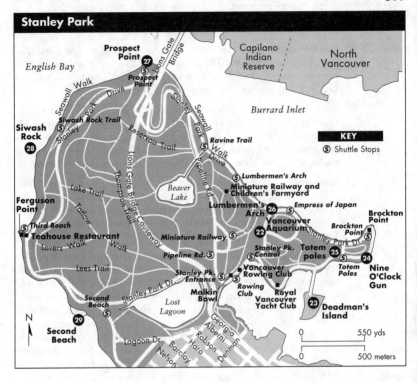

Stanley Park

Prospect Point
27
Prospect Point

English Bay

Seawall Walk

Siwash Rock Trail

Stanley Park Drive

Lions Gate Bridge

Capilano Indian Reserve

North Vancouver

Burrard Inlet

KEY
Ⓢ Shuttle Stops

Siwash Rock
28

Reservoir Trail

Ravine Trail

Walk Drive

Lions Gate Bridge Causeway

Lake Trail

Tatlow Walk

Beaver Lake

Pipeline Rd.

Lumbermen's Arch
Miniature Railway and Children's Farmyard

Lumbermen's Arch
26

Empress of Japan

Brockton Point

Ferguson Point

Third Beach
Teahouse Restaurant

Lovers Walk

Thompson Trail

Miniature Railway Ⓢ

Pipeline Rd. Ⓢ

Vancouver Aquarium
22

Stanley Pk. Central Ⓢ

Brockton Point Ⓢ

Stanley Park Dr.

Totem poles
25

Totem Poles

Nine O'Clock Gun
24

Lees Trail

Stanley Pk. Entrance Ⓢ

Vancouver Rowing Club

Second Beach

Stanley Park Dr.

Malkin Bowl

Rowing Club

Royal Vancouver Yacht Club

Deadman's Island
23

N

Second Beach
29

Lost Lagoon

Lagoon Dr.

Georgia
Alberni
Robson
Haro
Denman
Barclay
Nelson

0 ——— 550 yds

0 ——— 500 meters

ing the day. The seawall can get crowded on summer weekends, but inside the park is a network of peaceful, usually deserted, walking and cycling paths through old growth forest. Take a map—they're available at park concession stands—and don't go into the woods alone or after dusk.

Sights to See

㉓ Deadman's Island. This former burial ground for the local Salish people and the early settlers is a small naval training base called HMCS *Discovery.* The island is not open to the public.

㉖ Lumbermen's Arch. Made of logs, this archway, erected in 1947, is dedicated to the workers in Vancouver's first industry. Beside the arch is an asphalt path that leads back to Lost Lagoon and the Vancouver Aquarium.

Miniature Railway and Children's Farmyard. A child-size steam train takes kids and adults on a ride through the woods. Next door there's a whole farmyard full of critters, including goats, rabbits, and guinea pigs. ⊠ *Off Pipeline Rd.,* ☎ *604/257–8531.* ⊉ *$2.50 for each.* ◷ *June–Sept., daily 11–4; Oct.–Dec. 4 and Jan. 4–Apr. 1, weekends 11–4 (weather permitting); Dec. 5–Dec. 12, daily 5–9; Dec. 13–Jan. 3, daily 2–9.*

㉔ Nine O'Clock Gun. This cannonlike apparatus by the water was installed in 1890 to alert fishermen to a curfew ending weekend fishing. Now it signals 9 o'clock every night.

㉗ Prospect Point. Cormorants build their seaweed nests along the cliff ledges here. The large black diving birds are distinguished by their long necks and beaks. When not nesting, they often perch atop floating logs or boulders. Another remarkable bird found along the park's shore is the beautiful great blue heron. Herons prey on fish. The oldest heron rookery in British Columbia is in the trees near the aquarium, where the birds like to horn in during feeding time for the whales.

🖐 ㉙ **Second Beach.** In summer a draw is the 50-meter pool, which has life-guards and water slides. The shallow end fills up on hot days, but the lap-swimming end of the pool is usually deserted. Nearby is a sandy beach, a playground, and covered picnic sites.

㉘ **Siwash Rock.** Legend tells of a young Native American who, about to become a father, bathed persistently to wash his sins away so that his son could be born pure. For his devotion he was blessed by the gods and immortalized in the shape of Siwash Rock, just offshore. Two small rocks, said to be his wife and child, are on the cliff above the site.

㉕ **Totem poles.** Totem poles were not made in the Vancouver area. These, carved of cedar by the Kwakiutl and Haida peoples late in the 19th century, were brought to the park from the north coast of British Columbia. The carvings of animals, fish, birds, and mythological crea-tures are like family coats-of-arms or crests.

★ 🖐 ㉒ **Vancouver Aquarium Marine Science Centre.** The humid Amazon rain-forest gallery here holds piranhas, tropical birds, and jungle vegeta-tion. Other displays show the underwater life of coastal British Columbia, the Canadian arctic, and the tropics. Huge tanks (populated with orca and beluga whales, and playful sea otters) have large win-dows for underwater viewing. There are whale shows several times a day. A Pacific Canada Pavilion, built in 1999, looks at the aquatic life in the waters near Vancouver, and a demonstration salmon stream flows through Stanley Park from Burrard Inlet to the aquarium. ⊠ ☎ 604/659–3474. 🖃 $12. ☉ *July–Labor Day, daily 9:30–7; Labor Day–June, daily 10–5:30.*

Granville Island

Granville Island was a sandbar until World War I, when the federal government dredged False Creek to provide access to the sawmills that lined the shore. The sludge from the creek was heaped onto the sand-bar to create the island and to house much-needed industrial and log-ging-equipment plants. By the late 1960s many of the businesses that had once flourished on Granville Island had deteriorated. Buildings were rotted, rat-infested, and dangerous. In 1971 the government bought up leases from businesses that wanted to leave and developed an imag-inative plan to refurbish the island with a public market, marine ac-tivities, and artisans' studios.

The small island's few residents live on houseboats. Most of the for-mer industrial buildings and tin sheds have been retained but are painted in upbeat reds, yellows, and blues. Through a committee of community representatives, the government regulates the types of busi-nesses on Granville Island. Most of the businesses permitted involve food, crafts, marine activities, and the arts.

Numbers in the text correspond to numbers in the margin and on the Granville Island map.

A Good Walk

To reach Granville Island on foot, make the 15-minute walk from down-town Vancouver to the south end of Hornby Street. **Aquabuses** (☎ 604/689–5858) depart here and deliver passengers across False Creek to the Granville Island Public Market. **False Creek Ferries** (☎ 604/684–7781), which leave every five minutes from a dock behind the Van-couver Aquatic Centre, are another option. Still another way to reach the island is to take a 20-minute ride on a **Buslink** (☎ 604/521–0400) bus. From Waterfront Station or stops on Granville Street take a False Creek South bus (No. 50) to the edge of the island. Or, from Granville and Broadway, catch Granville Island Bus 51 for direct service to Granville Island. Parking is free for one to three hours; paid parking is available in garages on the island.

Another way to travel is to hop the **Downtown Historic Railway** (604/ 665–3903) at Leg-in-Boot Square, near 6th Avenue and Moberly Street (where pay parking is available) and ride the 1½-km (1-mi) line to the island. Part of an experiment to revive streetcar service around False Creek, the 1905 electric tram ran, at press time, only on summer weekend and holiday afternoons, but service is expected to expand, and possibly extend to Science World (☞ Yaletown and False Creek, *below*) by 2000.

A short walk from the bus, ferry, or tram stop is the **Granville Island Public Market** ㉚.

Walk south on Johnston Street to begin a clockwise loop tour of the island. Ocean Cement is one of the last of the island's industries; its lease does not expire until the year 2004. Next door is the **Emily Carr Institute of Art and Design** ㉛. Follow a walkway along the south side of the art school to Sea Village, one of the only houseboat communities in Vancouver. Take the boardwalk that starts at the houseboats and continues partway around the island.

Walk around the Granville Island Hotel, and then turn right into Cartwright Street. This end of the island, home to an eclectic mix of craft galleries, studios, and workshops, is a fascinating place to watch artisans at work. You can see wooden boats being built at the Alder Bay Boat Company and watch printmakers in action at New Leaf Editions. The Federation of Canadian Artists Gallery and the Gallery of BC Ceramics both showcase local works. Also on Cartwright are the **Granville Island Water Park** ㉜ and the **Granville Island Information Centre** ㉝. A bit farther down the street is the **Kids' Market** ㉞. Adults can head for the microbrewery tour at **Granville Island Brewing** ㉟, across the street.

Cross Anderson Street and walk down Duranleau Street. On your left are the sea-oriented shops of the Maritime Market, and the fishing, train, and model boat displays at the **Granville Island Museums** ㊱. The last place to explore on Granville Island is the upscale **Net Loft** ㊲ shopping arcade. Once you have come full circle, you can either take the ferry back to downtown Vancouver or stay for dinner and catch a play at the Arts Club or the Waterfront Theatre (☞ Nightlife and the Arts, *below*).

TIMING
If your schedule is tight, you can tour Granville Island in three to four hours. If you're a shopping fanatic, you'll likely need a full day.

Sights to See

㉛ **Emily Carr Institute of Art and Design.** The institute's three main buildings—wooden structures formerly used for industrial purposes—were renovated in the 1970s. The **Charles H. Scott Gallery,** inside the front door to the right, hosts contemporary exhibitions in various media. ☒ *1399 Johnston St.,* ☏ *604/844–3811.* ☐ *Free.* ☉ *Weekdays noon– 5, weekends 10–5.*

㉟ **Granville Island Brewing.** Tours of Canada's first modern microbrewery last about a half hour and include a souvenir glass and a taste of four different brews, including some that aren't on the market yet. Kids are welcome—they get a taste of root beer. ☒ *1441 Cartwright St.,* ☏ *604/687–2739.* ☐ *$7.* ☉ *Daily 9:30–7 (call for tour times).*

Granville Island

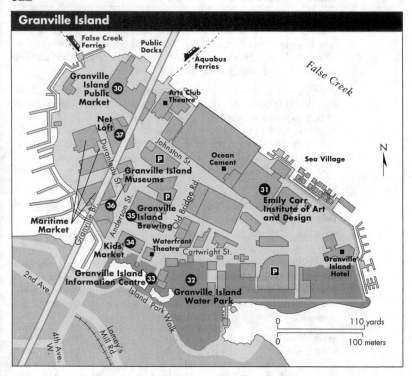

33 **Granville Island Information Centre.** You can pick up maps at the center, and find out about special events. Festivals, outdoor concerts, and dance performances often occur on the island. ✉ *1398 Cartwright St.,* ☎ *604/666–5784.* ⊙ *Daily 8–6.*

36 **Granville Island Museums.** Rods, reels, artwork, and a mounted salmon that at 97 pounds is the largest ever caught with a rod and reel are among the fishing artifacts at this facility. You can try your luck against the large game fish that inhabit the video fish-fighting simulator. The collection of the Model Ships Museum includes exquisitely detailed early 20th-century vessels. One of the museum's highlights is a cast-bronze replica of the HMS *Hood,* the British Royal Navy ship that dealt the final blows that sunk the German warship the *Bismarck* in 1941. Upstairs, the Model Train Museum lays claim to the world's largest toy train exhibit. Shops in the surrounding Maritime Market are all geared to the sea. ✉ *1502 Duranleau St.,* ☎ *604/683–1939.* ✏ *$3 for all three museums.* ⊙ *June–Aug., daily 10–5:30; Sept.–May, Tues.–Sun. 10–5:30.*

★ **30** **Granville Island Public Market.** Because no chain stores are allowed in this 50,000-square-ft building, each outlet is unique. Most sell high-quality merchandise. You can pick up a snack, espresso, or fixings for lunch on the wharf, and year-round you'll see crafts, exotic foods, and mounds of locally grown produce. There's plenty of outdoor seating on the water side of the market. ✉ *1669 Johnston St.,* ☎ *604/666–6477.* ⊙ *Daily 9–6.*

👆 **32** **Granville Island Water Park.** This kids' paradise has slides, sprinklers, and a fire hydrant made for children to shower one another. ✉ *1318 Cartwright St.,* ☎ *604/257–8195.* ✏ *Free.* ⊙ *Late May–early Sept., daily 10–6.*

⟲ ㉞ **Kids' Market.** Yet another slice of kids' heaven on Granville Island, the Kids' Market has two floors of small shops that sell toys, arts-and-crafts materials, dolls, records and tapes, chemistry sets, and other items. ⊠ *1496 Cartwright St.,* ☏ *604/689–8447.* ⊙ *Daily 10–6.*

㉗ **Net Loft.** In this blue and red building is a collection of high-quality boutiques, including a bookstore, a crafts store–gallery, a kitchenware shop, a postcard shop, a custom-made hat shop, a handmade paper store, a British Columbian native art gallery, and a café. ⊠ *1661 Johnston St., across from Public Market.* ⊙ *Daily 10–6.*

Kitsilano

The beachfront district of Kitsilano (popularly known as Kits), south of downtown Vancouver, is among the trendiest Canadian neighborhoods. Originally inhabited by the Squamish people, whose chief, Khahtsahlanough, gave the area its name, Kitsilano began to attract day-trippers from Vancouver in the early part of this century. Some stayed and built lavish waterfront mansions. Others built simpler Craftsman-style houses farther up the slope. After a period of decline in the mid-20th century, Kits, which contains many restored wood-frame Craftsman houses, is once again chic.

Kitsilano is home to three museums, some fashionable shops, and popular pubs and cafés. Kits has hidden treasures, too: rare boats moored at Heritage Harbour, stately mansions on forested lots, and, all along the waterfront, quiet coves and shady paths within a stone's throw of Canada's liveliest beach.

Numbers in the text correspond to numbers in the margin and on the Greater Vancouver map.

A Good Walk

Vanier Park, the grassy beachside setting for three museums and the best kite-flying venue in Vancouver, is the logical gateway to Kits. The most enjoyable way to get here is by **False Creek Ferries** (☏ 604/684–7781), from Granville Island or behind the Vancouver Aquatic Centre on Beach Avenue. The ferries dock at Heritage Harbour behind the Vancouver Maritime Museum. You can also walk or cycle about 1 km (½ mi) along the waterfront pathway from Granville Island (leave the island by Anderson Street and keep to your right along the waterfront). If you prefer to come by road, drive over the **Burrard Street Bridge,** turn right at Chestnut Street, and park in either of the museum parking lots, or take **Bus 2** or **22** from downtown, get off at Cypress Street and Cornwall Avenue, and walk down to the park.

Vancouver Museum ㊴, which showcases the city's natural and cultural history, shares a building with the **Pacific Space Centre** ㊳, a high-tech museum focusing on outer space. To the west and toward the water is the **Vancouver Maritime Museum** ㊵, which traces the maritime history of the West Coast. Each museum has hands-on exhibits that appeal to kids.

Behind the Maritime Museum, where you'll dock if you come in by ferry, is **Heritage Harbour,** home to a rotating series of boats of historical interest, including *BCP 45,* the picturesque fishing boat that used to appear on Canada's five-dollar bill. In summer the big tent set up in Vanier Park is the venue for the Bard on the Beach Shakespeare series (☞ Nightlife and the Arts, *below*).

West of the Maritime Museum is a quiet, grassy beach. A wooden staircase leads from the beach up to a paved walkway. Take a moment to look at the huge **Kwakiutl totem pole** in front of the museum, and then follow the walkway west to popular Kitsilano Beach. Ahead is **Point Grey.** Across the water you can see Stanley Park, and behind you is Vancouver's downtown core. Continue past the pool, keep to the water, and you'll enter a shady pathway lined with blackberry bushes running behind the **Kitsilano Yacht Club.** Soon the lane opens up to a viewpoint and gives access to another sandy cove.

About ½ km (¼ mi) from the yacht club, the path ends at another wooden staircase. This leads up to a viewpoint and a park on Point Grey Road. Across the street from the top of the staircase is an Edwardian era, **wood-turreted mansion** (⊠ 2590 Point Grey Rd.) built by a member of Kitsilano's early elite. Double back the way you came—heading east toward Kits Beach—but this time follow Point Grey Road for a look at the front of the waterfront homes you could see from the beach path. The **Logan House** (⊠ 2530 Point Grey Rd.), built in 1909, is an ivory-colored Edwardian dream home with a 180-degree curved balcony.

Follow Point Grey Road as it curves to the right, and cross Cornwall Avenue at the lights at Balsam Street. Turn left on First Avenue and walk two blocks to **Yew Street,** where in summer you'll find the biggest concentration of sidewalk pubs and cafés in Greater Vancouver. Alternatively, you can hike up the hill to **4th Avenue,** once the heart of the hippie district, and explore the shops between Maple and Arbutus streets. You can catch a bus back to downtown Vancouver on Cornwall or 4th Avenue, or cut across Kits Beach Park back to Vanier Park.

TIMING

The walk alone will take about an hour and a half. Add three hours to see the Pacific Space Centre and an hour for each of the other museums. With time out for shopping or swimming, a visit to Kitsilano could easily fill a whole day.

Sights to See

Kitsilano Beach. At Kits Beach (☞ Outdoor Activities and Sports, *below*) are picnic sites, a playground, Vancouver's biggest outdoor pool, and some fine people-watching. Inland from the pool, the Kitsilano Showboat hosts free performances, mostly of the children's dancing variety, during summer. ⊠ *Off Cornwall Ave.,* ☎ *604/738–8535 (summer only).*

38 Pacific Space Centre. The interactive exhibits and high-tech learning systems at this museum include a kinetic space-ride simulator and a theater showcasing Canada's achievements in space. During the day catch the astronomy show at the **H.R. MacMillan Star Theatre.** When the sky is clear, the ½-meter telescope at the **Gordon MacMillan Southam Observatory** (☎ 604/738–2855) is focused on whatever stars or planets are worth watching that night. Admission to the observatory is free, and it's open in the evening, weather permitting (call for hours). ⊠ *Vanier Park, 1100 Chestnut St.,* ☎ *604/738–7827.* ☎ *$12.* ☉ *July–Aug., daily 10–5; Sept.–June, Tues.–Sun. 10–5.*

40 Vancouver Maritime Museum. Fully half the museum has been turned over to kids, with touchable displays that provide a chance to drive a tug, build an underwater robot, or dress up as a seafarer. Toddlers and school-age children will appreciate the hands-on displays in Pirates' Cove and the Children's Maritime Discovery Centre. The museum also has an extensive collection of model ships and is the last moorage for the RCMP schooner the *St. Roch,* the first ship to sail in both directions through the treacherous Northwest Passage. Historic boats are moored at **Heritage Harbour,** behind the museum, and a huge Kwak-iutl totem pole stands out front. ⊠ *Vanier Park, 1905 Ogden Ave., north end of Cypress St.,* ☎ *604/257–8300.* ☎ *Museum $6, Heritage*

Harbour free. ☉ *Mid-May–Aug., daily 10–5; Sept.–mid-May, Tues.–Sat. 10–5; Sun. noon–5.*

🖐 ㊴ **Vancouver Museum.** Life-size replicas of a trading post, a Victorian parlor, and an 1897 Canadian Pacific Railway passenger car, as well as a real dugout canoe, are the highlights at this museum, whose exhibits focus on the city's natural history, its early history, and on First Nations art and culture. Plans are in place for a major expansion to be completed by 2001. ✉ *Vanier Park, 1100 Chestnut St.,* ☎ *604/736–4431.* 🎫 *$8.* ☉ *July–Aug., daily 10–5; Sept.–June, Tues.–Sun. 10–5.*

Greater Vancouver

Some of Vancouver's best gardens, natural sights, and museums, including the renowned Museum of Anthropology, are south of downtown, on the campus of the University of British Columbia and in the city's southern residential districts. Individual attractions are easily reached by Buslink buses (☎ 604/521–0400), but you'll need a car to see them all comfortably in a day.

Numbers in the text correspond to numbers in the margin and on the Greater Vancouver map.

A Good Drive

From downtown Vancouver, cross the **Burrard Street Bridge** and follow the marked scenic route. This will take you along Cornwall Avenue, which becomes Point Grey Road and follows the waterfront to Alma Street. The little wooden structure at the corner of Point Grey Road and Alma Street is the **Hastings Mill Museum,** Vancouver's first retail shop and now a museum.

The scenic route continues south on Alma Street and then west (to the right) on 4th Avenue. This flows into **Northwest Marine Drive,** which winds past Jericho, Locarno, and Spanish Banks beaches and up to the University of British Columbia. At the university are the **Museum of Anthropology** ㊶, which houses one of the world's best collections of Westcoast First Nations artifacts, and **Nitobe Memorial Garden** ㊷, a Japanese-style strolling garden. Three kilometers (2 mi) farther along Marine Drive is the **University of British Columbia Botanical Garden.**

For more gardens, follow Marine Drive through the university grounds and take the left fork onto 41st Avenue. Turn left again onto Oak Street to reach the entrance of the **VanDusen Botanical Garden** ㊸ on your left. The complex is planted with an English-style maze, water gardens, herb gardens, and more. Return to 41st Avenue, continue farther east, and then turn left on Cambie Street to reach **Queen Elizabeth Park** ㊹, which overlooks the city. To get back downtown, continue north on Cambie and over the Cambie Street Bridge.

TIMING

Except during rush hour, it takes about 30 minutes to drive from downtown to the University of British Columbia. You should add another 30 to 45 minutes' driving time for the rest of the tour, and about two hours to visit each of the main attractions.

Sights to See

Hastings Mill Museum. Vancouver's first store was built in 1865 at the foot of Dunlevy Street in Gastown and moved to this seaside spot in 1930. The only building to survive the 1886 Great Fire, the site is a museum, with displays of native artifacts and pioneer household goods. ✉ *1575 Alma Rd.,* ☎ *604/734–1212.* 🎫 *By donation.* ☉ *June–mid-Sept., daily 11–4; mid-Sept.–May, weekends 1–4.*

★ ㊶ **Museum of Anthropology.** Arthur Erickson designed the award-winning cliff-top structure that houses the Museum of Anthropology (MOA). Vancouver's most spectacular museum, the MOA focuses on the arts of Pacific Northwest First Nations and aboriginal peoples from around the world, among them the late Bill Reid, one of Canada's most respected Haida carvers. Reid's *The Raven and the First Men,* a highlight of the museum's collection, took five carvers more than three years to complete. In the Great Hall are large and dramatic totem poles, ceremonial archways, and dugout canoes—all adorned with carvings of frogs, eagles, ravens, bears, and salmon. You'll also find exquisite carvings of gold, silver, and argillite (a black stone found in the Queen Charlotte Islands), as well as masks, tools, and textiles from many other cultures. The ceramics wing contains several hundred pieces from 15th- to 19th-century Europe. To reach the museum by transit, take a UBC Bus 4 or UBC Bus 10 from Granville Street downtown to the university loop, which is a 10-minute walk from the museum. ⊠ *University of British Columbia, 6393 N.W. Marine Dr.,* ☎ *604/822–3825.* ⌧ *$6, free Tues. 5–9.* ☉ *Memorial Day–Labor Day, Tues. 10–9, Mon. and Wed.–Sun. 10–5; Labor Day–Memorial Day, Tues. 11–9, Wed.–Sun. 11–5.*

㊷ **Nitobe Memorial Garden.** This 2½-acre garden is considered one of the most authentic Japanese tea and strolling gardens outside Japan. The circular path around the park symbolizes the cycle of life and provides a tranquil view from every direction. In April and May cherry blossoms are the highlight, and in June the irises are magnificent. ⊠ *University of British Columbia, 1903 West Mall,* ☎ *604/822–9666.* ⌧ *Mid-Mar.–mid-Oct. $2.50; mid-Oct.–mid-Mar. free.* ☉ *Mid-Mar.–mid-Oct., daily 10–6; mid-Oct.–mid-Mar., weekdays 10–2:30.*

㊹ **Queen Elizabeth Park.** Besides views of downtown, the park has lavish sunken gardens brimming with roses and other flowers, an abundance of grassy picnicking spots, and illuminated fountains. Other park facilities include 20 tennis courts, pitch and putt, and a restaurant. In the **Bloedel Conservatory** you can see tropical and desert plants and 60 species of free-flying tropical birds in a glass geodesic dome. To reach the park by public transportation, take a Cambie Bus 15 from the corner of Robson and Burrard Streets downtown to 33rd Avenue. ⊠ *Cambie St. and 33rd Ave.,* ☎ *604/257–8570.* ⌧ *Conservatory $3.50.* ☉ *Apr.–Sept., weekdays 9–8, weekends 10–9; Oct.–Mar., daily 10–5.*

University of British Columbia Botanical Garden. Temperate plants—10,000 trees, shrubs, and flowers from around the world—thrive on this 70-acre site on the university campus. ⊠ *6804 S.W. Marine Dr.,* ☎ *604/822–9666.* ⌧ *Summer $4.50, winter free.* ☉ *Mid-Mar.–mid-Oct., daily 10–6; mid-Oct.–mid-Mar., daily 10–2:30.*

㊸ **VanDusen Botanical Garden.** On what was a 55-acre golf course grows one of the largest collections of ornamental plants in Canada. Displays from every continent include an Elizabethan maze, five lakes, and a Sino-Himalayan garden. There's also a shop, a library, and a restaurant (☎ 604/261–0011) on the grounds. The gardens are wheelchair accessible. An Oak Bus 17 will get you here from downtown. Queen Elizabeth Park is a ½-mi walk away, on 37th Avenue. ⊠ *5251 Oak St., at 37th Ave.,* ☎ *604/878–9274.* ⌧ *$6; ½ price Oct.–Mar.* ☉ *June–mid-Aug., daily 10–9; call for off-season hrs.*

Yaletown and False Creek

In 1985 and 1986 the provincial government cleared up a derelict industrial site on the north shore of False Creek, built a world's fair, and invited the world. Twenty million people showed up at Expo '86.

Finally, a travel companion that doesn't snore on the plane or eat all your peanuts.

When traveling, your MCI WorldCom Card is the best way to keep in touch. Our operators speak your language, so they'll be able to connect you back home—no matter where your travels take you. Plus, your MCI WorldCom Card is easy to use, and even earns you frequent flyer miles every time you use it. When you add in our great rates, you get something even more valuable: peace-of-mind. So go ahead. Travel the world. MCI WorldCom just brought it a whole lot closer.

You can even sign up today at www.mci.com/worldphone or ask your operator to make a collect call to 1-410-314-2938.

EASY TO CALL WORLDWIDE

1 Just dial the WorldPhone access number of the country you're calling from.
2 Dial or give the operator your MCI WorldCom Card number.
3 Dial or give the number you're calling.

Australia ◆	
To call using OPTUS	**1-800-551-111**
To call using TELSTRA	**1-800-881-100**
Bahamas/Bermuda	**1-800-888-8000**
British Virgin Islands	**1-800-888-8000**
Costa Rica ◆	**0-800-012-2222**
Denmark	**8001-0022**
Norway ◆	**800 -19912**
India	**000-127**
For collect access	**000-126**
United States/Canada	**1-800-888-8000**

For your complete WorldPhone calling guide, dial the WorldPhone access number for the country you're in and ask the operator for Customer Service. In the U.S. call 1-800-431-5402.

◆ Public phones may require deposit of coin or phone card for dial tone.

EARN FREQUENT FLYER MILES

AmericanAirlines®
AAdvantage®

Continental Airlines
OnePass

▲ Delta Air Lines
SkyMiles®

▬ MILEAGE PLUS®
United Airlines

US AIRWAYS
DIVIDEND MILES

Distinctive guides packed with up-to-date expert advice
and smart choices for every type of traveler.

Fodor's. For the world of ways you travel.

Now the site of the fair has become one of the largest urban redevelopment projects in North America, creating—and, in some cases, reclaiming—a whole new downtown district that Vancouverites themselves are only beginning to discover.

Tucked in among the forest of green-glass, high-rise condo towers is the old warehouse district of Yaletown. First settled by railroad workers who had followed the newly laid tracks down from the town of Yale in the Fraser Canyon, Yaletown in the 1880s and 1890s was probably the most lawless place in Canada. The Royal Canadian Mounted Police complained it was too far through the forest for them to police it. Yaletown is now one of the city's poshest neighborhoods, and the Victorian brick loading docks have become terraces for cappuccino bars. The area, which also holds restaurants, a brew pub, and galleries that sell art and avant-garde home decor, makes the most of its waterfront location, with a seaside walk and cycle path that runs completely around the shore of False Creek.

Numbers in the text correspond to numbers in the margin and on the Greater Vancouver map.

A Good Walk

Start at **Library Square** ㊺ at Homer and Georgia streets. Leave by the Robson Street (east) exit, cross Robson, and continue south on Hamilton Street. On your right you'll see a row of Victorian frame houses built between 1895 and 1900, all painted in candy-box colors and looking completely out of place among the surrounding high-rises. In 1995 these historic homes were plucked from the West End and moved here to protect them from the onslaught of development.

Cross Smithe Street, and continue down Mainland Street to Nelson Street—you're now in the heart of Yaletown. Stop for a coffee at one of Yaletown's loading-dock cafés or poke around the shops on Hamilton and Homer streets.

From the foot of Mainland Street, turn left on Davie Street and cross Pacific Boulevard. This takes you to the **Roundhouse.** Continue to the **waterfront** at the foot of Davie. Here you'll find an intriguing iron and concrete sculpture, with panels displaying archival images of events around False Creek. A few minutes' walk along the waterfront to your right is the Yaletown dock for **Aquabus Ferries** (☎ 604/689–5858), where you can catch a boat to Granville Island or Science World.

Turn left and follow the waterfront walkway. After about 1 km (½ mi) (possibly with some detours around construction sites), you'll reach the **Plaza of Nations,** the heart of the old Expo site, with pubs and cafés. Cross the plaza toward Pacific Boulevard and take the pedestrian overpass to B.C. Place Stadium. Walk around to Gate A, where you'll find the **B.C. Sports Hall of Fame and Museum** ㊻. To your left as you leave the museum you'll see the **Terry Fox Memorial.** This archway at the foot of Robson Street was built in honor of Terry Fox (1958–1981), a local student whose cross-Canada run raised millions for cancer research. From here you can walk two blocks north on Beatty Street and take the **SkyTrain** one stop east or retrace your steps to the waterfront and walk another 1 km (½ mi) east to **Science World** ㊼, a hands-on museum. From Science World, the SkyTrain will take you back downtown, or you can catch a ferry back to Yaletown or to other stops on False Creek.

TIMING

It takes about 1½ hours to walk around all the sights. Allow about an hour for the B.C. Sports Hall of Fame and museum and two hours for Science World. Shoppers may not make it past Yaletown.

Sights to See

🔅 **46** **B.C. Sports Hall of Fame and Museum.** Inside the B.C. Place Stadium complex, this museum celebrates the province's sports achievers. Visitors can test their own sprinting, rowing, climbing, and throwing prowess in the high-tech participation gallery. ⊠ *B.C. Place, 777 Pacific Blvd. S, Gate A,* ☎ *604/687–5520.* 🎫 *$6.* ⊙ *Daily 10–5.*

45 **Library Square.** The spiraling library building, open plazas, waterfall, and shaded atriums of Library Square, which was completed in the mid-1990s, were built to evoke images of the Colosseum in Rome. A high-tech library fills the core of the structure. The outer edge of the spiral houses boutiques, coffeehouses, and a fine book shop. ⊠ *350 W. Georgia St.,* ☎ *604/331–3600.* ⊙ *Mon.–Thurs. 10–8, Fri.–Sat. 10–5, Sun. hrs vary.*

Roundhouse. Originally the turnaround point for transcontinental trains reaching the end of the line at Vancouver, this round brick structure was built in 1888. A spirited local campaign helped create a home here for **Engine 374,** which pulled the first passenger train into Vancouver on May 24, 1887. The Roundhouse, a community center, hosts festivals and exhibitions. ⊠ *181 Roundhouse Mews,* ☎ *604/713–1800.* 🎫 *Free; admission may be charged to some events.* ⊙ *Weekdays 9 AM–10 PM, weekends 9–5.*

🔅 **47** **Science World.** In a gigantic shiny dome built over an Omnimax theater, this hands-on museum contains interactive exhibits. The special Search Gallery is aimed at younger children, as are the fun-filled demonstrations given in Center Stage. The 3-D laser theater appeals to older kids. ⊠ *1455 Quebec St.,* ☎ *604/268–6363.* 🎫 *Science World $11.25, Omnimax $9.75, combination ticket $14.50.* ⊙ *July–Aug., daily 10–6; Sept.–June, weekdays 10–5, weekends 10–6.*

DINING

Vancouver dining is fairly informal. Casual but neat dress is appropriate everywhere except a few expensive restaurants that require men to wear a jacket and tie (indicated in the text). Smoking is prohibited by law in all Vancouver restaurants. A 15% tip is expected. A 10% liquor tax is charged on wine, beer, and spirits. Some restaurants build this into the price of the beverage, but others add it to the bill.

CATEGORY	COST*
$$$$	over C$40
$$$	C$30–C$40
$$	C$20–C$30
$	under C$20

per person in Canadian dollars, for a three-course meal, excluding drinks, service, and sales tax

Cafés

$–$$ ✕ **Bread Garden Bakery, Café & Espresso Bar.** Salads, quiches, elaborate cakes and pies, giant muffins, and fine cappuccinos draw a steady stream of hungry locals to the five branches of this growing, Vancouver-based chain (☞ Greater Vancouver, *below*). All five locations are open six to midnight, and the Yaletown outlet shares space with Milestones, a popular burger bar. ⊠ *812 Bute St.,* ☎ *604/688–3213;* ⊠ *1040 Denman St.,* ☎ *604/685–2996;* ⊠ *1109 Hamilton St.,* ☎ *604/689–9500. AE, DC, MC, V.*

Chinese

$$–$$$$ ✕ **Imperial Chinese Seafood.** The two-story floor-to-ceiling windows at
★　　this Cantonese restaurant in the Art Deco Marine Building have stupendous

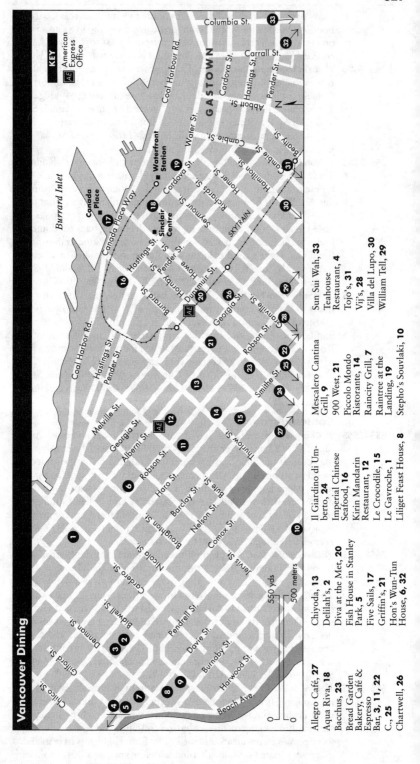

Vancouver Dining

329

KEY
AE American Express Office

Allegro Café, 27
Aqua Riva, 18
Bacchus, 23
Bread Garden Bakery, Café & Espresso Bar, 3, 11, 22
C., 25
Chartwell, 26

Chiyoda's, 13
Delilah's, 2
Diva at the Met, 20
Fish House in Stanley Park, 5
Five Sails, 17
Griffin's, 21
Hon's Wun-Tun House, 6, 32

Il Giardino di Umberto, 24
Imperial Chinese Seafood, 16
Kirin Mandarin Restaurant, 12
Le Crocodile, 15
Le Gavroche, 1
Liliget Feast House, 8

Mescalero Cantina Grill, 9
900 West, 21
Piccolo Mondo Ristorante, 14
Raincity Grill, 7
Raintree at the Landing, 19
Stepho's Souvlaki, 10

Sun Sui Wah, 33
Teahouse Restaurant, 4
Tojo's, 31
Vij's, 28
Villa del Lupo, 30
William Tell, 29

views of Stanley Park and the North Shore mountains across Coal Harbour. Any dish with lobster, crab, or shrimp from the live tanks is recommended, as is the dim sum, served from 11 AM to 2:30 PM. ⊠ *355 Burrard St.,* ☎ *604/688–8191. Reservations essential. AE, DC, MC, V.*

$$–$$$$ ✕ **Kirin Mandarin Restaurant.** This upscale restaurant, just two blocks from most of the major downtown hotels, offers a range of northern Chinese cuisines. Dishes include Shanghai-style smoked eel, Peking duck, and Szechuan hot-and-spicy scallops. A second location at Cambie Street and 12th Avenue focuses on milder Cantonese seafood creations. Kirin has a Richmond location as well. ⊠ *102–1166 Alberni St.,* ☎ *604/ 682–8833. Reservations essential. AE, DC, V.*

$$–$$$$ ✕ **Sun Sui Wah.** Sails in the ceiling reminiscent of Vancouver's landmark
★ Trade and Convention Centre add a lofty elegance to this East Side Cantonese restaurant. An offshoot of a popular Hong Kong establishment, Sun Sui Wah is best known for its dim sum, which ranges from traditional handmade dumplings to some highly adventurous offerings with little Japanese touches thrown in. It's worth coming back for dinner for house specialties like roasted squab and enormous king crab from the live tanks. There's another location in Richmond, the suburban heart of Vancouver's Chinese community. ⊠ *3888 Main St.,* ☎ *604/872–8822. ⊠ 4940 No. 3 Rd., Richmond* ☎ *604/273–8208. AE, MC, V.*

$ ✕ **Hon's Wun-Tun House.** Mr. Hon has been keeping Vancouver residents in Chinese comfort food since the 1970s. The best bets on the 300-item menu (nothing is over $10) are the pot stickers, the wonton and noodle dishes, and anything with barbecued beef. The shiny new Robson Street outlet has a separate kitchen for vegetarians and an army of fast-moving waitresses keeping your tea topped up. The original Keefer Street location is in the heart of Chinatown. ⊠ *1339 Robson St.,* ☎ *604/685–0871; ⊠ 268 Keefer St.,* ☎ *604/688–0871. Reservations not accepted. MC, V.*

Contemporary

$$$–$$$$ ✕ **Chartwell.** Named after Sir Winston Churchill's country home, a painting of which hangs over the green marble fireplace, the flagship dining room at the Four Seasons hotel (☞ Lodging, *below*), with its rich wood paneling and deep leather chairs, is the city's top spot for a power lunch. Menu highlights include a braised Salt Spring Island lamb shoulder served with truffled flageolet cassoulet and grilled salmon with smoked celery root and barley risotto. Men will feel more comfortable in jackets. ⊠ *Four Seasons, 791 W. Georgia St.,* ☎ *604/689–9333. Reservations essential. AE, DC, MC, V. No lunch Sat.*

$$$–$$$$ ✕ **Diva at the Met.** At this multitiered restaurant at the Metropolitan Hotel (☞ Lodging, *below*) the presentation of the innovative contemporary cuisine is as appealing as the modern art deco–style decor. The menu changes seasonally, but top creations from the open kitchen have included smoked Alaska black cod and porcini-crusted veal loin steak. The after-theater crowd heads here for late-evening snacks and desserts: Prawn tempura, vegetable chips, fresh sorbet, and Stilton cheesecake are served until midnight. The creative breakfasts and weekend brunches are also popular. ⊠ *Metropolitan Hotel, 645 Howe St.,* ☎ *604/602–7788. AE, DC, MC, V.*

$$$–$$$$ ✕ **Five Sails.** The special-occasion restaurant at the Pan Pacific Hotel (☞ Lodging, *below*) commands a sweeping view of Canada Place, Lions Gate Bridge, and the lights of the North Shore. The broad-reaching, seasonally changing menu emphasizes fresh fish and seafood and takes its inspiration from all around the Pacific Rim. Highlights have included ginger-marinated salmon, ahi tuna with foie gras, and Dover sole with Portobello mushrooms. ⊠ *Pan Pacific Hotel, 300–999 Canada Pl.,* ☎ *604/891–2892 or 604/662–8111. AE, DC, MC, V. No lunch.*

$$$-$$$$ ✕ **900 West.** Half of this lofty, elegant room in the Hotel Vancouver (☞ Lodging, *below*) is the city's most fashionable (to be fair, its only) wine bar. The other half is an elegant dining room serving innovative contemporary cuisine. Using European techniques, fresh and seasonal British Columbia produce, and ideas from around the globe, chef Dino Renaerts concocts dishes that are creative, sometimes complex, and very West Coast. The evolving menu has included roasted lobster and veal medallions with root vegetable gratin and sea urchin sabayon. An extensive wine list includes 55 varieties available by the glass. ⊠ *Hotel Vancouver, 900 W. Georgia St.,* ☎ *604/669–9378. AE, D, DC, MC, V. No lunch weekends.*

$$-$$$$ ✕ **Raintree at the Landing.** In a beautifully renovated historic building in Gastown, Vancouver's first Pacific Northwest restaurant has waterfront views, fireplaces, a local wine list, and cuisine based on fresh, often organic, regional ingredients. The seasonal menus and daily specials feature innovative treatments of such local bounty as Salt Spring Island lamb and Fraser Valley rabbit, as well as luxurious soups, breads baked in-house, and at least three vegetarian options. A favorite is the "Pacific Northwest Salmon Bounty," featuring several varieties of smoked salmon. The set menus are a good value, offering three courses for less than $30. ⊠ *375 Water St.,* ☎ *604/688–5570. Reservations essential. AE, DC, MC, V.*

$$-$$$ ✕ **Aqua Riva.** This lofty, lively modern room just yards from the Canada Place cruise ship terminal affords striking views over the harbor and the North Shore mountains. Food from the wood-fired oven, rotisserie, and grill include thin-crust pizzas with innovative toppings, grilled salmon, spit-roasted chicken, and a good selection of pastas, salads, and sandwiches. There's a long microbrewery beer and martini list, too. ⊠ *200 Granville St.,* ☎ *604/683–5599. Reservations essential. AE, D, DC, MC, V.*

$$-$$$ ✕ **Delilah's.** Cherubs dance on the ceiling, candles flicker on the tables, and martini glasses clink during toasts at this popular restaurant. The West Coast Continental cuisine prepared by chef Peg Montgomery is innovative and beautifully presented. Her menu, which changes seasonally, is divided into two- and five-course prix-fixe dinners. Try the pancetta, pine nut, Asiago, and mozzarella fritters with sun-dried tomato aioli and the grilled swordfish with blueberry-lemon compote if they're being served. ⊠ *1789 Comox St.,* ☎ *604/687–3424. AE, DC, MC, V. No lunch.*

$$-$$$ ✕ **Griffin's.** Squash-yellow walls, bold black and white tiles, an open kitchen, and splashy food art keep things lively at this high-energy Hotel Vancouver (☞ Lodging, *below*) bistro. The Pacific Northwest buffets—for breakfast, lunch, evening appetizers, and dessert—are the main attractions here. An à la carte menu features burgers, pizza, pasta, and seafood. A traditional afternoon tea, with a pastry buffet, is served from 2:30 to 4:30 daily. ⊠ *Hotel Vancouver, 900 W. Georgia St.,* ☎ *604/662–1900. AE, D, DC, MC, V.*

$$-$$$ ✕ **Raincity Grill.** This West End hot spot across the street from English Bay is a neighborhood favorite. The sophisticated candlelighted room and views of English Bay play second fiddle to a creative menu that highlights regional seafood, meats, and produce. Grilled romaine spears are used in the Caesar salad, giving it a delightful smoky flavor. Varying preparations of salmon and duck are usually available, as is at least one vegetarian selection. The exclusively Pacific Northwest wine list offers about 100 choices by the glass. ⊠ *1193 Denman St.,* ☎ *604/685–7337. AE, DC, MC, V.*

Continental

$$$–$$$$ ✕ **William Tell.** Silver service plates, embossed linen napkins, and a silver vase on each table set a tone of Swiss luxury at this establishment in the Georgian Court Hotel. Chef Todd Konrad prepares excellent sautéed veal sweetbreads with red-onion marmalade and marsala sauce and Swiss dishes like cheese fondue and thinly sliced veal with mushrooms in a light white-wine sauce. The bar-and-bistro area caters to a more casual crowd than the main restaurant. On Sunday night there's an all-you-can-eat buffet. ⊠ *Georgian Court Hotel, 765 Beatty St.,* ☎ *604/688–3504. Reservations essential. AE, DC, MC, V. Restaurant closed Mon. Lunch served in the bistro section only.*

$$$ ✕ **Teahouse Restaurant.** The former officers' mess in Stanley Park is perfectly poised for watching sunsets over the water, especially if you're in the glassed-in wing, which resembles a conservatory. In summer you can dine on the patio. The West Coast Continental menu includes roasted pear salad, morel-stuffed chicken, and rack of lamb with Dijon cream. ⊠ *7501 Stanley Park Dr., Ferguson Point,* ☎ *604/669–3281. Reservations essential. AE, MC, V.*

Eclectic

$$$–$$$$ ✕ **Mescalero Cantina Grill.** On weekends Mescalero becomes party central, but weekdays are more subdued. Tapas, many with European and Asian Pacific influences, are the main attraction—mussels with sun-dried tomato cream; roast pear puff pastry with Stilton and garlic pesto; and braised rabbit ravioli—but dinner selections, such as salmon fillet on spinach linguine, and grilled pork chops with sweet potato–pear gnocchi, are equally creative. Sunday brunch always draws a crowd. ⊠ *1215 Bidwell St.,* ☎ *604/669–2399. AE, DC, MC, V.*

French

$$$–$$$$ ✕ **Le Crocodile.** Chef and owner Michel Jacob specializes in traditional Alsatian food at this roomy and elegant location on Smithe Street off Burrard. Favorite dishes, many of which also appear at nicer prices at lunch, include caramel–sweet onion tart, Dover sole, calf's liver with garlic spinach butter, and venison with chanterelle mushroom sauce. ⊠ *100–909 Burrard St.,* ☎ *604/669–4298. Reservations essential. AE, DC, MC, V. Closed Sun. No lunch Sat.*

$$$–$$$$ ✕ **Le Gavroche.** Classic French cuisine receives contemporary accents but remains solidly authentic at this restaurant inside a century-old house. The smoked salmon with potato galette is among the simple dishes, but the chefs also prepare complex fare like the grilled pork tenderloin with Calvados and Stilton sauce. The excellent 30-page wine list stresses Bordeaux. ⊠ *1616 Alberni St.,* ☎ *604/685–3924. Reservations essential. AE, DC, MC, V. No lunch weekends.*

Greek

$ ✕ **Stepho's Souvlaki.** Regulars swear by, and are quite prepared to wait ★ in line for, Stepho's cheap and tasty roast lamb, moussaka, and souvlaki, served in a dark and bustling taverna. **Takis',** a few doors east at 1106 Davie Street (☎ 604/682–1336), serves equally good-value Greek Cypriot food, and there's usually no waiting. Both restaurants have take-out menus—handy for picnics on the beach just down the street. ⊠ *1124 Davie St.,* ☎ *604/683–2555. AE, MC, V.*

Indian

$$ ✕ **Vij's.** Vikram Vij calls his restaurant a curry art gallery, but he's not ★ talking about the bold Klimt-inspired murals on the walls. The art here is on the plate, with such haute-Punjabi creations as cinnamon-spiced buffalo meat with sweet corn; tiger prawns with cucumber salsa; and rockfish, spot prawns, and scallops in coconut curry. The dishes on the brief, seasonally changing menu are far from traditional, and the

spices are beautifully orchestrated to allow exotic flavors like mango, tamarind, and fenugreek to shine through. Vij's doesn't take reservations, but the inevitable lineups are events in themselves, as the attentive staff serve *papadum* and *chai* (spicy snacks and tea) to the waiting diners. ⊠ *1480 W. 11th Ave.,* ☎ *604/736–6664. Reservations not accepted. AE, MC, V. No lunch.*

Italian

$$$–$$$$ ✕ **Piccolo Mondo Ristorante.** Soft candlelight, bountiful flower arrangements, and fine European antiques create an intimate feel at this northern Italian restaurant on a quiet street a block off Robson. Start with an eggplant and tuna tart with pecorino cheese and basil oil, and follow it up with the classic osso buco or the linguine tossed with smoked Alaskan cod, capers, and red onions. In the award-winning wine cellar are more than 4,000 bottles (480 vintages). ⊠ *850 Thurlow St.,* ☎ *604/688–1633. Reservations essential. AE, DC, MC, V. Closed Sun. No lunch Sat.*

$$$–$$$$ ✕ **Villa del Lupo.** This Victorian heritage house on the edge of trendy Yaletown is home to one of Vancouver's most established Italian restaurants. Country-house-elegant decor sets a romantic tone, and the contemporary menu takes its inspiration from various regions of Italy. Sea bass wrapped with Parma prosciutto and sage and roasted with braised fennel-savoy cabbage as well as osso buco in a sauce of tomatoes, red wine, cinnamon, and lemon are favorites here. ⊠ *869 Hamilton St.,* ☎ *604/688–7436. Reservations essential. AE, DC, MC, V. No lunch.*

$$–$$$$ ✕ **Bacchus.** Low lighting, deep-velvet drapes, and Venetian glass lamps create a mildly decadent feel at this sensuous restaurant inside the Wedgwood Hotel (☞ Lodging, *below*). Live jazz music, a cigar room, and appropriately ornate northern Italian cuisine round out the mood. Bacchus is open until 1:30 AM six nights a week for after-theater refreshments, and for weekend brunch. Afternoon tea is served between 2 and 4 daily. ⊠ *Wedgwood Hotel, 845 Hornby St.,* ☎ *604/608–5319. Reservations essential. AE, D, DC, MC, V.*

$$–$$$$ ✕ **Il Giardino di Umberto.** This little yellow house at the end of Hornby
★ Street hides an attractive jumble of four terra-cotta-tiled rooms and a vine-draped courtyard with a wood-burning oven. For extreme romance, there's a Juliet balcony with its own table for two overlooking the main dining room. The Tuscan food served here features such dishes as smoked salmon with orange, fennel, and leeks; roasted reindeer loin with port peppercorn sauce; osso buco with saffron risotto; and duck with shallots. ⊠ *1382 Hornby St.,* ☎ *604/669–2422. Reservations essential. AE, DC, MC, V. Closed Sun. No lunch Sat.*

Japanese

$$$ ✕ **Tojo's.** Hidekazu Tojo is a sushi-making legend in Vancouver, with
★ more than 2,000 special preparations stored in his creative mind. His handsome tatami rooms, on the second floor of a modern green-glass tower on West Broadway, provide the proper ambience for intimate dining, but Tojo's 10-seat sushi bar provides a convivial ringside seat for watching the creation of edible art. Reserve the seat at the end for the best view. ⊠ *202–777 W. Broadway,* ☎ *604/872–8050. Reservations essential. AE, DC, MC, V. Closed Sun. No lunch.*

$$–$$$ ✕ **Chiyoda.** A sushi bar and a *robata* (grill) bar curve through Chiyoda's chic modern main room: On one side are the customers and an array of flat baskets full of the day's offerings; on the other side are the chefs and grills. There are usually more than 35 choices of things to grill, from black cod marinated in miso paste to squid, snapper, oysters, and shiitake mushrooms—all fresh from the market. ⊠ *205–1050 Alberni St.,* ☎ *604/688–5050. Reservations essential. AE, DC, MC, V. Closed Sun. No lunch Sat.*

Mediterranean

$$–$$$ ✕ **Allegro Café.** Cushy curved booths, low lighting, friendly staff, and a long martini menu give this downtown place near Robson Square a romantic—even flirtatious—feel. The menu is playful, too, with such rich and offbeat concoctions as pasta bundles with roasted butternut squash and Gorgonzola cream, and roasted breast of chicken with herbs, goat cheese, and peach and fig chutney. The rich daily soups and fair prices make this a good weekday lunch stop. ⊠ *888 Nelson St.,* ☎ *604/683–8485. AE, DC, MC, V. No lunch weekends.*

Native American

$$–$$$$ ✕ **Liliget Feast House.** This intimate downstairs room looks like the
★ interior of a native longhouse, with wooden walkways across pebble floors, contemporary native art on the walls, and cedar-plank tables with tatami-style benches. Liliget is one of the few places in the world serving the original Pacific Northwest Coast native cuisine. A feast or potlach (ceremonial-feast) platter lets you try most of the offerings, which include bannock bread, baked sweet potato with hazelnuts, alder-grilled salmon, toasted seaweed with rice, steamed fern shoots, barbecued venison, oysters, smoked mussels, and oolican oil, which is prepared from candlefish. ⊠ *1724 Davie St.,* ☎ *604/681–7044 or 888/ 681–7044. Reservations essential. AE, DC, MC, V. No lunch.*

Seafood

$$$–$$$$ ✕ **C.** With dishes like quince and ginger barbecued eel, roasted fresh-
★ water striped bass with yam and sour cream torte, and octopus-bacon-wrapped scallops, C injects a new excitement into Vancouver's seafood scene. Besides the full lunch and dinner menus, there's a raw bar offering sushi, sashimi, oysters, and caviar; an elaborate Sunday brunch; and, at weekday lunch, a West Coast seafood dim sum. The interior is done in cool, almost stark grays. Outside, a heated seaside patio has views of Granville Island. ⊠ *2–1600 Howe St.,* ☎ *604/681–1164. Reservations essential. AE, DC, MC, V. No lunch Sat.*

$$–$$$ ✕ **Fish House in Stanley Park.** Tucked between Stanley Park's tennis courts and putting green, this 1930s former sports pavilion with a conservatory, veranda, and fireplace has a relaxed country-house ambience. Chef Karen Barnaby writes cookbooks, and the titles—*Pacific Passions* and *Screamingly Good Food*—say a lot about the food here, which is hearty, flavorful, and unpretentious. Good choices are the ahi tuna steak Diane and the cornhusk-wrapped salmon with a maple glaze. Before dinner head straight for the oyster bar, or arrive between 5 and 6 to take advantage of the early-bird specials. ⊠ *8901 Stanley Park Dr., near Stanley Park's Beach Ave. entrance,* ☎ *604/681–7275. Reservations essential. AE, DC, MC, V.*

LODGING

Vancouver hotels, especially the more expensive properties downtown, contain fairly comparable facilities. Unless otherwise noted, expect to find the following amenities: minibars, in-room movies, no-smoking rooms and/or floors, room service, massage, baby-sitting, laundry service and dry cleaning, concierge, business services, meeting rooms, and parking (there is usually an additional fee). Lodgings in the inexpensive to moderate category do not generally provide much in the way of amenities (no in-room minibar, restaurant, room service, pool, exercise room, and so on). The chart below shows high-season prices, but from mid-October through May, rates throughout the city can drop as much as 50%.

CATEGORY	COST*
$$$$	over C$300
$$$	C$200–C$300
$$	C$125–C$200
$	under C$125

All prices are in Canadian dollars, for a standard double room, excluding 10% room tax and 7% GST.

$$$$ 🏨 **Four Seasons.** This 30-story luxury hotel in downtown Vancouver
★ is famous for pampering guests (kids and pets included). The lobby is lavish, with seemingly acres of couches and a fountain in the lounge. Standard rooms are elegantly furnished, as are the roomier corner rooms with sitting areas. The two opulent split-level suites are handy for putting up visiting royalty. Service at the Four Seasons is top notch, and the attention to detail is outstanding. The many amenities include free evening limousine service. The formal dining room, Chartwell (☞ *Dining, above*), is one of the best in the city. ⊠ *791 W. Georgia St., V6C 2T4,* ☎ *604/689–9333,* 📠 *604/684–4555. 318 rooms, 67 suites. Restaurant, café, lobby lounge, in-room data ports, indoor-outdoor pool, hot tub, saunas, exercise room, children's programs, business services. AE, D, DC, MC, V.*

$$$$ 🏨 **Hotel Vancouver.** The copper roof of this château-style hotel (☞ Rob-
★ son to the Waterfront *in* Exploring Vancouver, *above*), which opened in 1939, dominates Vancouver's skyline. Even the standard guest rooms have an air of prestige, with high ceilings, mahogany furniture, sitting areas, and down duvets. Rooms on the Entrée Gold floor have extra services and amenities, including a private lounge and their own concierge. A full-service salon and day spa add to the pampering. ⊠ *900 W. Georgia St., V6C 2W6,* ☎ *604/684–3131 or 800/441–1414,* 📠 *604/662–1937. 555 rooms, 42 suites. 2 restaurants, lobby lounge, in-room data ports, indoor lap pool, wading pool, beauty salon, hot tub, saunas, spa, health club, car rental. AE, D, DC, MC, V.*

$$$$ 🏨 **Metropolitan Hotel.** The structure was built in 1984 as the Mandarin Oriental Hotel, based on the principles of feng shui, and those precepts have been respected in all renovations since. The spacious, peaceful rooms are decorated in muted colors, and public areas show off Asian art. Business-class rooms come with printers, fax machines, and cordless phones. Standard rooms have bathrobes, newspapers, down comforters, and other luxury amenities. The popular studio suites are even bigger and only slightly more expensive than standard rooms. Through an etched glass wall in the lobby you can catch a glimpse of the hotel's restaurant, Diva at the Met (☞ Dining, *above*). ⊠ *645 Howe St., V6C 2Y9,* ☎ *604/687–1122 or 800/667–2300,* 📠 *604/643–7267. 179 rooms, 18 suites. Restaurant, bar, in-room data ports, indoor lap pool, hot tub, saunas, men's steam room, exercise room, racquetball, squash. AE, DC, MC, V.*

$$$$ 🏨 **Pan Pacific Hotel.** A centerpiece of the waterfront Canada Place, the
★ luxurious Pan Pacific is convenient to the Vancouver Trade and Convention Centre and a cruise-ship terminal. Among the dramatic features of the three-story atrium lobby are a totem pole and waterfall. The lounge, restaurant, and café all have huge windows with views of the harbor and mountains. Eighty percent of the rooms have water views, and 30 new Global Office rooms have in-room desktop computers and videoconferencing facilities. ⊠ *300–999 Canada Pl., V6C 3B5,* ☎ *604/662–8111, 800/663–1515 in Canada, 800/937–1515 in the U.S.;* 📠 *604/685–8690. 466 rooms, 40 suites. 3 restaurants, café, coffee shop, lobby lounge, in-room data ports, in-room safes, pool, beauty salon, hot tubs, outdoor hot tub, saunas, steam rooms, aerobics, health club,*

336

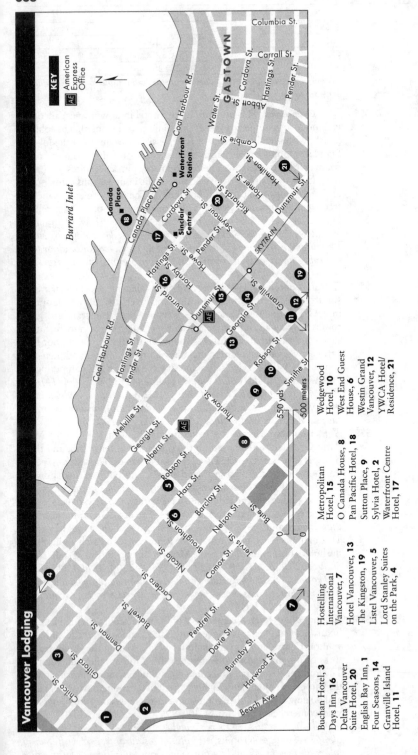

Vancouver Lodging

KEY

AE American Express Office

Burrard Inlet

GASTOWN

Columbia St.

Carrall St.

Cordova St.

Hastings St.

Pender St.

Canada Place

Waterfront Station

Sinclair Centre

SKYTRAIN

Buchan Hotel, **3**
Days Inn, **16**
Delta Vancouver Suite Hotel, **20**
English Bay Inn, **1**
Four Seasons, **14**
Granville Island Hotel, **11**

Hostelling International Vancouver, **7**
Hotel Vancouver, **13**
The Kingston, **19**
Listel Vancouver, **2**
Lord Stanley Suites on the Park, **4**

Metropolitan Hotel, **15**
O Canada House, **8**
Pan Pacific Hotel, **18**
Sutton Place, **9**
Sylvia Hotel, **2**
Waterfront Centre Hotel, **17**

Wedgewood Hotel, **10**
West End Guest House, **6**
Westin Grand Vancouver, **12**
YWCA Hotel/ Residence, **21**

indoor track, racquetball, squash, billiards, convention center, travel services. AE, DC, MC, V.

$$$$ 🏨 **Westin Grand Vancouver.** With its strikingly minimalist decor, cherry-wood and marble lobby, and all-suite layout, the Westin Grand—completed in April 1999—sets the tone for a new style of hotel springing up in fast-growing Vancouver. All the compact studio and one-bedroom suites have floor-to-ceiling windows with views of the skyline, and fully equipped kitchenettes, including microwaves and dishwashers, tucked into armoires. Corner suites are larger and have small balconies. Office suites come equipped with fax, photocopier, and laser printer. The hotel is close to Vancouver's main sports and entertainment district and to the fashionable shops and dining spots of the Yaletown district. ⊠ *433 Robson St., V6B 6L9,* ☎ *604/684–9393 or 888/680–9393,* 🖶 *604/684–9396. 23 rooms, 184 suites. Restaurant, bar, in-room data ports, kitchenettes, outdoor lap pool, outdoor hot tub, sauna, steam room, exercise room, nightclub, piano, children's programs (ages 0–12), travel services. AE, DC, MC, V.*

$$$–$$$$ 🏨 **Delta Vancouver Suite Hotel.** Vancouver's newest luxury hotel, attached to the city's newest conference center (the Simon Fraser University Centre for Dialogue), is a nice example of early millennial chic. The striking marble and cherry-wood lobby soars four stories high. The suites have blond art-deco furnishings, floor-to-ceiling windows, movable work tables, and sliding doors or Japanese screens to hide the bedroom. Slightly pricier Signature Club suites offer a private lounge, Continental breakfast, evening refreshments, and turndown service. The hotel's cozy restaurant, Manhattan, is hidden away from the madding crowd. ⊠ *550 W. Hastings St., V6B 1L6,* ☎ *604/689–8188,* 🖶 *604/ 605–8881. 7 rooms, 219 suites. Restaurant, lobby lounge, in-room data ports, indoor pool, hot tub, sauna, exercise room, convention center. AE, D, DC, MC, V.*

$$$–$$$$ 🏨 **Listel Vancouver.** This hotel on Vancouver's most vibrant shopping
★ street has reinvented itself as something of an art gallery. About half of the guest rooms display the original or limited-edition works of such contemporary artists as Carmelo Sortino, Bernard Cathelin, and Otto Rogers, and each is decorated with antiques or custom-made furniture to complement the art. Gallery-room guests are invited to a reception at the nearby Buschlen Mowatt Gallery (☞ Shopping, *below*) each evening. There's also live jazz and occasional opera performances in O'Doul's lounge downstairs. ⊠ *1300 Robson St., V6E 1C5,* ☎ *604/ 684–8461 or 800/663–5491,* 🖶 *604/684–7092. 119 rooms, 10 suites. Restaurant, lobby lounge, in-room data ports, indoor pool, hot tub, exercise room. AE, D, DC, MC, V.*

$$$–$$$$ 🏨 **Sutton Place.** The feel here is more exclusive European guest house
★ than large modern hotel. Guest rooms are furnished with rich, dark woods reminiscent of 19th-century France, and the service is gracious and attentive. The hotel's Fleuri Restaurant is known for its Continental cuisine, Sunday brunch, and weekend evening chocoholic bar. La Grande Residence (part of Sutton Place), a fully equipped apartment hotel, suitable for stays of at least a week, is next door at 855 Burrard. ⊠ *845 Burrard St., V6Z 2K6,* ☎ *604/682–5511 or 800/961–7555,* 🖶 *604/682–5513. 350 rooms, 47 suites, 162 apartments. Restaurant, bar, indoor lap pool, hot tub, women's sauna, spa, men's steam room, health club. AE, D, DC, MC, V.*

$$$–$$$$ 🏨 **Waterfront Centre Hotel.** An underground walkway leads from this striking 23-story glass hotel to Canada Place. Views from the lobby and from 70% of the guest rooms are of Burrard Inlet and Stanley Park. Other rooms look onto a terraced herb garden. The spacious rooms have big picture windows and are attractively furnished with blond wood furniture and contemporary Canadian artwork. Large corner rooms have the best views. Rooms on the Entrée Gold floor have extra amenities, including in-room safes, a private lounge, and their own concierge. ✉ *900 Canada Pl. Way, V6C 3L5,* ☎ *604/691–1991 or 800/441–1414,* FAX *604/ 691–1999. 460 rooms, 29 suites. Restaurant, lobby lounge, pool, hot tub, sauna, steam room, exercise room, car rental. AE, D, DC, MC, V.*

$$$–$$$$ 📺 **Wedgewood Hotel.** The small, elegant Wedgewood is run by an
   ★   owner who cares fervently about her guests. The lobby and guest rooms are decorated in a traditional European style with original artwork and antiques selected by the proprietor on her European travels. Guest rooms are spacious and each has a balcony, a bar, and a desk. The four penthouse suites have fireplaces. All the extra touches are here, too: afternoon ice delivery, dark-out drapes, robes, and a morning newspaper. The turndown service incudes homemade cookies and Evian water. In the lobby is the sensuous Bacchus restaurant and lounge (☞ Dining, *above*). ✉ *845 Hornby St., V6Z 1V1,* ☎ *604/689–7777 or 800/663–0666,* FAX *604/ 608–5348. 51 rooms, 38 suites. Restaurant, lobby lounge, in-room data ports, in-room safes, sauna, exercise room. AE, D, DC, MC, V.*

   $$$ 📺 **Granville Island Hotel.** Granville Island (☞ Exploring Vancouver, *above*) is one of Vancouver's more entertaining neighborhoods, but unless you've moored up in your own houseboat, the only overnight option is the Granville Island Hotel. This modern water's-edge hotel looks from the outside like it's made of Lego toy blocks. Inside, the decor is more elegant, with marble floors and Persian rugs in the lobby and guest rooms. Most rooms have water views, and all have big soaking tubs. Those on the top floor, the third, have small balconies. Step into the corridor and you'll overlook the vats brewing away for the fashionable brew pub and restaurant downstairs. Rooms not overlooking the pub's summertime patio are the quietest. ✉ *1253 Johnston St., V6H 3R9,* ☎ *604/683–7373 or 800/663–1840,* FAX *604/683–3061. 54 rooms. Restaurant, pub, in-room data ports, hot tub, sauna, billiards. AE, MC, V.*

$$–$$$ 📺 **English Bay Inn.** This renovated 1930s Tudor-style house one block
   ★   from the ocean and Stanley Park is elegantly furnished with museum-quality antiques. The parlor has wing chairs, a fireplace, a gilt Louis XV clock, and French doors overlooking the front garden. The guest rooms are equally sumptuous. Three have sleigh beds and one has a romantic four-poster. The suite has a loft bedroom with its own fireplace. Two double rooms in an equally beautiful house across the street have their own sitting and breakfast room. ✉ *1968 Comox St., V6G 1R4,* ☎ *604/683–8002,* FAX *604/899–1501. 6 rooms, 1 suite. Free parking. Full breakfast. No smoking. AE, MC, V.*

$$–$$$ 📺 **West End Guest House.** This Victorian house, built in 1906, is a true
   ★   "painted lady," from its front parlor, cozy fireplace, and early 1900s furniture to its bright-pink exterior. Most of the handsome rooms have high brass beds, antiques, and gorgeous linens, as well as TVs and phones; two larger rooms have gas fireplaces. The inn is in a residential neighborhood, a two-minute walk from Robson Street. Book by March for summer. A full breakfast is included. ✉ *1362 Haro St., V6E 1G2,* ☎ *604/681–2889,* FAX *604/688–8812. 8 rooms. Bicycles, free parking. No smoking. AE, D, MC, V.*

   $$ 📺 **Days Inn.** This six-story hotel, which opened as the Abbotsford in 1920, is one of the few moderately priced hotels in the business district. Rooms are bright, clean, and utilitarian, with phones, TVs, and refrigerators. The two-bedroom, one-bathroom units are a good value for groups and families. There is no room service or air-conditioning, although in-room data ports and voice mail are available. Guests have free use of the YWCA pool and fitness facilities, a half block away. ✉ *921 W. Pender St., V6C 1M2,* ☎ *604/681–4335,* FAX *604/681–7808. 80 rooms, 5 suites. Restaurant, lounge, pub, fans, in-room data ports, in-room safes, billiards, coin laundry. AE, D, DC, MC, V.*

$$ ⊞ **Lord Stanley Suites on the Park.** Here's a secret: These small, attractive, fully equipped suites built in 1998 on the edge of Stanley Park are privately owned and thus charge less than a comparable hotel for a nightly stay; the weekly rates are even better. Each suite incorporates an office nook as well as a sitting room, one or two bedrooms, a galley kitchen, and a washer/dryer. Those overlooking busy Georgia Street have an enclosed sunroom. Those backing onto quieter Alberni Street have balconies. You'll find many good restaurants on Denman Street, just a block away. The only catch: The vacant lot next door may, or may not, be under construction in 2000. Check before booking. ⊠ *1889 Alberni St.,* ☎ *604/688–9299 or 888/767–7829,* FAX *604/688–9297. 98 one-bedroom suites, 4 two-bedroom suites. In-room data ports, in-room VCRs, saunas, exercise room. AE, DC, MC, V.*

$$ ⊞ **O Canada House.** Beautifully restored, this 1897 Victorian within
★ walking distance of downtown was where the first version of *O Canada,* the national anthem, was written in 1909. Each spacious bedroom is appointed with late-Victorian antiques. Modern comforts, like in-room TVs, VCRs, phones, and bathrobes, help make things homey. The top-floor room is enormous, with two double beds and a private sitting area. A separate one-bedroom coach house in the garden is the most romantic option. Guests also have the use of a guest pantry and two parlors, both with fireplaces. A full breakfast is included. ⊠ *1114 Barclay St., V6E 1H1,* ☎ *604/688–0555,* FAX *604/488–0556. 6 rooms. Free parking. No smoking. MC, V.*

$ ⊞ **Buchan Hotel.** The three-story Buchan, built in the 1930s, sits on a tree-lined residential street a block from Stanley Park. The hotel's rooms have basic furnishings, ceiling fans, and color TVs but no telephones or air-conditioning. The lounge has a fireplace, and there's storage for bikes and skis. The 35 pension-style rooms with shared baths may be the most affordable accommodations near downtown. The Buchan has no elevator. ⊠ *1906 Haro St., V6G 1H7,* ☎ *604/685–5354 or 800/668–6654,* FAX *604/685–5367. 65 rooms, 30 with bath. Coin laundry. No smoking. AE, DC, MC, V.*

$ ⊞ **Hostelling International Vancouver.** Vancouver has two Hostelling
★ International locations: a big barracklike hostel at Jericho Beach in Kitsilano and a smaller, downtown hostel near English Bay and Stanley Park. Each has private rooms for two to four people; bunks in men's, women's, and coed dorms; a shared kitchen and dining room, coin laundry, TV lounge, bicycle rental, luggage and bike storage, and a range of low-cost tours and activities. The downtown hostel also has a meeting room, a games room, and a library and is wheelchair accessible. The Jericho Beach hostel has a licensed café open April–November. A free shuttle bus runs between the hostels and the bus and train station. ⊠ *Downtown: 1114 Burnaby St., V6E 1P1,* ☎ *604/684–4565,* FAX *604/ 684–4540. 23 rooms, 44 4-bed dorms.* ⊠ *Jericho Beach: 1515 Discovery St., V6R 4K5,* ☎ *604/224–3208,* FAX *604/224–4852. 10 rooms, 58 4-bed dorms.*

$ ⊞ **The Kingston.** Convenient to shopping, the Kingston is an old-style four-story building with no elevator—the type of establishment you'd find in Europe. Small and immaculate, the spartan rooms all have phones; some rooms have TVs and private baths. Guests with cars will have to find their own parking. A Continental breakfast is offered. ⊠ *757 Richards St., V6B 3A6,* ☎ *604/684–9024 or 888/713–3304,* FAX *604/ 684–9917. 56 rooms, 8 with bath. No-smoking floor, coin laundry. AE, MC, V.*

$ ⊞ **Sylvia Hotel.** To stay at the Sylvia from June through August you'll need to book six months to a year ahead. This ivy-covered 1912 building is popular because of its low rates and near-perfect location: about 25 ft from the beach on scenic English Bay, 200 ft from Stanley Park, and a 20-minute walk from Robson Street. The unadorned rooms all have private baths, phones, and TVs. Some suites are huge, and all have kitchens. ⊠ *1154 Gilford St., V6G 2P6,* ☎ *604/681–9321,* FAX *604/ 682–3551. 97 rooms, 22 suites. Restaurant, bar, room service, dry cleaning, laundry service, parking (fee). AE, DC, MC, V.*

$ ⊞ **YWCA Hotel/Residence.** A secure, 12-story building in the heart of
★ the entertainment district, the YWCA has bright comfortable rooms, some big enough to sleep five. All have cheery floral bedspreads, nightstands and desks, mini-refrigerators, telephones, and sinks. Some share a bath down the hall, some share a bath between two rooms, and others have private baths. The hotel is open to men and women and offers discounts for senior citizens, students, and YWCA members. Rates include use of the YWCA pool and fitness facility at 535 Hornby Street (☞ Health and Fitness Clubs *in* Outdoor Activities and Sports, *below*). ⊠ *733 Beatty St., V6B 2M4,* ☎ *604/895–5830, 800/663–1424 in Western Canada and the Pacific Northwest;* FAX *604/681–2550. 155 rooms. 3 shared kitchens, 2 shared kitchenettes, no-smoking floors, refrigerators, 3 shared TV lounges, 3 coin laundries, meeting rooms, parking (fee). MC, V.*

NIGHTLIFE AND THE ARTS

For **events information,** pick up a copy of the free *Georgia Straight* (available at cafés and bookstores around town) or look in the "Entertainment" section of the *Vancouver Sun* (Thursday's paper has listings in the "Queue" section). Call the **Arts Hotline** (☎ 604/684–2787) for the latest entertainment information. Book tickets through **Ticketmaster** (☎ 604/280–4444).

Nightlife

Bars and Lounges

DOWNTOWN

Musicians at the chic **Bacchus Lounge** (⊠ Wedgewood Hotel, 845 Hornby St., ☎ 604/608–5319) play mellow tunes to sip cocktails by. A waterfall and soft, comfy chairs make the airy **Garden Terrace** (⊠ Four Seasons, 791 W. Georgia St., ☎ 604/689–9333) a peaceful place to relax. The fireplaces, wing chairs, dark wood, and leather at the **Gerard Lounge** (⊠ Sutton Place Hotel, 845 Burrard St., ☎ 604/682–5511) provide a suitably stylish setting for the film-industry types who hang out here. The tenders of the wine bar at the **Hotel Vancouver** (⊠ 900 W. Georgia St., ☎ 604/669–9378) pour 55 wines by the glass.

GRANVILLE ISLAND

The **Backstage Lounge** (⊠ 1585 Johnston St., ☎ 604/687–1354) is a loud and popular hangout behind the main stage at the Arts Club Theatre. The after-work crowd heads to **Bridges** (⊠ 1696 Duranleau St., ☎ 604/687–4400), near the Public Market overlooking False Creek. The **Creek** (⊠ Granville Island Hotel, 1253 Johnston St., ☎ 604/685–7070) is a popular microbrewery lounge.

Brew Pubs

The brewmasters at **Steam Works** (⊠ 375 Water St., ☎ 604/689–2739), on the edge of Gastown, use an age-old steam process and large copper kettles (visible through glass walls in the dining room downstairs) to fashion several brews, including espresso ale. The **Yaletown Brewing Company** (⊠ 1111 Mainland St., ☎ 604/681–2739) occupies a renovated warehouse. The microbrewery turns out eight tasty concoctions and includes a darts and billiards pub and a restaurant.

Casinos

Vancouver has a few casinos; proceeds go to local charities and arts groups. No alcohol is served. The **Great Canadian Casino** (⊠ 1133 West Hastings St., ☎ 604/682–8415) is in the Renaissance Hotel. The **Royal Diamond Casino** (⊠ 106B-750 Pacific Blvd. S, ☎ 604/685–2340) is in the Plaza of Nations Expo site downtown.

Coffeehouses

A large European population and the shortage of pubs mean that coffeehouses play an even bigger role in Vancouver's social life than they do in Seattle's. The Starbucks invasion is complete—there are blocks in town with two branches—but there are other, more colorful places to have a cappuccino, write that novel, or watch the world go by.

There are many coffee places on Granville Island, but only the **Blue Parrot Café** (⊠ Granville Island Public Market, 1689 Johnston St., ☎ 604/688–5127) provides such sweeping views of the boats on False Creek. The Blue Parrot, like the public market, gets madly crowded on weekends. Cushy couches and wholesome goodies make **Bojangles Café** (⊠ 785 Denman St., ☎ 604/687–3622) a good place to rest up after a walk around Stanley Park. **Blake's on Carrall** (⊠ 221 Carrall St., ☎ 604/899–3354) is an atmospheric Gastown hangout, doubling as a mini–art gallery and performance space. Everyone seems to know everyone else at **Delaney's** (⊠ 1105 Denman St., ☎ 604/662–3344), a friendly and often crowded coffee bar near English Bay. Cozy wooden booths and stacks of magazines will tempt you to spend a rainy afternoon here.

Comedy Clubs

The **TheatreSports League** (☎ 604/738–7013), a hilarious improv troupe, performs at the Arts Club New Review Stage on Granville Island. The **Vancouver International Comedy Festival** (☎ 604/683–0883), held in late July and early August, brings an international collection of improv, stand-up, circus, and other acts to Granville Island. **Yuk Yuks** (⊠ 750 Pacific Blvd. S, in the Plaza of Nations Expo site, ☎ 604/687–5233) is Vancouver's main stand-up venue.

Gay and Lesbian Nightlife

Celebrities (⊠ 1022 Davie St., ☎ 604/689–3180) is a multilevel space with dancing, billiards, and Wednesday drag shows. **Denman Station** (⊠ 860 Denman St., ☎ 604/669–3448), a friendly and low-key pub, is patronized by gay men and lesbians. **Odyssey** (⊠ 1251 Howe St., ☎ 604/689–5256) is one of Vancouver's most popular gay discos.

Music

DANCE CLUBS

The **Gate** (⊠ 1176 Granville St., ☎ 604/608–4283) is a popular place with a big dance floor, live music on weekends, and Top 40 during the week. **Richard's on Richards** (⊠ 1036 Richards St., ☎ 604/687–6794) is one of Vancouver's most established dance clubs, with live bands on weekdays. **Sonar** (⊠ 66 Water St., ☎ 604/683–6695), in Gastown, has international dance sounds and frequent touring guest DJs.

FOLK

The **Vancouver Folk Music Festival** (☎ 604/602–9798 or 800/883–3655), one of the world's leading folk- and world-music events, takes place at Jericho Beach Park on the third weekend of July. For folk and traditional Celtic concerts year-round, call the **Rogue Folk Club** (☎ 604/736–3022).

JAZZ AND SOUL

The hot line of the **Coastal Jazz and Blues Society** (☎ 604/872–5200) has information about concerts and clubs. The society also runs the

Vancouver International Jazz Festival, which lights up 37 venues around town every June.

BaBalu (⊠ 654 Nelson St., ☎ 604/605–4343) leads the local lounge revival with its house band, the Smoking Section. The DJ at **Bar None** (⊠ 1222 Hamilton St., ☎ 604/689–7000) in Yaletown favors funk and soul. Bands perform on Monday and Tuesday. The **Cellar Jazz Café** (⊠ 3611 W. Broadway, ☎ 604/738–1959) presents everything from acid jazz to mainstream quartets, both live and recorded. Beatnik poetry readings would seem to fit right in at the **Chameleon Urban Lounge** (⊠ 801 W. Georgia St., ☎ 604/669–0806) in the basement of the Crowne Plaza Hotel Georgia, but it's the sophisticated jazz, R&B, and Latin tunes that draw the crowds. A big-band dance sound carries into the night at the **Hot Jazz Club** (⊠ 2120 Main St., ☎ 604/873–4131).

ROCK

The **Rage** (⊠ 750 Pacific Blvd. S, ☎ 604/685–5585) hosts touring acts on weeknights and has DJs on weekends. Two spots for local and alternative live bands are the **Railway Club** (⊠ 579 Dunsmuir St., ☎ 604/681–1625) and the **Starfish Room** (⊠ 1055 Homer St., ☎ 604/682–4171). The **Vogue Theatre** (⊠ 918 Granville St., ☎ 604/331–7909), a former movie palace, hosts a variety of concerts by visiting performers.

Pool Halls

Most of the city's hot pool halls are in Yaletown, including the **Automotive Billiards Club** (⊠ 1095 Homer St., ☎ 604/682–0040), **Cutters Billiard** (⊠ 1011 Hamilton St., ☎ 604/669–3533) , and **Soho Café and Billiards** (⊠ 1144 Homer St., ☎ 604/688–1180).

The Arts

Dance

The **Dance Centre** (☎ 604/606–6400) has information about dance in British Columbia.

Ballet British Columbia (☎ 604/732–5003), based at the **Queen Elizabeth Theatre** (⊠ 600 Hamilton St.), mounts productions and hosts out-of-town companies from November through April. A few of the many modern dance companies in town are Karen Jamieson, DanceArts Vancouver, and JumpStart; among the venues they perform at include **Firehall Arts Centre** and the **Vancouver East Cultural Centre** (☞ Theater, *below*).

Film

Tickets are half price on Tuesday at most Vancouver movie theaters. The **Vancouver International Film Festival** (☎ 604/685–0260) is held in late September and early October in several theaters around town.

FOREIGN/INDEPENDENT

Fifth Avenue Cinemas (⊠ 2110 Burrard St., ☎ 604/734–7469). **Park Theater** (⊠ 3440 Cambie St., ☎ 604/876–2747). **Pacific Cinématèque** (⊠ 1131 Howe St., ☎ 604/688–8202). **Ridge Theatre** (⊠ 3131 Arbutus St., ☎ 604/738–6311).

Music

CHAMBER MUSIC AND SMALL ENSEMBLES

Early Music Vancouver (☎ 604/732–1610) performs medieval, Renaissance, and Baroque music throughout the year and hosts the Vancouver Early Music Summer Festival. Concerts by the **Friends of Chamber Music** (☎ 604/437–5747) are worth watching for. Programs of the **Vancouver Recital Society** (☎ 604/602–0363) are always of excellent quality.

CHORAL GROUPS

Choral groups like the **Bach Choir** (☎ 604/921–8012), the **Vancouver Cantata Singers** (☎ 604/921–8588), and the **Vancouver Chamber Choir** (☎ 604/738–6822) play a major role in Vancouver's classical music scene.

ORCHESTRAS

The **Vancouver Symphony Orchestra** (☎ 604/876–3434) is the resident company at the **Orpheum Theatre** (✉ 601 Smithe St.).

Opera

Vancouver Opera (☎ 604/682–2871) stages several productions a year from October through May at the **Queen Elizabeth Theatre** (✉ 600 Hamilton St.).

Theater

Arts Club Theatre (✉ 1585 Johnston St., ☎ 604/687–1644) operates two stages on Granville Island and presents theatrical performances all year. **Bard on the Beach** (☎ 604/739–0559) is a summer series of Shakespeare's plays performed under a huge tent on the beach at Vanier Park. **Carousel Theatre** (☎ 604/669–3410) performs theater for children and young people at the **Waterfront Theatre** (✉ 1412 Cartwright St.) on Granville Island.

The **Chan Centre for the Performing Arts** (✉ 6265 Crescent Rd., on the University of British Columbia campus, ☎ 604/822–2697) contains a 1,400-seat concert hall, a theater, and a cinema. The **Firehall Arts Centre** (✉ 280 E. Cordova St., ☎ 604/689–0926) showcases Canadian works in an intimate downtown space. The **Fringe** (☎ 604/257–0350), Vancouver's annual live theatrical arts festival, is staged in September at various venues in Vancouver's east end.

The **Queen Elizabeth Theatre** (✉ 600 Hamilton St., ☎ 604/665–3050) is a major venue for ballet, opera, and other events. The **Stanley Theatre** (✉ 2750 Granville St., ☎ 604/687–1644), an elegant 1930s movie palace, reopened in 1998 as a live theater. **Theatre Under the Stars** (☎ 604/687–0174) performs musicals at Malkin Bowl, an outdoor amphitheater in Stanley Park, during July and August. **Vancouver East Cultural Centre** (✉ 1895 Venables St., ☎ 604/254–9578) is a multipurpose performance space. **Vancouver Playhouse** (✉ 649 Cambie St., ☎ 604/665–3050) is the leading venue in Vancouver for mainstream theatrical shows.

OUTDOOR ACTIVITIES AND SPORTS

Beaches

An almost continuous string of beaches runs from Stanley Park to the University of British Columbia. The water is cool, but the beaches are sandy, edged by grass. All have lifeguards, washrooms, concession stands, and limited parking, unless otherwise noted. Liquor is prohibited in parks and on beaches. For information, call the **Vancouver Board of Parks and Recreation** (☎ 604/738–8535, summer only).

Kitsilano Beach, over the Burrard Bridge from downtown, has a lifeguard and is the city's busiest beach. In-line skaters, volleyball games, and sleek young people are ever present. The part of the beach nearest the Vancouver Maritime Museum is the quietest. Facilities include a playground, tennis courts, a heated pool, concession stands, and nearby restaurants and cafés.

The **Point Grey beaches** provide a number of options. Jericho, Locarno, and Spanish Banks, which begin at the end of Point Grey Road, have huge expanses of sand, especially in summer and at low tide. The shallow water, warmed slightly by sun and sand, is good for swimming. Farther out, toward Spanish Banks, the beach becomes less crowded. Past Point Grey is Wreck Beach, Vancouver's nude beach.

Among the **West End beaches,** Second Beach and Third Beach, along Beach Drive in Stanley Park, draw families. Second Beach has a guarded pool. A water slide, kayak rentals, street performers, and artists keep things interesting all summer at English Bay Beach, at the foot of Denman Street. Farther along Beach Drive, Sunset Beach is a little too close to the downtown core for safe swimming.

Participant Sports

Biking

One of the best ways to see the city is to cycle along at least part of the **Seaside Bicycle Route.** This 15-km (10-mi), flat, car-free route starts at Canada Place downtown and follows the waterfront around **Stanley Park** (☞ Stanley Park *in* Exploring Vancouver, *above*) and continues, with a few detours, all the way around False Creek to Spanish Banks beach. Rentals are available from a number of places near Stanley Park, including **Bayshore Bicycles** (⊠ 745 Denman St., ☎ 604/688–2453), the **Westin Bayshore Hotel** (⊠ 1601 W. Georgia St., ☎ 604/689–5071), and **Spokes Bicycle Rentals & Espresso Bar** (⊠ 1798 W. Georgia St., ☎ 604/688–5141). Cycling helmets, a legal requirement in safety-conscious Vancouver, come with the rentals.

For guided biking and mountain bike tours, *see* Ecology Tours *in* Contacts and Resources, *below.*

Boating

Blue Pacific Yacht Charters (⊠ 1519 Foreshore Walk, Granville Island, ☎ 604/682–2161) is one of several boat charter companies on Granville Island. **Cooper Boating Centre** (⊠ 1620 Duranleau, Granville Island, ☎ 604/687–4110) has a three-hour introduction to sailing around English Bay, as well as longer cruise-and-learn trips lasting from five days to two weeks.

Golf

For a spur of the moment game, call **Last Minute Golf** (☎ 604/878–1833). The company matches golfers and courses at substantial greens-fee discounts. The half-day packages of **West Coast Golf Shuttle** (☎ 604/878–6800) include the greens fee, power cart, and hotel pickup.

The facilities of the 18-hole, par-71 public **McCleery Golf Course** (⊠ 7188 McDonald St., ☎ 604/257–8191) include a driving range. The greens fee is $34–$37; an optional cart costs $25. **Northview Golf and Country Club** (⊠ 6857 168th St., Surrey, ☎ 604/576–4653) has two Arnold Palmer–designed 18-hole courses (both par 72) and is the home of the Air Canada Championship (a PGA tour event). The greens fee for the Ridge course, where the PGA tour plays, ranges from $45 to $80, the fee for the Canal course from $35 to $60; an optional cart at either course costs $30. At the 18-hole, par-72 course (closed November–March) at the **Westwood Plateau Golf and Country Club** (⊠ 3251 Plateau Blvd., Coquitlam, ☎ 604/552–0777) the greens fee, which includes a cart, ranges from $90 to $125.

Health and Fitness Clubs

The **Bentall Centre Athletic Club** (⊠ 1055 Dunsmuir St., lower level, ☎ 604/689–4424) has racquetball and squash courts and weight rooms; aerobics classes are also given here. The **YMCA** (⊠ 955 Burrard St., ☎ 604/681–0221) downtown has daily rates. Facilities include a pool and weight rooms, as well as racquetball, squash, and handball courts. The **YWCA** (⊠ 535 Hornby St., ☎ 604/895–5800) has a pool, weight rooms, and fitness classes.

Hiking

Stanley Park, the more rugged **Pacific Spirit Park** near the University of B.C., and the seaside **Lighthouse Park** in West Vancouver all have fairly flat, forested trails.

Jogging

The **Running Room** (⊠ 1519 Robson St., ☎ 604/684–9771) is a good source for information about fun runs in the area.

The seawall around **Stanley Park** (☞ Stanley Park *in* Exploring Vancouver, *above*) is 9 km (5½ mi) long. Running it provides an excellent minitour of the city. You can take a shorter run of 4 km (2½ mi) in the park around Lost Lagoon.

Tennis

There are 180 free public courts around town. Contact the **Vancouver Board of Parks and Recreation** (☎ 604/257–8400) for locations. **Stanley Park** has 15 well-surfaced outdoor courts near English Bay Beach. Many of the other city parks have public courts as well.

Water Sports

KAYAKING

Kayaks are a fun way to explore the waters of False Creek and the shoreline of English Bay. **Ecomarine Ocean Kayak Center** (⊠ Granville Island, 1668 Duranleau St., ☎ 604/689–7575) and **Ocean West Expeditions** (⊠ English Bay Beach, ☎ 800/660–0051) rent kayaks and offer lessons and tours.

WINDSURFING

Sailboards and lessons are available at **Windsure Windsurfing School** (⊠ Jericho Beach, ☎ 604/224–0615). The winds aren't very heavy on English Bay, making it a perfect locale for learning the sport. You'll have to travel north to Squamish for more challenging high-wind conditions.

Spectator Sports

Vancouver's professional basketball and hockey teams play at **General Motors Place** (⊠ 800 Griffiths Way, ☎ 604/899–7400). **Ticketmaster** (☎ 604/280–4400) sells tickets to many local sports events.

Basketball

The **Vancouver Grizzlies** (☎ 604/899–7400) of the National Basketball Association play at General Motors Place.

Football

The **B.C. Lions** (☎ 604/930–5466) of the Canadian Football League play at B.C. Place Stadium (⊠ 777 Pacific Blvd. S, ☎ 604/661–7373).

Hockey

The **Vancouver Canucks** (☎ 604/899–7400) of the National Hockey League play at General Motors Place.

SHOPPING

Unlike many cities where suburban malls have taken over, Vancouver is full of individual boutiques and specialty shops. Antiques stores, ethnic markets, art galleries, high-fashion outlets, and fine department stores abound. Store hours are generally from 9:30 to 6 on Monday, Tuesday, Wednesday, and Saturday; from 9:30 to 9 on Thursday and Friday; and from noon to 5 on Sunday.

Shopping Districts and Malls

About two dozen high-end art galleries, antiques shops, and Oriental rug emporiums are packed end to end between 6th and 15th avenues on Granville Street, in an area known as **Gallery Row. Oakridge Shopping Centre** (⊠ 650 W. 41st Ave., at Cambie St., ☏ 604/261–2511) has chic, expensive stores that are fun to browse through. The immense **Pacific Centre Mall** (⊠ 550–700 W. Georgia St., ☏ 604/688–7236), on two levels and mostly underground, is in the heart of downtown. **Robson Street,** stretching from Burrard to Bute Street, contains boutiques and cafés. A commercial center has developed around **Sinclair Centre** (⊠ 757 W. Hastings St.), which caters to sophisticated and upscale tastes (☞ Robson to the Waterfront *in* Exploring Vancouver, *above*).

Ethnic Districts

Bustling **Chinatown**—centered on Pender and Main streets—holds restaurants and markets (☞ Gastown and Chinatown *in* Exploring Vancouver, *above*). **Commercial Drive** north of East 1st Avenue is the center of Vancouver's Italian and Latin American communities. You can sip cappuccino in coffee bars or buy sun-dried tomatoes or an espresso machine. **Little India** is on Main Street around 50th Avenue. Curry houses, sweetshops, grocery stores, discount jewelers, and silk shops abound.

Department Stores

Among Vancouver's top department stores is Canadian-owned **Eaton's** (⊠ 701 Granville St., ☏ 604/685–7112), which carries everything: clothing, appliances, furniture, jewelry, accessories, and souvenirs. Many malls have branches. **Holt Renfrew** (⊠ 633 Granville St., ☏ 604/681–3121) is smaller, focusing on high fashion for men and women.

Auction Houses

Love's (⊠ 1635 W. Broadway, ☏ 604/733–1157) holds auctions of collectibles and antiques on the last Wednesday and Thursday of each month at 6 PM. **Maynard's** (⊠ 415 W. 2nd Ave., ☏ 604/876–6787) auctions home furnishings every second Wednesday at 7 PM and holds occasional art and antiques auctions as well.

Specialty Stores

Antiques

Two key hunting grounds for antiques are Gallery Row on Granville Street (☞ Shopping Districts, *above*) and the stretch of antiques stores along Main Street from 16th to 25th Avenue. The **Vancouver Antique Center** (⊠ 422 Richards St., ☏ 604/669–7444) has two floors of antiques and collectibles dealers under one roof.

Treasure hunters enjoy the vintage clothing and curio shops clustered along the 300 block of **West Cordova Street,** between Cambie and Richards streets near Gastown.

Art Galleries

Buschlen Mowatt (⊠ 1445 W. Georgia St., ☎ 604/682–1234), one of the city's best galleries, exhibits the works of Canadian and international artists. **Diane Farris** (⊠ 1565 W. 7th Ave., ☎ 604/737–2629) often showcases hot new artists. The **Inuit Gallery of Vancouver** (⊠ 345 Water St., ☎ 604/688–7323) exhibits Pacific Northwest–coast native and Inuit art. The **Marion Scott Gallery** (⊠ 481 Howe St., ☎ 604/685–1934) specializes in Inuit art. The **Douglas Reynolds Gallery** (⊠ 2335 Granville St., ☎ 604/731–9292) has one of the city's finest collections of Pacific Northwest–coast native art.

Books

Vancouver's two **Chapters** stores (⊠ 788 Robson St., ☎ 604/682–4066; ⊠ 2505 Granville St., at Broadway, ☎ 604/731–7822) are enormous, with a café in each location and a series of author readings and other performances. **Duthie Books** (⊠ 710 Granville St., ☎ 604/689–1802; other locations) is a long-established homegrown favorite. **MacLeod's Books** (⊠ 455 W. Pender St., ☎ 604/681–7654) is one of the city's best antiquarian bookstores. Despite its name, **Manhattan Books and Magazines** (⊠ 1089 Robson St., ☎ 604/681–9074) specializes in European books and periodicals.

Clothes

For unique women's clothing, try **Dorothy Grant** (⊠ 757 W. Hastings St., ☎ 604/681–0201), where traditional Haida native designs meld with modern fashion. **Dream** (⊠ 311 W. Cordova, ☎ 604/683–7326) is where up-and-coming local designers sell their wares. European fashions for men and women meet locally designed furs at **Lauren Paris** (⊠ 377 Howe St., ☎ 604/681–6391). Handmade Italian suits and other upscale menswear is sold at stylish **E. A. Lee** (⊠ 466 Howe St., ☎ 604/683–2457). There are also a few women's items to browse through. **Leone** (⊠ 757 W. Hastings St., ☎ 604/683–1133) is an ultrachic boutique, dividing designer collections in themed areas. If your tastes are traditional, don't miss **Straith** (⊠ 900 W. Georgia St., ☎ 604/685–3301) in the Hotel Vancouver (☞ Lodging, *above*), offering tailored designer fashions for men and women. At **Versus** (⊠ 1008 W. Georgia St., ☎ 604/688–8938) boutique, ladies and gents sip cappuccino as they browse through fashionable Italian designs.

Gifts

Museum and gallery gift shops are among the best places to buy high-quality souvenirs—West Coast native art, books, music, jewelry, and other items. Four noteworthy stores are the **Clamshell Gift Shop** (⊠ Vancouver Aquarium, ☎ 604/659–3413) in Stanley Park, the **Gallery Shop** (⊠ 750 Hornby St., ☎ 604/662–4706) in the Vancouver Art Gallery, the **Museum of Anthropology Gift Shop** (⊠ 6393 N.W. Marine Dr., ☎ 604/822–3825) on the University of British Columbia campus, and the **Museum Shop** (⊠ 639 Hornby St., ☎ 604/687–8266) in the Canadian Craft Museum.

Hill's Indian Crafts (⊠ 165 Water St., ☎ 604/685–4249), in Gastown, sells Pacific Northwest native art. **Leona Lattimer Gallery** (⊠ 1590 W. 2nd Ave., ☎ 604/732–4556), near Granville Island and built like a longhouse, is full of native arts and crafts in all price ranges. At the **Salmon Shop** (☎ 604/669–3474) in the Granville Island Public Market you can pick up smoked salmon wrapped for travel.

VANCOUVER A TO Z

Arriving and Departing

By Bus

Greyhound Lines (☎ 604/482–8747; 800/661–8747 in Canada; 800/231–2222 in the U.S.) is the largest bus line serving Vancouver. The **Pacific Central Station** (⊠ 1150 Station St.) is the depot for Greyhound. **Quick Shuttle** (☎ 604/940–4428 or 800/665–2122) bus service runs between downtown Vancouver, Vancouver Airport, Seattle (Sea-Tac) Airport, and downtown Seattle five times a day in winter and up to eight times a day in summer. The downtown Vancouver depot is at the **Sandman Hotel** (⊠ 180 W. Georgia St.).

By Car

Interstate 5 in Washington State becomes **Highway 99** at the U.S.–Canada border. Vancouver is a three-hour drive (226 km/140 mi) from Seattle. It's best to avoid border crossings during peak times such as holidays and weekends. Highway 1, the **Trans-Canada Highway,** enters Vancouver from the east. To avoid traffic, arrive after rush hour (8:30 AM).

By Ferry

B.C. Ferries (☎ 250/386–3431; 888/223–3779 in British Columbia only) serves Vancouver, Victoria, and other parts of coastal British Columbia. For more information about the system and other ferries that serve the area, *see* Ferry Travel *in* Smart Travel Tips A to Z.

By Plane

Vancouver International Airport (⊠ Grant McConachie Way, Richmond, ☎ 604/276–6101) is on Sea Island, about 14 km (9 mi) south of downtown off Highway 99. An airport improvement fee is assessed on all flight departures: $5 for flights within British Columbia or the Yukon, $10 for other flights within North America, and $15 for overseas flights. Alaska, America West, American, British Airways, Continental, Northwest, Reno, and United serve the airport. The two major domestic carriers are Air Canada and Canadian Airlines. *See* Air Travel *in* Smart Travel Tips A to Z for airline numbers.

Air B.C. (☎ 604/688–5515 or 800/663–3721) serves destinations around the province including Vancouver airport and Victoria airport. **West Coast Air** (☎ 604/688–9115 or 800/347–2222) and **Harbour Air** (☎ 604/688–1277 or 800/665–0212) both operate 35-minute harbor-to-harbor service (downtown Vancouver to downtown Victoria) several times a day. Planes leave from near the **Pan Pacific Hotel** (⊠ 300–999 Canada Pl.). **Helijet Airways** (☎ 604/273–1414 or 800/665–4354) has helicopter service between downtown Vancouver, downtown Seattle, and downtown Victoria. The heliport is near Vancouver's Pan Pacific Hotel (☞ *above*).

BETWEEN THE AIRPORT AND DOWNTOWN

The drive from the airport to downtown takes 20 to 45 minutes, depending on the time of day. Airport hotels provide free shuttle service to and from the airport. If you're driving, go over the Arthur Lang Bridge and north on Granville Street (also signposted as Highway 99). Signs will direct you to Vancouver City Centre.

The **Vancouver Airporter Service** (☎ 604/946–8866) bus leaves the international and domestic arrivals levels of the terminal building about every half hour, stopping at major downtown hotels. It operates from 5:23 AM until midnight. The fare is $10 one-way and $17 round-trip.

Taxi stands are in front of the terminal building on domestic and international arrivals levels. The taxi fare to downtown is about $22. Area cab companies include **Black Top** (☎ 604/681–2181) and **Yellow** (☎ 604/681–1111).

Limousine service from **Airlimo** (☎ 604/273–1331) costs a bit more than the taxi fare to downtown, about $30.

By Train

The **Pacific Central Station** (⊠ 1150 Station St.), at Main Street and Terminal Avenue, near the Main Street SkyTrain station, is the hub for rail service. **Amtrak** (☎ 800/872–7245) operates the *Mt. Baker International* train between Seattle and Vancouver, and is scheduled to begin its *Cascades* high-speed train service between Vancouver and Eugene, Oregon. **VIA Rail** (☎ 800/561–8630 in Canada; 800/561–3949 in the U.S.) provides transcontinental service through Jasper to Toronto three times a week. Passenger trains leave the **BC Rail Station** (⊠ 1311 W. 1st St., ☎ 604/631–3500; 800/339–8752 in British Columbia; 800/663–8238 from outside British Columbia) in North Vancouver for Whistler and the interior of British Columbia.

Getting Around

Ride a bike, walk, take a cab, or take the bus, SeaBus, SkyTrain, or False Creek Ferry, but if at all possible avoid using a car in downtown Vancouver. The congested downtown core is all of about 2 square mi. There is very little parking and many one-way streets, all of which makes driving difficult. There's really no advantage to bringing a car downtown, unless you're staying there, in which case your hotel will have parking. Even then, you'll still be better off using public transportation to tour the area.

By Bus

Exact change is needed to ride **Translink** (☎ 604/521–0400) buses. Buslink buses are run by Translink. The fare is $1.50 for normal rides, and $2.25 for weekday trips to the suburbs, including the SeaBus to the North Shore. Books of 10 tickets are sold at convenience stores and newsstands; look for a red, white, and blue FARE DEALER sign. Day passes, good for unlimited travel all day, cost $6. They are available from fare dealers and at any SeaBus or SkyTrain station. Transfers are valid for 90 minutes, allow travel in both directions, and are good on buses, SkyTrain, and SeaBus. A guide called "Discover Vancouver on Transit" is available free at the Tourist Info Centre (☞ Visitor Information *in* Important Contacts, *below*).

By Car

Vancouver rush-hour traffic can be horrendous. The worst bottlenecks outside the city center are the North Shore bridges, the George Massey Tunnel on Highway 99 south of Vancouver, and Highway 1 through Coquitlam and Surrey. Parking downtown is expensive and tricky to find; metered street parking is scarce. Two large underground pay parking lots that usually have space are at **Library Square** (⊠ 800 block of Hamilton St., off Robson St.) and **Pacific Centre** (⊠ 700 block Howe St., east side). Parking fees vary, running from about $6 to $10 a day. Don't leave anything in your car, even in the trunk. Car break-ins are quite common downtown (hotel parking tends to be more secure than public lots). Parking outside the downtown core is an easier proposition. Right turns are allowed on most red lights after you've come to a full stop.

By Ferry

The **SeaBus** is a 400-passenger commuter ferry that crosses Burrard Inlet from the foot of Lonsdale (North Vancouver) to downtown. The ride takes 13 minutes and costs the same as the Buslink bus (and it's much faster). With a transfer, connection can be made to any Buslink bus or SkyTrain. **Aquabus Ferries** (☎ 604/689–5858) and **False Creek Ferries** (☎ 604/684–7781), which are not part of the Translink system, connect several stations on False Creek including Science World, Granville Island, Stamp's Landing, Yaletown, Vanier Park, and the Hornby Street dock. Aquabus Ferries can take bicycles.

By Rapid Transit

Vancouver has a one-line, 25-km (16-mi) rapid transit system called **SkyTrain,** which travels underground downtown and is elevated for the rest of its route to New Westminster and Surrey. Trains leave about every five minutes. Tickets, sold at each station from machines (correct change is not necessary), must be carried with you as proof of payment. You may use transfers from SkyTrain to SeaBus (☞ *above*) and Buslink buses and vice versa. The SkyTrain is convenient for transit between downtown, BC Place Stadium, Pacific Central Station, and Science World.

By Taxi

It is difficult to hail a cab in Vancouver. Unless you're near a hotel, you'll have better luck calling a taxi service. Try **Black Top** (☎ 604/683–4567) or **Yellow** (☎ 604/681–1111).

Contacts and Resources

B&B Reservation Agencies

Super, Natural British Columbia (✉ 601–1166 Alberni St., V6E 3Z3, ☎ 604/663–6000 or 800/663–6000) can book accommodation anywhere in British Columbia. **Town & Country Bed and Breakfast Reservation Service** (✉ Box 74542, 2803 W. 4th Ave., V6K 1K2, ☎ FAX 604/731–5942) specializes in B&Bs.

Car Rental

Avis (☎ 604/606–2847 or 800/331–1212). **Budget** (☎ 604/668–7000 or 800/527–0700). **Thrifty** (☎ 604/606–1666 or 800/367–2277).

Consulates

Australia (✉ 1225-888 Dunsmuir St., ☎ 604/684–1177). **New Zealand** (✉ 1200-888 Dunsmuir St., ☎ 604/684–7388). **United Kingdom** (✉ 800-1111 Melville St., ☎ 604/683–4421). **United States** (✉ 1095 W. Pender St., ☎ 604/685–4311).

Emergencies

Ambulance (☎ 911). **Fire** (☎ 911). **Police** (☎ 911).

Medicentre (✉ 1055 Dunsmuir St., lower level, ☎ 604/683–8138), a drop-in clinic in the Bentall Centre, is open weekdays. Doctors are on call through the emergency ward at **St. Paul's Hospital** (✉ 1081 Burrard St., ☎ 604/682–2344), a downtown facility open around the clock.

Guided Tours

Tour prices fluctuate, so inquire about rates when booking tours. Kids are generally charged half the adult fare.

AIR

Tour Vancouver, the harbor, or the mountains of the North Shore by helicopter. For around $200 per person (minimum of three people) for 45 minutes, **Vancouver Helicopters** (☎ 604/270–1484) flies from the Harbour Heliport downtown. You can see Vancouver from the air for $72 for 30 minutes, or take a 90-minute flight over nearby mountains and glaciers with **Harbour Air Seaplanes** (☎ 604/688–1277), which leaves from beside the Pan Pacific Hotel.

BOAT

Aquabus Ferries (☎ 604/689–5858) and **False Creek Ferries** (☎ 604/684–7781) both operate 25-minute minicruises around False Creek for about $6. You can also take a one-hour tour of False Creek on a vintage wooden ferry with **Aquabus Ferries.** The tours cost $10 and leave hourly from the Aquabus dock on Granville Island.

Harbour Cruises (✉ 1 N. Denman St., ☎ 604/688–7246), at the foot of Denman Street on Coal Harbour, operates a 1¼-hour narrated tour of Burrard Inlet aboard the paddle wheeler MPV *Constitution.* Tours, which cost less than $20, take place from April through October. Harbour Cruises also offers sunset dinner cruises, four-hour lunch cruises up scenic Indian Arm, and links with the Royal Hudson Steam Train (☞ Train Tours, *below*) to make a daylong boat-train excursion to Howe Sound.

Paddlewheeler River Adventures (✉ 810 Quayside Dr., New Westminster, ☎ 604/525–4465), in the Information Centre at Westminster Quay, will take you out on the Fraser River in an 1800s-style paddle wheeler. Choose from a three-hour tour of the working river, a day trip to historic Fort Langley, a sunset dinner cruise, or a Friday-night martini cruise.

FIRST NATIONS

West Coast City and Nature Sightseeing (☎ 604/451–1600) offers a daily, four-hour Native Culture tour, with expert guides offering insights into the history and culture of Vancouver-area First Nations peoples. The tours take in the Stanley Park totem poles, the Museum of Anthropology, and two First Nations community facilities: the First Nations House of Learning and the Native Education Centre. The $41 fee includes admission to the Museum of Anthropology.

ORIENTATION

Gray Line (☎ 604/879–3363 or 800/667–0882) offers a 3½-hour Grand City bus tour year-round. The tour picks up at all major downtown hotels and includes Stanley Park, Chinatown, Gastown, English Bay, and Queen Elizabeth Park. The fee is about $39. From May through October, Gray Line also has a narrated city tour aboard double-decker buses. Passengers can get on and off as they choose and can travel free the next day. Adult fare is about $22. The one-hour **Stanley Park Horse Drawn Tours** (☎ 604/681–5115) cost about $14 per person ($43 for a family of four). The tours leave every 20 to 30 minutes from the information booth on Stanley Park Drive. The **Vancouver Trolley Company** (☎ 604/801–5515 or 888/451–5581) runs old-style trolleys through Vancouver from mid-March through October on a two-hour narrated tour of Stanley Park, Gastown, English Bay, Granville Island, and Chinatown, among other sights. A day pass allows you to complete one full circuit, getting off and on as often as you like. Start the trip at any of the 16 sights and buy a ticket on board. The adult fare is $22. **West Coast City and Nature Sightseeing** (☎ 604/451–1600) runs a four-hour City Highlights tour for about $40. Pickup is available from all major hotels downtown.

PERSONAL GUIDES

Early Motion Tours (☎ 604/687–5088) will pick you up at your hotel for a spin through Vancouver in a Model-A Ford convertible. Individualized tours in six European languages are available from **VIP Tourguide Services** (☎ 604/214–4677).

WALKING

During the summer, students from the **Architectural Institute of British Columbia** (☎ 604/683–8588) lead free walking tours of the city's top heritage sites. The **Gastown Business Improvement Society** (☎ 604/683–5650) sponsors free 90-minute historical and architectural walking tours daily June–August. Meet the guide at 2 PM at the statue of "Gassy" Jack in Maple Tree Square. Ninety-minute walking tours of Chinatown leave from the **Chinese Cultural Centre** (✉ 50 E. Pender St., ☎ 604/687–0729) daily on the hour from 10 to 4 and cost $5. **Rockwood Adventures** (☎ 604/926–7705) has guided walks around Vancouver neighborhoods, including Gastown, Granville Island, and Chinatown, and a special walk for art lovers. Guides with **Walkabout Historic Vancouver** (☎ 604/720–0006) take on the costume and the character of early residents for their two-hour historical walking tours around Downtown and Gastown or Granville Island. Tours run year-round.

Late-Night Pharmacy

Shopper's Drug Mart (✉ 1125 Davie St., ☎ 604/669–2424) is open around the clock.

Road Emergencies

The **British Columbia Automobile Association** (☎ 604/293–2222) provides 24-hour emergency road service for members of the American Automobile Association and the Canadian Automobile Association.

Visitor Information

Super, Natural British Columbia (☎ 800/663–6000). **Vancouver Tourist Info Centre** (✉ 200 Burrard St., V6C 3L6, ☎ 604/683–2000).

7 BRITISH COLUMBIA

From lush inland valleys and rugged
mountains to magnificent beaches
and forested islands, this Canadian
province north of Washington State has
an abundance of natural beauty. There
are plenty of opportunities for whale- and
nature-watching, as well as for skiing,
golfing, fishing, and kayaking, or you can
simply relax in a peaceful country inn. Your
visit may take you to places as different
as small coastal and island towns, the
Anglophile city of Victoria, and majestic
national parks in the Rockies.

BRITISH COLUMBIA, CANADA'S WESTERNMOST province, harbors Pacific beaches, verdant islands, the awesome Rocky Mountains, year-round skiing, and world-class fishing—a wealth of outdoor action and beauty. The people of the province are a similarly heterogeneous mix: descendants of the original Native American peoples and 19th-century British, European, and Asian settlers, and more recent immigrants from all corners of the earth.

Updated by
Sue Kernaghan

Canada's third-largest province (only Québec and Ontario are bigger), British Columbia occupies almost 10% of Canada's total surface area, stretching from the Pacific Ocean eastward to the province of Alberta and from the U.S. border north to Alaska, the Yukon, and Northwest Territories. It spans more than 930,000 square km (360,000 square mi), making it larger than every American state except Alaska.

British Columbia's appeal as a vacation destination stems from its status as the most spectacular part of the nation, with abundant coastal scenery and stretches of snowcapped peaks. Outdoor enthusiasts have gravitated here for sports including fishing, golfing, hiking, kayaking, rafting, and skiing. Whale-watching adventures, whether by charter boat or in a kayak, are increasingly popular.

Most of British Columbia's population clusters in two coastal cities. Vancouver (☞ Chapter 6) is an international city whose relaxed lifestyle is spiced by a varied cultural scene embracing large ethnic communities. Victoria, the provincial capital on Vancouver Island, is a smaller, more subdued town of 19th-century brick and well-tended gardens, although it, too, has undergone an international metamorphosis in recent years.

Pleasures and Pastimes

Dining

Although Vancouver and Victoria have the most varied and cosmopolitan cuisine, some excellent restaurants in smaller towns and several fine country inns have helped define a local cuisine based on the best of regional fare, including seafood, lamb, organic produce, and increasingly good wine. Attire is generally casual in the region. Victoria, southern Vancouver Island, and the Gulf Islands ban smoking in restaurants and all public places; regulations vary in other towns.

CATEGORY	COST*
$$$$	over $C35
$$$	$C25–$C35
$$	$C15–$C25
$	under $C15

per person, in Canadian dollars, for a three-course meal, excluding drinks, service, and 7% GST

Lodging

Accommodations range from bed-and-breakfasts and rustic cabins to deluxe chain hotels. In the cities you'll find an abundance of lodgings, but outside the major centers, especially in summer, it's a good idea to reserve ahead, even for campsites. In winter, many backcountry resorts close, and city hotels drop prices by as much as 50%. All Victoria hotels have no-smoking rooms, and smoking is banned in public areas. Most small inns and B&Bs in the province ban smoking indoors.

CATEGORY	COST*
$$$$	over $C200
$$$	$C150–$C200
$$	$C90–$C150
$	under $C90

All prices are in Canadian dollars, for a standard double room, excluding 10% provincial accommodation tax and 7% GST.

Outdoor Activities and Sports

GOLF

There are more than 230 golf courses in British Columbia, and the number is growing. The province is now an official golf destination of both the Canadian and American PGA tours. The topography here tends to be mountainous and forested, and many courses have fine views as well as treacherous approaches to greens.

HIKING

Virtually all of British Columbia's provincial parks have fine hiking-trail networks. Heli-hiking is also very popular here; helicopters deliver hikers to high alpine meadows and verdant mountaintops.

SKIING

With more than half the province higher than 4,200 ft above sea level, new downhill areas are constantly opening. Currently, more than 40 resorts in the province have downhill facilities. The Columbia Mountains in particular offer exceptional deep-powder skiing. British Columbia also has hundreds of miles of groomed cross-country (Nordic) ski trails in the provincial parks and more than 40 cross-country resorts.

WATER SPORTS

The Inside Passage, Queen Charlotte Strait, the Strait of Georgia, and the other island-dotted straits and sounds that border the mainland, plus thousands of lakes, rivers, and streams, offer plentiful opportunities for canoeing, fishing, rafting, and sea kayaking. You can explore the waters of British Columbia on your own or join one of the many day trips and expeditions offered by outfitters.

WHALE-WATCHING

Three resident and several transient pods of orcas (killer whales) travel the province's coastal waters. These, and the gray whales living along the west coast of Vancouver Island, are the primary focus of the many whale-watching boat tours conducted during the summer. July, August, and September are the best time to see orcas; in March and April thousands of migrating gray whales pass close to the west coast of Vancouver Island on their way from Baja California to Alaska.

First Nations Culture

Before the arrival of Europeans, the lush landscapes of the Pacific Northwest gave rise to one of the richest and most artistically prolific cultures on the continent. Visit archaeological sights and museums, or share a living culture through music, dance, and food at attractions run by First Nations people, including the re-created villages at Duncan on Vancouver Island, 'Ksan (near Hazelton), and Secwepemc, in Kamloops.

Exploring British Columbia

Vancouver Island, off the province's west coast, is effectively a small offshore mountain range, its gentle, rural east coast and wild, rain-lashed west separated by a hilly, forested spine. Victoria, the provincial capital at the island's southern tip, and the rural Gulf Islands sprinkled off the mainland side have long attracted escapists of every kind. These days, though, travelers are also seeking out the deep, temperate rain forests and dramatic beaches of the island's west coast, as well as the migrating whales to be seen here. The mainland coast to the north of Vancouver can only be reached by ferry or floatplane.

Most of British Columbia's population clusters in a region known as the Lower Mainland, in and around Vancouver in the southwest corner of the province. From here, three highways and a rail line climb over the Coast Mountains to the rolling high plateau that forms the central interior. To the north are the Cariboo ranch country and, beyond that, the vast, sparsely inhabited northern half of the province. To the east are the Okanagan and Shuswap valleys, which hold the province's fruit- and wine-growing region and its lake district. Farther east are the mountainous Kootenays and the Columbia and Rocky mountains, where small towns hunker in valleys below the craggy peaks.

Amid the parallel mountain ranges of the Rockies and the Columbias, the national parks are somewhat far flung and the towns tend toward the functional rather than the touristy. Distances are great here, so you should allow plenty of time for driving from destination to destination. When you travel by car, keep in mind that more than three-quarters of British Columbia is mountainous terrain, which can be difficult to traverse in winter. Many areas, including most of the west coast of Vancouver Island, have no roads at all and are accessible only by air or sea.

Numbers in the text correspond to numbers in the margin and on the Southern British Columbia, Downtown Victoria, Vancouver Island, and British Columbia Rockies maps.

Great Itineraries

British Columbia is about the size of Western Europe, with as much geographical variety and substantially fewer roads. The good news is that many great sights, stunning scenery, and even wilderness lie within a few days' tour of Vancouver or the U.S. border.

IF YOU HAVE 1–3 DAYS

For a short trip, ⊡ **Victoria** ①–⑬ is a fine place to begin. There's plenty to explore, from the flower-fringed Inner Harbour and the museums and attractions nearby to Bastion Square and the red gates of Chinatown. World-famous Butchart Gardens is only half an hour away by car, and you might take a full day to explore the beautiful grounds. On Day 3, head out to ⊡ **Sooke** ⑭ or to one of the Gulf Islands—⊡ **Galiano** ㉘, ⊡ **Mayne** ㉙, or ⊡ **Salt Spring** ㉚—to stay at a romantic country inn for a night.

A mainland alternative is to take the Coast Mountain Circle tour, driving north from Vancouver to the resort town of ⊡ **Whistler** ㉛ and over the scenic Duffy Lake Road to the gold-rush town of **Lillooet.** You can then return to Vancouver through the steep gorges of the **Fraser Canyon,** with stops at Hell's Gate on the Fraser River and ⊡ **Harrison Hot Springs** ㉜.

IF YOU HAVE 4–6 DAYS

A brief stay in ⊡ **Victoria** ①–⑬ can be followed by either a tour of Vancouver Island or a drive into the mainland. If you plan to stay on Vancouver Island, Day 4 allows time to see the Cowichan Native Village in **Duncan** ⑮ and the murals and restored Victorian buildings of ⊡ **Chemainus** ⑯. On Day 5, one alternative is to trek across the island to the scenic west coast to visit ⊡ **Ucluelet** ⑲ and ⊡ **Tofino** ⑳ (pick one for your overnight) and spend some time whale-watching or hiking around **Pacific Rim National Park Reserve** ㉑. Another choice is to continue up the east coast to do some salmon fishing in ⊡ **Campbell River** ㉓ or to visit ⊡ **Port Hardy** ㉕ to see the resident whale pods near Telegraph Cove.

If you've gone the eastern route, Day 6 will take you by ferry from 🔟 **Comox** ㉒ across the Strait of Georgia to **Powell River** ㉗ on the Sunshine Coast. Ferries and short highway jaunts will carry you down the scenic coast to Vancouver. If you've crossed to Vancouver's west coast, you can spend Day 6 backtracking to **Victoria** or making your way to **Nanaimo** ⑰ to catch the ferry to Vancouver and the mainland. A mainland itinerary takes you from Victoria to one of the Gulf Islands on Day 4, then along the Coast Mountain Circle on Days 5 and 6.

IF YOU HAVE 7–10 DAYS

A longer trip will allow time to see Vancouver Island, as described above, then cruise the breathtaking **Inside Passage** ㉝ from Port Hardy to 🔟 **Prince Rupert** ㉟, where you can catch another ferry to see the old-growth forest and abandoned Haida villages of the 🔟 **Queen Charlotte Islands (Haida Gwaii)** ㊱. From Port Hardy you could also take the scenic **Discovery Coast Passage** ㉞ to Bella Coola. You can then complete the circle back to **Vancouver** by air, ferry, road, or, from Prince Rupert, train.

Another option, after a visit to Vancouver Island, is to tour British Columbia's mainland. Day 7 takes you into the interior, either over the mountains via 🔟 **Whistler** ㉛ and **Lillooet,** or through the **Fraser Canyon.** A good choice for Days 8–10 is to make the loop through the Okanagan Valley, the fruit-growing and wine-producing region of the province. You can make stops in 🔟 **Kamloops** ㊳ to fish or visit the Secwepemc Native Heritage Museum, **Vernon** ㊵ to enjoy the O'Keefe Historic Ranch, or 🔟 **Kelowna** ㊶ or 🔟 **Penticton** ㊷ to relax at a beach or tour the vineyards.

If you want to head to the Rockies, 🔟 **Kimberley** ㊺ and 🔟 **Radium Hot Springs** ㊽ make convenient overnight stops. Spend Days 7–10 visiting mountain highlights such as **Mt. Revelstoke National Park** ㊾ (overnight in 🔟 **Revelstoke** ㊿), 🔟 **Glacier National Park** ㊼, and the town of 🔟 **Golden** ㊿. In **Yoho National Park,** visit the famous **Burgess Shale** ㊾ fossil beds.

When to Tour British Columbia

The coast and islands, touched by Pacific currents, have relatively mild winters and summers (usually above 32°F in winter, below 80°F in summer), although winter brings frequent rains. The North Coast, Queen Charlotte Islands, and the west coast of Vancouver Island can be wet year-round. The interior is drier, with greater extremes, including hot summers and reliably snowy winters. Temperatures here drop below freezing in winter and sometimes reach 90°F in summer.

During summer, main attractions can be crowded, while in winter, some tourist facilities close down. Although the weather is best during the mid-June–mid-September period, you can avoid crowds and make substantial savings on lodgings by scheduling your visit outside this period. Check on rates, though, as many hotel operators are now aware that they can keep rates high from mid-May to early October and still fill their rooms.

VICTORIA

Originally Fort Victoria, Victoria was the first European settlement on Vancouver Island and is the oldest city on Canada's west coast. It was chosen in 1843 by James Douglas to be the Hudson's Bay Company's westernmost outpost, and it became the capital of British Columbia in 1868. The city has since evolved into a walkable, livable seaside town of gardens, waterfront walks, and restored 19th-century architecture. Victoria is often (some say too often) called the most British city in

Canada. These days, though, except for the odd red phone box, good beer, and well-mannered drivers, this very Canadian town is working to shed its tea-cozy image, preferring to celebrate its combined native, Asian, and European heritage.

After dark, there are more than enough quasi-British pubs in which to watch a hockey game, but Victoria also has thriving dining, music, art, and theater scenes, all on an accessible scale. A visit to the stunning Butchart Gardens (☞ Side Trip from Victoria, *below*), north of the city, is a great way to enjoy the area's outdoors.

The city is 71 km (44 mi), and about three hours by car and ferry, south of Vancouver; it's about 2½ hours by high-speed passenger ferry from Seattle. A bylaw bans smoking in all Victoria public places, including hotels, restaurants, and pubs.

Downtown Victoria

Great waterfront views, historic buildings, funky shopping areas, lush gardens, and fine museums are the highlights of a visit to Victoria's walkable downtown.

A Good Walk and Tour

For some wonderful views, begin your tour of Victoria on the waterfront at the **Visitor Information Centre** ①. Just across the way is the **Empress** ②, a majestic railroad hotel that originally opened in 1908. A short walk around the harbor along the Inner Harbour Walk (take any of the staircases from Government Street down to the water level) will take you to the **Parliament Buildings** ③, seat of the provincial government. The colonnaded building to your right is the former train station, now a wax museum.

Follow Government Street four blocks south to **Emily Carr House** ④, the birthplace of one of British Columbia's best-known artists; then take Simcoe Street east to **Beacon Hill Park** ⑤, a beautiful green space. Follow Douglas Street north or wander through the park to Blanshard Street, where, just past Academy Close, you'll see the entrance to **St. Ann's Academy** ⑥, a former convent school with parklike grounds. (There's also a footpath to the academy from Southgate Street.) From St. Ann's, follow Belleville Street west. The next stop, at the corner of Douglas and Belleville streets, is the glass-roofed **Crystal Garden** ⑦, a former swimming pool where you can see 75 varieties of tropical flowers, birds, and mammals. Across Douglas Street is the **Royal British Columbia Museum** ⑧, one of the most impressive museums in Canada. Just behind the museum and bordering Douglas Street is Thunderbird Park, where totem poles and a ceremonial longhouse stand in one corner of the garden of **Helmcken House,** the oldest house in British Columbia.

From Helmcken House, continue five blocks north on Douglas Street to View Street and turn left, walking three blocks to **Bastion Square** ⑨, with its restaurants, cobblestone streets, and small shops. While you're here, you can stop in at the **Maritime Museum of British Columbia** ⑩ and learn about an important part of the province's history. Just around the corner on Wharf Street is the **Victoria Bug Zoo,** a creepy-crawly attraction popular with kids. North of Bastion Square, west of Government Street between Johnson Street and Pandora Avenue, is **Market Square** ⑪, one of the most picturesque shopping districts in the city. You can then cross Pandora Avenue and walk up the narrow, shop-lined Fan Tan Alley to Fisgard Street, the heart of **Chinatown** ⑫.

A 25-minute walk or a short drive east on Fort Street will take you to Joan Crescent and lavish **Craigdarroch Castle** ⑬ and, five minutes down the hill on Moss Street, to the **Art Gallery of Greater Victoria.** In summer, a ride on Victoria Harbour Ferries (☞ Victoria Essentials, *below*) from the Inner Harbour will take you to **Point Ellice House,** a historic waterside home and garden.

TIMING

Many sights are within easy walking distance of one another, but there's so much to see at the Royal British Columbia Museum and the other museums that you could easily fill two days. This would allow time for some shopping and visiting Craigdarroch Castle, too. The walk alone takes about 1½ hours.

Sights to See

Art Gallery of Greater Victoria. This fine museum is home to large collections of Chinese and Japanese ceramics and other art and to the only authentic Shinto shrine in North America. The gallery also has a permanent exhibit of British Columbia native Emily Carr's work and numerous temporary exhibitions yearly. It's a few blocks west of Craigdarroch Castle (☞ *below*), off Fort Street. ⊠ *1040 Moss St.,* ☎ *250/384–4101.* ☞ *$5; Mon. by donation.* ☺ *Mon.–Wed. and Fri.–Sat. 10–5, Thurs. 10–9, Sun. 1–5.*

➒ **Bastion Square.** James Douglas chose this spot for the original Fort Victoria in 1843 and the original Hudson's Bay Company trading post. Today boutiques and restaurants occupy the old buildings.

★ ☝ ➎ **Beacon Hill Park.** The southern lawns of this spacious haven for joggers, walkers, and cyclists have one of the best views of the Olympic Mountains and the Strait of Juan de Fuca. The park has lakes, walking paths, gardens, a wading pool, a petting zoo, a cricket pitch, and an outdoor amphitheater for Sunday afternoon concerts. It is also home to the world's tallest freestanding totem pole (127 ft) and to Mile Zero of the Trans-Canada Highway. ⊠ *East of Douglas St.*

⑫ **Chinatown.** The Chinese built much of the Canadian Pacific Railway in the 19th century, and their influences still mark the region. If you enter Chinatown (one of the oldest in Canada) from Government Street, you'll walk under the elaborate **Gate of Harmonious Interest,** made from Taiwanese ceramic tiles and decorative panels. Along the street, merchants display paper lanterns, silks, fruits, and vegetables. **Fan Tan Alley,** off Fisgard Street, holds claim not only to being the narrowest street in Canada but also to having been the gambling and opium center of Chinatown. Look for it between Numbers 545½ and 549½ on the south side of the street.

⑬ **Craigdarroch Castle.** This magnificent mansion was built as the home of one of British Columbia's wealthiest men, coal baron Robert Dunsmuir, who died in 1889 just a few months before its completion. Converted into a museum depicting turn-of-the-century life, the castle has ornate Victorian furnishings, stained-glass windows, carved woodwork (precut in Chicago for Dunsmuir and sent by train), and a beautifully restored ceiling frieze in the drawing room. A winding staircase climbs four floors to a ballroom and a tower overlooking Victoria and the Olympic Mountains. ⊠ *1050 Joan Crescent,* ☎ *250/592–5323.* ☞ *$7.50.* ☺ *Mid-June–early Sept., daily 9–7; mid-Sept.–mid-June, daily 10–4:30.*

Southern British Columbia

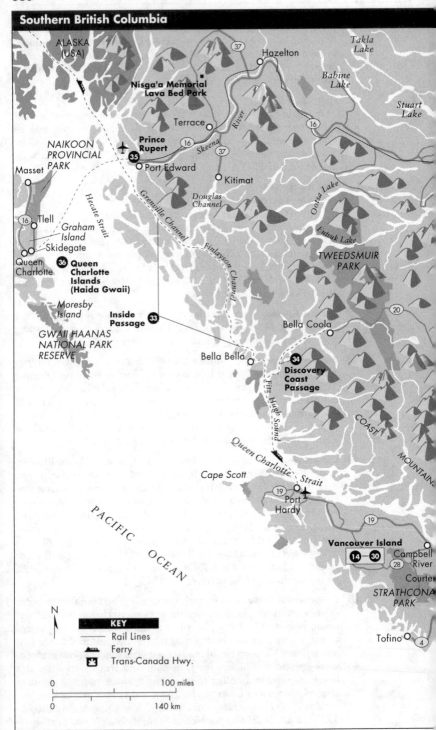

ALASKA
(USA)

Takla
Lake

Hazelton

Babine
Lake

Nisga'a Memorial
Lava Bed Park

Stuart
Lake

Terrace

16

Skeena River

37

Prince
Rupert

35

16

Port Edward

Kitimat

Douglas
Channel

Ootsa Lake

Eutsuk Lake

TWEEDSMUIR
PARK

Masset

NAIKOON
PROVINCIAL
PARK

Hecate Strait

Grenville Channel

16

Tlell

Graham
Island

Skidegate

Finlayson Channel

Queen
Charlotte

36

Queen
Charlotte
Islands
(Haida Gwaii)

20

Moresby
Island

Inside
Passage

33

Bella Coola

GWAII HAANAS
NATIONAL PARK
RESERVE

Bella Bella

34

Discovery
Coast
Passage

COAST

Fitz Hugh Sound

MOUNTAINS

Queen Charlotte Strait

Cape Scott

19

Port
Hardy

19

PACIFIC OCEAN

Vancouver Island

14 — 30

Campbell
River

28

Courtenay

STRATHCONA
PARK

Tofino

4

N

KEY
— Rail Lines
⚓ Ferry
🍁 Trans-Canada Hwy.

0   100 miles
0   140 km

Downtown Victoria

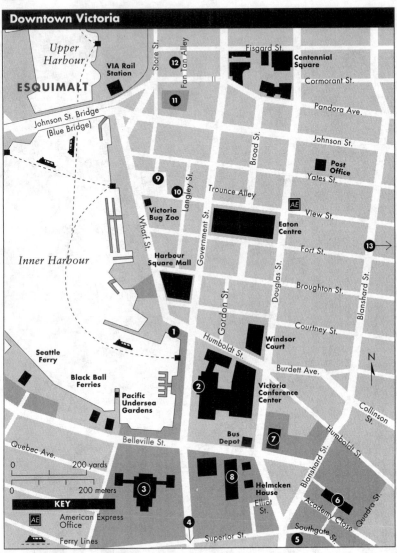

Bastion Square, **9**

Beacon Hill Park, **5**

Chinatown, **12**

Craigdarroch
Castle, **13**

Crystal Gardens
Conservatory, **7**

Emily Carr House, **4**

Empress Hotel, **2**

Maritime Museum of
British Columbia, **10**

Market Square, **11**

Parliament
Buildings, **3**

Royal British
Columbia Museum, **8**

St. Ann's Academy, **6**

Visitor Information
Centre, **1**

OFF THE
BEATEN PATH **CRAIGFLOWER MANOR –** This historic site has an 1853 Georgian-style manor and the first farm on Vancouver Island. It's about 10 km (6 mi) west of Victoria off Highway 1A. ✉ *2709 Shoreline Dr.,* ☎ *250/383–4627.* 🎫 *Manor and schoolhouse $5.* ⊙ *Mid-June–early Sept., daily noon–4.*

⑦ **Crystal Garden.** Opened in 1925 as the largest saltwater swimming pool in the British Empire, this glass-roof building, owned by the provincial government, now serves as a home for exotic flora and endangered tropical mammals, reptiles, and birds, including flamingos, tortoises, macaws, lemurs, bats, and, in summer, butterflies. ✉ *713 Douglas St.,* ☎ *250/381–1213.* 🎫 *$7.* ⊙ *Daily; call for seasonal hrs.*

④ **Emily Carr House.** Emily Carr (1871–1945), one of Canada's most celebrated artists and a respected writer as well, was born and raised in this very proper wooden Victorian house before she abandoned her middle-class life to live in, and paint, the wilds of British Columbia. Carr's own descriptions, from her autobiography, *Book of the Small,* were used to restore the house. ✉ *207 Government St.,* ☎ *250/383–5843.* 🎫 *$5.* ⊙ *Mid-May–mid-Oct., daily 10–5; Dec., daily 11–4. At other times, tours by prearrangement.*

★ ② **The Empress.** Originally opened in 1908, the Empress is a symbol of both the city and the Canadian Pacific Railway. Designed by Francis Rattenbury, who also designed the Parliament Buildings (☞ *below*), the property is another of the great châteaus built by Canadian Pacific, still the owners. The ingredients that made the 460-room hotel a tourist attraction in the past—Old World architecture and ornate decor, a commanding view of the Inner Harbour—are still here. Stop in for afternoon tea, served at hour-and-a-half intervals during the afternoon (a dress code calls for smart-casual wear, and reservations are recommended). Hotel staff run tours daily at 10 AM in summer, and the archives, a historical photo display, are open to the public anytime. **Miniature World** (☎ 250/385–9731), a display of doll-size dioramas including one of the world's longest model railroads, is on the Humboldt Street side. ✉ *721 Government St.,* ☎ *250/384–8111.* 🎫 *Free; historical tours $6; afternoon tea $21; Miniature World $8.*

OFF THE
BEATEN PATH **FORT RODD HILL AND FISGARD LIGHTHOUSE –** An 1895 coastal artillery fort and the oldest (and still functioning) lighthouse on Canada's west coast are National Historic Sites. Next door is Hatley Castle, a Victorian mansion and former military college. The grounds are open to the public. These sites are about 15 km (9 mi) west of Victoria, off Highway 1A. ✉ *603 Fort Rodd Hill Rd.,* ☎ *250/478–5849.* 🎫 *$3.* ⊙ *Mar.–Oct., daily 10–5:30; Nov.–Feb., daily 9–4:30.*

Helmcken House. The oldest house in British Columbia, built in 1852 by pioneer doctor and statesman John Sebastian Helmcken, is a treasure trove of history, from the early Victorian furnishings to an unnerving collection of 19th-century medical tools. Audio tours last 20 minutes. Next door is **St. Ann's Schoolhouse,** one of the first schools in British Columbia (not open to the public). **Thunderbird Park,** with totem poles and a ceremonial longhouse constructed by Kwakiutl chief Mungo Martin, occupies one corner of the garden; it's part of the ☞ **Royal British Columbia Museum.** ✉ *10 Elliot St.,* ☎ *250/361–0021.* 🎫 *$4.* ⊙ *May–Sept., daily 10–5; Feb.–Apr. and Oct.–mid-Nov., Thurs.–Mon. 11–4; call for special Christmas programs.*

⑩ **Maritime Museum of British Columbia.** Dugout canoes, model ships, Royal Navy charts, photographs, uniforms, and ship's bells, now housed in Victoria's original courthouse, chronicle the province's seafaring history. A seldom-used 100-year-old birdcage elevator, believed to be the oldest in North America, ascends to the third floor, where an 1888 vice-admiralty courtroom looks set for a court-martial. ☒ *28 Bastion Sq.,* ☎ *250/385–4222.* 🎟 *$5.* ⊘ *Daily 9:30–4:30.*

⑪ **Market Square.** During Victoria's late-19th-century heyday, this two-level square, built like an old inn courtyard, provided everything a sailor, miner, or up-country lumberjack could want. Now, beautifully restored to its original architectural, if not commercial, character, it's a traffic-free, café- and boutique-lined hangout—now, as then, a great spot for people-watching. ☒ *West of Government St. between Johnson St. and Pandora Ave.*

★ ❸ **Parliament Buildings.** These massive stone structures, designed by Francis Rattenbury and completed in 1898, are flanked by statues of two men: Sir James Douglas, who chose the site where Victoria was built, and Sir Matthew Baille Begbie, the man in charge of law and order during the gold-rush era. Atop the central dome is a gilded statue of Captain George Vancouver, the first European to sail around Vancouver Island. A statue of Queen Victoria stands in front of the complex; more than 3,000 lights outline the buildings at night. When the legislature is in session, you can sit in the public gallery and watch British Columbian democracy at work (tradition has the opposing parties sitting 2½ sword lengths apart). Free, informative half-hour tours are obligatory on summer weekends and optional the rest of the time. ☒ *501 Belleville St.,* ☎ *250/387–3046.* 🎟 *Free.* ⊘ *June–Aug., daily 9–5; Sept.–May, weekdays 8:30–5.*

Point Ellice House. The restored O'Reilly family home, an 1867 Italianate villa overlooking the Upper Harbour, holds the largest collection of Victorian furnishings in western Canada. Tea, served with home-baked goodies, is again served on the lawn. You can also take an audio tour of the house, stroll in the gardens, or try your hand at croquet. Point Ellice House is a few minutes' drive north of downtown, but it's much more fun to come by sea. Victoria Harbour Ferries (☞ Getting Around *in* Victoria Essentials, *below*) leave from a dock in front of the Empress hotel. ☒ *2616 Pleasant St.,* ☎ *250/380–6506.* 🎟 *$4; tea $13.* ⊘ *Mid-May–mid-Sept., daily 10–5. Tea served daily noon–4; reservations recommended. Also open for Halloween and Christmas events.*

★ ☾ ❽ **Royal British Columbia Museum.** The museum, easily the best attraction in Victoria, is as much a research and educational center as a draw for the public. The definitive First Peoples exhibit includes a genuine Kwakwaka'wakw longhouse (the builders retain rights to its ceremonial use) and provides insights into the daily life, art, and mythology of both coastal and lesser-known interior peoples, before and after the arrival of Europeans. The Modern History Gallery re-creates most of a frontier town, complete with cobblestone streets, silent movies, and rumbling train sounds. The Natural History Gallery realistically reproduces the sights, sounds, and smells of many of the province's natural habitats, and the Open Ocean mimics, all too realistically, a submarine journey. An on-site IMAX theater shows National Geographic films on a six-story-high screen. ☒ *675 Belleville St.,* ☎ *250/387–3701 or 800/661–5411.* 🎟 *$8, some surcharges for special exhibits; IMAX theater $9.* ⊘ *Museum daily 9–5; theater daily 10–8.*

❻ **St. Ann's Academy.** This former convent and school, founded in 1858, played a central role in Victoria's pioneer life. Closed in 1974, it was restored and reopened as a historic site in 1997. The academy's little chapel, the first Roman Catholic cathedral in Victoria, now looks just as it did in the 1920s. The 6-acre grounds, with their fruit trees and herb and flower gardens, are also being restored as historic landscapes. ⊠ *835 Humboldt St.,* ☎ *250/386–1428.* 🎟 *Free.* ⊘ *July–Aug., daily 10–4; May–June and Sept.–Oct., Wed.–Sun. 10–4. Call for winter hrs.*

☾ **Victoria Bug Zoo.** Kids love bugs, and this offbeat minizoo, opened in 1997, is drawing kids big and little to its two small rooms displaying at least 35 insects—mostly large tropical varieties such as stick insects, scorpions, and centipedes. Many bugs can be held, and staff are always on hand with scientific information. ⊠ *1107 Wharf St.,* ☎ *250/ 384–2847.* 🎟 *$6.* ⊘ *Daily 9:30–6.*

❶ **Visitor Information Centre.** The friendly staff here can help you out with maps, theater and concert tickets, room reservations, and outdoor adventure day trips. ⊠ *812 Wharf St.,* ☎ *250/953–2033.* ⊘ *July–Aug., daily 8:30–8; May–June and Sept., daily 9–7; Oct.–Apr., daily 9–5.*

Dining

$$$$ ✕ **Empress Room.** A fireside table in the elegant restaurant of the Em-
★ press hotel is one choice for a special-occasion dinner. Innovative and beautifully presented Pacific Northwest cuisine vies for attention with the setting when candlelight dances on the tapestried walls. Fresh local ingredients go into seasonal dishes such as wild mushroom and chicken terrine, veal tenderloin with wild rice–herb crust and black currant sauce, and Fraser Valley smoked marinated duck breast. The wine list is excellent, as are the popular table d'hôte menus. ⊠ *The Empress, 721 Government St.,* ☎ *250/389–2727 or 800/644–6611. Reservations essential. AE, D, DC, MC, V. No lunch.*

$$$–$$$$ ✕ **Camille's.** Quiet and intimate, Camille's is tucked away in a historic
★ building off Bastion Square. The menu concentrates on fresh local products, and such exotica as ostrich, quail, and emu often appear, too. These, and popular dishes like roast venison with wild mushroom polenta and grainy Dijon-and-mint-crusted lamb, are served in generous portions. The 300-variety wine list is one of the island's best. ⊠ *45 Bastion Sq.,* ☎ *250/381–3433. AE, MC, V. No lunch.*

$$$–$$$$ ✕ **Il Terrazzo.** A charming redbrick terrace edged by potted greenery
★ and warmed by fireplaces and overhead heaters makes Il Terrazzo— tucked away off Waddington Alley near Market Square and not visible from the street—the locals' choice for romantic alfresco dining. Scallops dipped in roasted pistachios and garnished with arugula, Belgian endive, and mango salsa; grilled lamb chops on angel-hair pasta with tomatoes, garlic, mint, and black pepper; and other hearty northern Italian dishes come piping hot from the restaurant's wood oven. ⊠ *555 Johnson St., off Waddington Alley (call for directions),* ☎ *250/ 361–0028. Reservations essential. AE, MC, V. No lunch Sun., no lunch Sat. mid-Oct.–mid-Apr.*

$$–$$$$ ✕ **Café Brio.** A little north of the Inner Harbour, a building resembling
★ an Italian villa is the setting for one of Victoria's most enjoyable restaurants. Candlelight, hardwood floors, lush Modigliani nudes, and rich gold walls create a warm glow. The daily menu depends on what's fresh that day. Very fresh—the café works in partnership with a local organic farm and serves the produce the same day it's harvested. Favorites have included confit of duck with three-bean, pancetta, and tomato braise, and a melt-in-the-mouth lamb sirloin with leeks and chanterelles. The vegetarian options are always good, and the extensive wine list goes easy on the markups. ⊠ *944 Fort St.,* ☎ *250/383–0009. AE, MC, V. No lunch weekends.*

$$–$$$$ ✕ **Marina Restaurant.** This lovely, round restaurant with deep semicircular booths and a 180-degree view over the Oak Bay Marina is pop-

ular with locals and visitors alike. The extensive menu usually lists creative appetizers such as warm salmon and spinach salad and a variety of pastas, grills, and seafood entrées. If you don't have reservations and the dining room and sushi bar are full, head downstairs to the Café Deli for picnic foods to eat on the patio or take out. The Marina is also a prime spot for Sunday brunch. ⊠ *1327 Beach Dr.,* ☎ *250/598–8555. AE, DC, MC, V.*

$$–$$$ ✕ **Don Mee's.** A large neon sign invites you inside this traditional Chinese restaurant, with its long staircase that leads to an expansive, comfortable dining room. Some of the Szechuan and Cantonese entrées are sweet-and-sour chicken, Peking duck, and bean curd with broccoli. Dim sum is served daily during lunch hours. ⊠ *538 Fisgard St.,* ☎ *250/383–1032. AE, DC, MC, V.*

$$–$$$ ✕ **Herald Street Caffe.** An established favorite, this jazz- and art-filled
★ bistro in Victoria's warehouse district has been open since 1982. Inventive taste combinations and intriguing Asian touches are notable on a menu that changes seasonally but always lists fresh local cuisine, daily fish grills, great pastas, and good vegetarian selections. Try, if available, either calamari in tomato-dill ratatouille with crumbled feta or free-range beef tenderloin stuffed with a wild mushroom chestnut pâté. The wine list is excellent and the staff knowledgeable. ⊠ *546 Herald St.,* ☎ *250/381–1441. Reservations essential. AE, DC, MC, V. No lunch Mon.–Tues.*

$$–$$$ ✕ **Le Petit Saigon.** An intimate café-style restaurant offers quiet dining with beautifully presented Vietnamese fare with a touch of French influence. The crab, asparagus, and egg swirl soup is a specialty, and combination meals are a good value and tasty. ⊠ *1010 Langley St.,* ☎ *250/386–1412. AE, MC, V. No lunch Sun.*

$$–$$$ ✕ **Siam Thai.** The Thai chefs here work wonders with both hot and mild Thai dishes. The *phad Thai goong* (fried rice noodles with prawns, tofu, peanuts, eggs, bean sprouts, and green onions) and *satays* (grilled, marinated cubes of meat served with a spicy peanut sauce) are good options. This family-run restaurant is spacious and conveniently near the Inner Harbour. Its well-stocked bar has a variety of beers. ⊠ *512 Fort St.,* ☎ *250/383–9911. AE, DC, MC, V. No lunch Sun.*

$–$$ ✕ **Re-Bar Modern Foods.** Bright and casual, this kid-friendly café in Bastion Square is *the* place for vegetarians in Victoria, although the almond burgers, wild mushroom ravioli, decadent home-baked goodies, and big breakfasts will keep omnivores happy, too. A large selection of teas and fresh juices shares space with espresso, microbrews, and local wines on the drinks list. ⊠ *50 Bastion Sq.,* ☎ *250/361–9223. AE, DC, MC, V.*

$ ✕ **Barb's Place.** This funky, blue-painted take-out shack is on Fisherman's Wharf, on the south side of Victoria Harbour just off Erie Street, where the fishing boats come in. It has become an institution in Victoria, and locals consider the authentic fish-and-chips (halibut) to be the best. You can catch a ferry to Fisherman's Wharf from the Inner Harbour, pick up an order, and take another ferry to Songhees Point for a picnic. ⊠ *310 St. Lawrence St.,* ☎ *250/384–6515. No credit cards. Closed Nov.–Mar.*

Lodging

$$$$ ▥ **The Aerie.** The million-dollar view of Finlayson Arm and the Gulf
★ Islands persuaded Maria Schuster to build her luxury resort here, 30 km (19 mi) north of Victoria. Ten acres of parkland surround the sprawling Mediterranean-style villa, in which most rooms have a patio, a fireplace, and a whirlpool tub. Three large suites have leather sleigh beds, gas fireplaces, soaker tubs, steam showers, and balconies. The dining

room is open to the public from 6 PM for stunning views and outstanding cuisine. The herb-crusted pheasant breast and the chanterelle, potato, and rosemary bisque are worth the drive from Victoria. A full breakfast is included, and a full-service Aveda spa adds to guests' comfort. ✉ *600 Ebedora La., Box 108, Malahat V0R 2L0,* ☎ *250/743–7115 or 800/518–1933,* FAX *250/743–4766. 11 rooms, 12 suites. Restaurant, lounge, fans, indoor pool, indoor and outdoor hot tubs, sauna, spa, tennis court, hiking, library, meeting rooms, helipad. AE, DC, MC, V.*

$$$$ 🏨 **Beaconsfield Inn.** Built in 1905, the Beaconsfield has retained its Old World charm. Mahogany appears throughout the house; down comforters and canopy beds adorn some rooms, reinforcing its Edwardian style. Some rooms have fireplaces and whirlpool baths. Added pluses are the guest library and the conservatory-sunroom. Full breakfast and afternoon tea are included in the room rates. The inn is on a quiet residential street nine blocks from the Inner Harbour. The owners also operate a newer one-bedroom beach cottage about 10 minutes away. ✉ *998 Humboldt St., V8V 2Z8,* ☎ *250/384–4044,* FAX *250/384–4052. 5 rooms, 4 suites. Breakfast room, library, free parking. MC, V.*

$$$$ 🏨 **The Empress.** For titled ladies, empire builders, movie stars, and a
★ great many others, the exquisitely comfortable Empress (☞ Downtown Victoria, *above*) is the only place to stay in Victoria. Opened in 1908, this Canadian Pacific château has aged gracefully, with sympathetically restored Edwardian decor, discreet modern amenities, and service standards from a more gracious age. Nonguests can stop by the Empress for a traditional afternoon tea, meet for a curry buffet under the tiger skin in the Bengal Lounge, or sample superb regional cuisine in the Empress Room (☞ Dining, *above*). ✉ *721 Government St., V8W 1W5,* ☎ *250/384–8111 or 800/441–1414,* FAX *250/381–4334. 474 rooms, 36 suites. 2 restaurants, lounge, fans, minibars, room service, indoor pool, wading pool, hot tub, sauna, exercise room, laundry service and dry cleaning, concierge, concierge floor, business services, convention center, parking (fee). AE, D, DC, MC, V.*

$$$$ 🏨 **Ocean Pointe Resort Hotel and Spa.** Across the "blue bridge" (John-
★ son Street Bridge) from downtown Victoria, the waterfront Ocean Pointe has a resort's worth of pampering amenities, including a full European aesthetics spa. The hotel's striking two-story lobby and half of its guest rooms have views of the Inner Harbour and the lights of the Parliament Buildings across the water. Standard rooms are spacious and airy, decorated in rich greens and burgundies and dark woods, and the apartment-size suites have kitchenettes and separate living and dining areas. The Victoria restaurant serves fine Pacific Northwest cuisine in a scenic setting. The Ocean Pointe offers some very deep discounts in the off-season. ✉ *45 Songhees Rd., V9A 6T3,* ☎ *250/ 360–2999 or 800/667–4677,* FAX *250/360–5856. 212 rooms, 34 suites. 2 restaurants, lounge, in-room data ports, minibars, room service, indoor pool, hot tub, sauna, spa, 2 tennis courts, health club, jogging, racquetball, squash, shops, baby-sitting, laundry service and dry cleaning, concierge, business services, meeting rooms, travel services, airport shuttle, parking (fee). AE, DC, MC, V.*

$$$–$$$$ 🏨 **Abigail's Hotel.** A Tudor-style inn built in 1930, Abigail's is both
★ lovely and convenient—it's within walking distance of the shops and restaurants downtown. Guest rooms are attractively furnished in an English Arts and Crafts style, and down comforters, together with whirlpool tubs and fireplaces in many, add to the pampering atmosphere. Six large rooms in the new (1998) Coach House building are especially lavish, with king-size four-poster beds. All of Abigail's rooms have phones but, for romance's sake, no TVs. A lavish hot breakfast is included (breakfast in bed is an option), and in the evening guests can gather for sherry

and hors d'oeuvres by the fire in the library. ⊠ *906 McClure St., V8V 3E7,* ☏ *250/388–5363 or 800/561–6565,* FAX *250/388–7787. 22 rooms. Breakfast room, library, laundry service and dry cleaning, concierge, free parking. AE, MC, V.*

$$–$$$$ 🏨 **Laurel Point Inn.** Set on a parklike 6-acre peninsula in the Inner Harbour, a few minutes' walk from the Victoria Clipper dock and the town center, this modern resort and convention hotel has water views from every room. The decor, especially in the newer, Arthur Erickson–designed suites, is modern, light, and airy, with a strong Asian influence. Historic Chinese art decorates many public areas, and the Terrace Room lounge looks out over a Japanese garden. Most rooms are wheelchair accessible; all have balconies, hair dryers, and coffeemakers. ⊠ *680 Montreal St., V8V 1Z8,* ☏ *250/386–8721 or 800/663–7667,* FAX *250/386–9547. 120 rooms, 80 suites. Restaurant, 2 lounges, room service, indoor pool, sauna, hot tub, laundry service and dry cleaning, business services, meeting rooms, free parking. AE, DC, MC, V.*

$$–$$$$ 🏨 **Prior House Bed & Breakfast Inn.** This beautifully restored 1912 manor home, on a quiet street near Craigdarroch Castle, was originally built for the king's representative in British Columbia. Guests can relax on flower-decked terraces overlooking a pretty garden; a library and two parlors have antique furniture, leaded-glass windows, and oak paneling. Guest rooms, all with TVs and fireplaces and some with whirlpool tubs, vary from cozy to opulent. The Garden Suite, with a private entrance, two bedrooms, and a full kitchen, is an especially good value. A lavish breakfast and afternoon tea are included. ⊠ *620 St. Charles St., V8S 3N7,* ☏ *250/592–8847,* FAX *250/592–8223. 4 rooms, 2 suites. Breakfast room, refrigerators, library, free parking. MC, V.*

$$$ 🏨 **Swans.** When English-born shepherd Michael Williams bought supplies for his kennel at the Buckerfield Company Feed Store during the 1950s, he never dreamed he would one day own the building and turn it into a waterfront hotel. Extensive renovations have given the 1913 brick warehouse a new look: there's a brewery, bistro, and pub on the first floor and a jazz bar in the cellar; large, apartment-like suites with full kitchens and Pacific Northwest art fill the upper floors. ⊠ *506 Pandora Ave., V8W 1N6,* ☏ *250/361–3310 or 800/668–7926,* FAX *250/361–3491. 5 studios, 11 1-bedroom suites, 13 2-bedroom suites. Restaurant, wine shop, room service, coin laundry, meeting rooms, parking (fee). AE, DC, MC, V.*

$$–$$$ 🏨 **Mulberry Manor.** The last building designed by Victoria architect
★ Samuel McClure has been restored and decorated to magazine-cover perfection with antiques, sumptuous linens, and tile baths. The Tudor-style mansion sits behind a high stone wall on an acre of carefully manicured grounds. Charming hosts Susan and Tony Temple serve expansive breakfasts with homemade jams, and sherry in the sitting room in the early evening. The inn is a five-minute drive from the Inner Harbour, among the mansions of the Rockland neighborhood. ⊠ *611 Foul Bay Rd., V8S 1H2,* ☏ *250/370–1918,* FAX *250/370–1968. 2 rooms, 1 suite. Breakfast room, free parking. MC, V.*

$$ 🏨 **Carberry Gardens.** A 1907 gambrel-roof, board-and-shingle home in the historic Rocklands neighborhood, Carberry Gardens is tucked away on a quiet lane just blocks from Craigdarroch Castle. Bright and airy, the house has a veranda and a striking 30-ft-high entryway. The pretty Victorian-themed guest rooms are stocked with bathrobes and sherry. One bedroom has a detached bathroom, but that bathroom is fun, with French doors that open to a little balcony. The inn has a guest pantry and a parlor with a fireplace and TV, and a three-course breakfast is included. ⊠ *1008 Carberry Gardens, V8S 3R7,* ☏ *250/595–8906,* FAX *250/595–8185. 3 rooms. Refrigerator. MC, V.*

$ 🏨 **The Cherry Bank.** Inside this 1897 Victorian house with a modern restaurant attached is a warren of red wallpapered corridors that give the place the look of a wholesome Wild West brothel. No matter—this wacky-looking budget hotel a few blocks from the Inner Harbour is clean and friendly and is a good value, especially for groups and families; one room has a kitchenette, and another is large enough to sleep six. There are no phones or TVs in the rooms, but a bacon-and-egg breakfast is included. ⊠ *825 Burdett Ave., V8W 1B3,* ☎ *250/385–5380,* FAX *250/383–0949. 25 rooms, 19 with bath; 1 suite. Restaurant, pub, free parking. AE, MC, V.*

Nightlife and the Arts

For entertainment listings, pick up a free copy of *Monday Magazine* (it comes out every Thursday) or call the Talking Yellow Pages (☎ 250/953–9000).

The Arts

MUSIC

The **Pacific Opera Victoria** (☎ 250/385–0222) stages three productions a year in the 900-seat McPherson Playhouse (⊠ 3 Centennial Sq., ☎ 250/386–6121), adjoining the Victoria City Hall. The **Victoria Symphony** (☎ 250/385–6515) has a winter schedule and a summer season, playing in the recently refurbished Royal Theatre (⊠ 805 Broughton St., ☎ 250/386–6121) and at the University Centre Auditorium (⊠ Finnerty Rd., ☎ 250/721–8480).

Thursday to Saturday, the **Millennium Jazz Club** (⊠ Under Swan's Hotel at 1601 Store St., ☎ 250/360–9098) has live music from big band to funk, bebop to rumba. The **TerriVic Jazz Party** (☎ 250/953–2011) showcases internationally acclaimed musicians every April. The **Victoria Jazz Society** (☎ 250/388–4423) organizes an annual JazzFest International in late June and the Vancouver Island Blues Bash, held every Labor Day weekend.

THEATER

Live productions can be seen at the **Belfry Theatre** (⊠ 1291 Gladstone Ave., ☎ 250/385–6815), **Langham Court Theatre** (⊠ 805 Langham Ct., ☎ 250/384–2142), **McPherson Playhouse** (⊠ 3 Centennial Sq., ☎ 250/386–6121), and the **Phoenix Theatre** (⊠ Finnerty Rd., ☎ 250/721–8000) at the University of Victoria.

Nightlife

Chic and arty **Hugo's** (⊠ Magnolia Hotel, 627 Courtney St., ☎ 250/920–4844) serves lunch, dinner, and four of its own brews. The **Planet** (⊠ 15 Bastion Sq., ☎ 250/385–2626) has live rock, blues, and jazz, DJs, and visits from internationally recognized bands. In addition to live music, darts, and brewery tours, **Spinnakers Brew Pub** (⊠ 308 Catherine St., ☎ 250/386–2739), a short ferry ride across the harbor, pours plenty of British Columbian microbrewery beer. **Steamers Public House** (⊠ 570 Yates St., ☎ 250/381–4340) has four pool tables and live music every night.

The **Strathcona Hotel** (⊠ 919 Douglas St., ☎ 250/383–7137) is something of an entertainment complex, with the Sticky Wicket Pub on the main floor and Legends nightclub in the basement. Its biggest draw, though, is the beach volleyball played on the roof in summer. **Swan's Pub** (⊠ 1601 Store St., ☎ 250/361–3310) is a popular brew pub and café with live folk and jazz five nights a week. For dancing to Top 40 tunes, head to **Sweetwater's** (⊠ 27–560 Johnson St., in Market Sq., ☎ 250/383–7844). **Uforia** (⊠ 1208 Wharf St., ☎ 250/381–2331) is a waterfront spot for dancing to today's hits.

Outdoor Activities and Sports

Golf

Golf Central provides a transportation and booking service for golfers all over southern Vancouver Island (☎ 250/380–4653). The **Cordova Bay Golf Course** (✉ 5333 Cordova Bay Rd., ☎ 250/658–4075) is an 18-hole, par-72 course set on the shoreline. The 18-hole, par-72 **Olympic View Golf Club** (✉ 643 Latoria Rd., ☎ 250/474–3673), 25 minutes from downtown, offers both challenging and forgiving tees and stunning views. Although the 18-hole, par-70 **Victoria Golf Club** (✉ 1110 Beach Dr., ☎ 250/598–4321) is private, it's open to other private-club members (have your pro shop book ahead); the windy course is the oldest (1893) in British Columbia and has spectacular views.

Hiking

The **Galloping Goose Regional Trail** (☎ 250/478–3344), an old railroad line reclaimed for walkers, cyclists, and equestrians, runs 100 scenic km (62 mi) from Swartz Bay through downtown Victoria and on to just east of Sooke. **Goldstream Provincial Park** (✉ Hwy. 1 at Finlayson Arm Rd., ☎ 250/478–9414), 19 km (12 mi) northwest of Victoria, has an extensive trail system, old-growth forest, waterfalls, a salt marsh, and a river. Park staff lead walks. Goldstream is a prime site for viewing bald eagles in December and January.

Swan Lake Christmas Hill Nature Sanctuary, a few miles from downtown, has a 23-acre lake set in 143 acres of fields and wetlands. From the 2½-km (1½-mi) trail and floating boardwalk, birders can spot a variety of waterfowl even in winter, as well as nesting birds in the tall grass. ✉ 3873 Swan Lake Rd. (Bus 26, 70, or 75), ☎ 250/479–0211. ▣ Free. ✆ Nature House weekdays 8:30–4, weekends noon–4.

Whale-Watching

To see the pods of orcas that travel in the waters around Vancouver Island, you can take charter boat tours from Victoria from May through October. Half-day tours in Zodiacs (motor-powered inflatable boats) and covered speed boats cost about $75–$80 per person. **Great Pacific Adventures** (☎ 250/386–2277), **Ocean Explorations** (☎ 250/383–6722), and **Seacoast Expeditions** (☎ 250/383–2254) are among the many operators in town. To book just about any kind of marine activity, including whale-watching, seaplane touring, fishing, and kayaking, contact the **Victoria Marine Adventure Centre** (✉ 950 Wharf St., ☎ 250/995–2211 or 800/575–6700). It's open May–September, daily 7 AM–10 PM; October–April, daily 9–5.

Shopping

Shopping Centers

For a wide selection, head to the larger shopping centers downtown, such as **Eaton Centre** (✉ 1 Victoria Eaton Centre, at Government and Fort Sts., ☎ 250/382–7141), a department store and mall with about 100 boutiques and restaurants. **Market Square** (✉ 560 Johnson St., ☎ 250/386–2441) has everything from fudge, music, and comic books to jewelry, local arts, and New Age accoutrements.

Specialty Stores

Shopping in Victoria is easy: Virtually everything can be found in the downtown area on or near Government Street stretching north from the Empress hotel. The city has more than 60 antiques shops, most of them along Fort Street between Blanshard and Cook streets, in a area known as Antique Row. You will also find antiques on the west side of Government Street near the Old Town.

The **Cowichan Trading Co., Ltd.** (⊠ 1328 Government St., ☎ 250/383–0321) sells native jewelry, art, moccasins, and Cowichan Indian sweaters. The **Fran Willis Gallery** (⊠ Upstairs, 1619 Store St., ☎ 250/381–3422) shows contemporary Canadian paintings and sculpture. **Hill's Indian Crafts** (⊠ 1008 Government St., ☎ 250/385–3911) has souvenirs and original West Coast native art. As the name suggests, **Irish Linen Stores** (⊠ 1019 Government St., ☎ 250/383–6812) stocks fine linen and lace items—hankies, napkins, tablecloths, and place mats. **Munro's Books** (⊠ 1108 Government St., ☎ 250/382–2464), in a 1909 building with a high ceiling, elaborate moldings, and murals, is one of Canada's prettiest bookstores, with a well-rounded selection. If the British spirit of Victoria has you searching for fine teas, head to **Murchie's** (⊠ 1110 Government St., ☎ 250/383–3112) for a choice of 40 varieties, plus coffees, tarts, and cakes. Original art and fine Canadian crafts are the focus at the **Northern Passage Gallery** (⊠ 1020 Government St., ☎ 250/381–3380).

Side Trip from Victoria

Butchart Gardens

★ *21 km (13 mi) north of downtown Victoria.*

Originally a private estate and still family-run, this stunning 50-acre garden has been drawing visitors since it was planted in a limestone quarry in 1904. The site's Japanese, Italian, rose, and sunken gardens now grow 700 varieties of flowers in a setting that looks beautiful year-round. Butchart is a display rather than a horticultural garden, but the knowledgeable staff can handle most gardening queries. From mid-June to mid-September many exhibits are illuminated at night, and musicians and other entertainers perform in the afternoons and evenings. In July and August, fireworks light the sky over the gardens every Saturday night; picnickers are welcome. Also on the premises are a conservatory, seed and gift shop, and restaurants. A million people visit every year, most on summer mornings. Come in the afternoon if you can. ⊠ *800 Benvenuto Ave., Brentwood Bay,* ☎ *250/652–5256 or 250/652–4422; 250/652–8222 for dining reservations.* 🖼 *$15.75; discounts in winter.* ⊙ *June 15–Sept. 4, daily 9 AM–10:30 PM; Sept. 5–Sept. 15, daily 9 AM–9 PM; Sept. 16–June 14, daily 9 AM–dusk.*

Victoria Essentials

Arriving and Departing

BY BUS

Pacific Coach Lines (☎ 250/385–4411 in Victoria; 604/662–8074 in Vancouver; 800/661–1725 elsewhere) operates daily service between downtown Vancouver and downtown Victoria on BC Ferries.

BY CAR

Highway 17 connects Swartz Bay ferry terminal on the Saanich Peninsula with downtown Victoria. **Highway 1** (also known as the Trans-Canada Highway) runs south from Nanaimo to Victoria. **Highway 14** connects Sooke and Port Renfrew, on the west coast of Vancouver Island, with Victoria.

BY FERRY

BC Ferries (☎ 250/386–3431 in Victoria or outside B.C.; 888/223–3779 from elsewhere in B.C.) provides frequent year-round passenger and vehicle service between Vancouver and Vancouver Island. The Vancouver terminal is in Tsawwassen, 38 km (24 mi) or about an hour's drive southwest of downtown at the end of Highway 17. In Victoria, ferries arrive at and depart from the Swartz Bay Terminal (30 minutes' drive from Victoria) at the end of Pat Bay Highway, 32 km (20 mi) north of downtown. Sailing time is 1 hour, 35 minutes. Fares vary by day and season but run about $40, one-way, for a car and driver ($9 for foot passenger). Vehicle reservations (☎ 888/724–5223 in B.C.; 604/444–2890 from outside the province) on Vancouver-to-Victoria routes are optional and a $15 reservation fee applies.

Year-round passenger-only service between Victoria and Seattle on jet catamarans is operated by **Clipper Navigation** (☎ 250/382–8100 in Victoria; 206/448–5000 in Seattle; 800/888–2535 elsewhere). Between mid-May and mid-September Clipper Navigation also provides direct passenger and vehicle service between Seattle and Victoria on the *Princess Marguerite III.* Reservations are advised on both services.

Black Ball Transport (☎ 250/386–2202; 360/457–4491 in the U.S.) operates a car ferry between Victoria and Port Angeles, Washington. **Washington State Ferries** (☎ 250/381–1551; 206/464–6400 in the U.S.; 888/808–7977 in WA only) cross daily, year-round, between Sidney, just north of Victoria, and Anacortes, Washington.

BY PLANE

Among the airlines serving **Victoria International Airport** (⊠ Willingdon Rd. off Hwy. 17, Sidney, ☎ 250/953–7500), Air B.C., Canadian Airlines, and Horizon Air (☞ Air Travel *in* Smart Travel Tips A to Z for telephone numbers) provide service between Vancouver, Seattle, and Victoria airports. The **Airporter** service (☎ 250/386–2525) leaves from the Empress and other downtown hotels and meets all flights at Victoria airport; fee is $13. **Taxi fare** to or from the airport is about $38.

West Coast Air (☎ 604/688–9115 or 800/347–2222) and **Harbour Air** (☎ 604/688–1277 or 800/665–0212) both offer 35-minute harbor-to-harbor service (downtown Vancouver to downtown Victoria) several times a day. **Kenmore Air** (☎ 425/486–1257 or 800/543–9595) offers direct daily floatplane service from Seattle to Victoria's Inner Harbour.

Getting Around
BY BUS

BC Transit (☎ 250/382–6161) runs a fairly extensive service in Victoria and the surrounding areas, with an all-day pass that costs $5.50.

BY FERRY

Victoria Harbour Ferries (☎ 250/708–0201) makes eight stops around the Inner Harbour, including the Empress hotel, Point Ellice House, Spinnaker's Brew Pub, Ocean Pointe Resort, and Fisherman's Wharf. Fares start at $3; harbor tours are $12 to $14. There's service every 12–20 minutes daily, mid-March–October, and on sunny weekends the rest of the year.

BY TAXI

Taxis are available from **Empress Taxi** (☎ 250/381–2222) and **Victoria Taxi** (☎ 250/383–7111).

Contacts and Resources
CAR RENTALS

Avis (☎ 250/386–8468). **Budget** (☎ 250/953–5300). **Enterprise** (☎ 250/475–6900). **Island Autos** (☎ 250/384–4881). **National Tilden** (☎ 250/386–1213). **Rent-a-Wreck** (☎ 250/413–4638).

EMERGENCIES

Ambulance, fire, police (☎ 911).

GUIDED TOURS

Gray Line (☎ 250/388–5248) offers city tours on double-decker buses. **Tally-Ho Horsedrawn Tours** (☎ 250/383–5067) offers a get-acquainted session with downtown Victoria that includes Beacon Hill Park. **Victoria Carriage Tours** (☎ 250/383–2207) has horse-drawn tours of the city. The best way to see the sights of the Inner Harbour is by **Victoria Harbour Ferries** (☞ Getting Around, *above*).

HOSPITAL
Victoria General Hospital (✉ 1 Hospital Way, off Helmcken Rd., ☎ 250/727–4212).

LATE-NIGHT PHARMACY
London Drugs (✉ 911 Yates St., ☎ 250/381–1113) is open daily until 10 PM.

LODGING RESERVATION SERVICE
Super, Natural British Columbia (☎ 800/663–6000) and **Tourism Victoria** (☎ 800/663–3883) can assist with reservations year-round. **Garden City B&B Reservation Service** (✉ 660 Jones Terr., V8Z 2L7, ☎ 250/479–1986, FAX 250/479–9999) can book B&B accommodations throughout Vancouver Island.

VISITOR INFORMATION
Tourism Victoria (✉ 812 Wharf St., V8W 1T3, ☎ 250/953–2033 or 800/663–3883, FAX 250/382–6539).

VANCOUVER ISLAND

The largest island on Canada's west coast, Vancouver Island stretches 564 km (350 mi) from Victoria in the south to Cape Scott in the north. Some 97% of the island's population of 684,000 live on its sheltered eastern side, between Victoria and Campbell River; 50% live in Victoria itself. A ridge of mountains, blanketed in spruce, cedar, and Douglas fir, crowns the island's center, providing opportunities for skiing, climbing, and hiking.

The island's west coast, facing the open ocean, is wild and often inhospitable, with few roads and only a handful of small settlements. Nevertheless, the west coast is invaded every summer by campers, hikers, kayakers, and even surfers drawn by the magnificent stretch of beach, old-growth forests, and challenging hiking trails of Pacific Rim National Park Reserve, as well as the chance to see whales offshore.

The cultural heritage of the island is from the Kwakiutl, Nootka, and Coastal Salish native groups. Native art and cultural centers flourish throughout the region.

Mining, logging, and tourism are the important island industries, although tourism, and especially ecotourism, has become increasingly important in recent years.

Sooke

⑭ *42 km (26 mi) west of Victoria on Hwy. 14.*

The village of Sooke provides a peaceful seaside escape, with rugged beaches, hiking trails through the surrounding rain forest, and views of Washington's Olympic Mountains across the Strait of Juan de Fuca. **East Sooke Park,** on the east side of the harbor, has 350 acres of beaches, hiking trails, and wildflower-dotted meadows. A popular hiking and biking route, the **Galloping Goose Regional Trail** (☎ 250/478–3344) is a former railway line that runs all the way to Victoria. The **Sooke Potholes** (✉ End of Sooke River Rd., off Hwy. 14), along the Galloping Goose Regional Trail, are a series of swimming holes carved out of the sandstone by the Sooke River.

Vancouver Island

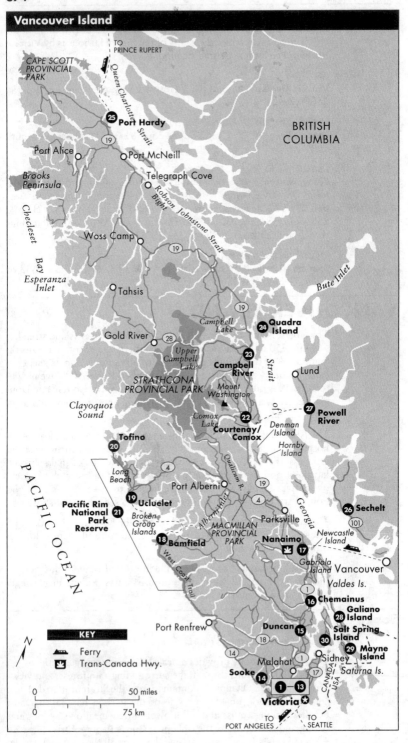

TO
PRINCE RUPERT

*CAPE SCOTT
PROVINCIAL
PARK*

Queen Charlotte Strait

25 Port Hardy

Port Alice

Port McNeill

*Brooks
Peninsula*

Telegraph Cove

Robson Johnstone Bight

*Checleset
Bay*

Woss Camp

**BRITISH
COLUMBIA**

*Esperanza
Inlet*

Tahsis

Robson Johnstone Strait

(19)

Bute Inlet

Gold River

(28)

*Campbell
Lake*

24 Quadra
Island

*Upper
Campbell
Lake*

23 Campbell
River

Strait

Lund

*STRATHCONA
PROVINCIAL PARK*

▲ Mount
Washington

*Clayoquot
Sound*

*Comox
Lake*

22 Courtenay/
Comox

of

*Denman
Island*

27 Powell
River

20 Tofino

*Hornby
Island*

*Long
Beach*

(4)

Port Alberni

Qualicum R.

(19)

Georgia

**Pacific Rim
National
Park
Reserve**

19 Ucluelet

*Broken
Group
Islands*

(4)

Parksville

26 Sechelt

(101)

21

*MACMILLAN
PROVINCIAL
PARK*

Alberni Inlet

*Newcastle
Island*

18 Bamfield

Nanaimo 17

West Coast Trail

*Gabriola
Island* Vancouver

Valdes Is.

(1)

16 Chemainus

**Galiano
28 Island**

Port Renfrew

Duncan **15**

**Salt Spring
30 Island**

PACIFIC OCEAN

(18)

Saturna Is.

(14)

Malahat

(1)

Sidney

**29 Mayne
Island**

Sooke 14

(17)

CANADA
USA

1 — 13

Victoria ✪

KEY

⛴ Ferry
🛥 Trans-Canada Hwy.

N

0 —————— 50 miles
0 —————— 75 km

TO
PORT ANGELES

TO
SEATTLE

The **Sooke Region Museum and Visitor Information Centre** displays Salish and Nootka crafts and artifacts from 19th-century Sooke. ⊠ *2070 Phillips Rd., Box 774, V0S 1N0,* ☎ *250/642–6351,* ⅢAX *250/642–7089.* 🖭 *Donations accepted.* ☉ *July–Aug., daily 9–6; Sept.–June, Tues.–Sun. 9–5.*

OFF THE BEATEN PATH	**JUAN DE FUCA PROVINCIAL PARK** – This park between Jordan River and Port Renfrew has campsites and a long series of beaches, including Botanical Beach with its amazing tide pools. The **Juan de Fuca Marine Trail** is a tough 47-km (30-mi) hike set up as an alternative to the overly popular West Coast Trail (☞ Pacific Rim National Park Reserve, *below*) and begins in Port Renfrew. ⊠ *Hwy. 14,* ☎ *250/391–2300.*

Dining and Lodging

$$–$$$ ✕ **Seventeen Mile House.** Originally built as a hotel, this 1894 house is a study in turn-of-the-century island architecture. This is a good place for pub fare, a beer, or fresh local seafood on the road between Sooke and Victoria. ⊠ *5126 Sooke Rd.,* ☎ *250/642–5942. MC, V.*

$$$$ ✕🖾 **Sooke Harbour House.** People (including incognito movie stars) ★ who are discerning about their R&R are drawn to this 1929 ocean-front clapboard inn with its elegant yet relaxed ambience and one of Canada's finest dining rooms. Dining here is an event: The Pacific Northwest menu changes daily, the seafood is just-caught fresh, and much of the produce—including herbs, mushrooms, and edible flowers—is grown on the property. The guest rooms, each with a sitting area and fireplace, are individually decorated (some with fish, bird, or seaside themes) and photo-shoot perfect. The Victor Newman Longhouse room displays impressive First Nations art, and the bi-level Blue Heron room has a summer cottage feel, with a private deck overlooking the ocean. Breakfast (delivered to your room) is included in the room rates year-round, and lunch is included between May and October and on weekends the rest of the year. ⊠ *1528 Whiffen Spit Rd., V0S 1N0,* ☎ *250/642–3421 or 800/889–9688,* ⅢAX *250/642–6988. 28 rooms. Restaurant, in-room data ports, refrigerators, room service, massage, hiking, snorkeling, boating, bicycles, piano, laundry service and dry cleaning, business services, meeting room. AE, DC, MC, V.*

$$–$$$ 🖾 **Point No Point.** Here's a place for your inner Robinson Crusoe. Twenty-two cabins sit on the edge of a cliff, overlooking 2 km (1 mi) of sandy private beach and the open Pacific. The one- and two-bedroom cabins, in single, duplex, and quad units, range from rustic to romantic. Seven newer cabins have tall windows, loft bedrooms, and hot tubs; the older, cheaper cabins are basic, with the original 1960s furniture (pets allowed in two of these). Every unit has a kitchen, a fireplace or woodstove, and a deck. The lodge restaurant serves lunch, afternoon tea, and dinner from a seafood-oriented menu. Each table has a pair of binoculars for spotting whales and ships on the open sea. ⊠ *1505 West Coast Rd., 24 km (15 mi) west of Sooke, V0S 1N0,* ☎ *250/646–2020,* ⅢAX *250/646–2294. 22 cabins. Restaurant, hiking. AE, MC, V. Restaurant closed for dinner Mon. and Tues.; check for winter closures.*

Shopping

At the **Blue Raven Gallery** (⊠ 1971 Kaltasin Rd., ☎ 250/881–0528), Victor and Carey Newman, a father-and-son team of Kwakiutl and Salish artists, display traditional and modern prints, masks, and jewelry.

Duncan

⑮   *60 km (37 mi) north of Victoria on the Trans-Canada Hwy. (Hwy. 1).*

★ ᙚ   Duncan is nicknamed City of Totems for the many totem poles that dot the small community. The **Cowichan Native Village,** covering 6 acres on the banks of the tree-lined Cowichan River, is one of Canada's leading First Nations cultural and educational facilities. You can see the work (including a stunning whaling canoe diorama) of some of the Pacific Northwest's most renowned artists in a lofty longhouse-style gallery, learn about the history of the Cowichan people during a multimedia show, and sample traditional foods at the Riverwalk Café. You can also watch artisans at work in the world's largest carving house and even try your hand at carving on a visitors' pole. Crafts demonstrations and performances take place in summer. ✉ *200 Cowichan Way,* ☎ *250/746–8119.* ☞ *$8.* ☉ *Daily 9–5. Café closed Nov.–Apr.*

The **British Columbia Forest Museum,** more a park than a museum, spans some 100 acres, combining indoor and outdoor exhibits that focus on the history of forestry in the province. In the summer you can ride an original steam locomotive around the property. The "Forest Renewal B.C." exhibition has a theater, computer games, aquariums, and hands-on displays about the province's ecosystems. There are also nature trails on the property. ✉ *2892 Drinkwater Rd. (Trans-Canada Hwy.),* ☎ *250/715–1113,* ℻ *250/715–1170.* ☞ *$8.* ☉ *May–early Sept., daily 9:30–6; early Sept.–Apr., call for seasonal hrs.*

Shopping
Duncan is the home of Cowichan wool sweaters, hand-knit by the Cowichan people. Sweaters are available at the **Cowichan Native Village** (☞ *above*) and from **Hill's Indian Crafts** (☎ 250/746–6731) on the main highway, about 1½ km (1 mi) south of Duncan.

Chemainus

★ **⑯**   *25 km (16 mi) north of Duncan, 27 km (17 mi) south of Nanaimo.*

Chemainus is known for the bold epic **murals** that decorate its townscape, as well as its beautifully restored Victorian homes. Once dependent on the lumber industry, the small community began to revitalize itself in the early 1980s when its mill closed down. Since then, the town has brought in international artists to paint more than 30 murals depicting local historical events around town. Footprints on the sidewalk lead you on a self-guided tour of the murals. Restaurants, shops, tearooms, coffee bars, art galleries, a mini–train line, several B&Bs, and antiques dealers have helped create one of the prettiest little towns on Vancouver Island. The **Chemainus Dinner Theatre** (✉ 9737 Chemainus Rd., ☎ 250/246–9820 or 800/565–7738) presents family-oriented fare along with dinner.

Lodging
$$ ⊞ **Bird Song Cottage.** This whimsical white-and-lavender Victorian cot-
★   tage, an easy walk from the beach and town, has been playfully decorated with antiques and collectibles, including a grand piano, a Celtic harp, and Victorian hats. A full breakfast (often with piano accompaniment) is served on the sunporch. The Nightingale room has a private garden and a claw-foot tub, and the other two have baths with showers; every room has a window seat. Castlebury Inn, a more expensive ($$$) one-bedroom, medieval-theme castle-cottage behind the inn, has a kitchen, a two-sided fireplace, and a small balcony with an ocean view. ✉ *9909 Maple St., Box 1432, V0R 1K0,* ☎ *250/246–9910,* ℻ *250/246–2909. 3 rooms, 1 cottage. AE, MC, V.*

Nanaimo

17 *25 km (16 mi) north of Chemainus, 110 km (68 mi) northwest of Victoria, 115 km (71 mi) southeast of Courtenay, 23 km (14 mi) on land plus 38 nautical mi west of Vancouver.*

Nanaimo is the primary commercial and transport link for the mid-island, with direct ferry service to the mainland. The **Nanaimo District Museum** (✉ 100 Cameron Rd., ☎ 250/753–1821) has reproductions of petroglyphs (rock carvings) that have been found in the area. The carvings represent human and animal spirit figures. At **Petroglyph Provincial Park** (✉ Hwy. 1 south of Nanaimo, ☎ 250/391–2300), 8 km (5 mi) south of town, marked trails begin at the parking lot and lead to designs carved thousands of years ago.

From Nanaimo, you can take a 10-minute ferry ride (☎ 250/753–5141) to **Newcastle Island,** a provincial park where you can picnic, ride your bicycle, walk on trails leading past old mines and quarries, and catch glimpses of deer, rabbits, and eagles.

Dining and Lodging

$$–$$$$ ✕ **The Grotto.** The owners of this offbeat seafood and sushi place near the Departure Bay ferry terminal have been adding to their supply of nautical paraphernalia since 1960. Inside and out, the place looks like a sea shanty, full of driftwood, fishing floats, and weathered pillars borrowed from a dock. The five-page Japanese-Canadian menu has enough options to keep everyone happy. Try the sushi, charred tuna, teriyaki spareribs, Cajun pasta, or the Japanese platter for two. ✉ *1511 Stewart Ave.,* ☎ *250/753–3303. AE, MC, V. Closed Mon. No lunch.*

$$$ ✕ **Mahle House.** Much of the innovative Pacific Northwest cuisine served
★ at this cozy 1904 farmhouse is raised on site or in the neighborhood. Highlights on the seasonal menu include different versions of rabbit, venison, mussels, and salmon, as well as good vegetarian options. On Wednesday night, you can try the Adventure Dining Experience: For $25 you get five courses chosen by the chef, and your dinner companions (up to a party of four) each get something different. Mahle House is about 12 km (7 mi) south of Nanaimo. ✉ *Cedar and Hemer Rds.,* ☎ *250/722–3621. AE, MC, V. Closed Mon.–Tues. and Jan. No lunch.*

$$–$$$ ☷ **Coast Bastion Inn Nanaimo.** This convenient business hotel downtown overlooks the harbor. The rooms are large and modern, and all have water views. Corner rooms on the seventh floor and up are larger and have sitting areas and panoramic ocean views. ✉ *11 Bastion St., V9R 2Z9,* ☎ *250/753–6601,* ⅏ *250/753–4155. 171 rooms, 4 suites. Restaurant, lounge, air-conditioning, no-smoking floor, room service, hot tub, sauna, exercise room, laundry service and dry cleaning, business services, meeting rooms. AE, D, DC, MC, V.*

$$–$$$ ☷ **Yellow Point Lodge.** Since the 1930s, this lodge on a spit of land 24
★ km (15 mi) south of Nanaimo has been a kind of adults-only summer camp. Everything's included, from the use of kayaks, bicycles, and tennis courts to the three full meals and snacks served communally in the dining room. Accommodations range from comfortable lodge rooms to cozy new cottages with minirefrigerators and bed frames made with logs; there are also some very basic summer-only cabins with no running water and a shared bathhouse. The main lodge, with its great stone fireplace and ocean views, is a wonderful place to unwind; you can also stroll the resort's 165 acres, lounge on its secluded beaches, or take a tour on the owner's cutter. Guests must be over 16. ✉ *3700 Yellow Point Rd., Ladysmith V0R 2E0,* ☎ *250/245–7422,* ⅏ *250/245–7411. 9 lodge rooms, 25 rooms with no running water, 10 units in shared cabins, 12 private cabins. Dining room, outdoor saltwater pool, out-*

door hot tub, sauna, 2 tennis courts, badminton, jogging, volleyball, boating, mountain bikes. AE, MC, V. AP.

Outdoor Activities and Sports

GOLF

Fairwinds Golf and Country Club (⊠ 3730 Fairwinds Dr., Nanoose Bay, ☎ 250/468–7666 or 800/663–7060) is an 18-hole, par-71 course.

KAYAKING

Kayak rentals and one- to four-day guided sea-kayak expeditions are offered by **Wild Heart Adventure Tours** (⊠ 2774 Barnes Rd., ☎ 250/722–3683, ℻ 250/722–2175).

Bamfield

🔞 *100 km (62 mi) southwest of Port Alberni by gravel road.*

In Bamfield, a remote village of about 200, the seaside boardwalk affords an uninterrupted view of ships heading up the inlet to Port Alberni. The town is well equipped to handle overnight visitors. Bamfield is also a good base for boating trips to the Broken Islands Group and hikes along the West Coast Trail (☞ Pacific Rim National Park Reserve, *below*). From Port Alberni, you can take a breathtaking $40 trip to Bamfield aboard the **Lady Rose** (⊠ Argyle Pier, 5425 Argyle St., ☎ 250/723–8313; 800/663–7192 for reservations Apr.–Sept.), a Scottish ship built in 1937.

Dining and Lodging

$$$$ ✕▥ **Eagle Nook Ocean Wilderness Resort.** This wilderness country inn,
★   accessible only by sea or air, sits on a narrow strip of land in Barkley Sound. For all its blissful isolation, Eagle Nook offers some highly civilized comforts. Every spacious room has a water view, and the lounge has leather chairs and a stone fireplace. The dining room serves fine Pacific Northwest cuisine, which you can enjoy inside or alfresco. Hiking trails lace the woods, and many activities, including fishing, kayaking, and whale-watching, can be prebooked. Getting here, by floatplane, by water taxi from China Creek near Port Alberni, or by prearrangement on the *Lady Rose* ferry (☞ Port Alberni, *above*), is a scenic adventure in its own right. There's a two-night minimum stay; prices are per person and include meals and nonguided activities. ⊠ *Box 575, Port Alberni V9Y 7M9, ☎ 250/723–1000 or 800/760–2777, ℻ 250/723–9842. 23 rooms. Restaurant, lounge, outdoor hot tub, exercise room, hiking, dock, boating, fishing, laundry services, meeting room, helipad. AE, MC, V. Closed Nov.–May. AP.*

Ucluelet

🔞 *100 km (62 mi) west of Port Alberni, 295 km (183 mi) northwest of Victoria.*

Ucluelet, which in the native language means "people with a safe landing place," is, along with Bamfield and Tofino, one of the towns serving Pacific Rim National Park Reserve (☞ *below*). Until 1999 it was a tiny roadside fishing village; a new development, **Reef Point Adventure Station** (*see* Dining and Lodging, *below*), may well turn it into a leading resort destination for those who like adventure.

A variety of charter companies (☞ Outdoor Activities and Sports, *below, and* Contacts and Resources *in* British Columbia A to Z, *below*) take boats to greet the 20,000 gray whales that pass close to Ucluelet on their migration to the Bering Sea every March and April. Sometimes the whales can even be seen from the Ucluelet shore. Increasingly, people are coming in the off-season to watch the dramatic winter storms that pound the coast here. The **MV *Francis Barkley*** (✉ Argyle Pier, 5425 Argyle St., ☎ 250/723–8313; 800/663–7192 for reservations Apr.–Sept.) sails to Ucluelet from Port Alberni for $45.

Amphitrite Point Lighthouse (✉ end of Coast Guard Rd.), which has a panoramic view of the beach, is the starting point for the **Wild Pacific Trail**, a level, part-boardwalk, wheelchair-accessible path along the coast and through the rain forest. When completed (in about 2003), the trail will link Ucluelet to Long Beach in Pacific Rim National Park Reserve.

Dining and Lodging

$$-$$$ ✕ **Matterson House.** In a tiny 1931 cottage with just seven tables and an outdoor deck in summer, husband-and-wife team Sandy and Jennifer Clark serve up generous portions of seafood, burgers, pasta, and filling standards like prime rib and roast beef. It's simple food, prepared well with fresh local ingredients; everything, including soups, desserts, and the wonderful bread, is homemade. The wine list has local island wines unavailable elsewhere and worth trying. ✉ *1682 Peninsula Rd.,* ☎ *250/726–2200. MC, V. Closed part of Nov.*

$$$$ 🏨 **Reef Point Adventure Station.** This environmentally sensitive resort, opened in 1999 on Ucluelet's harbor, resembles a west-coast fishing village of the early 1900s. The whole woodsy complex is built on posts and linked by raised boardwalks and bridges running through the rain forest. Unlike a fishing village, though, it has a spa, upscale shops and restaurants, and an IMAX theater. The accommodation options are a 20-room seaside lodge, beachfront cabins, and a 100-room hotel. Soft adventure activities such as sea kayaking, hiking, diving, sailing, biking, and surfing are available on or near the 60-acre site. Reef Point was under construction at press time, and some facilities may still be under construction in 2000. Call ahead to confirm details and prices. ✉ *131 Seabridge Way, Box 730, V0R 3A0,* ☎ *250/726–2700, 888/594–7333 in B.C.,* 🗚 *250/726–2701. 120 rooms, 70 cottages. Restaurant, pub, spa, boating, bicycles, cinema. AE, DC, MC, V.*

$$$-$$$$ 🏨 **A Snug Harbour Inn.** Set on a cliff above the Pacific, this couples-oriented B&B offers some of the most dramatic views anywhere. The rooms, all with fireplaces, private balconies or decks, whirlpool baths, and ocean views, are decorated in a highly individual style. The Sawadee room reflects hosts Skip and Denise Rowland's time in Thailand, and the Atlantis is done in ultramodern yellow and black. Eagles nest nearby, and trails through the woods lead to the seaside. Skip can organize helicopter trips from here. A full breakfast is included. ✉ *460 Marine Dr., Box 367, V0R 3A0,* ☎ *250/726–2686 or 888/936–5222,* 🗚 *250/726–2685. 4 rooms. Breakfast room, outdoor hot tub, hiking, helipad. MC, V.*

$-$$$ 🏨 **Canadian Princess Fishing Resort.** If vintage ships are to your liking, you may want to book a cabin on this converted 230-ft, steam-powered survey ship, which has comfortable but hardly opulent staterooms. Each has one to four berths, and all share bathrooms. Larger than the ship cabins, the resort's deluxe shoreside rooms have more contemporary furnishings; a few have fireplaces. This unique resort appeals to nature enthusiasts and anglers, and whale-watching can be arranged. The Stewart Room Restaurant is open to nonguests; the specialty is (no surprise here) seafood. ✉ *Boat Basin, 1943 Peninsula Rd., Box 939, V0R 3A0,* ☎ *250/726–7771 or 800/663–7090,* 🗚 *250/726–7121. 46 shoreside rooms, 30 shipboard sleeping units. Restaurant, 2 bars, boating, fishing. AE, DC, MC, V. Closed late Sept.–early Mar.*

Outdoor Activities and Sports

Most Ucluelet operators offer a variety of whale-watching, fishing, or cruising options. The **Canadian Princess Fishing Resort** (☎ 250/726–7771 or 800/663–7090) has 10 comfortable fishing and whale-watching boats with heated cabins and bathrooms. **Subtidal Adventures** (☎ 250/726–7336) specializes in whale-watching and nature tours; there's a choice of an inflatable Zodiac or a 36-ft former coast guard rescue boat. Some local operators include **Island West Fishing Resort** (☎ 250/726–7515), **Quest Charters** (☎ 250/726–7532), and **Viking Charters** (☎ 250/726–4410).

Tofino

★ ⑳ *42 km (26 mi) northwest of Ucluelet, 337 km (209 mi) northwest of Victoria, 130 km (81 mi) west of Port Alberni.*

The end of the road makes a great stage—and Tofino is certainly that. On a narrow peninsula just beyond the north end of the Pacific Rim National Park Reserve (☞ *below*), this is as far west as you can go on Vancouver Island by paved road. One look at the pounding Pacific surf and the old-growth forest along the shoreline convinces many people that they've reached not just the end of the road but the end of the earth.

Tofino's tiny number of year-round residents know what they like and have made what could have been a tourist trap into a funky little town with nine art galleries, an excellent bookstore, several sociable cafés, and plenty of opportunity to get out to the surrounding wilds—to see the old-growth forests of Meares Island, the natural hot springs at Hot Springs Cove, the long stretches of beach, and, of course, the whales and other wildlife. Tofino has plenty of accommodations and campsites in and around town; at press time, plans were in place to open a Hostelling International hostel.

Dining and Lodging

$$$$ ✕▨ **Wickaninnish Inn.** Set on a rocky promontory above Chesterman
★   Beach, with open ocean on three sides and old-growth forest as a backdrop, the three-story weathered-cedar building is a comfortable place to enjoy the area's dramatic wilderness scenery, summer or winter. The whole inn is no-smoking, and every spacious room has a sitting area, an ocean view, and its own balcony, fireplace, and soaker tub. The staff takes very good care of guests, and the new full-service Ancient Cedars Spa (also open to nonguests) adds to the pampering. Chef Rodney Butters of the Pointe Restaurant selects his catch personally at the Tofino docks. The menu has featured scallops in Rainforest Ale broth, venison and hazelnut pâté, and steamed Long Beach Dungeness crabs. If you can, try the chef's special seven-course dinner, available with a day's notice. ✉ *Osprey La. at Chesterman Beach, Box 250, 5 km (3 mi) south of Tofino, V0R 2Z0,* ☎ *250/725–3100 or 800/333–4604,* ℻ *250/725–3110. 46 rooms. Restaurant, lounge, in-room data ports, minibars, room service, massage, spa, steam room, hiking, beach, fishing, laundry services, meeting room. AE, D, DC, MC, V.*

$$$$ ▨ **Clayoquot Wilderness Resort.** The accommodations and restaurant at this resort float on a barge in Quait Bay, moored next to 127 acres of wilderness park; Tofino is 25 minutes away by water taxi. The property, part of the pristine wilderness of Clayoquot Sound, includes two lakes, hiking trails, and acres of old-growth forest. Host Randy Goddard, who describes the informal, family-oriented resort as an "adult kids' camp," offers fresh- and saltwater fishing, whale-watching, kayaking, horseback riding, and nature cruising. The comfortable rooms all have water or forest views (but no phones or TVs) and open

onto a wraparound veranda. Room rates include all meals and free water-taxi pickup from Tofino. ⊠ *Box 728, V0R 2Z0,* ☎ *250/726–8235 or 888/333–5405,* FAX *250/726–8558. 16 rooms. Dining room, lounge, fans, outdoor hot tub, sauna, exercise room, dock, boating, meeting rooms, helipad. MC, V. AP.*

$$–$$$$ 🏨 **Middle Beach Lodge.** A longtime favorite on the beach 3 km (2 mi) south of Tofino has a choice of two lodges. A rustic wooden, adults-only building on the forest edge has basic rooms (no phones or TVs), some with sea views, and a path down to the beach. The newer (1996) Headlands complex, made with recycled timber and perched on an ocean-front bluff, offers larger, more luxurious rooms, some with fireplaces and ocean-view balconies, and family-size cabins with kitchenettes and fireplaces. Each lodge has a lounge with a floor-to-ceiling stone fireplace and ocean views. Dinners are available during high season at this no-smoking inn. ⊠ *400 McKenzie Beach Rd., Box 100, V0R 2Z0,* ☎ *250/725–2900,* FAX *250/725–2901. 35 rooms, 4 suites, 19 cabins. Dining room, beach, coin laundry, meeting rooms. AE, MC, V. CP.*

$ 🏨 **Paddlers' Inn.** This multiple-business inn on the waterfront in the center of Tofino covers all the bases. Downstairs, an espresso bar and bookstore overlook a kayaking outlet. Upstairs, five clean, fresh rooms have Scandinavian furniture and futons but no phones or TVs. The rooms share two bathrooms, and the one-bedroom suite has its own bath, kitchenette, and deck. The inn is completely no-smoking. ⊠ *320 Main St., Box 620, V0R 2Z0,* ☎ *250/725–4222 or 800/863–4664,* FAX *250/ 725–2070. 5 rooms with shared bath, 1 suite. Café, boating. MC, V. Closed Nov.–Feb. CP.*

Outdoor Activities and Sports

FISHING

Local charter companies include **Weigh West Marine Resort** (☎ 250/ 725–3277 or 800/665–8922).

GOLF

Long Beach Golf Course (⊠ Pacific Rim Hwy., ☎ 250/725–3332) is a nine-hole, par-36 course.

KAYAKING

Remote Passages Sea Kayaking (⊠ 71 Wharf St., ☎ 250/725–3330 or 800/666–9833) has guided day and evening paddles; no experience is necessary. **Tofino Sea-Kayaking Company** (⊠ 320 Main St., ☎ 250/ 725–4222 or 800/863–4664) rents kayaks and runs wilderness trips.

WHALE-WATCHING

Between March and May, gray whales migrate along the coast here; resident grays can be seen anytime between May and November. Humpback whales, sea otters, and other wildlife are increasingly seen in the area. Most whale-watching operators also offer trips to Meares Island and Hot Springs Cove. **Jamie's Whaling Station** (⊠ 606 Campbell St., ☎ 250/725–3919; 800/667–9913 in Canada) is one of the most established operators on the coast and has both Zodiacs and more comfortable 65-ft tour boats. **Remote Passages Marine Excursions** (⊠ 71 Wharf St., ☎ 250/725–3330 or 800/666–9833), a well-established operator, offers whale-watching and other wildlife-viewing trips with an ecological focus. The **Whale Centre** (⊠ 411 Campbell St., ☎ 250/725–2132) has a museum with a 40-ft whale skeleton you can study while waiting for your boat. **Chinook Charters** (☎ 250/725–3431 or 800/665–3646) and **Sea Trek Tours and Expeditions** (☎ 250/725–4412 or 800/811–9155) have trips in the area.

Shopping

The magnificent **Eagle Aerie Gallery** (⊠ 350 Campbell St., ☎ 250/725–3235) houses a collection of prints, paintings, and carvings by the renowned native artist Roy Henry Vickers. **House of Himwitsa** (⊠ 300 Main St., ☎ 250/725–2017) sells native crafts, jewelry, and clothing. The complex has a seafood restaurant and lodge rooms, too. Local artists display their work at **Islandfolk Gallery** (⊠ 120 4th St., ☎ 250/725–3130), **Reflecting Spirit** (⊠ 411 Campbell St., ☎ 250/725–2472), and **Village Gallery** (⊠ 321 Main St., ☎ 250/725–4229). **Wildside Booksellers** (⊠ 320 Main St., ☎ 250/725–4222) has an extensive selection and an espresso bar.

Pacific Rim National Park Reserve

★ ㉑ *85 km (53 mi) west of Port Alberni.*

This national park (⊠ Box 280, Ucluelet V0R 3A0, ☎ 250/726–7721, FAX 250/726–4720) has some of Canada's most stunning coastal and rain-forest scenery, abundant wildlife, and a unique marine environment. It comprises three separate areas—Long Beach, the Broken Group Islands, and the West Coast Trail—for a combined area of 20,243 acres, including 130 km (81 mi) of shoreline. The **Park Information Centre** (2 km/1 mi north of the Tofino-Ucluelet junction on Hwy. 4, ☎ 250/726–4212) is open mid-June to mid-September, daily 9:30–5. Park-use fees apply in all sections of the park. In the Long Beach section, an $8 daily group pass, available from dispensers in the parking lots, admits up to 10 people in one vehicle for a day and includes admission to the Wickaninnish Centre (☞ *below*).

The **Long Beach** unit gets its name from an 18-km (11-mi) strip of hard-packed sand strewn with driftwood, shells, and the occasional Japanese glass fishing float. Long Beach is the most accessible part of the park and roads can get busy in summer. People come in the off-season to watch winter storms and to see migrating whales in early spring.

A first stop for many visitors, the **Wickaninnish Centre** is the park's visitor and interpretive center, right on the ocean edge about 16 km (10 mi) north of Ucluelet. It's a great place to learn about the wilderness; theater programs and exhibits provide information about the park's marine ecology and rain-forest environment. The center is also a good lunch stop—it was originally an inn, and its restaurant still serves up hearty seafood lunches and dinners. ⊠ *Hwy. 4,* ☎ *250/726–4701 for center; 250/726–7706 for restaurant.* ☑ *Free with park- use fee.* ☽ *Mid-Mar.–mid-Oct., daily 10:30–6.*

The 100-plus islands of the **Broken Group Islands** can be reached only by boat. Many commercial charter tours are available from Ucluelet, at the southern end of Long Beach, and from Bamfield and Port Alberni. The islands and their waters are alive with sea lions, seals, and whales. The inner waters near Gibraltar, Jacques, and Hand islands offer protection and good boating conditions, but go with a guide if it's your first trip.

The third element of the park, the **West Coast Trail,** stretches along the coast from Bamfield to Port Renfrew. This extremely rugged 75-km (47-mi) trail is for experienced hikers. It can be traveled only on foot, takes an average of six days to complete, and is open May–September. A permit ($115 with the registration and ferry fees) is necessary, and a quota system is in place. Advance reservations are recommended and can be made with **Super, Natural British Columbia** (☎ 250/387–1642 or 800/663–6000) between March and September.

En Route Heading back to the east coast from Port Alberni, stop off at **Cathedral Grove** in MacMillan Provincial Park on Highway 4. Walking trails lead past Douglas fir trees and western red cedars, some as much as 800 years old. Their remarkable height creates a spiritual effect, as though you were gazing at a cathedral ceiling.

Courtenay and Comox

㉒ *220 km (136 mi) northwest of Victoria, 17 nautical mi west of Powell River, 46 km (29 mi) southeast of Campbell River; Comox is 6 km (4 mi) east of Courtenay.*

Courtenay and Comox are commercial towns that also provide a base for Mt. Washington and Forbidden Plateau skiers. In Courtenay you can catch the **Esquimalt & Nanaimo** small-gauge railway to Nanaimo, Victoria, and other South Island stops (☞ Getting Around *in* British Columbia A to Z, *below*). **BC Ferries** (☎ 888/223–3779) sails from Comox to Powell River on the Sunshine Coast (☞ *below*).

Dining and Lodging

$$–$$$ ✕ **Old House Restaurant.** This riverside restaurant set among gardens
★ (though also overlooking a pulp mill across the way) provides casual dining in a restored 1938 house with cedar beams, four stone fireplaces, and a patio for dining. People flock here for the West Coast home-style cuisine—pastas, salads, and sandwiches, along with fancier, more innovative dishes (seafood stir-fry, peppered Fanny Bay oysters)—and the fresh daily specials. ⊠ *1760 Riverside La., Courtenay,* ☎ *250/338–5406. AE, DC, MC, V.*

$$–$$$ ▥ **Kingfisher Oceanside Resort and Spa.** Soothing is the word to de-
★ scribe this seaside resort 10 minutes south of Courtenay. Thirty-two new beachfront units, all with balconies or patios, kitchens, gas fireplaces, and expansive ocean views, are decorated in rich sea blues and greens. A full-service spa (also open to nonguests) offers the works, including beauty treatments, aromatherapy, hydrotherapy, and massage (for two, if you like). The steam room looks like a mermaid's cave, and the exercise room has an ocean view. The original, lower-price rooms, set a little farther back from the water, are also modern and spacious, and some have kitchens. ⊠ *4330 S. Island Hwy., R.R. 6, Site 672, C-1, Courtenay V9N 8H9,* ☎ *250/338–1323 or 800/663–7929,* ᵮᴬˣ *250/338–0058. 38 rooms, 22 suites. Restaurant, lounge, no-smoking floors, room service, pool, outdoor hot tub, sauna, tennis court, beach, boating, fishing, bicycles, library, baby-sitting, laundry service, business services, meeting rooms. AE, D, DC, MC, V.*

$ ▥ **Greystone Manor.** This 1918 house about 3 km (2 mi) south of Courtenay has a lovingly tended 1½-acre English garden and views over Comox Bay, where seals are often visible. Inside, period furnishings and a woodstove make things cozy. Two rooms have baths with showers; one has a claw-foot tub in a room across the hall. Breakfast, which includes fresh fruit, muffins, and fruit pancakes, is included in the rates. ⊠ *4014 Haas Rd., R.R. 6, Site 684, C-2, Courtenay V9N 8H9,* ☎ *250/338–1422. 3 rooms. Breakfast room, piano. MC, V.*

Outdoor Activities and Sports

Forbidden Plateau (⊠ Forbidden Plateau Rd., Courtenay, ☎ 250/334–4744), about 20 minutes from Courtenay, has 22 downhill ski runs, one chairlift, night skiing, and a vertical drop of 1,050 ft. **Mt. Washington Ski Resort Ltd.** (⊠ Strathcona Park Way, Courtenay, ☎ 250/338–1386), 19 km (12 mi) from Courtenay, with nearly 50 downhill runs, a 1,657-ft vertical drop, five chairlifts, and an elevation of 5,200 ft, is the island's largest ski area. The resort also has 29 km (18 mi) of double track–set cross-country trails.

Campbell River

㉓ *50 km (31 mi) north of Courtenay and Comox, 155 km (96 mi) north-west of Nanaimo, 270 km (167 mi) northwest of Victoria.*

Campbell River draws people who want to fish; some of the biggest salmon ever caught on a line have been landed just off the coast here. Coho salmon and cutthroat trout are also plentiful in the river.

The primary access to Strathcona Provincial Park (☞ *below*) is on High-way 28 west from town. Other recreational activities include diving in **Discovery Passage,** where a battleship has been sunk; kayaking; or taking a summer whale-watching tour. For information, contact **Campbell River Visitor Information Centre** (✉ 1235 Shoppers Row, Box 400, V9W 5B6, ☎ 250/287–4636, ℻ 250/286–6490).

OFF THE BEATEN PATH
M.V. Uchuck – From Gold River at the west end of Highway 28, 100 km (62 mi) from Campbell River, the M.V. *Uchuck* (✉ ☎ 250/283–2515), a 100-passenger packet freighter, takes everything from tourists to groceries to isolated west-coast settlements. Day and overnight trips are available year-round; reservations (and good sea legs) are essential.

Dining and Lodging

$–$$ ✕ **Royal Coachman Neighbourhood Pub.** Informal, blackboard-menu restaurants like this one dot the landscape of the island. The menu, which changes daily, is surprisingly daring for what is essentially a high-end pub, and the inn draws crowds nightly, especially on Tuesday and Saturday (prime rib nights). Come early for both lunch and dinner to avoid a wait. ✉ *84 Dogwood St.,* ☎ *250/286–0231. Reservations essential. AE, MC, V.*

$$$–$$$$ ⌂ **Painter's Lodge.** Bob Hope, John Wayne, and their fishing buddies came to this lodge overlooking Discovery Passage to catch big Tyee (spring salmon) in the 1940s and '50s. Rebuilt in 1988, the attractive cedar complex now lures nature-oriented visitors and whale-watchers as well as anglers; the resort's own fleet runs guided fishing and nature cruises. The 15 lodge rooms and the rooms, suites, and one- to three-bedroom cabins spread around the property all have balconies or patios, and some have kitchens, fireplaces, and whirlpool baths. The owners, the Oak Bay Marine Group, also run a water taxi to Painter's sister resort, April Point Lodge, on Quadra Island (☞ *below*), where you can kayak or explore biking and hiking trails. Painter's Lodge is 8 km (5 mi) north of Campbell River. ✉ *1625 McDonald Rd., Box 460, V9W 5C1,* ☎ *250/286–1102 or 800/663–7090,* ℻ *250/286–0158. 90 rooms, 4 cabins. Restaurant, lounge, pub, pool, 2 outdoor hot tubs, 2 tennis courts, exercise room, fishing, bicycles, playground, meeting rooms. AE, D, DC, MC, V. Closed mid-Oct.–mid-Mar.*

Outdoor Activities and Sports

Storey Creek Golf Club (✉ 300 McGimpsey Rd., ☎ 250/923–3673) is an 18-hole, par-72 course 20 minutes south of Campbell River.

Quadra Island

㉔ *10 mins by ferry from Campbell River.*

Quadra is a thickly forested island, rich with wildlife and laced with hiking trails. The **Kwagiulth Museum and Cultural Centre** (✉ 34 Weway Rd., ☎ 250/285–3733) in Cape Mudge Village houses a collection of potlatch (ceremonial feast) regalia and historical photos.

Dining and Lodging

$$ ✕▣ **Tsa-Kwa-Luten Lodge.** Authentic Pacific Coast native food and cultural activities are highlights of this resort operated by members of the Cape Mudge First Nations band. The main lodge, standing on a high bluff amid 1,100 acres of forest, is striking, with a lofty foyer built in the style of a native longhouse. The guest rooms, decorated with modern furniture and Kwagiulth artwork (but no TVs), all overlook Discovery Passage; many have decks, fireplaces, or lofts. Three two-bedroom beachfront cottages have gas fireplaces, whirlpool baths, kitchenettes, and private verandas. A four-bedroom guest house is great for groups. You can visit nearby petroglyphs, kayak, bike, hike, take a whale-watching cruise, or even try archery here. The restaurant, serving traditional Kwagiulth cuisine, is open to nonguests by reservation. ✉ *Lighthouse Rd., Box 460, Quathiaski Cove V0P 1N0,* ☎ *250/285–2042 or 800/ 665–7745,* ℻ *250/285–2532. 29 rooms, 4 cottages. Restaurant, lounge, no-smoking rooms, outdoor hot tub, sauna, archery, boccie, boating, fishing, mountain bikes, laundry service, business services, meeting rooms. AE, DC, MC, V.*

Strathcona Provincial Park

★ *40 km (25 mi) west of Campbell River.*

Strathcona Provincial Park (☎ 250/954–4600), the largest provincial park on Vancouver Island, encompasses **Mt. Golden Hinde,** at 7,220 ft the island's highest mountain, and **Della Falls,** Canada's highest waterfall, reaching 1,440 ft. This wilderness park's lakes and 161 campsites attract summer canoeists, hikers, anglers, and campers. The main access is by Highway 28 from Campbell River; **Mt. Washington** and Forbidden Plateau ski areas, also in the park, can be reached by roads out of Courtenay (☞ *above*).

The **Strathcona Park Lodge and Outdoor Education Centre** (✉ Hwy. 28, ☎ 250/286–3122), a privately owned resort on the park outskirts, has reasonably priced lodge rooms, lakefront cabins, and a variety of outdoor adventure programs available to the public in summer. It's about 45 km (28 mi) west of Highway 19.

Johnstone Strait

East side of Vancouver Island, roughly between Campbell River and Telegraph Cove.

Pods of resident orcas live year-round in the Inside Passage and around Vancouver Island; in **Robson Bight Provincial Park** they like rubbing against the beaches. Whales are most often seen during the salmon runs of July, August, and September. Because of their presence, Robson Bight has been made into an ecological preserve: Whales there must not be disturbed by human observers. Some of the island's best whale-watching tours, however, are conducted nearby, out of **Telegraph Cove,** a village built on pilings over water.

There are other things to do in the area, too. From Port McNeill, a 30-minute ferry ride will take you to Alert Bay, where you can see the First Nations artifacts at the **U'mista Cultural Centre** (☎ 250/974–5403), or to Sointula to visit the remains of a Finnish Utopian community.

Outdoor Activities and Sports

KAYAKING

In Telegraph Cove, **North Island Kayak Rentals** (☎ 250/949–7707) rents canoes and kayaks.

WHALE-WATCHING

Most trips run between June and October. Half- and full-day whale-watching expeditions are available through **Seasmoke/Sea Orca Whale Watching** (☎ 250/974–5225 or 800/668–6722) in Alert Bay and **Stubbs Island Whale Watching** (☎ 250/928–3185 or 800/665–3066) in Telegraph Cove.

Port Hardy

㉕ *238 km (148 mi) northwest of Campbell River, 499 km (309 mi) northwest of Victoria, 274 nautical mi southeast of Prince Rupert.*

Port Hardy is the departure and arrival point for BC Ferries' (☞ Getting Around *in* British Columbia A to Z, *below*) year-round trips through the scenic Inside Passage to and from Prince Rupert, the coastal port serving the Queen Charlotte Islands, and, in summer, to Bella Coola and other small communities along the midcoast. (For more information about these areas, *see* North Coast, *below*.) In summer Port Hardy can be crowded, so book your accommodations early. Ferry reservations for the trip between Port Hardy and Prince Rupert and Port Hardy and Bella Coola should also be made well in advance.

Lodging

$$ 🏨 **Glen Lyon Inn.** The rooms have a full ocean view of Hardy Bay and, like most other area motels, have clean, modern amenities. Eagles can often be spotted eyeing the water for fish to prey on. The inn is one of the closest to the ferry terminal, which is 7 km (4 mi) away. Fishing and whale-watching charters can be arranged. ⊠ *6435 Hardy Bay Rd., Box 103, V0N 2P0,* ☎ *250/949–7115,* 🆋 *250/949–7415. 29 rooms, 1 suite. Restaurant, lounge, no-smoking rooms. AE, DC, MC, V.*

SUNSHINE COAST

The stretch of mainland coast north of Vancouver, backed by mountains and accessible only by sea or air (☞ Getting Around *in* British Columbia A to Z, *below*), is so deeply cut with fjords that it has the look and feel of an island—or rather, two islands. The Sechelt Peninsula to the south has long been popular with artists, writers, and Vancouver weekenders. The Malaspina Peninsula, a ferry ride across Jervis Inlet to the north, is wilder and more densely forested; it is focused on the pulp mill town of Powell River. Highway 101, the one paved road running the length of the coast, forms the last (or the first) 139 km (86 mi) of the Pan-American Highway, connecting the village of Lund, British Columbia, to Puerto Mont, Chile, 24,000 km (14,880 mi) away.

The coast is a bit sunnier than the more exposed coastline to the north (hence its name), and its many provincial parks, marinas, lakes, and walking trails are popular with outdoorspeople and families, though not, as yet, with mass tourism or luxury resort developers. The Sunshine Coast remains one of the quieter, more affordable places to travel in southern British Columbia.

Sechelt

㉖ *37 km (22 mi) plus 12 nautical mi northwest of Vancouver.*

Sechelt, the largest town on the scenic peninsula of the same name, suffers a bit from sprawl but has several interesting shops and restaurants. It's home to many artists and writers as well as a strong First Nations community, the Sechelt Nation. The town is a good place to stock up on supplies.

To the south of Sechelt, in and around the seaside community of Gibsons and the 1930s-era village of Roberts Creek, are attractive parks, beaches, shops, B&Bs, and restaurants. (The Gumboot Garden and the Creekhouse restaurant are two good picks in Roberts Creek.) The best scenery, though, is to the north of Sechelt, around and beyond the little marinas of Madiera Park, Garden Bay, and Irvine's Landing, collectively known as **Pender Harbour.** Here Highway 101 winds past forests, mountains, and a delightful confusion of freshwater lakes and ocean inlets.

You can experience a dramatic natural sight at **Skookumchuk Narrows Provincial Park** (⊠ Egmont Rd. off Hwy. 101, ☎ 604/898–3678), 5 km (3 mi) inland from the Earls Cove ferry terminal and 45 km (28 mi) northwest of Sechelt. A 4-km (2½-mi) walk through the forest comes out at a viewpoint where, at the turn of the tide, seawater churning through the narrow channel creates one of the world's fastest tidal rapids. Tide tables are posted at the trailhead and at the **Pender Harbour Info Centre** (☎ 604/883–2561) in Madiera Park.

Princess Louisa Inlet is a narrow fjord at the top of Jervis Inlet; more than 60 waterfalls tumble down its steep walls. The fjord is accessible only by boat, and a number of local companies, including **Princess Louisa Tours** (☎ 604/512–7611 or 888/566–7778) and **Sunshine Coast Tours** (☎ 604/883–2456 or 800/870–9055), offer summer day trips.

Dining and Lodging

$–$$ ✕🏨 **Bonniebrook Lodge.** A seaside lodge 5 km (3 mi) north of Gib-
★ sons covers all the bases. Four rooms in the original 1922 building (three rooms share two baths) are freshly done in a Victorian style and share an ocean-view deck. Three larger, more luxurious rooms in a 1998 addition have all the romantic prerequisites: fireplaces, VCRs, minirefrigerators, and whirlpool baths for two. Chez Philippe ($$$), a fine French restaurant in the lodge, is open to the public for dinner; the $26 four-course set menu is an excellent value. A full breakfast is included at this no-smoking inn. The lodge is 20 km (12 mi) southeast of Sechelt. ⊠ *Foot of Gower Point Rd., R.R. 4, S-10, C-34, Gibsons V0N 1V0, ☎ 604/886–2887, 604/886–2188 for dinner reservations; ℻ 604/886–8853. 7 rooms, 4 with bath. Beach, camping. AE, DC, MC, V. Restaurant closed Tues.–Thurs. mid-Sept.–mid-May.*

$ 🏨 **Sundowner Inn.** This 1929 clapboard building, perched on a hill overlooking Garden Bay, was once a mission hospital. Now it's an atmospheric, family-run budget hotel, with basic rooms, 1950s furniture, and a stunning setting. You can take a boat trip to Princess Louisa Inlet and Desolation Sound from here, or join in the occasional dinner theater and murder mystery weekends. Garden Bay is 8 km (5 mi) off Highway 101, 30 km (19 mi) north of Sechelt. ⊠ *4339 Garden Bay Rd., Box 113, Garden Bay V0N 1S0, ☎ 604/883–9676, ℻ 604/883–9886. 10 rooms, 7 with bath. Restaurant, fans, outdoor hot tub, fishing, boating, dock, meeting rooms. DC, MC, V. Closed Nov.–Apr.*

Powell River

27 *70 km (43 mi) plus 12 nautical mi by ferry northwest of Sechelt, 121 km (75 mi) plus 12½ nautical mi northwest of Vancouver, 17 nautical mi (75-min ferry ride) east across Strait of Georgia from Comox.*

The main town on the Malaspina Peninsula, Powell River was established around a pulp-and-paper mill in 1912, and the forestry industry continues to have a strong presence in the area. The town has several B&Bs and restaurants, as well as a park with oceanfront camping and

RV hookups. The **Powell River Townsite,** one of the oldest function-ing mill towns in the province, is a national historic site. Thirty kilo-meters (19 mi) north of Powell River is the historic boardwalked village of **Lund,** the start (or end) of the Pan-American Highway.

Renowned as a year-round salmon-fishing destination, Powell River also has 30 regional lakes with exceptional trout fishing and is in-creasingly popular as a winter scuba diving destination. Nearby, the 80-km (50-mi) **Powell Forest Canoe Route** and **Desolation Sound Ma-rine Park** attract boaters. The **Powell River Visitors Bureau** (✉ 4690 Marine Ave., ☎ 604/485–4701) has information about the many ac-tivities and hiking trails in the area.

THE GULF ISLANDS

Of the hundreds of islands sprinkled across the Georgia Strait be-tween Vancouver Island and the mainland, the most popular and ac-cessible are Galiano, Mayne, and Salt Spring. A temperate climate (warmer, with half the rainfall of Vancouver), white shell beaches, rolling pasturelands, and virgin forests are common to all, but each island has its unique flavor. Marine birds are numerous, and there is unusual veg-etation such as arbutus trees (also known as madrones, a leafy ever-green with red peeling bark) and Garry oaks. Writers, artists, craftspeople, weekend cottagers, and retirees take full advantage of the undeveloped islands.

These islands are rustic (only Salt Spring has a bank machine) but not undiscovered: they are popular escapes from Vancouver and Victoria, and in summer it's a good idea to reserve accommodations. If you're bringing a car from mainland British Columbia, ferry reservations are required (☞ Getting Around *in* British Columbia A to Z, *below*). A bylaw bans smoking in all southern Gulf Island public places, includ-ing lodgings, restaurants, and pubs.

Galiano Island

28 *20 nautical mi (almost 2 hrs by ferry due to interisland stops) from Swartz Bay (32 km/20 mi north of Victoria), 13 nautical mi (a 50-min ferry ride) from Tsawwassen (39 km/24 mi south of Vancouver).*

Galiano's long, unbroken eastern shoreline is perfect for leisurely beach walks, and the numerous coves and inlets along the western coast make it a prime area for kayaking. **Montague Harbour Provincial Ma-rine Park** has camping and boating facilities. Miles of trails through Douglas-fir forest beg for exploration by foot or bike. Hikers can climb to the top of **Mt. Galiano** for a view of the Olympic Mountains in Washington or trek the length of **Bodega Ridge.** The best spots to view Active Pass and the surrounding islands are Bluffs Park and Bell-house Park; these are also good for picnicking and bird-watching.

Biological studies show that the straits between Vancouver Island and the mainland of British Columbia are home to the largest variety of marine life in North America. The frigid waters offer superb visibility, especially in winter. Alcala Point, Porlier Pass, and Active Pass are top locations for scuba diving. Anglers head to the point at Bellhouse Park to spin cast for salmon from shore or head by boat to Porlier Pass and Trincomali Channel.

Go Galiano (☎ 250/539–0202) provides year-round taxi, bus, ferry pickup, and sightseeing services on the island. In summer, **Dionisio Ex-press** (☎ 250/539–3109) runs a boat service to Dionisio Marine Park.

Dining and Lodging

$$–$$$ ✕⊞ **Woodstone Country Inn.** This serene inn sits on the edge of a for-
★ est overlooking a meadow that's fantastic for bird-watching. Stenciled
walls and tall windows bring the pastoral setting into spacious bedrooms. Most of the rooms have fireplaces, patios, and oversize soaker
tubs. A hearty gourmet breakfast and afternoon tea are included in the
cost. Woodstone's elegant restaurant serves French-influenced Pacific
Northwest fare, such as yam soup with toasted almonds and herb-crusted
rack of lamb with pear-tomato chutney and mustard-seed sauce. Guests
and nonguests can have four-course dinners here by advance reservation. ✉ *Georgeson Bay Rd., R.R. 1, V0N 1P0,* ☏ *250/539–2022 or
888/339–2022,* ⊞ *250/539–5198. 13 rooms. Restaurant, piano, meeting room. AE, MC, V. Closed Jan.*

$–$$ ⊞ **Sutil Lodge.** Family photos from the 1920s and Art Deco furnish-
★ ings re-create a sense of lodge life in an earlier era at this 1928 bungalow set on 20 wooded acres on Montague Bay. The simple guest rooms
have throw rugs on dark hardwood floors and beds tucked under
window nooks. The kayak center on the property attracts folks from
around the world (rentals and guided trips are available). Another option is a catamaran cruise with a gourmet picnic lunch. A full breakfast, served in the lodge's old dance hall, and afternoon tea are included
in the rate at this friendly, no-smoking inn. ✉ *637 Southwind Rd., V0N
1P0,* ☏ *250/539–2930 or 888/539–2930,* ⊞ *250/539–5390. 7 rooms
share 3 baths. Breakfast room, hiking. AE, MC, V. Closed Oct.–Mar.*

Outdoor Activities and Sports

BIKING

Biking is a fun way to explore the island's miles of trails. Bike rentals
are available from **Galiano Bicycle** (✉ 36 Burrill Rd., ☏ 250/539–9906),
within walking distance of the Sturdies Bay ferry terminal.

DIVING

For dive charters, contact **Galiano Diving** (☏ 250/539–3109) or **Gulf
Islands Diving & Boat Charters** (☏ 250/539–5341).

FISHING

Bert's Charters (☏ 250/539–3181), **Mel-n-i Fishing Charters** (☏ 250/
539–3171), and **Retreat Cove Charters** (☏ 250/539–9981) are some
of the many fishing operators on the island.

GOLF

The **Galiano Golf and Country Club** (✉ 24 St. Andrew Crescent, ☏
250/539–5533) is a nine-hole, par-32 course in a forest clearing.

KAYAKING

Galiano Island Sea Kayak and Catamaran (☏ 250/539–2930 or 888/
539–2930) has rentals and tours; it also offers catamaran cruises with
a gourmet picnic lunch. **Gulf Islands Kayaking** (☏ 250/539–2442) has
equipment rentals and guided kayak tours.

Mayne Island

㉙ *28 nautical mi from Swartz Bay (32 km/20 mi north of Victoria), 22
nautical mi from Tsawwassen (39 km/24 mi south of Vancouver).*

Middens of clam and oyster shells give evidence that tiny Mayne Island—only 21 square km (8 square mi)—was inhabited as early as 5,000
years ago. It later became the stopover point for miners headed from
Victoria to the gold fields of the Fraser River and Barkerville. By the
mid-1800s it had developed into the communal center of the inhabited Gulf Islands, with the first school, post office, police lockup,
church, and hotel. Farm tracts and orchards established in the 1930s

and 1940s and worked by Japanese farmers until their internment during World War II continue to thrive today. Mayne's mild hills and wonderful scenery make it great territory for a vigorous bike ride.

Mount Parke was declared a wilderness park in 1989. A 45-minute hike leads to the highest point on the island and a stunning, almost 360° view of Vancouver, Active Pass, and Vancouver Island.

The small town of **Miners Bay** is home to Plumbers Pass Lockup (closed September–June), built in 1896 as a jail but now a minuscule museum chronicling the island's history. You could also stop for a drink at the seaside **Springwater Lodge,** one of the oldest hotels in the province. From Miners Bay head north on Georgina Point Road to **St. Mary Magdalene Church,** a pretty stone chapel built in 1898. Across the road, a stairway leads down to the beach.

Active Pass Lighthouse, at the end of Georgina Point Road, is part of Georgina Point Heritage Park. It was built in 1855 and still signals ships into the busy waterway. The grassy grounds are great for picnicking. There's a pebble beach for beachcombing at shallow (and therefore warmer) **Campbell Bay.**

Dining and Lodging

$$$–$$$$ ✗🖬 **Oceanwood Country Inn.** This Tudor-style house on 10 quiet,
★   forested acres overlooking Navy Channel has English country decor throughout. Fireplaces, French doors opening onto ocean-view balconies, and whirlpool baths make several rooms deluxe. The waterfront restaurant serves four-course table d'hôte dinners of outstanding regional cuisine such as pan-seared Fraser Valley turkey breast and potato-crusted sea bass. Afternoon tea and breakfast are included in the room rates. ⊠ *630 Dinner Bay Rd., V0N 2J0,* ☎ *250/539–5074,* ℻ *250/539–3002. 12 rooms. Restaurant, hot tub, sauna, hiking, jogging, bicycles, library, meeting room. MC, V. Closed Dec.–Feb.*

$$ ✗🖬 **Fernhill Lodge.** This 1983 west-coast cedar contemporary has fantastical theme rooms—Moroccan, East Indian, and Old English. Two of them have outdoor hot tubs. On the 5-acre grounds are an herb garden and a rustic gazebo with a meditation loft. Hosts Mary and Brian Crumblehulme offer, on request, historical four-course dinners (Roman, medieval, and Renaissance, to name a few themes) for guests and nonguests. Full breakfasts are included in the room rate. ⊠ *Fernhill Rd., R.R. 1, C-4, V0N 2J0,* ☎℻ *250/539–2544. 3 rooms. Dining room, sauna, piano, library. MC, V.*

Outdoor Activities and Sports

Bay View Bike Rentals (⊠ 764 Steward Rd., Miners Bay, ☎ 250/539–2924) rents bicycles. For kayak rentals, try **Mayne Island Kayaking** (⊠ 359 Maple Dr., Miners Bay, ☎ 250/539–2667).

Salt Spring Island

③⓪   *28 nautical mi from Swartz Bay (32 km/20 mi north of Victoria), 22 nautical mi from Tsawwassen (39 km/24 mi south of Vancouver).*

Named for the saltwater springs at its north end, Salt Spring is the largest and most developed of the Gulf Islands. Among its first nonnative settlers were black Americans who came here to escape slavery in the 1850s. The agrarian tradition they and other immigrants established remains strong (a Fall Fair has been held every September since 1896), but tourism and art now support the local economy. A government wharf, three marinas, and a waterfront shopping complex at Ganges serve a community of more than 10,000 residents.

Ganges, a pedestrian-oriented seaside village and the island's cultural and commercial center, has dozens of smart boutiques, galleries, and restaurants. Mouat's Trading Company (⊠ Fulford–Ganges Rd.), built in 1912, was the original village general store. It's now a hardware store but still houses a display of historical photographs.

Ganges is also the site of **ArtCraft,** a summer-long arts-and-craft sale featuring the work of more than 200 artisans, and the **Salt Spring Festival of the Arts,** a festival of international music, theater, and dance held in July. Dozens of working **artists' studios** are open to the public here; pick up a studio tour map at the **Visitor Information Centre** (⊠ 121 Lower Ganges Rd., ☎ 250/537–5252).

St. Mary Lake, on North End Road, and **Cusheon Lake,** south of Ganges, are the best bets for warm-water swimming.

Near the center of Salt Spring, the summit of **Mt. Maxwell Provincial Park** (⊠ Mt. Maxwell Rd., off Fulford–Ganges Rd.) has spectacular views of south Salt Spring, Vancouver Island, and other Gulf Islands. It's also a great picnic spot. The last portion of the drive is steep, winding, and unpaved.

Ruckle Provincial Park (⊠ Beaver Point Rd., ☎ 250/653–4115) is the site of an 1872 homestead and extensive fields still farmed by the Ruckle family. The park also has camping and picnic spots, 11 km (7 mi) of coastline, a beach, and trails leading to rocky headlands.

Dining and Lodging

The **Visitor Information Centre** (☞ *above*) can direct you to many of Salt Spring's lodging options. The island also has a number of provincial campsites and a **youth hostel** (☎ 250/537–4149) that has tepees and tree houses as well as dorms and tenting on the island.

$$$–$$$$ ✕ **House Piccolo.** Blue-and-white tablecloths and framed pastel prints on whitewashed walls give this cozy restaurant a casual feel. Broiled sea scallop brochette, roasted British Columbia venison with juniper berries, and the salmon du jour are good choices from the dinner menu, but save room for homemade ice cream or the signature chocolate terrine. ⊠ *108 Hereford Ave., Ganges,* ☎ *250/537–1844. Reservations essential. AE, DC, MC, V. No lunch.*

$–$$ ✕ **Moby's Marine Pub.** Big portions of great food such as warm salmon or scallop salad and lamb burgers, a harborside deck, a cozy room with fireplaces, and Sunday evening jazz make this friendly, no-smoking pub a favorite among visitors and islanders alike. ⊠ *124 Upper Ganges Rd.,* ☎ *250/537–5559. MC, V.*

$$$$ ✕▦ **Hastings House.** The centerpiece of this luxurious 25-acre seaside farm estate is a Tudor-style manor built in 1939. Guest quarters are in the manor or in beautifully renovated buildings around the property. All are furnished with antiques in an English country theme; all have fireplaces or woodstoves. The rates, among the highest in the province, include a full breakfast and afternoon tea. In-room spa services are also available. Five-course prix-fixe dinners in the manor house are open to the public (reservations essential); some typical entrées are peppered venison medallions and grilled leg of lamb with garlic potato puree. A jacket is required in the formal dining room but not in the more casual lower-floor dining area. ⊠ *160 Upper Ganges Rd., V8K 2S2,* ☎ *250/537–2362 or 800/661–9255,* FAX *250/537–5333. 3 rooms, 7 suites. Restaurant, minibars, massage, croquet, mountain bikes. AE, MC, V. Closed Jan.–early Mar.*

$$$–$$$$ ▦ **Anne's Oceanfront Hideaway.** Perched on a steep slope above the sea, 6 km (4 mi) north of the Vesuvius ferry terminal, this modern, wa-

terfront home has panoramic ocean views, a cozy library, a sitting room, an elevator, and two covered verandas. A lavish hot breakfast is included in the price, and one room is wheelchair accessible. Every room has a hydromassage tub; three have private balconies. The Douglas Fir and Garry Oak rooms have the best views. Luxurious details, like morning coffee in the rooms, robes, and a welcoming bottle of wine, make this a comfortable place to unwind. ⊠ *168 Simson Rd., V8K 1E2,* ☎ *250/537–0851 or 888/474–2663,* FAX *250/537–0861. 4 rooms. Breakfast room, air-conditioning, outdoor hot tub, boating, bicycles, library. AE, MC, V.*

$$$–$$$$ ⌂ **Beach House on Sunset.** The sunsets are stunning from this Mediterranean-style house set on a waterfront slope 5 km (3 mi) north of the Vesuvius ferry terminal. Three upstairs rooms in the B&B have private entrances and balconies; one has French doors framing sea views, a fireplace, a claw-foot tub, and a private deck with an outdoor shower. A one-bedroom cedar cottage with a wraparound porch and a kitchen sits over the boathouse at water's edge. Extras include down comforters, terry robes, slippers, fruit platters, decanters of sherry, and a bountiful breakfast. You can also arrange boat charters and kayak tours here. ⊠ *930 Sunset Dr., V8K 1E6,* ☎ *250/537–2879,* FAX *250/537–4747. 3 rooms, 1 cottage. Breakfast room, boating. MC, V. Closed Dec.–Feb.*

$$–$$$$ ⌂ **Salty Springs Spa Resort.** The only property to take advantage of the island's natural mineral springs has a full-service spa offering beauty treatments, herbal wraps, massage, and more for guests and nonguests. Accommodations at this adult-oriented resort include a new four-room B&B and one- and two-bedroom chalet-style pine cabins with Gothic-arch ceilings, fireplaces, kitchenettes, hot mineral-springs baths for two, and private decks with gas barbecues. Most of the cabins are set close together but have unobstructed ocean views; two chalets tucked away in the woods are more private. ⊠ *1460 N. Beach Rd., V8K 1J4,* ☎ *250/537–4111,* FAX *250/537–2939. 4 rooms, 13 cabins. Sauna, spa, steam room, badminton, boating, bicycles, recreation room, coin laundry, meeting room. AE, MC, V.*

Outdoor Activities and Sports

Cycling and kayaking are the main activities on Salt Spring, and operators tend to double up. For kayaking trips, lessons, and rentals, as well as bike rentals and repairs, try **Salt Spring Kayaking** (⊠ 2923 Fulford–Ganges Rd., Ganges, ☎ 250/653–4222). **Salt Spring Marine Rentals** (⊠ At the head of Ganges Harbour, ☎ 250/537–9100) has fishing charters, nature cruises, and boat, bicycle, and scooter rentals. A source for kayak rentals, tours, and lessons is **Sea Otter Kayaking** (⊠ 1186 North End Rd., Ganges, ☎ 250/537–5678). **Island Escapades** (⊠ 163 Fulford–Ganges Rd., Ganges, ☎ 250/537–2537 or 888/529–2567) offers kayaking, sailing, hiking, and climbing tours.

GOLF

Blackburn Meadows Golf Course (⊠ 269 Blackburn Rd., ☎ 250/537–1707) and **Salt Spring Island Golf and Country Club** (⊠ 805 Lower Ganges Rd., ☎ 250/537–2121) are both pleasant nine-hole courses.

COAST MOUNTAIN CIRCLE

A stunning sampler of mainland British Columbia, a drive into the Coast Mountains from Vancouver follows the Sea to Sky Highway (Highway 99) past fjordlike Howe Sound and Whistler, world famous for its skiing. The route then continues on a quiet back road to the gold-rush town of Lillooet, where you can either head into the High Country or return to Vancouver. The latter choice will take you along Highways 12 and 1 through the gorges of the Fraser Canyon; you can stop for a soak at the spa town of Harrison Hot Springs on the way. This is a scenic two- to three-day drive; the roads are good but are best avoided in snow past Whistler. A BC Rail line also cuts a dramatic swath through the mountains from North Vancouver to Lillooet, on its way north to Prince George.

Whistler

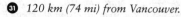 *120 km (74 mi) from Vancouver.*

If you think of skiing when you hear mention of Whistler, British Columbia, your thinking is on track. Whistler and Blackcomb mountains, part of Whistler Resort, are the two largest ski mountains in North America and are consistently ranked the first- or second-best ski destinations on the continent. The resort has winter and summer glacier skiing, the longest vertical drop in North America, and one of the most advanced lift systems in the world. Whistler has also grown in popularity as a summer destination, with a range of outdoor activities and events to fill the warm, sunny months. Even if you don't want to roam much farther than the village, there are five lakes for canoeing, fishing, swimming, and windsurfing; five golf courses; and many hiking and mountain-bike trails. All this action is just a couple of hours from Vancouver.

At the base of Whistler and Blackcomb mountains are Whistler Village, Village North (also called Marketplace), and Upper Village—a rapidly expanding, interconnected community of lodgings, restaurants, pubs, gift shops, and boutiques. Culinary options in the resort range from burgers to French food, Japanese fare to deli cuisine; nightly entertainment runs the gamut from sophisticated piano bars to casual pubs. With all of the recent expansion in Whistler, there is now space to rest 15,200 sleepy heads within 1,500 ft of the lifts. Dozens of hotels and condos stand within a five-minute walk of the mountains, and the site is frenzied with activity. In winter, the village buzzes with skiers and snowboarders from all over the world; in summer the pace is more relaxed, as the focus shifts to cycling, hiking, and boating around the Whistler Valley.

Streets in Whistler Village, Village North, and Upper Village are all pedestrian-only; pay parking is readily available on the village outskirts. But anywhere you want to go within the resort is at most five minutes away. The bases of Whistler and Blackcomb mountains are just at the edge of town; in fact, you can ski right into the lower level of the Chateau Whistler Resort. Whistler Municipality operates a free **public transit system** that loops throughout the village, and paid public transit serves the whole valley; call ☎ 604/932–4020 for information and schedules. For a cab, call **Sea to Sky Taxi** (☎ 604/932–3333).

Dining

Dining at Whistler is informal; casual dress is appropriate everywhere. Prices tend to be higher than in the surrounding region. Many restaurants close for a week or two between late October and late November. In the winter or summer, you'll need dinner reservations in all but the fast-food joints.

$$$$ ✕ **Val d'Isère.** Chef-owner Roland Pfaff satisfies a skier's craving for fine French food with traditional dishes from his native Alsace and with Gallic takes on Canadian produce. Some specialties served in this elegant but welcoming room overlooking the Town Plaza are goat cheese and roasted chestnut salad, braised duck legs with endives, and roast rabbit with dried fruit crumbs and polenta. ⊠ *8–4314 Main St.*, ☎

604/932–4666. Reservations essential. AE, DC, MC, V. No lunch Nov.–May.

$$$–$$$$ ✗ **Il Caminetto di Umberto, Trattoria di Umberto.** Umberto offers home-style Italian cooking in a relaxed atmosphere; he specializes in such pasta dishes as seafood-and-spinach-stuffed cannelloni. Il Caminetto is known for its veal, osso buco, and game dishes. The Trattoria is the more casual and slightly less expensive of the two. ✉ *Il Caminetto: 4242 Village Stroll,* ☎ *604/932–4442;* ✉ *Trattoria: Mountainside Lodge, 4417 Sundial Pl.,* ☎ *604/932–5858. Reservations essential at both restaurants. AE, DC, MC, V. No lunch at Il Caminetto di Umberto.*

$$$–$$$$ ✗ **La Rúa.** One of the brightest lights on the Whistler dining scene is on the ground floor of Le Chamois (☞ Lodging, *below*). Reddish flagstone floors and sponge-painted walls, a wine cellar behind a wrought-iron door, modern oil paintings, and sconce lighting give the restaurant an intimate, Mediterranean ambience. Favorites from the Continental menu include charred rare tuna, loin of deer, rack of lamb, and baked sea bass fillet in red wine and herb sauce. ✉ *4557 Blackcomb Way,* ☎ *604/932–5011. Reservations essential. AE, DC, MC, V. No lunch.*

$$–$$$$ ✗ **Zeuski's.** This friendly taverna in Village North brings big portions of tasty Greek fare to Whistler. Wall murals of the Greek islands surround candlelit tables, helping create a Mediterranean atmosphere. There's also a patio for alfresco dining. It's hard to pass on the spanakopita, souvlaki, and other standards, but the house special, *kotapoulo* (chicken breast rolled in pistachios and roasted), is not to be missed, nor are the tender, delicately herb-battered calamari. ✉ *4314 Main St.,* ☎ *604/932–6009. Reservations essential. AE, DC, MC, V.*

$$–$$$ ✗ **The Brewhouse.** Whistler's first brew pub serves up six of its own ales and lagers, with names like Big Wolf Bitter and Dirty Miner Stout, in a cozy setting in Village North. The restaurant's open kitchen serves wood-oven pizza, rotisserie prime rib, and spit-roast chicken; the casual pub on the same premises has pool tables, TV screens, and some creative pub grub. ✉ *4355 Blackcomb Way,* ☎ *604/905–2739. AE, MC, V.*

Lodging

Lodgings, including B&B inns, pensions, and hundreds of time-share condos, can be booked through **Whistler Central Reservations** (☎ 604/932–4222; 604/664–5625 in Vancouver; 800/944–7853 in the U.S. and Canada).

Price categories are based on January–April ski season rates; rates are somewhat higher during Christmas and spring break and can be slightly lower in the summer. Many Whistler lodgings require minimum stays, especially during the Christmas season. Also be aware that Whistler Village has some serious nightlife. If peace and quiet are important to you, ask for a room away from the main pedestrian thoroughfares or consider staying outside the village in one of Whistler's residential neighborhoods.

$$$$ 🏨 **Chateau Whistler Resort.** This family-friendly fortress just steps
★ from the Blackcomb ski lifts is a self-contained, ski-in, ski-out resort-within-a-resort, with its own shopping arcade and other amenities. The marvelous lobby is filled with rustic Canadiana, handmade Mennonite rugs, a grand stone fireplace, and enticing overstuffed sofas. The standard rooms are comfortably furnished and of average size, but the suites are fit for royalty, with antique furnishings and specially commissioned quilts and artwork. Rooms and suites on the Entrée Gold floors have fireplaces, whirlpool tubs, and their own concierge and private lounge. Wildflower, the rustic main dining room, features an à la carte menu starring fresh, often organic British Columbia fare. ✉

4599 Chateau Blvd., V0N 1B4, ☎ *604/938–8000 or 800/606–8244,* FAX *604/938–2099. 558 rooms, 47 suites. 2 restaurants, lobby lounge, indoor-outdoor pool, beauty salon, hot tub, sauna, spa, steam room, 18-hole golf course, 3 tennis courts, health club, ski shop, ski storage, children's programs (ages 5–12), concierge, concierge floor, convention center. AE, D, DC, MC, V.*

$$$$ 🏨 **Le Chamois.** At the foot of the Blackcomb ski runs, the Chamois has a prime location in the Upper Village. Of the spacious rooms with convenience kitchens, the most romantic are the executive studios with whirlpool baths set in front of the living room's windows, overlooking the slopes and lifts. The one-bedroom suites with kitchenettes and two full baths are great for families; the three- and four-bedroom suites with gas fireplaces, fully equipped kitchens, and washer/dryers are a good bet for groups. ⊠ *4557 Blackcomb Way, V0N 1B4,* ☎ *604/ 932–8700 or 800/777–0185,* FAX *604/905–2576. 47 suites, 6 studios. Restaurant, café, kitchenettes, room service, exercise room, coin laundry, meeting rooms. AE, DC, MC, V.*

$$$–$$$$ 🏨 **Durlacher Hof.** Custom fir woodwork and doors, exposed ceiling beams, a *kachelofen* (traditional farmhouse fireplace-oven), and antler chandeliers hung over fir benches and tables carry out the rustic European theme of this fancy Tyrolean inn a few minutes' walk outside the village. The green and maroon bedrooms contain more custom-crafted furniture but no phones or TVs to disturb the peace. Four upgraded rooms are very spacious and have such added amenities as whirlpool tubs; smaller rooms have showers rather than tubs. A hearty European breakfast and afternoon tea are included in the tariff, and occasional dinners are also available at this no-smoking inn. German is spoken here. ⊠ *7055 Nesters Rd., Box 1125, V0N 1B0,* ☎ *604/ 932–1924,* FAX *604/938–1980. 8 rooms. Breakfast room, massage, outdoor hot tub, sauna, ski storage. MC, V.*

$$–$$$ 🏨 **Edgewater Lodge.** This modern cedar lodge lies along glacier-fed Green Lake on 45 acres of private forested land, about 3 km (2 mi) north of the village. All rooms have private entrances, TVs, phones, and expansive water and mountain views. A bit removed from Whistler's ski slopes and nightlife, Edgewater is perfectly placed for peace, quiet, and the resort's myriad other activities. Biking, hiking, and cross-country ski trails run past the lodge, and the Nicklaus North Golf Course (☞ Golf *in* Outdoor Activities and Sports, *below*) is nearby. The Whistler Outdoor Experience (☞ Boating *in* Outdoor Activities and Sports, *below*) runs an activity center here, offering fishing, hiking, canoeing, kayaking, and trail riding in summer, and snowshoeing, sleigh rides, and cross-country skiing in winter; these activities are also available to nonguests. Breakfast is included in the tariff at this no-smoking inn, and highly rated evening meals are also available. ⊠ *8841 Hwy. 99, Box 369, V0N 1B0,* ☎ *604/932–0688 or 888/870–9065,* FAX *604/ 932–0686. 6 rooms, 6 suites. Restaurant, bar, outdoor hot tub, meeting room. AE, MC, V. CP.*

$ 🏨 **Hostelling International Whistler.** One of the nicest hostels in Canada is also the cheapest sleep in the area. Beds in men's or women's four-bunked dorms, a shared kitchen, and a games room with a pool table and fireplace make up the basic accommodations of this hostel overlooking Alta Lake. The hostel is next to the swimming beach at Rainbow Park and is 15 km (10 mi) by road, or 4 km (2½ mi) by footpath, from the village. About four Buslink buses a day serve the hostel, and BC Rail will make a request stop here. ⊠ *5678 Alta Lake Rd., V0N 1B0,* ☎ *604/932–5492,* FAX *604/932–4687. 32 beds in 7 dorms, 1 private room (no bath). Ski storage. MC, V.*

Outdoor Activities and Sports

The best first stop for any Whistler outdoor activity is the **Whistler Activity and Information Center** (⌂ 4010 Whistler Way, ☏ 604/932–2394) in the conference center at the edge of the village, where you can book activities and pick up hiking and biking maps.

Adjacent to the Whistler area is the 78,000-acre **Garibaldi Provincial Park** (⌂ off Hwy. 99, ☏ 604/898–3678), with dense mountainous forests splashed with hospitable lakes and streams.

BOATING

Canoe and kayak rentals are available at **Alta Lake** at both Lakeside Park and Wayside Park. A spot that's perfect for canoeing is the **River of Golden Dreams,** from Alta Lake to Green Lake. For guided canoeing and kayaking trips, as well as sailing and water-skiing, call **Whistler Outdoor Experience** (☏ 604/932–3389) at the Edgewater Lodge on Green Lake.

There are several rivers with rapids around Whistler, and **Whistler River Adventures** (☏ 604/932–3532 or 888/932–3532) offers a variety of half- and full-day rafting and jet-boating trips.

FISHING

All five of the lakes around Whistler are stocked with trout. **Whistler Backcountry Adventures** (☏ 604/932–3474), **Whistler Fishing Guides** (☏ 604/932–4267), and **Whistler River Adventures** (☏ 604/932–3532 or 888/932–3532) will take care of anything you need—equipment, guides, and transportation.

GOLF

Chateau Whistler Golf Club (⌂ 4612 Blackcomb Way, ☏ 604/938–2092) is an excellent 18-hole, par-72 course designed by Robert Trent Jones II. The **Nicklaus North Golf Course** (⌂ 8080 Nicklaus North Blvd., ☏ 604/938–9898 or 800/386–9898) is a challenging 18-hole, par-71 course designed by Jack Nicklaus. Arnold Palmer designed the 18-hole, par-72 championship course at the **Whistler Golf Club** (⌂ 4010 Whistler Way, ☏ 604/932–4544 or 800/376–1777).

HIKING

In summer, Whistler and Blackcomb's ski lifts whisk hikers up to the alpine, where marked trails are graded by difficulty. Pick up a map at the **Whistler Activity and Information Center** (☞ *above*) in the village, or join a guided hike or nature walk with **Outdoor Adventures@Whistler** (☏ 604/932–0647) or **Whistler Outdoor Experience** (☏ 604/932–3389).

HORSEBACK RIDING

The **Adventure Ranch** (☏ 604/894–5020, 604/932–3532, or 888/932–3532), north of Whistler, **Sea to Sky Stables** (☏ 604/898–3908), south of Whistler, and **Whistler Outdoor Experience** (☏ 604/932–3389) at Green Lake run trail rides.

INDOOR SPORTS

Meadow Park Sports Centre (⌂ 8107 Camino Dr., ☏ 604/938–3133), about 6 km (4 mi) north of Whistler Village, has a six-lane pool, children's wading pool, hockey–ice-skating rink, hot tub, sauna, steam room, and two squash courts. **Mountain World** (⌂ 4010A Whistler Way, ☏ 604/932–5000), in the village, has an indoor climbing wall, golf and ski simulators, and a whole range of virtual reality games.

SIGHTSEEING

Blackcomb Helicopters (☏ 604/938–1700 or 800/330–4354) is one of several local operators that fly year-round flightseeing tours over Whistler's stunning mountains and glaciers. In summer, the company offers heli-hiking, heli-fishing, heli-picnics, and even heli-weddings. Several companies, including **Outdoor Adventures@Whistler** (☎ 604/932–0647) and **Whistler ATV Tours** (☎ 604/932–6681), have guided rides through the backcountry in all-terrain vehicles.

SKIING AND SNOW SPORTS

The meandering trail around the Whistler Golf Course in the village is an ideal beginners' route for cross-country skiing. For more advanced skiing, try the 28 km (17 mi) of track-set trails that wind around scenic Lost Lake, Chateau Whistler Golf Course, the Nicklaus North Golf Course, and Green Lake. Cross-country trail maps and equipment rental information are available at the **Whistler Activity and Information Center** (☞ *above*) in the village.

The vertical drops and elevations at **Blackcomb** and **Whistler** (☎ 604/932–3434 or 800/766–0449, FAX 604/938–9174) mountains are perhaps the most impressive features to downhill skiers and snowboarders here. Blackcomb has a 5,280-ft vertical drop, North America's longest, although Whistler comes in second, with a 5,020-ft drop. The top elevation is 7,494 ft on Blackcomb and 7,160 on Whistler. Blackcomb and Whistler receive an average of 360 inches of snow per year; Blackcomb is open June–early August for summer glacier skiing. The resort covers 7,071 acres of skiable terrain in 12 alpine bowls and on three glaciers and has more than 200 marked trails. It is served by the most advanced high-speed lift system on the continent.

For a primer on the ski facilities here, drop by the free **Whistler Welcome Night** (☎ 604/932–3434 or 800/766–0449), held at 6:30 every Thursday and Sunday evening during the ski season at the Chateau Whistler Resort or the Whistler Conference Centre. First-timers at Whistler, whether beginners or experienced skiers, may want to try **Ski Esprit** (☎ 604/932–3434 or 800/766–0449). Run by the resort, these three- to four-day programs combine lessons, après-ski activities, and an insider's guide to the mountains. **Whistler/Blackcomb Ski and Snowboard School** (☎ 604/932–3434 or 800/766–0449) provides lessons to skiers of all levels. Equipment rentals are available at the **Whistler Gondola Base** (☎ 604/905–2252) and at several outlets in the village. The **Mountain Adventure Centre** (☎ 604/905–2295) in the Pan Pacific Hotel, at the Blackcomb Day Lodge, and at two alpine locations, rents high-performance gear and lets you swap equipment during the day.

Whistler Heli-Skiing (☎ 604/932–4105 or 888/435–4754) has guided day trips with up to three glacier runs, or 8,000 to 10,000 ft of skiing, for intermediate to expert skiers; the cost is about $430.

Whistler has plenty of options for nonskiing days, too. **Blackcomb Snowmobile** (☎ 604/932–8484) runs guided snowmobile trips into the backcountry. **Outdoor Adventures@Whistler** (☎ 604/932–0647) can take you for walks in the deep powder on snowshoes. **Whistler Outdoor Experience** (☎ 604/932–3389) runs romantic horse-drawn sleigh rides as well as snowshoeing and cross-country ski trips. **Whistler Snowmobile** (☎ 604/932–4086) has dogsled trips as well as snowmobiling and snowshoeing.

Lillooet

131 km (81 mi) northeast of Whistler.

Past Whistler, Highway 99 is much less traveled as it makes its way around lakes and glaciers, through the Mount Currie native reserve, and over the mountains to Lillooet. The arid gullies and Wild West landscape around Lillooet may come as a surprise after the greenery of the coast and mountains. During the 1850s and 1860s this was Mile Zero of the Cariboo Wagon Road, which took prospectors to the gold fields. There are several motels in Lillooet and a BC Rail station. The **Lillooet Museum** (⊠ 790 Main St., ☎ 250/256–4308), open May–August, presents native and gold-rush history.

Fraser Canyon

Highway 1, the Trans-Canada Highway, follows the Fraser River as it cuts its way from the High Country through the Coast Mountains to Vancouver. The deepest, most dramatic cut is the 38-km (24-mi) gorge between Yale and Boston Bar, where the road and rail line cling to the hillside high above the water.

At **Hell's Gate,** about 40 km (25 mi) south of Lytton, an airtram (cable car) carries passengers across the foaming canyon above the fishways, where millions of sockeye salmon fight their way upriver to spawning grounds. The lower airtram terminal has displays on the life cycle of the salmon, a fudge factory, a gift shop, and a restaurant. This site is about 2½ hours east of Vancouver. ⊠ *Hell's Gate Airtram, Exit 170 off Hwy. 1, Hope,* ☎ *604/867–9277.* ☜ *$10.* ☉ *Apr. and Oct., daily 10–4; May–June and Sept., daily 9–5; July–Aug., daily 9–6.*

Harrison Hot Springs

③² *128 km (79 mi) northeast of Vancouver.*

The small resort community of Harrison Hot Springs lies at the southern tip of picturesque Harrison Lake, off Highway 7 in the Fraser Valley. Mountains surround the 64-km-long (40-mi-long) lake, which is ringed by pretty beaches. Besides the hot springs, boating and swimming are popular here.

The **Harrison Public Pool,** across from the beach, is an indoor hot spring–fed pool. ⊠ *224 Esplanade,* ☎ *604/796–2244.* ☜ *$7.* ☉ *Daily 9 AM–9 PM.*

☾ **Kilby Historic Store and Farm,** a 20-minute drive west of Harrison Hot Springs, re-creates a rural British Columbian village of the 1920s with some original buildings and some replicas, farm animals, costumed interpreters, and 1920s-style home cooking in the **Harrison River Tearoom.** ⊠ *215 Kilby Rd. (off Hwy. 7), Harrison Mills,* ☎ *604/796–3859.* ☜ *$5.* ☉ *Mid-Apr.–mid-Nov.; call for hrs.*

Minter Gardens, 8 km (5 mi) southwest of Harrison Hot Springs, is a 27-acre compound with 11 beautifully presented theme gardens (Chinese, English, and rose, for example), playgrounds, and a giant evergreen maze. ⊠ *Exit 135 off Hwy. 1, 52892 Bunker Rd., Rosedale,* ☎ *604/794–7191 or 888/646–8377.* ☜ *$9.50.* ☉ *Apr.–Oct., daily 9–dusk.*

Dining and Lodging

$$$ ✕ **Black Forest.** A charming Bavarian dining room overlooking the lake serves German standards from schnitzels to Black Forest cake, with a few Continental dishes (mainly steaks and seafood) for good measure. Hearty German beer and an array of wines round out the selection. ⊠ *180 Esplanade,* ☎ *604/796–9343. AE, MC, V. No lunch Oct.–Apr.*

$$–$$$$ ⊞ **Harrison Hot Springs Resort.** Built beside the lake in 1926, this hotel has expanded over the years with two modern high-rise additions. Rooms are freshly renovated, and amenities include a new, 6,000-ft outdoor hot spring–fed pool with waterfalls, an outdoor freshwater pool, and a children's water park. ⊠ *100 Esplanade, V0M 1K0,* ☎ *604/796–2244 or 800/663–2266,* ₣ₐₓ *604/796–3682. 302 rooms, 11 cottages. 2 restaurants, coffee bar, lounge, no-smoking floors, room* *service, 2 indoor and 3 outdoor pools, massage, sauna, 9-hole golf course, 2 tennis courts, exercise room, hiking, jogging, bicycles, billiards, playground, laundry service, convention center. AE, D, MC, V.*

En Route Off Highway 1, about an hour west of Harrison Hot Springs on the way back to Vancouver, is **Ft. Langley National Historic Site,** a re-created 1850s Hudson's Bay trading post. ✉ *23433 Mavis St., Fort Langley,* ☎ *604/513–4777.* 🎫 *$4.* ⊙ *Mar.–Oct., daily 10–5.*

NORTH COAST

Gateway to Alaska and the Yukon, this vast, rugged region is marked by soaring, snowcapped mountain ranges, scenic fjords, primordial islands, and towering rain forests. Once the center of a vast trading network, the mid- and north coasts are home to First Nations peoples who have lived here for 10,000 years and to more recent immigrants drawn by the natural resources of fur, fish, and forest. The region is thin on roads, but you can travel by ferry, sailboat, cruise ship, plane, or kayak to explore the ancient native villages of the coast and the Queen Charlotte Islands (☞ Getting Around *in* British Columbia A to Z, *below*). The climate of this mist-shrouded coast is among the wettest in the world; winters are a time for torrential rains, summers are damp, and rain gear is essential year-round.

Inside Passage

★ ㉝ *507 km (314 mi), or 274 nautical mi, between Port Hardy on northern Vancouver Island and Prince Rupert.*

The Inside Passage, a sheltered marine highway, follows a series of natural channels behind protective islands along the green-and-blue-shaded British Columbia coast. The undisturbed landscape of rising mountains and humpbacked islands has a striking, prehistoric look. You can take a ferry cruise along the Inside Passage or see it on one of the more expensive luxury liners that sail along the British Columbia coast from Vancouver to Alaska.

The comfortable ferry **Queen of the North,** carrying up to 650 passengers and 157 vehicles, takes 15 hours (almost all in daylight during summer sailings) to make the trip from Port Hardy on Vancouver Island to Prince Rupert. Reservations are required for the cruise and advised for hotel accommodations at ports of call. ✉ *BC Ferries, 1112 Fort St., Victoria V8V 4V2,* ☎ *250/386–3431 in Victoria or outside B.C.; 888/223–3779 elsewhere in B.C.* 🎫 *One-way summer passage for car and driver $318; $104 for each adult passenger.* ⊙ *Sailings Oct.–Apr., once weekly; May, twice weekly; June–Sept., daily, departing on alternate days from Port Hardy and Prince Rupert; departure time 7:30 AM, arrival time 10:30 PM; call to verify schedule.*

Discovery Coast Passage

★ ㉞ *258 km (161 mi), or 138 nautical mi, between Port Hardy on northern Vancouver Island and Bella Coola.*

BC Ferries service travels up the Inside Passage to the native community of Bella Bella and then turns up Dean Channel to the mainland town of Bella Coola. The scenery is stunning, and the route allows passengers to visit communities along the way, including Namu, Shearwater, Klemtu, and Ocean Falls. It also provides an alternative route into the Cariboo region, via Highway 20 from Bella Coola to Williams Lake. Lodging at ports of call varies from luxury fishing lodges to rough camping, but it is limited and must be booked in advance. BC Ferries can arrange travel, activity, and accommodations packages.

The **Queen of Chilliwack,** carrying up to 375 passengers and 115 ve-hicles, takes from 17 to 33 hours (depending on the number of stops) to make the trip from Port Hardy on Vancouver Island to Bella Coola. Reservations are required for vehicles and advised for foot passengers. One cabin is available. ⊠ *BC Ferries, 1112 Fort St., Victoria V8V 4V2,* ☎ *250/386–3431 in Victoria or outside B.C.; 888/223–3779 else-where in B.C.* ☒ *One-way fares between Port Hardy and Bella Coola are approximately $110 for a passenger, $220 for a vehicle.* ☉ *Mid-June–mid-Sept., departing Port Hardy on Tues., Thurs., and Sat.; leav-ing Bella Coola on Mon., Wed., and Fri.*

Prince Rupert

❸❺ *1,502 km (931 mi) by highway and 750 km (465 mi) by air northwest of Vancouver; 15 hrs by ferry northwest of Port Hardy on Vancouver Island.*

The fishing and logging town of Prince Rupert is the largest town on the north coast. It's the final stop on the BC Ferries route through the Inside Passage, as well as the home base for ferries to the Queen Char-lotte Islands. The ferry terminal is about 2 km (1 mi) from town; in summer, a downtown shuttle bus ($3) meets each ferry.

The **Museum of Northern British Columbia** has one of the province's finest collections of coastal native art, with some artifacts that date back 10,000 years. Native artisans work on totem poles in the carving shed, and in summer the museum runs walking tours of the town and a 2½-hour boat tour of the harbor and Metlakatla native village. Prince Ru-pert's **Visitor Info Centre** (☎ 250/624–5637) is on site, and the museum also operates the **Kwinista Railway Museum**, a five-minute walk away on the waterfront. ⊠ *100 1st Ave. W,* ☎ *250/624–3207.* ☒ *$5.* ☉ *Sept.–May, Mon.–Sat. 9–5; June–Aug., Mon.–Sat. 9–8, Sun. 9–5.*

The **North Pacific Cannery Village Museum** in Port Edward, 20 km (12 mi) south of Prince Rupert, is the oldest salmon cannery on the west coast. You can tour the cannery, mess hall, and managers' houses, where interpretive displays about the canning process and village life are set up. ⊠ *Off Hwy. 16, Port Edward,* ☎ *250/628–3538,* FAX *250/628–3540.* ☒ *$6.* ☉ *May–Sept., daily 9–6; call for off-season hrs.*

Dining and Lodging

$$$ ✕ 🏨 **Crest Hotel.** Warm and modern, the Crest is a block from the two shopping centers but stands on a bluff overlooking the harbor. Some rooms have minibars and whirlpool baths. The restaurant, pleasantly decorated with brass rails and beam ceilings, has a view of the water-front. Among the seafood specialties are some outstanding salmon dishes. ⊠ *222 1st Ave. W, V8J 3P6,* ☎ *250/624–6771 or 800/663–8150,* FAX *250/627–7666. 101 rooms, 1 suite. Restaurant, coffee shop, lounge, in-room data ports, no-smoking floor, room service, outdoor hot tub, steam room, exercise room, fishing, baby-sitting, laundry service and dry cleaning, business services, meeting rooms. AE, D, DC, MC, V.*

$$ 🏨 **Highliner Inn.** This modern high-rise near the waterfront is conve-niently situated in the downtown shopping district, only one block from the airline terminal building. Ask for a room with a balcony and view of the harbor. ⊠ *815 1st Ave. W, V8J 1B3,* ☎ *250/624–9060 or 800/668–3115,* FAX *250/627–7759. 94 rooms. Restaurant, lounge, no-smok-ing floors, room service, beauty salon, coin laundry, business services, meeting room. AE, D, DC, MC, V.*

Shopping

Native art and other local crafts are for sale at **Studio 9** (⌷ 105–515 3rd Ave. W, ☎ 250/624–2366). The historic **Cow Bay** area on the waterfront has a number of interesting shops.

Queen Charlotte Islands

★ ㊱ *93 nautical mi southwest of Prince Rupert, 367 nautical mi northwest of Port Hardy.*

The Queen Charlotte Islands, or Haida Gwaii ("Islands of the People"), have been called the Canadian Galápagos. Their long isolation off the province's north coast has given rise to subspecies of wildlife found nowhere else in the world. The islands are also the preserve of the Haida people, who make up half the population. Their vibrant culture is undergoing a renaissance, evident throughout the islands.

Most of the islands' 6,000 permanent residents live on Graham Island (the northernmost and largest of the group of 150 islands), where 120 km (75 mi) of paved road connects the town of Queen Charlotte in the south to Masset in the north. Moresby Island, to the south, is the second largest of the islands and is largely taken up by the Gwaii Haanas National Park Reserve (☞ *below*), an ecological reserve with restricted access. The wildlife (including bears, eagles, and otters), old-growth forest, and stunning scenery make the islands a nature lover's delight, and kayaking enthusiasts from around the world are drawn to waterways here.

Three **Visitor Information Centres,** in Queen Charlotte (⌷ Wharf St., ☎ 250/559–8316), Sandspit (⌷ 1 Airport Rd., ☎ 250/637–5362), and Masset (⌷ Main St., ☎ 250/626–3982), are open during the summer. For information about the islands' ancient Haida villages, contact the **Haida Gwaii Watchmen** (⌷ Museum Rd., Skidegate, ☎ 250/559–8225).

Naikoon Provincial Park (☎ 250/557–4390), in the northeast corner of Graham, preserves a large section of unique wilderness with swamps, pine and cedar forests, lakes, and wildlife. The 5-km (3-mi) walk leads from the Tlell Picnic Site to a beach and onto the wreck of a 1928 logging vessel, the *Pezuta*. At the north end of the park, a climb up the 400-ft Tow Hill gives the best views of McIntyre Bay. A 20-km (12-mi) hike along the Fife Trail will take you from the Tow Hill parking lot to East Beach. There are also two drive-in campgrounds in the park.

On the southern end of Graham Island, the **Haida Gwaii Museum** has an impressive display of Haida totem poles, masks, and carvings of both silver and argillite (hard black slate). A gift shop sells Haida art, and a natural history exhibit gives interesting background on the wildlife of the islands. ⌷ *2nd Beach Rd., Skidegate,* ☎ *250/559–4643.* ⌷ *$3.* ☉ *Apr.–Oct., weekdays 9–5, weekends 1–5; Nov.–Mar., Mon. and Wed.–Fri. 10–5, Sat. 1–5.*

The 4,942-square-km (1,907-square-mi) **Gwaii Haanas National Park Reserve/Haida Heritage Site,** managed jointly by the government of Canada and the Council of the Haida Nation, protects a vast tract of wilderness, unique species of flora and fauna, and many historic and cultural sites including **Nunsting,** a UNESCO World Heritage Site that contains some of the finest heraldic poles found anywhere. The reserve is on Moresby Island and numerous smaller islands at the southern end of the archipelago. The protected area, accessible only by air or sea, is both ecologically and culturally sensitive. The best way to visit, and highly recommended for those unfamiliar with the area, is with a licensed operator. Parks Canada has a list, or *see* Outdoor Activities and Sports, *below*. To visit on your own (without a licensed operator), you must make a reservation, register for each trip, and attend a mandatory orientation session. ✉ *Parks Canada, Box 37, Queen Charlotte V0T 1S0,* ☎ *250/559–8818, 800/663–6000 for an information pack;* FAX *250/559–8366.*

Lodging

Accommodation is available in Sandspit, Queen Charlotte, Tlell, Port Clements, and Masset. Reservations are recommended. **Super, Natural British Columbia** (☎ 800/663–6000) can be of assistance. The islands also have numerous campgrounds.

$ ▦ **Alaska View Lodge.** On a clear day, you can see the mountains of Alaska from the large front deck of this B&B, 13 km (8 mi) east of Masset. A 10-km-long (6-mi-long) sandy beach borders the lodge on one side and woods on the other. Eagles are a familiar sight, and in winter you can often catch glimpses of the northern lights. Every room in this no-smoking B&B has two queen beds. A full breakfast is included. ✉ *Tow Hill Rd., Box 227, Masset V0T 1M0,* ☎ *250/626–3333 or 800/661–0019,* FAX *250/626–3303. 4 rooms, 2 with bath. Breakfast room, hiking, beach. MC, V.*

$ ▦ **Spruce Point Lodge.** This cedar-sided building, encircled by a balcony, is right on the beach, about 5½ km (3½ mi) from the ferry terminal at Skidegate. Like many other Queen Charlotte accommodations, it has pine furnishings and a rustic, down-home feel. A Continental breakfast, delivered to your room, is included. Three rooms have kitchenettes. ✉ *609 6th Ave., Box 735, Queen Charlotte V0T 1S0,* ☎ FAX *250/559–8234. 7 rooms. Boating, fishing. MC, V. CP.*

Outdoor Activities and Sports

GUIDED TOURS

Bluewater Adventures (☎ 604/980–3800 or 888/877–1770, FAX 604/980–1800) has eight- and nine-day sailboat tours around the Charlottes; trips start and end in Sandspit. Vancouver-based **Ecosummer Expeditions** (☎ 604/214–7484 or 800/465–8884, FAX 604/214–7485) runs kayak and sailing tours of the islands. **Pacific International Cruises Inc.** (☎ 604/683–2174 or 888/357–7111, FAX 604/608–1058) has a 44-passenger cruise ship that visits Gwaii Haanas National Park Reserve and other sites. **Queen Charlotte Adventures** (☎ 250/559–8990 or 800/668–4288, FAX 250/559–8983) leads multiday kayak, power boat, fishing, and llama-trekking tours around the islands. **Parks Canada, Gwaii Haanas** (☎ 250/559–8818) has a list of tour companies licensed to operate in Gwaii Haanas.

KAYAKING

Moresby Explorers (✉ 469 Alliford Bay Rd., Sandspit, ☎ 250/637–2215 or 800/806–7633) in Sandspit is a source for kayak rentals.

Shopping

The Haida carve valuable figurines from argillite, a variety of hard, black slate. Other island specialties are silk-screen prints and silver jewelry. A number of shops in Queen Charlotte City are on **3rd Avenue.** The **Haida Gwaii Museum** (☞ *above*) has an excellent gift shop. Some shops around the islands are **Haida Arts and Jewellery** (✉ 387 Eagle Rd., Old Masset, ☎ 250/626–5560) and the **Long House Gift Shop** (✉ 107A Front St., Skidegate, ☎ 250/559–8013).

THE CARIBOO AND THE NORTH

This is British Columbia's wild west, a vast, thinly populated plateau stretching from the dense spruce and fir forests of the north to the ranching country of the south. The Cariboo covers an area roughly bordered by Bella Coola on the west, Lillooet in the south, Wells Gray Park on the east, and Prince George in the north. In the 19th century, thousands came here looking for—and finding—gold. Those times are remembered throughout the region, most vividly at the re-created gold-rush town of Barkerville. You can still pan for gold here, but these days visitors are more likely to come for ranch vacationing, horseback riding, fly-fishing, mountain biking, and cross-country skiing.

From Prince Rupert on the coast, Highway 16 heads east to interior British Columbia. It passes through Terrace, which has a hot-springs complex at the Mt. Layton Resort, hiking and skiing at Shames Mountain, and excellent fishing in the Skeena River. About 100 km (80 mi) north of Terrace, partly by gravel road, is the Nisga'a Memorial Lava Bed Provincial Park, the site of Canada's most recent volcanic eruption. Kitimat (Highway 37, south of Terrace), at the head of the Douglas Channel, has superb fishing.

Hazelton

293 km (182 mi) northeast of Prince Rupert, 439 km (272 mi) northwest of Prince George, 1,217 km (755 mi) northwest of Vancouver.

★ Hazelton is rich in the culture of the Gitxsan and Wet'suwet'en peoples. **'Ksan Historical Village and Museum,** about a 15-minute drive from Hazelton, is a re-created Gitxsan village. The elaborately painted community of seven longhouses is a replica of the one that stood on the site when the first European explorers arrived in the 19th century. The carving shed, often used by 'Ksan artists, is open to the public, and three other longhouses can be visited: One displays modern masks and robes, another has song-and-dance performances on Friday evenings in summer, and the third exhibits both original items and copies of tools, household goods, and artifacts from before the time of European contact. A restaurant serves traditional Gitxsan food. ⊠ *Hwy. 62,* ☎ *250/842–5544 or 877/842–5518.* ▣ *$2; $8 with tour.* ☉ *June–Sept., daily 9–6, with site tours on the hr; Oct.–May, museum and gift shop only, weekdays 9–5.*

Prince George

③⑦ *440 mi (273 mi) southeast of Hazelton, 721 km (447 mi) east of Prince Rupert, 786 km (487 mi) north of Vancouver.*

At the crossroads of two railways and two highways, Prince George has grown to become the capital of northern British Columbia and the third-largest city in the province. In Ft. George Park, you can visit the **Fraser–Ft. George Regional Museum** to see the fine collection of artifacts illustrating local history. ⊠ *333 Gorse St.,* ☎ *250/562–1612.* ▣ *$4.25.* ☉ *May–Sept., daily 10–5; Oct.–Apr., Tues.–Sun. noon–5.*

A collection of photos, rail cars, and logging and sawmill equipment at the **Prince George Railway and Forestry Museum** traces the history of the town and the region from the arrival of the railroad. ⊠ *850 River Rd., next to Cottonwood Park,* ☎ *250/563–7351.* ▣ *$4.50.* ☉ *May–Oct. daily, 10–5; call for winter hrs.*

Shopping

The **Prince George Native Art Gallery** (⊠ 1600 3rd Ave., ☎ 250/614–7726) sells traditional and contemporary works, including carvings, sculpture, jewelry, and literature.

Gold Rush Trail

Begins at Prince George and ends at Lillooet, 170 km (105 mi) west of Kamloops, 131 km (81 mi) northeast of Whistler.

From Prince George, Highway 97 heads south toward Kamloops and the Okanagan Valley, following the 640-km (397-mi) Gold Rush Trail, along which frontiersmen traveled in search of gold in the 19th and early 20th centuries. The trail goes through Quesnel, Williams Lake, Wells, and Barkerville, and along the Fraser Canyon and Cache Creek. Many communities have historic sites that help tell the story of the gold-rush era. The **Cariboo, Chilcotin, Coast Tourism Association** (⊠ 266 Oliver St., Williams Lake V2G 1M1, ☎ 250/392–2226 or 800/663–5885, ℻ 250/392–2838) has information about the trail.

★   The most vivid re-creation of the gold rush is at **Barkerville Historic Town,** 90 km (56 mi) east of Quesnel on Highway 26. Once the biggest town west of Chicago and north of San Francisco, it is now a provincial historic site with more than 120 restored and reconstructed buildings. Actors in period costume, merchants vending 19th-century goods, stagecoach rides, and live musical revues capture the town's heyday. The town is open year-round, but most of the theatrical fun happens in summer. There are B&Bs in Barkerville and a campground nearby. ⊠ *Hwy. 26, Barkerville,* ☎ *250/994–3302.* ⊡ *Mid-May–mid-Sept., $5.50 for a 2-day pass; free in winter.* ☉ *Mid-May–mid-Sept., daily 8 AM–8 PM; mid-Sept.–mid-May, daily dawn–dusk.*

Bowron Lakes Provincial Park (⊠ end of Hwy. 26), 30 km (19 mi) west of Barkerville by gravel road, has a 116-km (72-mi) chain of rivers, lakes, and portage that makes up a popular canoe route. Canoeists must reserve ahead (☎ 800/663–6000) and pay a fee of $50 per person.

Lodging

$$$$ ▦ **Echo Valley Ranch Resort.** At the base of Mt. Bowman, 50 km (31 mi) northwest of Clinton, this adult-oriented ranch makes the most of its scenic setting. Included in the rates are a range of activities and three hearty country meals using the ranch's own organic produce. You can indulge in spa and beauty treatments or hike, bike, fish, or ride. Tennessee Walker horses and experienced Cariboo cowboys take riders on day and overnight trips. White-water rafting, flightseeing, and staying at a First Nations tepee village can be arranged, too. ⊠ *Box 16, Jesmond V0K 1K0,* ☎ *250/459–2386 or 800/253–8831,* ℻ *250/459–0086. 20 rooms, 3 cabins. Dining room, indoor pool, lake, outdoor hot tub, sauna, massage, hiking, horseback riding, fishing, bicycles, cross-country skiing, sleigh rides, recreation room, business services, meeting rooms. MC, V. AP.*

$–$$ ▦ **Wells Hotel.** This faithfully refurbished 1930s hotel makes a good base for visiting nearby Barkerville (8 km/5 mi away) and the Bowron Lakes canoeing area and for accessing the 80 km (50 mi) of hiking, biking, and cross-country ski trails nearby. Rooms are simple, comfortable, and freshly decorated. Wells is 74 km (46 mi) east of Quesnel on Highway 26; the hotel can arrange pickups from Quesnel. A 23-room addition is planned for 2000. The hotel is no-smoking. ⊠ *2341 Pooley St., Box 39, Wells V0K 2R0,* ☎ *250/994–3427 or 800/860–2299,* ℻ *250/994–3494. 17 rooms, 8 with bath. Restaurant, pub, outdoor hot tub, hiking, bicycles, meeting rooms. AE, MC, V.*

THE HIGH COUNTRY AND THE OKANAGAN VALLEY

South-central British Columbia (often simply called the "Interior" by Vancouverites) encompasses the high arid plateau between the Coast Mountains on the west and the Monashees on the east. The Okanagan Valley, five hours east of Vancouver by car, or one hour by air, contains the interior's largest concentration of people. The region's sandy lake beaches and hot, dry climate have long made it a family holiday magnet for Vancouverites and Albertans, and rooms and campsites can be hard to come by in summer.

The Okanagan Valley is also the fruit-growing capital of Canada and a major wine-producing area. Many of the region's more than 30 wineries are in scenic spots and welcome visitors with tastings, tours, and restaurants. The B.C. Wine Information Centre (☞ Penticton, *below*) can help you create a winery tour and can provide details about annual wine festivals.

Throughout the Okanagan you'll see depictions of a smiling green lizard that looks a bit like the Loch Ness Monster without the tartan cap. This is Ogopogo, a harmless, shy, and probably mythical creature said to live in Okanagan Lake.

Kamloops

38 *355 km (220 mi) northeast of Vancouver, 163 km (101 mi) northwest of Kelowna.*

Virtually all roads meet at Kamloops, the High Country's sprawling transport hub. From here, highways fan out to Vancouver, the Okanagan, the Cariboo, and Jasper in the Rockies. Kamloops is also the closest town to Sun Peaks, one of the province's leading ski resorts (☞ Outdoor Activities and Sports, *below*).

The **Secwepemc Museum and Native Heritage Park,** a reconstructed village set on a traditional gathering site, interprets and celebrates the culture and lifestyle of the Secwepemc people, who have lived in this area for thousands of years. Displays include winter houses and summer lodges; the museum holds recorded oral history, photographs, artifacts, and artwork. ✉ *355 Yellowhead Hwy.,* ☎ *250/828–9801.* ✉ *$5.* ۞ *June–Sept. 7, weekdays 9–8, weekends noon–8; Sept. 8–May, weekdays 8:30–4:30.*

Lodging

$$ 🏨 **Woody Life Village.** This complex has modern duplex log cabins and a lodge with such unwoodsy amenities as an indoor pool and an exercise room. You also have access to the fishing and boating at Lac Le Jeune resort, a five-minute drive away. Woody Life is 25 km (16 mi) south of Kamloops, just off Highway 5. ✉ *Lac le Jeune Rd. (650 Victoria St.), V2C 2B4,* ☎ *250/374–3833 or 800/561–5253,* ℻ *250/ 374–9997. 30 rooms. Dining room, kitchenettes, indoor pool, hot tub, sauna, exercise room, meeting rooms. AE, DC, MC, V. Closed Nov.– mid-Apr.*

Outdoor Activities and Sports

GOLF

Rivershore Golf Links (✉ 330 Rivershore Dr., ☎ 250/573–4211) is an 18-hole, par-72 course designed by Robert Trent Jones Sr. There's an 18-hole course at **Sun Peaks Resort** (☞ *below*).

SKIING

With a 2,953-ft vertical drop, **Sun Peaks Resort** (✉ 50 Creekside Way, Sun Peaks, ☎ 250/578–7222 or 800/807–3257) has developed into a leading ski resort, with many hotels, restaurants, and a golf course. It has 64 downhill runs, five chairlifts, and 12 groomed and tracked cross-country trails.

Salmon Arm

③ *108 km (67 mi) east of Kamloops, 106 km (64 mi) north of Kelowna.*

Salmon Arm is the commercial center of the Shushwap (named for Shuswap Lake), a greener and less-visited region than the Okanagan to the south. From Sicamous, 27 km (17 mi) northeast of Salmon Arm, you can take a summer day trip on Shushwap Lake on the **Phoebe Anne** (☎ 250/836–2200), a mini–paddle wheeler. **Roderick Haig-Brown Provincial Park** (✉ off Hwy. 1 at Squilax, ☎ 250/851–3000) is where thousands of salmon come to spawn in the Adams River in late September and October; the park is about 40 km (25 mi) northwest of Salmon Arm.

Dining and Lodging

$$–$$$ ✕▥ **Quaaout Lodge.** Owned by the Little Shuswap First Nations band, this modern cedar hotel on Little Shuswap Lake provides an opportunity to experience the culture of interior native peoples. Some of the well-appointed rooms have fireplaces and whirlpool baths for two set under windows overlooking the lake; the restaurant serves native cuisine. The lodge has a ceremonial sweat lodge and a traditional *kekuli,* or winter shelter, as well as a sandy beach and trails through hundreds of acres of forested land. The hotel is 43 km (27 mi) northwest of Salmon Arm. ✉ *Off Hwy. 1, Box 1215, Chase V0E 1M0,* ☎ *250/679–3090 or 800/663–4303,* FAX *250/679–3039. 72 rooms. Restaurant, indoor pool, hot tub, sauna, exercise room, horseback riding, jogging, dock, boating, fishing, bicycles, meeting rooms. AE, DC, V.*

Outdoor Activities and Sports

Sicamous on Shushwap Lake is a mecca for houseboat holidays. Several operators, including **Three Buoys** (☎ 250/836–2403 or 800/663–2333) and **Twin Anchors** (☎ 250/836–2450 or 800/663–4026), rent fully equipped floating homes that are a fun way to explore the lake.

Vernon

④ *117 km (73 mi) southeast of Kamloops.*

Because Vernon has no public access to Okanagan Lake, it's less of a tourist draw than other towns in the area. Nearby are two other lakes and the all-season, gaslight era–themed village resort atop Silver Star Mountain.

Kalamalka Lake Provincial Park (✉ Kidston Rd., ☎ 250/494–6500) has warm-water beaches and some of the most scenic viewpoints and hiking trails in the region.

North of Vernon, the 50-acre **O'Keefe Historic Ranch** provides a window on 19th-century cattle-ranch life. Among the many restored ranch buildings are a mansion, a church, a working blacksmith's shop, and a general store. The restaurant serves ranchers' fare. ✉ *9380 Hwy. 97, 12 km (7 mi) north of Vernon,* ☎ *250/542–7868.* ⌑ *$6.* ☉ *Mid-May–mid-Oct., daily 9–5.*

Outdoor Activities and Sports

Predator Ridge Golf Resort (✉ 360 Commonage Rd., ☎ 250/542–3436) is an 18-hole, par-73 course.

Silver Star Mountain Resort (✉ Silver Star Rd., Silver Star Mountain, ☎ 250/542–0224 or 800/663–4431, FAX 250/542–1236), 30 km (19 mi) east of Vernon, has eight lifts, a vertical drop of 2,500 ft, 84 runs, and night skiing. The resort also has 35 km (22 mi) of groomed, track-set cross-country trails, hotels and restaurants, and hiking trails.

Kelowna

㊶ *46 km (29 mi) south of Vernon, 68 km (42 mi) north of Penticton.*

The largest town in the Okanagan Valley, Kelowna is growing rapidly, like many other interior towns. Although its edges are looking untidily urban these days, the town still has an attractive, walkable core and a restful beachside park. On the **Okanagan Valley Wine Train** (☎ 780/ 488–8725 or 888/674–8725), you can take a day trip to Vernon along Kalamalka Lake and taste wines on board the 1950s vintage train. The train runs mid-May–mid-October.

Dining and Lodging

$$$ ✕ **De Montreuil.** This cozy downtown restaurant makes the most of the regional bounty, serving dishes—such as quenelles of Okanagan goat cheese, duck breast with raspberry and shallot confit, and locally raised rack of lamb with rosemary, garlic, and mint—that the owners (two local brothers) have dubbed Cascadian cuisine. The menu, priced by the number of courses rather than by the dish, encourages experimentation; the warm yellow decor encourages lingering. ✉ *368 Bernard Ave.,* ☎ *250/860–5508. AE, DC, MC, V. No lunch weekends.*

$$$$ 🏨 **Grand Okanagan Lakefront Resort and Conference Centre.** On the shore of Okanagan Lake, this modern hotel is a five-minute stroll from downtown Kelowna. About half the rooms in the original high-rise tower and in the 1999 addition have views of the lake and surrounding hills. Two- and three-bedroom waterfront condo suites have fully equipped kitchens, washer/dryers, and whirlpool baths. At press time, a full-service spa was set to open by 2000. ✉ *1310 Water St., V1Y 9P3,* ☎ *250/763–4500 or 800/465–4651,* FAX *250/763–4565. 261 rooms, 64 suites. 3 restaurants, lounge, pub, café, indoor-outdoor pool, outdoor pool, hot tubs, sauna, exercise room, dock, baby-sitting, laundry service and dry cleaning, business services, convention center. AE, DC, MC, V.*

$$$ 🏨 **Lake Okanagan Resort.** This self-contained, kid-friendly resort, 16
★ km (10 mi) from Kelowna, spreads across a 300-acre hill on the un-developed west side of Okanagan Lake. The units, ranging from one-bedroom suites in the main hotel to three-bedroom chalets, all have lake views and kitchens or kitchenettes, and most have balconies or decks. There are abundant activities, including lake cruises, and a resort shuttle scoots guests up and down the hillside. ✉ *2751 Westside Rd., V1Z 3T1,* ☎ *250/769–3511 or 800/663–3273,* FAX *250/769–6665. 113 suites and chalets. Restaurant, bar, café, kitchenettes, no-smoking rooms, 2 pools, indoor and outdoor hot tubs, saunas, 9-hole golf course, 7 tennis courts, exercise room, hiking, horseback riding, beach, dock, boating, jet skiing, waterskiing, mountain bikes, video games, children's programs (ages 6–16), playground, laundry service, meeting rooms, helipad. AE, DC, MC, V.*

Outdoor Activities and Sports
BIKING AND HIKING

Bikers and hikers can try the rail bed of the **Kettle Valley Railway** between Penticton and Kelowna. The Visitors Bureau for Kelowna (☎ 250/861–1515) can provide maps and information.

GOLF

Gallagher's Canyon Golf and Country Club (⊠ 4320 Gallagher's Dr. W, ☎ 250/861–4240) is an 18-hole, par-72 course. **Harvest Golf Club** (⊠ 2725 KLO Rd., ☎ 250/862–3103) has 18 holes and is a par-72 course.

SKIING

Big White Ski Resort (⊠ Big White Rd., off Hwy. 33, ☎ 250/765–3101 or 800/663–2772) has nine lifts and more than 100 runs on 2,075 acres of skiable terrain, and night skiing five nights a week. The resort, which also has three snowboard parks and 25 km (16 mi) of cross-country trails, is expanding rapidly; at last count it had 6,000 beds in 16 hotels.

Penticton

⓵ *395 km (245 mi) east of Vancouver.*

Penticton, with its long, sandy beach backed by pink motels and cruising pickup trucks, is a nostalgia-inducing family holiday spot. The arid hills around town are full of orchards, vineyards, and small farms. The **S.S. *Sicamous*** (⊠ 1099 Lakeshore Dr. W, ☎ 250/492–0403), a paddle wheeler moored at the lakeside, is now a museum. Sixteen kilometers (10 mi) north of town, you can ride the historic **Kettle Valley Steam Railway** (⊠ 10112 S. Victoria Rd., Summerland, ☎ 250/494–8422), which has summer trips along 10 km (6 mi) of a 1915 rail line.

The **B.C. Wine Information Centre** (⊠ 888 Westminster Ave., ☎ 250/490–2006) will help you plan a self-drive winery tour and can provide details about the annual wine festivals in April and October.

Dining and Lodging

$$$–$$$$ ✕ **Granny Bogner's.** The granny in question is chef Hans Strobel's Alsatian ancestor, whose hearty French recipes are featured in this homey restaurant, set in a 1912 house full of antique furniture and fresh flowers. The poached salmon and roast duckling help make this one of the best restaurants in the Okanagan. ⊠ *302 Eckhardt Ave. W, ☎ 250/493–2711. Reservations essential. AE, MC, V. Closed Sun.–Mon. and Jan. No lunch.*

$$$ ▨ **Penticton Lakeside Resort and Conference Center.** On the shore of Okanagan Lake, this modern resort hotel is within walking distance of Penticton's beachfront. The resort has spacious rooms with balconies and all the amenities, including a full-size health club, a private beach, and a lakeside outdoor café. ⊠ *21 Lakeshore Dr. W, V2A 7M5, ☎ 250/493–8221 or 800/663–9400, FAX 250/493–0607. 197 rooms, 7 suites. Restaurant, bar, in-room data ports, no-smoking floors, room service, indoor pool, beauty salon, hot tub, massage, sauna, 2 tennis courts, aerobics, health club, volleyball, beach, dock, bicycles, baby-sitting, children's programs (ages 5–12), dry cleaning, concierge, convention center. AE, D, DC, MC, V.*

Outdoor Activities and Sports

For downhill skiing, **Apex Mountain Resort** (⊠ Apex Mountain Rd. off Green Mountain Rd., ☎ 250/292–8111 or 877/777–2739) has 56 trails, two chairlifts, a vertical drop of 2,000 ft, and a peak elevation of 7,187 ft. The resort also has night skiing as well as cross-country trails and snowmobile and dogsled tours. Apex is 40 km (25 mi) northwest of Penticton.

En Route   Following Highway 3 to Vancouver, you'll pass right through **Manning Provincial Park,** which has camping, hiking, swimming, boating, and trail riding, in addition to downhill and cross-country skiing. Also on the highway are the year-round **visitor center** (☎ 250/840–8836) and accommodations and a restaurant at **Manning Park Resort** (☎ 250/840–8822).

THE KOOTENAYS

Tucked between Highways 1 and 3, along which most travelers rush to and from the Rockies, the Kootenays are an idyllic backwater of mountains, lakes, natural hot springs, ghost towns, and prettily preserved Victorian villages. Kootenay Lake and Lower Arrow Lake define the region. A century ago this area was booming because of the discovery of silver in the hills, and with the prospectors came vestiges of European society: stately homes, an elegant paddle wheeler, and the town of Nelson, built in respectable Victorian brick. These days the Kootenays are filled with fine restaurants and historic country inns; a wealth of opportunities for hiking, fishing, boating, and skiing; and some of the best scenery in the province.

Nelson

★ ㊃   *321 km (200 mi) east of Penticton, 657 km (407 mi) east of Vancouver.*

Bypassed a little by history, this city of 10,000, with its Victorian architecture, lake and mountain setting, and college-town ambience, is one of the most attractive towns in British Columbia. Nelson has a wealth of crafts shops and coffee bars, several B&Bs, a youth hostel, and a restored 1906 streetcar running along the lakeshore. The **Visitor Info Centre** (✉ 225 Hall St., ☎ 250/352–3433) can direct you on a self-guided tour around the town's art and crafts galleries and its more than 355 historic buildings.

About 45 km (30 mi) north of Nelson is **Ainsworth Hot Springs Resort** (✉ Hwy. 31, Ainsworth Hot Springs, ☎ 250/229–4212 or 800/668–1171), where you can stroll through a network of caves and plunge into hot and cold spring-fed pools.

OFF THE BEATEN PATH   **KASLO –** On the west side of Kootenay Lake, as you head north from Nelson on Highway 31, is this very pretty village. An 1898 sternwheeler, the S.S. *Moyie* (☎ 250/353–2525), is moored on the lakeshore, its interior restored to *Titanic*-era opulence. It's open mid-May to mid-September for tours. If you head west from Kaslo on scenic, winding Highway 31A, you'll pass the turnoff to **Sandon** (☎ 250/358–2247 for tours), the one silver-mining ghost town that's open for business with a few stores and a visitor center.

Dining and Lodging

$$–$$$ ✕ **All Season's Café.** Tucked into an alley between Baker and Victoria streets, this former family cottage serves innovative cuisine that its owners have dubbed (because people kept asking) Left Coast Inland Cuisine. In practice, this means a seasonally changing menu that uses fresh, local, often organic produce and lists lots of vegetarian creations. Among the good choices are the baked goat cheese soufflé on greens with maple-walnut vinaigrette and the seared salmon, scallops, and prawns with summer squash risotto. ✉ *620 Herridge La.,* ☎ *250/352–0101. MC, V. No lunch Sat., no lunch weekdays Sept.–May.*

$-$$ 🏠 **Willow Point Lodge.** This three-story 1920 country inn is perched
★   on 3½ acres of forested mountainside, about 3 km (2 mi) north of Nelson. The views from the broad, covered veranda and most of the
rooms take in Kootenay Lake, the Selkirk Mountains, and the inn's
own extensive gardens. All the rooms are beautifully decorated, but a
favorite is the Oak Room, with its big stone fireplace, red velvet bed
canopy, and a private entrance. One room has a detached bath. A lavish breakfast is included in the rate, and trails lead from the property
to waterfalls nearby. ⊠ *2211 Taylor Dr., R.R. 1, S-21, C-31, V1L 5P4,*
☎ *250/825–9411 or 800/949–2211,* FAX *250/825–3432. 6 rooms. Outdoor hot tub, hiking. MC, V.*

Outdoor Activities and Sports

HIKING

Kokanee Creek Provincial Park and **Kokanee Glacier Provincial Park**
(☎ 250/422–4200 for both), north of Nelson off Highway 3A, have
extensive trail networks. Kokanee Creek also has lake swimming, picnic sites, and nearby boat rentals.

SKIING

Red Mountain Resorts (⊠ 1000 Red Mountain Rd., Rossland, ☎ 250/
362–7384 or 800/663–0105), which spans two mountains and three
mountain faces, has 83 marked runs, five lifts, and a vertical drop of 2,900
ft. **Whitewater** (⊠ Off Hwy. 6, ☎ 250/354–4944 or 800/666–9420) has
38 runs, three lifts, a 1,300-ft vertical drop, and plenty of powder skiing.

Crawford Bay

40 km (25 mi) northeast of Nelson, including ferry ride.

This peaceful backwater has pastoral scenery framed by snowcapped
mountains. On the east side of Kootenay Lake, Crawford Bay can be
accessed by a scenic, 45-minute free **car ferry** (☎ 250/229–4215) from
Balfour, north of Nelson. By car, it's off Highway 3 on Route 3A.

Lodging

$-$$ 🏠 **Wedgwood Manor.** Built for the daughter of the famous china mag-
★   nate, this 1909 country manor with a wide veranda has been restored
to its Edwardian beauty. The rooms are elegant: Two have whirlpool
baths, and several have canopy beds and their original fine woodwork.
Much of the 50-acre estate is forested, walking trails lead through the
woods, and the Purcell Mountains form a striking backdrop to croquet
games on the lawn. A full breakfast, included in the rates, is served by
the fire in the breakfast room. ⊠ *16002 Crawford Creek Rd., Box 135,*
V0B 1E0, ☎ FAX *250/227–9233 or 800/862–0022. 6 rooms. Breakfast*
room, badminton, croquet, hiking. MC, V. Closed mid-Oct.–early Apr.

Outdoor Activities and Sports

The 18-hole, par-72 **Kokanee Springs Golf Resort** (⊠ 16082 Woolgar
Rd., ☎ 250/227–9226 or 800/979–7999) is one of western Canada's
most scenic courses, with views of Kokanee Glacier, accommodations,
and a restaurant.

BRITISH COLUMBIA ROCKIES

It is obvious how the Rocky Mountains got their name. Wildly folded
sedimentary and metamorphic rocks thrust up by awesome forces of
nature form ragged peaks and high cliffs. Add glaciers and snowfields
to the high peaks, carpet the valleys with forests, mix in a generous
helping of large mammals, wildflowers, rivers, and lakes, and you've
got the recipe for the mountains of eastern British Columbia.

"British Columbia Rockies" is in part a misnomer. The term is often used to refer to the Columbia Mountains of southeastern British Columbia, a series of parallel ranges that flank the western slope of the Rockies but geologically are not a part of the Rockies. As the first ranges to capture storms moving from the west across the plains of interior British Columbia, the Columbias get much more rain and snow than do the Rockies. In the Monashees, the most westerly of the subranges, annual snowfalls can exceed 65 ft. This precipitation has helped create the large, deep glaciers that add to the high-alpine beauty of the Columbias. Lower down, the moist climate creates lusher forests than those in the Rockies to the east.

Recognizing early the region's exceptional natural beauty, the Canadian government began shielding the area from human development and resource exploitation in the 1880s. Today, about 25,000 square km (roughly 10,000 square mi) straddling the Alberta–British Columbia border—an area larger than the state of New Hampshire—are protected in seven national parks in the Rockies and the Columbias. The parks of the Rockies—Waterton Lakes, Banff, Jasper in Alberta, and Kootenay and Yoho in British Columbia—have large areas that remain untouched by human development. Several thousand more square miles are also protected as wilderness areas and provincial parks.

Most of the facilities and roads of the Rockies and Columbias are concentrated in the valleys, where the elevations are 3,000 to 4,500 ft. All the roads offer stunning scenery. Entering British Columbia from Montana to the south, Highway 93 cuts through the southern British Columbia Rockies and Kootenay National Park, passing Fernie, Cranbrook, Fort Steele, Kimberley, Fairmont Hot Springs, Invermere, and Radium Hot Springs. The Trans-Canada Highway (Highway 1) travels from the west through Revelstoke, Mt. Revelstoke National Park, Glacier National Park, Golden, and Yoho National Park.

Fort Steele

44 *40 km (25 mi) east of Kimberley, 94 km (58 mi) south of Fairmont Hot Springs.*

Fort Steele and nearby Kimberley were home to many German and Swiss immigrants who arrived in the late 19th century to work as miners and loggers. Southeastern British Columbia was not unlike the Tyrol region they had left, so it was comfortable to settle here. Later, a demand for experienced alpinists to guide and teach hikers, climbers, and skiers brought more settlers from the Alpine countries, and a Tyrolean influence is evident throughout southeastern British Columbia. Schnitzels and fondues appear on menus as often as burgers and fries.

★ ☺ **Fort Steele Heritage Town,** a reconstructed 19th-century mining outpost consisting of more than 60 buildings, is a step back to the silver- and lead-mining days of the 1890s. Its theater, millinery store, barbershop, and dry-goods store breathe authenticity, preserving the flavor of a bygone era. There's enough here to hold the interest of children and adults alike for a half day or more. ⊠ *3 km (2 mi) south of Fort Steele on Hwy. 93/95,* ☎ *250/489–3351; 250/426–6923 for taped information.* ☜ *$5.50; grounds free Sept.–May.* ☺ *Concessions and museum June–early Sept., daily 9:30–8; grounds daily 9:30–dusk.*

Kimberley

- **45** *40 km (25 mi) west of Fort Steele, 98 km (61 mi) south of Fairmont Hot Springs.*

A cross between quaint and kitschy, Kimberley is rich with Tyrolean character. The Platzl ("small plaza," in German) is a pedestrian mall of shops and restaurants modeled after a Bavarian village. Chalet-style buildings are as common here as log cabins are in the national parks. In summer Kimberley plays its alpine theme to the hilt: Merchants dress up in lederhosen and dirndls, and promotional gimmicks abound.

Dining and Lodging

$$-$$$ ✕ **Chef Bernard's Kitchen.** Eating in this small, homey storefront
  ★   restaurant on the Kimberley pedestrian mall is like dining in someone's pantry. The menu is international, ranging from German and Thai to Cajun. Homemade desserts are always a favorite. Breakfast is served in summer. ⊠ *170 Spokane St.,* ☎ *250/427–4820. Reservations essential. AE, D, DC, MC, V.*

  $ ⌸ **Inn of the Rockies.** In keeping with downtown Kimberley's Bavarian theme, the hotel (part of the Quality Inn chain) has an exterior of exposed-wood beams and stucco. Large rooms have a small sitting area and are plainly furnished with dark brown wood-veneer furniture. The restaurant serves good, reasonably priced food. Just a block from the Platzl, this is the best of the rather plain hotels in Kimberley. There is a minimal rate decrease during the off-season. ⊠ *300 Wallinger Ave., V1A 1Z4,* ☎ *250/427–2266 or 800/661–7559,* 𝖥𝖠𝖷 *250/427–7621. 43 rooms. Restaurant, lounge, hot tubs, exercise room, coin laundry. AE, DC, MC, V.*

Nightlife and the Arts

In summer Bavarian bands in Kimberley strike up with oompah music on the Platzl, especially when festivals are in swing. The **Old Time Accordion Championships,** in early July, are a Kimberley highlight.

Outdoor Activities and Sports

Kimberley Ski Resort (⊠ Kimberly Ski Area Rd., ☎ 250/427–4881 or 800/667–0871) has a vertical drop of 2,300 ft, 47 runs, six lifts, and on-mountain facilities.

Fairmont Hot Springs

- **46** *20 km (12 mi) south of Invermere, 94 km (58 mi) north of Fort Steele.*

Fairmont Hot Springs is named for the hot springs and the resort that has sprouted around it. The "town" is little more than a service strip along the highway, but turn in to the resort and things become more impressive. The town is also close to Columbia Lake, popular with boaters and board sailors. Golf is a growing attraction at several fine courses in the area.

Lodging

$$-$$$ ⌸ **Fairmont Hot Springs Resort.** The wide selection of activities from golf to heli-hiking makes vacationing here feel somewhat like being at camp, but don't overlook the hot springs and spa. Inside the attractive, low-slung bungalow-style structure, rooms are contemporary, many with wood paneling; some are equipped with kitchens and have balconies or patios. The RV sites are popular. Golf, ski, and spa packages are available. Rates decrease by 40% off-season. ⊠ *Hwy. 93/95, Box 10, V0B 1L0,* ☎ *250/345–6311; 800/663–4979 in Canada,* 𝖥𝖠𝖷 *250/345–6616. 140 rooms, 294 RV sites. 7 restaurants, lobby lounge, snack bar, 4 pools, hot springs, spa, 2 18-hole golf courses, 2 tennis courts, private airstrip. AE, D, DC, MC, V.*

Invermere

47 *18 km (11 mi) south of Radium Hot Springs.*

Invermere, one of the many highway service towns in the British Columbia Rockies, is the central access point for Windermere Lake, Panorama Resort, and the Purcell Wilderness area.

For summer water sports, **Windermere Lake**—actually an extrawide stretch of the Columbia River—is popular among swimmers, boaters, and board sailors. Invermere has a good beach on the lake.

One of the best area museums is the **Windermere Valley Pioneer Museum,** which depicts the life of 19th-century settlers through artifacts and other memorabilia in seven pioneer buildings. ⊠ *622 3rd St.,* ☎ *250/342–9769.* ⊠ *$2.* ⊙ *June, Tues.–Sat. 1–4; July–early Sept., Tues.–Sat. 10:30–4:30.*

The **Pynelogs Cultural Centre** (⊠ 1720 4th Ave., at Kinsmen Beach, ☎ 250/342–4423) showcases and sells all types of local crafts: paintings, pottery, photographs, jewelry, and sculptures. Occasional evening concerts usually have a folk or jazz theme.

Panorama Resort (☞ Dining and Lodging *and* Outdoor Activities and Sports, *below*) is a year-round accommodation known best for skiing in winter. For summer visitors it has tennis courts, an outdoor pool, golf, and hiking and biking trails. The resort is on the edge of the **Purcell Wilderness**—a large section of the southern British Columbia Rockies devoted to backcountry hiking, camping, and fishing, with relatively few facilities.

Dining and Lodging

$$–$$$$ ✕ **Strand's Old House Restaurant.** An gem amid the usual pizza and
★ burger joints, this eatery seems somewhat out of place in Invermere. The five rooms seat 8 to 48 people, providing varied levels of coziness. In summer, the outdoor gazebo seats additional guests in an attractive courtyard setting. The menu is deliciously international, with dishes such as Thai shrimp salad, snails in garlic butter and red wine, pheasant with shiitake mushroom sauce, and rack of lamb flavored with Dijon mustard and herbs. ⊠ *818 12th St.,* ☎ *250/342–6344. Reservations essential in summer. AE, MC, V. Closed Sun.–Tues. Oct.–mid-May. No lunch.*

$$–$$$$ ✕ **Toby Creek Dining Lounge.** This ski-lodge restaurant at the Panorama Resort (☞ *below*) is something of a chameleon. Between late May and mid-December, it's a family restaurant, serving three meals a day. From mid-December to late May, it morphs into an elegant fine-dining establishment, open for dinner only. The menu then showcases superior steaks, chicken, seafood, and fondues, but more adventurous diners may opt for the ostrich, pheasant, venison, caribou, or musk ox. ⊠ *Panorama Resort Rd., 18 km (11 mi) west of Invermere,* ☎ *250/342–6941. Reservations essential mid-Dec.–May. AE, D, MC, V.*

$$ ☷ **Best Western Invermere Inn.** The familiar red and turquoise decor of this hotel chain means there are few surprises here, although rooms are on the large side. The hotel is conveniently located at a quiet end of the main shopping and dining area in town. It's the nearest major hotel to the town beach, but still about 2 km (1 mi) away. Rates drop 20% off-season. ⊠ *1310 7th Ave., V0A 1K0,* ☎ *250/342–9246 or 800/661–8911,* ℻ *250/342–6079. 42 rooms. Restaurant, lounge, outdoor hot tub, exercise room. AE, D, MC, V.*

$$ ☷ **Panorama Resort.** Near the edge of the Purcell Wilderness, the lodge at the base of the ski lift conveys a college-dorm atmosphere; other accommodations are in condo villas that resemble part of a mountainside suburb. Many have fireplaces, patios, or balconies. Skiing, hiking,

British Columbia Rockies

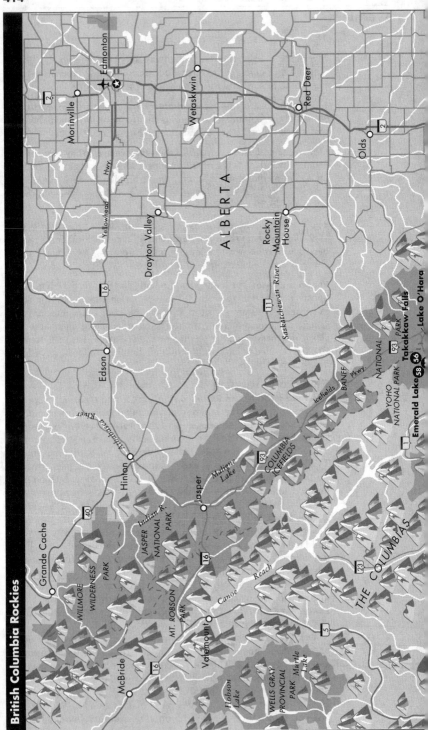

Edmonton

Morinville

Wetaskiwin

Red Deer

Olds

ALBERTA

Drayton Valley

Rocky Mountain House

Yellowhead Hwy.

Saskatchewan River

Edson

Athabasca River

Grande Cache

WILLMORE WILDERNESS PARK

JASPER NATIONAL PARK

Indian R.

Hinton

Jasper

Maligne Lake

COLUMBIA ICEFIELDS

Icefields

BANFF

Pkwy.

YOHO NATIONAL PARK

PARK

Takakkaw Falls

Emerald Lake

Lake O'Hara

McBride

MT. ROBSON PARK

Valemount

Canoe

Reach

THE COLUMBIAS

Hobson Lake

WELLS GRAY PROVINCIAL PARK

Murtle Lake

biking, an outdoor pool, and tennis courts are available, depending on the season. The Greywolf at Panorama golf course (☞ *below*), opened in 1999, is part of Panorama's drive to become a year-round resort. Only one restaurant (☞ Toby Creek Dining Lounge, *above*) is open during summer. Rates decrease by 25% off-season. ⊠ *Toby Creek Rd., 18 km (11 mi) west of Invermere, V0A 1T0,* ☎ *250/342–6941 or 800/ 663–2929,* ℻ *250/342–3395. 105 lodge rooms, 250 condo units. 2 restaurants, 3 bars, cafeteria, pool, sauna, golf, 8 tennis courts, hiking, downhill skiing, nightclub. AE, D, MC, V.*

Outdoor Activities and Sports

HELI-SKIING

R. K. Heli-Ski (☎ 250/342–3889 or 800/661–6060), based at the Panorama Resort ski area, has daily tours.

SPORTING GEAR

Columbia Cycle and Motorsports (⊠ 375 Laurier St., ☎ 250/342–6164) has bicycle rentals. **D. R. Sports** (⊠ 2755 13th St., ☎ 250/342–3517) rents bikes for kids and adults in summer (hourly or daily) and snowboards in winter. **Invermere Sales & Rentals** (⊠ 403 7th Ave., ☎ 250/ 342–6336; 250/342–3311 for lakeside location May–Sept.) sells and rents canoes, boats, and personal watercraft. **Nipika Outdoors** (⊠ 375 Laurier St., ☎ 250/342–8643) rents skis, snowboards, and snowshoes in winter, kayaks and canoes in summer.

Radium Hot Springs

48   *103 km (64 mi) south of Golden, at junction of Hwys. 93 and 95.*

Radium Hot Springs is little more than a service town for the busy highway traffic passing through it, but the town makes a convenient access point for Kootenay National Park and has lower prices than the national parks.

☾ **Radium Hot Springs,** the springs that give the town its name, are the town's longest-standing attraction and the summer lifeblood for the numerous motels in the area. Two outdoor pools are tucked at the bottom of the spectacular Sinclair Canyon. The hot pool is maintained at 41°C (106°F); in a cooler pool the hot mineral water is diluted to 28°C (82°F). Lockers, towels, and suits (period and modern) can be rented. ⊠ *Hwy. 93, 2 km (1 mi) northeast of Hwy. 95,* ☎ *250/347–9485 or 800/767–1611.* 🖾 *$5 per soak; day passes $7.* ☉ *Hot pool summer, daily 9 AM–10:30 PM; mid-Oct.–Apr., daily noon–9; cooler pool schedule varies with weather.*

Dining and Lodging

$$$–$$$$ ✕ **Old Salzburg Restaurant.** This is one of the few restaurants that prepare quality food reflecting the pervasive Bavarian theme of the region. The ambience of the dining room lends itself to more formal attire, but casual dress is also acceptable. The excellent food avoids the heavy greasiness so common to other restaurants of its type. You can choose from schnitzels, spaetzles, and bratwurst, as well as chicken, beef, venison, and lamb entrées. Steaks, seafood, and pastas are also available. ⊠ *4943 Hwy. 93, at junction of Hwys. 95 and 93,* ☎ *250/347–6553. Reservations essential. MC, V. No lunch mid-Sept.–mid-May.*

$$ 🏨 **Radium Hot Springs Resort.** Recreational facilities and activities bring this resort to life. Accommodations are in hotel rooms or one-, two-, or three-bedroom condo units. Rooms are modern, with hardwood furnishings and sponge-painted walls, and each has a sundeck, a wet bar, and a view overlooking the golf fairways. Condos have full kitchens. Golf is the main attraction, along with the proximity to the hot springs, and golf packages are available. There's a small rate reduction off-season. ⊠ *8100 Golf Course Rd., Hwy. 93/95, Box 310, V0A 1M0,* ☎ *250/347–9311 or 800/665–3585,* ℻ *250/347–6299. 90 rooms, 30 condo units. Dining room, indoor pool, hot tub, sauna, 18-hole golf course, 2 tennis courts, exercise room, racquetball, squash, mountain bikes, cross-country skiing. AE, D, DC, MC, V. Closed late Oct.–late Mar.*

$–$$ ⬧ **The Chalet.** The hotel sits on a crest above town, and all rooms have
★ expansive views of the Columbia River valley from 300 to 600 ft above the town and valley. Each room comes with a sitting area and kitchenette (microwave oven, refrigerator, sink); all have balconies. Rooms are gradually being upgraded from the old wood-veneer furniture and dark colors to much brighter colors and better-quality furnishings. Ask for a renovated room. The best views are from the top floor. Rates drop one-third off-season. ⊠ *Madsen Rd., Box 456, V0A 1M0,* ☎ *250/347–9305,* ℻ *250/347–9306. 17 suites. Kitchenettes, sauna, hot tub, exercise room. AE, D, DC, MC, V.*

Kootenay National Park

525 km (326 mi) east of Vancouver, 103 km (64 mi) south of Golden.

Named for the Kootenai people who settled in the area, Kootenay National Park touches the west side of Banff National Park in Alberta and the south end of Yoho National Park. When the tourist population of Banff swells during the busy summer months, Kootenay Park remains surprisingly quiet, although not for lack of natural beauty. Facilities are few here; most people see the park only as they drive through on Highway 93, which traverses the length of the park. For park fees, *see* Contacts and Resources *in* British Columbia A to Z, *below.*

For local information, contact the **Kootenay National Park Visitor Centre** (⊠ Aquacourt at Radium Hot Springs pools, Box 220, Radium Hot Springs V0E 1M0, ☎ 250/347–9505 in summer; 403/292–4401 or 250/347–9551 in winter). The center is open to visitors only from late May to early October.

㊾ Floe Lake, at the base of a 3,300-ft-high cliff called the Rockwall, is one of the most popular hiking destinations in Kootenay. The 10-km (6-mi) trail from the highway passes through characteristic Kootenay backcountry terrain. Plan a full day for this one. ⊠ *Trailhead, 22 km (14 mi) from east gate of Kootenay Park.*

The trail that best characterizes the hiking in Kootenay is the strenuous **Rockwall Trail,** which runs along the series of steep rock facades that are the park's predominant feature. Floe Lake (☞ *above*) marks the trail's southern terminus; it then runs north for 30 km (19 mi) to join up with the **Helmet Creek Trail,** which runs for 14 km (9 mi) back to the highway. The total hiking distance, counting the Floe Lake and Helmet Creek trails, is 54 km (35 mi). Several other long day-hike spurs give hikers the option of doing less than the full distance. ⊠ *Trailheads: Floe Lake trailhead for southern end, 22 km (14 mi) from east gate of park; Helmet Creek trailhead for northern end, 9½ km (6 mi) west of the east gate of park.*

㊿ At 5,416 ft, **Vermilion Pass** is not one of the highest passes in the Canadian Rockies, but it marks the boundary between Alberta and British Columbia, as well as the Continental Divide—rivers east of here flow to the Atlantic Ocean; rivers to the west flow to the Pacific Ocean. The pass is at the juncture of Banff and Kootenay national parks, on Highway 93.

En Route The 105-km (65-mi) drive north from Radium Hot Springs, where Highway 93 joins Highway 95, to Golden is a pleasant one, rambling along the rolling **flood plain of the Columbia River.** To the left are the river and the Purcell Mountains; more immediately to the right are the Rockies, although the major peaks are hidden by the ranges in the foreground. Resorts catering to RVs abound here.

Revelstoke

(51) *148 km (92 mi) west of Golden, on western edge of Mt. Revelstoke National Park.*

The little town of Revelstoke offers both summer and winter activities for visitors. The attractive downtown district has spruced-up buildings from the turn of the century that house modern shops, restaurants, and businesses.

Dining and Lodging

$$–$$$$ ✕ **Black Forest Restaurant.** A Bavarian theme pervades the region, and this is a good place to sample the cuisine. Exposed wood, Bavarian pottery, and big-game trophies decorate the interior, creating something of a cross between a hunting lodge and a Bavarian mountain chalet. Fondues and schnitzels are the specialties, but the adventuresome can try the "Viking Pot," a selection of German sausages, smoked pork loin, and sauerkraut. Other options are seafood, chicken, ribs, and steak. Save room for the elaborate cheesecake desserts. ✉ *Trans-Canada Hwy. W (Hwy. 1), 5 km (3 mi) west of town,* ☎ *250/837–3495. AE, DC, MC, V. Closed mid-Oct.–early Dec. and Tues. No lunch.*

$$–$$$$ ★ ✕ **One-Twelve.** In the Regent Inn (☞ *below*), this restaurant has low cedar ceilings and an abundance of historic photos that lend warmth to the atmosphere. Fine seafood dishes make up about half the menu; Continental favorites such as chicken cordon bleu and beef brochette complete the choices. The blue-ribbon menu selection is lamb broiled with rosemary and red wine. ✉ *112 1st St. E,* ☎ *250/837–2107. Reservations essential. AE, DC, MC, V.*

$$ 🏨 **Regent Inn.** This hotel is a Revelstoke landmark, set in the heart of downtown. It mixes many styles: colonial, with its brick-arcade facade; true Canadian, in its pine-trimmed lobby area and restaurant (☞ One-Twelve, *above*); and Scandinavian, in the angular, low-slung wood furnishings of the guest rooms. Rooms are on the large side but have no spectacular views. ✉ *112 1st St. E, Box 450, V0E 2S0,* ☎ *250/837–2107,* FAX *250/837–9669. 43 rooms. Restaurant, pub, outdoor hot tub, sauna. AE, D, DC, MC, V. CP.*

Outdoor Activities and Sports

BIKING

High Country Cycle & Sports (✉ 118 Mackenzie Ave., ☎ 250/814–0090) has bikes for rent.

SKIING

Cat Powder Skiing (☎ 250/837–5151) organizes two-, three-, and five-day all-inclusive packages that run into the Selkirks and on the upper slopes of Mt. MacKenzie in Revelstoke. **Selkirk Tangiers Helicopter Skiing** (☎ 250/344–5016 or 800/663–7080) runs three-, five-, and seven-day all-inclusive packages in the Selkirk and Monashee mountains near Revelstoke.

Mt. Revelstoke National Park

52 *Western edge adjacent to town of Revelstoke, eastern border 20 km (12 mi) west of Glacier National Park.*

On the western flanks of the Selkirks, this park has smaller mountains than those in the Rocky Mountains to the east, and lusher vegetation, thanks to the additional rain and snow on the west-facing slopes. Conceived primarily as a day-use park, Mt. Revelstoke National Park covers just 260 square km (100 square mi). The park's main attraction is the 26-km (16-mi) **Summit Road** to a mountaintop at 6,395 ft. The gravel road begins from Highway 1, 1½ km (1 mi) before the turnoff to the town of Revelstoke, and the last couple of miles may be closed by melting snows until July. Several easy hikes from the summit parking lot meander past small lakes and have excellent views of the Selkirk and Monashee ranges. For park fees, *see* Contacts and Resources *in* British Columbia A to Z, *below.* For information, contact **Mt. Revelstoke and Glacier National Parks Visitor Centre** (⊠ Box 350, Revelstoke V0E 2S0, ☎ 250/837–7500).

Canyon Hot Springs

53 *35 km (22 mi) east of Revelstoke.*

The two pools at Canyon Hot Springs, tucked between Mt. Revelstoke and Glacier national parks about 35 km (22 mi) east of Revelstoke, take advantage of the hot springs and make a good rest stop. A 15,000-gallon hot pool is naturally heated to 40°C (104°F), and a 60,000-gallon cooler pool is mixed with cool water to maintain a temperature of 27°C (80°F). **Albert Canyon** ghost town, site of the original hot-spring facility built by railroad workers at the turn of the century, is a short distance south of the present facility. ⊠ *Off Hwy. 1,* ☎ *205/837–2420.* ≡ *$4.50.* ☉ *May, June, and Sept., daily 9–9; July–Aug., daily 9 AM–10 PM.*

Glacier National Park

54 *58 km (36 mi) west of Golden, 45 km (28 mi) east of Revelstoke.*

Glacier National Park is known for rugged mountains and, not surprisingly, an abundance of glaciers (more than 400). The glaciers result not because of the exceptionally high elevation—although some peaks here do exceed 10,000 ft—but because of the high winter snowfalls in the park. Many of the glaciers can be seen from the highway, but to appreciate Glacier National Park fully, you must take to the trail (☞ Outdoor Activities and Sports, *below*). For park fees, *see* Contacts and Resources *in* British Columbia A to Z, *below.* For local information, contact **Mt. Revelstoke and Glacier National Parks Visitor Centre** (⊠ Box 350, Revelstoke V0E 2S0, ☎ 250/837–7500).

At **Rogers Pass,** near the center of Glacier National Park along Highway 1, the heavy winter snowfalls made rail and road construction exceedingly difficult. Avalanches claimed the lives of hundreds of railway-construction workers in the early 1900s and continued to be a threat during highway construction in the 1950s.

Today, the Rogers Pass war against avalanches is both active and passive. Heavy artillery—105-mm howitzers—is used to shoot down snow buildups before they become so severe as to threaten a major avalanche. (If you're traveling in the backcountry, always be alert to unexploded howitzer shells that pose a potential hazard.) On the passive side, train tunnels and long snow sheds along the highway shield travelers from major slide paths.

The **Rogers Pass Centre** documents Glacier National Park's history and is well worth a visit even if you are just passing through. Open year-round, the center has exhibits about geology and wildlife and screens 30-minute movies on subjects from avalanches to bears. ✉ *Hwy. 1,* ☎ *250/837–6274.* *Park pass required.* ⏲ *May–mid-June and mid-Sept.–Oct., daily 9–5; mid-June–mid-Sept., daily 7 AM–9 PM; Nov.–Apr., daily 7–5.*

Lodging

$$ **Glacier Park Lodge.** This modern, two-story Best Western at the top of Rogers Pass offers ambience in familiar chain-hotel style: wood-veneer tables and chairs and pink carpeting. The steep-sloping A-frame roof is a design concession to the heavy winter snows. The lodge accommodates travelers with its 24-hour service station, 24-hour coffee shop, and gift shop. Rates drop 40% off-season. ✉ *The Summit, Rogers Pass, Hwy. 1, Glacier National Park V0E 2S0,* ☎ *250/837–2126 or 800/528–1234,* FAX *250/837–2126. 51 rooms. Restaurant, cafeteria, indoor pool, outdoor hot tub. AE, D, DC, MC, V.*

Outdoor Activities and Sports

From the Ilecillewaet Campground, a few miles west of the park's Rogers Pass Centre, several **hiking** trails lead to good overlooks and glacier tongues, offering day-hiking opportunities. One of the best, although fairly strenuous, is the **Asulkan Valley trail.** This 13-km (8-mi) loop passes waterfalls and yields views of the Asulkan Glacier and three massifs—the Ramparts, the Dome, and Mt. Jupiter. A much easier hike is the 1½-km (1-mi) loop **Brook trail** (6 km/4 mi west of the Rogers Pass Centre), with views of the glaciers of Mt. Bonney.

Golden

(55) *105 km (65 mi) north of Radium Hot Springs.*

Little more than a truck-stop town a decade ago, Golden has a new emphasis on tourism. Although the town remains an active service center for the lumber and trucking industries, new hotels, restaurants, and tour operators have sprung up. Many fine alpine lodges, most offering hiking and cross-country skiing right out the door, dot the hills and mountains around Golden. At press time the local ski hill, **Golden Peaks Resort,** was planning upgrades, including a summer gondola and summit hotels and a teahouse.

Dining and Lodging

$–$$$$ ★ ✕ **Sisters & Beans.** Local artwork (for sale) adorns the walls of this turn-of-the-century house partitioned into numerous cozy dining rooms. The international menu lists appetizers such as hummus and nachos; entrées include Thai curry, pasta, steaks, seafood, and bratwurst. The homemade breads are delectable, as are the fondues served in winter. ✉ *1122 10th Ave. S, at the corner of Hwy. 95 and 12 St.,* ☎ *250/344–2443. MC, V. Closed late Oct.–mid-Nov. and late Apr.–mid-May.*

$$–$$$ ✕ **La Cabrina.** Dark brown wood dominates this Italian restaurant, from the chairs and tables to the exposed log beams and walls. Pastas are a highlight, but don't overlook the chicken, steak, veal, and salmon, served with vegetables and the potato of the day. You might try the *pollo sud* (grilled chicken with sun-dried tomatoes and olives, topped with herb butter) or the veal saltimbocca. ✉ *1105 9th St. S,* ☎ *250/344–2330. MC, V.*

$$–$$$ ★ **Kapristo Lodge.** An oasis of pampering service, the Kapristo lies 14 km (9 mi) south of Golden. From 600 ft above the Columbia River valley, the view is impressive enough, but the lodge's real charm is its unabashed effort to spoil the guests. The rate includes breakfast; lunch

and dinner are extra and must be booked in advance. The lodge can also set up three- and seven-day adventure packages with local outfitters. Reserve well in advance for peak-season accommodation. Rates drop 20% off-season. ⊠ *1297 Campbell Rd., Box 90, Golden V0A 1H0,* ☎ *250/344–6048,* FAX *250/344–6755. 6 rooms, 4 with bath. Dining room, outdoor hot tub, sauna, travel services. MC, V.*

$$ 🖬 **Prestige Inn.** Furnishings and amenities make this three-story motel the pick of the lot along the busy Trans-Canada Highway (Highway 1), just up the hill from the main part of town. Queen-size beds, large rooms, and 10-ft ceilings create a very spacious feel. Ten rooms have kitchenettes, and the suites have whirlpool baths. Ask for a room overlooking town—there's no extra charge, the room faces away from the highway, and the view is far more pleasing. ⊠ *1049 Trans-Canada Hwy., Box 9, Golden V0A 1H0,* ☎ *250/344–7990. 82 rooms, 3 suites. Restaurant, lounge, indoor pool, hot tub, exercise room, meeting rooms. AE, D, MC, V.*

Outdoor Activities and Sports

HELI-HIKING AND HELI-SKIING

Golden Alpine Holidays (☎ FAX 250/344–7273) offers heli-tours in the Selkirk Mountains, with accommodation in rustic mountain lodges (propane lights, woodstoves and saunas, full kitchen, no running water or electricity, outhouse toilets) near the tree line. You can hire a guide and move between lodges or stay at a single lodge. Heli-skiing season is from December through April; heli-hiking is offered from early July to mid-September. Packages are three to seven days.

Purcell Heli-Ski/Hiking (☎ 250/344–5410) has two- to seven-day heli-skiing/snowboarding packages in the Purcell Mountains, with day use of a modern mountain lodge. Overnight accommodations are in Golden. Heli-skiing is available from December to mid-May, and one-half or full-day heli-hiking from mid-June to September.

RAFTING

The Kicking Horse River has excellent white-water rafting. Half-day excursions run about $50, full-day excursions about $80–$100 per person. Rafting season is generally May–September, but high-water conditions, especially in spring, may force cancellation of the wilder trips. **Alpine Rafting** (☎ 250/344–6778 or 888/599–5299) runs mild to extreme white-water trips on the Kicking Horse, including multiday trips. **Glacier Raft Company** (☎ 250/344–6521) specializes in extreme white water (Class IV and up) but also runs more serene trips for those of fainter heart. **Rocky Mountain Rafting** (☎ 250/344–6979 or 888/518–7238) runs half- to full-day trips ranging from calm and scenic to wild white water. **Whitewater Voyageurs** (☎ 250/344–7335 or 800/667–7238) specializes in the extreme white water of the lower Kicking Horse. **Wet 'N' Wild Adventures** (☎ 250/344–6546 or 800/668–9119) conducts moderate to wild one-half- to two-day trips on mild to severe Kicking Horse white water.

EQUIPMENT

Selkirk Source for Sports (⊠ 504 9th Ave. N, ☎ 250/344–2966) has a large selection of winter and summer sportswear, sports equipment, and accessories. **Summit Cycle** (⊠ 3–1007 11th Ave., ☎ 250/344–6600) offers bicycle rentals.

Shopping

Canyon Creek Pottery (⊠ 917 10th Ave. N, ☎ 250/344–5678) sells a wide range of western Canadian arts, crafts, and jewelry, but pottery crafted on-site is the focus. You can walk in the studio and view future gallery items being created.

Yoho National Park

16 km (10 mi) east of Golden.

The name "Yoho" is a native word that translates, approximately, to "awe inspiring." Indeed, Yoho National Park contains some of the most outstanding scenery in the Canadian Rockies. The park adjoins Alberta's Banff National Park to the east, but it is quieter than its neighbor. Highway 1 divides Yoho into the northern half, which includes Takakkaw Falls, the Burgess Shale fossil site, the Yoho River valley, and Emerald Lake; and the southern half, of which Lake O'Hara is the physical and spiritual epicenter. For park fees, *see* Contacts and Resources *in* British Colombia A to Z, *below.* For park and local information, contact the **Yoho National Park Visitor Centre** (✉ Hwy. 1, at the intersection of Field, Box 99, Field, British Columbia V0A 1G0, ☎ 250/343–6783).

56 **Takakkaw Falls,** in the northern half of Yoho park, is 833 ft high—the highest waterfall in Canada. The falls are spectacular in early summer, when melting snow and ice provide ample runoff. The road to the falls is not recommended for vehicles over 22 ft long; there is a drop-off area for trailers. ✉ *Access from 13-km (8-mi) Yoho Valley Rd., off Hwy. 1.*

57 The **Burgess Shale site,** halfway between the Takakkaw Falls road and the Emerald Lake Lodge road, contains the fossilized remains of 120 marine species dating back 515 million years. It was designated a World Heritage Site in 1981. Guided hikes are the only way to see the actual fossil sites, and they're popular, so make reservations. The hikes are conducted July–mid-September, and the going is fairly strenuous; the round-trip distance is 20 km (12 mi). A shorter, steeper hike leads to the Mt. Stevens trilobite fossil beds. Guided hikes are also offered to extensions of the Burgess Shale fossils in Kootenay and Banff national parks. Allow a full day for any of the hikes. ✉ *East of Golden on Hwy. 1. Reservations for guided hikes,* ✉ *Yoho-Burgess Shale Research Foundation, Box 148, Field, British Columbia V0A 1G0,* ☎ *800/343–3006.* 🎫 *Guided hike $35–$45.*

58 At **Emerald Lake,** a vivid turquoise shimmer at the base of the President Range, you can rent a canoe, have a cup of tea at the teahouse by Emerald Lake Lodge (☞ Dining and Lodging, *below*), or take a stroll around the lake. The lake is a trailhead for hikers, as well as a haunt of cross-country and backcountry skiers. ✉ *Access from 8-km (5-mi) road off Hwy. 1.*

59 **Lake O'Hara,** in Yoho's southern half, is widely regarded as one of *the* ultimate destinations for outdoor enthusiasts in the Canadian Rockies. For summer, Lake O'Hara Lodge (☞ Dining and Lodging, *below*) is booked months in advance. Although the forest-lined fire road between Highway 1 and the lake can be hiked, it makes more sense to ride the lodge-run bus. (Call the lodge for times and space availability.) Save your legs for hiking any of several moderately strenuous trails that radiate from the lodge into a high-alpine world of small lakes surrounded by escarpments of rock and patches of year-round snow. Keep in mind, however, that the bus makes the Lake O'Hara area accessible to many other people, so solitude may be hard to find. ✉ *Access from 11-km (7-mi) Lake O'Hara Fire Rd. off Lake Louise–Great Divide Dr.*

Dining and Lodging

$$$$ ✕🏨 **Emerald Lake Lodge.** This enchanted place at the edge of a secluded, ★ glacier-fed lake has a log-cabin main lodge with a large stone hearth. The main dining room is a glass-enclosed terrace, with views of the

lake through tall stands of evergreens. The menu mixes traditional Canadian and American fare—steaks, game, and fish—with such nouvelle sauces as ginger-tangerine glaze. All guest rooms have fireplaces and balconies, and pleasant though unspectacular interiors. The awe-inspiring setting is what commands premium rates. Request a lakefront cottage with a balcony overlooking the lake. Room rates drop by 40% off-season. ⊠ *Yoho National Park, 9½ km (6 mi) north of Field, Box 10, Field, British Columbia V0A 1G0,* ☎ *250/343–6321 or 800/663–6336,* ℻ *250/343–6724. 85 units in 2- and 4-room cottages. 2 restaurants, bar, sauna, outdoor hot tub, exercise room, horseback riding, boating, recreation room. AE, DC, MC, V.*

$$$$ ▣ **Lake O'Hara Lodge.** In summer guests are ferried by a lodge-operated bus along an 11-km (7-mi) fire road between Highway 1 and the grounds. In winter guests must ski the distance. The lodge and lakeside cabins offer fairly luxurious backcountry living; cabins have private baths (rooms share baths), and a dining room serves three meals a day, included in the room rate. Reservations for the high summer season (mid-June–September) should be booked far in advance. The minimum stay is two nights, and rates are based on double-occupancy rooms. ⊠ *Off Hwy. 1, Yoho National Park; mail: Box 55, Lake Louise, Alberta T0L 1E0,* ☎ *250/343–6418 in season; 403/678–4110. 23 rooms with shared bath. Dining room, hiking, cross-country skiing, boating. No credit cards. Closed mid-Apr.–mid-June and Oct.–mid-Jan. AP.*

BRITISH COLUMBIA A TO Z

Arriving and Departing

By Bus
Greyhound (☎ 604/482–8747; 800/661–8747 in Canada; 800/231–2222 in the U.S.) connects destinations throughout British Columbia with cities and towns all along the Pacific Northwest Coast.

By Car
Driving time from Seattle to Vancouver is about three hours by **I–5** and **Highway 99.** From there, **Highway 1,** the Trans-Canada Highway, is the principal east–west route across the province into the Rockies. The other major east–west routes are **Highway 16** to the north and **Highway 3** to the south. **Highways 97** and **5** are the main north–south routes.

By Ferry
For information, *see* Victoria Essentials, *above.*

By Plane
British Columbia is served by **Victoria International Airport** (☞ Victoria Essentials, *above*) and **Vancouver International Airport** (☞ Vancouver A to Z *in* Chapter 6). There are domestic airports in most cities. **Air Canada** and **Canadian Airlines** (☞ Air Travel *in* Smart Travel Tips A to Z) are the two dominant carriers. **Kenmore Air** (☎ 425/486–1257 or 800/543–9595) offers direct daily flights from Seattle to Victoria year-round, and summer service from Seattle to Nanaimo, Campbell River, and Port Hardy. **North Vancouver Air** (☎ 604/278–1608 or 800/228–6608) links Seattle and Vancouver.

By Train
VIA Rail (☎ 800/561–3949 or 800/561–8630) trains arrive in Vancouver and Prince Rupert from Jasper (Alberta), where they connect with trains to and from Toronto and Edmonton.

Getting Around

By Bus

MAINLAND

BC Transit (☎ 604/885–3234) serves towns between Langdale and Halfmoon Bay on the Sunshine Coast. **Greyhound Lines of Canada** (☎ 604/482–8747; 800/661–8747 in Canada) serves most towns on the mainland. **Malaspina Coach Lines** (☎ 604/682–6511) has routes from Vancouver to towns on the Sunshine Coast. **Perimeter Whistler Express** (☎ 604/266–5386 in Vancouver; 604/905–0041 in Whistler) has daily service from Vancouver International Airport to Whistler.

VICTORIA AND VANCOUVER ISLAND

Island Coach Lines (☎ 250/385–4411) serves most towns on Vancouver Island. **Pacific Coach Lines** (☎ 250/385–4411 in Victoria; 604/662–8074 in Vancouver; 800/661–1725 elsewhere) operates daily connecting service between Victoria and Vancouver on BC Ferries.

By Car

Major roads in British Columbia, and most secondary roads, are paved and well engineered, although snow tires and chains are needed for winter travel. Many wilderness and park access roads are unpaved, and there are no roads on the mainland coast once you leave the populated areas of the southwest corner near Vancouver. Inquire locally about logging activity before using logging or forestry service roads. **B.C. Highways** (☎ 604/660–9770) has 24-hour highway reports.

MAINLAND

Highway 99, also known as the Sea to Sky Highway, connects Vancouver to Whistler and continues to Lillooet in the interior. The **Trans-Canada Highway** (Highway 1) connects Vancouver with Kamloops and points east via the Fraser Canyon. The **Coquihalla Highway** (Highway 5), a toll road ($10 for cars and vans) linking Hope and Kamloops, is the fastest route to the interior. **Highway 101,** the Pan-American Highway, serves the Sunshine Coast from Langdale to Lund.

In the Canadian Rockies, keep in mind that snow arrives in early fall and remains until late spring. When traveling between October and April, stay informed of local road conditions, especially if you're traveling over mountain passes. A few roads are closed in winter.

VANCOUVER ISLAND

The **Trans-Canada Highway** (Highway 1) runs from Victoria to Nanaimo. The **Island Highway** (Highway 19) is a fast route connecting Nanaimo to Campbell River. On occasion it joins the old road, now called Highway 19A. **Highway 14** connects Victoria to Sooke and Port Renfrew on the west coast. **Highway 4** crosses the island from Parksville to Tofino and Pacific Rim National Park Reserve.

By Ferry

BC Ferries (☎ 250/386–3431 in Victoria or outside B.C.; 888/223–3779 from elsewhere in B.C.) provides frequent, year-round passenger and vehicle service between Vancouver and Vancouver Island, the Gulf Islands, and along the Sunshine Coast and the Inside Passage. If you're planning to combine travel to the Sunshine Coast and Vancouver Island, ask about discount packages.

In the Queen Charlotte Islands, the *Queen of Prince Rupert,* a BC Ferries ship, sails six times a week between late May and September (three times a week the rest of the year). The crossing from Prince Rupert to Skidegate, near Queen Charlotte on Graham Island, takes about seven hours.

A few B.C. Ferries routes are seasonal. Vehicle reservations (☎ 604/444–2890 from outside B.C.; 888/724–5223 in B.C.), not accepted on all routes, require a reservation fee. You can also make reservations on BC Ferries' Web site (www.bcferries.bc.ca), which has up-to-date fare and schedule information on all routes.

Pender Harbour Ferries (☎ 604/883–0083) run summer-only passenger services between Garden Bay, Madeira Park, and Irvine's Landing on the Sunshine Coast.

By Plane
Air B.C. and **Canadian Airlines** serve towns around the province (☞ Air Travel *in* Smart Travel Trips A to Z for phone numbers). **North Vancouver Air** (☎ 604/278–1608 or 800/228–6608) serves Vancouver, Victoria, Tofino, Nelson, and Creston.

GULF ISLANDS
Harbour Air Ltd. (☎ 604/688–1277 in Vancouver; 250/385–2203 in Victoria; 800/665–0212 from elsewhere) provides regular service from Victoria, Nanaimo, and Vancouver to Salt Spring, Thetis, Mayne, Saturna, Galiano, and South Pender islands. **Pacific Spirit Air** (☎ FAX 250/537–9359, ☎ 800/665–2359) provides scheduled floatplane service from Vancouver Harbour and Vancouver International Airport to all southern Gulf Islands.

QUEEN CHARLOTTE ISLANDS
Harbour Air Ltd. (☎ 250/627–1341 or 800/689–4234) runs scheduled floatplanes between Sandspit, Masset, Queen Charlotte City, and Prince Rupert year-round.

By Train
MAINLAND
BC Rail (☎ 604/631–3500; 800/339–8752 in B.C.; 800/663–8238 from outside B.C.) travels from Vancouver to Prince George, a route of 747 km (463 mi), and offers daily service to Whistler. A specialty train-tour service, **Rocky Mountaineer RailTours** (☎ 604/606–7200 or 800/665–7245, FAX 604/606–7201) connects Vancouver and Kamloops with Banff, Jasper, and Calgary in Alberta. Dome cars allow panoramic mountain views, and food and service are excellent. A luxury bilevel dome coach has two spiral staircases, a private dining area, an open-air observation platform, and onboard hosts. **VIA Rail** (☎ 800/561–8630 in Canada; 800/561–3949 in the U.S.) provides service between Prince Rupert and Prince George.

VANCOUVER ISLAND
Esquimalt & Nanaimo Rail Liner (✉ 450 Pandora Ave., Victoria V8W 3L5, ☎ 800/561–8630 in Canada; 800/561–3949 in the U.S.), operated by VIA Rail, runs a narrow-gauge rail line from Victoria's Pandora Street Station to Courtenay, with stops that include Duncan, Chemainus, and Nanaimo. Schedules vary seasonally.

Contacts and Resources
B&B, Camping, and Lodging Reservation Agencies
Reservations for lodging anywhere in the province can be made through **Super, Natural British Columbia**'s reservation service (☎ 800/663–6000). Between March and October, the provincial government runs a toll-free **Campground Reservation Line** (☎ 800/689–9025).

Best Canadian Bed and Breakfast Network (✉ 1064 Balfour Ave., V6H 1X1, ☎ 604/738–7207, FAX 604/732–4998) can book B&Bs across the province. For B&Bs in the British Columbia Rockies, contact the **British Columbia Bed-and-Breakfast Association** (☎ 604/276–8616).

Garden City B&B Reservation Service (⊠ 660 Jones Terr., Victoria V8Z 2L7, ☎ 250/479–1986, FAX 250/479–9999) can book B&B accommodations throughout Vancouver Island. The **Gourmet Trail** books packages at five of the province's finest inns (☞ Guided Tours, *below*). **Gulf Islands Reservation Service** (☎ 888/539–2930) can book about 150 Gulf Island B&Bs and holiday homes.

Car Rentals

Most major agencies, including Avis, Budget, Enterprise, National Tilden, and Hertz, serve cities in the province (☞ Car Rentals *in* Smart Travel Tips A to Z). Car rentals are available on Salt Spring Island through **Heritage Rentals** (☎ 250/537–4225, FAX 250/537–4226).

Emergencies

Ambulance, fire, poison control, police (☎ 911). Some outlying areas do not have 911 service. If you don't get immediate response, dial 0.

Guided Tours

Town listings also have information about cruises, outfitters, and tour operators, including whale-watching tours.

AIRPLANE

Alpenglow Aviation (⊠ 210 Fisher Rd., at the airport, Golden, British Columbia, ☎ 250/344–7117 or 888/244–7177) runs one- to two-hour tours of the British Columbia Rockies. **Golden Falcon Aviation** (⊠ 250 Fisher Rd., at the airport, Golden, British Columbia, ☎ 250/344–2534 or 888/909–8687) runs one- to four-hour tours in the Rockies. Prices begin at $100 per person; a two-passenger minimum is required.

BIKING

Rocky Mountain Cycle Tours (⊠ 333 Baker St., Nelson, British Columbia, ☎ 250/354–1241 or 800/661–2453) runs seven-day tours in the Rockies. Prices begin at U.S. $795.

CRUISES

Bluewater Adventures (☎ 604/980–3800 or 888/877–1770, FAX 604/980–1800) has multiday natural history sailboat cruises to the Queen Charlotte Islands, Vancouver Island, and the Inside Passage. You can cruise the Queen Charlotte Islands and the Inside Passage on a sailboat with **Ecosummer Expeditions** (☎ 604/214–7484 or 800/465–8884, FAX 604/214–7485). **Pacific International Cruises** (☎ 604/683–2174 or 888/357–7111, FAX 604/608–1058) runs four- and five-day natural history–oriented Inside Passage and Queen Charlotte cruises aboard the 44-passenger M.V. *Pacific.* **Silver Challenger Marine Eco Tours** (☎ 604/943–3343 or 877/943–3343) can take small groups around the Gulf Islands on a commercial fishing boat; chefs on board cook your shellfish catch as you go.

ECOLOGY TOURS

Near Victoria, **Island Outings** (☎ 250/642–4469 or 888/345–4469) offers soft adventure trips year-round, including hiking, river touring, and whale-watching. **Nature Calls Eco-Tours** (☎ 250/361–4453) leads half- and full-day guided hikes in wilderness areas near Victoria. Experts from the **Royal British Columbia Museum** (☎ 250/387–5745) lead day trips to study Vancouver Island's natural and cultural history.

FOOD AND WINE

The **Gourmet Trail** (⊠ 304–1913 Sooke Rd., Victoria V9B 1V9, ☎ 250/478–9505 or 800/970–7722) offers self-drive and all-inclusive escorted tours linking five hotels and country inns on Vancouver Island and Salt Spring Island famous for their cuisine.

Gray Line of Vancouver (☎ 604/879–3363 or 800/667–0882) has tours from Vancouver to Victoria, and to Whistler. **West Coast City and Nature Sightseeing** (☎ 604/451–1600) offers a sightseeing tour from Vancouver to Whistler that allows passengers to stay over and return on their date of choice.

TRAIN

You can sample West Coast cuisine in the vintage rail coaches of the **Pacific Starlight Dinner Train** (☎ 604/631–3500; 800/339–8752 in British Columbia; 800/663–8238 from outside British Columbia), which leaves the North Vancouver B.C. Rail station at 6:15 PM, stops at scenic Porteau Cove on Howe Sound, and returns to the station at 10 PM. The *Royal Hudson* (☎ 604/631–3500; 800/339–8752 in British Columbia; 800/663–8238 from outside British Columbia), Canada's only functioning main-line steam train, leaves the North Vancouver B.C. Rail station for a trip along the mountainous coast up Howe Sound to the logging town of Squamish. After a break there, you can return by train or sail back to Vancouver on the M.V. *Britannia*.

Hospitals

British Columbia has hospitals in many towns: **Kelowna General Hospital** (✉ 2268 Pandosy St., ☎ 250/862–4000); on the Gulf Islands, **Lady Minto Hospital** (☎ 250/538–4800) in Ganges on Salt Spring Island; **Prince George Regional Hospital** (✉ 2000 15th Ave., ☎ 250/565–2000; 250/565–2444 emergencies); in Kamloops, **Royal Inland Hospital** (✉ 311 Columbia St., ☎ 250/374–5111).

National Parks

If you are planning to visit the national parks for a week or more, it makes sense to purchase the **Western Canada Annual Pass.** The cost is $35 per adult, or $70 per group of two to seven people, and the pass is valid one year from the month of purchase for all seven mountain parks (Banff, Jasper, Yoho, Kootenay, Waterton Lakes, Mt. Revelstoke, and Glacier), as well as for Riding Mountain and Prince Albert national parks in Saskatchewan, Elk Island National Park in Alberta, and Pacific Rim National Park in British Columbia. A **day pass** for Kootenay and Yoho parks is $5 per adult per day, or $10 per day for a group of two to seven people, and is valid for both parks. A pass for Mt. Revelstoke and Glacier parks (valid for both parks) is $4 per adult per day, or $10 per group in a private vehicle; an annual pass costs $28 per adult, $50 per group.

Additional fees are charged for backcountry camping permits ($6 per person per night, or $42 annually, maximum $30 per trip), firewood ($3 per night), fishing ($6 weekly, $13 annual), campsites, national historic sites, and related activities. The parks are open daily, 24 hours a day. **National historic sites** generally charge a $2 or $3 entry fee. For more information, contact **Parks Canada** (✉ Canadian Heritage-Parks Canada, 220 4th St. SE, Room 552, Calgary, Alberta T2G 4X3, ☎ 403/292–4401 or 800/651–7959, FAX 403/292–6004).

Outdoor Activities and Sports

For whale-watching and other outdoor adventure operators, *also see* the listings under individual towns.

BACKPACKING AND HIKING

Backpackers need to register with the nearest park warden for **permits.** This is principally for safety reasons, so you can be tracked down in case of emergency, as well as for trail-usage records. The fee is $6 per person per night (to a maximum of $30 per person per trip or $42 annually) for the use of backcountry campsites. You can make **reserva-**

tions up to three weeks in advance ($10 reservation fee) by contacting the park office. The park warden can also supply trail and topographical maps and information on current trail conditions. **B.C. Parks** (⊠ 800 Johnson St., 2nd floor, Victoria V8V 1X5, ☎ 250/387–5002) offers detailed information.

FISHING

A **saltwater-fishing license** for one day costs $7.50 for nonresidents and is available at most fishing lodges and charter boat companies in the province. For information about saltwater fishing regulations, contact the **Department of Fisheries and Oceans** (☎ 604/666–2828).

You can buy a **freshwater fishing license** at visitor information centers, sports shops, and many gas stations in the region. If you are fishing in the national parks, you need a **national parks license** (but not provincial licenses). The fees for one-day, eight-day, and annual licenses for nonresident Canadians are $10, $20, and $28, respectively; for non-Canadians the fees are $10, $25, and $40. A seven-day national park license is $6; an annual license is $13.

Fishing regulations vary between jurisdictions, so ask for a copy of relevant regulations when you purchase a license. Note that all lead weights weighing less than 50 grams (2 ounces) were banned from use in the national parks; steel shot is an acceptable substitute. For freshwater fishing information, contact the provincial **Department of Environment and Lands** (☎ 604/582–5200).

HORSEBACK RIDING AND GUEST RANCHES

Super, Natural British Columbia (☞ B&B, Camping, and Lodging Reservation Agencies, *above*) can provide listings of pack-trip outfitters. It also has information about guest ranches; riding is generally a major part of a stay. Information is also available from the **Guide-Outfitters Association** (☎ 250/278–2688).

KAYAKING

The **Canadian Outback Adventure Company** (☎ 604/921–7250 or 800/565–8735) schedules sea-kayaking trips to Johnstone Strait, Desolation Sound, and the Gulf Islands. **Ecosummer Expeditions** (☎ 604/214–7484 or 800/465–8884, ℻ 604/214–7485) and **Gabriola Cycle and Kayak Tours** (☎ 250/247–8277) run multiday paddles to the Queen Charlottes, the Inside Passage, and other parts of the coast. **Wild Heart Adventure Tours** (☎ 250/722–3683, ℻ 250/722–2175) offers multiday paddles around Vancouver Island and the Gulf Islands.

MULTIACTIVITY

Fresh Tracks (☎ 604/737–8743 or 800/667–4744) has 55 different outdoor adventure trips, including hiking, kayaking, river rafting, and sailing adventures, all over the province and Canada. **Go Green Eco Adventures Tours** (☎ 250/336–8706 or 888/324–7336) has multiday, multiactivity trips, including kayaking, hiking, and whale-watching, on Vancouver Island and the Gulf Islands.

RAFTING

The following companies provide options from lazy half-day floats to exhilarating white-water journeys of up to a week: **Canadian Outback Adventure Company** (☞ Kayaking, *above*), **Canadian River Expeditions** (☎ 604/938–6651; 800/898–7238 in Canada), **Fraser River Raft Expeditions Ltd.** (☎ 604/863–2336 or 800/363–7238, ℻ 604/863–2355), **Hyak Wilderness Adventures** (☎ 604/734–8622 or 800/663–7238, ℻ 604/734–5718), **Suskwa Adventure Outfitters** (☎ ℻ 250/847–2885 or 888/546–7832), and **Whistler River Adventures** (☎ 604/932–3532 or 888/932–3532).

SKIING

For cross-country and downhill ski area information, *see* listings under individual towns. For information about helicopter and snowcat skiing, contact the **B.C. Helicopter and Snowcat Skiing Operators Association** (☎ 250/542–9020, FAX 250/542–5070). The largest heli-skiing operator in the Rockies region is **Canadian Mountain Holidays** (☎ 403/762–7100 or 800/661–0252, FAX 403/762–5879). It has heli-skiing (and, in summer, heli-hiking) packages in the Cariboo and Purcell ranges, with accommodation at remote lodges. Reserve several months in advance.

SNOWMOBILING

Great Canadian Snowmobile Tours (☎ 250/837–6500 or 800/668–0330, FAX 250/837–6577), based in Revelstoke, runs three-hour to full-week trips in the Columbias, starting at $60 per person. The company also rents snowmobiles. **Revelstoke Snowmobile Tours** (☎ 250/837–5200, FAX 250/837–5210), in Revelstoke, offers half- to full-day tours in the Columbia Mountains that start at $75 and also rents snowmobiles without a guide.

Safety

Very few of the natural hazards in remote locales are marked with warning signs. Be wary of slippery rocks and vegetation near rivers and canyons, snow-covered crevasses on glaciers, avalanche conditions in winter, and potentially aggressive animals. Each year there are several fatalities from natural hazards in the mountains.

Visitor Information

For information about the province, contact **Tourism B.C.** (✉ 802–865 Hornby St., Vancouver V6Z 2G3, ☎ 604/660–2861 or 800/663–6000). More than 140 communities have **Travel Infocentres.**

The principal regional tourist offices are as follows: **Cariboo, Chilcotin, Coast Tourism Association** (✉ 266 Oliver St., Williams Lake V2G 1M1, ☎ 250/392–2226 or 800/663–5885, FAX 250/392–2838); **Northern British Columbia Tourism Association** (✉ 3167 Tatlow Rd., Box 1030, Smithers V0J 2N0, ☎ 250/847–5227 or 800/663–8843, FAX 250/847–4321), for information on the Queen Charlotte Islands and northern British Columbia; **Northern Rockies, Alaska Highway Tourism Association** (✉ 9923 96th Ave., Box 6850, Fort St. John V1J 4J3, ☎ 250/785–2544 or 888/785–2544, FAX 250/785–4424) for information on northeastern British Columbia; **Rocky Mountain Visitors Association** (✉ Box 10, Kimberley, British Columbia V1A 2Y5, ☎ 250/427–4838); **Thompson Okanagan Tourism Association** (✉ 1332 Water St., Kelowna V1Y 9P4, ☎ 250/860–5999 or 800/567–2275, FAX 250/860–9993); **Tourism Vancouver Island** (✉ 302–45 Bastion Sq., Victoria V8W 1J1, ☎ 250/382–3551, FAX 250/382–3523), for information on Vancouver Island and the Gulf Islands; and **Vancouver, Coast & Mountains Tourism Region** (✉ 250–1508 W. 2nd Ave., Vancouver V6J 1H2, ☎ 604/739–0823 or 800/667–3306, FAX 604/739–0153) for information about the Coast Mountain Circle and the Sunshine Coast.

Galiano Island Visitor Information Centre (✉ Box 73, Galiano V0N 1P0, ☎ FAX 250/539–2233) and **Salt Spring Island Visitor Information Centre** (✉ 121 Lower Ganges Rd., Ganges V8K 2T1, ☎ 250/537–5252, FAX 250/537–4276) provide information on the Gulf Islands.

The **Prince Rupert Infocentre** (✉ 100 1st Ave. W, Box 669, Prince Rupert V8J 3S1, ☎ 250/624–5637 or 800/667–1994, FAX 250/627–8009) has information about that town. For information on the Queen Charlotte Islands, contact the **Queen Charlotte Visitor Information Centre** (✉ Box 819, Queen Charlotte V0T 1S0, ☎ 250/559–8316, FAX 250/

559–8952). For information and accommodation reservations for towns serving Pacific Rim National Park Reserve, contact the **Tofino Chamber of Commerce** (⊠ Box 476, V0R 2Z0, ☎ 250/725–3414) or the **Ucluelet Chamber of Commerce** (⊠ 100 Main St., Box 428, V0R 3A0, ☎ 250/726–4641). For information about Prince George, contact **Tourism Prince George** (⊠ 1198 Victoria St., V2L 2L2, ☎ 250/562–3700 or 800/668–7646, FAX 250/563–3584). **Whistler Resort Association** (⊠ 4010 Whistler Way, Whistler V0N 1B4, ☎ 604/932–4222; 604/664–5625 in Vancouver; 800/944–7853 in the U.S. and Canada, FAX 604/938–5758) can help with accommodations and other information about the town.

8 SOUTHEAST ALASKA

INCLUDING KETCHIKAN, WRANGELL, JUNEAU, AND SITKA

Carved out of a corner of British Columbia, Alaska's Southeast is defined by the Inside Passage—once the traditional route to the Klondike goldfields and today the centerpiece of many Alaskan cruises. Here are densely forested islands, cliff-rimmed fjords, and Glacier Bay National Park. Juneau, the capital, is also here, as are fishing towns such as Petersburg and Ketchikan, which is known for its totem-pole carving. An onion-dome cathedral accents Sitka, the onetime capital of Russian America.

By Mike Miller

Updated by
Don Pitcher

SOUTHEAST ALASKA STRETCHES below the bulk of the state along the northwest border of British Columbia like the tail of a kite. It is a world of massive glaciers, fjords, and snowcapped peaks. The largest concentration of coastal glaciers on earth can be viewed at Glacier Bay National Park and Preserve, one of the region's most prized attractions. Thousands of islands are blanketed with lush stands of spruce, hemlock, and cedar. Bays, coves, lakes of all sizes, and swift, icy rivers provide some of the continent's best fishing grounds—and scenery as majestic and unspoiled as any in North America. Many of Southeast Alaska's wildest and most pristine landscapes are within Tongass National Forest, which encompasses nearly 17 million acres—or 73% of the Panhandle's land.

Like anywhere else, Southeast Alaska has its drawbacks. For one thing, it rains a lot—even more than in other parts of the Pacific Northwest. If you plan to spend a week or more here, you can count on showers during at least a few of those days. Die-hard Southeasterners simply throw on a slicker and rubber boots and shrug off the rain. Their attitude is philosophical: Without the rain, there would be no forests, no lakes, no streams running with world-class salmon and trout, and no healthy populations of brown and black bears, moose, deer, mountain goats, and wolves. Locals also know that the rain keeps people from moving in; without it in such profusion Southeast Alaska would probably look more like Seattle.

Another disadvantage—or advantage, depending on your point of view—is an almost total lack of connecting roads between the area's communities. To fill this void, Alaskans created the Marine Highway System of passenger and vehicle ferries that have staterooms, observation decks, cafeterias, cocktail lounges, and heated, glass-enclosed solariums.

The Southeast's natural beauty and abundance of wildlife have made it one of the world's fastest-growing cruise destinations. About 20 big cruise ships ply the Inside Passage during the height of the summer. Regular air service to the Southeast flies from the lower 48 states and from other parts of Alaska.

The native peoples in the Southeast coastal region are Tlingit, Haida, and Tsimshian. These peoples, like their coastal neighbors in British Columbia, preserve a culture rich in totemic art forms, including deeply carved poles, masks, baskets, and ceremonial objects. Many live among non-natives in modern towns and continue their own traditions.

A pioneer spirit dominates the towns of Southeast Alaska. Residents—some from other states, some with roots in the "old country," some who can trace their ancestors back to the gold-rush days, and some whose ancestors came over the Bering Land Bridge from Asia tens of thousands of years ago—are an adventurous lot. The rough-and-tumble spirit of the Southeast often combines with a worldly sophistication: those who fish are also artists, loggers are often business entrepreneurs, and homemakers may be native dance performers.

Pleasures and Pastimes

Dining

Seafood, both fish and shellfish, is the lynchpin of Southeast Alaskan cuisine, and it appears in fresh abundance at virtually every dining establishment. Most often it is prepared simply and shares space on the

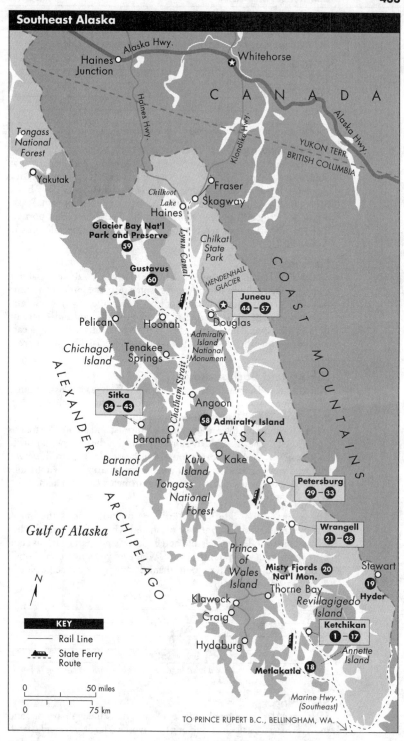

Southeast Alaska

CANADA

Alaska Hwy.

Haines Junction

Whitehorse

Tongass National Forest

Yakutat

Haines Hwy.

Klondike Hwy.

Fraser

Skagway

Chilkoot Lake

YUKON TERR.
BRITISH COLUMBIA

Alaska Hwy.

Glacier Bay Nat'l Park and Preserve **59**

Haines

Chilkat State Park

MENDENHALL GLACIER

Lynn Canal

Gustavus **60**

Juneau **44 – 57**

C O A S T

Pelican

Hoonah

Douglas

Chichagof Island

Tenakee Springs

Admiralty Island National Monument

M O U N T A I N S

A L E X A N D E R

Chatham Strait

Sitka **34 – 43**

Angoon

Baranof

Admiralty Island **58**

A L A S K A

Baranof Island

Kuiu Island

Kake

Petersburg **29 – 33**

Tongass National Forest

A R C H I P E L A G O

Gulf of Alaska

Wrangell **21 – 28**

N

Prince of Wales Island

Misty Fjords Nat'l Mon. **20**

Stewart

Thorne Bay

19 Hyder

Revillagigedo Island

KEY

Klawock

Craig

Ketchikan **1 – 17**

Hydaburg

Annette Island

—— Rail Line

State Ferry Route

Metlakatla **18**

0   50 miles

0   75 km

Marine Hwy. (Southeast)

TO PRINCE RUPERT B.C., BELLINGHAM, WA.

menu with steaks and unfussy American-style pastas, salads, and sandwiches. Except, perhaps, in Juneau, you won't find much by way of trendy food: The fare here is designed to stick to your ribs.

CATEGORY	COST*
$$$$	over $40
$$$	$25–$40
$$	$10–$25
$	under $10

*per person for a three-course meal, excluding drinks, service, and tax

Ferry-Hopping

The Alaska Marine Highway System (☞ Arriving and Departing *in* Southeast Alaska A to Z, *below*) is a primary means of transportation along the Inside Passage, with service to most towns on a daily basis. Most northbound travelers hop aboard the ferry in Bellingham, Washington, or Prince Rupert, British Columbia. Ferries can transport vehicles of all sizes, but reservations are necessary, especially out of Bellingham.

Fishing

Southeast Alaska is an angler's paradise. There are saltwater salmon charter boats, salmon fishing lodges (some near the larger communities, others remote and accessible only by floatplane), fly-in mountain-lake lodges where the fishing is for trout and char, and—bargain hunters take special note—more than 150 remote but weather-tight cabins operated by the U.S. Forest Service (☞ Tongass National Forest, *below*).

Hiking and Backpacking

Trekking woods, mountains, and beaches is Southeast Alaska's unofficial regional sport. Many of the trails are abandoned mining and logging roads. Others are natural routes—in some sections, even game trails—meandering over ridges, through forests, and alongside streams and glaciers. The Alaska Division of Parks Southeast regional office in Juneau (☞ Visitor Information *in* Southeast Alaska A to Z, *below*) will send you a list of state-maintained trails and parks in the Panhandle; local visitor bureaus and recreation departments can also help.

Lodging

The quintessential Southeast Alaska accommodation is the lodge, whether rustic and outdoorsy or plush and sybaritic. Historic old hotels and inns, modern motels and hotels, B&Bs, and spartan cabins complete the Alaskan hospitality picture. Wherever you stay, you're bound to find pleasing decorative accents themed on indigenous Pacific Northwest–coast art and nature.

CATEGORY	COST*
$$$$	over $120
$$$	$90–$120
$$	$50–$90
$	under $50

*All prices are for a standard double room in high season, excluding tax and service.

Shopping

Southeast Alaska has an abundance of fine artists and craftspeople, and most towns have galleries exhibiting their works. Tlingit and Haida handicrafts include wooden masks, paddles, bentwood boxes, and button blankets. You'll find these items at gift shops up and down the coast. If you want to be sure of authenticity, buy items tagged with the state-approved AUTHENTIC NATIVE HANDICRAFT FROM ALASKA label. Virtually every community has at least one canning and/or smoking operation that packs and ships local seafood, smoked and canned salmon included.

Tongass National Forest

The country's largest national forest, the Tongass (✉ Centennial Hall, 101 Egan Dr., Juneau 99801, ☎ 907/586–8751) stretches the length of Alaska's Panhandle and encompasses nearly 17 million acres, or three-fourths of the Southeast region. Much of the forest is covered by old-growth, temperate rain forest, but it also includes rugged mountains, steep fjords, glaciers, and ice fields within its boundaries. Its lands and waters are home to a wide variety of animals: black and brown bears, bald eagles, Sitka black-tailed deer, mountain goats, wolves, marine mammals, and dozens of sea- and shorebird species. Two national monuments, Admiralty Island near Juneau and Misty Fjords near Ketchikan, are within its borders.

Exploring Southeast Alaska

The Southeast Panhandle stretches some 500 mi from Yakutat at its northernmost point to Ketchikan and Metlakatla at its southern end. At its widest the region measures only 140 mi, and in the upper Panhandle just south of Yakutat, it's a skinny 30 mi across. Most of the Panhandle consists of a sliver of mainland buffered by nearby islands.

More than a thousand islands line the Inside Passage—most of them mountainous with lush covers of timber (though large clear-cuts are also common). Collectively they constitute the Alexander Archipelago. On the mainland to the east of the United States–Canada border lies British Columbia. Most communities are on islands rather than on the mainland. The principal exceptions are Juneau, Gustavus, and Hyder. Island outposts include Ketchikan, Wrangell, Petersburg, Sitka, and the villages of Craig, Pelican, Metlakatla, Kake, Angoon, and Hoonah.

You can get to and around the area by ship or by plane, but forget arriving by car or RV unless your destination is Hyder, which is connected by road to the Alaska Highway. Elsewhere in the Southeast, the roadways in these parts run at most a few dozen miles out from towns and villages; then they dead-end. (If you wish to drive up the Alaska Highway and then visit road-isolated communities, you can reserve vehicle space on Alaska's state ferries.)

Numbers in the text correspond to numbers in the margin and on the Ketchikan, Wrangell, Petersburg, Sitka, Juneau, and Glacier Bay Park and Preserve maps.

Great Itineraries

Like all of Alaska's regions, the Southeast covers a vast area (even though it represents a thin slice of the state), and most of its communities, as well as its parks, national forest lands, and other wildlands, are accessible only by boat or plane. You should therefore allow yourself at least a week here. If you have only a few days, it might be best to fly into one of Southeast Alaska's larger communities—like Juneau, Sitka, or Ketchikan—and then take a state ferry to other Panhandle communities. Or, fly to a remote destination. Most visitors explore the Southeast on cruise ships, which generate their own schedules. But there are plenty of adventures awaiting ambitious independent travelers who plan ahead and ride state ferries instead of cruise ships.

IF YOU HAVE 5 DAYS

Spend two or three days in 🏛 **Juneau** ㊹–㊿. Go south via the state ferry to 🏛 **Sitka** ㉞–㊸, ancestral home of the Tlingit and once the capital of Russian America. Spend the next two days exploring this picturesque town and nearby sights, possibly taking in a performances by Russian-style dancers at Centennial Hall in Sitka. Active travelers can go sea kayaking, hiking, and wildlife cruising. Or instead of going south from Juneau, another good bet is to travel north to ⊞ **Gustavus** ⑥⓪ and nearby **Glacier Bay National Park and Preserve** ⑤⑨, one of America's premier parklands, where tidewater glaciers, rugged mountain scenery, and abundant marine wildlife await.

IF YOU HAVE 7 DAYS

Many cruises to Southeast Alaska last seven days, and a week is also sufficient time for independent travelers to see at least a cross section of the region by traveling aboard state ferries and aircraft. Starting at ⊞ **Ketchikan** ①–⑰, known for its totem poles, the Alaska Marine Highway regularly makes stops at all of the region's larger communities: **Wrangell** ㉑–㉘, with its ancient petroglyphs; ⊞ **Petersburg** ㉙–㉝, which has a strong Norwegian influence; ⊞ **Sitka** ㉞–㊸, former capital of Russian Alaska, and ⊞ **Juneau** ㊹–㊼, the state capital. It also serves several smaller communities like **Kake, Angoon, Tenakee Springs,** and **Hoonah.** Give yourself time to see local sights and visit some out-of-town destinations, like Alaska Chilkat Bald Eagle Preserve, **Admiralty Island** ⑤⑧, and **Glacier Bay National Park and Preserve** ⑤⑨.

When to Tour the Southeast

The best time to visit is May–September, when the weather is mildest, daylight hours are longest, wildlife is most abundant, the fishing is best, and festivals and tourist-oriented activities are in full swing.

KETCHIKAN

Ketchikan, which has more totem poles than anywhere else in the world, is perched on a large island at the foot of Deer Mountain (3,000 ft). The site at the mouth of Ketchikan Creek was a summer fish camp of the Tlingit until white miners and fishermen came to settle the town in 1885. Gold discoveries just before the turn of the 20th century brought more immigrants, and valuable timber and commercial fishing resources spurred new industries. By the 1930s the town bragged it was the "salmon-canning capital of the world." You will still find some of the Southeast's best salmon fishing here.

Exploring Ketchikan

There's a lot to be seen on foot in Ketchikan's compact downtown. For many travelers, the town offers the first taste of Alaska. If this is true for you, you will not be disappointed. Ketchikan rises steeply from the busy fishing docks, with staircases climbing to hillside homes. Downtown's favorite stops include the Spruce Mill Development shops and Creek Street. A bit farther away you'll find the Totem Heritage Center and Deer Mountain Hatchery. Out of town (but included on most bus tours) are two longtime favorites: Totem Bight State Historical Park and Saxman Native Village.

On the highway in either direction, you won't go far before you run out of road. The North Tongass Highway ends about 18 mi from downtown, at Settler's Cove Campground. The South Tongass Highway terminates at a power plant about 8 mi from town. Side roads soon end at campgrounds and at trailheads, viewing points, lakes, boat-launching ramps, and private property.

A Good Walk

The best place to begin a walking tour of Ketchikan is from the helpful **Ketchikan Visitors Bureau** ①. Just a few steps up Mill Street is the

Spruce Mill Development ②, filled with shops and restaurants. Next door, the **Southeast Alaska Visitor Center** ③ is a fine place to learn about Southeast's wild places. Continue up Mill Street past minuscule **Whale Park** ④, with its Chief Kyan totem pole, and turn right on Stedman Street. Cross the bridge to **Thomas Street** ⑤, overlooking a busy boat harbor. Continue walking along Stedman to the **Return of the Eagle** ⑥ mural before turning left on Deermont Street. Follow it uphill several blocks to the **Totem Heritage Center** ⑦ and its collection of ancient totem poles. Just across the footbridge are **Deer Mountain Hatchery** ⑧ and **City Park** ⑨. From here, Park Avenue runs parallel to Ketchikan Creek, heading downhill to the fish ladder and Salmon Carving next to **Salmon Falls** ⑩. Look uphill to see the historic **Grant Street Trestle** ⑪; it's about a 20-minute walk down Park Avenue, or you can call a cab from the hatchery.

From the fish ladder, a boardwalk path parallels Ketchikan Creek and leads to the infamous **Creek Street** ⑫. For a side trip, take the funicular to **Westmark Cape Fox Lodge** ⑬ and back before continuing down Creek Street boardwalk to **Dolly's House** ⑭. Retrace your steps up the boardwalk and cross the **Creek Street Footbridge** ⑮, where you can watch salmon heading upstream in the summer. In front of you is the Chief Johnson Totem Pole, carved in 1989, and just to your right is the **Tongass Historical Museum** ⑯, with interesting relics from the early days of mining and fishing. Turn left on Bawden Street to pass historic **St. John's Church** ⑰.

TIMING

This walking tour should take around two or three hours, stops included. If you are looking for an easier and shorter version (approximately one hour), omit the leg of the walk that leads to Totem Heritage Center, Deer Mountain Hatchery, and City Park. (These sights are typically included in local bus tours that also take in Totem Bight State Historical Park and Saxman Native Village.)

Sights to See

❾ **City Park.** The Deer Mountain Hatchery and Heritage Center lead into this small park, which has picnic tables and paved paths and is bisected by the creek. ⊠ *Park and Fair Sts.*

⑫ **Creek Street.** Ketchikan's infamous red-light district once existed here. Today the small, quaint houses, built on stilts over the creek waters, have been restored as trendy shops.

⑮ **Creek Street Footbridge.** Stand over Ketchikan Creek for good salmon viewing when the fish are running in midsummer.

❽ **Deer Mountain Hatchery.** Tens of thousands of salmon are annually dispersed into local waters at the hatchery on Park Avenue. The hatchery, owned by the Ketchikan Indian Corporation, has exhibits on traditional native fishing and gives guided tours. The hatchery is also a good place to see and photograph bald eagles up close. ⊠ *429 Deermount St.,* ☎ *907/225–5158.* ☜ *$5.95.* ⊙ *Mid-May–Sept., daily 8:30–4:30.*

⑭ **Dolly's House.** The street's most famous brothel has been preserved as a museum, complete with furnishings, beds, and a short history of the life and times of Ketchikan's best-known madam. ⊠ *Creek St.,* ☎ *907/225–6329.* ☜ *$4.* ⊙ *Open when cruise ships are in port (ask at the Visitors Bureau;* ☞ *below).*

⑪ **Grant Street Trestle.** At one time virtually all of Ketchikan's walkways and streets were made from wooden trestles. Now only one remains, constructed in 1908.

438

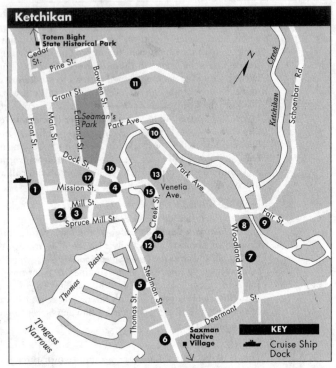

Ketchikan

① Ketchikan Visitors Bureau. The helpful visitors bureau is right next to the cruise ship docks. A third of its space is occupied by day-tour, flight-seeing, and boat-tour operators. ⊠ *131 Front St., Ketchikan 99901,* ☎ *907/225–6166 or 800/770–3300.* ⊙ *Weekdays 8–5.*

⑥ *Return of the Eagle.* Twenty-one native artists created this colorful mural on a wall of the Robertson Building on the Ketchikan campus of the University of Alaska–Southeast. ⊠ *Stedman St.*

⑰ St. John's Church. Built in 1903, this church is the oldest remaining house of worship in Ketchikan. Its interior is formed from red cedar cut in the native-operated sawmill in nearby Saxman. ⊠ *Bawden St.*

⑩ Salmon Falls. Get out your camera and set it for fast speed at the falls, **fish ladder,** and wooden **Salmon Carving,** just off Park Avenue on Married Man's Trail. When the salmon start running in midsummer, thousands leap the falls (or take the easier fish ladder route) to spawn in Ketchikan Creek's waters farther upstream. Many can also be seen in the creek below the falls. ⊠ *Married Man's Trail, off Park Ave.*

③ Southeast Alaska Visitor Center. Museum-quality exhibits, including one on the rain forest, focus on the resources, native cultures, and ecosystems of Southeast Alaska at this impressive visitor center. The U.S. Forest Service and other federal agencies provide information on Alaska's public lands. Especially helpful for independent travelers is the inviting "trip-planning room," where you can relax on Mission-style furniture while consulting books, maps, and videos about the sights in Ketchikan and the Southeast. A multimedia show, "Mystical Southeast Alaska," is shown every 30 minutes during the summer in the center's theater. ⊠ *50 Main St.,* ☎ *907/228–6220.* ⊠ *$4 May–Sept.; free Oct.–Apr.* ⊙ *May–Sept., daily 8–5; Oct.–Apr., Tues.–Sat. 8:30–4:30.*

❷ **Spruce Mill Development.** The new complex on Mill Street is modeled after 1920s-style cannery architecture. Spread over 6½ acres along the waterfront, five buildings contain a mix of retail stores, souvenir shops, and restaurants, plus a covered fish and crafts market. A new "immersive theater" with a screen that surrounds viewers is expected to open here in 2000. Films will emphasize Southeast Alaska and native legends. ⊠ *Spruce Mill and Front Sts.*

❺ **Thomas Street.** From this street is a nice view of Thomas Basin, one of four harbors in Ketchikan and home port to a variety of pleasure and commercial fishing boats.

⑯ **Tongass Historical Museum.** Native artifacts and pioneer relics revisit the mining and fishing eras at this museum. Among the rotating exhibits are a big and brilliantly polished lens from Tree Point Lighthouse, the bullet-riddled skull of a notorious brown bear called Old Groaner, native ceremonial objects, and a 14-ft model of a typical Alaskan salmon-fishing seine boat. ⊠ *629 Dock St.,* ☎ *907/225–5600.* ⊡ *$3.* ☉ *Mid-May–Sept., daily 8–5; Oct.–May 14, Wed.–Fri. 1–5, weekends 1–4.*

❼ **Totem Heritage Center.** An amazing collection of original totems dating from almost two centuries ago is displayed for up-close viewing. ⊠ *Deermount St.,* ☎ *907/225–5900.* ⊡ *$4.* ☉ *May–Sept., daily 8–5; Oct.–Apr., weekdays 1–5.*

⑬ **Westmark Cape Fox Lodge.** For a stunning view of the harbor and fine dining (☞ Dining and Lodging, *below*), walk to the top of steep Venetia Avenue or take the funicular ($1) ride up from Creek Street. ⊠ *800 Venetia Way,* ☎ *907/225–8001.*

❹ **Whale Park.** This park, catercorner from St. John's Church (☞ *above*), is the site of the **Chief Kyan Totem Pole.** Just up the street is the **Chief Johnson Totem Pole,** raised in 1989 and a replica of the 1901 totem on the same site.

OFF THE BEATEN PATH

TOTEM BIGHT STATE HISTORICAL PARK – The poles at Ketchikan's two most famous totem-pole parks (the other is at Saxman Native Village) are, for the most part, 60-year-old replicas of older totem poles brought in from outlying villages as part of a federal works–cultural project during the 1930s. Totem Bight has many totem poles and a hand-hewn native tribal house and sits on a scenic spit of land facing the waters of Tongass Narrows. ⊠ *North Tongass Hwy., 10 mi north of town,* ☎ *907/247–8574.*

SAXMAN NATIVE VILLAGE – A paved walking path–bike trail parallels the road to Saxman Village, named for a missionary who helped Native Alaskans settle here before 1900. The village's tribal house is believed to be the largest in the world. There's a carver's shed nearby where totem poles and totemic art objects are created, and there's also a theater where a multimedia presentation tells the story of Southeast Alaska's native peoples. You can see the **Totem Park** if you drive out on your own, but to visit the tribal house you must take a tour (☞ Cape Fox Tours in Guided Tours, *below*). ⊠ *South Tongass Hwy., 2 mi south of town,* ☎ *907/225–5163.*

Dining and Lodging

$$$–$$$$ ✕ **Salmon Falls Resort.** This huge, octagonal restaurant is a half-hour drive from town, but the local seafood and steaks make the trip more than worthwhile. The restaurant is built of pine logs, and at the center of the dining room, supporting the roof, rises a 40-ft section of 48-

inch pipe manufactured to be part of the Alaska pipeline. The dining area overlooks the waters of Clover Passage, where sunsets can be vivid red. Specialties include blackened salmon and prawns stuffed with crabmeat. ⊠ *Mile 17, N. Tongass Hwy., 99901, ☎ 907/225–2752, 800/247–9059 outside Alaska. AE, MC, V. Closed Oct.–Apr.*

$$$–$$$$ ✕ **Steamers.** Anchoring the new Spruce Mill Mall, part of the Spruce Mill Development, this spacious restaurant has an extensive menu of fresh seafood, pasta, and steaks. It has also rigged more beer taps than any one establishment in all of the Southeast and offers more types of liquor than you ever knew existed. Along with steamer clams, a favorite among locals, seafood dominates the menu. Try the captain's platter: salmon, halibut, prawns, and scallops cooked any way you like. ⊠ *76 Front St., ☎ 907/225–1600, AE, D, DC, MC, V.*

$$ ✕ **Kay's Kitchen.** Big windows face the water from this homey little restaurant 1½ mi north of downtown Ketchikan. Kay's is known for homemade soups, generous sandwiches, barbecued ribs, and homemade desserts, including ice cream. ⊠ *2813 Tongass Ave., ☎ 907/225–5860. MC, V.*

$$$$ 🏨 **Waterfall Resort.** Remote, but boasting the ultimate in creature
★ comforts, this upscale fishing lodge is on Prince of Wales Island near Ketchikan. At this former commercial salmon cannery you sleep in the lodge or in Cape Cod–style cottages (formerly cannery workers' cabins, but they never had it so good); eat bountiful meals of salmon, halibut steak, and all the trimmings; and fish from your own private cabin cruiser under the care of your own private fishing guide. A three-night minimum stay with all meals and floatplane fare from Ketchikan comes to around $2,900 per person. ⊠ *320 Dock St., Suite 222, Box 6440, Prince of Wales, 99901, ☎ 907/225–9461, 800/544–5125 outside Alaska,* ℻ *907/225–8530. 10 lodge rooms, 4 suites, 26 cabins. Restaurant, boating, fishing. AE, D, MC, V.*

$$$$ 🏨 **Westmark Cape Fox Lodge.** One of Ketchikan's poshest properties offers fantastic views of the town and harbor from 135 ft above the village. An open ski lodge–style lobby with roaring fire and grand piano make for a cozy, luxurious setting. Rooms are quite spacious, with Shaker-style furnishings, the traditional Tlingit tribal colors (red, black, and white), and watercolors of Native Alaskan birds. All rooms provide views of either Tongass Narrows or Deer Mountain (and the parking lot). Heen Kahidi Restaurant at the Cape Fox serves seafood, pasta, chicken, steaks, and a big Sunday brunch buffet. Make reservations for the window tables that overlook Ketchikan. ⊠ *800 Venetia Way, 99901, ☎ 907/225–8001, 800/544–0970 for reservations,* ℻ *907/225–8286. 72 rooms. Restaurant, lobby lounge, no-smoking rooms, room service, meeting rooms. AE, D, DC, MC, V.*

$$$–$$$$ 🏨 **Cedars Lodge.** Nothing in the plain, square exterior of this hotel or in its spartan lobby hints at the deluxe accommodations within. Two of the guest rooms are split-level with circular stairways, and many rooms have a full kitchen and whirlpool bath. Windows are large and some give views of the busy water and air traffic in Tongass Narrows. Simple American fare is served at a buffet dinner and breakfast (summer only). A variety of fishing and lodging packages are on offer. ⊠ *1471 Tongass Ave., Box 8331, 99901, ☎ 907/225–1900 or 800/813–4363,* ℻ *907/225–8604. 13 rooms. Restaurant, room service, fishing. AE, D, DC, MC, V.*

$$$–$$$$ 🏨 **The Landing.** This Best Western property is named for the state ferry landing directly across the road. Decor is modern, with standard motel furnishings. The small lobby contains a fireplace and Mission-style furniture. Some rooms have microwaves and kitchenettes; suites have all the comforts of home. The Landing Restaurant is always packed with a hungry breakfast clientele and with families. Upstairs, Jeremiah's Fine

Food and Spirits offers fine dining in cozy digs and a relaxing no-smoking lounge built around a stone fireplace. ⊠ *3434 Tongass Ave.,* ☎ *907/225–5166 or 800/428–8304,* FAX *907/225–6900. 76 rooms. 2 restaurants, café, exercise room, airport shuttle. AE, D, DC, MC, V.*

$$$ 🏨 **The Narrows Inn.** Four miles from town, the Narrows is a modern lodge with an on-the-premises steak and seafood restaurant. The small hotel rooms are bright, with natural wood trim and themed prints on the walls. Waterside rooms have balconies overlooking Tongass Narrows—a good place to watch seals, otters, and eagles. A Continental breakfast is included. For a more urban experience, take the Narrows shuttle to town to shop or dine. ⊠ *Box 8660, 99901,* ☎ *907/247–2600 or 888/686–2600,* FAX *907/247–2602. 44 rooms. AE, D, MC, V.*

$$ 🏨 **Gilmore Hotel.** The Gilmore has a European feel, and because of such features as a 1930s-style lobby, it's on the National Register of Historic Places. There are some welcome modern touches but no elevator in this three-story building, and the rooms are quite small. All the same, everything is well maintained, and courtesy van service is offered. Annabelle's Keg and Chowder House features a delightful 1920s-style decor, with a menu that includes seafood, pasta, and prime rib. You can choose among five kinds of seafood chowder or steamer clams. There's also an espresso bar and Annabelle's, a semiformal lounge with a jukebox. ⊠ *326 Front St., 99901,* ☎ *907/225–9423 or 800/275–9423,* FAX *907/225–7442. 38 rooms. Restaurant, bar, café, ice cream parlor. AE, D, DC, MC, V.*

Guided Tours

You can book local tours of all types at the Ketchikan Visitors Bureau. **Alaska Cruises** (☎ 907/225–6044, 800/228–1905 for a brochure, FAX 907/225–8636) runs harbor tours of the Ketchikan waterfront. It also provides cruise or fly-cruise one-day excursions from downtown Ketchikan to Misty Fjords. **Cape Fox Tours** (☎ 907/225–4846, FAX 907/225–3137) conducts tours of Saxman Native Village, rafting trips down the White River, helicopter hiking, and visits to the historic George Inlet Cannery.

Nightlife and the Arts

Bars

Ketchikan is a party town, so you won't have any trouble finding something going on at several downtown bars. For a spacious, no-smoking venue head to **Kingfisher Bar** (⊠ upstairs in the Salmon Landing Mall, ☎ 907/247–5227), with a dozen microbrews on tap and live bands on weekends. Big windows face the cruise ship dock and Tongass Narrows. **1st City Saloon** (⊠ 830 Water St., ☎ 907/225–1494) is the main dance spot, with live rock, blues, or jazz Wednesday–Saturday. **Pioneer Bar** (⊠ 122 Front St., ☎ 907/225–3210) delivers a more countrified mix of rock and country and western on weekends.

Outdoor Activities and Sports

Fishing

Sportfishing for salmon and trout is excellent in the Ketchikan area, in either saltwater or freshwater lakes and streams. Contact the **Ketchikan Visitors Bureau** (☞ Visitor Information *in* Southeast Alaska A to Z, *below*) for information on guide services and locations.

Hiking

If you're a tough hiker, the 3-mi trail from downtown to the top of **Deer Mountain** will repay your efforts with a spectacular panorama of the city below and the wilderness behind. The trail begins at the corner of Fair and Deermount streets. **Ward Cove Recreation Area,** about 6 mi north of town, offers easier hiking next to lakes and streams and beneath towering spruce and hemlock trees; it also has several designated picnic spots.

Scuba Diving

Alaska Diving Service (⊠ 4845 N. Tongass Ave., ☎ 907/225–4667) rents tanks and equipment and guides you to the best places to dive.

Sea Kayaking

Locals and visitors alike enjoy paddling around the nearby protected waters, especially those in Misty Fjords National Monument (☞ *below*). **Southeast Exposure** (☎ 907/225–8829 in summer) rents canoes and kayaks, gives kayaking classes, and guides trips. **Southeast Sea Kayaks** (☎ 907/225–1258 or 800/287–1607) leads kayak tours of Ketchikan's historic waterfront.

Shopping

Art Galleries

Among the best of Southeast Alaska's galleries is the **Scanlon Gallery** (⊠ 318 Mission St., ☎ 907/247–4730 or 800/690–4730), with a location in downtown Ketchikan. It handles not only major Alaska artists (Byron Birdsall, Rie Muñoz, John Fehringer, Jon Van Zyle) and local talent but also traditional and contemporary native art, including soapstone sculptures.

Design, art, and clothing converge in the stylish **Soho Coho Contemporary Art and Craft Gallery** (⊠ 5 Creek St., ☎ 907/225–5954 or 800/888–4070), where you'll find an eclectic collection of art and T-shirts featuring the work of owner Ray Troll—best known for his wacky fish art—as well as that of other Southeast Alaskan artists.

Books

Upstairs from the Soho Coho Gallery (☞ *above*), **Parnassus** (⊠ 5 Creek St., ☎ 907/225–7960) is a book lover's bookstore with many Alaskan titles and a knowledgeable staff.

Seafood

For some of the Southeast's best canned or smoked salmon and halibut, and all kinds of other seafood such as clams and crab, try either of the two locations of **Ketchikan's Salmon Etc.** (⊠ 10 Creek St.; ⊠ 322 Mission St.; ☎ 907/225–6008; 800/354–7256 outside Alaska).

AROUND KETCHIKAN

Metlakatla

⑱ *12 mi south of Ketchikan.*

The village of Metlakatla is on Annette Island, just a dozen miles from busy Ketchikan, but a world away culturally. A visit to this quiet and conservative place offers the chance to learn about life in a small Inside Passage native community. Local taxis can take visitors to other sights around the island, including Yellow Hill and the old Air Force Base (☞ *below*).

In most Southeast native villages, the people are Tlingit or Haida in heritage. Metlakatla is the exception; here most folks are Tsimshian. They moved to the island from British Columbia in 1887, led by William Duncan, an Anglican missionary from Scotland. The new town grew rapidly and soon included dozens of buildings laid out on a grid of streets—a cannery, a sawmill, and a church that could seat a thousand people. Congress declared Annette Island a federal Indian reservation in 1891, and it remains the only reservation in Alaska today. Father Duncan continued to control life in Metlakatla for decades, until the government finally stepped in shortly before his death in 1918.

During World War II the U.S. Army built a major **Air Force Base** 7 mi from Metlakatla that included observation towers for Japanese subs, airplane hangars, gun emplacements, and housing for 10,000 soldiers. After the war, it served as Ketchikan's airport for many years, but today the long runways are virtually abandoned save for a few private flights.

Metlakatla's religious heritage still shows through today. The clapboard **William Duncan Memorial Church,** topped with two steeples, burned in 1948 but was rebuilt several years later. **Father Duncan's Cottage** is maintained as it was when he was alive and includes numerous artifacts and historic photographs. ✉ *Corner of 4th Ave. and Church St.,* ☎ *907/886–4441, ext. 232.* ◷ *Apr.–Sept., daily 10–2.*

Father Duncan worked hard to eliminate traditional Tsimshian beliefs and dances, so he would probably not approve of recent efforts to relearn the old ways. Today the people of Metlakatla proudly perform these old dances and stories. The best place to see this is at the traditional **Longhouse,** which faces Metlakatla's boat harbor. Three totem poles stand on the back side of the building, and the front is covered with a Tsimshian design. Inside are displays of native crafts and a model of the fish traps that were once common throughout the Inside Passage. Native dance groups perform here on Wednesday and Friday in summer (☞ Metlakatla Tours *in* Guided Tours, *below*). ☎ *907/886–8688.* ◷ *May–mid-Sept., Wed. 7–noon, Fri. 3–7:30.*

Two miles from town is a boardwalk path that leads up the 540-ft **Yellow Hill.** Distinctive yellow sandstone rocks and panoramic vistas make this a worthwhile detour on clear days.

Dining and Lodging

$$ ✕ **Uncle Fred's Cafe.** Housed in a new building across from the Tsimshian Longhouse (☞ *above*), Uncle Fred's has the best meals in town. The lunches and dinners include daily specials, along with old-fashioned burgers, hand-cut fries, fresh-baked breads and pies, and homemade soups. Fresh fish is cooked up in season. ✉ *Across from Longhouse,* ☎ *907/886–5007. No credit cards. Closed Sun.–Mon.*

$$–$$$$ 🏨 **Metlakatla Hotel and Suites.** This two-story building features both standard motel accommodations and three spacious apartments with full kitchens and one, two, or three bedrooms. All rooms include private baths, TVs, and VCRs, and two have Internet hookups. Private decks have been added to the upstairs rooms. Family-style meals are served. ✉ *3rd Ave. and Lower Milton St., 99926,* ☎ *907/886–3456,* 📠 *907/886–3455. 8 rooms, 3 apartments. Dining room. AE, D, MC, V.*

Guided Tours

Metlakatla Tours (☎ 907/886–4441 or 877/886–8687) offers a variety of local tours in the summer, including one with a dance performance, a visit to the cannery, and a salmon bake. **Taquan Air** (☎ 907/225–8800 or 800/770–8800) has scheduled floatplane flights between Ketchikan and Metlakatla, or you can catch a ferry operated by the **Alaska Marine Highway System** (☞ Arriving and Departing *in* Southeast Alaska A to Z, *below*).

Hyder

⑲ *70 mi northeast of Ketchikan.*

The tiny town of Hyder sits at the head of narrow Portland Canal, a 70-mi-long fjord northeast of Ketchikan. The fjord marks the border between Canada and the United States, and Hyder sits just 2 mi from the larger town of Stewart, British Columbia. Highway 37A continues over spectacular Bear Pass from Stewart, connecting these towns with the rest of Canada.

The 1898 discovery of gold and silver in the surrounding mountains brought a flood of miners to the Hyder area, and the town eventually became a major shipping port. Mining remained important for decades, but a devastating 1948 fire destroyed much of the town, which had been built on pilings over the water. Mining still takes place here, but the beauty of the area is now attracting increasing numbers of tourists. Today, quiet Hyder calls itself "the friendliest ghost town in Alaska."

There isn't much to the town of Hyder, just a dirt road with a handful of tourist-oriented businesses, a post office, and library. Nearby Stewart has more to offer, including a bank, museum, hotels, restaurants, and camping. You will need to check in at Canadian customs (open 24 hours) before crossing the border from Hyder into Stewart. Canadian money is primarily used in Hyder, but greenbacks are certainly accepted.

The **Stewart Historical Society Museum** (⌂ 6th and Columbia Sts., ☎ 250/636–2568) contains wildlife displays and exhibits on the region's mining history. It's open June–September.

The **Toastworks Museum** in Stewart has more than 600 antique kitchen appliances, some more than a century old. The same building houses a juice and coffee bar with smoothies, espresso, and Internet access. ⌂ *306 5th St.,* ☎ *250/636–2344.* ⊡ *$3.* ☉ *May–Sept., daily 10–6.*

An **old stone storehouse** stands along the road as you enter Hyder. Built in 1896, this is the oldest masonry building in Alaska.

Six miles north of Hyder out Salmon River Road is the **Fish Creek Wildlife Observation Site.** In July and August, the salmon attract black and brown bears here, which, in turn, attract more than a few photographers. The creek produces some of the largest chum salmon anywhere. Farther away—25 mi east of Stewart on Highway 37A—is the imposing **Bear Glacier.** The glacier sits across a small lake that is often crowded with icebergs. A dirt road from Hyder leads to remote **Salmon Glacier.**

Getting "Hyderized" is a term that you will hear upon arrival in the area. The tradition supposedly began when prospectors would tack a dollar bill on the wall in case they were broke when they returned. The walls of Hyder's **Glacier Inn** (Main St., ☎ 250/636–9248) are papered with thousands of signed bills, including those of countless tourists.

Dining and Lodging

$$ ✗ **Bitter Creek Cafe.** This bustling Stewart café has a wide variety of food, including gourmet pizza, lasagna, burgers, seafood, and even Mexican. The quirky interior features a fun collection of antiques, including a 1930 Pontiac. The outside deck is a fine place to relax on a summer afternoon. ⌂ *5th Ave., Stewart, B.C., Canada,* ☎ *250/636–2166. MC, V. Closed Oct.–Apr.*

$$ ⊞ **Grandview Inn.** This modern two-story hotel is Hyder's nicest place to stay. All rooms are pretty standard, with private baths and TVs but no phones. Six of the rooms have two double beds; the others include one bed and a fully equipped kitchenette. ⌂ *Box 49, 99923,* ☎ *250/*

636–9174, ⨳ 250/636–2673. 10 rooms. AE, DC, MC, V. Closed Nov.–Mar.

Guided Tours

Seaport Limousine (☎ 250/636–2622) leads guided tours of the Hyder area, including Fish Creek and Salmon Glacier. Get to Hyder aboard a ferry operated by the **Alaska Marine Highway System** (☞ Arriving and Departing *in* Southeast Alaska A to Z, *below*). Service is once a week (on Saturday) in the summer only, and the ferry stays in Hyder for four hours before returning to Ketchikan. **Taquan Air** (☎ 907/225–8800 or 800/770–8800) has year-round service between Ketchikan and Hyder every Monday and Thursday.

Misty Fjords National Monument

⓴ *40 mi east of Ketchikan by air.*

Misty Fjords National Monument is a wilderness of cliff-faced fjords, mountains, and islands with an abundance of spectacular coastal scenery, wildlife, and recreational opportunities. Misty Fjords offers breathtaking vistas when viewed up close in small boats. Travel on these waters can be an almost mystical experience, with the greens of the forest reflected in waters as still as black mirrors. You may find yourself in the company of a whale, see a bear fishing for salmon along the shore, or even pull in your own salmon for an evening meal. Note, however, that the name Misty refers to the weather you're likely to encounter in this rainy part of Alaska. For boat and plane tours, *see* Guided Tours *in* Ketchikan, *above*. ⊠ *3031 Tongass Ave., Ketchikan 99901,* ☎ *907/225–2148.*

WRANGELL

Next up the line is the town of Wrangell, on an island near the mouth of the fast-flowing Stikine River. A small, unassuming timber and fishing community, Wrangell has existed under three flags. Known as Redoubt St. Dionysius when it was part of Russian America, the town was renamed Fort Stikine under the British.

Exploring Wrangell

The rough-around-the-edges town of Wrangell is off the track of the larger cruise ships, so it does not suffer from tourist invasions to the degree that Ketchikan and Juneau do. The town is fairly compact, and most sights are within walking distance of the city dock or ferry terminal.

A Good Walk

A good place to start your tour is at the stalls selling local goods and souvenirs outside the **Wrangell Visitor Center** ㉑, close to the city docks in the Stikine Inn. Head through town along Front Street, stopping at **Kiksetti Totem Park** ㉒ before turning onto Shakes Street to see Wrangell's most interesting sight, **Chief Shakes Island** ㉓. You will probably want to spend time here just soaking in the harbor view and examining the old totem poles. **Chief Shakes's grave site** ㉔ is on the hill overlooking Wrangell Harbor. Get there from Chief Shakes Island by turning right on Case Avenue and then left onto Church Street. From the grave site, head back up Church Street to the **Wrangell Museum** ㉕ for another taste of the past. Get to the **Irene Ingle Public Library** ㉖ by continuing up Church Street and turning right on 2nd Street. The next stop is the private little museum called **Our Collections** ㉗, on Evergreen Avenue approximately ⅓ mi north of the ferry terminal. Keep going an-

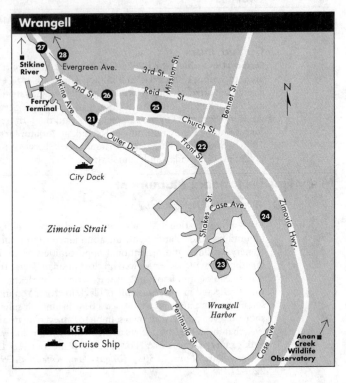

other ⅓ mi out Evergreen Avenue to **Petroglyph Beach** ㉘, where ancient etchings are visible along the shore.

TIMING

It is a 1½-mi walk between Petroglyph Beach and Chief Shakes Island, so you should plan on two hours to complete the walk and sightseeing around town.

Sights to See

㉔ **Chief Shakes's grave site.** Buried here is Shakes V, who led the local Tlingits during the first half of the 19th century. The site is on Case Avenue, marked by two killer-whale totem poles. ⊠ *Case Ave.*

㉓ **Chief Shakes Island.** Some of the finest totem poles in Alaska are preserved on the island, Wrangell's number one visitor attraction. Walk over the footbridge off the harbor dock to also see a tribal house constructed in the 1930s as a replica of one that was home to many of the various Shakes and their peoples. ⊠ *Off Shakes St.,* ☎ *907/874–3747.* ⊠ *$1.50 donation requested.* ☉ *When cruise ships are in port (ask at the Wrangell Visitor Center;* ☞ *below) or by appointment.*

㉖ **Irene Ingle Public Library.** The library, behind the post office, has two ancient petroglyphs out front. ⊠ *124 2nd St.,* ☎ *907/874–3535.*

㉒ **Kiksetti Totem Park.** This is a pocket-size park of Alaska greenery and impressive totem poles. ⊠ *Front St.*

㉗ **Our Collections.** The private museum displays thousands of items—clocks, animal traps, waffle irons, tools—that the Bigelows have gathered and used themselves over the past 60 years of Alaska living. The collection, run by Elva Bigelow, is in a large metal building on the water side of Evergreen Avenue. ⊠ *Evergreen Ave.,* ☎ *907/874–3646.* ⊠ *Donations* *accepted.* ✆ *Open for groups of cruise-ship and ferry passengers or by appointment.*

㉘ Petroglyph Beach. Scattered among other rocks at this public beach are three dozen or more large stones bearing designs and pictures chiseled by unknown, ancient artists. No one knows why the rocks at this curious site were etched the way they were; perhaps they were boundary markers or messages. Because the petroglyphs can be damaged by physical contact, the state discourages visitors from creating a rubbing off the rocks with rice paper and crayons. Instead, you can purchase a rubber stamp duplicate of selected petroglyphs from the city museum or from a Forest Service interpreter at the cruise dock. Do not, of course, attempt to move any of the petroglyph stones. ⊠ *Off Evergreen Ave.*

㉕ Wrangell Museum. A bootlegger's still and aviation and communication memorabilia are some of the historical artifacts composing this collection. The original house totem poles from Chief Shakes's clan house (believed to have been carved in the late 1700s), petroglyphs, woven native baskets from the turn of the 20th century, and other local relics round it out. It's on the lower floor of the community center, between the Presbyterian church and the high school. ⊠ *318 Church St.,* ☎ *907/874–3770.* ⊑ *$2.* ✆ *May–late Sept., weekdays 10–5, Sat. 1–4, Sun. when the ferry or cruise ships arrive; late Sept.–Apr., Tues.–Fri. 10–4 or by appointment.*

㉑ Wrangell Visitor Center. This tourist office is close to the city docks in the Stikine Inn. ⊠ *107 Stikine Ave.,* ☎ *907/874–3901 or 800/367–9745,* ℻ *907/874–3905.* ✆ *Weekdays 10–4.*

OFF THE
BEATEN PATH **ANAN CREEK WILDLIFE OBSERVATORY –** About 30 mi southeast of Wrangell in the Tongass National Forest, Anan is one of Alaska's premier black- and brown-bear viewing areas. Each summer, from early July to mid-August, as many as 30 or 40 black bears gather at this Southeast stream to feed on pink salmon. On an average visit of about two hours, you might spot two to four bears. Forest Service interpreters are on hand to answer questions from July through September. The site is accessible only by boat or floatplane (☞ Guided Tours, *below*).

Lodging

$$–$$$ 🏨 **Stikine Inn.** On the dock in the main part of town, this inn has great views of Wrangell's harbor. Rooms are simply decorated with basic, older furnishings. The Waterfront Grill has large windows from which you'll enjoy good views of the harbor. Gourmet burgers, cross-cut waffle fries, pasta, and homemade pizzas are staples. ⊠ *107 Stikine Ave., 2 blocks from the ferry terminal, Box 990, 99929,* ☎ *907/874–3388 or 888/874–3388,* ℻ *907/874–3923. 33 rooms. Restaurant. AE, D, MC, V.*

$$ 🏨 **Grand View Bed & Breakfast.** Two miles from town, this contemporary hillside home provides spectacular views of the Inside Passage. Rooms, some with antiques and some decorated Alaskan style, have private baths and entrances, along with TVs and phones. The friendly owners, John and Judy Baker, make delectable breakfast specials, including freshly baked rolls. ⊠ *Box 927, 99929,* ☎ ℻ *907/874–3225. 3 rooms. No credit cards.*

$$ 🏨 **Harding's Old Sourdough Lodge.** This lodge made of hand-milled cedar sits on the docks in a beautifully converted construction camp. The Harding family welcomes you with home-baked sourdough breads and local seafood in the big, open dining-living room. Guest rooms have rustic paneling and modest country-style furnishings. A new private suite has a luxuriously large bathroom with a heated floor and a hot tub. ✉ *1104 Peninsula St., Box 1062, 99929,* ☎ *907/874–3613 or 800/874–3613,* FAX *907/874–3455. 16 rooms. Dining room, sauna, steam room, boating, meeting room, travel services, airport shuttle. AE, D, DC, MC, V.*

$$ 🏠 **Roadhouse Lodge.** This homestead-style waterfront lodge 4½ mi from downtown has a collection of relics from all over the state that gives the place the feel of a museum of early Alaska. The lodge's restaurant is a hangout for locals and visitors alike and serves wholesome, tasty, and ample meals. Specialties include steaks, fresh halibut, local prawns (sautéed, deep-fried, or boiled in the shell), and Indian fry bread. The guest rooms have dark wood paneling and are eclectically furnished. ✉ *Mile 4, Zimovia Hwy., Box 1199, 99929,* ☎ *907/874–2335,* FAX *907/ 874–3104. 10 rooms. Restaurant, bar, travel services, airport shuttle. MC, V.*

$ 🏠 **Shakes Slough Cabins.** If you're a hot-springs or hot-tub enthusiast, these Forest Service cabins on the Stikine River, accessible from Wrangell, are worth checking out. Reservations are required; request details from the Forest Service office in Wrangell or make reservations by calling ☎ 877/444–6777. You can also get details on the Web at www.ReserveUSA.com. ✉ *Forest Service: 525 Bennett St., Wrangell 99929,* ☎ *907/874–2323,* FAX *907/874–7595;* ✉ *U.S. Forest Service Information Center: 101 Egan Dr., Juneau 99801,* ☎ *907/586–8751. 2 cabins. Hot springs. AE, D, MC, V.*

Guided Tours

Alaska Tugboat Tours (☎ 907/874–3101 or 888/488–4386) takes groups of four to six guests through the Inside Passage aboard a vintage 1967 tugboat that's been transformed into a comfortable floating resort. **Sunrise Aviation** (☎ 907/874–2319 or 800/874–2311, FAX 907/874–2546) is a charter-only air carrier that offers trips to the Anan Creek Wildlife Observatory (☞ *above*), LeConte Glacier (☞ *below*), or Forest Service cabins. Van tours of the Wrangell area are offered by **Roadhouse Lodge** (☞ Lodging, *above*).

Outdoor Activities and Sports

Fishing
Numerous companies schedule salmon and trout fishing excursions ranging in length from an afternoon to a week. Contact the **Wrangell Visitor Center** (☞ Visitor Information *in* Exploring Wrangell, *above*) for information on guide services and locations.

Golf
Muskeg Meadows Golf Course (☎ 907/874–2538), in a wooded area ½ mi from town, is a new nine-hole course with woodchip fairways, artificial greens, and a driving range. Golf clubs and pull carts can be rented.

Hiking
Rain Walker Expeditions (☎ 907/874–2549) offers two-hour, half-, or full-day guided natural history, botany, wildlife, and bird-watching tours of wild places near Wrangell.

Shopping

You'll find vendors selling local crafts, including children selling garnets from a nearby quarry, at covered shelters near the Wrangell city dock. **River's Edge Fine Arts and Gifts** (107 Stikine Ave., ☎ 907/874–3330 or 888/278–4753), just off the lobby of the Stikine Inn (☞ Lodging, *above*), carries a selection of prints, hand-carved wood bowls, furniture, jewelry, and pottery. A local marine artist, Brenda Schwartz, often works in her studio inside this shop.

PETERSBURG

Getting to Petersburg is an experience, whether you take the "high road" by air or the "low road" by sea. Alaska Airlines claims the shortest jet flight in the world, from takeoff at Wrangell to landing at Petersburg. The schedule calls for 20 minutes of flying, but it's usually more like 15. At sea level only ferries and smaller cruisers can squeak through Wrangell Narrows, with the aid of more than 50 buoys and range markers along the 22-mi crossing. The inaccessibility of Petersburg is part of its off-the-beaten-path charm. Unlike in several other Southeast communities, you'll never be overwhelmed here by hordes of cruise passengers.

At first sight Petersburg may make you think you're in the old country, with neat, white, Scandinavian-style homes and storefronts with steep roofs and bright-colored swirls of leaf and flower designs (called rosemaling). Row upon row of sturdy fishing vessels in the harbor invoke the spirit of Norway. No wonder. This prosperous fishing community was founded by Norwegian Peter Buschmann in 1897.

You may occasionally even hear some Norwegian spoken, especially during the Little Norway Festival held here each year on the weekend closest to May 17. If you're in town during the festival, be sure to partake in one of the fish feeds that highlight the Norwegian Independence Day celebration. You won't find better beer-batter halibut and folk dancing outside Norway.

One of the most pleasant things to do in Petersburg is to roam among the fishing vessels tied up at dockside in the town's expanding harbor. This is one of Alaska's busiest, most prosperous fishing communities, and the variety of seacraft is enormous. You'll see small trollers, big halibut vessels, and sleek pleasure craft. Wander, too, around the fish-processing structures (though be prepared for the pungent aroma). By watching shrimp, salmon, or halibut catches being brought ashore, you can get a real appreciation for this industry and the people who engage in it.

Exploring Petersburg

Although Petersburg is a pretty enough town to explore, here the workaday world of commercial fishing is more important than rolling out the red carpet for tourists. The main attractions are the town's Norwegian heritage and its magnificent mountain-backed setting.

A Good Walk

The **Petersburg Visitor Information Center** ㉙ at 1st and Fram streets is a logical spot to begin any walking (or biking) tour of Petersburg. Just a block up the hill, the **Clausen Memorial Museum** ㉚ is a testimony to life in Petersburg. From here, head back downhill to Nordic Drive (Main Street), turning left and then right onto historic Sing Lee Alley. Follow it to the **Sons of Norway Hall** ㉛ along scenic **Hammer Slough** ㉜. Walk back through the center of town on Nordic Drive. On the north side of downtown, steps lead down to the water at scenic **Eagle's Roost Park** ㉝.

TIMING

Petersburg is small enough to walk around in an hour, but you may want to spend more time biking around the back roads farther from town.

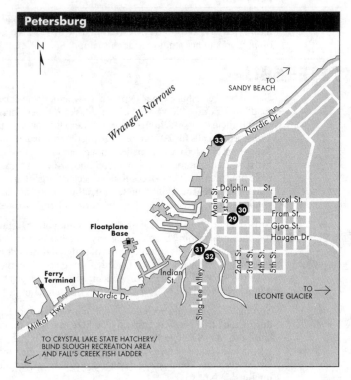

Sights to See

30 Clausen Memorial Museum. The museum interprets commercial fishing and the cannery industry, the era of fish traps, the social life of Petersburg, and Tlingit culture. Don't miss the 126½-pound king salmon, the largest ever caught, as well as the Tlingit dugout canoe, two fish-trap anchors, the Cape Decision lighthouse station lens, and *Earth, Sea and Sky,* a 3-D sculptured wall mural outside. ⊠ *203 Fram St., 99833,* ☎ *907/772–3598.* ☞ *$2.* ⊙ *May–mid-Sept., Mon.–Sat. 9:30–4:30, Sun. 12:30–4:30; mid-Sept.–Apr., opening hrs vary.*

33 Eagle's Roost Park. Just north of the Petersburg Fisheries cannery, this park is a great place to spot eagles, especially at low tide. On a clear day you will also discover dramatic views of the sharp-edged Coast Range, including the 9,077-ft summit of Devils Thumb.

32 Hammer Slough. Stop along this pool for a vision of houses and buildings on high stilts reflected perfectly in still waters; it's best seen at high tide.

29 Petersburg Visitor Information Center. This office is a good source for local information. ⊠ *1st and Fram Sts., Box 649,* ☎ *907/772–4636.* ⊙ *May–Sept., Mon.–Sat. 9–5, Sun. noon–4; Oct.–Apr., weekdays 10–2.*

31 Sons of Norway Hall. The large, white barnlike structure that stands just south of the Hammer Slough is the headquarters of an organization devoted to keeping alive the traditions and culture of the old country. Scandinavian-style arts and crafts are sold inside. At **Tonka Seafoods** across the street you can tour the plant and sample smoked halibut and salmon. ⊠ *Sing Lee Alley,* ☎ *907/772–3662.* ⊙ *Hrs vary (call ahead).*

OFF THE
BEATEN PATH

FALL'S CREEK FISH LADDER – Coho and pink salmon migrate upstream in late summer and fall at this fish ladder. *Mile 10.8 of the Mitkof Hwy.*

CRYSTAL LAKE STATE HATCHERY/ BLIND SLOUGH RECREATION AREA –
More than 60,000 pounds of salmon and trout are produced each year at the hatchery, at Mile 17.5 of the Mitkof Highway. A bird-viewing area can be found at Blind Slough, 16 mi south of town. A dozen or so swans overwinter here, and in the summer you're likely to see many ducks and other waterfowl.

LECONTE GLACIER – Petersburg's biggest draw lies about 25 mi east of town and is accessible only by water or air. LeConte Glacier is the continent's southernmost tidewater glacier and one of its most active, often calving off so many icebergs that the tidewater bay at its face is carpeted shore to shore with floating bergs. Ferries and cruise ships pass it at a distance. For tour information, *see* Guided Tours, *below.*

Dining and Lodging

$$-$$$$ ✕ **The Homestead.** There's nothing fancy at your standard country town restaurant, just basic American fare: steaks, local prawns and halibut, a salad bar, and generous breakfasts. Special favorites are the homemade peach, blackberry, and rhubarb pies. ⊠ *217 Main St.,* ☎ *907/772–3900. AE, MC, V.* ☺ *Weekdays 24 hrs, Sat. until 10 PM. Closed Sun.*

$$-$$ ✕ **Alaskafe.** This comfortable coffeehouse and lunch spot in downtown Petersburg, above Coastal Cold Storage, serves vegetarian soups, colorful salads, pastries, and filling Italian-style panini sandwiches grilled to order. You can browse through a selection of books and magazines, or even rent their computer for Internet access while you're waiting for your meal. ⊠ *306B Nordic Dr.,* ☎ *907/772–5282. No credit cards.*

$$-$$ ✕ **Pellerito's Pizza.** Although it has a few tables, this always-crowded pizza joint primarily specializes in take-out pizzas, giant calzones, and hero sandwiches. You'll also find ice cream, cinnamon rolls, and espresso. ⊠ *1105 S. Nordic Dr., across from the ferry terminal,* ☎ *907/772–3727. MC, V.*

$$$-$$$$ ▥ **Scandia House.** Exuding an old-country, Norwegian atmosphere, this hotel on Petersburg's main street, a fixture since 1910, was rebuilt following a 1995 fire. Rosemaling designs adorn the exterior. The interior is squeaky-clean, with contemporary oak furniture, and some rooms have kitchenettes or king-size beds and a view of the harbor. A Continental breakfast of homemade muffins and coffee warms the small but relaxing lobby in the morning. ⊠ *110 Nordic Dr., Box 689, 99833,* ☎ *907/772–4281 or 800/722–5006,* FAX *907/772–4301. 33 rooms, 3 suites. Kitchenettes, minibars, beauty salon, boating, bicycles, car rental. AE, D, DC, MC, V.*

$$-$$$ ▥ **Water's Edge Bed & Breakfast.** Located along the shore of Frederick Sound 1½ mi north of Petersburg, this family-run B&B features either a creekside or waterside room. Seals, eagles, and whales are often seen just outside the door. A deluxe Continental breakfast is served, and the library is stocked with books on Alaska and natural history. Take advantage of the owners' Kaleidoscope Cruises (☞ Guided Tours, *below*) or borrow the bikes or canoe to explore on your own. Lodging-cruise packages are on offer. ⊠ *3705 Sandy Beach Rd., Box 1201, 99833,* ☎ *907/772–3736 or 800/868–4373,* FAX *907/772–4286. 2 rooms. Bicycles, boating, library, airport shuttle. No credit cards.*

$$ ▥ **Tides Inn.** This is the largest hotel in town, a block uphill from Petersburg's main thoroughfare. Room furnishings are standard, but comfortable nonetheless; some rooms have kitchens. Rooms in the newer wing have views of the boat harbor. The coffee is always on in the small

lobby, and in the morning you're welcome to complimentary juices, muffins, and pastries. ✉ *307 N. 1st St., Box 1048, 99833,* ☎ *907/772–4288 or 800/665–8433,* FAX *907/772–4286. 48 rooms. Car rental. AE, D, DC, MC, V.*

Guided Tours

Stop by the visitor center (☞ Exploring Petersburg, *above*) for a complete listing of local tour companies. **Kaleidoscope Cruises** (☎ 907/772–3736 or 800/868–4373) offers whale-watching and glacier-ecology boat tours led by professional biologists and naturalists. **Tongass Kayak Adventures** (☎ 907/772–4600) leads half-day sea kayak trips from Petersburg, along with longer trips to LeConte Bay and elsewhere in the area.

Pacific Wing, Inc. (✉ Airport on Hagen Dr., ☎ 907/772–9258) is an air-taxi operator that gets high marks from locals for its flightseeing tours over the Stikine River and LeConte Glacier. **Viking Travel** (✉ 101 Nordic Dr., ☎ 907/772–9258 or 907/772–3818, FAX 907/772–3940) books whale-watching, glacier, sea kayaking, and other charters with local operators.

Nightlife and the Arts

Bars and Nightclubs

Sample the brew and blasting tunes at the smoky **Kito's Kave** (✉ Sing Lee Alley, ☎ 907/772–3207) and examine the outrageous wall decor— a Mexican painting on black velvet, a mounted Alaska king salmon, and two stuffed sailfish from a tropical fishing expedition. The **Harbor Bar** (✉ Nordic Dr., ☎ 907/772–4526), with ship's wheels, ship pictures, and a mounted red snapper, is true to the town's seafaring spirit.

Outdoor Activities and Sports

Bicycling

Because of its small size, most of Petersburg can be covered by bicycle. A good route to ride is along the coast on Nordic Drive past the lovely homes and to Sandy Beach. Coming back to town, take the interior route (Haugen Drive) and you'll pass the airport, "Tent City" (housing for cannery workers), and some pretty churches before returning to the waterfront. **Northern Bikes** (✉ 110 Nordic Dr., ☎ 907/772–3978) rents bicycles.

Diving

If you're feeling adventurous, spend an afternoon with **Southeast Diving** (✉ 208 Haugen Dr., ☎ 907/772–2446). Some of the best Alaskan souvenirs and marine life can be found under the waters of Frederick Sound.

Shopping

Art Galleries

Several local shops sell handcrafted items and artwork. For whalebone carvings try **Petersburg Gallery** (✉ Harbor Way, ☎ 907/772–2244). A stroll down Sing Lee Alley at the south end of Nordic Drive will take you past stores and galleries with local artists' work. Of note is **Ravens Nest Gallery** (✉ Sing Lee Alley, ☎ 907/772–3400).

Bookstore

Set back off the alley in a beautiful big white house that served as a boardinghouse to fishermen and schoolteachers is **Sing Lee Alley Book**

Store (⊠ Sing Lee Alley, ☎ 907/772–4440), with a good supply of books on Alaska, best-sellers, cards, and gifts.

SITKA

Sitka was the home to Tlingit people for centuries prior to the 18th-century arrival of the Russians. In canoes up to 60 ft long, the Tlingits fished and traded the Alaskan Panhandle. Unfortunately for them, Russian territorial governor Alexander Baranof coveted the Sitka site for its beauty, mild climate, and economic potential. In the island's massive timber forests he saw raw materials for shipbuilding. Its location offered trading routes as far west as Asia and as far south as California and Hawaii. In 1799 Baranof negotiated with the local chief to build a wooden fort and trading post some 6 mi north of the present town. He called the outpost St. Michael Archangel and moved a large number of his Russian and Aleut fur hunters there from their former base on Kodiak Island.

The Tlingits soon took exception to the ambitions of their new neighbors. Reluctant to pledge allegiance to the czar and provide free labor, in 1802 they attacked Baranof's people and burned his buildings. Baranof, however, was away on Kodiak at the time. He returned in 1804 with a formidable force, including shipboard cannons. He attacked the Tlingits at their fort near Indian River, site of the present-day 105-acre Sitka National Historical Park, and forced them to flee to Chichagof Island.

In 1821 the Tlingits returned to Sitka to trade with the Russians, who were happy to benefit from the tribe's hunting skills. Under Baranof and succeeding managers, the Russian-American Company and the town prospered, becoming known as "the Paris of the Pacific." Besides the fur trade, the community built a major shipbuilding and repair facility, sawmills, and forges, and even initiated an ice industry. The Russians shipped blocks of ice from nearby Swan Lake to the booming San Francisco market. In 1800 Baranof shifted the capital of Russian America to Sitka from Kodiak.

The town declined after its 1867 transfer from Russia to the United States but became prosperous again during World War II, when it served as a base for the U.S. effort to drive the Japanese from the Aleutian Islands. Today its most important industries are fishing, government, and tourism.

Exploring Sitka

It is hard not to like Sitka, with its eclectic blending of native, Russian, and American history and a setting that is both dramatic and beautiful. This is one of the best Inside Passage towns to explore on foot, with such sights as St. Michael's Cathedral, Sheldon Jackson Museum, Sitka National Historical Park, and the Alaska Raptor Rehabilitation Center topping the town's must-see list.

A Good Walk

A good place to begin a tour of Sitka is the distinctive onion-dome **St. Michael's Cathedral** ㉞, right in town center. Next, head to **Centennial Hall** ㉟, a block behind the cathedral along Harbor Drive. Inside are the interesting Isabel Miller Museum and the Sitka Convention and Visitors Bureau. From Centennial Hall, turn right on Lincoln Street and continue a block to the **Russian Bishop's House** ㊱, one of the symbols of Russian rule, dating from 1842. Continue out Lincoln Street along the harbor to Sheldon Jackson College, where the **Sheldon Jackson Mu-**

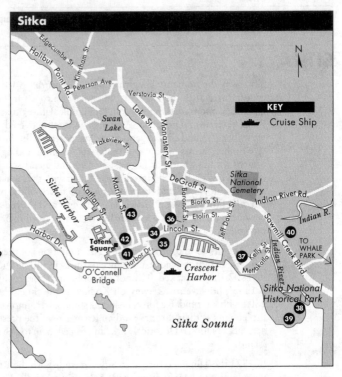

Sitka

KEY
Cruise Ship

seum ㊲ is packed with native cultural artifacts. Another ½ mi up is the **Sitka National Historical Park** ㊳, where you can watch native artisans and learn about 19th-century conflicts between Tlingits and Russians. Paths take you through the rain forest past tall totem poles and to the site of a **Tlingit Fort** ㊴ from the battle of 1804. A signed trail crosses the Indian River (watch for spawning salmon) and heads to the **Alaska Raptor Rehabilitation Center** ㊵, for an up-close look at bald eagles.

Return to town along Sawmill Creek Road to the small Sitka National Cemetery, where you turn left on Jeff Davis Street. Continue downhill to Lincoln Street and turn right, following it back to Centennial Hall. From here, walk along Harbor Drive for two blocks and take the gentle path to the summit of **Castle Hill** ㊶, where Russia transferred Alaska to American hands. Follow the path down the other side of the hill to view the impressive **Sitka State Pioneers' Home** ㊷, the statue of pioneer "Skagway Bill" Fonda, and the new Sheet'ka Kwaan Naa Kahidi Community House cultural center. Native dances take place here in the summer (☞ Dance *in* Nightlife and the Arts, *below*). Turn right at the center and pass the reconstructed Russian block house that tops a nearby hill. End your walk at the **Russian and Lutheran cemeteries** ㊸, along Marine Street a block from the block house. The grave of Princess Maksutoff, a member of the Russian royal family, is here.

TIMING

Sitka has many attractions, and you could easily spend a full day exploring this culturally rich area. You can accomplish the walk in two to three hours if you do not spend much time at each stop.

Sights to See

㊵ **Alaska Raptor Rehabilitation Center.** You have the unique experience of viewing American bald eagles and other wild Alaskan birds up close at this center set on a beautiful tract of land crisscrossed by hiking trails. This nonprofit organization rescues dozens of birds a year and houses those unable to return to the wild. Informative tours and a video are offered. ☎ *907/747–8662.* 🖾 *$10 mid-May–Sept.; free Oct–mid-May.* ⊘ *Mid-May–Sept., when cruise ships are in port; Oct.–mid-May, Sun. 2–4.*

④① **Castle Hill.** On this hill Alaska was formally handed over to the United States on October 18, 1867, and the first 49-star U.S. flag was flown on January 3, 1959, signifying Alaska's statehood. To reach the hill and get one of Sitka's best views, take the first right off Harbor Drive just before the John O'Connell Bridge, and then go into the **Baranof Castle Hill State Historic Site** entrance. A paved path takes you to the top of the hill, overlooking Crescent Harbor. Several Russian residences on the hill, including Baranof's castle, burned down in 1894.

③⑤ **Centennial Hall.** Out front of this contemporary brick building behind St. Michael's Cathedral is a replica of a Tlingit war canoe. Inside, you'll find the **Isabel Miller Museum,** a small art gallery, and an auditorium for Russian dance performances (☞ Dance *in* Nightlife and the Arts, *below*). The **Sitka Convention and Visitors Bureau** is also inside. ⊠ *Harbor Dr.,* ☎ *907/747–6455 museum, 907/747–5940 Visitors Bureau.* ⊘ *Museum May–Sept., daily 8–6; Oct.–Apr., Tues.–Sat. 10–4. Visitors Bureau May–Sept., daily 8–5; Oct.–Apr., weekdays 8–5.*

④③ **Russian and Lutheran cemeteries.** Most of Sitka's Russian dignitaries are buried in these sites off Marine Street. The most distinctive grave belongs to Princess Maksutoff (died 1862), wife of the last Russian governor and one of the most illustrious members of the Russian royal family to be buried on Alaskan soil.

③⑥ **Russian Bishop's House.** Now a registered historic landmark, this house facing the harbor was constructed by the Russian-American Company for Bishop Innocent Veniaminov in 1842. Inside the house, one of the few remaining Russian-built log structures in Alaska, are exhibits on the history of Russian America, including a room where a portion of the house's structure is peeled away to expose Russian building techniques. *501 Lincoln St.,* ☎ *907/747–6281.* 🖾 *$3.* ⊘ *May–Sept., daily 9–1 and 2–5; Oct.–Apr., by appointment.*

③④ **St. Michael's Cathedral.** One of Southeast Alaska's best-known national landmarks had its origins in a log structure erected between 1844 and 1848. In 1966 the church was destroyed in a fire that swept through the downtown business district. As the fire engulfed the building, townspeople risked their lives and rushed inside to rescue the cathedral's precious icons, religious objects, vestments, and other treasures brought to the church from Russia. Using original measurements and blueprints, an almost exact replica of onion-domed St. Michael's was built and dedicated in 1976. Today, visitors can see what could possibly be the largest collection of Russian icons in the United States, among them the much-prized *Our Lady of Sitka* (also known as the *Sitka Madonna*) and the *Christ Pantocrator* (*Christ the Judge*) on either side of the doors of the interior altar screen. Other objects include ornate Gospel books, chalices, crucifixes, much-used silver-gilt wedding crowns dating to 1866, and an altar cloth made by Princess Maksutoff. ⊠ *Lincoln St.,* ☎ *907/747–8120.* 🖾 *$1 donation requested.* ⊘ *May–Sept., daily 7:30–5:30; Oct.–Apr., daily 1:30–5:30.*

③⑦ **Sheldon Jackson Museum.** On Lincoln Street is **Sheldon Jackson College,** founded in 1878. Of particular interest here is the octagonal museum, which dates from 1895 and contains priceless Indian, Aleut, and Eskimo items collected by Dr. Sheldon Jackson (1834–1909) in the remote regions of Alaska he traveled as an educator and missionary. Carved masks, Chilkat blankets, dogsleds, kayaks—even the helmet worn by Chief Katlean during the 1804 battle against the Russians—are on display. ⊠ *801 Lincoln St.,* ☎ *907/747–8981.* ☞ *$3.* ☼ *Mid-May–mid-Sept., daily 8–5; mid-Sept.–mid-May, Tues.–Sat. 10–4.*

㊳ Sitka National Historical Park. The information center here contains audiovisual programs and historical exhibits, plus native and Russian artifacts. In the cultural center, native artists and craftspeople are on hand to demonstrate silversmithing, weaving, wood carving, and basket making. ⊠ *106 Metlakatla St.,* ☎ *907/747–6281.* ☞ *Free.* ☼ *June–Sept., daily 8–5; Oct.–May, weekdays 8–5.*

㊷ Sitka State Pioneers' Home. The large, four-level, red-roof structure on the northeast side of the hill, with the imposing 14-ft statue in front, is the first of several state-run retirement homes for Alaska's senior citizens. The statue, symbolizing Alaska's frontier sourdough spirit, was modeled by an authentic pioneer, William "Skagway Bill" Fonda. It portrays a determined prospector with pack, pick, rifle, and supplies on his back heading for the gold country. ⊠ *Castle Hill.*

★ ㊴ Tlingit Fort. Follow the self-guided trail in **Sitka National Historical Park** (☞ *above*) to this grassy meadow, the site of the 1804 battle. The path passes some of the most skillfully carved totem poles in Alaska. Several of these date from the early 1930s, and all were made and raised by natives in accordance with Tlingit traditions. ⊠ *Sitka National Historical Park,* ☎ *907/747–6281.* ☞ *Free.* ☼ *June–Sept., daily 8 AM–10 PM; Oct.–May, weekdays 8–5.*

Totem Square. On this square below Castle Hill are three anchors discovered in local waters that are believed to be of 19th-century British origin. Look for the double-headed eagle of czarist Russia carved into the cedar of the totem pole in the park.

Dining and Lodging

$$–$$$ ✕ **Channel Club.** Once you've surveyed the dozens of salads arrayed on the salad bar, you might not even make it to the steak and seafood for which this restaurant, festooned with fishnet, floats, and whalebone carvings, is known. A courtesy van provides door-to-door service if you're without transportation. ⊠ *Mile 3.5, 2906 Halibut Point Rd.,* ☎ *907/747–9916. AE, DC, MC, V.*

$$$$ ⌂ **Rockwell Lighthouse.** On an island ¾ mi from town, Burgess Bauder rents out his 1,600-square-ft, four-story lighthouse, hand-built in the 1980s with coastal woods and brass lights. The light at the top is built to coast guard specifications. There are accommodations for four couples, including a modern kitchen. The house features a curving staircase that wraps up the inside of the lighthouse. Decor is—not surprisingly—nautical. The price includes transportation to and from the lighthouse. In summer, you have use of a small motorboat. ⊠ *Box 277, 99835,* ☎ FAX *907/747–3056. 4 rooms. Dining room, boating. No credit cards.*

$$$–$$$$ ⌂ **Cascade Inn.** A few miles out of town and oh-so-conveniently attached to a grocery, video, and liquor store, this motel is the newest in town. The large rooms all feature standard hotel furniture and balconies that face the water and the extinct Mt. Edgecumbe volcano. A deck with a hot tub and a barbecue pit sits just above the water. ⊠ *2035 Halibut Point Rd., 99835,* ☎ *907/747–6804 or 800/532–0908,* FAX *907/747–6572. 10 rooms. Grocery, kitchenettes, hot tub, bicycles, laundry service, travel services. D, MC, V.*

$$$–$$$$ ⚏ **Westmark Shee Atika.** If you stay here for a night or two, you will
★ surely come away with an increased appreciation for Southeast Alaskan
native art and culture. Artwork illustrates the history, legends, and ex-
ploits of the Tlingit people. Many rooms overlook Crescent Harbor
and the islands in the waters beyond; others have mountain and for-
est views. The Raven Room Restaurant offers seafood, pasta, and
steak. Fried halibut nuggets are a top draw; or return at breakfast for
delicious eggs Benedict. ✉ *330 Seward St., 99835,* ☎ *907/747–6241,*
FAX *907/747–5486. 101 rooms. Restaurant, bar. AE, D, DC, MC, V.*

$$ ⚏ **Sitka Hotel.** Built in 1939, this friendly, old-fashioned hotel with a
Victorian-style lobby is right in downtown. The rooms are a quaint
mix of Victorian-style brass beds and wallpaper and contemporary furniture. A cozy no-smoking lounge and off-street parking are bonuses.
✉ *118 Lincoln St., 99835,* ☎ *907/747–3288,* FAX *907/747–8499. 110
rooms. MC, V.*

$ ⚏ **White Sulphur Springs Cabin.** This Tongass National Forest pub-
lic-use cabin 65 mi outside Sitka has nearby hot springs. Like many
other Forest Service cabins, this cabin sleeps four (bring your own sleep-
ing bags) and has bunk beds, a wood stove, table, and outhouse. It does
not have mattresses, cooking utensils, or any services, so you must bring
all of your supplies. The cabin faces the Pacific Ocean and has a nearby
hot springs bathhouse. Access is by boat (you'll need to walk in from
a nearby cove) or helicopter. You can make reservations over the phone
or on the Internet (www.ReserveUSA.com). ☎ *907/747–6671 information, 877/444–6777 reservations. 1 cabin. AE, D, MC, V.*

Guided Tours

Sitka Tours (☎ 907/747–8443, FAX 907/747–7510) meets state ferries
and provides short city tours while vessels are in port.

Nightlife and the Arts
Bars and Nightclubs

As far as the locals are concerned, a spot in one of the massive green-
and-white vinyl booths at **Pioneer Bar** (✉ 212 Katlean St., ☎ 907/747–
3456), across from the harbor, is a destination unto itself. It's vintage
Alaska, with hundreds of pictures of local fishing boats, and has occasional live music and pick-up pool games. A bit out of the way, **Rook-
ies** (✉ 1617 Sawmill Creek Rd., ☎ 907/747–3285) is a sports bar with
pool, air hockey, darts, and a DJ playing dance music. A free shuttle
will make sure you get home safe and sound.

Dance

The **New Archangel Dancers of Sitka** (☎ 907/747–5516) perform authentic Russian Cossack–type dances whenever cruise ships are in
port. Tickets are sold a half hour before performances; a recorded mes-
sage gives the schedule a week in advance. **Sheet'ka Kwaan Naa Kahidi
Dancers** (☎ 907/747–7290) perform Tlingit dances in full native re-
galia at the new Sheet'ka Kwaan Naa Kahidi Community House on
Katlian Street.

Festivals

Southeast Alaska's major classical chamber-music festival is the annual
Sitka Summer Music Festival (✉ Box 3333, 99835, ☎ 907/747–6774),
a three-week June celebration of concerts and special events held in
Centennial Hall. The **Sitka WhaleFest** (✉ Box 1226, 99835, ☎ 907/
747–5940, FAX 907/747–3739) is held around town in early November when the whales are plentiful (as many as 80) and tourists are not.

Outdoor Activities and Sports

Bird-Watching and Hiking

Seven miles north of Sitka along Halibut Point Road are two bird-watching and hiking trails. The **Starrigavan Estuary Life Interpretive Trail** provides views of spawning salmon and waterfowl and has a platform for bird-watchers. Not far away, the **Starrigavan Forest & Muskeg Interpretive Trail** has great views of the valley.

Canoeing and Kayaking

Above Old Harbor Books (☞ Shopping, *below*), **Baidarka Boats** (☎ 907/747–8996, ⅨⅩ 907/747–4801) rents sea kayaks and guides trips in the Sitka area. **Alaska Travel Adventures** (☎ 907/789–0052 in Juneau) does a three-hour kayaking tour in protected waters south of Sitka; instruction is provided and no experience is necessary.

Shopping

Art Galleries

Impressions (✉ 239 Lincoln St., ☎ 907/747–5502 or 888/747–5502) is a fine downtown gallery with art prints and limited editions from Southeast Alaskan artists, including Evon Zerbetz and Rie Muñoz. **Fairweather Prints** (✉ 209 Lincoln St., ☎ 907/747–8677) is not your standard gallery. Instead of paintings, the artwork here consists of beautifully printed "wearable art" with Alaskan designs.

Bookstore

Old Harbor Books (✉ 201 Lincoln St., ☎ 907/747–8808) is a fine place to buy Alaskan books. Located directly behind the bookstore is Back Door Cafe, with espresso and pastries.

JUNEAU

Juneau, Alaska's capital and third-largest city, is on the North American mainland but can't be reached by road. The city owes its origins to two colorful sourdoughs, Joe Juneau and Dick Harris, and to a Tlingit chief named Kowee. The chief led the two men to rich reserves of gold in the outwash of the stream that now runs through the middle of town and in quartz rock formations back in the gulches and valleys. That was in 1880, and shortly after the discovery a modest stampede resulted in the formation of first a camp, then a town, then finally the Alaska district government capital in 1906.

For 60 years or so after Juneau's founding, gold was the mainstay of the economy. In its heyday the AJ (for Alaska Juneau) gold mine was the biggest low-grade ore mine in the world. It was not until World War II, when the government decided it needed Juneau's manpower for the war effort, that the AJ and other mines in the area ceased operations. After the war, mining failed to start up again, and government became the city's principal employer.

Juneau is full of contrasts. The historic downtown buildings and dramatic hillside position provide a frontier feeling, but the city's cosmopolitan nature comes through in fine museums, noteworthy restaurants, and a literate and outdoorsy populace. In addition to the city itself, you will discover a tramway to alpine trails atop Mt. Roberts, densely forested wilderness areas, quiet bays for sea kayaking, and even a famous drive-up glacier. Juneau has one of the best museums in Alaska, is surrounded by beautiful wilderness, and has a glacier in its backyard.

Exploring Juneau

Juneau is an obligatory stop on the Inside Passage cruise and ferry circuit and enjoys an overabundance of tourists in mid-summer. Downtown Juneau is compact enough so that most of its main attractions are within walking distance of one another. Note, however, that the city is very hilly, so your legs will get a real workout. Along with the Alaska State Museum and Mt. Roberts Tramway, be sure to make time for a tour to Mendenhall Glacier and the Gastineau Salmon Hatchery.

A Good Walk

A good starting point is **Marine Park** ㊹, right along the cruise ship dock. For an introduction to public lands in the area, walk up Marine Way to Willoughby Avenue, where **Centennial Hall** ㊺ houses a Forest Service/Park Service information center. Continue another block up Marine Way and turn right on Whittier Street to reach the engaging **Alaska State Museum** ㊻, filled with artifacts and art from around the state. From here, circle back along Willoughby Avenue to the **State Office Building** ㊼. Catch the elevator to the eighth-floor atrium and head out onto the observation deck for vistas across Gastineau Channel. Then continue out the east side of the building onto 4th Street. The small but informative **Juneau-Douglas City Museum** ㊽ sits a short distance away at 4th and Calhoun streets. The unimpressive banklike building across the street is the **Alaska State Capitol** ㊾. Next stop is the **Governor's Mansion** ㊿, a few minutes uphill on Calhoun Street. If you have the time and energy, you may want to continue along Calhoun, across the Gold Creek Bridge, and then down along 12th Street to the quiet **Evergreen Cemetery** (51), where town fathers Joe Juneau and Dick Harris are buried.

Backtrack to the Governor's Mansion and retrace your steps down Calhoun Street to the overpass. Climb the steps and cross the footbridge to 5th Street, and turn left up Main Street, followed by a right on 7th Street. Next stop is the artifacts-filled old home of Judge Wickersham, the **House of Wickersham** (52) on 7th and Seward streets. From here on, you will be working your way back downhill, so the walking gets easier. The **St. Nicholas Russian Orthodox Church** (53) occupies the corner of 5th and Gold streets, and the **Log Cabin Visitor Center** (54) is just a couple of blocks away at 3rd and Seward streets. By now you probably have a good taste of Juneau; step inside for the complete details.

Now it's time to explore the historic buildings and busy shops of downtown Juneau, particularly those along **South Franklin Street** (55). Check out the Alaskan Hotel, the Alaska Steam Laundry Building, and the Senate Building before dipping inside the always crowded **Red Dog Saloon** (56) at the intersection of South Franklin and Admiral Way. A few more minutes' walking will take you to the **Mt. Roberts Tramway** (57), a great way to reach alpine country for a hike overlooking Juneau and Gastineau Channel.

TIMING

To cover downtown Juneau's many interesting sights, you should budget at least three or four hours for exploring. Add more time for a ride on the Mt. Roberts Tramway or for the side trip to Evergreen Cemetery.

Sights to See

㊾ **Alaska State Capitol.** Constructed in 1930, this building has pillars of Southeast Alaska marble. The building now houses the governor's office, and the state legislature meets here during the winter months. ✉ *Corner of Seward and 4th Sts.,* ☎ *907/465–2479.* ⏲ *Tours mid-May–*

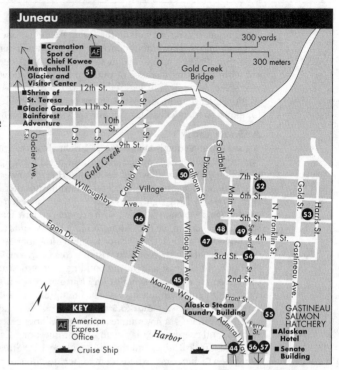

mid-Sept., Sun.–Fri. 9–4:30; tours can also be arranged when legislature is in session.

46 **Alaska State Museum.** Alaska's finest museum is certain to appeal to all tastes. Native Alaskan buffs will enjoy examining the 38-ft walrus-hide umiak constructed by Eskimos and a re-created interior of a Tlingit tribal house. Natural-history exhibits include stuffed brown bears and a two-story-high eagle nesting tree. Mining displays and contemporary art complete the collection. ☒ *395 Whittier St.,* ☎ *907/465–2901.* ☞ *$4.* ☾ *Mid-May–mid-Sept., weekdays 9–6, weekends 10–6; Sept. 16–May 14, Tues.–Sat. 10–4.*

45 **Centennial Hall.** The helpful on-site **information center** is operated jointly by the U.S. Forest Service and the National Park Service. The center provides movies, slide shows, and information about recreation in the surrounding Tongass National Forest (☞ *above*) and the nearby Glacier Bay National Park and Preserve (☞ *below*). ☒ *101 Egan Dr.,* ☎ *907/ 586–8751.* ☾ *Weekdays 8–5; may be open weekends.*

51 **Evergreen Cemetery.** Many Juneau pioneers, including Joe Juneau and Dick Harris, are buried here. A meandering gravel path leads through the graveyard, and at the end of it is the monument commemorating the cremation spot of Chief Kowee.

50 **Governor's Mansion.** The three-level colonial-style home on Calhoun Street was completed in 1912. Tours of the residence are, unfortunately, not permitted. ☒ *Calhoun St.*

52 **House of Wickersham.** At the top of the hill behind the Capitol stands the former residence of James Wickersham, pioneer judge and delegate to Congress. The home, constructed in 1898, contains memorabilia from the judge's travels throughout Alaska—from rare native basketry and ivory carvings to historic photos and a Chickering grand piano that came " 'round the Horn" to Alaska while the Russians still ruled here. The tour includes full narration by costumed guides and tea and sourdough bread with "the judge." ⊠ *213 7th St., ☎ 907/586–9001. ☜ $7.50. ☉ May–Sept., Tues.–Sun. 10–3, tours on the hr; Oct.–Apr., by appointment.*

48 Juneau-Douglas City Museum. Among the exhibits interpreting local mining and Tlingit history are old mining equipment, historic photos, and pioneer artifacts, including a turn-of-the-20th-century store and kitchen. Also of interest are a Juneau time line, exhibits on commercial fishing and steamships, historic paintings, a hands-on area for children, and a half-hour video of Juneau's history. ⊠ *114 4th St., ☎ 907/586–3572. ☜ $2. ☉ May–Sept., weekdays 9–5, weekends 10–5; Oct.–Apr., Fri.–Sat. noon–4 or by appointment.*

54 Log Cabin Visitor Center. Modeled after a 19th-century structure, this building served first as a Presbyterian church, then as a brewery. Stop in for a walking-tour map and information on all the tours in Juneau and the surrounding areas. ⊠ *134 3rd St., at Seward St., ☎ 907/586–2201 or 888/581–2201. ☉ May–Sept., weekdays 8:30–5, weekends 9–5; Oct.–Apr., weekdays 9–5.*

44 Marine Park. On the dock where the cruise ships tie up is a little urban oasis with benches, shade trees, and shelter. It's a great place to enjoy an outdoor meal purchased from one of Juneau's many street vendors. A **visitor kiosk** is staffed according to cruise-ship schedules.

57 Mt. Roberts Tramway. The tram whisks you from the cruise terminal 2,000 ft up the side of Mt. Roberts. After the six-minute ride, passengers can take in an award-winning film on the history and legends of the Tlingits, visit the nature center, go for a walk on hiking trails, purchase native crafts, or experience fine mountain-view dining from the decks. The smoke-free bar serves locally brewed beers. ☎ *907/463–3412 or 888/461–8726. ☜ $19.75. ☉ May–Sept., Sun.–Fri. 9–9, Sat. 9 AM–10 PM.*

★ **56 Red Dog Saloon.** The frontierish quarters of the Red Dog have housed an infamous Juneau watering hole since 1890. Every conceivable surface in this two-story bar is cluttered with life preservers, business cards, and college banners; and when tourist season hits, a little atmospheric sawdust covers the floor as well (☞ Nightlife and the Arts, *below*). ⊠ *278 S. Franklin St., ☎ 907/463–9954.*

53 St. Nicholas Russian Orthodox Church. Quaint, onion-domed, and constructed in 1894, St. Nicholas is the oldest Russian church building in Southeast Alaska. ⊠ *326 5th St., ☎ 907/586–1023. ☜ $1 donation. ☉ Tours mid-May–Sept., daily 9–6.*

55 South Franklin Street. Buildings on South Franklin Street (and Front as well) are among the oldest and most interesting structures in the city, housing curio and crafts shops, snack shops, and two salmon shops. Many reflect the architecture of the 1920s and '30s, and some are even older. The small **Alaskan Hotel** (☞ Dining and Lodging *and* Nightlife and the Arts, *below*) opened in 1913 and retains its period trappings. The barroom's massive, mirrored, oak back bar is accented by Tiffany lights and panels. The 1901 **Alaska Steam Laundry Building**, with a windowed turret, now houses a coffeehouse, film processor, and other stores. The **Senate Building** is across the street.

47 State Office Building. At this government building you can have a picnic lunch with the state workers on the eighth-floor patio. On Friday at noon, stop by for concerts played inside the four-story atrium on a grand old theater pipe organ, a veteran of the silent-movie era. ⊠ *4th St.*

OFF THE
BEATEN PATH

GASTINEAU SALMON HATCHERY – Watch through an underwater window as salmon fight their way up a fish ladder. Inside the hatchery you will learn about commercial fishing and the lives of salmon. A retail shop sells gifts and salmon products. ✉ 2697 Channel Dr., ☎ 907/463–4810. 🖭 $3 (includes tour). ⊙ May–Sept., weekdays 10–6, weekends noon–6.

GLACIER GARDENS RAINFOREST ADVENTURE – Spread over 50 acres of rain forest 8 mi north of Juneau are ponds, waterfalls, hiking paths, and gardens with cascades of flowers growing atop unique tree formations. Covered golf carts carry you along the 4 mi of paved paths, and a 520-ft-high overlook provides dramatic views across Mendenhall Glacier (☞ below). ✉ 7600 Glacier Hwy., ☎ 907/790–3377. 🖭 $14 (includes guided tour). ⊙ May–Sept., daily 9–6.

MENDENHALL GLACIER – Juneau's famous drive-up glacier, 13 mi north of downtown, spans 12 mi and is fed by the massive Juneau Icefield. Like many other Alaskan glaciers, it is slowly retreating up the valley, losing 100 ft a year as massive chunks of ice calve into the small lake separating Mendenhall from the **Mendenhall Visitor Center.** Nature trails lead along Mendenhall Lake and into the mountains overlooking Mendenhall Glacier. ✉ End of Glacier Spur Rd., off Mendenhall Loop Rd., ☎ 907/789–0097. ⊙ May–Sept., daily 8:30–5; Oct.–Apr., weekends 8:30–5.

SHRINE OF ST. TERESA – A self-guided pilgrimage to the shrine is well worth the 23-mi journey from downtown Juneau (a taxi should cost at least $45). Built in the 1930s, this stone church and its 14 stations of the cross are the only inhabitants of a serene tiny island that is accessible via a 400-ft-long pedestrian causeway. Sunday services are held at 1 PM June–August. The "honesty-box" gift shop sells crucifixes, books, T-shirts, and souvenirs. ✉ 5933 Lund St., ☎ 907/780–6112.

NATIVE VILLAGES – If you hanker to know how the Native Alaskan village peoples of Southeast Alaska live today, you can fly or take the state ferry *LeConte* to Kake, Angoon, or Hoonah. You won't find much organized touring in any of these communities, but you will find hotels (advance reservations are strongly suggested), and guided fishing, natural-history, and wildlife-watching trips can be arranged by asking around. In Kake, contact the **Waterfront Lodge** (✉ Box 222, Kake 99830, ☎ 907/785–3472); in Angoon, try the **Whalers' Cove Lodge** (✉ Box 101, Angoon 99820, ☎ 907/788–3123 or 800/423–3123); in Hoonah is the **Hoonah Lodge** (✉ Box 320, Hoonah 99829, ☎ 907/945–3636).

Dining and Lodging

$$–$$$ ✕ **The Fiddlehead.** Juneau's favorite restaurant is actually two restau-
   ★   rants in one, both smoke free. Downstairs you can get a casual breakfast, lunch, or dinner in a somewhat generic setting of light wood, gently patterned wallpaper, stained glass, and historic photos. The food is healthy, generously served, and eclectic, ranging from black beans and rice to the rich pasta Greta Garbo (fettuccine with smoked salmon and cream sauce). Homemade bread and cookies from the restaurant's bakery are delicious. The Fireweed Room upstairs has a full bar and a pricier menu: Here you can sample baked Alaskan oysters on the half-shell, grilled halibut, or seafood linguine while rubbing elbows with the legislative elite. ✉ 429 Willoughby Ave., ☎ 907/586–3150. AE, D, DC, MC, V.

$$–$$$ ✕ **Hangar on the Wharf.** Crowded with both locals and travelers, the Hangar is housed in the building where Alaska Airlines started business. The whitewashed wood, stainless-steel accents, and vintage air-

plane parts and photos create a casual dining experience. Expansive views of Gastineau Channel and Douglas Island can be enjoyed from the bar and restaurant. A wide selection of entrées, including locally caught halibut and salmon, filet mignon, and prawn linguine, make this a Juneau hot spot. ⊠ *2 Marine Way, Merchants Wharf Mall,* ☎ *907/586–5018. AE, D, MC, V.*

$$–$$$ ✕ **Mike's Place.** For decades, Mike's, in the former mining community of Douglas, across the bridge from Juneau, has been serving up seafood, steak, pasta, and salads. Locals come here for the best steaks in the area, but Mike's treatment of tiny Petersburg shrimp—fried and sautéed—is also noteworthy. Lunch specials are reasonably priced. It's a romantic spot, with white linens on the tables and live jazz on summer weekends. ⊠ *1102 2nd St., Douglas,* ☎ *907/364–3271. AE, D, DC, MC, V. Closed Mon. No lunch weekends.*

$$ ✕ **Gold Creek Salmon Bake.** Trees, mountains, and the rushing water
★ of Salmon Creek surround the comfortable, canopy-covered benches and tables at this salmon bake. Fresh-caught salmon is cooked over an alder fire and served with a simple but succulent sauce of brown sugar, margarine, and lemon juice. For $24 you are served salmon, ribs, and chicken along with hot baked beans, rice pilaf, salad, corn bread, and blueberry cake. Wine and local Alaskan Amber beer are extra. After dinner you can pan for gold in the stream or wander up the hill to explore the remains of the Wagner Gold Mine. A free round-trip bus ride from downtown hotels is included. ⊠ *1061 Salmon Lane Rd.,* ☎ *907/789–0052 or 800/323–5757. AE, D, MC, V. Closed Oct.–Apr.*

$$$$ 🏠 **Baranof Hotel.** For half a century the Baranof has been the city's best address, though this designation has been challenged in recent years by the Goldbelt Hotel Juneau (☞ *below*). The Art Deco lobby and most rooms in this nine-story hostelry have tasteful woods and period lamps creating an atmosphere reminiscent of 1939, when the hotel first opened. Twenty rooms are equipped with either a treadmill or an exercise bike. ⊠ *127 N. Franklin St., 99801,* ☎ *907/586–2660, 800/544–0970 for reservations,* 𝔽𝔸𝕏 *907/586–8315. 179 rooms, 17 suites. Restaurant, coffee shop, lobby lounge, beauty salon, meeting rooms, travel services. AE, D, DC, MC, V.*

$$$$ 🏠 **Frontier Suites Airport Hotel.** Located near the airport in Mendenhall Valley, 9 mi from Juneau, this new hotel is great for families. All rooms are suites, with modern and functional furniture and full kitchens with a stove, refrigerator, microwave, dishes, silverware, and pans. Most suites feature separate bedrooms and living rooms (with sleeper sofas) and two televisions. Two bunk rooms include a mini-loft for older children. Downstairs, the River Rock Restaurant and Lounge serves seafood, pasta, prime rib, and steak. ⊠ *9400 Glacier Hwy., 99801,* ☎ *907/790–6600 or 800/544–2250,* 𝔽𝔸𝕏 *907/790–6612. 40 suites. Restaurant, bar, kitchenettes. AE, D, DC, MC, V.*

$$$$ 🏠 **Goldbelt Hotel Juneau.** A high-rise by Juneau standards, the seven-story Goldbelt is across Main Street from Centennial Hall and across Egan Drive from the docks. A Chilkat blanket and other native artifacts are displayed in the lobby. Deluxe suites have king-size beds, and 15 rooms are equipped with treadmills or stationary bikes. The Gold Room Restaurant is just off the lobby. ⊠ *51 W. Egan Dr., 99801,* ☎ *907/586–6900 or 888/478–6909,* 𝔽𝔸𝕏 *907/463–3567. 105 rooms. Restaurant, lobby lounge, meeting rooms. AE, D, DC, MC, V.*

$$$$ 🏠 **Grandma's Feather Bed.** A diamond in the rough of suburban Juneau, this hotel has a warm and inviting atmosphere that makes you feel as if you're visiting someone's home. Each of the spacious rooms in the Victorian-style farmhouse is painted with cheerful, bright colors and is outfitted with jetted bathtubs and feather comforters; some have fireplaces and kitchen nooks. The complimentary breakfast features all-you-can-eat pancakes, omelets, French toast, and more. ⊠ *2348 Mendenhall Loop Rd., 99801,* ☎ *907/789–5566,* FAX *907/789–2818. 14 rooms. Restaurant, airport shuttle. AE, D, DC, MC, V.*

$$$$ 🏨 **Juneau Airport TraveLodge.** The rooms and furnishings here are pretty standard, but this is the only motel in Juneau with an indoor pool (small) and whirlpool tub—a plus if you want to unwind after a day of touring. The structure, like the Mi Casa Restaurant inside, is Mexican in design and decor. ⊠ *9200 Glacier Hwy., 99801,* ☎ *907/ 789–9700 or 800/255–3050,* FAX *907/789–1969. 86 rooms. Restaurant, lobby lounge, in-room data ports, indoor pool, hot tub, airport shuttle. AE, D, MC, V.*

$$$$ 🏨 **Pearson's Pond Luxury Inn and Garden Spa.** Guests at this luxurious private retreat can enjoy an amazing view of the great blue Mendenhall Glacier. Built on a small lake, the large home has a three-tier deck with two hot tubs and a barbecue grill. The rooms are private and set up for business travelers or families. Efficiency kitchens are stocked with breakfast essentials. Activities include taking part in yoga on the deck, hiking or cross-country skiing, or relaxing in the hot tub with wine and cheese. You can also bob around the lake in the rowboat, paddleboat, and kayaks. Computers and data ports are available. ⊠ *4541 Sawa Circle, 99801,* ☎ *907/789–3772 or 888/658–6328,* FAX *907/ 789–6722. 3 suites. In-room data ports, kitchenettes, massage, boating, fishing, bicycles, laundry service. AE, D, DC, MC, V.*

$$$–$$$$ 🏨 **The Prospector.** A short walk west of downtown and next door to ★ the State Museum, this small but modern hotel is frequented by business travelers and legislators. Rooms are large, with contemporary furnishings and bright Alaskan watercolors. T. K. McGuire's dining room and lounge serves prime rib, steaks, and seafood. ⊠ *375 Whittier St., 99801,* ☎ *907/586–3737, 800/331–2711 outside Alaska, 800/478–5866 in Alaska;* FAX *907/586–1204. 58 rooms. Restaurant, lobby lounge. AE, D, DC, MC, V.*

$$–$$$$ 🏨 **Inn at the Waterfront.** Built in 1889, this inn mixes antiques with ★ modern amenities. Rooms are clean and bright, with simple, comfortable furniture. The inn was a brothel until 1958, and the Summit, an intimate candlelit restaurant with a copper-top bar area, is reminiscent of those days. Seafood, including prawns, king crab, and halibut, dominates, but meat lovers will enjoy the big porterhouse steaks and roasted rack of lamb. Meal reservations are essential. ⊠ *455 S. Franklin St., 99801,* ☎ *907/586–2050,* FAX *907/586–2999. 17 rooms. Restaurant. AE, D, DC, MC, V.*

$$ 🏨 **Alaskan Hotel.** This historic 1913 hotel in the heart of downtown Juneau ★ sits over the popular bar of the same name; rooms can be a bit noisy when bands are playing. Guest rooms are on three floors and have antiques and iron beds. The flocked wallpaper, floral carpets, and Tiffany windows are reminiscent of the hotel's original gold rush–era opulence. ⊠ *167 S. Franklin St.,* ☎ *907/586–1000 or 800/327–9347,* FAX *907/463– 3775. 42 rooms, 22 with bath. Bar, hot tubs. D, DC, MC, V.*

$ 🏨 **U.S. Forest Service Cabins.** Scattered throughout Tongass National Forest, these rustic cabins offer a charming and cheap escape for just $25–$45 per cabin. Most are fly-in units, accessible by floatplanes from virtually any community in the Southeast. These public-use cabins have bunks for six to eight occupants, tables, stoves, and outdoor privies, but no electricity or running water. You provide your own sleeping bag, food, and cooking utensils. Bedside reading in most cabins includes a diary kept by visitors—add your own adventure. ⊠ *U.S. Forest Service Information Center, Centennial Hall, 101 Egan Dr., Juneau 99801,* ☎ *907/586–8751; 877/444–6777 for reservations; www.ReserveUSA.com. 150 cabins. AE, D, MC, V.*

$ ⚠ **U.S. Forest Service Campgrounds.** Eight Forest Service–maintained campgrounds are scattered around Tongass National Forest and are accessible from the communities of Juneau, Sitka, Ketchikan, Petersburg, and Thorne Bay. All have pit toilets and sites for RVs and tents, but not all provide drinking water. ✉ *U.S. Forest Service Information Center, 101 Egan Dr., Juneau 99801,* ☎ *907/586–8751, 877/444–6777 for reservations. D, MC, V.*

Guided Tours

Boating and Kayaking
Auk Ta Shaa Discovery (☎ 907/586–8687 or 800/820–2628) leads canoe excursions on Mendenhall Lake, along with raft and kayak trips down the Mendenhall River. **Alaska Travel Adventures** (☎ 907/789–0052) also leads Mendenhall River floats. **Auk Nu Tours** (☎ 907/586–8687 or 800/820–2628) has all-day catamaran tours to the beautiful glaciers of Tracy Arm Fjord.

Helicopter Flightseeing
Several local companies offer helicopter flightseeing trips that take you to the spectacular glaciers flowing from Juneau Icefield. Most have booths along the downtown cruise ship dock. All include a touchdown on a glacier, with a chance to romp on these rivers of ice. The companies include **ERA Helicopters** (☎ 907/586–2030 or 800/843–1947), **Coastal Helicopters** (☎ 907/789–5600), **Northstar Trekking** (☎ 907/790–4530), and **Temsco Helicopters** (☎ 907/789–9501).

Sightseeing
Juneau Trolley Car Company (☎ 907/789–4342) makes stops at a dozen or so of Juneau's historic and shopping attractions. **Goldbelt Tours** (☎ 907/463–3231 or 800/820–2628) provides bus tours of downtown Juneau and nearby sights, including a stop at Mendenhall Glacier.

Wilderness Lodge
Taku Glacier Lodge (☎ 907/586–8258, ℻ 907/789–2021) is a remote historic lodge along Taku Inlet south of Juneau that faces Hole-in-the-Wall Glacier.

Nightlife and the Arts

Bars
The **Alaskan Hotel Bar** (✉ 167 S. Franklin St., ☎ 907/586–1000) is about as funky a place as you'll find in Juneau: flocked-velvet walls, antique chandeliers above the bar, and vintage Alaskan frontier brothel decor. Sit back and enjoy the live music or take turns with the locals at the open mike.

When the ships are in, the music at **Red Dog Saloon** (✉ 278 S. Franklin St., ☎ 907/463–9954) is live and the crowd gets livelier. One wonders if the sometimes rough-and-tumble fishing crowd even knows that the bar's namesake is actually a small shadow of a Scottie dog.

If you're a beer fan, look for **Alaskan Brewing Company**'s award-winning Alaskan Amber, Pale, Frontier, and Smoked Porter beer, brewed and bottled in Juneau. Visitors are welcome at the microbrewery (✉ 5429 Shaune Dr., ☎ 907/780–5866) and can sample the brews after watching the bottling operation.

Music Festivals
The annual weeklong **Alaska Folk Festival** (✉ Box 21748, 99802, ☎ 907/364–2658) is staged each April in Juneau, drawing singers, banjo masters, fiddlers, and even cloggers from all over the state. During the last week of May, Juneau is the scene of **Juneau Jazz 'n Classics** (✉

Box 22152, 99802, ☎ 907/463–3378), which celebrates music from Bach to Brubeck.

Theater

Southeast Alaska's only professional theater company, **Perseverance Theater** (✉ 914 3rd St., Douglas, ☎ 907/364–2421) presents everything from Broadway plays to Shakespeare to locally written material.

Outdoor Activities and Sports

Cross-Country Skiing

During the winter, the **Parks and Recreation Department** (☎ 907/586–5226) sponsors a group ski and snowshoe outing each Wednesday and Saturday morning when there's sufficient snow. You can rent skis and get advice about touring the trails and ridges around town from **Foggy Mountain Shop** (✉ 134 N. Franklin St., ☎ 907/586–6780).

Downhill Skiing

The only downhill area in the Southeast, **Eaglecrest** (✉ 155 S. Seward St., Juneau 99801, ☎ 907/790–2000, 907/586–5330 for recorded ski information), on Douglas Island, just 30 minutes from downtown Juneau, offers late-November to mid-April skiing and snowboarding on a well-groomed mountain with two double chairlifts, cross-country trails, a beginner's platter pull, ski school, ski-rental shop, cafeteria, and tri-level day lodge. Enjoy the northern lights while you night ski from January through mid-March.

Fitness Clubs

The **Juneau Racquet Club** (✉ 2841 Riverside Dr., ☎ 907/789–2181), about 10 mi north of downtown, adjacent to Mendenhall Mall, will accommodate out-of-towners at its first-class indoor tennis and racquetball courts. Facilities include sauna, hot tub, exercise equipment, massage tables, sports shop, and snack bar. **JRC Downtown** (✉ W. Willoughby Ave., ☎ 907/586–5773) is a smaller version of the club. Both charge $12 per day for nonmembers.

Gold Panning

Gold panning is fun, especially for children, and Juneau is one of the Southeast's best-known gold-panning towns. Sometimes you actually uncover a few flecks of the precious metal in the bottom of your pan. You can buy a pan at almost any Alaska hardware or sporting-goods store. Look for schedules of gold-panning tours at the **Log Cabin Visitor Center** (☞ Exploring Juneau, *above*).

Golf

Juneau's par-3, nine-hole **Mendenhall Golf Course** (✉ 2101 Industrial Blvd., ☎ 907/789–1221) is pretty modest but does rent clubs and have spectacular vistas.

Hiking

The **Parks and Recreation Department** (☎ 907/586–5226) in Juneau sponsors a group hike each Wednesday morning and on Saturday in summer. Contact the **U.S. Forest Service** (☎ 907/586–8751) for trail books and maps.

Sea Kayaking

Alaska Discovery (✉ 5449 Shaune Dr., Suite 4, Juneau, ☎ 907/780–6226 or 800/586–1911) offers all-day kayak trips in nearby Berners Bay. Experienced kayakers can rent boats and equipment from **Juneau Outdoor Center** (☎ 907/586–8220) in Douglas or from **Adventure Sports** (☎ 907/789–5696) in Mendenhall Valley.

Shopping

Art Galleries

Rie Muñoz of the **Rie Muñoz Gallery** (✉ 2101 Jordan Ave., ☎ 907/
789–7411) in Mendenhall Valley is one of Alaska's best-known artists,
creator of a stylized, simple, and colorful design technique that is
much copied but rarely equaled. Other artists' work is also on sale at
the Muñoz Gallery, including wood-block prints by nationally recognized artist Dale DeArmond. Various books illustrated by Rie Muñoz
and written by Alaskan children's author Jean Rogers are for sale. In
downtown Juneau, see Rie Muñoz's art at **Decker Gallery** (✉ 233 S.
Franklin St., ☎ 907/463–5536 or 800/463–5536).

Seafood

Taku Smokeries (✉ 550 S. Franklin St., ☎ 800/582–5122), at the south
end of town near the cruise ship docks, processes nearly 6 million pounds
of fish, mostly salmon, a year. You can view the smoking process
through large windows and then purchase the packaged fish in the deli-
style gift shop or have some shipped back home.

ADMIRALTY ISLAND AND GLACIER BAY NATIONAL PARK AND PRESERVE

Admiralty Island

🟡 *10–35 mi west of Juneau.*

The island is famous for its lush rain forests and abundant wildlife, including one of the largest concentrations of brown bears anywhere on
the planet. The island's Tlingit inhabitants called it Kootznoowoo, mean-
ing "fortress of the bears." Ninety-six miles long, with 678 mi of
coastline, Admiralty—the second-largest island in the Southeast—is home
to an estimated 1,500 bears, or almost one per square mile. **Admiralty
Island National Monument** has a system of public-use cabins, a canoe
route that crosses the island via a chain of lakes and trails, the world's
highest density of nesting bald eagles, large concentrations of humpback whales, and some of the region's best sea kayaking and sportfishing. ✉ *8461 Old Dairy Rd., Juneau 99801,* ☎ *907/586–8790.*

More than 90% of Admiralty Island is preserved within the
Kootznoowoo Wilderness. Its chief attraction is **Pack Creek,** where you
can watch brown bears feeding on salmon. One of Alaska's premier
bear-viewing sites, Pack Creek is comanaged by the U.S. Forest Service and the Alaska Department of Fish and Game. Permits are required
during the main viewing season, June 1–September 10, and only 24
people per day are allowed to visit Pack Creek from July 5 through
August 25. Reservations are made through the Forest Service's Centennial Hall Information Center beginning March 1. ✉ *Centennial Hall
Information Center,* ☎ *907/586–8751.* 🎫 *$50.*

Lodging

$$$$ 🏠 **Thayer Lake Lodge.** One of Southeast Alaska's oldest lodges, Thayer
★ Lake is on private land within Admiralty Island National Monument.
Bob and Edith Nelson built this small, rustic lodge-and-cabins operation, which houses up to 10 people (5 in each cabin), after World War
II. They built it mostly with their own labor and used local timber. Lake
fishing is unsurpassed for cutthroat and Dolly Varden trout (though
they're not overly large). You can take a canoe or motorboat on the
9-mi-long lake that laps the sandy beach fronting the lodge. Simple family-style meals are served in the lodge. Many visitors opt for a complete package that includes a floatplane flight from Juneau, lodging,

and meals, plus a guided trip to Pack Creek. ✉ *Box 8897, Ketchikan 99901,* ☎ *907/247–8897 or 907/225–3343,* FAX *907/247–7053. 2 cabins. Dining room, kitchenettes, hiking, boating, fishing. No credit cards. Closed mid-Sept.–May.*

Guided Tours

Alaska Discovery (✉ 5449 Shaune Dr., Suite 4, Juneau, ☎ 907/780–6226 or 800/586–1911, FAX 907/780–4220) leads single and multi-day trips to Pack Creek that include going on a floatplane, sea kayaking, and guided bear viewing. You'll need a permit from the **U.S. Forest Service** (✉ 101 Egan Dr., Juneau 99801, ☎ 907/586–8751) before visiting Pack Creek. Two good companies are **Ward Air** (☎ 907/789–9150) and **Alaska Coastal Airlines** (☎ 907/789–7818).

Glacier Bay National Park and Preserve

★ ⑤⑨ *60 mi northwest of Juneau.*

Near the northern end of the Inside Passage, Glacier Bay National Park and Preserve (✉ Box 140, Gustavus 99826, ☎ 907/697–2230) is one of the jewels of the entire national park system. Visiting Glacier Bay is like stepping back into the Little Ice Age—it's one of the few places in the world where you can approach massive tidewater glaciers. With a noise that sounds like cannons firing, bergs the size of 10-story office buildings sometimes come crashing from the "snout" of a glacier. The crash sends tons of water and spray skyward, and it propels mini–tidal waves outward from the point of impact. **Johns Hopkins Glacier** calves so often and with such volume that the large cruise ships can seldom come within 2 mi of its face.

Glacier Bay is a recently formed (and still forming) body of water fed by the runoff of the ice fields, glaciers, and mountains that surround it. Captain James Cook and then Captain George Vancouver sailed by Glacier Bay and didn't even know it. At the time of Vancouver's sailing in 1794, the bay was hidden behind and beneath a vast glacial wall of ice. The glacier face was more than 20 mi across and in places more than 4,000 ft in depth. It extended more than 100 mi to its origins in the St. Elias Mountain Range. Since then, due to warming weather and other factors not fully understood, the face of the glacial ice has melted and retreated with amazing speed, exposing 65 mi of fjords, islands, and inlets.

It was Vancouver who named the magnificent snow-clad **Mt. Fairweather** that towers over the head of the bay. Legend has it that Vancouver named Fairweather on one of the Southeast's most beautiful blue days—and the mountain was not seen again during the following century. An exaggeration, to be sure, but overcast, rainy weather is certainly the norm here.

In 1879, about a century after Vancouver's sail-by, one of the earliest white visitors to what is now Glacier Bay National Park and Preserve came calling. He was naturalist John Muir, drawn by the flora and fauna that had followed in the wake of glacial withdrawals, and fascinated by the vast ice rivers that descended from the mountains to tidewater. Today, the naturalist's namesake glacier, like others in the park, continues to retreat dramatically. Its terminus is now scores of miles farther up the bay from the small cabin he built at its face during his time there.

Glacier Bay is a marvelous laboratory for naturalists of all persuasions. Glaciologists, of course, can have a field day. Animal lovers can hope to see the rare glacial "blue" bears of the area, a variation of the black

Glacier Bay National Park and Preserve

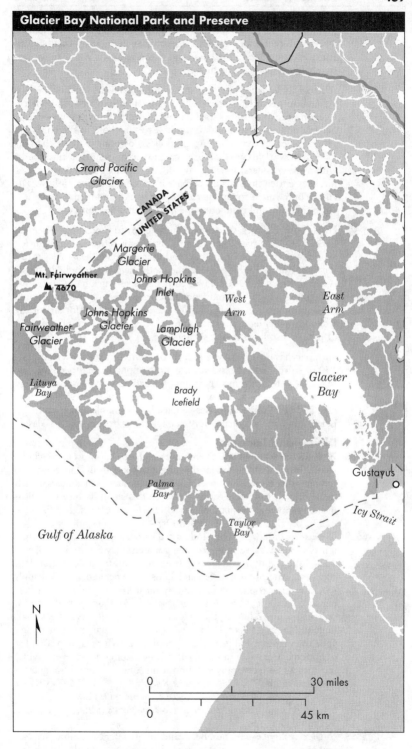

Grand Pacific
Glacier

CANADA
UNITED STATES

Margerie
Glacier

Johns Hopkins
Inlet

Mt. Fairweather
▲ 4670

West
Arm

East
Arm

Johns Hopkins
Glacier

Fairweather
Glacier

Lamplugh
Glacier

Lituya
Bay

Brady
Icefield

Glacier
Bay

Gustavus

Palma
Bay

Icy Strait

Gulf of Alaska

Taylor
Bay

N

0   30 miles

0   45 km

bear, which is here along with the brown bear; whales feasting on krill; mountain goats in late spring and early summer; and seals on floating icebergs. Birders can look for the more than 200 species that have already been spotted in the park, and if you're lucky, you may witness two bald eagles engaging in aerobatics.

A remarkable panorama of plants unfolds from the head of the bay, which is just emerging from the ice, to the mouth, which has been ice-free for more than 200 years. In between, the primitive plants—algae, lichens, and mosses—that are the first to take hold of the bare, wet ground give way to more complex species: flowering plants such as the magenta dwarf fireweed and the creamy dryas, which in turn merge with willows, alders, and cottonwood. As the living plants mature and die, they enrich the soil and prepare it for new species to follow. The climax of the plant community is the lush spruce-and-hemlock rain forest, rich in life and blanketing the land around **Bartlett Cove.**

⑥ For airborne visitors, **Gustavus** is the gateway to Glacier Bay National Park. The long, paved jet airport, built as a refueling strip during World War II, is one of the best and longest in Southeast Alaska, all the more impressive because facilities at the field are so limited. Alaska Airlines, which serves Gustavus daily in the summer, has a large, rustic terminal at the site, and from a free telephone on the front porch of the terminal you can call any of the local hostelries for a courtesy pickup. Smaller light-aircraft companies that serve the community out of Juneau also have on-site shelters.

Gustavus has no downtown. In fact, Gustavus is not a town at all. The 150 or so year-round residents are most emphatic on this point; they regularly vote down incorporation. Instead, Gustavus is a scattering of homes, farmsteads, arts-and-crafts studios, fishing and guiding charters, and other tiny enterprises peopled by hospitable individualists. It is, in many ways, a contemporary example of the frontier spirit in Alaska.

Dining and Lodging

$-$$ ✕ **Strawberry Point Cafe.** There's nothing fancy here, just good wholesome cooking that features locally caught seafood, from Dungeness crab to king salmon and shrimp. Alaskan antiques and knickknacks, such as an eclectic bottle collection, enhance this small, homey establishment. Friday night is pizza night. ✉ *On the dock road,* ☎ *907/697–2227. AE, D, DC, MC, V. Closed Oct.–Apr.*

$$$$ ▦ **Bear Track Inn.** Built of handcrafted spruce logs, this family-owned inn sits on a 17-acre property facing majestic Icy Strait. The soaring 30-ft lobby contains a central fireplace, comfortable overstuffed couches, rustic wooden tables, and moose-antler chandeliers. The inn's spacious guest rooms are luxuriously furnished. In addition to offering such local specialties as Dungeness crab, Alaskan spotted prawns, or salmon in parchment, the full-service restaurant serves steak, halibut, and salmon fillets. The knowledgeable staff will help you design your own customized itinerary of outdoor activities from a long list of options. The room rate (packages range from one to seven nights) includes air or ferry transportation from Juneau, ground transportation, and meals. ✉ *255 Rink Creek Rd., 99826,* ☎ *907/697–3017 or 888/697–2284,* ℻ *907/697–2284. 14 rooms with bath. Restaurant, hiking, boating, fishing, travel services, airport shuttle. AE, D, MC, V. Closed Oct.–Jan.*

$$$$ ▦ **Glacier Bay Country Inn.** Bears and moose might peek into this pic-
★   turesque rambling log structure with marvelous cupolas, dormers, gables, and porches, which was built from local hand-logged timbers yet has modern amenities. Some rooms have antiques and open log-beam ceilings. Innkeepers Ponch and Sandi Marchbanks charter their

three boats, each of which sleeps four to six. Gourmet meals are included in the room rate (about $24 for nonguests). Among the guests' favorites: steamed Dungeness crab, homemade fettuccine, and rhubarb custard pie. ✉ *Halfway between the airport and Bartlett Cove, Box 5, 99826,* ☎ *907/697–2288 or 800/628–0912,* ℻ *907/697–2289. 6 rooms with bath, 4 cabins. Restaurant, boating, travel services. AE, MC, V. Closed Oct.–Mar.*

$$$$ ⬚ **Glacier Bay Lodge.** This lodge within the national park is constructed of massive timbers and blends well into the thick rain forest surrounding it on three sides. The modern yet rustic rooms are accessible by boardwalks. If it swims or crawls in the sea hereabouts, you'll find it on the menu in the rustic dining room. A guest favorite is the halibut baked *aleyeska,* a fillet baked in a rich sauce of sour cream, cheese, and onions. Activities include whale-watching, kayaking, and hiking with a naturalist. ✉ *Bartlett Cove, Box 199, 99826 (mailing: 520 Pike Tower, Suite 1400, Seattle, WA 98101),* ☎ *907/697–2226 in summer, 800/451–5952,* ℻ *206/623–7809. 56 rooms. Restaurant, boating, travel services. AE, D, MC, V. Closed mid-Sept.–mid-May.*

$$$$ ⬚ **Gustavus Inn.** Built in 1928 and established as an inn in 1965, Gustavus Inn continues a tradition of gracious Alaska rural living. In the
★ remodeled original homestead building, rooms are decorated in New England–farmhouse style. Glacier trips, fishing expeditions, bicycle rides around the community, and berry picking in season are offered here. Hosts David and Jo Ann Lesh heap bountiful servings of seafood and fresh vegetables on the plates of overnight guests and others who reserve for family-style meals in the cozy farmhouse-style dining room in advance ($22.50). Dinnertime is 6:30 sharp. ✉ *Mile 1, Gustavus Rd., Box 60, 99826,* ☎ *907/697–2254 or 800/649–5220, 913/649–5220 in winter;* ℻ *907/697–2255, 913/649–5220 in winter. 11 rooms with bath, 2 rooms share a bath. Restaurant, fishing, travel services, airport shuttle. AE, MC, V. Closed mid-Sept.–mid-May.*

$$–$$$$ ⬚ **Puffin Bed & Breakfast.** These attractive cabins are in a wooded homestead and are decorated with Alaskan crafts. There's also a main lodge with a social area and kitchen for the guests. A full breakfast is included. The owners also operate Puffin Travel for fishing, kayaking, sightseeing charters, and Glacier Bay cruises. There's also a two-bedroom house for rent that's not part of the B&B. ✉ *¼ mi off Wilson Rd., Box 3, 99826,* ☎ *907/697–2260,* ℻ *907/697–2258. 6 cabins, 4 with bath. Breakfast room, boating, fishing, travel services, airport shuttle. No credit cards. Closed mid-Sept.–mid-May.*

Guided Tours

Glacier Bay is best experienced from the water, whether from the deck of a cruise ship, on a tour boat, or from the level of a sea kayak. National Park Service naturalists come aboard to explain the great glaciers; to point out features of the forests, islands, and mountains; and to help spot black bears, brown bears, mountain goats, whales, porpoises, and birds.

The boat *Spirit of Adventure,* which operates daily from the dock at Bartlett Cove, near Glacier Bay Lodge (☞ Dining and Lodging, *above*), is smaller than the cruise ships but also has uniformed Park Service naturalists aboard. **Air Excursions** (☎ 907/697–2375 or 800/354–2479) offers Glacier Bay flightseeing tours from Gustavus.

Outdoor Activities and Sports

SEA KAYAKING

The most adventurous way to explore Glacier Bay is by paddling your own kayak through the bay's icy waters and inlets. But unless you're an expert, you're better off signing on with the guided tours. You can book one of **Alaska Discovery**'s (✉ 5449 Shaune Dr., Suite 4, Juneau, ☎ 907/780–6226 or 800/586–1911) five- or eight-day guided expeditions. Alaska Discovery provides safe, seaworthy kayaks and tents, gear, and food. Its guides are tough, knowledgeable Alaskans, and they've spent enough time in Glacier Bay's wild country to know what's safe and what's not. **Spirit Walker Expeditions, Inc.** (✉ Box 240, 99826, ☎ 907/697–2266 or 800/529–2537, ℻ 907/697–2701) leads one- to eight-day sea kayaking trips to various parts of Icy Strait (but not within Glacier Bay itself).

Kayak rentals for unescorted Glacier Bay exploring and camping can be arranged through **Glacier Bay Sea Kayaks** (✉ Bartlett Cove, Box 26, 99826, ☎ 907/697–2257). Prior to going out, you will be given instructions on handling the craft plus camping and routing suggestions. **Sea Otter Kayak Glacier Bay** (✉ Box 228, 99826, ☎ 907/697–3007, ℻ 907/697–2338) rents kayaks, gives instructions on their use, and supplies the essentials.

SOUTHEAST ALASKA A TO Z

Arriving and Departing

By Car

Only tiny **Hyder,** just across the border from Stewart, British Columbia, is accessible by conventional highway. You can reach Hyder on British Columbia's Cassiar Highway, which can be reached, in turn, from Highway 16 just north of Prince Rupert.

By Ferry

From the south, the **Alaska Marine Highway System** (✉ Box 25535, Juneau 99802, ☎ 907/465–3941 or 800/642–0066) operates stateroom-equipped vehicle and passenger ferries from Bellingham, Washington, and from Prince Rupert, British Columbia. The vessels call at Ketchikan, Wrangell, Petersburg, Sitka, and Juneau, and they connect with smaller vessels serving bush communities; in all, 14 Southeast towns are served by state ferries. One of the smaller ferries also operates between Hyder and Ketchikan. In the summer, staterooms on the ferries are always sold out before sailing time; reserve months in advance. If you are planning to take a car on the ferry, early reservations for vehicle space are also highly recommended. This is particularly true for recreation vehicles.

B.C. Ferries (✉ 1112 Fort St., Victoria, B.C., Canada V8V 4V2, ☎ 250/386–3431) operates similar passenger and vehicle ferries from Vancouver Island, British Columbia, to Prince Rupert. From here, travelers can connect with the Alaska Marine Highway System.

By Plane

Alaska Airlines operates several flights daily from Seattle and other Pacific Coast and southwestern cities to Ketchikan, Wrangell, Petersburg, Sitka, Glacier Bay, and Juneau. The carrier connects Juneau to the northern Alaskan cities of Yakutat, Cordova, Anchorage, Fairbanks, Nome, Kotzebue, and Prudhoe Bay. In summer, **Delta Airlines** has at least one flight daily from Seattle to Juneau. **Wings of Alaska** can connect you from Juneau to several towns.

Getting Around

By Ferry

The **Alaska Marine Highway System** (☞ Arriving and Departing, *above*) will not only bring you into Southeast Alaska but will also ferry you from town to town.

By Plane

Every large community in Southeast Alaska, and many smaller ones, have **air-taxi services** that fly you from town to town and, if you're seeking backcountry adventures, into remote wilderness cabins. Local chambers of commerce (☞ Visitor Information, *below*) can provide lists of bush-plane services.

Contacts and Resources

B&B Reservation Service

The **Alaska Bed & Breakfast Association's Inside Passage Chapter** (✉ Box 22800, Juneau 99802, ☎ 907/789–8822 or 877/252–2959, FAX 907/780–4673) books B&B accommodations in most Southeast communities.

Guided Tours

ADVENTURE

Alaska Discovery (✉ 5449 Shaune Dr., Suite 4, Juneau, ☎ 907/780–6226 or 800/586–1911, FAX 907/780–4220). **Alaska Tugboat Tours** (☎ 907/874–3101 or 888/488–4386). **Cape Fox Tours** (☎ 907/225–4846, FAX 907/225–3137). **Tongass Kayak Adventures** (☎ 907/772–4600).

BICYCLING

Sockeye Cycle Company (✉ 24 Portage St., Box 829, 99827, ☎ 907/766–2869).

BOATING

Alaska Cross-Country Guiding and Rafting (☎ FAX 907/767–5522). **Alaska Travel Adventures** (☎ 907/789–0052). **Auk Nu Tours** (☎ 907/586–8687 or 800/820–2628). **Auk Ta Shaa Discovery** (☎ 907/586–8687 or 800/820–2628). **Spirit Walker Expeditions, Inc.** (✉ Box 240, Gustavus 99826, ☎ 907/697–2266 or 800/529–2537, FAX 907/697–2701).

CHARTERS AND FLIGHTSEEING

Coastal Helicopters (☎ 907/789–5600). **ERA Helicopters** (☎ 907/586–2030 or 800/843–1947). **Mountain Flying Service** (☎ 907/766–3007 or 800/766–4007). **Northstar Trekking** (☎ 907/790–4530). **Pacific Wing** (☎ 907/772–9258). **Sunrise Aviation** (☎ 907/874–2319 or 800/874–2311, FAX 907/874–2546). **Temsco Helicopters** (☎ 907/789–9501). **Wings of Alaska** (☎ 907/789–0790).

CRUISES

Alaska Cruises (☎ 907/225–6044, 800/228–1905 for a brochure, FAX 907/225–8636) provides cruises from Ketchikan.

NATURE

Kaleidoscope Cruises (☎ 907/772–3736 or 800/868–4373) runs whale-watching and glacier ecology boat tours from Petersburg.

SIGHTSEEING

Goldbelt Tours (☎ 907/463–3231 or 800/820–2628) gives bus tours of Juneau that include Mendenhall Glacier. **Juneau Trolley Car Company** (☎ 907/789–4342) makes stops at a dozen or so of Juneau's sights. **Metlakatla Tours** (☎ 907/886–4441 or 877/886–8687) offers a variety of tours from Metlakatla. **Seaport Limousine** (☎ 250/636–2622) leads guided tours of the Hyder area. **Sitka Tours** (☎ 907/747–8443, FAX 907/747–7510) runs sightseeing, historical, and raptor tours in Sitka.

Hospitals

Bartlett Memorial Hospital (✉ 3260 Hospital Dr., Juneau, ☎ 907/586–2611). **Ketchikan General Hospital** (✉ 3011 Tongass Ave., ☎ 907/225–5171). **Petersburg Medical Center** (✉ 103 Fram St., ☎ 907/772–

4291). **Sitka Community Hospital** (⊠ 209 Moller Dr., ☎ 907/747–3241). **Wrangell General Hospital** (⊠ 310 Bennett St., ☎ 907/874–7000).

Emergencies
Police, fire, or **ambulance** (☎ 911).

Pharmacies
Juneau:Juneau Drug Co. (⊠ 202 Front St., ☎ 907/586–1233). **Ron's Apothecary** (⊠ 9101 Mendenhall Mall Rd., about 10 mi north of downtown in Mendenhall Valley, next to the Super Bear market, ☎ 907/789–0458; 907/789–9522 after-hours number for prescription emergencies).

Ketchikan:Downtown Drugstore (⊠ 300 Front St., ☎ 907/225–3144). **Race Avenue Drugs** (⊠ 2300 Tongass Ave., across from the Plaza Portwest shopping mall, ☎ 907/225–4151). After hours, call **Ketchikan General Hospital** (☎ 907/225–5171).

Petersburg:Rexall Drugs (⊠ 215 N. Nordic Dr., ☎ 907/772–3265). After hours, call **Petersburg Medical Center** (☎ 907/772–4291).

Sitka:Harry Race Pharmacy (⊠ 106 Lincoln St., ☎ 907/747–8006). **White's Pharmacy** (⊠ 705 Halibut Point Rd., ☎ 907/747–5755). After hours, call **Sitka Community Hospital** (⊠ 209 Moller Dr., ☎ 907/747–3241).

Wrangell:Stikine Drugs (⊠ 202 Front St., ☎ 907/874–3422). After hours, call **Wrangell General Hospital** (⊠ 310 Bennett St., ☎ 907/874–7000).

Travel Agency
Viking Travel (101 Nordic Dr., ☎ 907/772–9258 or 907/772–3818, FAX 907/772–3940) books adventure tours out of Petersburg.

Visitor Information
Hours of operation of the following visitor information centers are generally mid-May–August, daily 8–5 and later when cruise ships are in port; September–April, weekdays 8–5.

Southeast Alaska Tourism Council (⊠ Box 20710, Juneau 99802, ☎ 907/586–4777 or 800/423–0568; for a travel planner, www.alaskainfo.org). **Juneau Convention and Visitors Bureau** (⊠ 134 3rd St., Juneau, ☎ 907/586–2201 or 888/581–2201, www.juneaualaska.com). **Ketchikan Visitors Bureau** (⊠ 131 Front St., Ketchikan 99901, ☎ 907/225–6166 or 800/770–3300, www.visit-ketchikan.com). **Petersburg Visitor Information Center** (⊠ 1st and Fram Sts., Box 649, Petersburg 99833, ☎ 907/772–4636, www.petersburg.com). **Sitka Convention and Visitors Bureau** (⊠ 303 Lincoln St., Box 1226, Sitka 99835, ☎ 907/747–5940, www.sitka.org) also has a booth in the Centennial Building on Harbor Street. **Stewart-Hyder Chamber of Commerce** (⊠ Box 306, Stewart, British Columbia, Canada V0T 1W0, ☎ 250/636–9224, FAX 250/636–2199). **Wrangell Chamber of Commerce Visitors Center** (⊠ 107 Stikine Ave., Box 49, Wrangell 99929, ☎ 907/874–3901 or 800/367–9745).

Alaska Department of Fish and Game (⊠ Box 25526, Juneau 99802, ☎ 907/465–4112; 907/465–4180 for sportfishing seasons and regulations; 907/465–2376 for license information). **Alaska Division of Parks** (⊠ 400 Willoughby Ave., Suite 400, Juneau 99801, ☎ 907/465–4563). **U.S. Forest Service** (⊠ 101 Egan Dr., Juneau 99801, ☎ 907/586–8751).

INDEX